DR SARAH LOWNDES is a lecturer, curator and writer based in Glasgow. Lowndes lectures in the Historical and Critical Studies Department at Glasgow School of Art, where her research focuses on artist-led projects, interdisciplinary and performance-related practice and contemporary art. Her PhD analysed concrete performance art in Southern California in the 1960's and '70s, and she has contributed to *Frieze*, *The Frieze Yearbook*, *Artforum*, *Art on Paper*, *Untitled*, *Circa*, *MAP*, *2HB*, *Spike Art Quarterly* and *Afterall* and to catalogues for international institutions. She curated Three Blows, a weekend of all-sound acoustic performance by contemporary visual artists and musicians, set in St Cecilia's Hall in Edinburgh (2008), co-organised the symposium Subject in Process: Feminism and Art (2009), curated the international group exhibition Votive at CCA, Glasgow (2009) in co-operation with Glasgow Museums, and curated the all-women performance event "Urlibido: A Night of Magic" for Glasgow International 2010.

# SOCIAL SCULPTURE

## THE RISE OF THE GLASGOW ART SCENE

### SARAH LOWNDES

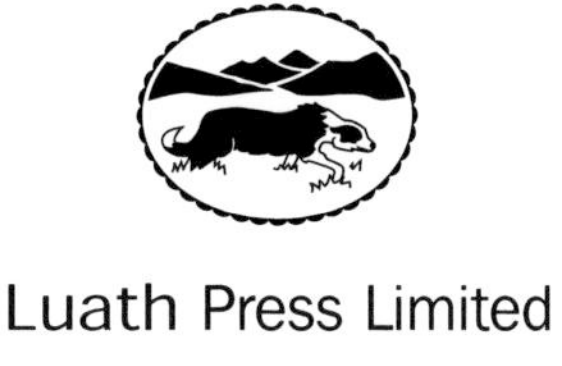

**Luath Press Limited**

EDINBURGH

www.luath.co.uk

First published 2003 by STOPSTOP, Glasgow.
This new revised edition published 2010.
Reprinted 2011, 2012, 2013, 2015, 2016, 2019, 2021, 2024, 2025

ISBN: 978-1-906817-59-6

The paper used in this book is recyclable. It is made
from low chlorine pulps produced in a low energy,
low emissions manner from renewable forests.

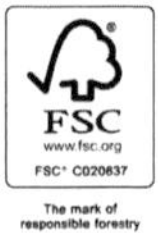 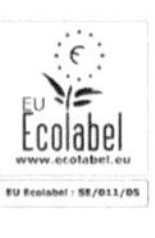 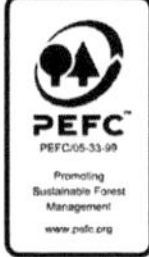

Printed and bound by
Robertson Printers, Forfar




Front cover image: Richard Wright, installing No Title
(2009), The Turner Prize, Tate Britain, 2009.
Photograph: Arthur Lambert, reproduced courtesy of
Richard Wright.

Back cover image: Cathy Wilkes, (installation detail),
I Give You All My Money, The Turner Prize, Tate Britain,
London, 2008. Photograph: Andy Keate, reproduced
courtesy of The Modern Institute / Toby Webster Ltd.

# CONTENTS

# ACKNOWLEDGEMENTS

I am very grateful to Gavin MacDougall at Luath Press for giving me this great opportunity to revisit *Social Sculpture* some seven years after it was first published, and to bring a revised and updated version of the book back into print. My thanks go also to Leila Cruickshank and Tom Bee at Luath Press for their sensitive redesign of the previous edition.

Much of the evidence for this history has been gathered from interviews with members of the local art and music communities. Heartfelt thanks are due to the following individuals, who generously gave their time to be interviewed or responded in writing to questions during the course of my research, either back in 2001–2002 or during my more recent round of interviews in 2009–2010. Some of these people consented to being interviewed during both rounds of interviews – and they deserve especial thanks for their generosity.

Sam Ainsley, Christine Borland, Martin Boyce, Will Bradley, Stuart Braithwaite, Katrina Brown, Adrian Burns, Lucy Byatt, Amanda Catto, Billy Clark, David Cook, Anne-Marie Copestake, Pat Crook, Sorcha Dallas, Kathryn Elkin, Charles Esche, Patricia Fleming, Luke Fowler, Mark Francis, Alex Frost, Douglas Gordon, Rebecca Gordon-Nesbitt, Marianne Greated, Colin Hardie, David Harding, Simon Herbert, Alexia Holt, M.P. Lancaster, Tom Laurie, Keith McIvor, Francis McKee, Graham McKenzie, Lucy McKenzie, Aidan Moffat, Alexander Moffat, Mutley, Scott Myles, Mark O'Neill, Tom O'Sullivan, Toby Paterson, Adele Patrick, Neil Robertson, Hannah Robinson, Louise Shelley, Jens Strandberg, Craig Tannock, Joanne Tatham, James Thornhill, Hayley Tompkins, Tom Varley, Toby Webster, Nicola White, Cathy Wilkes, Michael Wilkinson, John Williamson and Sinead Young.

I would also like to thank the following people, who have given me advice, encouragement, information, and/or loaned images and memorabilia:

Jane Allen, Kitty Anderson, Giles Bailey, Alice Bain, Marc Baines, Bridget Baird, Rosslyn Baird, Nerea Bello, Jon Bewley, Karla Black, Simon Bolton, Jorn Botnagel, Sheelagh Boyce, Ross Birrell, Fiona Bradley, Martin Clark, Miranda Cameron, Caroline and Justin Carter, John and Anne Claudet, Nathan Coley, April Crichton, Paola Cumiskey, Jeremy Cutler, Abraham Cruzvillegas, Kate Davis, Thea Djordjadze, Alan Dimmick, Chris Evans, Anna Johnston, Stevie Jones, Alhena Katsof, Torsten Lauschmann, Leigh Ferguson, Dan Fox, Rosalind Furness, Bill Gillham, Kirsty Gordon, Robert Dallas Gray, Melissa Gronlund, Andrew Hamilton, Keith Hartley, Jennifer Higgie, Robert Hubbert, Florence and Richard Ingleby, Vassiliki Kolocotroni, Tom Lawson, Torsten Lauschmann, Camilla Low, Dominic Lowndes, Joan Lowndes, Michael Lowndes, Peter Lowndes, Peter McArthur, Peter McCaughey, Ray McKenzie, Anna McLaughlan, Bruce McLean, Andrew Miller, Susan Morgan, Garry Morrison, Shelly Nadashi, Ken Neil, Paul Nesbitt, Katie Nicoll, Elizabeth O'Brien, Kay Pallister, Fred Pedersen, Gillian Purvis, Yvonne Quirmbach, Andreas Reihse, Gordon Robertson, Derek and Isabel Roberts, Julie Roberts, Gordon Robertson, Kath Roper-Caldbeck, Wouter Rummens, Vicky Rutherford, Claire and Danny Saunders, David Shrigley, Ross Sinclair, Polly Staple, Sally Swadell, Tony Swain, Finbarr Taylor, Sue Tompkins, Esther and Paul Thomson, Rob Tuffnell, Mark Vernon, Beata Veszely, Rebecca Wilcox, Jonnie Wilkes, Jill Wilson, Lorraine Wilson, Caroline Woodley, Ealan Wingate, Annie Wright, Bill Wright, Dominic Wright, Graham Wright, Helga Wright, Robin Wright and Stuart Wright.

I would also like to thank my colleagues and students in the Historical and Critical Studies Department at Glasgow School of Art who have been a frequent source of inspiration.

Most of all I want to thank my husband, Richard Wright, who has constantly encouraged and supported me throughout the two writings of this book. I would like to dedicate this book to you and to our daughter Violet and our son Raymond.

This book is a social history, which charts the emergence of performance and conceptual-related practice in Glasgow from the early 1970s onwards. The '70s saw the collapse of Scotland's industrial infrastructure and soaring unemployment, and ended with the failure of the first referendum on Scots devolution and the start of eighteen years of Tory rule in Scotland in 1979. The '70s, however, were also the point at which an undeniable upsurge in grassroots activity in the areas of theatre, literature, art and music production was also occurring in Glasgow. Although this history covers the work of both public institutions and grassroots arts initiatives, the emphasis throughout is on artist-led projects, and in particular, on the under-documented ephemeral projects and events that have done so much to bolster the Glasgow art scene.

During the mid-1980s the Glasgow art scene began to attract significant critical attention for the first time since the early twentieth century work of the first Glasgow Boys and Charles Rennie Mackintosh. The work of the Glasgow-based New Image painters Steven Campbell, Ken Currie, Peter Howson and Adrian Wiszniewski, who came to prominence during this time, has been substantially documented in a number of publications. By contrast, at the time that the first edition of *Social Sculpture* was published in 2003, no comprehensive analysis of the emergence of neo-conceptual practice in Glasgow in the late '80s and early '90s had yet been published, although several excellent catalogues and monographs did exist at that time on the work of individual artists such as 1996 Turner Prize winner Douglas Gordon and 1997 Turner Prize nominee Christine Borland. Since the early '90s a different approach to making work had been apparent in the practice of another generation of Glasgow-based artists like Jim Lambie, David Shrigley, Richard Wright and Cathy Wilkes – yet by 2003 still no sustained critical attention had been given to the connections between the artists, nor to the social context in which their work had developed. I wrote the first edition of Social Sculpture partly in response to existing histories of Scottish art, which tended to focus on the more traditional work of earlier generations of Scottish artists. This was the case with Duncan MacMillan's survey text Scottish Art in the 20th Century 1890–2001, which was described as "definitive" by Maria Vaizey in The Times but devoted just three pages to a very brief analysis of neo-conceptual art in Scotland. Similarly, Murdo Macdonald's otherwise comprehensive Scottish Art (2000) made only brief reference to four of the artists making neo-conceptual work in Scotland in the early '90s: Christine Borland, Douglas Gordon, Callum Innes and Ross Sinclair. Neither of these texts provided a sufficiently detailed or balanced account of the work that had emerged in the last twenty years in Scotland, which was something that the first edition of Social Sculpture aimed to redress.

Up until ten years ago, catalogues and monographs relating to the recent work of Glasgow-based artists were mainly funded by institutions outside Glasgow, and most often, outside the UK. Amongst the few critical texts published relating to the Glasgow art scene in the '90s were catalogues for group shows such as New Art in Scotland, Glasgow and Nettverk Glasgow.[1] Extended texts on the subject were few but included an unpublished collection of essays by artists, curators and critics commissioned by Transmission in the mid-'90s, as the first stage in attempting to compile a history of the city's first artist-run gallery.[2] Other key texts included Rebecca Gordon Nesbitt's MA thesis for The Courtauld Institute, When Bad Men Conspire, Good Men Should Associate, Transmission Gallery,

---

1   Held at CCA, Glasgow (1994), the Kunsthalle, Bern (1997) and the Museet for Samtidskunst, Oslo (1998) respectively.
2   Excerpts from this collection of essays in this text are identified by the phrase "unpublished essay on Transmission, 1995".

*Glasgow. 1983–1995* and *Glasgow: A Presentation of the Art Scene in the '90s* (1997) by Oslo based critic and curator Kari J. Brandtzaeg. Around 2001, a number of UK based institutions began to publish books relating to the Scottish contemporary art scene, perhaps the most notable of which have been the catalogue for Katrina Brown and Rob Tuffnell's Scottish art survey show, *Here and Now* (2001),[3] the long-awaited *Transmission* book (2002)[4] and *Justified Sinners: an archaeology of Scottish counter-culture (1960–2000)* (2002).[5] All of these texts were extremely useful in my attempt to build a comprehensive overview of the busy thirty-year period covered by the first edition of this book.

However, the attempt to trace the key emergent trends of Glasgow's recent contemporary art scene was both aided and complicated by the presence of these existing histories. In an effort to avoid replicating existing texts, I gathered new interview material from a wide range of individuals with specialist knowledge of Glasgow's key contemporary arts organisations, few of whom had been consulted for earlier texts on the subject. As the art being produced in Glasgow since the early '70s had been increasingly influenced by the parallel growth of the grassroots music scene in the city, I also interviewed a number of people involved in the network of local independent labels, live music venues, nightclubs and musicians' co-operatives. In order to balance the evidence of the city's artists and musicians within a wider framework, a number of professionals involved in curating, criticism or funding of the arts were also inter-viewed. To produce this new revised edition, I interviewed those artists, musicians and art professionals whom I considered to be best placed to give an inside account of how the Glasgow art scene has developed and changed in the last seven years.

As I have been updating the book to reflect the developments of the last seven years, it has been very gratifying to realise how many more excellent publications now exist on the work of Glasgow-based artists such as Karla Black, Martin Boyce, Luke Fowler, Alex Frost, Toby Paterson,

---

3   Katrina Brown and Rob Tuffnell, ed.s, Dundee Contemporary Arts, Dundee, 2001.
4   Anna McLaughlan and Claire Stephenson, ed.s, Black Dog Publishing, London, 2002.
5   Alec Finlay and Ross Birrell, ed.s, Pocketbooks, Edinburgh, 2002.

Tony Swain, Joanne Tatham and Tom O'Sullivan, Cathy Wilkes and Richard Wright. These magazine and journal articles, catalogues and monographs are an endorsement of the quality of their work, but are also indicative of something else – which is the transition the Glasgow art scene has made, from "emergent" in the '80s and '90s to "established" as it has been for the last decade. The recent exceptional media interest in the Glasgow scene has partly stemmed from the success of people associated with the Glasgow scene, such as Franz Ferdinand, who in the first edition of *Social Sculpture* were referred to only as "local 'kraut disco' band Franz Ferdinand", but who just a few months later became international stars when their second single, *Take Me Out* (2004) was released. Between 2005 and 2009 six Glasgow-based artists have been nominated for The Turner Prize, and two have won – Simon Starling in 2005, and Richard Wright in 2009.[6] Between 2000 and 2006, when Beck's Futures ended, no fewer than thirteen Glasgow-based artists were nominated for the prize, and three won – Roderick Buchanan (2000), Toby Paterson (2002) and Rosalind Nashashibi (2003).[7] In 2008, Glasgow-based artist-film makers and colleagues Duncan Campbell and Luke Fowler were both nominated for the inaugural Derek Jarman Prize, which Fowler went on to win. The 2003 launch of the Scotland Pavilion at the Venice Biennale has been followed in 2005, 2007 and 2009 with exhibitions of work that have been largely by Glasgow-based artists and for the most part, critically acclaimed. Meanwhile, Glasgow International has grown from a small event sustained by the goodwill of the local art community when it launched in 2005, to an ambitious and highly anticipated festival, described by *The Guardian* as "the UK's best annual visual arts festival."[8] All of these things combined have increased dramatically the degree to which Glasgow is now regarded as occupying an important position in the international art scene.

6    The six artists were: Jim Lambie, Simon Starling (both 2005), Nathan Coley (2007), Cathy Wilkes (2008), Lucy Skaer and Richard Wright (both 2009). Simon Starling now lives and works in Copenhagen.

7    The thirteen artists were: Roderick Buchanan, Lucy McKenzie, Cathy Wilkes, Martin Boyce, David Shrigley (all 2000), Toby Paterson (2002), Rosalind Nashashibi, Alan Currall, David Sherry, Lucy Skaer (all 2003), Hayley Tompkins (2004), Luke Fowler (2005) and Sue Tompkins (2006).

8    "What to see in 2010", *The Guardian*, 31st December 2009, http://www.guardian.co.uk/culture/2009/dec/31/what-to-see-in-2010.

There have also been notable increases in the range of venues, galleries, studio complexes, commissioning bodies and institutional support that have emerged in Glasgow over the last seven years. Although for many years the scene that emanated from Transmission, the city's oldest artist-led gallery, went about its business largely unremarked and (in the opinions of some) unsupported, that situation has gone about a sea-change in recent years, with Transmission (along with other arts organisations such as Street Level Photoworks, Glasgow Print Studio, Glasgow Independent Studio and Project Room, and Glasgow Media Access Centre (GMAC)) being incorporated into the mainly Glasgow City Council and Culture and Sport Glasgow funded Trongate 103 arts centre. When the city's Gallery of Modern Art (GoMA) opened in 1996, works by Glasgow-based "post-conceptual" artists such as Douglas Gordon and Christine Borland were notable by their absence – yet in the last decade their work, plus those of contemporaries including Toby Paterson and Graham Fagen, has been acquired by the GoMA.

Many of the individuals and organisations described in the first edition of this book were distinguished by their active determination to forge links with other artists and musicians and artist-led organisations outside Glasgow. The lack of consistent institutional and media support for the work being made in Glasgow up until the late '90s helped to create a uniquely resistant strain of cultural activity that was supported by a network of outside alliances. Until the late '90s the lack of a defined commercial market was another of the city's key characteristics, which undoubtedly influenced the nature of the music and art that is made here and the non-profit organisations that showed and distributed the work. Much of the most notable work that has emerged from the predominantly self-organised and autonomous arts infrastructure in the city since the early '90s has been deliberately non-permanent, short term and ephemeral. It happened in one-room galleries in tenement flats, in stairwells, on bits of wasteground, on rooftops, down alleyways, in derelict buildings. Much of this most interesting work has been, both literally and metaphorically, made in a corner – but the corner provides possibilities as well as limitations. As Gaston Bachelard noted in *The Poetics of Space* (1958), "The corner is a sort of half-box, part walls, part door. It will serve as an illustration for the dialectics of inside and outside…"[9]

The establishment of The Modern Institute by Will Bradley, Charles Esche and Toby Webster in 1998 has been followed more recently by the young commercial galleries Sorcha Dallas and Mary Mary, and the emergence of artist-led projects such as Market, Lowsalt, SWG3, Dias, Southside Studios and Gallery, Washington Garcia and The Duchy, but Glasgow remains a city in which many artists make work that they do not expect to sell. However, the relative absence of a commercial scene has also allowed the development of an art scene built with an economy of means and materials, and this "make do and mend" approach has stood the city's artists in good stead, particularly during the recent economic crisis. Despite the significant recent changes in Glasgow's international profile, the city still lacks the established infrastructure and opportunities of a major centre like New York or London. Collectors of contemporary art in Glasgow are few, and the city certainly has no equal to London gallerist Charles Saatchi, who is often credited with creating much of the hype around the young British artists (yBas) in the early '90s. Likewise, no major record label has a headquarters in Glasgow, although numerous independent labels, such as Chemikal Underground and Rock Action, sustain operations here. The combination of social co-operation and interest in process-based practices that characterise the Glasgow art scene helped to shield the city's artists from the collapse of the art market in autumn 2008, simply because most of them were never in it for the money in the first place.

Although many of the grassroots projects that take place in the city are only seen by a small number of people, the impact of such projects resonates more widely, either through reports in specialist journals, websites or of course, the less easily traced "trickle down" effect such initiatives can have on other artists and musicians. The recent advent of digital technologies and Web 2.0 platforms such as YouTube, MySpace,

---

9   Gaston Bachelard, *The Poetics of Space* (1958), this edition (Boston Massachusetts: The Beacon Press, 1994), p.137. Some of my observations in this paragraph appear in a modified version in an essay I wrote for Public Art Scotland (PAR +RS), entitled "I Am the Space Where I Am" (2010).

Vimeo, Flickr, Wordpress and Facebook has made it possible for artists and musicians to reach much wider audiences and at far greater speed, and can be viewed as descendants of open access forms such as demos recorded on cassette and photocopied fanzines. Perhaps ironically, the increased collaborative and distribution possibilities brought by these innovations could be said to have been most revolutionary for artists whose work is engaged not with virtual reality but with social reality – as it is now far easier, faster and less expensive to share documentation and to publicise events than at any other point in history.[10] The psycho-geography of Glasgow, of particular galleries, studios, bars and clubs now extends internationally, through personal recommendations and mutual interest, through global internet and media networks, to galleries, venues, studios and bedrooms across the world. This text is an attempt to document that evolving conversation across disciplines, what Joseph Beuys called "social sculpture".

10 Again, some of my observations in this paragraph appear in a modified version in an essay I wrote for Public Art Scotland (PAR +RS), entitled "I Am the Space Where I Am" (2010).

# CHAPTER 1

# IMAGINING GLASGOW
## (1855–1970)

Glasgow grew from a small town to a polluted, overcrowded metropolis in the space of a hundred years.[1] The speed of that expansion, fuelled by the city's advantageous position on the shores of the river Clyde, set in place the many oppositions that have subsequently informed the unique character of the city. As the Clyde flowed westwards towards America, it provided a highly profitable trade route for the passage of tobacco, sugar and cotton after the Union of the Crowns (1707) and the removal of the English Navigation Laws. The enormous wealth generated by this new transatlantic trade opened up one of the key divisions of the city: that between the rich and the poor. The wealth of the city was concentrated close to the river, in the Trongate in the East End, where the University was located, and where all the goods that were brought into Glasgow were weighed and taxed. The merchant class in the city were largely Protestant, resulting in a long-running association between fiscal power and religious orientation in Glasgow.

The economic and ideological domination of the merchant class in Glasgow in the 18th century is perhaps most visible in the many buildings in the city which physically consolidated their position.[2] This is most obviously seen in the Necropolis at the East End, where various elaborate tombs and monuments to Glasgow merchants are located on a hillside overlooking the city. The tallest statue in the graveyard, of the 16th century

---

1   In 1800 the city's population was estimated at 77,000 – by 1900 this had increased tenfold to 762,000.
2   The Merchant City area of Glasgow contains many mansions built for tobacco lords, while several city centre street names (Virginia Street, Jamaica Street, etc.) also point to the source of the city's 18th century prosperity.

religious reformer John Knox, was erected at the highest point in the Necropolis, and at public expense, in 1832. It has often been said that Knox and Mary Queen of Scots are the two figures who define the extremes of Scotland's religious history, but in Glasgow it is Knox who presides over the skyline, and there is no comparable statue of the Stuart queen. Glasgow has also been the focal point of the Scottish Orange Order since 1872, when a walk of 1,500 people took place there to commemorate Protestant victory in the 1690 Battle of the Boyne.

The existing divisions between wealthier Protestant and poorer Catholic communities in Glasgow increased dramatically as the Industrial Revolution brought new industries and new settlers to the city. By the late 19th century the city's population had swelled enormously, mainly due to the massive influx of settlers displaced by the Highland Clearances and the Irish Potato Famine. The majority of the first Irish settlers were Catholic, and worked mainly as sweated labour in the new industries – textiles, chemical and dyeing works – and as casual construction workers and dock labourers. The smaller (and more easily assimilated) community of Protestant Irish immigrant workers were more concentrated in the textile trades and later in engineering and shipbuilding. The influx of Catholic communities into the city contributed to a marked increase in the number of Protestants joining Orange Lodges in Glasgow during the 19th century, and in 1875 there was a great public meeting at the City Hall to protest against Vaticanism. The different trades of the two Irish settlers groups led to the formation of specifically "Protestant" areas in the city such as Govan and "Catholic" areas like the Saltmarket, which compounded the divisions between these rival religious communities.

As rapid industrialisation pushed the monied classes westwards into less polluted and overcrowded areas of the city, many entrepreneurial Catholic immigrants set up East End businesses as second-hand dealers, grocers, pawnbrokers, publicans and as proprietors of lodging houses and betting shops. Most of the inns, taverns and shebeens around the Bridgegate, Saltmarket and Gallowgate were Catholic-run. The passing of the Forbes Mackenzie Act in 1855, which closed Scotland's pubs on Sundays and introduced 11pm closing times, encouraged the growth of these illicit drinking dens. The late-night singing and dancing contests held at these establishments, however, offended the sensibilities of some Glaswegians. As one resident of the Calton district remarked in the 1880s, "The less we had to do with them the better. Their religion was not our religion, which was the best; and their customs were different from ours, as was their speech. Doubtless there were good folk among them, but the unruly and turbulent ones showed us what we might become if we did not keep to our own people."[3] The existing discrepancy between different regions of the city widened when in 1880 the Town Council decided to exclude pubs from new streets formed in connection with the City Improvement Act – a ruling which was applauded by The Scottish Temperance League. The rivalry of the Protestant and Catholic communities then polarised further in the late 19th century around support for two rival football teams: Rangers (established 1872) and Celtic (established 1888).[4] By the late 19th century, then, the key oppositions which would govern the unstable character of Glasgow were in place: wealth/poverty, Protestant/Catholic and temperance/dissolution.

The influx of Jewish settlers[5] from Russia, Poland, Lithuania and Hungary during the 19th century also contributed to another notable change in the cultural climate of the city, especially in the areas of the Gorbals and Shawlands, on the South side of the city. European-style bakeries and delicatessens opened in these neighbourhoods, and there was also a notable rise in public entertainments. Between 1862 and the outbreak of the Great War, 18 major theatres were built in Glasgow to satisfy demand.[6] The Scotia Music Hall on Stockwell Street presented *"mesmeric manifestations, freakshows and musical entertainments"*, while at Brittania Music Hall on the Trongate ventriloquists and hypnotists were amongst the most popular attractions. The first recorded Italian settlers,

---

3   Quoted in I.G.C. Hutchison, "Politics and Society in Mid-Victorian Glasgow, 1846–1886", unpublished PhD thesis, University of Edinburgh, 1974, pp.485–6.
4   A third team, Partick Thistle FC (established 1868), known as "the friendly team", represent neither religious group.
5   The first recorded Jewish settlers in Glasgow had arrived in the 1810s and in 1879 the first purpose-built synagogue in Scotland was built on the corner of Hill Street and Garnet Street, in Garnethill.
6   Four of these theatres still remain – The King's, The Pavilion, The Theatre Royal and the Royal Princess, known since 1945 as the Citizen's Theatre.

from the areas of Barga and Piscinisco, arrived in Glasgow at the end of the 19th century, and also quickly made a visible impact upon the city, as Glasgow-based writer and curator Francis McKee relates:

"In the mid-nineteenth century, Italian immigrants introduced ice cream as a street food to Glasgow. By the late nineteenth and early twentieth century, they graduated from rudimentary shops in slum quarters to more luxurious establishments in the city centre. At this time, Glasgow, a city which had for so long accepted the stricture of Presbyterianism, was beginning to enjoy itself. Both its prosperous middle-classes and its large workforce were seeking new entertainments – cinemas were opening, music-halls and dance-halls flourished. The conservative forces that controlled the city were made anxious by this growing entertainment industry. For them, the Italian ice cream shops epitomised the evil of luxury being smuggled into the soul of Glaswegians. The Italians were very obviously Roman Catholics, 'aliens' or foreigners, Sunday traders, and finally, they were purveyors of ice cream. When all these attributes were linked to the sale of something so obviously luxurious, unnecessary, and ephemeral as ice cream the forces of conservatism had found the embodiment of all they had feared."[7]

Glasgow was also a city of marked architectural contrasts. Unlike Scotland's capital city of Edinburgh, which lay 50 miles to the East and had recently imposed a pattern of architectural uniformity,[8] Glasgow's architecture even in this age of prosperity continued to reflect the rapid growth of the city, and the range of standards of living amongst different communities. This is not to suggest that rebuilding did not take place – in fact the Age of Improvement[9] had been so zealous that only four pre-18th century buildings were left standing.[10] Among the many architectural casualties

---

7   "Ice Cream and Immorality", by Francis McKee, Oxford Symposium on Food and Cookery: Public Eating, London, 1992, quoted in Women on Art, CCA, Glasgow, 1997.

8   The New Town of Edinburgh, laid out according to an award winning 1766 design by James Craig, had subsequently earned the city the title "The Athens of the North".

9   Between 1870 and the outbreak of the First World War, Glasgow was considered to be a model of how a modern industrial city should operate – boasting more open spaces and parkland than any other European city of comparable size, and a municipal water, gas, tram and telephone system.

10  Glasgow Cathedral, built between the 12th and 15th centuries, 15th century Provand's Lordship, and the 17th-century Tolbooth and Merchant's Hospital Steeple.

was the 16th century University near the High Street, which was demolished after the North British Railway Company made an offer for the land. By 1870 the new Gothic style university campus had opened in the West End, consolidating the general move westwards, away from the traditional city centre of the High Street and Trongate. Around this time the worst slum areas were cleared and numerous ostentatious buildings were commissioned for the city centre and West End, several of which were the handiwork of Glasgow-based architect Alexander 'Greek' Thomson (1817-1875), who incorporated motifs drawn from Egyptian, Greek and Roman architecture into his imaginative buildings. Other noted highlights of Glasgow's ambitious nineteenth-century architecture include the Parisian-style Charing Cross Mansions (1891) and the elaborate brickwork of Templeton's Carpet Factory (1889) which was inspired by the Doge's Palace in Venice.

Cultural provision in the city during this period was greatly enhanced by the establishment of the first municipal art gallery in Britain, McLellan Galleries, on Sauchiehall Street in 1856, followed by the establishment of the People's Palace Museum on Glasgow Green in 1898, to collect and exhibit artefacts of local cultural history. In 1901 the Kelvingrove Art Gallery and Museum was erected close to the University in the West End. The building, which was funded from the proceeds of Glasgow's second Great Exhibition in 1888, featured two massive towers derived from those of the Cathedral of Santiago de Compostela, while the steep angle of the roof resembles a Gothic town hall such as those found in Northern Europe. The holdings of Scottish contemporary art held in these public collections were dominated by the work of the "Glasgow Boys", a group of artists including George Henry (1858–1943), John Lavery (1856–1941), James Guthrie (1859–1930) and Edward Atkinson Hornel (1864–1933) who painted primarily landscapes and portraits. These artists were influenced by the loose style, bright colours and open-air painting favoured by their French contemporaries Matisse and Derain, and by the work of American born painter James Abott McNeill Whistler (1834–1903). Whistler's portrait of Thomas Carlyle was acquired by Glasgow's municipal collection in 1891, and his interest in Japanese culture would influence the work of both

Guthrie and Hornel, who undertook a trip to Japan subsidised by influential Glasgow art dealer Alexander Reid (1854–1924) and shipyard owner and art collector William Burrell.

The work of the Glasgow Boys, which looked to Europe and the Far East for inspiration, ushered in a new movement in Scottish art that would have lasting international significance. Glasgow School of Art graduates Charles Rennie Mackintosh (1868–1928) and Herbert McNair (1870–1945) and their respective wives, the sisters Margaret (1865–1933) and Frances Macdonald (1874–1921) were collectively known as "The Four". Their work drew on a blend of Celtic iconography, Japanese forms and curvilinear Art Nouveau design for inspiration. However, works associated with the group could be distinguished from those of most other European fine artists and designers by their use of clean vertical lines, attention to scale and use of modern materials – an influence possibly drawn from the local shipbuilding industry. Mackintosh, McNair and the Macdonald sisters worked in a variety of mediums, ranging from illustrations for books and magazines to decorative panels, furniture and wrought iron pieces. Mackintosh's architectural commissions, which fused the disparate traditions of Scottish baronial architecture, Italian Renaissance styles and Japanese influences, remain the most influential work associated with the group.[11]

Gleeson White, editor of the London-based periodical *The Studio* saw the group's work in London in 1890, where it was included in that year's Arts and Crafts Exhibition. In the article which helped to establish the reputation of The Glasgow Four, Gleeson wrote "Probably nothing in the gallery has provoked more decided censure than these works, and that fact alone should cause a thoughtful observer of art to pause before he joins the opponents." Gleeson continued perceptively, "The probability would seem to be that those who laugh at them today will be eager to eulogize them a few years hence."[12] Mackintosh subsequently received a number of important commissions, notably for the new Glasgow School of Art

---

11 "The Four" also inspired a younger generation of mainly female graphic and applied artists at Glasgow School of Art, who became known as the Glasgow Girls, among them Jessie M. King (1875–1949), Katherine Cameron (1874–1965) and Jessie Newbery (1864–1948).

12 Gleeson White, from the series Some Glasgow Designers, The Studio, London, 1896–7.

building on Renfrew Street (1897) and for Kate Cranston's famous Tearooms.[13] In 1899 Mackintosh was invited to exhibit at the Venice Biennale, and the following year both he and Margaret Macdonald were invited to exhibit with the Secessionists[14] in Vienna. After winning second prize in a German publisher's competition to design a "House for an Art Lover" in 1901, he exhibited in Turin (1902) and designed the Hill House at Helensburgh (1902) for the family of the publisher Walter Blackie. Over the next decade Mackintosh continued to exhibit throughout Europe and became particularly influential in Vienna and Germany, but he was constantly frustrated by the lukewarm reception to his work in Britain.[15]

## SHIPBUILDING AND POLITICAL PROTEST

The phrase "the Clyde made Glasgow and Glasgow made the Clyde" dates from the turn of the century, when the river was artificially widened and deepened to allow for the passage of larger vessels. "There is now a deep artificial channel which will take ships of the deepest draught, great ocean-going liners. It is now spanned by bridges of steel and grey granite. We are now in the heart of the industrial world; not just the mercantile, commercial, industrial metropolis that is Glasgow, but at the heart of industry itself, for in this spot was cradled the great movement, the Industrial Revolution, which transformed the face of the World."[16] Between 1870 and 1914 the Clyde shipyards built 18% of the world's steamships. Shipbuilding would generate the greatest wealth of all the new industries

13  The Glasgow and West of Scotland Temperance Society had opened its first temperance coffee house in 1832, under the aegis of publisher William Collins. Glasgow businesswoman Kate Cranston was a enthusiastic supporter of the Temperance movement and aimed to elevate the aesthetics of the temperance coffee house in her numerous Miss Cranston's Tea Rooms. Between 1897 and 1910 she commissioned Mackintosh to design a number of tea rooms in Glasgow, including the Buchanan Street Tea Rooms and the Willow Tea Room.

14  The association of Austrian Artists Vienna Secession was established in 1897 as an alternative to the conservative art establishment in the city by a group of artists and architects including Gustav Klimt.

15  In 1913 Mackintosh left the Glasgow architectural firm of Honeyman and Keppie, where he had worked since 1890, to devote himself to painting. He pursued an itinerant lifestyle in Walberswick, London and Port Vendres, France (where he produced a series of remarkable oil paintings and watercolours of the local landscape). Mackintosh had been a heavy drinker for most of his adult life, but his alcoholism worsened towards the end of his career. He was never able to realise plans drawn up in the 1920s for a theatre and died of cancer of the mouth in London in 1928.

16  Archie Hind, *The Dear Green Place*, New Authors Ltd., Glasgow, 1966, p12.

and make the most lasting impression on the city's identity. However, almost from its inception the success of the industry rested upon the exploitation of the shipyard workers, who laboured long hours with terrible pay and conditions. These problems intensified when the outbreak of World War I brought a deluge of orders[17] to the new European centre of Allied shipping.

This period of great activity on the Clyde was also the first period of unified political protest by the working classes in Glasgow.[18] The sudden immigration of thousands of munitions, steel and shipyard workers into the city strained the already over-stretched housing supplies on Clydeside, in the areas of Partick, Govan, Ibrox, Whiteinch, Shettleston, Clydebank, Dalmuir, Greenock and Port Glasgow. Social problems in these over-crowded areas intensified as landlords began neglecting repairs and improvements to properties while demanding inflated rents which aged tenants and the wives and children of soldiers[19] struggled to meet. The Glasgow Association for Women's Suffrage had been founded in 1913, and local women involved in the Votes for Women campaign,[20] such as Helen Waddell and members of the Labour Party, were quick to lend support to the beleaguered tenants. In February 1915 The Glasgow Women's Housing Association was formed to lobby against rent increases and in favour of municipal housing. Public meetings built support for tenants threatened with eviction and placards and billboards stating "we are not removing" forced home the message of resistance. By the end of 1915 the rent strike by 25,000, mainly women, tenants had successfully forced a state-imposed freeze on house rents.

The success of the Rent Strikes lent momentum to widespread unrest amongst the local workers, and the period later known as "Red Clydeside".

---

17  Between June 1913 and June 1914 6.9 million tons of shipping passed through the harbour. At the outbreak of WWI, 70,000 men worked on the Clyde.

18  James Keir Hardie (1856–1915) who became the first Independent Labour MP in 1892 and later the first leader of the Labour Party, was born in Lanarkshire but spent part of his childhood living in the Partick area of Glasgow, where he worked as a baker's delivery boy. In 1867 he moved back to Lanarkshire where he worked as a miner for thirteen years, before becoming increasingly involved in journalism and politics. Keir Hardie was a self-educated man and a committed pacifist, who worked tirelessly in his attempts to secure "Votes for Women and Socialism for All".

19  30,000 Glaswegian men volunteered for service in 1914 – by the end of the war 20,000 of them had been killed in action.

20  Women over 30 were given the vote in Britain in 1918, but another decade passed before women over 21 could participate in elections.

Sporadic industrial strikes took place from 1915 onwards, but it was January 1919 before the Scottish Trade Union Congress (TUC) and Clyde Workers Committee called for a forty-hour week with no loss of pay.[21] On January 31st, socialist leaders Emanuel Shinwell, James Maxton, Harry McShane and John McLean[22] joined 60,000 workers in Scotland's first mass picket, and 100,000 demonstrated in George Square as the red flag was raised. The government sent in troops and tanks to forcibly restore state control. In the wake of "Bloody Friday" widespread dissatisfaction with pay and working conditions rumbled on, intensifying once post-war orders to replenish ship supplies had been met. The post-war depression in the shipbuilding industry led to widespread unemployment and in 1921 John McLean led a march on the City Chambers by thousands of unemployed Glaswegians, one of many public protests that took place in the city in the years leading to the General Strike of 1926.

During the early 1920s a number of important union mergers took place, resulting in the emergence of the Transport and General Workers Union, the National Union of General and Municipal workers, and the Amalgamated Engineering Union. The TUC established itself at the head of the unions, and helped to co-ordinate a series of protests over wage cuts and job losses – between 1919 and 1925 nearly 28 million man-days were taken in strikes or lockouts. When in 1925 the Conservative Prime Minister Stanley Baldwin stated that generalised wage reductions were the only way to inject new life into the mining industry, workers from many other industries decided to come out in support of the miners. The government backed down, offering mine owners a subsidy to avoid wage cuts on 'Red Friday', July 31st 1925. But by mid-April the subsidy had run out and the mine owners announced wage cuts or lockouts starting on May 1st.

The TUC then called a nine day national strike, co-ordinated into two waves: transport, printing, iron and steel, metal and heavy chemicals workers were to go on strike on May 3rd; engineering and shipyard workers a week later. On May 4th 1926, dozens of pipe, brass and flute

---

21  A 54 hour working week was the norm at this time, although a 47 hour week was eventually negotiated.

22  John McLean (1879–1923) was a revolutionary socialist and nationalist. He was a committed supporter of the Russian Revolution, and in February 1918 Lenin appointed him the first Scottish consul to the new Bolshevik government in Russia.

bands led a huge May Day procession to Glasgow Green.[23] Just as the second wave of workers was called out, however, the TUC General Council resolved to end the strike, without having won any concessions from the government. In the aftermath of the strike employers imposed returns to work on their own terms and union members returning to work in the docks, engineering, transport and other industries had to sign "good behaviour" pledges. The government reacted to the General Strike by introducing punitive new legislation in the form of the Trade Disputes Act (1927), which curtailed picketing rights. Large numbers of the unemployed were struck off benefit on the pretext they were not "genuinely seeking work"[24] and trade union activity declined over the next few years. The history of political protest in the city would form another key aspect to Glasgow's cultural identity – which would later be consolidated by the actions of anti-nuclear protestors, striking shipyard workers, anti-Thatcher demonstrators and peace lobbies.

The Depression reached Britain within months of the 1929 Wall St Crash, but the effects of the economic downturn were more localised in Britain than in America, where most states and industries were affected. In Britain the hardest-hit areas were the coalfields of the Midlands and Wales and the ports and shipyards of the North. The late '20s and early '30s were a time of intense social deprivation in many areas of Glasgow, and outbreaks of gang violence now came to public attention as gangs such as the Southside Stickers and the Calton Entry ran pitched battles on the city streets. William McArthur and H. Kingsley Long's 1935 novel *No Mean City* has provided a lasting testament to the widespread hardship of the period preceding the Second World War. "What happens to them aw? They get married and they have kids. An' the wages doesny grow with the family. An' they take to drink a little later instead of sooner. An' the shop shuts or the yard shuts or there's a bliddy strike. An' there they go, back to the dung

---

23  Glasgow Green is perhaps the most famous of Glasgow's 74 public parks. This area of parkland, which lies along the north bank of the Clyde behind the Saltmarket and Trongate was acquired for public use in 1662. Glasgow Green was used for public hangings – between 1814 and 1865 67 men and 5 women were executed there – but was also traditionally used for washing and drying laundry, and for sporting matches of various kinds. As well as being a site for public recreation the Green has long been famous as a meeting place for political marches and rallies.

24  Steven Cherry, *Our History*, University of East Anglia, Norwich, 1981, p76.

heap, haudin' up the street corners, drawin' their money from the parish, an' keepin' awa oot the hoose all day, awa frae the old wife's tongue and the kids that go crawlin' and messin' aroon the floor."[25] Between the wars, the Glasgow Corporation built 50,000 council houses, but still failed to meet the demands of the growing population. In 1927 13% of Glaswegians lived in a "single end" (a one room apartment) and 27% lived three to a room.

## DEPRESSION, DANCE HALLS AND PICTURE PALACES

The increasing gulf between working-class Glaswegians and the city's leisured classes was emphasised when, despite the noticeable slump in the city's post-war economy, the corporation began to make plans for a fifth International Exhibition. Although the first four Exhibitions of 1881, 1888, 1901 and 1911 had taken place in quick succession, a break of twenty-seven years would stretch before the final exhibition was staged at Bellahouston Park in 1938. This exhibition can be seen as the last gasp of Glasgow's years as "the second city of the Empire", when a flurry of modish art deco restaurants, exclusive shops and hotels opened to cater for the influx of exhibition visitors. Amongst the new attractions was the Rogano seafood restaurant at Royal Exchange Square, where the Spanish sherry bar was presided over by Jack, a cocktail expert formerly on the Empress of Britain, and the opulent red and black Beresford Hotel on Sauchiehall Street, named after the cinema magnate W. Beresford Inglis, which came complete with kennels on the roof for the guests' pampered pets.[26]

By the Depression years of the 1930s, Glasgow had over 130 cinemas, more per head of population than any city outside the USA. One of the city's best-loved picture houses was the stylish Cosmo cinema (1939) on Rose Street, which fused '20s-style expressionist brickwork with a Deco-Moderne interior.[27] Probably as a result of the many picturehouses, the

---

25  Arthur McArthur and H. Kingsley Long, *No Mean City*, Longmans, Green, London,1935, p92.
26  Rogano still trades as one of the city's best seafood restaurants, but the Beresford Hotel on Sauchiehall Street has been used in recent years as Strathclyde University's Baird Halls of Residence.
27  Now known as the Glasgow Film Theatre (GFT), it is the only 1930s cinema still in operation in the city.

language and imagery of classic Hollywood cinema has had a palpable effect on the behaviour and speech of Glaswegians. For example, it has been suggested that James Cagney's roles in *Public Enemy* (1931) and *Angels With Dirty Faces* (1938) provided a model for aspiring gangsters in the city.[28] As Michael Munro notes in *The Patter*, his irreverent popular guide to local idioms, "Guy, meaning man or boy is in much greater use in Glasgow than anywhere else in Britain. Perhaps this is an indication of the deep influence of American films, particularly on the generation that grew up in the '30s and '40s."[29]

The outbreak of World War II brought mixed blessings for the city, in that the conflict briefly revived the fortunes of the numerous shipyards while heavy bombing in Clydebank and Greenock in 1941 worsened living conditions in already deprived areas. Although 1,500 people were killed in these attacks, they proved to be isolated, as Glasgow was too far removed from occupied Europe to be a regular enemy target. The harbour was in constant use throughout the war, with two of the most famous Glasgow-built ships, the Queen Mary (1934) and the Queen Elizabeth (1938) carrying over a million troops between them in the years 1943–5. This period of constant industry was captured in the large-scale paintings of English artist Stanley Spencer (1891–1959), who was commissioned by the War Artist's Advisory Committee to produce a series of paintings based on the Lithgow shipyard at Port Glasgow between 1940 and 1947. Unlike Glasgow born artist Muirhead Bone (1876–1953), who produced a series of bold monochrome prints of Clyde cranes in the years preceding and during the Great War, Spencer's large scale paintings concentrated on the human face of shipbuilding. Spencer's compositions were inspired by Italian predellas (altar paintings) and recast the welders and sail menders as semi-religious figures bathed in arcs of industrial light.

Wartime rationing was introduced across the nation in 1940, leading to a black market for "luxury" goods like tea, stockings and chocolate. But

28  This is not to imply a simple causal link between violent films and violent behaviour. The social conditions in Glasgow during the 1930s made outbreaks of street violence almost inevitable – the influence of Cagney and other actors of his generation extended only as far as providing a style in which to perpetrate violent crime.
29  Michael Munro, *The Patter*, Glasgow District Libraries, Glasgow,1985.

despite the real hardships endured by many working-class people in Glasgow, popular entertainments like the eleven big cinemas, nine theatres and ten dance halls in the central city centre strip made Glasgow "one of the hoppingest, skippingest, Pallais Gliding cities in Europe between the wars."[30] By 1946, Glasgow had 93 dance halls, almost three times as many as London per head of population. The Dennistoun Pallais, with a capacity of 1700, was Glasgow's largest dance hall, but Green's Playhouse on Renfrew Street and the Locarno on Sauchiehall Street were two of the most popular places to go. The dancehall was a place where young people could elevate their social standing through their dancing skills alone, which may account for the popularity of the pastime amongst working-class people in the city. Of course, the dance hall was also a place to "see and be seen" and the influence of American movie stars showed itself again in the elaborate costume and grooming of the young dancers. One Glasgow shop-girl remembered, "On Saturday night I went to the dancing. You were working late in the shop so you went straight there … you had your dancing shoes at work with you, and something for your tea. The plaza was nice with the coloured fountains and the wee tables. John and I liked it there. But we went to the F and F Palais in Partick too, and Green's Playhouse, the Locarno, and the Albert … I loved the dancing."[31]

Glaswegian William Brown remembers, "The young ladies stood up one side of the hall and the men stood up the other and at the first beat a' the drum you ran over and got a hold. The procedure for dancing was stereotyped in all dance halls at that time. The lassies took one side of the hall and the aspirants to love took the other side."[32] Dance hall etiquette changed dramatically when American servicemen began introducing risque new steps in the city's dance halls during the Second World War.[33] Before long the tango and the foxtrot were considered old hat, and the resultant craze for jiving and jitterbugging brought by the American GIs consolidated the pattern of young Glaswegians looking to America for the latest fashions.

30  Anna Blair, *More Tea at Miss Cranston's*, Shepheard-Walwyn Ltd. Edinburgh, 1991, p419.
31  Interview with Bunty Angles, Anna Blair, *More Tea at Miss Cranston's*, Ibid.
32  William Brown, interview from the archives of the People's Palace Museum, Glasgow.
33  An estimated 95% of all Americans on leave in Britain during the war came at some time to Glasgow.

In 1941, three damaged bronze statues had been removed from the Kelvingrove Museum and Art Gallery which were later melted down to help the war effort. The figures representing immortality, fame and victory disappeared just as Glasgow's reputation as "workshop of the world" was also on the wane. New trades, new methods of cargo handling, a huge growth in the size of ships and competition from foreign vessels all contributed to the increasing decline of the local shipbuilding industry. In 1942 Sir William Beveridge's report on the need for a comprehensive system of state-sponsored social insurance was published. Beveridge's recommendations for a series of reforms to check the persistent problems of squalor, disease and unemployment which had worsened during the '30s were taken up by Labour candidate Clement Atlee in his post-war election campaign against Churchill. In July 1945 Atlee won a landslide victory, and later the same year implemented the cornerstones of the modern Welfare State – the National Health Service and the National Insurance Act.

However, these social reforms came too late for many Glaswegians. In addition to the significant number of "GI brides" who left the city for new lives in America after the war, whole families of Scots emigrated to America, Canada, Australia and New Zealand from the late '40s onwards. In 1948, 900 people left Glasgow's King George V Dock on the Empire Brent, the first Australia-bound post-war emigrant ship, and by 1949 there were 100,000 UK emigrants in Australia alone. The post-war labour shortages at all levels prompted the British Government to recruit large numbers of workers from the Commonwealth and former Empire in the early '50s. In Glasgow, the presence of these new migrant communities was signalled publicly by the opening of the first mosque in the Gorbals in 1944, and the opening of the city's first Chinese restaurant by Hong Kong-born Mr. Wong Chong on Sauchiehall Street in 1959.


## UNBUILDING

Despite the decline in Glasgow's key industry, the city's population continued to grow, although by 1951 Birmingham had overtaken Glasgow as the second largest city in the UK. In 1946 the Clyde Valley Plan was drawn up to look at possible ways of reducing housing demand in the city, resulting in the now notorious overspill policy. Tenements in poverty-stricken areas of the city like the Gorbals were torn down in the 1950s and '60s, displacing families into the surrounding new towns of East Kilbride, Livingston, Cumbernauld, Glenrothes and Irvine and into peripheral high-rise schemes like Castlemilk, Pollok, Drumchapel and Easterhouse.[34] Most of the new estates were badly designed, lacked community facilities[35] and suffered from problems linked to moving "problem families" en masse. Unemployment, ill health and crime rates were high, and poor transport links increased the sense of isolation felt by many of the residents.

The widespread demolition of the tenements largely removed the style of Glasgow architecture which had been the norm for over a hundred years, although examples of this type of building can still be seen in several areas of the city including Garnethill, Partick, Hillhead and Shawlands. The slum tenements had been overcrowded and insanitary but they had afforded a particularly sociable way of life, with shared communal closes and back greens where children played and neighbours gathered. The Gorbals in particular had been known as a hive of social and cultural activity where workers' theatre and cine movements, music halls, pubs and clubs had flourished. There is some justification for the belief that the forced relocation of much of the inner city population of Glasgow during the '50s and '60s significantly contributed to the 'low' cultural status of the city in the post-war period. This pivotal time in Glasgow's social history was captured in the evocative black and white photographs of Oscar Marzaroli (1933–1988) and the paintings of Joan Eardley (1921–1963), both of whom focussed on slum children in areas like the Gorbals and Castlemilk in the late '50s and early '60s.

English-born Eardley had trained at Goldsmiths in London, before settling in Scotland in 1956 and beginning to use urban areas of Glasgow

---

34 55% of the inner city population was involuntarily relocated into these high rise public housing estates on the four corner peripheries of the city.

35 One controversial aspect of the new schemes was the ban on public houses imposed there between 1955 and 1964. As the folk music scene relied upon public houses, this legislation effectively undermined the continuation of the folk music tradition in local working-class communities.

and the beaches of the Kincardineshire coast as the focus for her work. Eardley's paintings of Glasgow tenements and street children often featured lettering based on graffiti and fly-posters, indicating how popular culture was beginning to influence fine art practice. In London, the Independent Group of artists and designers including Leith-born artist Eduardo Paolozzi,[36] Victor Pasmore, Peter Smithson and Nigel Henderson had now established their name with a series of controversial exhibitions at the ICA. Their 1953 exhibition, Parallel of Life and Art was panned by the critic Reyner Banham, who dubbed their approach 'the New Brutalism'. Banham wrote that "students at the Architectural Association complained of the deliberate flouting of the traditional concepts of photographic beauty, of the cult of ugliness and denying the spiritual in Man." In Glasgow, there had been no significant advances in increasing the level of cultural provision. The 1952 acquisition of Salvador Dali's Christ of Saint John of the Cross (1951) for the public collection had met with local outrage. Students at Glasgow School of Art protested that the money (£8,200) would have been better spent on setting up a gallery where young artists could exhibit in the city. And in 1955 the Corporation's finance committee rejected a proposal to convert the former Miss Cranston's tea rooms on Ingram Street – designed by Charles Rennie Mackintosh – into a restaurant and dedicated arts centre.

## TEENAGE KICKS

Despite continuing problems of social deprivation, Glasgow retained its reputation as a good-time city in the '50s and '60s. A fire in August of 1958 had closed down the popular Barrowlands Ballroom, but the renovated ballroom was open again by Christmas 1960. Resident bandleader Billy McGregor and his Gaybirds played the ballroom six or seven nights a week, entertaining the crowd with lively dance numbers interspersed with comic turns and raffle prize draws. In addition to the Hollywood movies that

---

36  Paolozzi (b.1924) along with two other Scottish artists, William Turnbull (b.1922) and painter Alan Davie (b.1920), was employed during the '50s by William Johnstone, principle of the Central School of Arts and Crafts in London.

had long formed a staple of the Glaswegians' cultural diet, R'n'B and soul music was now the popular choice in most dance clubs around the city. It was also around this period that the expression teenager or teen-ager seems to have become current on both sides of the Atlantic.[37] Rationing had finally been lifted in 1955, and a broader cultural awareness of activities specifically associated with youth now crossed from sociological studies and into the language of marketing and advertising.

The identification of the teenager as a potentially lucrative target market was primarily a result of the growing wealth of Western societies, and the increased leisure time and spending power of young people. However, the growth of the concept of "youth-as-fun", frequenting specifically teenage locales (the coffee shop, the picture house, the dance hall, the fashion boutique) and buying specifically teenage products (brylcreem, bobby-sox, rock 'n' roll records) did not entirely eclipse the idea of "youth-as-trouble",[38] expounded in the rebellious film roles of Marlon Brando in *The Wild One* (1953) and James Dean in *Rebel Without a Cause* (1955). Both films had been produced in a carefully monitored cultural climate, and thus could be seen as essentially unthreatening products designed to sate the vaguely rebellious yearnings of the teenage market. However, audience responses could be unpredictable, as screenings of "the first rock 'n' roll film" *The Blackboard Jungle* (1955) proved when British Teds[39] were inspired to slash cinema seats. In 1956, Glasgow residents were shocked when hundreds of teddy boys and girls danced in Keith Street outside the Tivoli cinema, Partick after a screening of the film, which opened with *Rock Around the Clock* by Bill Haley and the Comets. Near the Embassy Cinema, Shawlands, "young couples were whirling madly under the sway of the rhythm-provoking chanting of the crowd." At the Gaumount, King's Park, "A number of regular patrons were disgusted at

---

37  Use of the adjective "teenage" in America dates back to the 1920s, although the expression "teenager" does not seem to have come into popular use until after World War II.

38  Dick Hebdige (*Hiding in the Light*, 1988) uses these two terms to describe the two trajectories of discourse concerning youth culture: youth-as-trouble is associated with social policy and the documentary tradition, youth-as-fun with the language of popular culture, specifically advertising.

39  Teddy boys adopted an Edwardian style of dress, with draped coats, tapered "drainpipe" trousers and heavily Brylcreemed quiffs. One of the first post-war subcultures, they were later superceded by mods, rockers and skinheads.

the shouting and stamping during the screening."[40]

Like the Northern English towns of Stoke-on-Trent, Sheffield and Wigan, Glasgow would remain a stronghold of the North American soul sound for many years to come. "Sweet soul music. It lit something in him. It was something he wanted to spill out. He wanted to flail his arms and sing and laugh, sharing it. But he just stood, watching, bobbing his head, tapping his foot, looking now at the girls dancing, now at the group pounding out the music."[41] But the '60s were also a time when gang culture rose again as the demise of the shipbuilding industry brought deepening unemployment. The Calton Tongs, Gorbals Cumbie, Maryhill Fleet and Possilpark Uncle were just a few of the notorious gangs that roamed the dancehalls, cinemas and bars looking for fights. As with the '30s and '40s gangs, the use of razors (a "malky" or "chib" in popular parlance) to administer facial wounds (the "Glasgow smile") persisted throughout this period.[42]

However, the treatment of violent criminals was slowly changing, in part due to the influence of Glaswegian psychologist RD Laing (b.1927). Laing pioneered experimental treatment of patients with mental illness in various hospitals, including Gartnavel in Glasgow between 1953–6. He believed that society was responsible for the symptoms of madness that were presented by some patients. He wrote that, "The condition of alienation, of being asleep, of being unconscious, of being out of one's mind, is the condition of the normal man. Society values its normal men."[43] Laing advocated breaking down the divisions between patients and hospital staff, and using cookery and art as a way of treating mental disorders, instead of more conventional therapies like ECT and medication. His most famous book was *The Divided Self* (1960),[44] although *Madness and the Family* (1964), written with Aaron Esterson and *The Politics of Experience* and *The Bird of*

---


40   Rudolph Mckenna and Ian Sutherland, *They Belonged to Glasgow*, NWP, Glasgow, p110.

41   Alan Spence, *Its Colours They Are Fine*, William Collins Sons & Co Ltd., London, 1977, p107.

42   Between 1963 and 1968 Glasgow accounted for 41% of violent crime in Scotland.

43   RD Laing, *The Politics of Experience and The Bird of Paradise*, Penguin, London, 1967, p24.

44   Laing's ideas relating to the "splitting" of the self could be related to a Scottish literary tradition dating from the publication of James Hogg's *The Private Memoirs and Confessions of a Justified Sinner* in 1824, and the late 19th century work of Edinburgh-born writer Robert Louis Stevenson. Stevenson is often described as an early modernist, as his work explored psychological ideas that would not be widely circulated for another twenty years, in the writings of Sigmund Freud. Stevenson significantly developed the idea of the uncanny and the double in *The Strange Case of Doctor Jekyll and Mr Hyde* (1886) and his novels and children's verse were often concerned with dreams and the world of the imagination.

Paradise (1967) were also bestsellers. He later achieved a degree of notoriety for his experimentation with LSD and his turbulent love life, although the influence of his writings has endured beyond the scandals attached to his lifestyle. Laing's use of art as a means of addressing social problems was an approach that would later be implemented by art therapists and community arts workers in Scotland from the '60s onwards.

Glasgow-based poet Edwin Morgan (1920–2010) was another literary figure who propagated a different atmosphere in the rather stagnant cultural scene of 1950s Glasgow. Morgan wrote that, "Glasgow is very interesting for a writer. The absence of a strong literary tradition in Glasgow meant that for a long time it was hard to write about the reality of things."[45] Morgan was both politically outspoken, and unrepentant about his sexual inclinations (he was an early member of the Bachelor Clan, one of the first semi-public gay organisations in Scotland). He had an abiding interest in concrete and visual poetry and was renowned for his translations of Mayakovsky, Racine and Neruda into Scots. Morgan's proudly Scottish yet international outlook provided an interesting template for many younger writers emerging in the city such as young Glaswegian writers Alexander Trocchi (1925–1984), Archie Hind (b.1928) and William McIlvanney (b.1936).[46] Morgan taught in the English Literature Department at Glasgow University where he first encountered the young Alexander Trocchi – "Brilliant, wayward, charming, alarming, passing exams on Benzedrine, starting up a pig farm shortly before his finals. Everyone knew he would make his mark sometime, somehow, somewhere."[47] Trocchi's novels Young Adam (1954), Cain's Book (1960) and the essay The Invisible Resurrection of a Million Minds (1963) showcased a furious writing style and expressed his demands for a cultural revolt. "There is in fact no permanence anywhere. There is only becoming"[48] he wrote.

Trocchi's colourful career encompassed some years in Paris in the late

45  Edwin Morgan, *Footsteps and Witnesses, Lesbian and Gay Life Stories from Scotland*, Polygon, Edinburgh, 1993.
46  McIlvanney was born in Kilmarnock, but moved to nearby Glasgow to attend university. Many of his books have been set in Glasgow, and he is usually described as a "Glasgow writer".
47  Edwin Muir, "Letter 3", *Justified Sinners An Archaeology of Scottish Counter Culture* (1960–2000), Pocketbooks, Edinburgh, 2002.
48  Alexander Trocchi, *Invisible Insurrection of a Million Minds*, first published in New Saltire Review, 1963.

'50s, where he formed friendships with both Samuel Beckett and the Situationist Guy Debord, founded the literary magazine *Merlin* and penned erotica for the Olympia Press.[49] Later he lived and worked in New York, where he was remanded in custody on drugs charges in 1960. Guy Debord, Jacqueline de Jorg and Asger Jorn defended him in an article entitled "Hands Off Alexander Trocchi", pleading that as an artist his experimentation with drugs should be granted special dispensation. *Cain's Book* was widely considered to be one of the most important counter-culture novels of the '60s, and William Burroughs himself described Trocchi as a "unique and pivotal figure." However, "the Scottish Beat" always remained on the outside of the established Scottish literary scene. In 1962 he had a notorious spat with elder poet statesman Hugh McDiarmid at the Writer's Conference in Edinburgh.[50] Trocchi resented McDiarmid's Communist leanings and, in a spirited outburst, he advocated a more Dada-ist approach. After declaring that he was "only interested in sodomy and lesbianism" he was barred for life from the conference.


## YOU'VE NEVER HAD IT SO GOOD?


In October 1964 the Labour Party won election victory for the first time in 13 years. However, new Prime Minister Harold Wilson's "you've never had it so good" speech failed to ring true for many Scots. Although the work of young authors like Trocchi, Hind and McIlvanney represented a definite upturn in artistic production in Glasgow, these young authors were writing about the suffocating atmosphere in the city brought about by the collapse of the heavy industries. Hind's *The Dear Green Place* (1966), which won *The Guardian* Fiction prize, dramatised the problems that faced a young working class author and articulated the idea (still prevalent in Scotland) that creative activity is a luxury. The protagonist, Mat Craig, feels torn between "real work" (and wages) and his literary ambitions. "It had all

---

49  William Burroughs and Henry Miller were amongst the other authors published by the Olympia Press.
50  Organised by Jim Haynes and the publisher John Calder, the conference attracted many high-profile guests including Kenneth Tynan.

started when he had stayed up writing too late one night. The next morning he had lain over long in bed and had been late for work. This had made him feel unpleasant. From the day he had left school he had never been late for work, nor had he ever taken a day off."[51] In his second novel *A Gift From Nessus* (1968) William McIlvanney wrote about the devastating social effects of widespread unemployment in the city and the post-war peripheral housing schemes that had replaced the inner city slums. "The lights going up and down made the whole area resemble a vast computer, winking and shuttering out its inhuman formula, balancing time and space and capital in neat economy."[52] These novels, and other works by these young writers, lent credence to the belief that the artistic life of a city directly impacted on the health of the city as a whole, and significantly advanced the debate surrounding cultural provision in Glasgow.

## FAR AWAY, SO CLOSE

Several commentators have claimed that the establishment of the Edinburgh Festival in 1947 had conclusively shifted the cultural focus from Glasgow to Edinburgh during the late '40s, as Glasgow struggled to re-establish a position of prominence after World War II. Edinburgh had built upon its position of cultural pre-eminence in Scotland[53] in the inter-war period, and that stature had been bolstered further with the establishment of the new Gallery of Modern Art in the Royal Botanical Gardens during 1960.[54] Curators at the new gallery had also begun to assemble a permanent collection of works of international stature made after 1890, which was where the National Gallery of Scotland's collection tapered off. Previously an unwritten policy had existed that an artist had to be dead for at least ten years to qualify for inclusion in the collection. By the early '60s Edinburgh

---

51  Archie Hind, *The Dear Green Place*, New Authors Ltd., Glasgow, 1966, p58.
52  William McIlvanney, *A Gift From Nessus*, Eyre & Spottiswood, London, 1968, Part I Chpt 3.
53  Both The National Gallery and Scottish National Portrait Gallery had opened in the capital city in the 19th century. These galleries' permanent collections included works by Van Gogh, Gauguin, Monet and Cezanne which undoubtedly influenced the work of the Scottish Colourists – an Edinburgh-based group of painters active during the early years of the 20th century including Cadell, J. D. Fergusson, Hunter and Peploe.
54  The Scottish National Gallery of Modern Art's first exhibition, in 1961, was of the work of Henry Moore.

was also home to an exciting literary scene, where Hugh McDiarmid played host in the bars around Rose Street. Poets Norman McCaig (1910–1996), George Mackay Brown (1917–96) and Sorley McLean (1926–2001) were regulars in Milne's Bar and the Abbotsford, as was Edinburgh University student Alan Bold, and his friend and collaborator, the young Alexander (Sandy) Moffat. Moffat (b.1943) studied in the painting department of Edinburgh College of Art in the sixties where he was in the same class as the painter John Bellany (b.1942).[55]

"When I went to school no-one told you anything about Scotland. It was just a place where nothing happened. The thing you would aspire to was speaking English properly and maybe one day you would go to London. When I was a young guy I wasn't interested in anything Scottish – it was embarrassing and a thousand years out of date. But when I got through to art school I got friendly with a guy who lived a couple of hundred yards away from me called Alan Bold who became quite a well-known poet and proselytiser. He introduced me to Marxism and to Scottish art and literature. Bold went to Edinburgh University and became editor of a kind of literary magazine called *Gamba* they had there. He turned it into a very left-wing publication – he even got an interview with Mao Tse-tung through the Chinese Embassy in London. He was the original angry young guy.

Bellany and I were in an art school which was very old-fashioned and moribund and Alan Bold was the link between the intellectual scene at the university and the poets we were starting to find out about. We thought that you couldn't be an artist unless you knew all about that stuff – we were more educated in the pubs of Rose Street in intellectual terms than we were at the art school. On a nightly basis you would be arguing with all the poets, the university librarians, people who came to the Edinburgh Festival would pass through – musicians, film makers. So that's where it all began. Bellany and Bold and myself were determined to make what we did not parochial and we wanted to add to all these interesting things that had happened and

---

55  John Bellany was born in the fishing port of Port Seton and his large scale allegorical paintings often featured imagery relating to the sea and fishermen. Other Scottish artists of the period who were also making works alluding to maritime themes included Ian Hamilton Finlay (b.1925), George Wyllie (b.1921), Will McLean (b.1941) and Elizabeth Ogilvie (b.1946).

were happening in Scotland. We had to be in dialogue with Europe and what was happening elsewhere, and raise the stakes and that was our manifesto."[56] From 1963 onwards, Moffat and Bellany held several outdoor exhibitions of their paintings during the Edinburgh Festival, once on Castle Terrace, and twice on the railings of the National Gallery on the Mound.

For several young artists, however, the cultural scene in Scotland in the '60s simply could not compete with the frenetic cultural activity taking place in London. Karel Reisz, Tony Richardson and Lindsay Anderson's Free Cinema movement, the new directions in fashion brought by Vidal Sassoon and Mary Quant, and the emergence of British rock'n'roll in the form of The Beatles, The Who and The Rolling Stones[57] had combined to make London the "swinging" centre of fashionable Europe. London art college St. Martin's, where John Latham (b.1921) taught between 1965–67 was another site of considerable interest during this time. Latham co-founded the Artists' Placement Group (APG) with Barbara Stefani in 1965, which placed artists in non-gallery work environments such as factories and areas of dockland. In 1967 he was dismissed from St. Martin's after he invited a group of students and friends to chew a copy of Clement Greenberg's *Art and Culture* into a pulp, spit it into a bottle and return it to the college library. However, before his dismissal Latham came into contact with Glasgow-born artist Bruce McLean (b.1944), who had studied sculpture at Glasgow School of Art between 1961–63, before moving south to complete his studies at St. Martin's between 1963 and 1966. Like Gilbert & George, who began working on collaborative performance works while studying at the school in 1967, McLean's time at St. Martin's developed his interest in performance-related work.[58]

Back in Edinburgh, art teacher Richard Demarco (b.1930) was also working relentlessly to establish a local infrastructure for experimental theatre and

---

56 Alexander Moffat, in conversation with the author, May 2002. Moffat's painting *Poet's Pub* (1980) represents the Rose Street scene.

57 Glasgow's Barrowlands Ballroom played host to most of the major bands of the '60s, including The Who and The Rolling Stones. When the Beatles appeared at the Odeon Cinema on Renfield Street in 1964, fans ran riot smashing windows and overturning cars in the street outside the cinema.

58 McLean would later form the artist's collective Nice Style, the "World's First Pose Band", which parodied the posturing of contemporary rock stars such as Mick Jagger in a series of performances given between 1971–1974.

visual art. Demarco and his associate Jim Haynes (b.1933) were frustrated with the dullness and sobriety of Edinburgh, and were determined to try to sustain the vitality of the festival all year round. Louisiana-born Haynes was one of the founders of the political journal *The International Times* and ran the Paperback Bookshop, where controversial texts like *Lolita* and *Lady Chatterley's Lover* could be purchased. Haynes also co-hosted many bohemian gatherings with Demarco at the shop premises, including happenings and exhibitions. In the summer of 1962, Demarco and Haynes' intentions had begun to take clearer shape when actor/director Terry Lane and actor John Malcolm agreed to lend their support. Malcolm then managed to persuade the property developer Tom Mitchell to let them have the use of a dilapidated Lawnmarket property for a private theatrical club that would showcase experimental local and international productions.

As Joyce McMillan records in her fascinating history of the Traverse, "The Traverse Theatre opened in James Court, just off the Edinburgh Lawnmarket, on the night of 2 January 1963. The place was Kelly's Paradise, a crumbling former doss-house and brothel barely a stone's throw from the Castle; the play was Sartre's *Huis Clos*, presented in a double bill with Fernando Arrabal's *Orisons*; the weather was icy, so much so that the capacity audience of 60 invited guests shivered their way through supper in evening dress and heavy overcoats. At the second performance, the actress Colette O'Neil was accidentally stabbed on stage with a paperknife, and almost bled to death; the publicity was tremendous, advance bookings soared, and the theatre, in the words of its first director Terry Lane, 'never looked back'."[59] Four years later, Richard Demarco was still Vice-Chairman of the Traverse, but was working increasingly in the visual arts. He set up his first gallery in Melville Crescent in the West End in 1966, which supported photography, installation and performance work, at that time underexposed in Scotland.

In London the previous year, Anthony d'Offay[60] had set up his first

59 Joyce McMillan, *The Traverse Theatre Story*, Methuen, London, 1988, p9.
60 Anthony d'Offay's career had begun in Edinburgh where he had studied Modern Languages at the University. In 1961, using compensation money awarded for a swimming pool accident, he bought up Carvon Grey's library, which contained many art books and illustrated works and produced a meticulous catalogue to sell the work on.

premises in a small first-floor flat in Picadilly. By 1967, Slade student Nicholas Logsdail had opened the Lisson Gallery in a dilapidated building near Marylebone Station with help from friends including Derek Jarman. While d'Offay and Logsdail would quickly become key figures on the London art scene, Demarco's position in Edinburgh was considerably more isolated. In Glasgow, Cyril Gerber, Bet Low, Tom McDonald and John Taylor had founded the Charing Cross Gallery in 1963, directed towards the promotion of Scottish artists within Scotland. The gallery closed in 1968, although Cyril Gerber's new Compass Gallery on West Regent Street then continued in a similar vein. However, the main remit of these two west coast galleries was to extend the audience and market for art within Scotland, and both were perhaps less concerned than Demarco with the need to forge international links.

From the beginning, Demarco struggled to secure public funding for his projects and often relied upon donations from wellwishers and sales of work to local collectors in order to continue. He collaborated with Scottish actors, artists and writers, including the young Sean Connery and Ian Hamilton Finlay, but also extended invitations to international artists to visit the capital, such as Canadian installation artist Les Levine, for Canada 101 (1968) and Irish actor Stephen Rea, who performed in *Antigone* at the gallery in the late '60s. The Traverse continued to attract plaudits for a programme packed with plays by Ibsen, Chekhov, Pinter and Beckett, and Demarco's creative isolation was somewhat eased when in 1967 the first open access print workshop in Britain was established by American artist Bob Cox, and local artists Philip Reeves, Roy Wood and Kim Hempshall, on the second floor of a tenement flat in Edinburgh. The Edinburgh Printmakers Workshop provided a model on which later print studios in Glasgow, Aberdeen and Dundee would be based.

Artist and poet Ian Hamilton Finlay, who had trained briefly at Glasgow School of Art before the outbreak of WWII, was a key figure in Scottish art and literature of this period. After the war he lived on Orkney for a time before co-founding the Wild Hawthorn Press with his wife, Jessie McGuffie in 1961 and the magazine *Poor.Old.Tired.Horse.* (1962–1968), both of which contributed much to the alternative poetry scene of the '60s, and in particular, to the emergence of concrete poetry in Scotland. In 1967, Hamilton Finlay moved to Stonypath, a farmhouse above Dunsyre in Lanarkshire which he renamed Little Sparta, in opposition to Edinburgh, the so-called "Athens of the North". He installed numerous sculptures and carved text pieces there and applied for rates relief on the basis that the Temple to Apollo at Stonypath was a building of artistic and spiritual significance. He said, "I was tired of being a stateless person. It was obviously no good being Scottish. I don't think that any of the excuses will do – Calvinism, or The English, that's just nonsense. They are, quite simply, an inferior race. Something is up with them. They are hopeless, quite incapable of acting. Culture isn't a passive element. There is no culture where no culture is in operation. So long as it doesn't act, it doesn't exist."[61] Strathclyde Regional Council refused to grant Hamilton Finlay discretionary rates, and in 1972 sent sheriff officers to seize sculptures from the property in lieu of the unpaid bills. The ensuing struggle by Hamilton Finlay and supporters like Richard Demarco to repel the sheriff officers was later dubbed The Battle of Little Sparta.

Despite the vibrant scene in the Rose Street pubs and the pioneering activities of the Traverse, the Printmakers Workshop and individuals like Demarco and Hamilton Finlay, no solid infrastructure or funding existed for emerging artists in Scotland at that time. Tom Laurie, a young surveyor-planner, who moved from Glasgow to the new town of Cumbernauld in the 1960s remembers that there was an even greater lack of cultural resources available there. "We formed the Cumbernauld Theatre Group because there was nothing to do. We'd go round to each other's houses and somebody had a collection of Huddie Ledbetter records and we'd have evenings of poetry and plays."[62]

Alexander Moffat remembers: "I graduated in 1964, then worked in an engineering factory for a couple of years – shovelling shit as they used to say. There wasn't much happening in Scotland in those days – it's difficult to describe it. There was a desert. There was something called the Arts

61  Elizabeth Lyon, *The Art Work Interviews*, Famedram Publishers, Ellon, Scotland, 1993, p93.
62  Tom Laurie, in conversation with the author, November 2002.

Council of Great Britain,[63] but they were very middle class and respectable. The Labour government came into power in '64, and the Scottish Arts Council (SAC) proper was set up in 1967 by Jenny Lee, the Minister for the Arts at the time. A lot of things began to happen in Scotland after that date which were truly indigenous. About 1969 I started running this little gallery in Edinburgh called the New 57 Gallery[64], and I think we got £500 a year from the SAC to set up in what had been an old cobbler's shop in Rose Street, with tiny wee rooms. Really the aim was to show every young artist in Scotland who had some kind of ambition. Every now and again, at festival time we would do some kind of historic or international show. It was quite a simple policy – everybody on the committee was an artist – it was a prototype Transmission."[65]

The Richard Demarco Gallery continued to host many ground-breaking exhibitions and events in the early '70s and '80s, most notably perhaps the Strategy: Get Arts exhibition in the summer of 1970, which brought numerous international artists, including Joseph Beuys and Blinky Palermo, to exhibit in Scotland for the first time. Palermo installed a wall painting in the main stairway at Edinburgh College of Art, which was painted over by the somewhat rash College authorities later that same year.[66] Gunther Uecker showed his *Banging Door* piece, which opened and closed non-stop for the three weeks of the Edinburgh festival, creating a sound that was incorporated into the music of Friedhelm Dohl. In this, the first of many visits by Beuys to Scotland, he presented his sled sculpture *The Pack* with his four-hour-long Action called *Celtic (Kinloch Rannoch) Scottish Symphony* twice a day during a four day period in August. One of the many entranced witnesses to these events, Alistair Mackintosh, later recalled, "All the defences I had prepared caved in as I turned a corner in the Edinburgh College of Art to find a herd of sleds pouring out of the back of a Volks-

---

63  The Arts Council of Great Britain, with history going back to World War II, was established as a Body Corporate in 1946, and gave financial support to London's Tate Gallery and the Institute for Contemporary Arts (est. 1947) amongst other organisations.
64  From 1957 to 1965 the 57 Gallery was run from the George Street studio of Daphne Dyce-Sharp. In December 1965 a seven year lease was obtained from 105 Rose Street and the New 57 Gallery opened there in July 1966. Alexander Moffat played an important role in the gallery from 1964 onwards, becoming chairman in 1969.
65  Alexander Moffat, Ibid.
66  In the late 1990s a proposal to have the work restored was rejected by the Estate of Blinky Palermo.

wagen bus. Each had its blanket (neatly rolled), a torch and a lump of wax: they looked very happy, as if they were all about to set out on a picnic, although there was just the possibility that they might take over the world instead."[67]

The marriage of social consciousness[68] and fine art practice in Beuys' work would make a lasting impression on several artists working in Scotland during this period, notably Glasgow-based artist George Wyllie and younger Edinburgh-based artists including Glen Onwin (b.1947). This first visit by Beuys to Scotland heightened the growing interest in 'ideas-based' art practice in Scotland, and contributed directly to the growth of performance and conceptual practice in both Edinburgh and Glasgow. Beuys' use of "everyday" materials and his insistence that "every human being is an artist"[69] made a particularly potent impression on Scottish artists looking to incorporate recent social history into their practice. In Glasgow in particular, artists would begin to consider their practice as a place where some of the divisions and contradictions of their city's history could be exposed, if not resolved.

---

67  John F. Moffit, *Occultism in Avant-Garde Art: The case of Joseph Beuys*, UMI Research Press, Michigan, 1988, p13.
68  Beuys believed in "free democratic socialism" and was a founder member of the Green Party.
69  Joseph Beuys, "I am Searching for Field Character", *Art into Society, Society into Art*, Institute of Contemporary Arts, London, 1974.

# CHAPTER 2

# TRYING TO PLANT A SEED ON CONCRETE
## (1971–1985)

By 1971 the jobs of some 8,500 Clydeside shipbuilders were under threat from the newly elected Conservative government, which was unwilling to continue under-writing the industry's debts to the level of the previous Labour administration. At a mass protest held on Glasgow Green that summer Clydeside shipbuilder Jimmy Reid stood before an audience of thousands and said, "We are not wildcats. We want to work. The real wildcats are in No. 10 Downing Street. We don't only build ships on the Clyde, we build men. They have taken on the wrong people and we will fight." Opposition leader Harold Wilson, TUC leader Vic Feather and Tony Benn, the Shadow Trade and Industry Minister lent their support to the consortium of Clydeside shipbuilders from five separate yards as they began their 14-month work-in. By the autumn of 1972 the Upper Clyde Shipbuilders' (UCS) work-in had resulted in a government U-turn, and an injection of £35m into yards at Govan, Scotstoun and Linthouse, although this would later be seen as a temporary reprieve for an industry in terminal decline.

The collapse of the heavy industries in Glasgow had not eroded the rather Calvinist work ethic which still pervaded – or the idea that cultural endeavours were not "real work". Much of the cultural activity in Glasgow in the early '70s drew upon the social history of the city, informed by a desire to celebrate working-class history, but also perhaps by a sense of guilt. The post-war welfare state had created certain opportunities that had been denied to working-class people in the past, contributing to the emergence of artforms that were more socially engaged and more accessible, that recognisably connected the old industries and the new creative initiatives. One of the clearest examples of this social shift can be seen in the work of Billy Connolly (b. 1942), who had trained as a welder in the Glasgow shipyards before making a name on the folk music scene as The Humblebums with musical partner Gerry Rafferty. He later shot to fame with *The Great Northern Welly Boot Show* (1972) which told the thinly-disguised story of the workforce's 1971 occupation of the UCS yards, using lively sketches, pantomimes, music-hall routines and original Connolly compositions. The show was a huge hit both in Glasgow and at the Edinburgh Fringe, and indicated a marked change in Scottish theatrical productions as it dealt with situations specific to the working classes, and featured local songs and vernacular speech. *The Scottish National Dictionary* had previously proclaimed that "owing to the influx of Irish and foreign immigrants to the industrial area near Glasgow, the dialect has become hopelessly corrupt."

*The Great Northern Welly Boot Show* contributed significantly to the cultural rehabilitation of both the debased music-hall tradition and of the "corrupt" Glasgow dialect – themes that would be consolidated in the work of other playwrights, notably John McGrath. John McGrath (b.1936) had established the 7:84 theatre company in Scotland and England in 1971, which set a precedent for subsequent politically engaged Scottish theatre companies like Wildcat, Clyde Unity, Fifth Estate, TAG (Theatre-About-Glasgow) and Gerry Mulgrew's Communicado. 7:84 was named after statistics that had been published in *The Economist* in 1966, revealing that 7% of the population of the United Kingdom owned 84% of the wealth.[1] McGrath's numerous plays included *The Cheviot, The Stag and the Black Black Oil* (1973), which drew historical parallels between the Highland Clearances, and the economic crisis of the '70s and its "solution" – British North Sea oil.[2] Subsequent plays *The Game's A Bogey* (1974) and *Little Red*

---

1   The statistic was later used by conceptual artist Victor Burgin in a public work in Newcastle Upon Tyne called Possession (1976). Burgin posted 500 posters on bus shelters that lampooned the language of advertising. The work featured the question 'What does possession mean to you?' above a soft focus photograph of a man and woman embracing. The Economist statistic was reprinted beneath.

2   North Sea Oil and natural gas were first discovered in waters lying between Scotland and Norway in the late '60s, but these resources were not fully exploited until the '80s and '90s as major discoveries continued. In the 1970s the Scottish Nationalist Party launched a campaign, 'It's Scotland's Oil' to draw attention to the British government's use of oil-derived revenue to rectify the financial problems of the UK as a whole.

*Hen* (1975) were equally political, examining the socialist legacy of "Red Clydeside". McGrath said, "Working-class people usually don't go to the theatre because most theatre is not aimed at them. It's not about them. It speaks a language they don't speak."[3] 7:84 worked to change that, reaching a working-class audience through their much-imitated strategy of touring their productions around community centres, factories, working men's clubs and church halls. Glasgow's cultural landscape was slowly shifting, as artist's initiatives began to spring up in buildings around the city, the first of which was Glasgow Print Studio, which opened in St. Vincent's Crescent in Finnieston in 1972.[4] The facilities at the new print studio were soon being utilised by several of the most prominent Scottish artists, including Elizabeth Blackadder, John Byrne, John Bellany, John Taylor and Philip Reeves, who had been appointed Head of Printmaking at Glasgow School of Art in 1970.

Edinburgh, however, was still considerably ahead of Glasgow in terms of arts venues and activities. Mark Francis[5] first visited Edinburgh in the early '70s, after hearing Richard Demarco give a talk about his Edinburgh Arts activities at Oxford University, where Francis was an undergraduate. He remembers, "I came up to Edinburgh twice to attend the Edinburgh Arts summer schools, and in the summer of 1973 I attended Joseph Beuys' 12 Hour lecture in the Melville College gymnasium."[6] Beuys' *12 Hour Lecture* for Edinburgh Arts in the summer of 1973, intended to honour Anarcharsis Cloots, a German aristocrat who influenced the French Revolution, has acquired almost mythic status through the years. Other artists who participated in Demarco's Edinburgh Arts summer programme that year included Marina Abramovic, who gave a durational performance entitled *Rhythm 2* in the Meville College. Earlier that year Abramovic had performed *Rhythm 0*, one of her most seminal works, in Naples – the audience attending the performance were invited to use various objects (including a

3   Elizabeth Lyon, The Artwork Interviews, Famedram Publishers, Ellon, Scotland, 1993, p131.
4   The Peacock Printmaker's in Aberdeen opened the following year.
5   Mark Francis was formerly the Director of the Fruitmarket in Edinburgh (between 1984 and 1987), The Andy Warhol Museum in Pittsburg and co-founded the experimental exhibition space Fig-1 with Jay Jopling in London in 2000. He now works for Gagosian Gallery in London.
6   Mark Francis, in conversation with the author, August 2002.

loaded gun) upon her. For her Edinburgh Arts performance Abramovic took two pills used in curing acute schizophrenia, which brought her body into an unpredictable condition, the outcome being recorded by two fixed cameras (one facing Abramovic, one trained on the audience)[7].

Through attending the Edinburgh Arts summer schools Mark Francis formed a friendship with Richard Demarco, which fed his growing interest in contemporary art practice. After graduating from Oxford, he worked for various art organisations, including Kettle's Yard in Cambridge and with Nigel Greenwood in London. It was while working with Greenwood that he met the Edinburgh-based minimalist painter Alan Johnston (b.1947). Along with a few other Edinburgh-based artists including Glen Onwin and Kenneth Dingwall (b.1938), Johnston was making stripped-down, mono-chrome works that were at odds with the new Scottish figurative tradition represented by John Bellany and Alexander Moffat. Moffat remembers, "The Americans, the most powerful Western nation, had adopted abstraction as the expression of their democratic liberalism. That kind of war had started in the '50s and was still present in the '70s. One of the problems with abstract painting was that it could deal with a certain set of ideas, but there were all sorts of other things like politics that it just couldn't deal with. So I think that's why in the early '70s you had the first signs of what we now call conceptual art, because a lot of young artists wanted to deal with different types of reality."[8]

Conceptual art had evolved during the 1960s as a logical development of minimal art, and questioned the validity of the traditional art object, primarily through the use of concepts as the key "material" informing the work. By the early '70s the exhibitions *When Attitudes Become Form* (Kunsthalle Berne, 1969), Information (MoMA, New York, 1970) and *The New Art* (Hayward Gallery, London, 1972) had consolidated the inter-national reputation of conceptual artists like Carl Andre, Art & Language, John Baldessari, Douglas Heubler, Joseph Kosuth, Sol LeWitt, Robert

---

7   The following year Sir Roland Penrose and Buckminster Fuller accepted Demarco's invitation to appear as guest speakers for Edinburgh Arts. Demarco also forged links with Polish, Irish, French and Yugoslavian artists, and in 1980 Edinburgh Arts circumnavigated the British Isles with poets Sorley MacLean and George Mackay Brown on board for part of the route.
8   Alexander Moffat, in conversation with the author, May 2002.

Morris and Lawrence Weiner. Traditional media and physical manifestations were rejected by US based artists such as Huebler, Kosuth and Weiner in favour of written proposals and statements and various kinds of documentary evidence (photographs, films, charts and maps). In Lucy R. Lippard's *Six Years*, a critical overview of minimal, anti-form, systems, earth or process art made between 1966 and 1972, she had identified conceptual art as, "work in which the idea is paramount and the material form is secondary, lightweight, ephemeral, cheap, unpretentious and/or dematerialized."[9]

This kind of 'dematerialized' work found supporters within the Edinburgh art scene in both Richard Demarco and Graeme Murray, an Edinburgh College of Art graduate who set up a gallery in his home in the mid '70s. Murray showed the work of numerous artists experimenting with non-traditional techniques, including Ian Hamilton Finlay and Alan Johnston. The established international interest in conceptual art practice was also reflected in an exhibition by American artist Sol LeWitt[10] at Edinburgh's Gallery of Modern Art in the mid '70s, and the subsequent purchase of his work for inclusion in the permanent collection. Works by Joseph Beuys, Alan Johnston and Glen Onwin were also added to the growing collection of the Gallery of Modern Art in the mid to late '70s. However, some members of the city's art establishment were less convinced by this new style of work as Mark Francis recalls. "Alan Johnston was teaching at the art school at that time, but he was still quite a marginalised figure in Edinburgh, as he was always away travelling and doing shows elsewhere, which I think certain people resented."[11]

The Edinburgh Festival continued to draw international influences into

---

9   Lucy R. Lippard, *Six Years*, Praeger, New York, 1973, p vii.

10  The publication of LeWitt's "Paragraphs on Conceptual Art" in Artforum in the summer of 1967 provided the first public grounds for recognition of the conceptual art movement, although the term had been in circulation since the early '60s. In 1967 LeWitt was producing series of open-framed rectangular sculptures, indicating his interest in the repetition of forms and in the exclusion of signs of individual authorship (e.g. gestural marks, brushstrokes etc.). The following year he began developing proposals for wall drawings that could be executed according to sets of instructions. By May of 1969, when his "Sentences on Conceptual Art" were published in the first issue of Coventry-based art journal *Art-Language*, conceptual art had been widely recognized as an international avant-garde movement. The 1969 publication of Joseph Kosuth's essay "Art after Philosophy", which identified a conceptual tradition in art making that stemmed from Duchamp's *Readymades*, also significantly substantiated the theoretical positions associated with conceptual art.

11  Mark Francis, Ibid.

the city each summer, often attracting artists working in new mediums, such as video. During the Edinburgh Festival of 1971 several London-based artists, including David Hall, came to Edinburgh to present new works. Hall made a series of short television works, which were broadcast on Scottish Television instead of advertising during the Festival period, as part of Locations Edinburgh, curated by Alistair Mackintosh at the Scottish Arts Council for the Edinburgh Festival. Shot in and around Edinburgh, the works were a landmark both for UK television and moving image art in Scotland. Mick Hartney records in his essay "Int/ventions in Diverse Practices: A Critical Reader on British Video Art" that "the central idea of the project was that the artists should deploy the various communication networks of the city to make their work or to make it visible." Other artists in the show included Stuart Brisley, David Parsons and Jeffrey Shaw, who, like Hall were part of John Latham's conceptual art collective Artists' Placement Group. The group carried out a number of public interventions during the Festival, including Brisley's apparent staging of a slow-motion car crash in a disused car showroom, Ed Herring's playing back of ambient sounds into the environment, Parsons' street banners, and the inflatable sculptures made by Shaw and others.[12]

By 1974 Joseph Beuys' summer visits to Edinburgh had come to wider public attention as a result of the unlikely friendship he formed with Barlinnie[13] inmate Jimmy Boyle. Former debt collector Boyle is probably Glasgow's most infamous violent criminal: the Lord Advocate described his behaviour as being of "almost unimaginable ferocity." He was imprisoned in Barlinnie between 1967 and 1982, undergoing rehabilitation from 1973 onwards in the experimental Special Unit at the prison, resulting in his post-release career as an artist and writer. Art therapy formed part of the Special Unit's approach, which attracted the attention of Richard Demarco

---

12  For a more detailed discussion of the emergence of video art in Scotland, see Chris Byrne and Malcolm Dickson, "Moving History", *Variant* Issue 6, Glasgow.

13  Barlinnie, or Bar-L as it is known locally, is a high security prison for remand or short-stay prisoners located in the East End of Glasgow. The prison has a segregation unit and a specialist drug reduction unit, but is perhaps best known for the Special Unit, an experimental rehabilitation centre which operated there between 1973 and 1994. The Special Unit removed especially disruptive prisoners from the general system while obviating the need to condemn them to long periods of segregation or solitary confinement. In the first year that the Special Unit operated assaults were reduced from an expected 105 to 2.

and poet and playwright Tom McGrath (b.1940, Rutherglen). Demarco initiated Boyle's day release to meet Beuys in 1974, culminating in Beuys introducing the 1976 exhibition of Boyle's work at the Demarco gallery, *In Defence of the Innocent*. McGrath had been one of the founder editors of the underground magazine *The International Times* in 1966 and by 1974 was appointed director of the newly established Third Eye Centre in Glasgow, the establishment of which he had been instrumental in achieving. Amongst his many diverse projects, McGrath collaborated with Jimmy Boyle on the play *The Hard Man* (1977), which was premiered in Edinburgh at the Traverse.

Glasgow's Third Eye Centre was the first dedicated contemporary arts centre in the city, and was established in 1974 after protracted lobbying of the Scottish Arts Council by Tom McGrath and others. Glasgow-based artist Richard Wright (b.1960), who lived in the new town of Cumbernauld in the early '70s, remembers that the Third Eye Centre made a big impression on him as a teenager. "Most of the cafes in Glasgow were quite traditional – for example, across the road from the Third Eye Centre was M & A Browns, an old-fashioned tea room that was renowned for its fish teas. There weren't that many alternative situations in Glasgow – for example there were no health food shops. So to go somewhere where you got coffee in a mug and hippy-ish home cooked food was quite unusual. And all the people who worked there seemed to have long hair and wear black clothes."[14] The Third Eye Centre established a locally engaged agenda from the inaugural 1975 exhibition, which opened with a performance by Billy Connolly and featured the paintings of two artists closely associated with the city, Joan Eardley and John Byrne.

John Byrne (b.1940) had established a reputation as both an artist and playwright after studying at Glasgow School of Art. He had trained initially in the '50s as a colour mixer in a Paisley[15] carpet factory, an experience he later dramatised in his 1978 *The Slab Boys Trilogy*. Although *The Slab Boys Trilogy* was essentially a comedy, it also emphasised that young people

---

14  Richard Wright, in conversation with the author, February 2003.
15  Paisley is geographically very close to Glasgow, and the relationship between the town and the city is comparable to that of Salford and Manchester.

growing up in the economically depressed Glasgow area dreamed of opportunities elsewhere. Most markedly perhaps, the character of Spanky is obsessed with "getting to the States" and often imagines an alternative existence there: "Just think if we'd been brought up in the States – if our maws had met a couple of GIs during the war … yankee comics, gabardine suits, our ain transport."[16] Byrne would later explore Glasgow's 1950s and '60s Americana obsession further in the BBC Scotland series *Tutti Frutti*, which starred Glasgow School of Art graduate Robbie Coltrane.

Although by the mid-'70s the Teddy boy phenomenon had subsided into an underground cult In Scotland, another music scene which also looked to America for inspiration was building in popularity. The Northern Soul movement was rapidly gaining adherents – and busloads of dedicated fans of the Detroit sound[17] were leaving Glasgow each weekend for "all-nighters" in Shotts, or further afield, to Northern English towns and cities. Scott Brown, who would later found Goodfoot, one of Glasgow's longest running Northern Soul nights, remembers, "I was a mod from the age of 12 onwards, during the ska revival of the late '70s, and so got into all sorts of quality black music. But Northern's just the best there is … there's so much variety. It can be big uptempo stomping tunes or it can be sad reflective tunes and it all makes you dance. I started off going to all-nighters in Leeds and Manchester, having come of age just at the tail-end of all the all-nighters staged in Shotts that used to attract busloads from England."[18]

Two of the leading commentators on the emerging scene were Scottish – Perth-born broadcaster Stuart Cosgrove and Dave Godin, from Falkirk, who had given the movement its name in a 1970 magazine article. Godin said, "Northern soul reached out from the ghettoes of black America to the ghettoes of Scotland or at least to the youth clubs on the council estates in Falkirk that I grew up on."[19] Detroit and Glasgow had more in common than initially met the eye – both were post-industrial cities that would

---

16  *The Slab Boys Trilogy* by John Byrne, Salamander Press, 1982.
17  The key record label associated with the Northern Soul scene was Berry Gordon's independent label Motown Records, which was established in Detroit in 1959. Motown scored numerous major US hits with acts like the Temptations, the Miracles, The Marvelettes, The Supremes and the Four Tops. In the early '60s Gordy coined the phrase "The Sound of Young America" to describe the label's output.
18  David Belcher, *The Glasgow Herald*, 7th April, 2001.
19  David Belcher, *The Glasgow Herald*, Ibid.

become centres of independent music production. Detroit had been famous as one of the biggest car manufacturing cities in the US before overseas competition had sent the city's key industry into a slump. John Sinclair, the manager of '60s Detroit rock band the MC5 remembers that, "when San Francisco had the Summer of Love in 67, we had the Detroit riots. We tried to have a Summer of Love but it didn't work. We did a love-in on 30th April 1967 and the police attacked it on horseback. That was what Detroit was like, they didn't want any hippies. In Detroit they wanted you to go and make cars. Any manifestation of anything that didn't point towards working class organisation was a threat to the system, because everything was centred on manufacturing those automobiles and the parts for them."[20]

The other dominant musical form of the period was prog-rock, and when big name acts like Lynyrd Skynyrd, Hawkwind and Deep Purple played Glasgow it would be at The Apollo on Renfield Street. The Apollo was a yawning 3,500 seat venue which in the dance hall days had gone by the name of Green's Playhouse. The many stairways and corridors were covered in stained purple carpets, and it also featured myriad passageways and alcoves suitable for surreptitious smoking of joints. The Apollo was also renowned outside of Glasgow for attracting a particularly tough audience, who would think nothing of firing volleys of verbal abuse at any act deemed to be lacklustre. Another popular haunt for the disaffected youth of the day was The Amphora on Sauchiehall Street, which was decorated in a pseudo-Grecian style, with turquoise patent leather booths and glass partitions etched with Grecian nymphs clutching urns. The front bar was divided into two separate rooms, which were linked with a larger backroom where hash and acid could often be purchased. It was said that the U-shaped formation of the bar facilitated easy escape when the drugs squad called – the police would enter through one bar, and advance to the back room just as the dealers were exiting through the door of the other bar.

20  John Sinclair, "Invisible Jukebox", *The Wire*, Issue 227, January 2003, pp16–19.

# COMMUNITY ARTS

By the end of the 1960s, 160 multistorey housing blocks were in use in Glasgow but the problems associated with the peripheral schemes had remained outstanding. The idea of using arts activity as a means of alleviating severe social deprivation began to take firm root, and in the late '70s large conferences were held in both Edinburgh and Glasgow to raise greater funding for community arts projects, which became increasingly prevalent in deprived areas of both cities. In Glasgow, thirty murals appeared on exposed tenement gables in a seven-year period, by artists including Jim Torrance, Tim Armstrong, John McColl, Stan Bell and John Byrne. Artist and writer Alasdair Gray (b.1934), who had studied at Glasgow School of Art during the '50s, was also active within the city's mural painting scene at this time. Gray had also worked as a scene painter at the Glasgow Pavilion and Citizen's theatres in the early '60s, before taking up a decade-long post as the resident artist for Glasgow's People's Palace museum in 1967. Gray painted cityscapes of Glasgow's East End, and portraits of citizens in their home surroundings, in addition to painting large murals in two local churches and for The Ubiquitous Chip restaurant in the city's West-End, a favourite haunt of BBC[21] employees and Glasgow University academics.

In the late '70s an unusual department had been set up at Glasgow School of Art, as an adjunct to the Department of Drawing and Painting. The Department of Mixed Media was run by tutor Roger Hoare to cater for the needs of a few students working outside the school's established disciplines. Ray McKenzie, who began teaching in the Historical and Critical Studies Department at the school in 1976 remembers, "It was a sort of ghetto for all the rebellious students, and was run in the Assembly Hall for a few years. You won't find much mention of it in official records, but several of the school's most well-known students worked in that department, including Steven Campbell and Adrian Wiszniewski."[22] Steven Campbell (b.1953) was born in Rutherglen and left

---

21  The BBC had broadcast from Glasgow since 1923. For several years the Radio Scotland headquarters were in Cranworth Street in the West End, but by 1952 radio and television programming was being co-ordinated from the new BBC Scotland headquarters on Queen Margaret Drive.
22  Ray McKenzie, in conversation with the author, February 2003.

school at the age of 16 to take up an apprenticeship with British Steel. In 1978, aged 25, Campbell decided to change career and applied to Glasgow School of Art. Roger Hoare remembers, "He must have come to the Drawing and Painting Department and I heard the other teachers talking about this difficult student who was talented but just couldn't work in the studio with other students. My ears pricked up because I was looking for distant types to work in my department."[23] In the Mixed Media Department Campbell was able to develop his interest in performance art as well as continuing to work on the large scale figurative paintings which would later make his name.

During this period Roger Hoare also initiated a mural project called *Public Image*, and three of the artists involved in that project, Willie Hamilton, Tommy Lyndon and George Massey, went on to work with Alan Kane on an ambitious mural project at Easterhouse. Leith-born artist David Harding (b.1937) who worked as the town artist in the Scottish new town of Glenrothes from 1968–1978 remembered, "Some artists offered their services to poor and underprivileged communities in an attempt to give form to the lived milieu. Mural paintings and sculpture offered ways to make art which was owned by the community, some of whom collaborated in the development of the ideas and the execution of works. These artists shared a commitment to serving working-class culture and the environmental improvement of the inner city, suburban and new town housing estates."[24] One such work was Harding's *Poetry Path* (1977) in Glenrothes, a collaborative work made with Alexander Moffat's close associate Alan Bold. The paths were constructed along "Desire Lines" chosen by residents rather than by town planners and were an attempt to give local residents a sense of connection to their rather barren surroundings. David Harding explains that, 'They are the paths, familiar to all of us, that intuitively we take across grass as the shortest distance between two points. Not the longer, right-angled, paved path that architects designed for us. They meander too as when they become too muddy and are not straight lines.'[25]

Surveyor-planner Tom Laurie was still active in building community arts

23  Roger Hoare, interviewed for Steven Campbell, Art Works Scotland, ITV, 18/8/02.
24  David Harding, *Decadent*, Foulis Press, Glasgow, 1997, p15.
25  David Harding, in response to question semt by the author, August 2009.

resources in the new town of Cumbernauld in the late '70s. He remembers, "I ran the folk club there and I also directed plays and got really interested in contemporary theatre. I was involved on the board of the Cottage Theatre in Cumbernauld and one day I was invited to join the board of the Traverse in Edinburgh."[26] Through his involvement with the Traverse, Laurie met Glaswegian accountant Joe Gerber, who was the Chairman of the Edinburgh theatre before Laurie took on the post in the late '70s. He remembers, "Both being Glaswegian we were saying, 'why doesn't Glasgow have a theatre which showcases contemporary writing like the Traverse does in Edinburgh?' In early 1977 Joe and I had a meeting at the Third Eye Centre with its director Tom McGrath, and decided that we would ask for a response from the general public in Glasgow. We advertised a general meeting at the Third Eye Centre to discuss theatre, and what happened then was that we were overwhelmed. The place was jumping. It was a Sunday afternoon and there was standing-room only. A young administrator called Linda Haase agreed to act as an unpaid secretary, and the Glasgow Theatre Club was formed. I think initially we had 500 members, and we were very pleased with that intellectual response although at that time we didn't have a home.

Then an architect called Peter McGunn, who also taught at the Mackintosh School of Architecture, said to us, 'Look, I know that the Tron church along the Trongate is owned by the city council and it's used at the moment by the direct works plumbing division.' It was an ancient 18th century church in a pretty deleterious state, and he said that he thought it might be our best bet. We had two or three councillors from the city council on the membership of the Glasgow Theatre Club and after a lot of beavering and getting support from the Provost, they agreed to dispose of the building to the Glasgow Theatre Club for £1. We started the Tron with volunteers and had Saturday and Sunday morning work parties to clean the place up. We got the licence and for the first year we had café theatre in the Victorian bar."[27] By May 1979, just over a year after the formation of

---

26  Tom Laurie, in conversation with the author, November 2002.
27  Tom Laurie, Ibid.

the Glasgow Theatre Club, Phyl Douglas and Linda Haase were working from a cramped office on the Parnie Street side of the Tron, organising fundraising events in the Third Eye Centre and other venues throughout Glasgow. Their first major project was a two-week run of Tom McGrath and Jimmy Boyle's play *The Hardman* at Glasgow's Pavilion Theatre.[28]

The area around the Trongate had been in decline ever since 1952, when plans had first been mooted for an East Flank Road that would carve past the Cathedral, down the High Street and over the river. Although funds had been found for the construction of the Kingston Bridge and the M8 towards the West End,[29] the motorway connection in the East End remained unrealised in the late '70s. However, the continued possibility of the development meant that the price of property around the Trongate had plummeted, as Tom Laurie recalls. "Buildings and warehouses were empty, and that's why we could get the Tron for so little and the rent for King Street Studios was also very very modest because there was no value in it."[30] King Street Studios was one of several properties in Glasgow that had been earmarked by the newly formed Workshops and Artist's Studio Provision Scotland (WASPS). WASPS was a non-profit making property company,[31] which provided cheap studios and shared amenities for artists and considerably extended the existing support structure for artists living and working in the city. The Glasgow Theatre Club and WASPS King Street Studios now formed a major focus for arts activity in the previously undesirable Trongate area. And from 1978, local writers James Kelman, Alasdair Gray, Tom Leonard, Liz Lochhead[32] and Alan Spence were printing booklets of their work nearby, at the new Ingram Street location of the

28  Not long after *The Hard Man* was staged at The Pavilion Theatre in Glasgow in 1979, the exhibition *The Art and Daily Living of the Special Unit, Barlinnie Prison* was held at The Third Eye Centre.

29  Glasgow is the only UK city to have a six-lane motorway passing through its centre. The demolition during the 1970s of much of Charing Cross and St. George's Cross to make way for the motorway has been widely condemned, although the juxtaposition of the remaining Victorian architecture with the concrete expressway also contributes to the unique architectural identity of Glasgow. In 2000, junctions 14 to 20 of the motorway, including the Kingston Bridge, were awarded Grade 1 listed status by the Scottish Executive's inner city heritage body.

30  Tom Laurie, Ibid.

31  In the late '70s and early '80s the WASPS Trust had architect and developer John Forbes, former Glasgow City Council estates surveyor Ron McChristie, developer Ian Wall and Tom Laurie as board members.

32  In 1971 James Kelman had joined a writing class run by lecturer Philip Hobsbaum at Glasgow University, which was also attended by Alasdair Gray, Tom Leonard, Liz Lochhead and Agnes Owen. The group fostered a dialogue between the authors, which was later referenced by Gray in his novel *Lanark* (1981).

Glasgow Print Studio with the encouragement of the director Calum MacKenzie. Unlike Mat Craig, the aspiring novelist of *The Dear Green Place*, the artists and writers emerging in the late '70s in Glasgow no longer had to make a choice between conventional labour and their artistic practice, given that there wasn't much traditional employment to be had. As local poet Donnie O'Rourke put it, this created "a whole generation of artists, who, absolved of the old polarity between employment and one's real work, just do it."[33]

By the late '70s economic recession was splintering the political allegiances of UK voters into a marked North-South divide. UK unemployment was climbing towards the two million mark, and a series of strikes by municipal workers had eroded support for Labour Prime Minister James Callaghan still further. The Conservative party had enlisted the services of London advertising firm Saatchi & Saatchi, who came up with a billboard campaign that touched a national nerve. Charles and Maurice Saatchi's slogan, "Labour isn't working" was accompanied by an image of a lengthy dole queue. But although the Conservatives were fast gaining on the ailing Labour administration south of the border, in Scotland the picture was very different. In every election from 1957 until 1974, the Conservatives' share of the vote had fallen in Scotland, while in each of those elections Labour did better than elsewhere in the United Kingdom, and a third party, the Scottish National Party, had grown in popularity. Since the end of World War II, third parties had never taken more than 7% of the vote at general elections in Scotland, but by the election of 1974 the SNP had taken 39% of the vote and the Conservatives were left in third place.

In late '78 the Labour government responded to this change in voting patterns by calling a referendum in Scotland and Wales on the increasingly pressing issue of devolution. But as Andrew Marr later wrote in *The Battle for Scotland*, "Devolution carried the stigma of a failing government. It had been imposed on a doubtful party by a London leadership for purely

---

33 Donnie O'Rourke, Real Life, Fruitmarket, Edinburgh, 1999, p51. Francis McKee made a similar point in his 1997 essay "The Eight Moves of the Submerged Dragon", "Guided by the hand of intellectual commerce, the contemporary generation of artists in Glasgow have evolved a new economy based on the production of thought." Made in Glasgow, Normal, Glasgow, 1997.

electoral reasons. It had been legislated for in a fog of internal dissent and confusion. It was campaigned for by divided parties at a time of economic chaos." The devolution campaign was not backed by all members of the Labour party – in fact, an active Labour "Vote No" campaign was launched, with Neil Kinnock fronting the Welsh campaign and Brian Wilson, Robin Cook and Tam Dalyell leading the Scottish opposition to reform. On March 1st 1979, the Welsh electorate voted "No" with a resounding 80% of the vote, while in Scotland the result was a 52% "Yes" vote in conventional electoral terms. However, there was a low turnout for the referendum, and owing to a unique attachment proposed by backbench Labour MP George Cunningham, requiring 40% of the Scottish electorate to vote "Yes", the result was deemed to be unrepresentative. The devolution process was halted in its tracks, along with James Callaghan's government, which was brought down by a vote of no confidence later that year.

Although the Conservatives had only won 31% of the vote in Scotland at the general election in 1979, Britain's "first past the post" system meant that Scotland was forced to accept the electoral choice of the rest of the UK. Over the next few years the policies of the new government, led by Margaret Thatcher, had numerous negative consequences on the already moribund Scottish industries. Thatcher was quick to sweep the devolution issue under the carpet, the first of many actions which did little to endear her to the Scottish electorate. Thatcher also made a series of attacks on the Welfare State, withdrawing free school milk and tightening benefits legislation. She had famously declared some years earlier that she did not envisage seeing a female prime minister in her lifetime, and her policies were largely unsympathetic to working mothers, benefit claimants and single-parent families.

The depressed economy and political upheavals of the '70s have often been cited as contributing factors in the emergence of punk rock in Britain.[34] The Kings Road scene had been brought to national attention in 1976 with the release of the Sex Pistols' debut single, *Anarchy in the UK*. Sex Pistols

---

34 It should be noted that similar developments had taken place in the late '70s at CBGBs and the Mudd Club in New York, where bands like Television, Blondie, Patti Smith, The Ramones and Talking Heads were regular guests. There is some controversy over whether punk 'began' in New York and was imported into London by Sex Pistols manager Malcolm McLaren, or whether the development of both scenes was simultaneous and part of a general cultural shift.

lead singer John Lydon remembers, "Around the time of the punks, social-ism wasn't working in England. The Labour party were unimpressive and tedious. The Conservatives, the same. It fluctuated from one party to another, four years of this, four years of that, and you wouldn't notice any change. Young people – in fact, most people – just walked clean away from politics as if it were a waste of time. A cloud of apathy had truly set in. Of course, that's exactly the environment the Conservatives want. That's when they can strut their stuff using prejudice, hate, family values, all the non-issues of political life."[35] A planned performance by the Sex Pistols at The Apollo in Glasgow on 15th December 1976 had been cancelled after Peter McCann, the Lord Provost of Glasgow, had seen the band's foul-mouthed antics on *The Bill Grundy Show*. Peter Daly, a musician and journalist who was a teenager in Glasgow during the '70s, remembers that, "Back then, there was just so little – almost nothing – to do. It's almost impossible to stress how boring and nullifying it was there. You have to understand that punk rock in Glasgow took place against a backdrop of total repression. There was no record industry. There was nowhere adequate to rehearse. There was no welcome. Nothing was accommodated or accepted. It was like trying to plant a seed on concrete."[36]

This atmosphere of boredom and political disillusionment provided a fertile breeding ground for the energy of the Scottish punk scene to bloom. The best-known product of Glasgow's punk scene is probably Johnny and the Self Abusers, although they released only one single under that name before splitting into two separate bands, Cuban Heels and Simple Minds in 1978. Edinburgh-based band The Rezillos, who had formed in 1976, left a more lasting legacy. The Rezillos originally had an eight piece line-up, including charismatic frontwoman Fay Fife, bassist Eugene Reynolds, saxophonist William Mysterious and backing singer Gail Warning. Their debut single, *I Can't Stand My Baby/I Wanna Be Your Man* was released in 1977 by Sensible Records and in September that year they toured the UK as a five-piece with labelmates The Ramones. The following year their debut

35  John Lydon, Rotten *No Irish No Blacks No Dogs*, Hodder & Stoughton, London, 1993, p327.
36  David Cavanagh, *The Creation Records Story*, Virgin, London, 2000, pp5–6.

album, *Can't Stand The Rezillos*, was promoted by another UK tour, this time with Irish punk band The Undertones. Despite a massive following and the allure of Fay Fife's sci-fi humorous lyrics, The Rezillos parted in 1979 after playing three farewell gigs at the Glasgow Apollo, which were released as a second and final album, *Mission Accomplished*.[37]

Other Scottish punk bands on the scene at the time included the Fire Engines, Scars and TV Art all of whom hailed from Edinburgh, although Glasgow's Orange Juice was also producing interesting music in the New Wave mould by 1979. At a double bill at the Vic bar at Glasgow School of Art in 1979, Orange Juice shared the bill with Edinburgh's TV Art, who were soon to change their name to Josef K. The two bands quickly built an alliance, taking it in turns to headline on each other's home turf, and releasing a split single, *Radio Drill Time* (Josef K)/*Crazy to Exist* (Orange Juice), in 1980 on Alan Horne's newly formed Postcard Records.[38] Douglas McIntyre, who was then playing in a band called Article 58, was an admirer of Josef K throughout this period. He remembers, "One gig with the Fire Engines in Edinburgh sticks out as particularly memorable, both groups were burning up at this point. The sound and fury fused with white light heat demanded total attention. Their guitars were on collision course with Venus, sparking electrical stimulation in their trail. The blank generation were left trying to decode the scrambled frequencies."[39] Both bands had memorable frontmen, in Josef K's monochrome-suited Paul Haig, who refused to do encores, sign autographs or talk to the audience, and Orange Juice's cherubic singer Edwyn Collins. Collins had moved to Glasgow from Edinburgh at the age of 14 and had formed his first band, Nu-Sonics, at the tender age of 17. Both Nu-sonics and Orange Juice were distinguishable from other local bands by their somewhat fey style and, like Paul Haig,

---

37  Eugene Reynolds and Faye Fife carried on under the new name The Revillos while their guitarist, Joe Callis later found fame as a member of The Human League.

38  Other independent labels existed in Scotland in the late '70s, notably Bob Last's Fast Product label, established in 1977 in Edinburgh, who released records by The Gang of Four and The Human League, amongst others. Postcard Records was established in Glasgow by Horne in 1979, releasing the Orange Juice single *Falling and Laughing* later that same year. Like other British independent labels Factory, 4AD and Mute, Horne was able to secure a distribution deal with London's Rough Trade Records (established by Geoff Travis in 1977) which significantly raised the profile of his label and the bands he represented.

39  Douglas McIntyre, Josef K, Endless Soul compilation sleeve notes, Marina Records.

Collins was dogged with a reputation for being "difficult", a situation that wasn't helped by the grandiose claims he made for his music. Josef K and Orange Juice's Glaswegian label boss Alan Horne was also not known for making understatements, and dubbed his stable of young acts, "the sound of Young Scotland", echoing Berry Gordy's 1959 description of Motown Records as "the sound of young America."

## MEETING THE NEW GLASGOW BOYS

By 1979, Alexander Moffat had given up his post at the New 57 Gallery and had taken up an invitation to teach at Glasgow School of Art offered by Bill Buchanan, the newly appointed Head of Fine Art. Moffat remembers, "The problem about doing something in Edinburgh, or trying to do something in Edinburgh, was that you were up against this kind of middle-class lethargy. No-one wanted to take on the world, and you were banging your head against a brick wall. There was no excitement. Then when I came through to Glasgow, every student I met seemed to be a revolutionary."[40] Among the students Moffat encountered were Steven Campbell, Adrian Wiszniewski (b.1958) a former architecture student, Peter Howson (b.1958) who had worked at various jobs including a spell in the Scottish Infantry, and ex-social science student Ken Currie (b.1960). Both Campbell and Wiszniewski were working between Roger Hoare's Department of Mixed Media and the Painting Department. Hoare remembers, "They became quite a pair – very difficult to deal with, very funny, quite anarchic and gave me and the other students a lot of trouble."[41] Currie and Howson were also fiercely competitive, vying to see who could spend the longest hours in the studio.

Moffat worked to introduce his students at the school to a wider frame of reference throughout the early '80s. Moffat encouraged Campbell, Wiszniewski and others to study the work of earlier German artists such as George Grosz and Jorg Immendorf, other international painters including Fernand Leger and RB Kitaj and muralists like Diego Rivera.

40  Alexander Moffat, in conversation with the author, May 2002.
41  Roger Hoare, Steven Campbell, Art Works Scotland, Ibid.

He remembers, "There were all these old guys running the art school, who had been there for about 50 years and were ensconced in the Glasgow Art Club. It was all very closed-down, and the way that art was being taught was bad. The teachers were being presented as heroes, and some of the students were in awe of them. They were more famous than Picasso or Matisse as far as the students were concerned because they weren't getting exposed to that kind of work. It wasn't just being behind the times, we weren't even in the picture. No-one had been to Berlin or New York, they just didn't know what was going on in contemporary art. There was a lot of work to be done here."[42]

In 1979, artist Pete Seddon had also moved to Glasgow to work. Seddon's large-scale pastel drawings often drew upon political and historical elements, such as the Highland Clearances or the Troubles in Northern Ireland,[43] and he taught at the art school in the Historical and Critical Studies Department from the early 1980s. It was while in contact with Seddon and Moffat that Ken Currie began to develop his outspoken political views, and publish them in the pages of *Stigma* magazine. Although he later became better known as a figurative painter, during this period Currie was also known as a filmmaker. He dismissed the landscapes and semi-abstract representations of previous generations as having, "No issues, no opinions, no protests, no convictions – there is only paint, formless masses of paint."[44]

In the late '70s and early '80s an Expressionist art revival was taking place in Germany, Italy and the USA. A resurgence in interest in figurative painting swept through the international art market, in part because of three influential painting shows, the first of which was *A New Spirit in Painting* (1981)[45] at London's Royal Academy, curated by Norman Rosenthal, Nicholas Serota and Christos M. Joachimides. Joachimides' catalogue essay

---

42  Alexander Moffat, Ibid.

43  The Troubles had begun in earnest in 1969 although media coverage had greatly increased in the wake of the Bloody Sunday massacre at Derry in 1972. In 1981, Bobby Sands and nine other men starved themselves to death while in custody, seeking political status for republican prisoners.

44  *Stigma*, No. 2, Glasgow, November 1982.

45  Exhibiting artists: Frank Auerbach, Francis Bacon, Balthus, Georg Baselitz, Pier Paolo Calzolari, Alan Charlton, Sandro Chia, Rainer Fetting, Lucian Freud, Gotthard Graubner, Philip Guston, Dieter Hacker, Jean Helion, David Hockney, Howard Hodgkin, KH Hodicke, Anselm Kiefer, Per Kirkeby, RB Kitaj, Bernd Koberling, Willem de Kooning, Jannis Kounellis, Markus Lupertz, Brice Marden, Gordon Matta-Clark, Bruce McLean, Mario Merz, Malcolm Morley, Mimmo Paladino, AR Penck, Pablo Picasso, Sigmar Polke, Gerhard Richter, Robert Ryman, Julian Schnabel, Frank Stella, Cy Twombly and Andy Warhol.

helped to feed the argument then in circulation regarding the relative merits of "expressive" painting as opposed to less object-based art forms. Claiming that "The overemphasis on the idea of autonomy in art which brought about Minimalism and its extreme appendix, conceptual art, was bound to be self defeating."[46] Joachimides posited as an alternative a "return" to expressive painting. He wrote, "This new concern with painting is related to a certain subjective vision, a vision that includes both an understanding of the artist himself as an individual engaged in a search for self-realisation and as an actor on the wider historical stage. The subjective view, the creative imagination, has come back into its own and is evident in a new approach to painting. Artists, no longer satisfied with the deliberately objective view, are beginning to respond to their environment, allowing these reactions to be expressed in the form of images."[47]

Rosenthal, Serota and Joachimides' exhibition found echoes in the selection for two major exhibitions in Germany the following year: Zeitgeist in Berlin and Documenta 7 at Kassel, curated by Rudi Fuchs. Both Zeitgeist and Documenta were heavily populated with new painting from German painters like Georg Baselitz and Anselm Kiefer and Italian artists Sandro Chia and Francesco Clemente. Meanwhile in New York, the art market had been swelled by private sector sales, which now greatly exceeded government sponsorship of the arts. Although the American economy in the late '70s and early '80s had buckled under high rates of inflation and a huge budgetary deficit, under Ronald Reagan a rosier picture emerged. Reagan's staunchly anti-communist position, coupled with his introduction of lower taxes and the promise of new defence measures in space won him massive popularity, and he was re-elected in his second term with the highest percentage of the popular vote in American history. Among the many American neo-expressionist painters to benefit from the newly booming American economy in the mid-'80s were Eric Fischl (b.1948), David Salle (b.1952) and Julian Schnabel (b.1951).[48]

---

46 Christos M. Joachimides, *A New Spirit in Painting*, Royal Academy of Arts, London, 1981, pp14–16.
47 Christos M. Joachimides, *A New Spirit in Painting*, Ibid.
48 In 1982, Schnabel travelled to London for a Tate solo show of his monumental compositions, encrusted with thick layers of paint and arrangements of broken crockery.

Despite Joachimides' claim that expressive painting was returning to the forefront of artistic practice, in Scotland the narrative tradition was already strong in the work of Alasdair Gray, Alexander Moffat, John Bellany and other painters active since the '60s. However, the recent developments on the international art scene undoubtedly lent weight to Moffat's attempts to revive the "discredited tradition" of figurative painting at Glasgow School of Art. He recalls, "At that stage any kind of figurative painting was deeply unfashionable almost everywhere in the Western world. There were all sorts of reasons for that – one being that the Cold War was still going on. Figuration had been totally contaminated by Socialist Realism, the official art of Russia and East Germany. It was difficult to think in terms of figuration as a serious language, but I had always remained interested in its potential for representing a concept of the world. It seemed to me that people like Steven Campbell and Ken Currie were capable of doing something with painting that really hadn't been done before. I said to them, you need to go to Berlin, you need to go to Documenta at Kassel to catch up with what's going on. A couple of days later I would get a phone call, 'I'm in Berlin'. That was one of the great things about students here: the Glaswegian mindset. Before you finished the sentence, they were away. They knew what needed to be done. I remember saying to Stevie Campbell, if you want to do things, you must go to New York. 'I'm off!' he said, and went out the door. 'Is that what I've got to dae? I'll dae it'. There was an unbelievable energy. Of course the old guys hated them."[49]

Over in Edinburgh, the New 57 gallery was still staging shows that met with mixed receptions. Alexander Moffat remembers, "After I stepped down Jim Birrell took over and he did some really explosive shows which would make a lot of sense in terms of what people are doing now in Glasgow – he brought Joseph Kosuth to do these huge billboards on Easter Road. Jim also did the first show of Gordon Matta-Clark after his death, which was hated, I can tell you. In 1982 Jim did a festival

49  Alexander Moffat, Ibid. Steven Campbell won a Fulbright scholarship in 1982 and lived and worked in New York until 1985, during this period he showed at PS1 on Long Island and at the Walker Art Center in Minneapolis.

show of all the young turks in Glasgow – including Steven Campbell and Scott Kilgour.[50] It was the first time that a curator anywhere in Scotland started to look at what was going on in Glasgow – it was the beginning of something happening."[51] The SAC gallery in the lower half of the building ran a concurrent exhibition, Scottish Art Now, which featured the work of more established local artists such as Jack Knox, Derek Roberts, Graham Derwood and John Kirkwood. Moffat recalls, "The English critics seized on what was upstairs and that gave us a bit of a boost. It was another signal things were going to change."[52]

The public art collection in Glasgow increased substantially in the early '80s when, in 1981, the Hunterian Art Gallery opened on the campus of Glasgow University. The new gallery held the world's largest collection of Whistler oils, pastels, prints and letters and the meticulously reassembled interiors of Charles Rennie Mackintosh and Margaret Macdonald's former home at 6 Florentine Terrace. Building was also well underway on the custom-built Burrell Collection at Pollock Park, designed to house the extensive collection of artefacts bequeathed to the city by millionaire shipyard-owner Sir William Burrell. Works in the collection included 22 Degas paintings and works by Gericault, Cezanne, Renoir, Manet, Pisarro and Millais, in addition to several paintings by the first Glasgow Boys. These developments helped to consolidate the reputation of the rich artistic culture that had existed in Glasgow prior to the First World War while, at the same time perhaps, also emphasising the comparative lack of developed arts infrastructure supporting the contemporary scene.

In 1981 Glasgow painter and writer Alasdair Gray's magnum opus *Lanark*, which had been 24 years in the making, was finally published. The book memorably recast Glasgow as the dystopian city of Unthank and featured a series of footnotes (diplags and implags) to plagiarise/promote the work of other emerging Glasgwegian authors including James Kelman, Liz Lochhead and Alan Spence. In one much-quoted passage, Gray wrote,

---

50 Expressive Images included work by Murdena Campbell, Steven Campbell, Simon Fraser, Alistair Hearsaum, Scott Kilgour, Mario Rossi and Andrew Walker.
51 Alexander Moffat, Ibid.
52 Alexander Moffat, Ibid.

"If a city hasn't been used by an artist not even the inhabitants live there imaginatively. [ … ] Imaginatively Glasgow exists as a music-hall song and a few bad novels. That's all we've given to the world outside. It's all we've given to ourselves."[53] The song which Gray is referring to is almost certainly *I Belong to Glasgow* by Will Fyfe (1855–1947), which mythologised the common working man and his escape from his harsh existence through drink.

*When Ah get a couple of drinks on a Saturday,*
*Glasgow belongs to me.*

Glaswegians remained renowned for their fondness for alcohol, which was reflected in numerous local slang expressions for drunkenness, including on the batter, bazooka'd, bevvied, birlin, bladdered, blitzed, blootered, fleein', miraculous (marockyoolus), mortalled, paralytic (paralettic), plootered, on the randan, ripped, skooshed, steaming, stotious, wellied and well on.[54] A series of damning reports in the mid-70s had revealed that rates of alcoholism, vandalism, worker absenteeism and infant mortality in Glasgow were well above those of other European cities. Glasgow also suffered from unusually high rates of cancer and heart disease, and glue-sniffing had recently become a serious problem amongst young people in Glasgow, and its surrounding schemes and new towns. The city formerly distinguished by its shipbuilding and engineering prowess was now often referred to as "the sick old man of Europe" or as one 1976 *Glasgow Herald* article put it "The Slum Capital of Europe".

Despite the continuing problems of social deprivation in the city, local cultural workers continued to press for investment in arts initiatives as a way of alleviating some of the effects of widespread unemployment and poverty. The establishment of Glasgow arts festival Mayfest in 1982 helped to propagate further the creative atmosphere fostered by the Third Eye Centre and other local arts initiatives like the Cranhill Arts Project. A

53  Alasdair Gray, *Lanark*, Book 2, Chapter 22, reprinted, Canongate, Edinburgh, 1981.
54  Taken from *The Patter* (Glasgow City Libraries, 1985) and *The Patter: Another Blast*, (Canongate, 1988) both by Michael Munro.

proposal for Mayfest was drawn up by Alex Clark, Ferelith Lean and David MacClellan from Wildcat Theatre Company, which attracted financial support from the Trade Unions, Glasgow District Council and the Scottish Arts Council. Alex Clark wrote, "Mayfest [ … ] has already created a feeling among many performers, writers, poets and painters that they have an important role in the community, and the community is responding."[55]

The 1983 Election came soon after the controversial Falklands conflict, and once again the Conservatives' position worsened in Scotland, where the war had been widely criticised. 1983 was the Conservatives' greatest election victory for 50 years in Britain as a whole, but their share of the vote dropped by 3% in Scotland, leaving them with only 21 seats. A marked rise in transport by air had added to the problems of the beleaguered shipbuilding industry, and by 1983 the Clyde Port Authority reported a loss for the second year in succession. Of that year's deficit of £1.4 million, £1.06 million was made up of redundancy payments. UK unemployment had now reached three million and the worst areas of unemployment were concentrated in Glasgow and other west coast ports such as Liverpool and Belfast, while the steel and mining industries across the country had already begun their slow downward spiral. Despite these grim statistics, this was the year that an attempt was launched to change Glasgow's public profile, with the punning slogan "Glasgow's miles better" accompanied by the Mr Men cartoon character Mr Happy. The accompanying publicity campaign revolved around the notion of Glasgow as "a friendly city", featuring photographs of smiling Glaswegians including Chinese and Asian people to indicate the city's ethnic diversity.[56]

In December 1983, in a derelict Trongate shop premises next door to Terry's Tattoo Parlour, a new artist-run initiative was putting up its first show. "Transmission is Glasgow's first artist-run gallery organised by the Committee for the Visual Arts (CVA), a non-profit-making organisation. A

---

55  Alex Clark, "Mayfest: Glasgow's Opportunity", *The Visual Arts in Glasgow, Tradition and Transformation*, The Third Eye Centre, 1985.

56  In 1953 there were only three Chinese families in Glasgow, but by the 1980s over 8,000 Chinese people had relocated from Hong Kong and the New Territories to live in the city. Other immigrant communities had also continued to grow, reflected in the establishment of four Gurdmaras (Sikh Temples) and the opening in 1984 of Glasgow Central Mosque – the largest Mosque in Europe.

varied group of young artists dedicated to the exhibition and promotion of contemporary art and the integration of art into community life."[57] Alexander Moffat gave an introductory speech at the opening of the Chisholm Street gallery, in which he described the artist-run space as being "far more important than the Burrell Collection." In the same week that Transmission opened, curator Nicola White moved from Belfast, where she had been working for the Arts Council, to Glasgow to take up a post as Exhibitions Co-ordinator at The Third Eye Centre. She remembers, "Alistair Strachan and Alistair Magee worked on the installation team at the Third Eye Centre and they said, 'there's this gallery opening that we've organised, come along to it'."[58] The first committee was comprised of painters John Rogan, Lesley Raeside, Alistair Magee, Michelle Baucke and Alistair Strachan and the first years of Transmission were characterised by heavily politicised exhibitions like Urban Life[59] and Winning Hearts and Minds.[60] Artists such as Peter Howson, Adrian Wiszniewski and Ken Currie were involved with the gallery at this time, and exhibitions of paintings in the 'expressionist New Image'[61] style were predominant. The title of Adrian Wiszniewski's work in Urban Life gives a fair indication of the politics associated with the gallery at this point: *Youth, Lenin and the Horn of Plenty*.

In Edinburgh, the groundbreaking activities of the New 57 gallery were drawing to a close. The gallery had been sharing the upstairs portion of the old Fruitmarket building on Market Street with the Printmaker's Workshop, while the SAC ran a gallery on the ground floor. Jim Birrell and others had been negotiating for some time for the entire building to become a separate independent art gallery. They argued that the Arts Council couldn't continue its current system of running two galleries (one downstairs in Market Street, and the other in Charlotte Square) where Arts

---

57  1983 Transmission press release.
58  Nicola White, in conversation with the author, November 2002.
59  2nd December–8th January 1983. Curated by Ken Currie, Matthew Inglis and Lesley Raeside, the first exhibition at Transmission featured painting, sculpture and photography on the theme of urban life by twenty artists including Ken Currie, Peter Howson, Matthew Inglis, Adrian Wiszniewski, Michelle Baucke, Lesley Raeside, Alistair Magee, Alistair Strachan, John Rogan and Andy Walker.
60  24th March–20th April 1984. Drawing and painting by Lesley Raeside, John Rogan, Ken Currie, Peter Howson, Helen Gibson, Andrew Squire, Alison Stirling, Stephen Barclay, Gordon Muir and Arlene Stewart.
61  Clare Henry, *Glasgow Herald* November 1984.

Council subsidy and curatorial decisions went hand in hand. Eventually the SAC agreed to give both galleries up, meaning that the entire premises in Market Street could be established as a separate independent gallery, The Fruitmarket, in early 1984. Jim Birrell was reluctant to take on the post of director of the new gallery, and so the board began to seek candidates for the post.[62] Curator Mark Francis, who was then working at London's Whitechapel gallery, came into the frame, partly as a result of lobbying by Richard Demarco and Alan Johnston. Francis' track record gave him an edge over the other candidates, as the board had decided they wanted a director who could organise shows by international artists, especially around the time of the Edinburgh Festival, when the new gallery would be scrutinised by visitors from around the world.

For his opening show, during the 1984 Edinburgh Festival, Francis invited 24-year-old Jean-Michel Basquiat to present his first solo European exhibition. Francis remembers having his first inkling of the potential problems of his new post when an Edinburgh matron suggested that the show might not be well received, "'as we don't have black people here'. At the time I just burst out laughing but later I realised that she was completely serious. That kind of attitude caused me a lot of problems, because although they said they wanted international shows, they complained constantly about everything I did."[63] During his first year as director, Francis' programme featured a show by John Cage and a major solo show by New British Sculptor Richard Deacon, both of which had a sizeable impact on local artists.

Running parallel with Francis' exhibition program were the activities of another contemporary art space, The Artist's Collective[64] in the Royal Mile. The Artist's Collective had been established in 1984 by graduates and tutors from the local art school frustrated by the lack of exhibition opportunities for young artists in their city. Edinburgh College of Art lecturer Iain Patterson solicited advice from Alistair Magee and Alistair Strachan, who had set up Transmission in Glasgow a few months earlier, and Richard Wright, who had graduated from the painting school at Edinburgh College of Art in

---

62   Jim Birrell joined Alexander Moffat as a tutor in the Painting Department at Glasgow School of Art in the early '80s.
63   Mark Francis, Ibid.
64   Now known as The Collective Gallery, and located in Cockburn Street.

1982, and had been involved in the activities of Transmission for some months. Magee, Strachan and Wright met up with Patterson and Edinburgh artist John Kirkwood to discuss how Edinburgh's new artist-run gallery should evolve, and in November 1984 an exchange with Transmission, entitled Artist's Collective, took place featuring work by Peter Howson, Alastair Strachan, Richard Wright and John Rogan. Establishing a visual art scene in a depressed economic climate was no easy task, as Richard Wright remembers, "There was a tremendous problem of justification. We were all artists on the dole, but many of us were from working-class backgrounds – our parents expected us to get a job, and I think that that strongly influenced the macho character of the work, not because these artists were all men – they weren't – but the work had this hard quality of being made, somehow dug out. I think that was connected to a certain sense of guilt or anxiety about having a trade or skill, about going to work and spending time at work. A lot of that early painting stemmed from this lack of confidence, about saying 'I am an artist' in this empty zone where there was no receptivity."[65]

Sectarian tensions in Northern Ireland had been escalating throughout the early '80s, and in the summer of 1984 the IRA bombing of the Conservative party conference at Brighton made headlines around the world. The Troubles had always had particular resonance in Glasgow because of the large Irish communities in the city, something Glaswegian author Alan Spence's collection of short stories, *Its Colours They Are Fine* (1977) had tapped into some years earlier. The stories vividly described the sympathies of Glaswegians on both sides of the religious divide. "He gestured towards the picture of King William III which hung on the wall – sword pointing forward, his white stallion bearing him across Boyne Water. In a million rooms like this he was hung in just that pose, doomed to be forever crossing the Boyne. This particular ikon had been bought one drunken afternoon at the Barrows and borne home reverently and miraculously in the teatime crowds. Its frame was a single sheet of glass, bound around with royal blue tape.

65  Richard Wright, in conversation with the author, September 2001.

Fastened on to one corner was a Rangers rosette which bore a card declaring NO SURRENDER."[66]

In 1984 the year-long Miner's Strike against proposed pit closures began, adding to the sense of disenfranchisement many felt with the Westminster government. Thatcher's government had been quick to undermine the power of the unions, and as the '80s progressed it became clear that more reforms were planned. One notable voice of dissent could be found in the writings of former shipbuilder Jimmy Reid, who had first come to prominence during the 1972 UCS work-in and had subsequently served as the rector of Glasgow University and as a candidate for the Communist party. By the mid-80s, Reid was working as a columnist for various newspapers and Thatcher was the subject of many of his polemical articles. In March 1983 he wrote, "You can only really judge a society by how it provides and cares for the underprivileged. This is why I recoil in horror from the philosophy of Mrs Margaret Thatcher. You will search in vain through all her speeches and public statements to find one word of genuine sympathy for the have-nots, for those who are down and almost out. Her every utterance is a hymn of praise, for the well-heeled, those whom she calls 'successful'. Thatcher wants the rich to be richer and her policies have made them so. Meanwhile the poor are getting poorer. Since her rise to power unemployment has trebled. Thousands of youngsters now in their late teens have been without a job since leaving school. No doubt one day they will be branded as Social Security scroungers by Mrs Thatcher's more fortunate young hatchet men. She also wants to dismantle the Welfare State, which was created to provide a safety net to ensure that no one could fall into what sociologists now call the poverty trap. It was by no means perfect, yet it brought a security unknown to previous generations of working men and women. Britain's finest social achievement, the National Health Service, is now also under attack."[67] Under Thatcher, Scotland became the biggest nuclear arsenal and nuclear "dumpsite" in Western Europe, with Trident nuclear submarines based at Faslane, and all British nuclear weapons stockpiled at Glen Douglas, less than twenty miles

66  Alan Spence, *Its Colours They Are Fine*, William Collins Son & Co Ltd, London, 1977, pp80–81.
67  Jimmy Reid, *The Daily Record*, 14th March 1983.

away from Glasgow. Dounreay nuclear processing plant near Thurso was not only handling Scotland's waste, but waste transported from Sellafield in England, and from Germany and the United States, all of which was transported through Scotland by road and rail.

Gang violence continued to flare periodically in the city, most prominently in the infamous Ice Cream Wars, which culminated in six members of the Doyle family being burnt to death in a Ruchazie flat in 1984. Scottish Television detective series Taggart (1983–) played upon the the reputation of the criminal underworld of Glasgow for dramatic effect, not least in the lyrics of the wailing theme tune: "this town it's so mean".[68] However, a series of film comedies released in the late '70s and early '80s by Scottish director Bill Forsyth, including *That Sinking Feeling* (1979), *Gregory's Girl* (1980), *Local Hero* (1983) and *Comfort and Joy* (1984) had promoted more varied images of Scotland. Several critics hailed *That Sinking Feeling* as representing a departure from the previous, hackneyed images of Glasgow. "The image of Scots in British films has been largely confined in the past to the wayward eccentrics of *Whisky Galore* or to Glaswegian thugs. Refreshingly, in his first feature (independently produced on a risibly small budget) Bill Forsyth successfully captured the subversively ironic optimism of the Glasgow streets and somehow managed to combine it with the good-humoured charm of the best Ealing comedies. It's a street-smart fairytale about a group of unemployed teenagers embarking enthusiastically but incompetently on a big heist, and is played with such relish by members of the Glasgow Youth Theatre that it's guaranteed to win any audience over to its side within minutes: the British dispossessed's version of *Rockers*."[69] The follow-up to *That Sinking Feeling*, *Gregory's Girl*, was another massive hit for Forsyth and his young cast. The film was set in the new town of Cumbernauld and starred Claire Grogan, the lead singer of Glasgow pop band Altered Images, who had scored a massive hit in 1981 with *Happy Birthday*.[70] *Local Hero*, the tale of a Texan oil

---

68  Taggart's Glasgow continues to be one of STV's most successful exports, and is currently sold to 25 different countries worldwide.

69  *The Time Out Film Guide*, Penguin, London, 1993 Edition.

70  Claire Grogan and Orange Juice leader singer Edwyn Collins featured on the front cover of the NME in 1981, providing the Scottish music scene with an undeniable seal of approval from the London music media.

man who tries (unsuccessfully) to buy up a small Scottish fishing village gave a light-hearted spin on topical issues of the day, as did *Comfort and Joy*, which told the tale of a radio DJ unwittingly caught up in the Ice Cream Wars.

## DO IT YOURSELF

In 1984 recent Glasgow School of Art graduates Steven Campbell and Adrian Wiszniewski were selected for inclusion in national touring exhibition The British Art Show, which was subtitled Old Allegiances and New Directions. One of the three selectors was Alexander Moffat, who argued convincingly for the work of his former pupils[71] to be placed in the company of Art & Language, Susan Hiller and Paula Rego. However, not all of the painters studying at the school were happy to follow in the New Image painters' footsteps. That year *Variant* magazine was set up by Malcolm Dickson (b.1962) and some other painting graduates from Glasgow School of Art. *Variant* had been conceived partly as a response to Currie's *Stigma* publication, which Dickson and his collaborators felt was overly concerned with Communist party politics. The first few photocopied issues were funded by the Students' Union at the art school, and had a punky, DIY aesthetic informed by Dickson's interest in the local music scene. Dickson's approach had been much-influenced by the sleeve of Leeds-based punk/reggae band Scritti Politti's 1978 debut single *Skank Bloc Bologna*. The single had been released using £500 borrowed from drummer Tom Morley's brother, and the band had attempted to de-mystify the workings of the record industry by printing a breakdown of the record's production costs on the sleeve. *Skank Bloc Bologna* became a significant milestone in the development of the independent music scene in Britain but also provided an inspiring template for people working in other contexts, including Dickson.

In the summer of 1985 Glasgow girl-band Strawberry Switchblade found

71 Another artist associated with the New Glasgow Boys, Steven Conroy (b.1964), was also beginning to attract considerable media attention. The influence of Glaswegian artist James Cowie (1886–1956) could be traced in the quiet colours and suppression of visible brushstrokes in Conroy's portraits.

fleeting fame when their single *Since Yesterday* became a top 40 hit. Glasgow School of Art graduates Rose McDowell and Jill Bryson had been followers of Nu-Sonics and later Orange Juice, and had been well known around town for several years for their distinctive polka dot clothing, beribboned and crimped hair and heavy eyeliner. Orange Juice were still active on the Glasgow scene, as were Aztec Camera, who were also signed to Alan Horne's Postcard Records. Aztec Camera lead singer Roddy Frame, who hailed from the nearby new town of East Kilbride, remembered, "Our attitude was: Haircut 100 are good, they're pop, we like them. It was a little rebellion, anti-authentic, against the gritty reality of rock. It was a camp take on it all. Paradoxically, it [Postcard Records] became a by-word for authenticity."[72] Other uptempo local pop bands included Altered Images and The Bluebells, who scored two top 40 hits in 1984 with *I'm Falling* and *Young at Heart*. The home of the New Romantic movement in Glasgow was the former Locarno on Sauchiehall Street. Then known as Tiffany's, it was the venue of choice for both local bands like Simple Minds and English acts like Adam Ant and Culture Club. By the end of the year, however, Tiffany's had closed down, leaving bars like Fixx on Miller Street and clubs like Maestro's[73] on Scott Street and Nightmoves[74] on Sauchiehall Street as the key venues for live indie music in Glasgow.

The closure of Tiffany's had left a definite gap in the market for an unseated medium-sized venue for bands who couldn't fill The Apollo – or who didn't want to play there, given that venue's association with rock acts like Kiss, Deep Purple and Van Halen. Newly launched central-belt events guide *The List* reported, "It was Simple Minds, starved of their regular and much-loved Tiffany's who had the bright idea of opening up the long since closed former haunt of Bible John [Barrowlands Ballroom], especially to shoot a video."[75] Simple Minds had originally been influenced by Roxy

---

72  Roddy Frame, "Home Entertainment", *The Guardian*, August 16, 2002, pp18–19.
73  Later renamed The Cotton Club, then The Lime, before being absorbed into the CCA buildings in 1999.
74  Later renamed Rooftops and now known as The Moon.
75  Andrea Miller, *The List*, 1st–17th October 1985. The Barrowlands acquired a degree of notoriety in the late '60s when it became the hunting ground for a predatory murderer of women known as Bible John. Bible John strangled three women he picked up at the popular Gallowgate venue during 1968 and 1969. No one was ever arrested in connection with these crimes.

Music and Bowie although shades of Can, Kraftwerk and Neu could also be discerned on releases like *Empires and Dance* (1980). However, by the mid-'80s the band was moving closer to the melodic 'stadium rock' for which they are now better known. Elsewhere, the legacy of punk could still be heard though, in the music of Paisley band Close Lobsters. Lead singer Andrew Burnett, when asked what went through his mind on stage, answered, "I wonder if the girl at the front with the eyes is on drugs and if her boyfriend is here or not, is our bassist going to keel over before the end of the show, if I remembered to leave my zip undone, if Scotland will ever achieve independence in my lifetime etcetera, etcetera."[76]

Craig Tannock, who is now best known as the man behind two of Glasgow's most notable live music venues, The Apollo[77] and the 13th Note, remembers of this period, "I was in this band called News from Nowhere, and I was kind of a player-manager in the band. We got quite a lot of gigs around Glasgow at the time. In Glasgow we'd play at Fixx [on Miller Street] and the Rock Garden [in Queen Street]. We used to rehearse at the Hellfire Club, which was the epicentre of music activity in Glasgow from the mid-'70s until the early '80s. The second incarnation of the Hellfire Club was in the basement of Cava studios, in Bentinck Street. It was run by a guy called Dave Henderson, who was the brother of one of the women in Sophisticated Boom Boom, who were like the next big thing of 1984. Dave Henderson used to do sound and road managing for Simple Minds, he was a good friend of Jim Kerr's. Everybody rehearsed there – Lloyd Cole, Strangers and Brothers, and a reggae/soul collective called Man at the Window. This wee studio was very laid back. It was ramshackle but nice ramshackle. Dave Henderson was a very relaxed guy who seemed to spend a lot of time just watching TV in the studio."[78]

The growing popularity of regional British bands in the 1980s was significantly aided and abetted by Radio 1 DJs John Peel and Janice Long, and their Evening Sessions. Peel, Long and bands like The Fall, The Wedding

---

76  From *Do It For Fun* fanzine, issue #2, self-published, Glasgow, 1985.
77  Tannock's Apollo, a bar/rehearsal suite that opened in 1987 at Renfrew Court, should be differentiated from the large concert venue The Apollo on Renfield Street, which was demolished in 1985.
78  Craig Tannock, in conversation with the author, August 2002.

Present and The Smiths represented both a new post-punk sound and the growing prominence of vernacular speech on British airwaves. The Fall's outspoken lead singer Mark E. Smith provided particularly wry and articulate accounts of the frustrated energy of young people in the North of England, while The Smiths' lead singer Morrissey also made no secret of his contempt for the British Prime Minister. In a 1984 interview with *Rolling Stone* magazine Morrissey opined, "The entire history of Margaret Thatcher is one of violence and oppression and horror. I think that we must not lie back and cry about it. She is only one person, and she can be destroyed."[79] The outspoken political opinions of figures like Mark E. Smith and Morrissey added to the sense that the independent music scene represented a kind of resistance to existing power structures – primarily major record labels but also by extension, the ideology associated with the right-wing government.

In 1985 another Glasgow band called the BMX Bandits formed in Belshill, on the outskirts of the city. The original BMX Bandits line-up included vocalist and composer Duglas T. Stewart, Norman Blake and Frances McKee, although over the next few years the band would have many changes of line-up and would spawn numerous spin offs including The Boy Hairdressers, Teenage Fanclub and Superstar. Another Glasgow band, The Pastels, had released their first single back in 1982, and sub-sequently worked with various independent labels including Creation, Rough Trade and Paper House throughout the '80s. Pastels frontman Stephen McRobbie also ran the Glasgow's premier indie nightclub, Kandy Klub, at the city's Lorne Hotel. Pastels fan Jean-Bernard Andre later wrote, "In the early '80s it seemed that no-one could resist their break-point vocals, languid melodies and exemplary freshness. It was good because they were so far from the fashion of the time, and fiercely aware of their independence."[80] What several of these local bands had in common was their debt to American soul music, in particular the sound of Tamla Motown: The Pastels and BMX Bandits in particular were known for their

79  Morrissey, quoted in *Rolling Stone*, June 7th, 1984.
80  Jean-Bernard Andre, *Les Inrockuptibles* #128 Paris, 1997.

melodic, classically structured songs, use of vocal harmonies and *shimmering* tambourine sounds.

Even East Kilbride band The Jesus and Mary Chain, who were known for their nihilistic lyrics and use of white noise, showed a deep attachment to melody on many albums, perhaps most notably *Darklands* (1987). The band's Velvet Underground-esque compositions had piqued the interest of Glaswegian impresario Alan McGee,[81] of London-based independent label Creation Records, after he had heard a rough 1983 demo tape. McGee commented, "They were either the best band in the world or the worst. I decided to put out a record by them in case they were the best." By 1984 The Jesus and Mary Chain line-up consisted of the two founder members, brothers William and Jim Reid, assisted by Douglas Hart on bass and Bobby Gillespie[82] on drums. The band were notorious for coming on stage late and drunk, as at one gig at North London Polytechnic in 1985 when they took to the stage two and a half hours late and then played an incoherent 20 minute set. The audience showed their appreciation by invading the stage as soon as the band left it and destroying £7000 of equipment.

Although McGee was quick to draw comparisons between his protégées and the earlier antics of the Sex Pistols, The Jesus and Mary Chain could more accurately be understood as part of a tradition of soul-inflected guitar music that had been emerging in Glasgow since the late '70s, that would be continued with bands such as Bobby Gillespie's Primal Scream and Teenage Fanclub as the '80s progressed. Splash 1, the cult nightclub run by members of Primal Scream in Glasgow, revealed the band's love of '60s R'n'B influenced music, ranging from the softer sound of The Byrds and Love to the Rolling Stones, Neil Young and The Beatles. Rhythm guitarist Paul Harte and tambourine player John "the Joogs" Martin shared a Glasgow

---

81  After playing in various bands and launching Communication Blur fanzine in 1983, Alan McGee had established Creation Records in London in 1985. Creation became one of the most successful independent labels of the '80s and '90s, releasing records by The Jesus and Mary Chain, Primal Scream, The House of Love, My Bloody Valentine, Ride and later, Oasis.

82  Bobby Gillespie had worked as roadie for Glasgow band Altered Images and as a bass guitarist for the Wake, before forming his own band, Primal Scream in 1983 with Jim Beattie. Gillespie also worked as a printer, and designed and printed Alan McGee's Communication Blur fanzine as well as the sleeves of several early Creation singles. By 1985 Primal Scream had expanded to become a five-piece band, with Gillespie and Beattie being joined by Robert Young, Paul Harte and John Martin, releasing their first single on Creation that year. In 1986 Gillespie left The Jesus and Mary Chain to concentrate on Primal Scream – he was replaced by John Foster-Moore.

tenement flat with Jim Lambie, who had briefly played in The Boy Hairdressers and would later become better known as a visual artist. One of Primal Scream's followers, Jeff Barrett, remembers that the kitchen of the flat had "a little recess with the width to hold a single mattress, and there'd be a net curtain. Suddenly it would open and there you'd see the Joogs, and the whole fucking thing would be lined with silver foil. He thought he was living in the Factory. The lot of them did."[83]

Another key influence on the Glasgow music scene of this period was Manchester's Factory Records, run by Granada television presenter Tony Wilson with the aim of giving complete artistic freedom to acts including Durutti Column, A Certain Ratio and Joy Division. After lead singer Ian Curtis' suicide in May of 1980, Joy Division's *She's Lost Control* and *Love Will Tear Us Apart* had become definitive anthems for disenfranchised youth.[84] The remainder of the band had released another Joy Division song, *Ceremony*, under the name New Order in 1981, which reached the UK top 40. After recruiting Gillian Gilbert to play keyboards, they began to exploit the possibilities of electronic equipment and by 1983 they had released the UK's biggest selling 12-inch single of all time, dancefloor smash *Blue Monday.*

*Blue Monday* is seen by some as the bridge between '70s disco and the ascension of house music at the end of the '80s, and was followed in 1985 by two more instant club classics, *A Perfect Kiss* and *Sub-Culture*. In Glasgow *Blue Monday* received heavy play at two nightclubs in particular: subterranean Lucifers on Jamaica Street, where DJs Sam Piacenti, Peter McKernnan, Nick Peacock and Euan Dale played funk, soul, jazz and hiphop tracks, and The Shimmy Club, held on Tuesday nights at gay club Bennet's on Glassford Street. The Shimmy Club had been set up in 1983 by Bobby Gibson and Craig Davis, who played an eclectic mix of rare groove '60s soul, '70s dance and funk, R'n'B, punk and the latest dance music tracks – particular favourites being Gill Scott Heron's *The Bottle*, The Clash's

---

83 Jeff Barrett, David Cavanagh, *The Creation Records Story*, Virgin Publishing Ltd., London, 2000, p162.
84 Legendary Manchester-based producer Martin Hannett produced the minimal mixes that were an integral part of the Joy Division sound. In 1981 Hannett would produce another seminal set of recordings, when New York-based all-girl band ESG released their debut 3 track EP on Factory. Hannett's mixes of ESG's Moody, UFO and You're No Good would become instant dance floor classics and lay the foundations of the music form later described as 'mutant disco'.

*Rock the Casbah* and Rose Royce's *Is It Love That You're After?* The club attracted an amiable mix of punks, art students and Bennet's regular gay crowd and, like Edinburgh's Hootchie Cootchie Club,[85] could be seen as the cradle of the early house music scene in Scotland.

85  The Hootchie Cootchie club was set up in Tollcross in 1985 by Edinburgh DJ Yogi Haughton. Guests in the first few years included Unique 3 and Nightmares on Wax.

# CHAPTER 3

# DEMAND THE IMPOSSIBLE
## (1985–1987)

A flood in December of 1984 had forced Transmission to close for five months, and when the gallery reopened in April 1985 it was with a new committee made up of Gordon Muir, Malcolm Dickson, Carol Rhodes, Peter Thompson, Graham Johnstone, Simon Brown and Douglas Aubrey. This second committee continued the politically engaged agenda of the first but a move away from the work of the New Image painters could already be detected in the gallery's programme, which began to feature performance-based work and new video art. The connections between Transmission, the left-wing bookshop Clyde Books on Parnie Street, the WASPS studios and the newly opened Victorian bar at the Tron also contributed to the changing direction of the gallery. The Tron bar had been built up from parts acquired from buildings that were being demolished or redecorated – for example the gantry had been salvaged from a pub in Paisley which had been partially destroyed by fire. Local artist John Taylor, who had remained closely involved in the Glasgow Print Studio, co-ordinated a project for the Tron around this time, asking artists working in WASPS and the Print Studio to paint a small wooden panel to be displayed in the bar. In 1984, two years after the main auditorium had opened, the Tron was able to appoint its first Artistic Director, Michael Boyd.[1] That summer Ian McKenzie had opened Café Gandolfi on Albion Street, with

---

1    Michael Boyd was Artistic Director of The Tron between 1984 and 1996, during which time the theatre won five Mayfest Paperboat Awards, performed twice at the Edinburgh International Festival, won an LWT Plays on Stage Award and toured five times to North America. Actors associated with the theatre include Ewan Bremner, Peter Capaldi, Alan Cumming, Craig Ferguson, Forbes Masson and Peter Mullan.

stained glass windows by John K. Clark and carved wooden furniture by Tim Stead. Tom Laurie remembers, "They didn't understand what Ian meant when he said he wanted a license for a café. The attitude was very much, 'Cafés sell pokey hats and ginger – you don't get wine in a café, son'. It took him ages to get his licence, but he got it."[2] Gandolfi was the first restaurant in the city to offer a menu of traditional Scottish dishes like cullenskink and haggis and neeps alongside mediterranean dishes, and added to the growing atmosphere in the former twilight zone of the Trongate.

The cultural activity at WASPS, the Tron and Transmission were soon supplemented by the establishment of another artist-run initiative in the city. The Glasgow Film and Video Workshop (GFVW) had formed in 1982, and was based at various art centres in the city, including the Dolphin Arts Centre in Bridgeton, throughout the '80s. The GFVW was an important resource for artists who were interested in film and video, and their work would soon begin to figure prominently in Transmission's programme alongside more traditional media. However, one of the artists associated with the gallery was dissatisfied with the direction Transmission was taking. Artist and writer Billy Clark remembers, "Ken Currie sent a letter to Transmission resigning because the gallery was 'bourgeois'. He said he was giving up painting to use film because Lenin had said that film was the greatest tool of the worker. It was rubbish – just an excuse to slag everyone off, and no-one took it that seriously."[3] However, Currie's reservations about painting as a means of expression were shared by many people, several of whom were involved with Transmission. In September 1985 British Situationist artist Ralph Rumney's exhibition of photographs, text, sculpture and reliefs The Map is Not the Territory made a major impact on local artists. Committee member Malcolm Dickson wrote in a press release that Rumney's "rejection of the pseudo-approval of the artworld was fermented by the belief that art had lost its function and that painting was a dishonest way of making a living."[4]

2   Tom Laurie, Ibid.
3   Billy Clark, in conversation with the author, June 2002. Ken Currie worked as the film Production Co-ordinator/Director of Cranhill Community Arts Project between 1983–5, producing *Glasgow 1984* and *The Clyde Film*.
4   1985 Transmission press release.

In London, contemporary painting was as popular as ever, as the inaugural year of the Turner Prize in 1984 proved. Britain's biggest art prize, at that time, had been established by the Tate to stimulate debate around contemporary British art and in the first year was awarded to expatriate painter Malcolm Morley, who beat fellow nominees Richard Deacon, Gilbert & George, Howard Hodgkin and Richard Long. In 1985 Hodgkin was re-nominated for his colourful semi-abstract works, and this time he won over Terry Atkinson, Tony Cragg, Ian Hamilton Finlay, John Walker and curator Milena Kalinovska. That year also saw the opening of Charles Saatchi's gallery in London, with an exhibition of the work of Donald Judd, Brice Marden, Cy Twombly and Andy Warhol. Having made a splash in advertising circles with his agency's campaigns for the Conservative party, Saatchi was already causing an even bigger stir in art circles by bulk-buying work by emerging artists, such as Italian "New Image" painter Sandro Chia and New Yorker Julian Schnabel.

By 1985 Ken Currie was working on a series of large-scale murals depicting the radical history of Glasgow for the City Council-run People's Palace Museum. Currie's murals represented events such as the 1787 Massacre of the Calton Weavers and the Great Reform Agitation. Currie used dramatic chiaroscuro effects, contrasting black shadows with fire toned highlights on the muscular bodies and anxious faces of his subjects. The compositions were packed with a confusion of bodies and faces, and wreathed with banners and slogans declaring Union is Strength and We Want Justice. As the boom in figurative painting continued, two of Currie's contemporaries, Steven Campbell and Peter Howson, both sold works to the Tate and Campbell, Howson and Currie were all invited to exhibit in the high profile exhibition New Image Glasgow at the Third Eye Centre in Glasgow.[5] Currie's new enthusiasm for painting had caused a breach with his collaborators at the Cranhill Community Arts Project, and he wrote an article in *The Edinburgh Review*[6] defending his volte-face. He wrote,

5    This exhibition was curated by Alexander Moffat and featured the work of three of the artists who had been included in Transmission's first show: Peter Howson, Ken Currie, and Adrian Wiszniewski, plus Steven Campbell, Mario Rossi and Stephen Barclay.
6    Cultural journal *The Edinburgh Review* was edited by Peter Kravitz between 1984 and 1990.

"Although we all despise how capitalism has enmeshed art with money, it boils down to simple economics: paint and sell or starve – principles will never pay the rent and this is called pragmatism, not an excuse."[7] By late summer, the "New Glasgow Boys" were being hailed in the national press as one of the most interesting group of artists to emerge in some years. The favourable review of New Image Glasgow ("The Glow that Came from Glasgow") by Waldemar Januszcak in *The Guardian* that August indicated burgeoning critical interest in the work being made in the city at this time. For a city that was usually singled out in the national press because of the attendant problems of post-industrial decline, the positive press coverage generated by these artists was no small matter.

Nicola White was working as Exhibitions Co-ordinator at the Third Eye Centre at the time of New Image Glasgow and says, "It was a very good time to be in Glasgow, with the way that things changed over that period. Steven Campbell had just come back from New York and he was like 'the first famous Glasgow artist'. He was the first person who went away and was a success somewhere like New York and it was quite an incredible thing at the time. Our circles of influence were much smaller then. I think there were people who were very influenced by Steven Campbell, many of whom were students of Roger Hoare, who was one of the most influential teachers at the Art School. Peter Howson and Ken Currie were also in the show, although Ken had only just started to do drawings and paintings – cynics used to say he had been influenced by how well Steven was doing with figurative painting. In the early '80s painting was interesting again in London and New York and Berlin, and New Image Glasgow was part of that zeitgeist. Suddenly Glasgow, which had been a painting kind of place for decades, was on the pulse, and so the spotlight shifted to here, which was quite novel. It raised the bar for a lot of people – who saw that kind of critical attention or a wider sphere of influence was possible."[8] Curator Andrew Nairne, who was then working at Kettle's Yard in Cambridge but would later become Exhibitions Co-ordinator at the Third Eye Centre,

---

7    Ken Currie, "New Glasgow Painting in Context", in the *Edinburgh Review*, no.72, 1985, pp71–72.
8    Nicola White, Ibid.

agrees. "I think the new generation of Scottish artists, who have been hugely successful, Douglas Gordon and many others, all owe something to Steven Campbell, because he showed that it was possible to stay in Scotland and have your roots in Scotland and be a huge success internationally."[9]

Transmission was still staging shows and projects that linked art and politics, such as War of Images: Art and the Battle of Ideas[10] – described in the gallery press release as "politically engaged artists acting in a variety of media." War of Images featured artists from London, Liverpool and Glasgow and was held at both Transmission and Glasgow School of Art, ensuring that the links between the school and the gallery remained current. Ralph Rumney was invited back to participate in this exhibition, along with more than twenty-five other artists working in media ranging from painting to experimental sound work. Billy Clark remembers of this early period: "I first became involved with Transmission around the time of War of Images. Peter Kravitz, the editor of *The Edinburgh Review* had seen this War of Images show that Malcolm Dickson and Helen Flockart had put up, and wrote about it, picking up on the zeitgeist and what was going on. He wrote that this work seemed quite different to the work being made by Ken Currie and Adrian Wiszniewski and Steven Campbell, who by then were quite well known. Ken Currie had also contributed to *The Edinburgh Review* in the past. Peter lived in the same street as Malcolm Dickson, and when Peter and Malcolm got together I would get together with them. So out of that Malcolm and I wrote a response to the New Image writing that had previously appeared in *The Edinburgh Review*."[11]

Malcolm Dickson lost no time in drawing attention to the weaknesses he perceived in Currie's work, or to his recent change of ideological stance. He wrote, "New Image presents the opportunity of catching up with the fashions in contemporary art whilst missing out completely late-modernist tendencies such as performance. It also offers international prestige, the artist as Romantic hero, accumulation of wealth, social and cultural power

---

9   Andrew Nairne, Steven Campbell, Art Works Scotland, Ibid.

10   13th–31st January 1986.

11   Billy Clark, Ibid. Peter Kravitz had identified the influence of the punk scene and the Situationist International in his review of "War of Images".

and a reassertion of the Marketplace. [Currie's] previous intransigence and hard-line stance was vulnerable and has been dropped ... Currie's work is more consumable and the man himself is no longer a threat."[12]

Clark and Dickson's articles prompted a series of letters to *The Edinburgh Review*, most of which accused the Transmission committee of elitism. Dickson's lengthy response maintained that the opposite was true, and that Currie was guilty of a narrow ideological outlook. He wrote, "Currie claims to speak on behalf of a class which is depicted as a formless mass of socialised humanity. Perhaps the greatest drawback in his work is that he tries to fit reality into ideological theory, as presented by the British Communist Party. Such outdated revolutionary phraseology corresponds with the form it has chosen. As epitaphs to the bereavement of Red Clydeside, his art is moving in a sincere way. In the present, however, there is no room for, or an understanding of, a situation of plurality in culture and in politics."[13]


## ENVIRONMENTAL ART


"To paraphrase a preface to Michel de Certeau's essay, 'Walking in the City', public art gives to walking that extra meaning and makes it different to the official, from the business of life, in the way that poetry is different from a planning manual. It slows down the pace and increases perception. It grants to the twentieth-century urban experience a kind of drifting and the glamour that Walter Benjamin found in the nineteenth-century 'leisured observer'. Everyday life has a special value when it takes place in the gaps of the larger power structures."[14]


In 1985, the new Environmental Art Department at Glasgow School of Art was formalised by the appointment of David Harding as the Head of

---

12 Malcolm Dickson, "Polemics: Glasgow Painting Now", *The Edinburgh Review* No.73, 1985, p61.
13 Malcolm Dickson, "Masses of Compromise or the Germs of Sedition", *The Edinburgh Review*, No. 74, 1985, pp172–175.
14 David Harding, "Decadent", Foulis Press, Glasgow, 1997, p17, referencing Michel de Certeau, *The Practice of Everyday Life*, University of California Press, Berkeley, 1984.

Department.[15] Harding had previously spent a decade as the town artist in the new town of Glenrothes, and worked for eight years as the developer of the "Art in Social Context" course at Dartington College. Harding's new course at Glasgow offered students at the school an alternative to the existing fine art categories of Painting, Printmaking and Sculpture, and was influenced by the New Genre public art writings of Suzanne Lacy and Lucy R. Lippard. Harding also responded favourably to some of the suggestions made by his students (some of whom later claimed to have written the course document). The department was located in the old Girl's High School on Scott Street, described as "perfect: isolated from the other departments, a good half of it decaying. The tower, toilets and the basement were installations waiting to happen."[16] In the late '80s and early '90s, the department included Christine Borland, Claire Barclay, Douglas Gordon, Craig Richardson, Roderick Buchanan, Ross Sinclair, Louise Scullion, Nathan Coley and Martin Boyce amongst its students.

David Harding remembers, "What amazed me was the sophistication of three or four of those particular students at that time. They seemed to have already articulated an opposition to painting, but particularly the figurative, expressionist, new painting of Wiszniewski, Campbell, and these people. Now they had done this in their first year! [ … ] To work with students who had such strongly held views – and amazingly coming out of West of Scotland comprehensives with a very developed view and knowledge of contemporary art practice – that was astonishing for me."[17]

It is important to remember that the collection of modern art in Glasgow's museums is limited in comparison to other major European cities, and that Glasgow's museums receive a substantially smaller rate of government subsidy than those in the capital, Edinburgh.[18] The red sandstone "Hispanic Baroque" Kelvingrove Art Gallery and Museum, erected in 1901 with the proceeds of the second Great Exhibition, holds works by

---

15  The course had already been running without a Head of Department or a definite structure for a year, when Christine Borland and Douglas Gordon had been amongst the intake of students.

16  A.J. Close, "Home Is Where the Art Is", *Scotsman*, 18th May, 2002, pp2–4.

17  David Harding, interviewed by John Calcutt, *Here + Now*, Dundee, 2001.

18  This continues to be the case – in 2002, Edinburgh's museums had an annual budget of £30m, whereas Glasgow's budget was £17m.

Monet, Cezanne, Van Gogh, Gauguin, Matisse, Picasso and Braque, several landscapes and portraits by the first Glasgow Boys and the French-influenced Scottish Colourists Cadell, Fergusson, Hunter and Peploe. There are also paintings by Cezanne and Manet at the Burrell Collection in Pollock Park, and Salvador Dali's *Christ of Saint John of the Cross* (1951) is on permanent display in the city,[19] but those seeking seminal recent art would have to head for the library to pore over reproductions. As Glasgow-based artist Martin Boyce notes, "If you've grown up in Glasgow you've never seen a Warhol – you've never seen any modern art of any great significance. My memory of going to Kelvingrove or the Hunterian or any of those places was that they were places where everything was very old – that a museum was a place with lots of really old brown things. My first experience of modern art was Rauschenberg and Warhol and Oldenburg in reproduction also of course there was a photo of Duchamp's urinal. I thought, this is what modern art looks like. It always felt like you had to go somewhere else to experience it."[20]

In addition to the limitations of the public art collections, there were also few artists producing "ideas-based" art in Scotland at this time, although Graeme Murray continued to support the work of artists like Ian Hamilton Finlay at the gallery he ran from his home in Edinburgh. In 1985, Fruitmarket director Mark Francis invited American conceptual artist Dan Graham and American feminist artist Nancy Spero to exhibit in Edinburgh, considerably widening the existing frame of reference for Scottish artists. By the mid-'80s a new strand of artistic practice had been identified in the work of American artists Jenny Holzer, Barbara Kruger, Jeff Koons, Cindy Sherman and Sherrie Levine. The work of these artists shared some formal strategies with the conceptual artists of the '70s but was differentiated by their use of themes and materials drawn from everyday life. Their work, which was described by a number of critics as neo-conceptual, also responded in various ways to critical theory relating to authorship, commodity culture and feminism. This new area of practice brought to an end the predominance of neo-expressionist painting, and heralded a new

---

19  This work was originally on display at Kelvingrove Museum and Art Gallery before being moved to the new St. Mungo's Museum of Religious Life in Glasgow in 1993.
20  Martin Boyce, in conversation with the author, February 2002.

emphasis on photography and installation in the art world.

The interdisciplinary nature of David Harding's Environmental Art course corresponded with the increasingly fluid nature of art internationally. Twenty years earlier Allan Kaprow had written, "The young artists of today need no longer say 'I am a painter' or 'a poet' or 'a dancer'. He is simply an artist. All of life will be open to him."[21] Kaprow's challenge to the assumption that art is based on the craftmanship and permanence of the object was actively explored in the Environmental Art department, as Harding and tutors Sam Ainsley, Brian Kelly and Stan Bonner reworked the old Murals and Stained Glass department into a challenging new discipline. The department adopted the unofficial motto "Context is half the work" drawn from John Latham and Barbara Stevini's 1965 Artists' Placement Group and the tutors supported the growth of site-specific and installation work, which encouraged a general shift away from the art school's legacy of figurative painting.[22] So much had the debate surrounding art in Glasgow moved on that some of the students in the Environmental Art department denied that the New Image painters had any relevance to their practice at all. Douglas Gordon (b.1966) later said, "People ask us if we were reacting against artists like Steven Campbell and Adrian Wiszniewski, who were prominent when we were at school. But really, nobody could be bothered. They were so far away from what we were trying to do, we didn't use them as a reference point at all."[23]

Martin Boyce (b.1967) elected to join the Environmental Art department at the end of his first year of studies at the art school, after noticing the work being made by Environmental Art students Douglas Gordon, Iain Kettles and Ross Sinclair. He remembers, "The reaction against figurative painting was something that was almost more easily articulated after the fact. Other processes had begun to happen, and probably as much


21  Allan Kaprow, "Assemblages, Events and Happenings", New York, 1965.
22  A parallel can be drawn between the Environmental Art Department and Goldsmiths College, London, where Jon Thompson had abolished divisions between departments while Head of Fine Art in the early '70s. In 1974 Thompson invited the Yale-trained conceptual artist Michael Craig-Martin to teach at the school. Craig-Martin worked as a tutor at the school until 1988, where he came into contact with students including Damien Hirst, Sarah Lucas, Simon Patterson and Gary Hume. His promotion of multi-media, ideas-based art has subsequently been credited as a key factor in the emergence of the Young British Artists of the late '80s and early '90s.
23  Matthew Slotover, "Northern Lights", frieze, Issue 1, 1991, p40.

as anything it was about a department identity. I was very conscious then of the idea that the sculpture guys looked a certain way and the painting guys looked a certain way – the painters wore overalls and the sculptors always had plaster dust all over their shoes. Environmental Art guys wore second-hand suits and had shaved heads and Doc Martens – there was a bit of a look going on between different departments. There was an attempt to identify yourself in relation or in opposition to other departments, so there was probably a sense of not wanting to relate to what had happened in painting, but also not being able to relate to it. The classic motifs of a lot of that work – of shipbuilding and dockers – just didn't have any real relation to us, or certainly not to me anyway. So you started to look at other things. In Environmental Art it was accepted that painting, sculpture, photography, performance and wall painting were all just options in making an artwork – they were all strategies or possibilities rather than there being a dominant medium or approach."[24]

Students were encouraged to undertake comprehensive research, to produce art outside studios and galleries ('with or through people')[25], and to seek permission to install their work in the public domain. One of the first students on the new course was Christine Borland (b.1965) who later said, "Environmental Art gave me the practical means of getting in touch with people and also the desire to do it."[26] Environmental Art students were required to produce and site a piece of public art every year from second year onwards, and this assignment encouraged students to become adept at writing proposals and approaching local authorities. Sam Ainsley says, "Quite often in the department people had to persuade people who either didn't know anything about art or even actively hated it, to allow them to site a work. Those powers of persuasion, negotiation and sheer stubbornness in terms of making projects happen did differentiate the students in the department from students in other departments where their only context was the gallery."[27]

24  Martin Boyce, in conversation with the author, February 2002.
25  Environmental Art course document, Glasgow School of Art, 1995.
26  Christine Borland interviewed for The Late Show, BBC Scotland, 2nd April 1994.
27  Sam Ainsley, in conversation with the author, May 2001. The establishment of public art commissioning agency Art in Partnership in Edinburgh during 1985 also brought increased support for Scottish artists who were interested in working outside the gallery.

Like Environmental Art, Fine Art Photography was a late addition to the curriculum, but by 1984 was running under the rigorous command of Thomas Joshua Cooper (b.1946), the respected American fine art photographer, who encouraged students to engage with current critical theory surrounding photography. Joshua Cooper had been born in San Francisco, trained in California and New Mexico, and had taught in Nottingham before moving to Glasgow. The opening of the new Photography department at the school chimed with a general increase of interest in contemporary photography – The Photographer's Gallery had opened in London in 1970, and Stills was established in Edinburgh in 1976. The Glasgow Photography Group, active within the city at this time, was also moving towards the establishment of the city's first photography-specific gallery, Streetlevel, which was founded in the High Street in late 1989. Ray McKenzie, of the Glasgow School of Art's Historical and Critical Studies Department, was closely involved with the earliest incarnations of Streetlevel, and also supported the emergence of the discipline within the school.

Changes were also afoot at Transmission, as Malcolm Dickson, Carol Rhodes and Billy Clark began to make some improvements to the way the gallery was run. Clark says, "The SAC weren't interested in supporting us, and at that point the council weren't that supportive either. The base economics of it was that the council gave us the Chisholm Street gallery rent free, and that was their contribution to the gallery. There wasn't any money to run it and initially the idea was of a temporary space – it was like a club – you joined it and sent in your slides, and you got a chance to show there. But you hung your paintings and printed your poster yourself. Malcolm changed that, but a lot of the work of running the gallery was also done by Carol Rhodes. I would go down and help Carol with the mail outs and hanging shows, and gradually because of the nature of the work, we started to work more closely with the artists and to want to get money for them. That sounds basic, but then it was quite an initiative to think that way. I had the idea that anyone could join Transmission, not just artists, and that the committee should run it properly, because sometimes no-one was coming down and opening it up.

There also wasn't a big audience, so we had to build one up from scratch, sending out leaflets, going up to the art school and putting up posters around town. The audience that we got became our next committee."[28]

Over the following two year period several people were involved in the running of Transmission for varying lengths of time including Billy Clark, Malcolm Dickson, Carol Rhodes, Richard Walker, Gillian Steel, Tommy Lydon, John Main, Scott Paterson, Karen Strang, Anne Vance, Anne Elliot, Gordon Muir and Jayne Taylor. This group of artist-organisers were particularly interested in time-based, installation, site specific and issue-based work, and they staged several events influenced by the alternative exhibition strategies of New York's Fluxus movement and the Parisian Situationist International. Besides art exhibitions, readings, performances and discussions also took place in and around Transmission. The level of visual art activity within the city was matched by a literary renaissance, much of which emanated from The Third Eye Centre, Transmission, and the magazines *Variant, Here & Now* and *The Edinburgh Review.* However, during these "Thatcher years", both Transmission and *Variant* represented a strand of thought that was decidedly unpopular with Timothy Mason, the conservative Scottish Arts Council director. The Transmission committee's steadfast refusal to appoint a paid administrator perplexed and irritated the SAC, who seemed unwilling at that time to understand the ideological framework of Transmission. An unrepentant Malcolm Dickson later wrote that "voluntary spaces [ … ] are fundamentally different in kind from those based on a hierarchy of paid administrators 'doing a job'. This approach is based upon trust and a sympathy to other peoples' points of view."[29]

In 1986, the video, film, performance and installation group shows Glasgow Event Space 1 and 2 were held at Transmission, which provided an opportunity for the gallery to forge links with other independent arts organisations. The inaugural Event Space in February was the first exhibition in Scotland of video work since the '70s,[30] and was influenced by the work of the Electronic Imaging department at Duncan of Jordanstone

---

28  Billy Clark, in conversation with the author, June 2002.
29  Malcom Dickson, "Hit the North", unpublished essay on Transmission, 1996.
30  Video: *Towards Defining an Aesthetic,* held at The Third Eye Centre in 1976.

art college in Dundee[31] and probably, indirectly, by the dominance of video and performance art in the London art scene of the period.[32] Malcolm Dickson remembers, "Event Space 1 [ … ] involved Stephen Partridge from Dundee, Doug Aubrey and Alan Robertson of Pictorial Heroes."[33] That event, held at Transmission in its early years, was the first exhibition in Scotland of video since the 1970s. Artists included were Kevin Atherton, Steve Littman, Zoe Redman, Partridge, Rigby and more."[34] Former Third Eye Centre director and writer Tom McGrath had been working as a writer in residence at Duncan of Jordanstone between 1985 and 86, and introduced the exhibition on the opening night. Event Space 1 featured contributions from Projects UK in Newcastle and from IKON, the video company affiliated to Manchester's Factory Records. The second Event Space featured a selection of video art spanning twenty years from the Federal Republic of Germany, a series of 16mm films by women artists and performances by Richard Layzell and Charlie Hooker.

Performance artist and Slade tutor Stuart Brisley (b.1933) also appeared at the second Event Space. Brisley had shown in Scotland before, notably during the 1971 Edinburgh Festival as part of Locations Edinburgh exhibition. He was famed for physically taxing durational performances, such as *And For Today, Nothing* (1972) which involved sitting in a bath of black liquid and rotting meat for two days and *10 Days* (1972). For *10 Days*, he was served with food which he refused every day over the festive period, finally crawling through the debris on New Year's Eve, and ending the performance with a vast meal. Although by the mid-80s Brisley had tired of the art world's preconceptions of his work, he viewed Transmission as a sympathetic and experimental space, and continued to present performance works there, such

---

31  Video artist Stephen Partridge began working as a tutor at Duncan of Jordanstone in the mid-1980s. He persuaded the college to invest significant resources in the video department, and it has subsequently become one of the UK's leading centres for video and media art teaching and production.

32  Perhaps the most prominent London-based artists working with performance and video were Gilbert & George, who in the summer of 1986 won The Turner Prize. That year they exhibited some of their early drawings at the Fruitmarket in Edinburgh at the invitation of director Mark Francis.

33  Doug Aubrey recently described the work of his production company Pictorial Heroes as, "Future film making from the land of bravehearts and trainspotters. Born out of the punk, do it yourself (DIY) and warehouse cultures of the eighties, Pictorial Heroes are one of Scotland's most progressive film/tv and web production companies. Maverick, renegade and fearlessly independent, their recent productions have been at the cutting edge of digital film making and the new documentary form in Scotland."

34  Chris Byrne and Malcolm Dickson, "Moving History", *Variant* Issue 6, Glasgow.

as *Red Army 2* (1986). This performance utilised broken glass, spoken word, gestural painting and chemical fire extinguishers to conjure up some of the contradictory ideas surrounding the Russian Revolution.

During this period Transmission remained committed to showing work that engaged with the local community, such as Community and Art (March 1986), an exhibition about the work of Community Visual Arts Projects undertaken by Kate Thomson, Katie Lorimer and Jayne Taylor around Glasgow. Katie Lorimer had been working since 1983 in the Glasgow Eastern Area Renewal (GEAR) zone, on a variety of projects, often working collaboratively with John Upton, former artist in residence for the new town of Irvine. One of Upton and Lorimers' joint projects was a Tollcross Park kite fly-past in which a hundred local children took part. Lorimer said, "Most of the children had never flown a kite before, so there was the added bonus of witnessing the joy on their faces as their achievements in making the kites were rewarded by learning how to fly them."[35] Many artists living in Glasgow shared Upton and Lorimer's commitment to making socially engaged art, although there was still a noticeable lack of the public funds needed to underpin this kind of work.

In contrast to Glasgow, the cultural scene in Edinburgh seemed to be extremely buoyant. Edinburgh's city centre architecture had remained impressive throughout the years, never suffering from bombing raids or ill-advised 1960s trends in town planning. Glasgow based poet Liz Lochhead[36] wrote in her 1984 *Poem On a Day Trip* that Edinburgh was:

*No mean city, but genteel, grey and clean city*
*you diminish me – make me feel my coat is cheap,*
*shabby, vulgar coloured.*
*You make me aware of your architecture,*
*conscious of history and the way it has*
*of imposing itself upon people.*

---

35  John Kraska, Public and "Community Visual Arts Projects in Glasgow", *The Visual Arts in Glasgow, Tradition and Transformation*, The Third Eye Centre, 1985.

36  Motherwell-born Lochhead (b.1947) had trained as a painter in Glasgow, before becoming better known as a poet. For Lochhead, Edwin Morgan's interest in "pure sound" and commitment to spoken Scots provided an inspiring point of departure and in 1985/6 she translated Moliere's Tartuffe into "a totally invented and, I hope, theatrical Scots" for Edinburgh's Lyceum.

Edinburgh's economy had remained relatively stable since the Second World War, and the International Festival had continued to attract increasing numbers of tourists to the city year on year. The Scottish National Gallery of Modern Art had moved from the Botanical Gardens to splendid new premises at Belford Road in 1984, and Mark Francis had continued to attract a steady stream of highly respected artists to exhibit at the Fruitmarket, including Gilbert & George, Mary Kelly,[37] Italian Arte Povera artist Luciano Fabro and American conceptual artist Lawrence Weiner. He remembers, "I brought Lawrence Weiner to do shows in Edinburgh and Orkney in 1986, which I'm sure had an influence on young artists studying in Glasgow at that time. [That same year] Donald Judd also came and did a very lengthy and involved talk."[38]

Meanwhile, the Traverse theatre that Richard Demarco had helped to establish now moved to larger premises in the Grassmarket, and boasted two auditoriums. Plays by young Scottish writers like Tom McGrath, Andrew Dallmeyer and John Byrne were now more common than the Ibsen and Chekhov classics that had filled the theatre's programme in the early '60s. As in the '60s, however, Edinburgh University continued to attract the bohemian-inclined sons and daughters of the wealthy.[39] In April 1986, the same year that Band Aid took place, three Edinburgh University graduates, Charles Booth Clibborn, Jay Jopling and Greville Worthington organised the New Art New World auction in the city. The event raised £500,000 for Save the Children by selling works donated by Keith Haring, Julian Schnabel and Jean-Michel Basquiat. The worthiness of the enterprise was not in doubt, but it did demonstrate that while charity in Glasgow still "began at home", fifty miles away in Edinburgh young arts events organisers were considerably more prosperous and internationally well-connected.

37  American artist Mary Kelly's *Post-partum Document* (1973–9) challenged the assumption that motherhood is an instinctive experience. For this ambitious 165 piece work, Kelly combined found objects (used nappies, stained cloths etc.) with language drawn from psychoanalysis, linguistics, archeology and science to chart her son's early development. Although the *Post-partum Document* was initially derided by many critics, it is now considered to rank alongside Judy Chicago's *The Dinner Party* (1974–9) as a cornerstone of feminist art practice.

38  Mark Francis, in conversation with the author, August 2002.

39  Recent figures show that 13% of the total entrants to Edinburgh University are working class, as opposed to 21% of the entrants to Glasgow University. Source: *The Guardian*, March 4th, 2003.

Back in Glasgow, new Transmission committee member Billy Clark was interested in further developing the conversations he and Malcolm Dickson had with *The Edinburgh Review* editor Peter Kravitz and local writer James Kelman further within the context of Transmission. Billy Clark recalls, "Most of the people who I had been most influenced by, I didn't really consider them to be in the art world. A guy like James Kelman, for instance – I met him through Peter Kravitz, who knew him because he had been involved in producing *The Busconductor Hines*. We met up in The Halt[40] occasionally and from that everyone would talk about doing something – we all had lots of ideas about what we should be doing. We were also putting on these readings, Transmission Goes Verbal."[41]

The first Transmission Goes Verbal, in August 1986 featured readings from poet Tom Leonard (b.1944) and James Kelman (b.1946). James Kelman's first short story collection *Not Not While the Giro* (1983) and 1984 debut novel *The Busconductor Hines* had forced vernacular speech and socialist thought to the forefront of the new Scottish literary scene, while Leonard was well known for his sharp satirical verse. His poem *ma language is disgraceful* (1980) was a list of all the people who had chastised him for his mode of speech, including "sum wee smout thit thoat ah hudny read Chomsky" and "a calvinistic community thit thoat ah wuz revisionist." Kelman and Leonard's Transmission Goes Verbal event also proved to be an important catalyst in bringing about another organisation that would support political discussion in the city. Billy Clark remembered, "After their readings there was a big discussion, about politics, and the spirit of that carried on into other events … out of that came the Free University, which began in January 1987."[42] The Free University was held in various flats around Glasgow over the next five years, and was run by Malcolm Dickson, Carol Rhodes, Nicola White, Billy Clark, James Kelman, Alasdair Gray and Keith Miller. The flyer for the inaugural meeting in West End Park Street, read: "part free university, part late/cheap café, unemployed centre, artspace etc. DEMAND THE IMPOSSIBLE."

---

40  In the '80s, when The Halt on the corner of West End Park Street and Woodlands Road was run by Jim McIntyre, it hosted large scale multiband events, various DJ nights and a lively bohemian clientele. The Halt has been under different management since the mid '90s, and has also been remodelled, resulting in the loss of much of the original atmosphere.
41  Billy Clark, Ibid.
42  Billy Clark, Ibid.

Third Eye Centre Exhibitions Co-ordinator Nicola White had been helping out informally at Transmission for some time, and she was also involved with the early meetings of the The Free University. She remembers, "First of all we met in various flats, including Carol Rhodes', but when we had events we would meet in places like Maryhill Community Halls, Govan Halls and for a while we all had weekly meetings in Charing Cross Housing association in Lynedoch Street because they lent us a room. It was great – a really unstructured education which is probably one of the best kinds. People would take it in turns to organise meetings and we had all different sorts of people along to speak. At one meeting we had Glasgow anarchists in their '60s who'd been through a lot of direct action stuff after the war – they talked about the Anarchist movement in Scotland and its roots. We also had Adele Patrick from Women in Profile giving a talk about architecture and feminism. It was an ideas forum, it was very loose and it fed off energy."[43]

Several of the grassroots initiatives in Glasgow, specifically The Free University, Transmission, *Variant* and the co-operative Green City Wholefoods[44] positioned themselves ideologically very much in opposition to the Thatcher government. It could be said that Thatcherism created a situation whereby a particularly resistant strain of cultural activity could flourish. Although several commentators have linked the DIY movement with the idea of the 'self-made man' the collective, profit-sharing framework of many of the enterprises in the city was decidedly at odds with Thatcher's ideology. In 1986, inspired by the example of the Hellfire Club, Craig Tannock and his News from Nowhere band-mate Lachlan McQuarrie decided to set up a rehearsal space and demo tape recording facility. Tower Studios opened in the basement of a building beside the old Trinity college towers near Park Circus in March 1987, although as Tannock remembers, there was a long process to go through first.

"Lachlan and I had this very naive idea that we could open a little rehearsal studio that would be a good facility for our band, and also give us something

---

43  Nicola White, in conversation with the author, November 2002.

44  Green City Wholefoods was set up as a co-operative by Martin Meatyard and others in Fleming Street in the East End of Glasgow in the late '70s. At one time the biggest wholefood wholesalers in Britain, it was affiliated with various other organisations, including the Campaign for Nuclear Disarmament and Grassroots health food shop (then on Great Western Road).

to do, and a small wage as opposed to the dole. We wanted to set up as a co-op so we went along to the Scottish Co-operative Development Committee because we didn't have a clue about anything. They helped us with a business plan and cash-flow forecast. We had proper recording equipment, but it was quite basic so we didn't make any grand claims for ourselves: we said the studio was strictly for demo tapes. In about '86 we had been joined by a friend called Davie Garrett, who was the drummer in a band called The Tremens, but we also had quite a few problems before it opened.

We had a cowboy builder so it ended up costing twice as much as it should've, so that meant we couldn't afford to renovate the whole space we were renting. The landlord also gave us a false indication of what the rates were going to be – they were double the amount he told us. When we opened the door we were actually insolvent, although we didn't realise that until a year and a half later when the accountant found out. We invited people we knew who had local bands to come and rehearse there, people like Pauline and the Perverts, Conduct of Pigeons, Painted Word and The Hummingbirds – they were Brian Toland's band, who had been in the first Del Amitri line-up. At that point everybody was in a band so it only took a few months for the studio to become quite busy."[45]

That year Scottish firm McEwans Lager had commissioned a couple of television adverts, one of which strongly resembled Duran Duran's video for *The Reflex*. In this advert, stone balls rolled down a fantastic Escher-like structure, manned by blue painted slaves. The other, less memorable, advert showed flames inside a railway carriage. The soundtracks to the adverts were provided by two then-unsigned Scottish bands, Hipsway and Win. The adverts gave Tannock an idea about approaching McEwans for financial backing for showcase gigs by the bands that used Tower Studios. He says, "By that point News from Nowhere had split up and Lachlan and I had formed a new band called The Repercussions. Our drummer had a brother who was a dodgy car salesman, and we had no confidence or

45 Craig Tannock, in conversation with the author, August 2002.

experience in dealing with people in suits, so we sent him instead. He went in with our proposal and got a deal with McEwans to support us for the first gig at Fury Murray's in September. It was called Tower Beat, and it became a monthly gig."[46]

Although guitar bands had been and would remain a key part of the Glasgow music scene, in the late '80s many young musicians were turning away from traditional instruments in favour of turntables and electronic synthesisers. The sound of Chicago house[47] had been slowly filtering into Britain for a couple of years, with Farley "Jackmaster" Funk and Steve "Silk" Hurley both scoring top 40 hits in 1986 and 87. The equipment that was required to make the new sound was quickly acquired by British dance acts Coldcut, S-Express, M/A/R/R/S and Bomb the Bass, who later mounted a series of successful raids on the Top 40 with heavily sampled tracks assembled in home studios. As former *i-D* editor Matthew Colin wrote, "The way music could now be composed on a four track recorder, assembled from samples and beatboxes, then cut to a white label 12-inch single and sold through independent dance record stores, was a democratisation of the creative process, just as desk-top publishing had opened up the publishing industry and enabled the rise of the fanzine. Its do-it-yourself, open-access strategy was repeatedly compared to the anti-musicianship ethics of punk rock, but samplers and drum computers also banished the need to learn to play instruments, to rehearse, to book recording studios, to organise gigs or even to seek a record contract."[48]

DJ Mike Pickering and his partner Martin Prendergast had been running Nude Night at Manchester's Haçienda every Friday since 1984, which had been one of the earliest clubs to play Chicago house tracks, not to mention new experimental recordings by local artists like *Pacific State* by 808 State and A Guy Called Gerald's *Voodoo Ray*. Glasgow had been a stronghold of successive youth culture movements since the 1920s, and was also quick to

---

46  Craig Tannock, Ibid.
47  House music had got its name from the warehouses where the first big Chicago parties were held, while its off-shoot, acid house, had developed from an unexpected squelchy sound effect derived from the Roland TB 303 bass machine.
48  Matthew Colin, *Altered State The Story of Ecstasy Culture and Acid House*, Serpent's Tail, London, 1997, p59.

take up the new music and the new drug, ecstasy,[49] that was lending momentum to the scene. As Simon Reynolds writes in *Energy Flash – A Journey Through Rave Music and Dance Culture*, "When large numbers of people took ecstasy together, the drug catalysed a strange and wondrous atmosphere of collective intimacy, an electric sense of connection between complete strangers. Even more significantly, MDMA turned out to have a uniquely synergistic/synaesthetic interaction with music, especially uptempo, repetitive, electronic dance music."[50] Inspired by house tracks like Fingers Inc.'s *Washing Machine* and Phuture's *Acid Trax*, enterprising Scots like Funk D'Void (Lars Sandberg), Harri and DJ duo Slam (Stuart McMillan and Orde Meikle) soon laid their hands on the necessary equipment and began producing their own electronic compositions.

The Shimmy Club was no longer the only place in the city to go to hear the new house music from America, as regular nights of 'black American music' were now being hosted by Radio Clyde DJ Segun, Slam and Harri at Fury Murray's on Maxwell Street, Joe Paparazzi on Sauchiehall Street and Tin Pan Alley off Argyle Street. Jamaica Street basement club Lucifers had recently been taken over by Graham Wilson and Gregg MacLeod, who had the interior remodelled by design firm The Cloth before reopening under a new name, the Sub Club. The club's DJ roster had changed too, as Harri, Yogi Haughton, Bob Jeffries, Segun and Michael McCrimmon introduced more new dance music alongside classic black roots music. Jonnie Wilkes, who had recently moved to the city to study at the art school, remembers that this new music changed the whole club experience. "It was the first thing that made people dance strangely. I didn't really understand it, because before in clubs people stood around the dancefloor drinking. The next week I threw away the lager and went dancing too."[51]

---

49  Ecstasy and speed were the two main "recreational" drugs initially associated with the scene, although cocaine would later also become extremely popular. Ecstasy or MDMA was rediscovered in the early '60s by Alexander Shulgin, a biochemist working for Dow Chemicals while also secretly experimenting with psychedelics. In the late '70s and early '80s, MDMA, then nicknamed Adam, because of the way it facilitated a rebirth of the trusting and innocent 'inner child' spread throughout a looseknit circuit of therapists in America. The drug proved particularly effective in marriage thearapy and psychoanalysis, and by the mid-'80s was also in popular use in American nightclubs, where it was popularly referred to as X. By 1988 it had been outlawed in America, while in the UK it was already classed as a Class A illegal drug, alongside heroin and cocaine.
50  Simon Reynolds, *Energy Flash*, Picador, London, 1998, p xxiv.
51  Jonnie Wilkes, in conversation with the author, May 1998.

# WOMEN IN PROFILE

In early 1987, an announcement was made that Glasgow had been successful in its bid to become European City of Culture 1990. The announcement was a catalyst for several more small organisations to form, in anticipation of their exclusion from the "official" celebrations. Glasgow-based women's art group Women in Profile was the first of these,[52] and was initiated by Barbara Littlewood, a sociologist working at Glasgow University. Littlewood contacted Sam Ainsley at the Environmental Art Department, who was well known for her political views. Ainsley (b.1950, North Shields) had trained in the North of England, before moving to Scotland to do a post-graduate course and then teach at Edinburgh College of Art in the late '70s. Since 1981 she had combined her art practice with her position as a full-time lecturer at Glasgow School of Art. Ainsley, a committed feminist, was also vocal in her condemnation of the British government's nuclear policies.[53] In 1986, Europe had been threatened by a radioactive cloud after the biggest technological disaster in European history had taken place at Chernobyl nuclear power station. The Chernobyl disaster refocussed attention in Scotland on the increasing store of nuclear weapons and waste that the Thatcher administration was sending to Scotland.[54] At a conference called that year on the nuclear arms debate, Sam Ainsley had commented that "It is up to women to take the initiative to improve the human condition (or even fight for the survival of the species!) the hand that rocks the cradle must also be the hand that rocks the boat – love and anger are very close … "[55]

In Edinburgh, Fruitmarket director Mark Francis was becoming frustrated with the negative feedback his ambitious exhibition programme was receiving. He remembers that, "No one was remotely impressed with

---

52  Activist group Worker's City was set up the following year, in August 1988.

53  In 1985, Ainsley had made a banner in tribute to the women of Greenham Common. The Greenham Common women had maintained a peace camp there since 1981, when thousands of women had marched from Cardiff to Greenham Common in Berkshire, encircling the RAF base in protest against the NATO decision to site cruise missiles there.

54  Faslane Peace Camp was established in 1982 beside the Naval base at Faslane, 30 miles away from Glasgow, to protest against nuclear weapons and waste being stored there.

55  The Eye of the Storm, Scottish Artists and the Nuclear Arms Debate, Smith Art Gallery, Stirling, 1986.

anything I did. Even when I did a show by a local artist, Steven Campbell [in 1985] people complained that he hadn't paid his dues, because he had just gone off to New York and made it big there. Eventually [in 1987] I said to the board that I couldn't continue working in this unsupported atmosphere any longer, and I left. My next job was at the Pompidou Centre in Paris so I consoled myself with the thought that at least some people believed I was doing something right."[56] At the time of Francis' departure, the gallery's funding was secure, although under the new director, Fiona McLeod, The Fruitmarket entered a period of financial instability which culminated in bankruptcy just over a year later.

In the same year as Mark Francis' departure from The Fruitmarket, a showcase exhibition of new Scottish art entitled The Vigorous Imagination opened at the Scottish National Gallery of Modern Art in Edinburgh. The exhibition was selected by *The Glasgow Herald*'s art critic Clare Henry, Henry Meyric Hughes from the British Council, and Keith Hartley, the Assistant Keeper of the Gallery of Modern Art. The Vigorous Imagination featured the work of the most prominent Scottish New Image painters (Steven Campbell, Adrian Wiszniewski, Ken Currie and Peter Howson), in addition to the "constructed photography" of Calum Colvin, the sculptural work of David Mach and the textile banners of Sam Ainsley. Keith Hartley wrote that, "what is particular to this Scottish Imagination, though, is its forthrightness, its lack of manners and its sheer ability to body 'forth the forms of things unknowne' (Shakespeare). The figures, objects and forms that these artists create have an unusual vivacity and tangible rightness."[57] The exhibition was also sponsored by Shell UK Ltd., which gave some of the artists included in the exhibition a degree of discomfiture, because of Shell's involvement in South Africa. Sam Ainsley was amongst the artists who debated pulling out of the exhibition before reluctantly deciding to participate. That year, Ainsley was also preparing for a solo show of her textile works at The Third Eye Centre called *Why I Choose Red* (Inspired by a line from a Hugh McDiarmid poem – "a man in a red coat can neither hide or retreat").

56 Mark Francis, Ibid.
57 Keith Hartley, *The Vigorous Imagination*, Scottish National Gallery of Modern Art, Edinburgh,1987, p14.

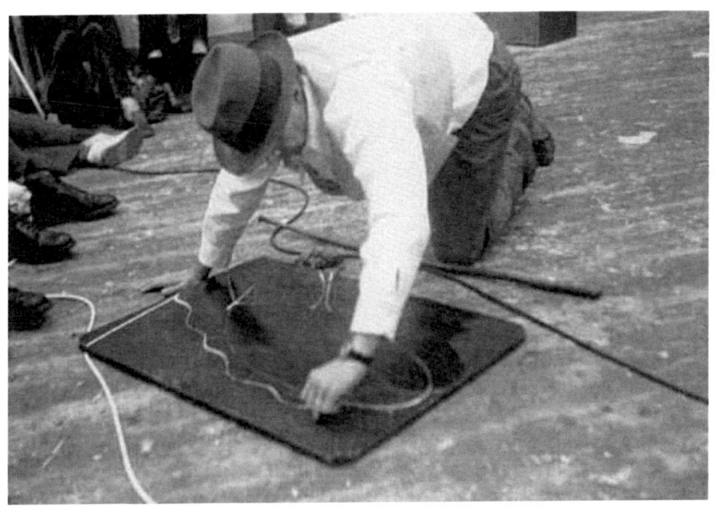

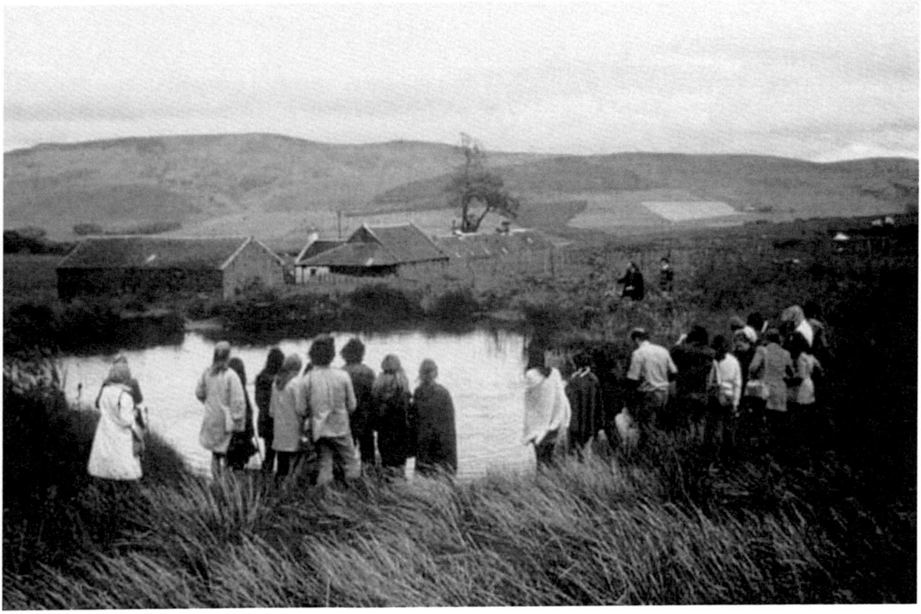

Joseph Beuys performs *Celtic* (*Kinloch Rannoch*) – the Scottish Symphony. Edinburgh, summer 1970.
Ian Hamilton Finlay welcomes Edinburgh Arts to Stonypath, summer 1972.

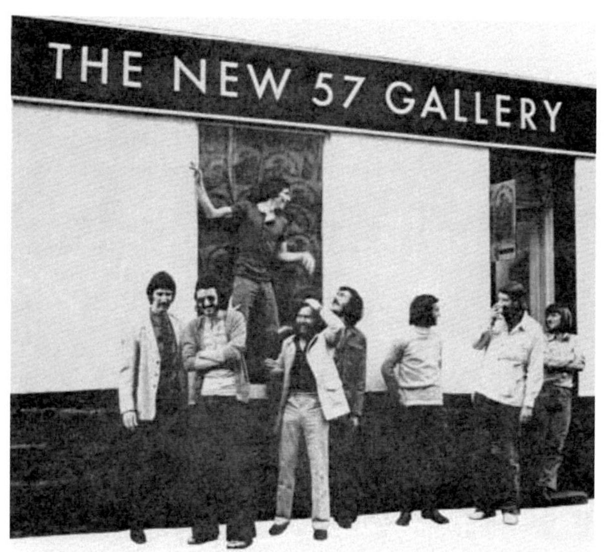


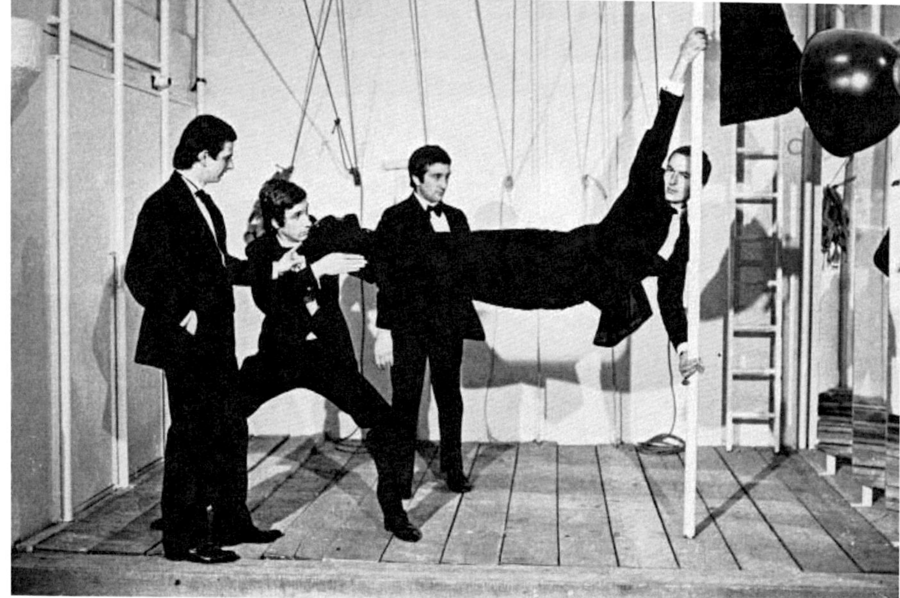

The New 57 committee, 1972, outside the gallery's premises at Rose Street, Edinburgh. Left to right: Alexander Moffat, Michael Doherty, Iain Patterson, Ian McLeod, Ian Paterson, Roger Askham, Kirkland Main and Jim Fairgrieve.
Artists' collective Nice Style, "the World's First Pose Band." Bruce McLean and other members carried out a series of performances in London between 1971–1974.

OPPOSITE
David Harding and Alan Bold, Poetry Path, Glenrothes, 1977.
Ivor Cutler photographed by son Jeremy c.1988.

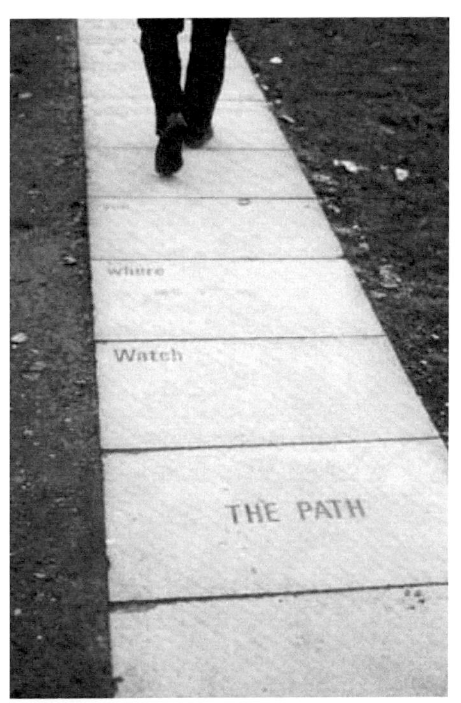
Where
Watch
THE PATH

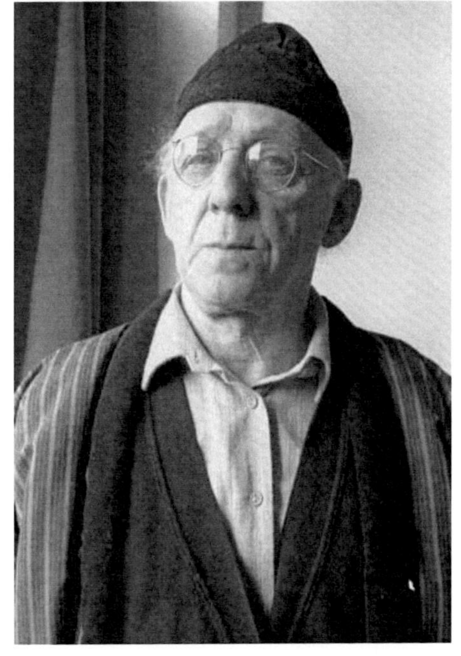

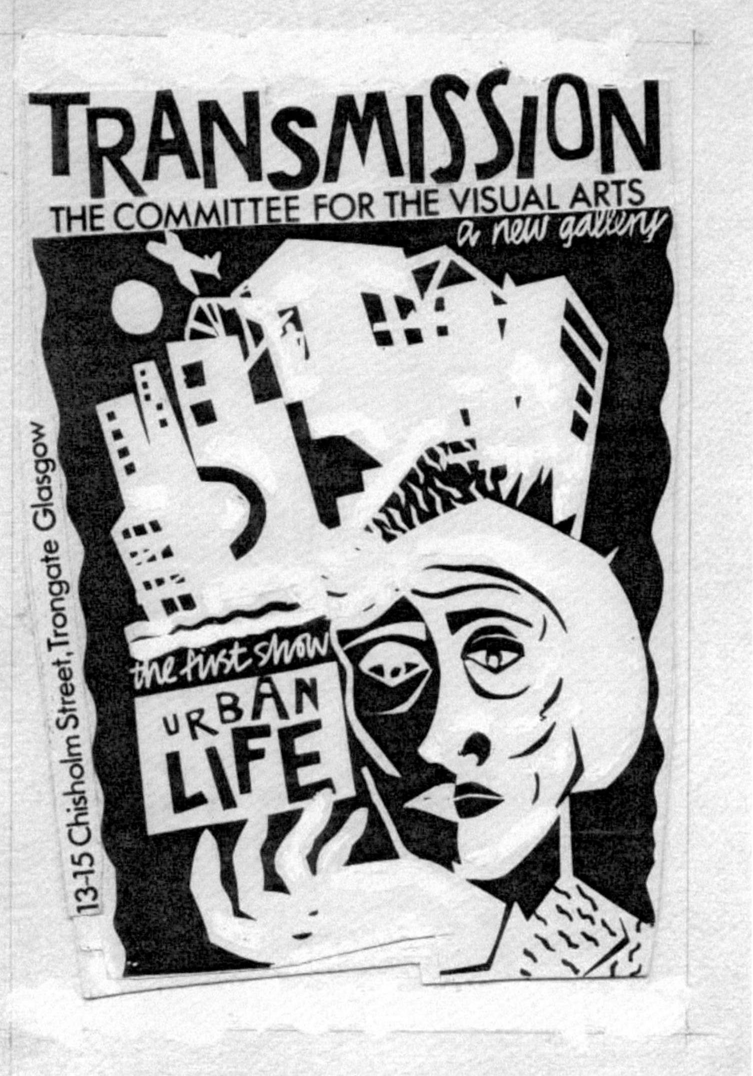



Invitation for Urban Life, inaugural exhibition at Transmission's Chisholm Street space, December 1983.

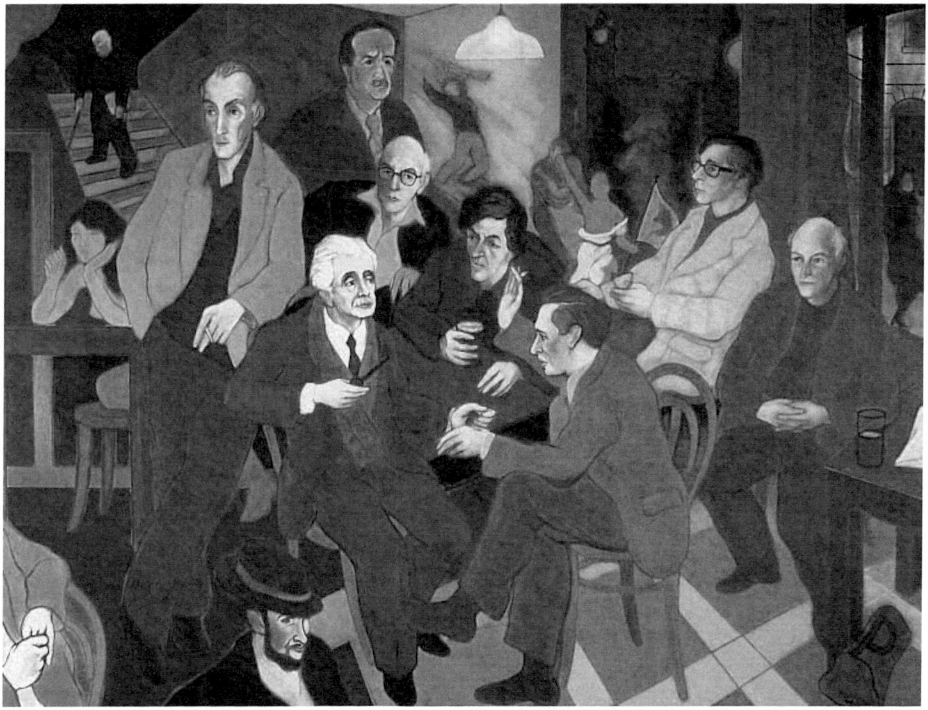

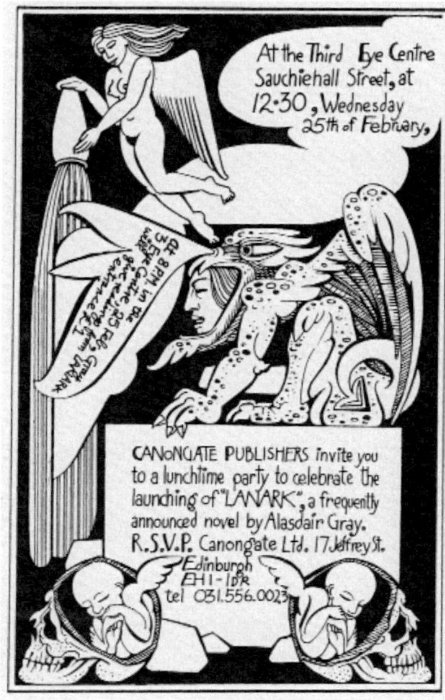


Alexander Moffat, *Poet's Pub*, 1980.
Alasdair Gray, *Lanark*, Third Eye Centre launch (1981).
Reproduced courtesy of the artist and Sorcha Dallas,
Glasgow.

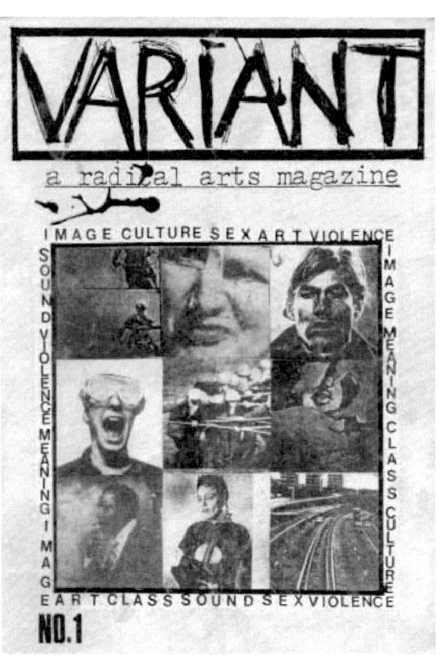
VARIANT
a radical arts magazine
IMAGE CULTURE SEX ART VIOLENCE
SOUND VIOLENCE MEANING IMAGE
IMAGE MEANING CLASS CULTURE
EART CLASS SOUND SEX VIOLENCE
NO.1

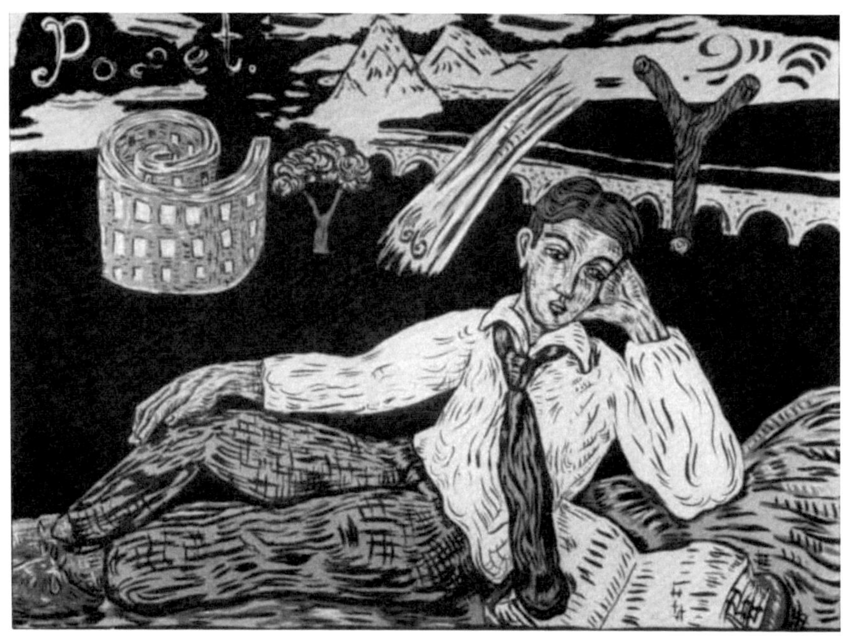
Poet.

*Slow Dazzle*, issue No.5, 1984. Cover features an early line-up of The Pastels.
*Since Yesterday*, Strawberry Switchblade, a Top 40 hit in the summer of 1984.

OPPOSITE
*Variant*, issue no.1, 1984.
Adrian Wiszniewski, *Po-et*, 1985.

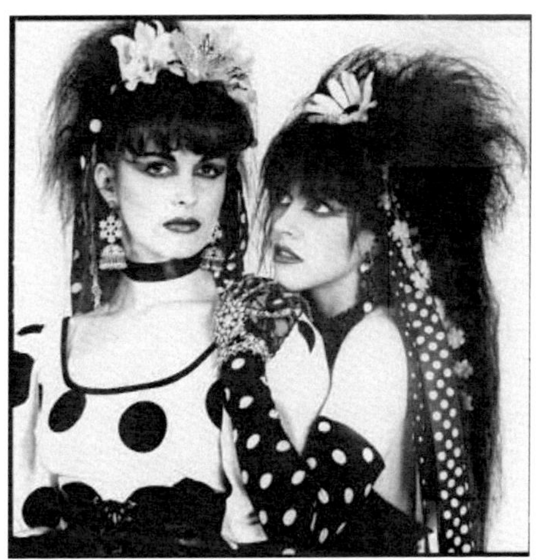

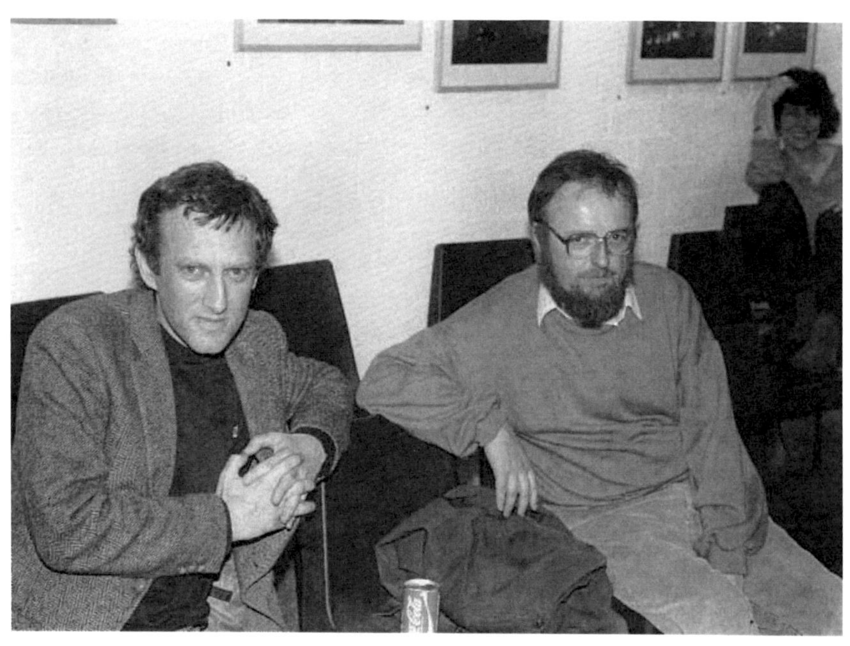

Transmission Goes Verbal, 1986. Left to right: James Kelman and Tom Leonard at the gallery.
Glasgow Events Space at Transmission, largest festival of film, installation and performance in Scotland for ten years, 1986.

OPPOSITE
Blackhill mural project (1987) by 3rd Year environmental art students Nathan Coley, Alan Dunn and Meg McLucas, directed by David Harding.
Exterior of the Mackintosh building at Glasgow School of Art, Renfrew Street.

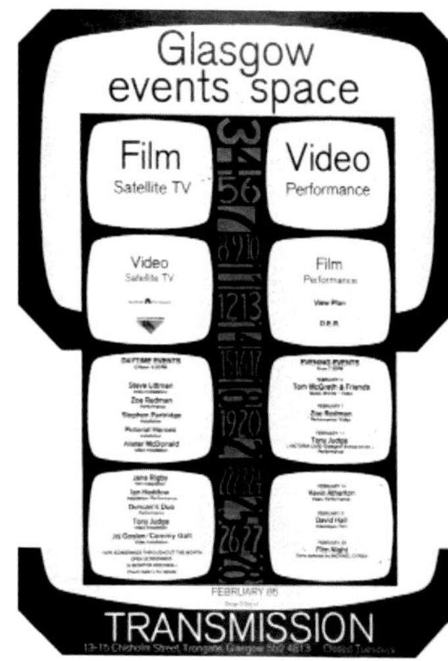

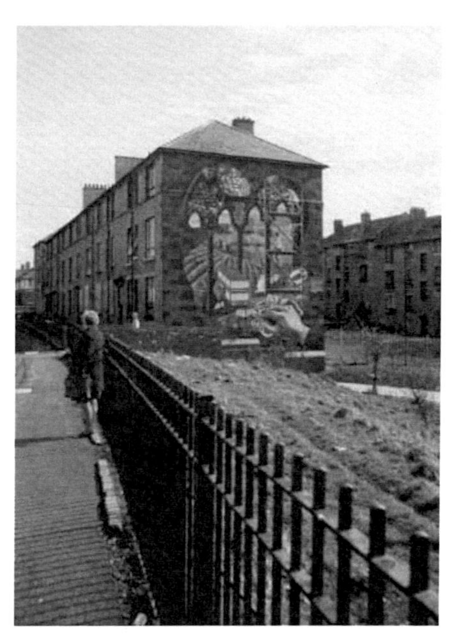

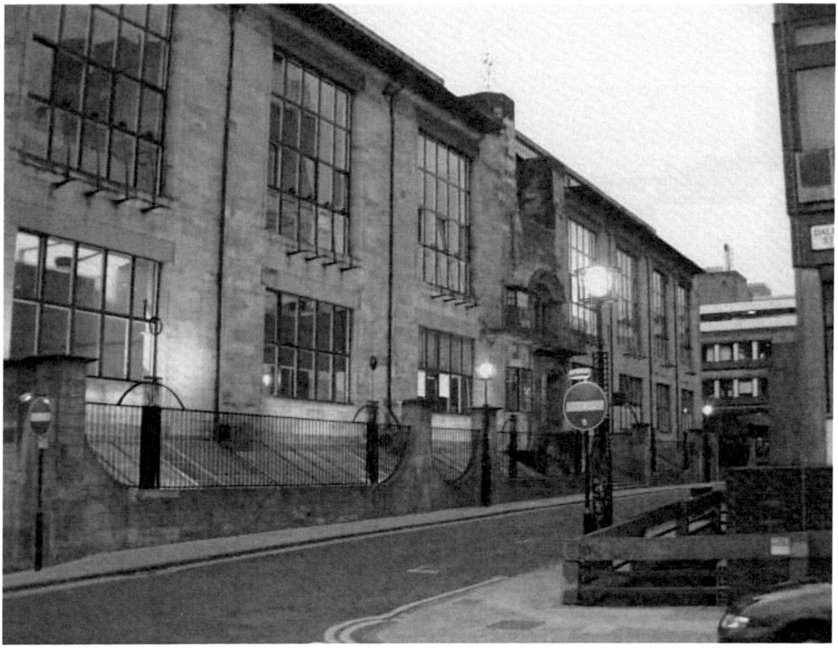

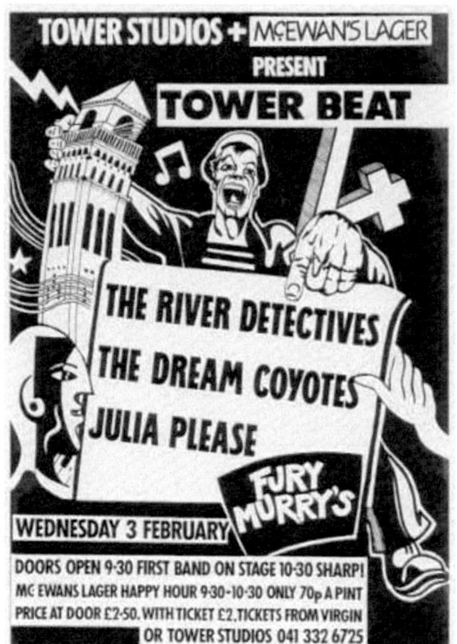


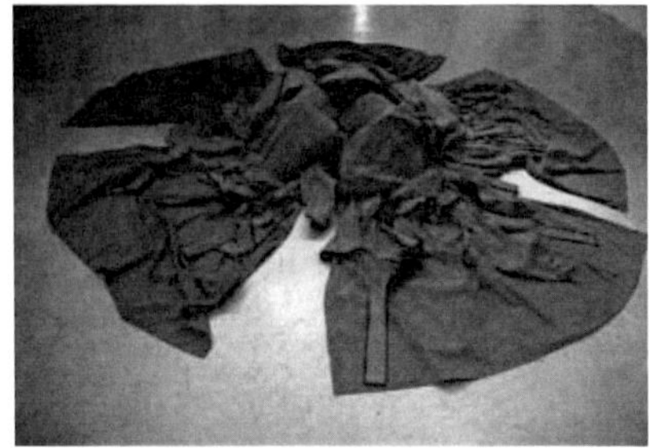

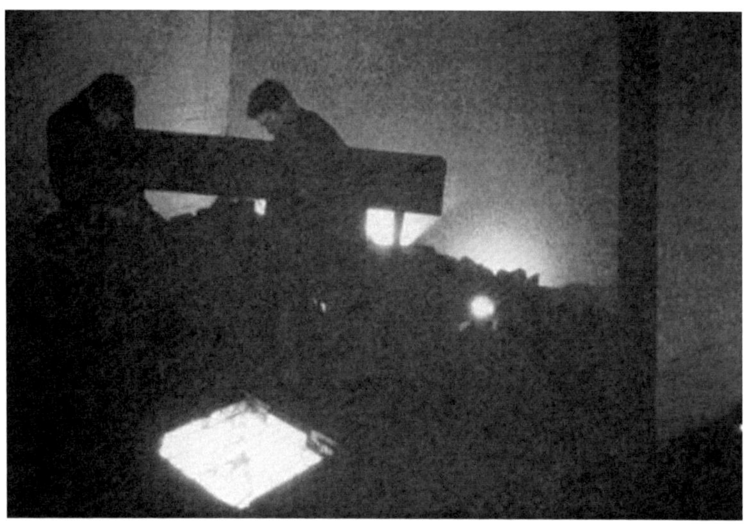

Sam Ainsley, *Circle of Strength*, Third Eye Centre, Glasgow, 1987.
Flyer for Tower Beat event at Fury Murry's, 1988.
The Puberty Institution (Douglas Gordon and Craig Richardson) present aNTEHYPERAESTHESIa at Transmission in December 1987.

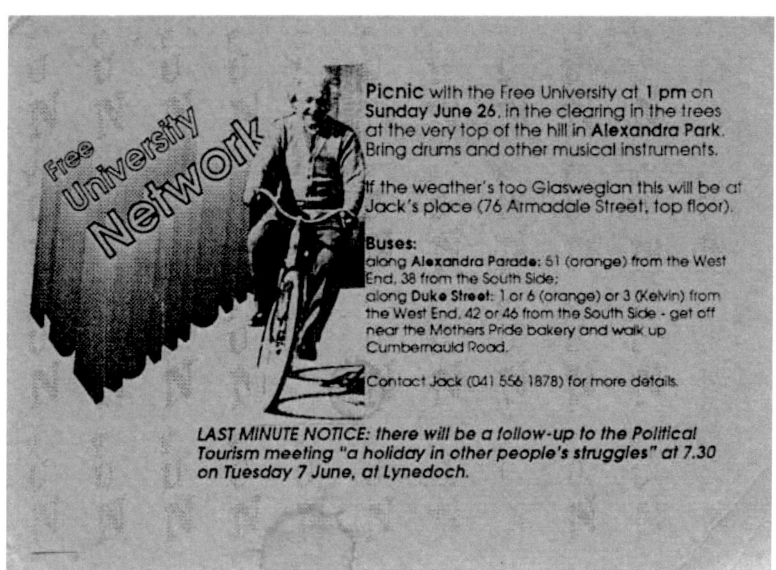



Free University Flyer, circa 1987.
*Desire in Ruins* installation at Transmission, May 1987. Installation and related events by Ed Baxter, Andy Hopton, Simon Dickson, Karen Elliot, Stefan Szczelkun, Glyn Banks and Hannah Vowles.

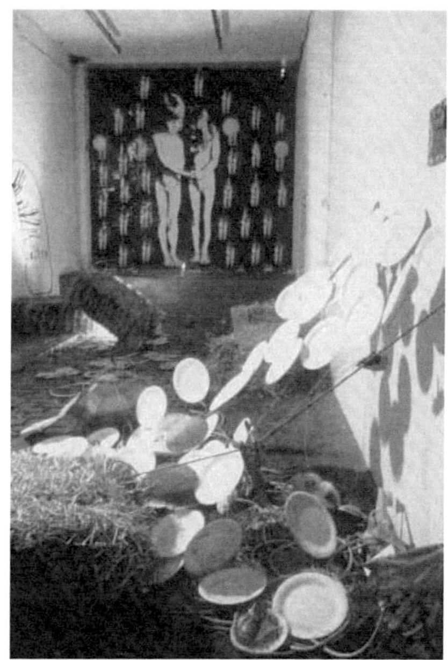

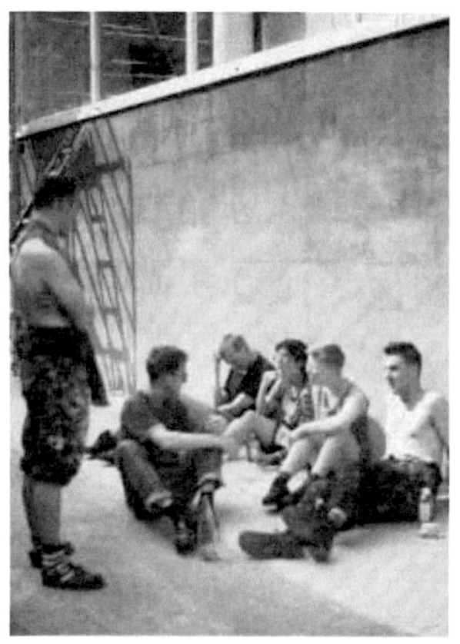

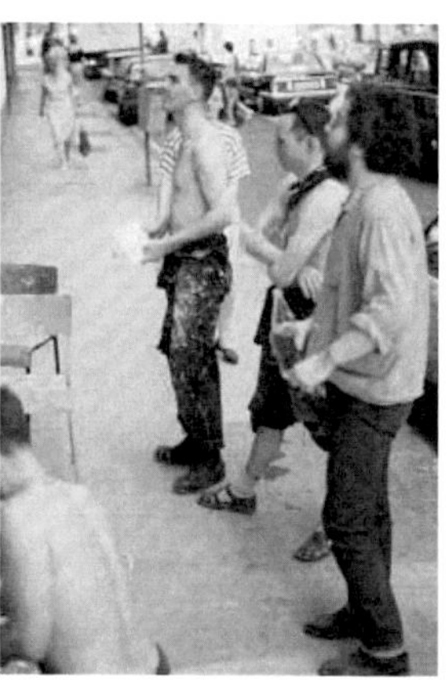

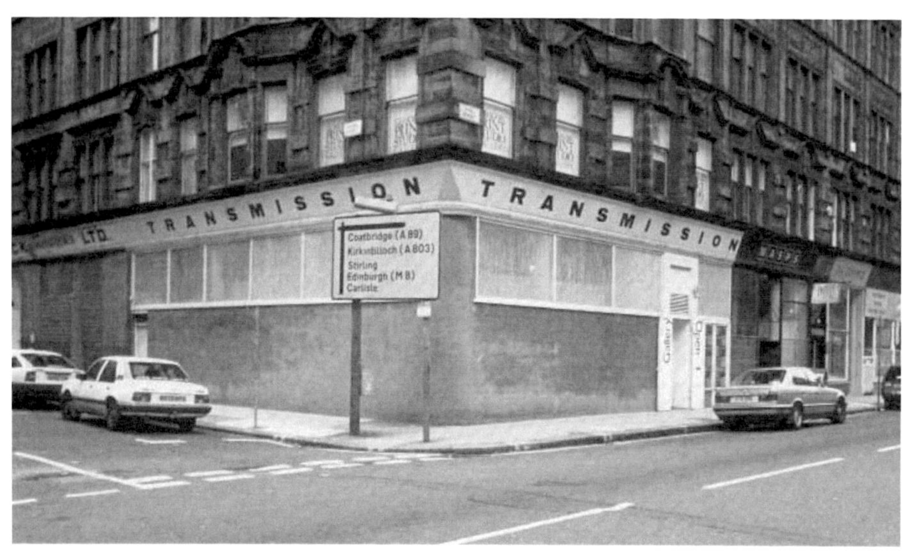

Renovations at Transmission's new King Street premises, summer of 1989. Left to right: Dave Allen, Euan Sutherland and Billy Clark.
Renovations at Transmission's new King Street premises, summer of 1989. Left to right: Euan Sutherland, Martin Boyce, Peter Gilmour, Helen-Marie Nugent, Karen Vaughan, Dave Allen.
Transmission's new King Street premises.

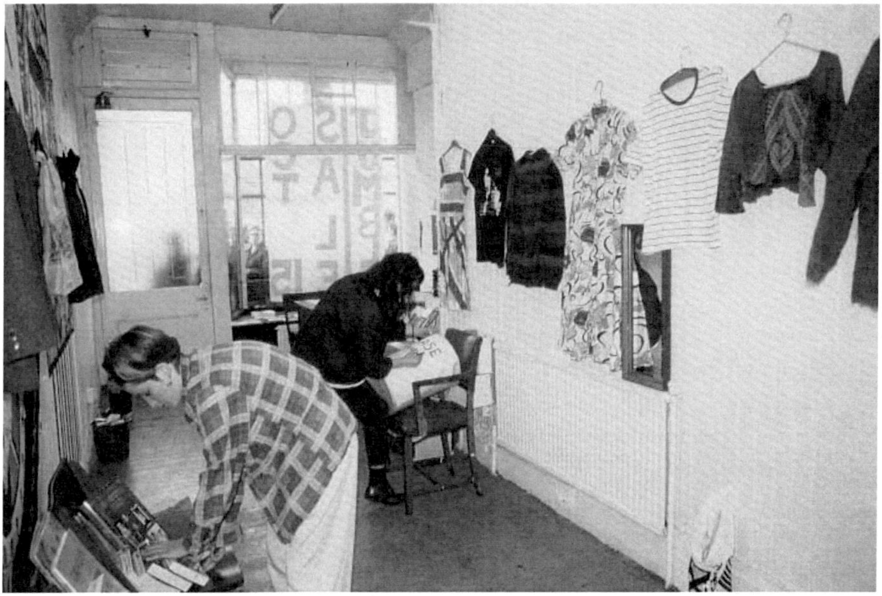

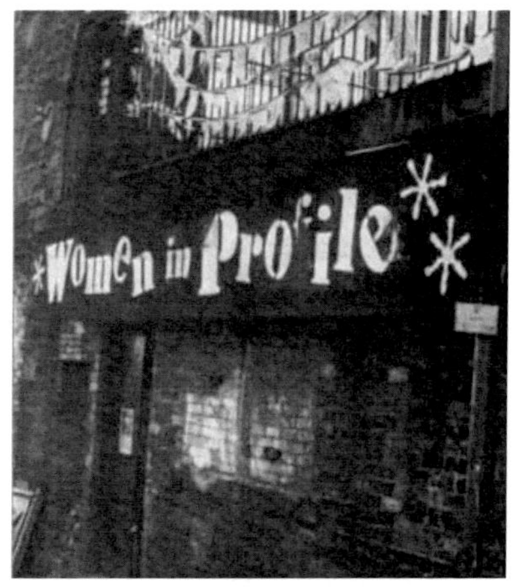

Jumble Sale at Transmission, October 1988.
Women in Profile headquarters, Dalhousie Lane, 1989.

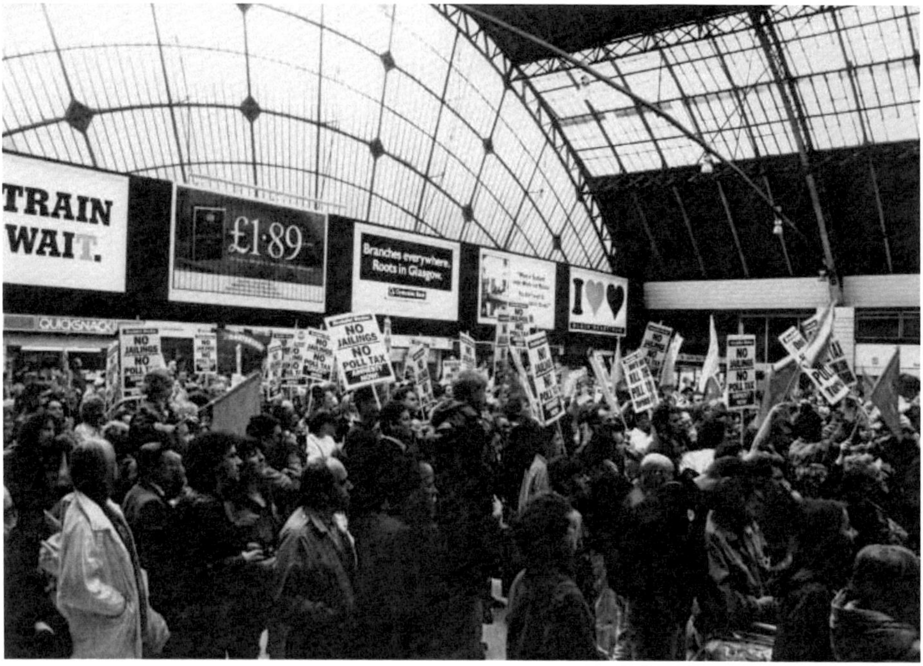

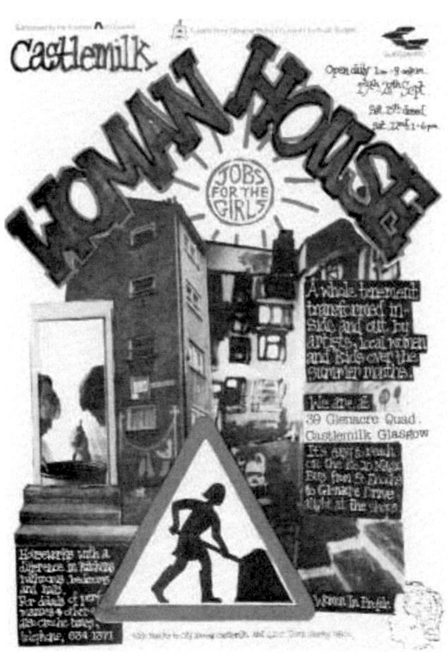
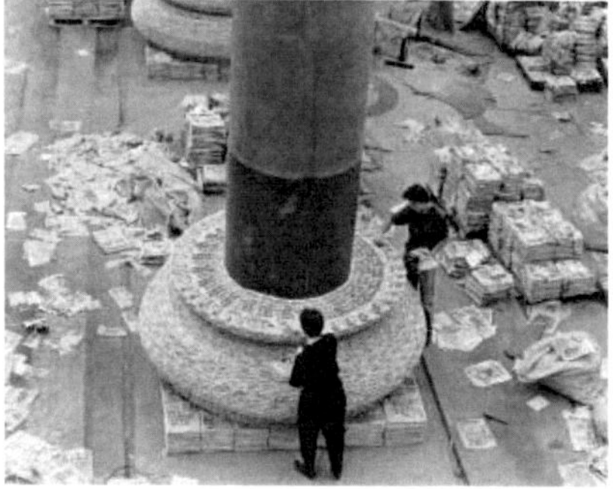

Anti Poll Tax demonstration, Queen Street Station, Glasgow, 1989.
Poster for Womanhouse, Castlemilk, 1990.
David Mach, *Here to Stay*, (installation view – work in progress), Tramway, 1990.

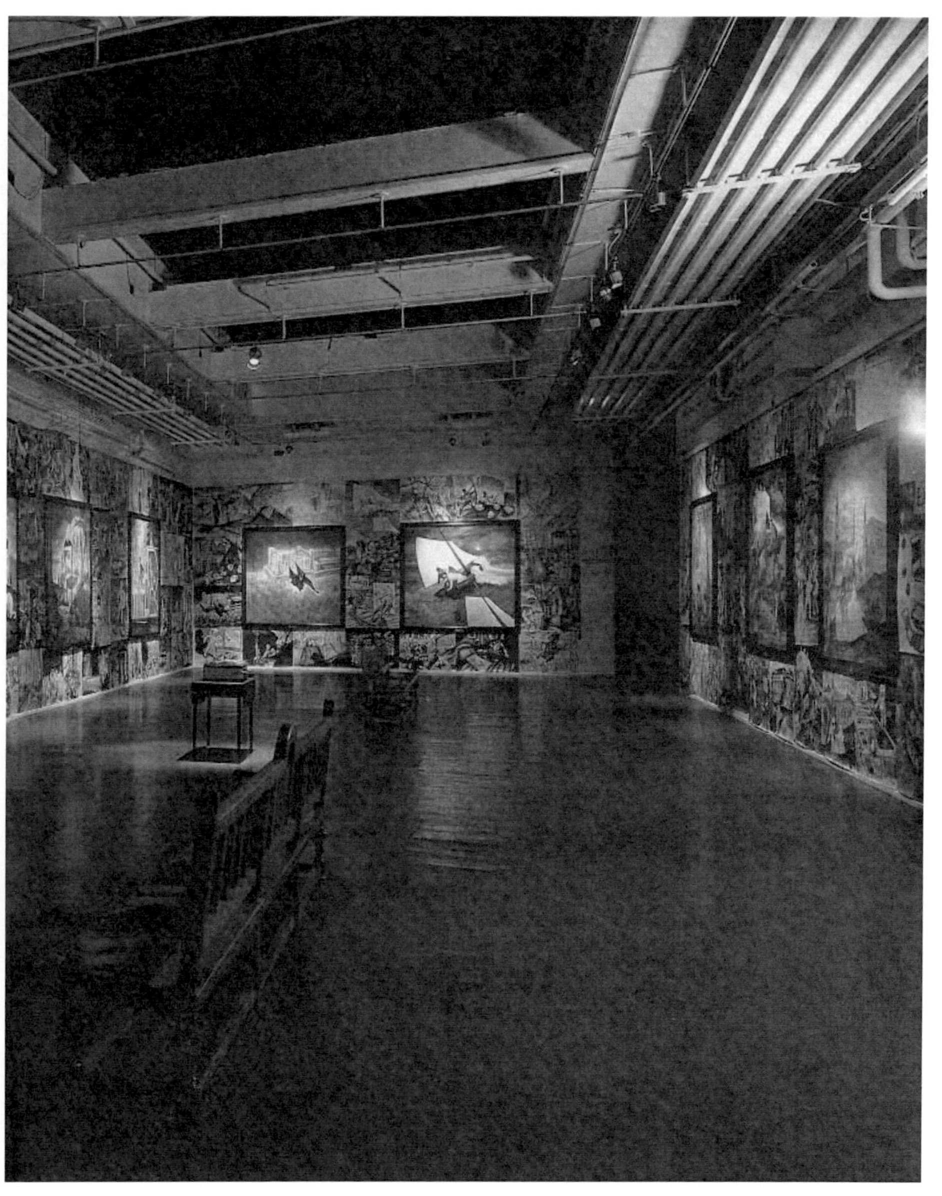

Steven Campbell, On Form & Fiction, Third Eye Centre, 1990.

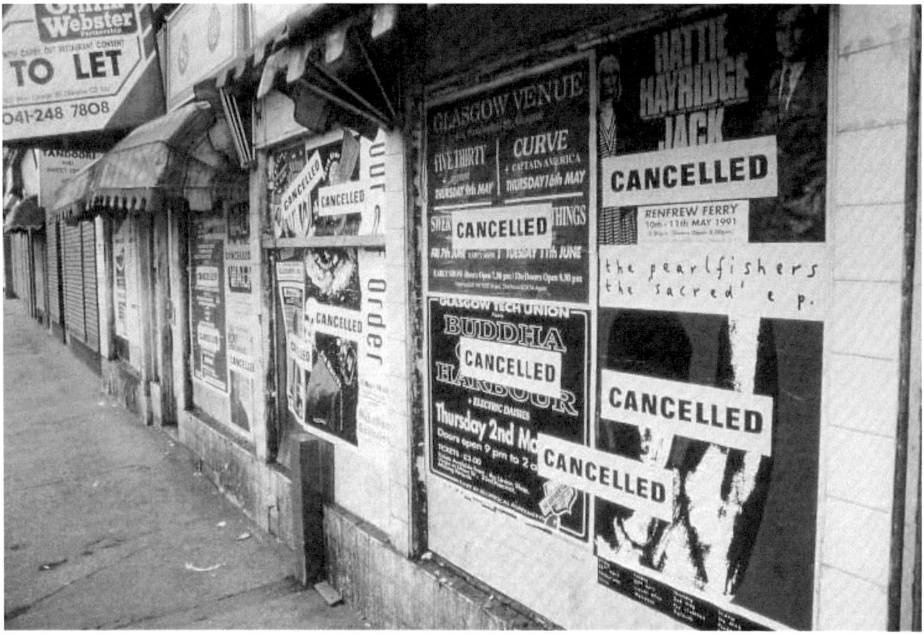

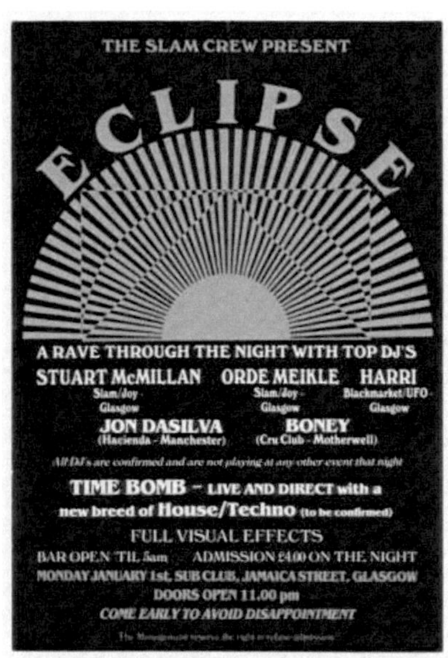


Jonathan Monk, *Cancelled*, 1990.
Slam flyer for event at the Sub Club, circa 1990.

Despite her busy workload, Ainsley was keen to help develop Barbara Littlewood's proposals for a series of Women in Profile events, but she also wanted to include students and graduates from the art school. First on Ainsley's list was recent graduate Adele Patrick (b.1961), who had moved from Doncaster to study embroidered and woven textiles at the school, and stayed on to do a masters in Design. Patrick had worked closely with fellow student Janice Kirkpatrick during their masters' course, and their degree show was a collaborative venture, which showcased the work of their fledgling design consultancy, Graven Images, beside text pieces relating to critical theory and feminist thought. Patrick remembers, "We had already fallen out with the guy who ran the course, Julian Gibb, because of his agenda. Postmodern theory was taught on the course but there was no gender stuff, so our work came about almost in spite of that. It was that kind of challenging context that sometimes gives rise to radical work."[58]

After taking advice from the Scottish Co-operative Development Committee, Graven Images[59] had set up shop that year in a cramped windowless office on Sauchiehall Lane, which they shared with a ceramics workshop. Patrick recalls of this period, "We were looking at issues to do with gender and how that manifested itself in objects. We had these idealistic notions of building things into objects that could then disrupt the other objects that might be around them. We had theoretical notions, and the objects themselves were arcane and dissident. You can imagine hairdressing salons, entrepreneurs, bar managers and the Troon RAC club were not interested so much in these things."[60] Patrick and Kirkpatrick had also remained involved in the art school, primarily through Sam Ainsley's invitation to teach seminars on the Environmental Art course. Patrick says, "I always thought she had such a lot of bottle to ask us to do it, because neither of us had any teaching experience whatsoever. I think she invited us because she had seen our degree show and thought that we had something to say. In fact we had too much to say. I remember that Christine Borland, Ross Sinclair, Douglas Gordon and Rachel Mimiec were amongst

---

58  Adele Patrick, in conversation with the author, August 2002.
59  Architecture graduate Ross Hunter later joined the partnership and Adele Patrick left Graven Images in 1989. The company has subsequently become well known for a wide range of design work, ranging from graphic design to restructuring whole buildings.
60  Adele Patrick, Ibid.

the students at those seminars. It was a phenomenal group to work with because they were all motivated and interested and all total individuals."[61]

Christine Borland remembers of this period, "Despite the woeful gender imbalance of staff, the enormous influence of the women who taught us (Sam Ainsley in particular, supported by seminars and gender work-shops from people she invited – sometimes very recent graduates like Adele Patrick and Janice Kirkpatrick) meant that body politics had a really high profile and were dealt with by both male and female students. In fact it was pretty rare, in Environmental Art, if you weren't engaged in this."[62] In this respect the Environmental Art Department stole the march on other departments in the school, especially the Painting Department. However, the Painting department had continued to enjoy a good international reputation during the late '80s, most notably perhaps for the work of the New Image painters, but also for later figurative painters such as Alison Watt (b.1965) and Jenny Saville (b.1970).

Both Alison Watt and Jenny Saville had had almost immediate success: Watt's self-portrait won the National Portrait Gallery's competition in 1987, while Charles Saatchi bought up all of Saville's degree show paintings. In a 1995 interview, however, Watt said the atmosphere in the Painting Department was less than completely supportive of women artists. She remembered, "One tutor became infamous for saying women can't paint because they don't have the balls for it." In the same programme, broadcaster Muriel Gray, who also attended the school in the 1980s, made a dig at the New Glasgow boys, saying, "There was always this real macho attitude at GSA – if you had a summer job as a spot welder at Brown's you'd get taken seriously. There was this idea that the real artists were the guys from the shipyards."[63]

The bias towards macho paintings identified by Watt and Gray was also prospering in the broadsheet newspapers of the period. Critic Andrew Graham Dickson wrote in *The Independent*, "Peter Howson's pastel *The Body Builder* (1986) is a powerful reminder that Glasgow School of Art maintains

61  Adele Patrick, Ibid.
62  Christine Borland, in response to questions sent by the author, June 2002.
63  Ex-S The School, BBC Scotland, March, 1995.

a strong tradition of life drawing. Howson's lonely, isolated figure is a proletarian hero hinting at the artist's stated ambition to revive – in modern Glasgow – the French Realist tradition of the 19th century." However, Saville's work in particular represented a new kind of figuration: her nude self-portraits were intended to attack prescriptive mass-media representations of female beauty. She said, "Nearly everyone I know is obsessed with dieting – from anorexics who end up in hospital to friends who take hundreds of laxatives a day. It's like an epidemic. Tabloids like *The Daily Record* are full of information on how to improve your body and hide unsightly areas.[ … ]Plastic surgeons use computers to achieve the perfect face, but this will all achieve such blandness. What would beauty be, if everyone were the same?"[64]

There were many female cultural workers in the city who felt that their work was being under-represented, and when Adele Patrick called a Women In Profile open meeting in the Assembly Hall at the art school, she was pleasantly surprised by the turnout. One of the first volunteers was Rachael Harris (b.1960), who was then still a student at the school. Harris was good friends with Belfast-born artist Cathy Wilkes (b.1966), then studying in the Sculpture Department at the school and painter Julie Roberts (b.1963), who had just moved up to Glasgow after a postgraduate year at St. Martin's in London, to join the first cohort of the new MA course at Glasgow School of Art. Harris, Wilkes and Roberts, and another GSA graduate also called Julie Roberts, agreed to help Patrick to develop the idea for a Womanhouse community art project, which was partly inspired by Judy Chicago and Miriam Shapiro's 1971 Womanhouse project in California.

Adele Patrick says, "Rachael was so scrupulous, she wouldn't do a project without consulting the people who had done a project under the name before. So she contacted Judy Chicago, who threatened to sue us, and then I went to London with Rachael to meet Kate Walker, who worked at the Women's Slide Library and had done a Womanhouse project in Leeds about ten years earlier. We tried to give credit for originating ideas but in fact our Womanhouse project had an absolutely independent trajectory.

64  Sarah Kent, Young British Artists III, Saatchi Gallery, London, 1994.

I think it was quite an amazing thing to do at the time, because it was quite a hostile environment. We also had all these huge, completely over-ambitious plans for an international conference of women in the arts, and a film festival, and an exhibition of lens-based work, called Photoworks."[65] The growing Women in Profile organisation was joined by other volunteers, including academics Susan Payne and Hilary Robinson[66,] and activist Kate Henderson, community arts workers Jane Alston and Sandra Gaffney, Laura Hudson and Jane Martin from the Glasgow Film and Video Workshop, and many local artists including Claire Barclay, Jayne Taylor, Susan Montford and Christine Borland and Transmission committee members Gillian Steel and Anne Vance.


## ART & POLITICS


The 1987 election had been another comfortable Conservative victory across Britain, but it was a disaster for the party in Scotland, where it was reduced to 24% of the vote and only 10 MPs, less than at any time since 1910. Support for the Scottish National Party had risen again, which led to a shock landslide defeat for Labour in their stronghold seat of Govan, by the SNP's Jim Sillars. Journalist Howell Raines wrote in *The New York Times* that year, "One effect [of the Thatcher administration] has been an uneven distribution along a North-South divide that cleaves Britain into two distinct regions of decline and prosperity. The old industrial cities of central and Northern Britain are pockets of decay, while London and 'the home counties' of South East England surf along on the lead wave of the Thatcher boom." The credibility of the Conservatives was at an all time low in Scotland, partly due to the controversial storing of nuclear weapons and waste at Faslane, and Thatcher's support for Ronald Reagan's bombing raids against Libya the previous year. The Arms-to-Iran scandal was also breaking that summer as Colonel Oliver North took the stand at a

65  Adele Patrick, Ibid.
66  Hilary Robinson taught in the Historical and Critical Studies Department at Glasgow School of Art between 1987 and 1992. Between 1990 and 1992 she was editor of arts magazine *Alba*, and she is also the author of several books on feminist art practice. Since 1992 she has taught at the University of Ulster at Belfast, becoming senior lecturer there in 2000.

congressional hearing. Although in America Reagan was still inspiring public confidence, in Britain Thatcher was increasingly attacked for her support of the eccentric ex-movie star president. A satirical poster published by environmental group Greenpeace superimposed the heads of Reagan and Thatcher on a *Gone With The Wind* poster, with a mushroom cloud blooming in the background. The tagline read, "She said she would follow him to the end of the earth … "

In July 1987, Transmission Goes Verbal 2 featured readings from emerging writers Janice Galloway, Ian Brotherhood and Jim Ferguson. The third and final installment in the series was in October, and staged in association with *The Edinburgh Review*. There were readings from the new Scottish poetry collection *Tower of Babble* by Bobby Christie, Ronald McNeil and Jim Ferguson. Malcolm Dickson left the Transmission committee soon afterwards, although he still contributed to Transmission shows like Event Space 3,[67] and later developed EventSpace into a separate host organisation. Dickson recalled, "When my tenure on the committee was up we formed EventSpace separately – Ken Gill, Doug Aubrey and Alan Robertson were the others. The model there as far as I was concerned was Projects UK in Newcastle – that of a non-venue based agency promoting innovative work in site-specific and non-gallery locations."[68] After leaving the committee, Dickson relaunched *Variant* which had lain dormant after the first two issues, this time subsidising the magazine through a mixture of private donations and advertising subscriptions. He remembered, '[We] relaunched with Issue 3 and a party at Alasdair Gray's[69] house. I don't remember much. There were three magazines that were all part of a broadening of culture for me at that time – *Variant*, *Here & Now* and *The Edinburgh Review*, *Variant* gave expression to a range of non-mainstream views on the arts, culture and politics – it included dissenting views and supported a diversity of creativity. Like the culture and scene it was part of, it was non-parochial,

67  11th–23rd April 1988. David Hall and John Latham of the Artist's Placement Group participated in Event Space 3, as did Paul Richards & Michael Nyman, JD Kelly, Lei Cox, Sven Harding and numerous others.
68  Chris Byrne and Malcolm Dickson, "Moving History", Ibid.
69  Gray was a stalwart supporter of the local art scene, and in 1987 used the advances for two books to organise a touring exhibition of four artists he felt had been neglected: John Connolly, Alan Fletcher, Carole Gibbins and Alasdair Taylor.

while still very much rooted in the place from where it emanated."[70]

Cathy Wilkes remembers, "At the end of the '80s and early '90s there was this idea that you were a cultural worker and that possibly involved writing, organising exhibitions, being politically involved, maybe making paintings. That was an idea that a large group of people all subscribed to. It was at the time when *Variant* was still a glossy magazine, run by a particular group of people, all writing under pseudonyms so they weren't professing their individuality or their identity as authors or artists. That was relatively common, and that probably rubbed off, to a certain extent, on the early committees at Transmission who moved very much as a group. I understood Transmission as an art and politics group, more to do with The Free University and the Anarchist movement, and the Anti-Nazi League. I didn't see Transmission as the same kind of gallery as Cyril Gerber or the Collins.[71] Most artists were making their work and not expecting to make any money out of it and probably, if they were involved in Transmission, had quite strong political motivations, for example people like Malcolm Dickson and Gordon Muir and Anne Vance."[72]

In 1987 Pete Seddon from the Historical and Critical Studies Department at Glasgow School of Art proposed that a Masters of Fine Art (MFA) course be set up at the school. The course took some time to reach a settled format[73] but despite some early complications, the MFA was clear in certain objectives, such as having a strong emphasis on research and current theory as explored in the Environmental Art Department, but being open to students from all disciplines.

Sam Ainsley remembers that the course set out to be "deliberately multi-specialist, multidisciplinary, and also tried to attract people who weren't

---

70  Malcolm Dickson, Letter 6, *Justified Sinners*, Pocketbooks, Edinburgh, 2002.

71  Cyril Gerber is a commercial gallery, which sells paintings, drawings and sculpture by Joan Eardley, William McTaggart, Anne Redpath, J.D. Fergusson, James Cowie, John Bellany and the first Glasgow Boys. Gerber also runs the Compass Gallery in West Regent Street, which promotes the work of younger, less established artists. The Collins Gallery is part of Strathclyde University – campus and is mainly associated with exhibitions of photography and painting. Ian Hamilton Finlay and Lys Hansen are amongst the artists who have exhibited there.

72  Cathy Wilkes, in conversation with the author, August 2001.

73  Initially the course was taught by the various heads of Department, who were David Harding (Environmental Art), Jack Knox (Painting), Cliff Bowen (Sculpture), Thomas Joshua Cooper (Photography), Phillip Reeves (Printmaking) and Bill Buchanan, Head of Fine Art, plus John Calcutt and Ray McKenzie from the Historical and Critical Studies Department. After two years had passed it was decided that the course needed to be streamlined, and Sam Ainsley, Roger Palmer and Alexander Moffat took over the running of the course. In 1989 Sam Ainsley was appointed the course leader and the course title changed from MA to MFA.

necessarily from our own undergraduate course. In these early years there were only 10 in each year group, who worked in dedicated MFA studios in the old Girl's High School. The course provided a framework for a postgraduate community of artists who were committed to being artists – they weren't going to do anything else. That group dynamic was very important."[74] The MFA provided a critical environment for developing the practice of the school's graduates but perhaps more importantly, also attracted graduates who had studied at art schools elsewhere. These graduates, who included Julie Roberts, Simon Starling, Louise Hopkins, Tom O'Sullivan, Joanne Tatham, Alan Currall, Fanni Niemi-Junkola, Anne Ooms, Lucy Byatt and Richard Wright, brought an important range of different approaches and experiences to the school, which widened the style of work being made within the city throughout the late '80s and '90s.

Malcolm Dickson had made sure that staff and students in the Environmental Art department were aware of Transmission's activities throughout his time on the committee, and the links between the artist-run gallery and the school extended to the MFA. The MFA tutors maintained that relationship with Transmission throughout the late '80s, as a conduit to activities outside the school. Sam Ainsley says, "The MFA is a small community of artists within a much bigger community of artists and I think that everyone who visited felt that there was much more interaction, discussion and debate than you would get in London, where everything was quite separate, where a social scene didn't exist so much as the working scene did. Lots of people found that community of artists very attractive. Being on the MFA wasn't the be all and end all, because through being on the MFA they met lots of other artists – going to openings, going to bars, going to parties. They then got a sense of a lively place where people were happy to talk to each other, to invite them to events and and generally make them feel welcomed."[75]

Transmission hit a funding crisis in the autumn of 1987 and, as no City Council or Scottish Arts Council aid was forthcoming, the gallery's collapse

74  Sam Ainsley, Ibid.
75  Sam Ainsley, Ibid.

was only averted by an auction of work by the membership. Seventy pieces of work were donated to the auction and sold at the Green Room at the RAC in Blytheswood Square, including works by art school staff Jack Knox and Sam Ainsley, established Scottish artists George Wyllie and Alasdair Gray and New Image painters Steven Campbell and Adrian Wiszniewski. The funds raised enabled Transmission to make a much-needed investment in their programme. Committee member Billy Clark later wrote, "As most of the money raised went towards promoting such art forms as time-based, installation, site-specific and issue-based work, which have had a considerable influence on todays artistic practice, it would be interesting to speculate what would have happened had we gone under."[76]

Other key events at Transmission during this year included an exhibition of Gordon Muir's graffiti-style paintings and Malcolm Dickson's installation *Beneath the Cobblestones the Sewer* in a show called Iconoclasm. Stefan Szczelkun also presented *How to Explain Glasgow Painting to a Dead Mackerel* – a performance after Joseph Beuys. Beuys' influence over the Scottish art scene had been greatly enhanced by his series of visits to Edinburgh from 1970 onwards and his death in 1986 had prompted a re-examination of seminal performance works such as *Explaining Painting to a Dead Hare* (1965) and *I like America and America likes Me* (1974). Beuys had also made visits to Ireland, twice giving lectures at the University of Ulster in Belfast. Irish contemporary art magazine *Circa* (est.1981) published an obituary which noted, "Beuys represents a strand of thinking in contemporary art which, with the current political drift further and further to the right, has been much maligned: ie the concept of a real interaction between art and society."[77]

Beuys' ideas had influenced artists working in Glasgow in a number of ways, from his use of low cost materials like felt and fat, to the ideas associated with his Free International University, which had already been adopted for local use by Malcolm Dickson, Billy Clark, Carol Rhodes, James Kelman and others. Beuys' idea of "social sculpture", which he used to

76  Billy Clark, "Tears for Souvenirs", unpublished essay on Transmission, 1995.
77  Circa 26, 1986, p45.

describe meaning that is generated between people involved in a variety of discourses, informed many of the debates around Transmission, *Variant*, the Environmental Art Department, and affiliated organisations. Beuys had also considered the process of conceptual art making to be at least as important as the finished work, if not more so. As he had remarked in 1969, "For me the formation of the thought is already sculpture."[78]

In the spring of 1987, Douglas Gordon and Craig Richardson (b.1966) had been working collaboratively with Euan Sutherland on performative pieces, under the name tradition:dehabilitation. Tradition:dehabilitiation had appeared at the National Review of Live Art at the Riverside Studios, London that year, but a few months later Douglas Gordon and Craig Richardson were performing as a duo under a new name, The Puberty Institution, at the Audio-Visual-Experimental Festival in Arnhem, Holland. Douglas Gordon remembered, "That was really the first experience of doing any kind of work in front of an audience that had no idea who you were, and that was incredible. It was nerve-wracking on the one hand because it was very public, you had an audience of a few hundred people, but on the other hand it was incredibly liberating because no-one knew who you were, you could escape that history you had in Scotland. So the idea of escaping to a kind of free space where you could become a different person, make different kind of work, was very appealing."[79]

---

78 Quoted in Lucy R. Lippard, *Six Years*, by Praeger, New York 1973 p xvii.

79 Douglas Gordon in conversation with Graham Fagen, Transcript, Volume 03, Issue 03, School of Fine Art, Duncan of Jordanstone, Dundee, 2001. In December 1987 The Puberty Institution gave their first durational performance on home turf. The performance, which was held at Transmission, was entitled aNTEHYPERAESTHESIa. A press release from the gallery said, "Their installation work has progressively adapted and evolved Scottish motifs which evoke an atmosphere of a forgotten past and hidden present. The installation utilizes a variety of materials and media and is enhanced by the physical presence of the durational performance."

CHAPTER 4

# SUBCULTURE
# (1988–1990)

In the late 1980s Transmission was increasingly showing video or performance-related work rather than the New Image painting popular with the local media and larger publicly funded galleries. The gallery's relative lack of public funding, which had necessitated the Fine Art Auction the previous year, consolidated the sense that the activities of Transmission were at odds with "the establishment". Figurative painter Adrian Wiszniewski later said that, "In the early '80s figurative art was very much get up and go. But by the end of the decade it was much less interesting. It became bourgeois, if you like. People were putting fat gold frames around everything even in their degree shows. But since the late 1980s and early 1990s there were another group of artists, especially around Transmission, who were more interesting. They were a reaction to the excesses of decorative art."[1]

The Transmission committee that year consisted of Billy Clark, Gillian Steel, Scott Paterson and Anne Elliot. The 1988 programme at Transmission included a postal art show, green-er evolution, sponsored by the Scottish Post Office and organised by Jayne Taylor, live performances by The Puberty Institution, Euan Sutherland and Tim Brennan and Residue Sputnik Activity, a performance, video, installation and film by Ivan Unwin. Residue Septik Activity was accompanied by another selection of videos from Manchester production company IKON for bands including The Fall, Joy Division and Big Flame. Billy Clark remembers, "We tried to

---

1   *The Glasgow Herald*, June 1996.

111

negotiate with the Estates Department at the Council over the rent, and got a letter back saying the rent had doubled. The auction money had all gone by then. The rats used to come into committee meetings. It was awful, absolutely disgusting. The rent in King Street was lower so it made sense to move."[2] Again, no Scottish Arts Council financial aid was forthcoming. Christine Borland remembers drily that the move "… was against the advice of the Scottish Arts Council, who felt Transmission should be content in its damp and rat-infested niche which was so suitable for all those atmospheric performances."[3] Fortunately, support was found from Glasgow District Council who may have viewed the project as a step towards the redevelopment of the Merchant City area of Glasgow.

Of the previous committee, only Billy Clark and Anne Elliot volunteered to take the work of the gallery on to the new, run-down premises in King Street. "For a while it was just me and Anne working away on the place, but we realised there were so many problems with it – it wasn't even connected to the National Grid. It had been a hairdresser's wholesale suppliers and the guy that had run it was a total crook, so there'd be guys coming up trying to serve me with writs, thinking I was him. WASPS had an office next door at the time, so the guy had bored a hole in the wall and connected up to their electricity supply. He had been doing this for years – it was a total death trap. The whole place had to be completely rewired."[4]

Craig Richardson and Douglas Gordon had just graduated from the Environmental Art Department at GSA, after staging their final fourth year project, a Puberty Institution performance in a derelict car park basement in Midland Street, underneath Central Station, which later became The Arches theatre and nightclub. This durational performance using hundreds of eggs showed the influence of Joseph Beuys on both the young artists.[5] After graduating from the Environmental Art Department the previous year, their close friend Christine Borland had undertaken masters studies at the University of Ulster in Belfast, where she had intended to stay. However,

2   Billy Clark, in conversation with the author, June 2002.
3   Christine Borland, "Dear Green Place No More", unpublished essay on Transmission, 1995.
4   Billy Clark, Ibid.
5   Gordon's undergraduate dissertation was titled, "From Anthropology to Performance Art – A Sensibility of Ritual", Richardson's "Joseph Beuys – the Sphere of Crisis".

after the close support network of Glasgow, Borland found the relative lack of a local arts infrastructure in Belfast too dispiriting, and was encouraged to return to Glasgow by Craig Richardson and Douglas Gordon.

Christine Borland's formal and conceptual strategies were closely related to those of some of the artists she had studied with in the Environmental Art Department, although her masters studies in Belfast seemed to develop her interest in underlying currents of violence, leading to later works exploring the frailty of human bodies and physical objects. Borland was also the first of her generation of Glasgow based artists to come into contact with charismatic performance artist Alistair MacLennan (b.1943, Blair Atholl), who taught on the MA at the University of Ulster. After completing an initial degree at Duncan of Jordanstone College of Art in Dundee in 1965, MacLennan had moved to America to study at the Art Institute of Chicago between 1966 and 1968. He was an eloquent and proactive artist/organiser, who performed durational actions revolving around ideas of decay and undermining existing political, social and cultural power structures. In the summer of 1988 MacLennan gave a performance called *Out the In* for the New Work/No Definition series at The Third Eye Centre, presented as part of The National Review of Live Art.[6] Malcolm Dickson and Billy Clark interviewed MacLennan for *Variant*, and asked him about his approach to making and showing his work. He responded, "If a gallery won't give me a show, I can put one on myself in my studio, where I live, or in the street. I'll invite friends. They can invite me to theirs. Before long, essential art may bypass official institutions and operate another circuit, run by artists. There are precedents. In numerical terms, an operation, though miniscule, can yet be effective. One simple network may yet map new worlds."[7]

In June 1988, Douglas Gordon moved to London to undertake MA studies at the Slade School of Art, where his tutors included Stuart Brisley,

---

6    The National Review of Live Art was established by Nikki Millican in Nottingham in 1984. Previous participants at the events in Nottingham and London included The Basement Group, Andre Stitt, Ivor Cutler, Paul McCarthy, Kathy Acker, John Byrne and tradition:dehabilitation (Craig Richardson, Douglas Gordon and Euan Sutherland). When Milican began working at The Third Eye Centre in 1988, The National Review of Live Art moved there. In 1988, Stephen Partridge from Duncan of Jordanstone and Steven Littman from Maidstone College organised the video section of The National Review of Live Art at the Third Eye Centre, which included installations by Mineo Aayamaguchi, Lei Cox, Paul Green, Daniel Reeves, Chris Rowland, and Jeremy Welsh.

7    *Variant*, issue 4, 1988, pp26–28.

Susan Hiller and Bruce McLean. That year in London Damien Hirst had organised a group show of 17 fellow Goldsmiths students, including Richard Patterson, Simon Patterson, Mat Collishaw, Ian Davenport, Angela Bullock, Michael Landy, Sarah Lucas, Gary Hume and Anya Gallachio, several of whom had been taught by tutor Michael Craig-Martin. Freeze was hailed by many commentators as evidence of the entrepreneurial spirit of young artists in the capital, and marked the beginning of the yBa phenomenon in the London art scene. However, not everyone was convinced that Freeze was really an attempt to forge independent working structures for emerging artists. Curator Simon Ford later wrote in Art Monthly that "these shows were easily assimilated into the prevailing dealer and gallery system which welcomed them as a form of research and development of new products and personalities."[8] Certainly several of the artists who showed in Freeze were approached by gallerists and dealers from London and New York, notably London's Charles Saatchi.


## DEMO DISCO


The Glasgow independent music scene was continuing to expand, thanks in part to Craig Tannock's activities. Lachlan McQuarrie had now been replaced at Tower Studios by newcomer Calum McLean, who brought an increased level of technical expertise to the studio and pushed for an upgrade of the existing equipment. Cashflow generated from the rehearsal rooms and recording sessions was diverted into new equipment and before long Tower had upgraded to 16 track recordings on two inch tape. McLean also came up with the germ of an idea that would catch the imagination of bands and gig-goers up and down the country. Tannock explains, "Before Calum joined us, one of the things he thought wasn't quite right at the Tower Beat gigs was that inbetween the three bands there would be some naff DJ playing totally inappropriate music. Again, none of us had thought it was remotely a problem. Calum thought it would be better to have some-thing more thematic, maybe the odd demo, someone more in tune with

8   Simon Ford, "Myth Making", *Art Monthly*, March 1996 pp3–9.

what was going on. I took that idea to an extreme and decided what we'd do, for this regular gig called Demo Disco at this bar called The Buck[9] in St. Vincent Street, would be to have two bands, one local and one from out of town. Through the Tower Beat gigs we had started to get more demo tapes sent in to us and more from further afield. The idea was to exclusively play demo tapes all night, inbetween the bands. No records at all. On top of that, we compiled a playlist that was initially 20 strong and between the two sets, excerpts would be played from each of the 20 tracks. Voting sheets would be placed on the tables and people voted for their top three and we compiled a demo Top 10 from that, which was sent out to all the A&R people and publishing companies in London. What happened then was that the previous week's Top 10 would go head to head with a new batch of 10 demos, and you could see the movement up and down the chart. It wasn't just a case of bands bringing all their friends along to vote for themselves. The band that proved that were from Newcastle and called Fish Turned Human, they ended up in the chart for 30 consecutive weeks with a song called *Soul Pollution*. Part of the reason for doing it was that all these bands were producing all these demo tapes and there seemed to be a huge leap between this demo culture and bands getting deals and getting on the radio."[10]

The do-it-yourself movement amongst local artists picked up speed in 1988 with the establishment of the WASPS studio complex in a former John Players cigarette factory off Alexandra Parade in the East End. David Cook, who has been director of WASPS since 1991, recalls, "A group of sculptors had found this building in Hanson Street, but it was too big for their needs. They approached WASPS, who took over the whole building, leased a third of it to the Glasgow Sculpture Studios and converted the rest into individual spaces. In the '70s and '80s there was no money for capital development in the arts – we converted Hanson Street for something ridiculous like £40,000. Then the government relaxed the betting levy on

---

9    The Buck became King Tut's Wah Wah Hut in 1990 under the ownership of DF Concerts promoter Stuart Clumpas.

10   Craig Tannock, in conversation with the author. By 1989, Demo Disco expanded nationwide, with eight week runs of the night happening concurrently in three different cities, for example Glasgow, Edinburgh and Newcastle, or Glasgow, Manchester and Nottingham.

the condition that a charitable trust would be set up, called the Foundation for Sport and the Arts. We benefited from that, and from the support of the Glasgow Development Agency, and in 1988 WASPS was able to buy Hanson Street and the other studios we had been leasing at East Campbell Street. Glasgow City Council was also very supportive, in a way that we've never seen repeated in our dealings with other local authorities throughout Scotland."[11]

Callum Sinclair, director of the Glasgow Sculpture Studios, remembers, "There were no facilities for people making sculpture, and it can be really expensive to get kitted out. A few of us had the idea to set up some shared facilities, and managed to get some money from the city council and SAC to get set up, then leased the premises from WASPS. Sybille Van Halem, Kate Thomson, Jim Buckley, Tracey McKenna, Linda Reddy and myself were the main people involved, although there were others who helped too. Suddenly, artists started appearing from all over the place – moving up from England and so on."[12] Renovations were slowly continuing at the new Transmission space on King Street although, as ever, the gallery was short on cash. The Scottish Arts Council suggested that the gallery hold a jumble sale to raise some funds, which took place in October that year at Chisholm Street, and attracted a long queue of bargain-hunting locals and young artists. The last major show to be held at Chisholm Street was a five-year retrospective, Land of Opportunity, which looked back over the gallery's greatest hits and provided a fitting close to that chapter in Transmission's history.

Cathy Wilkes was working towards the realisation of the Women in Profile Womanhouse project with Rachael Harris and Julie Roberts that year. She remembers of this time, "It was really common to sign on. I remember infuriating my parents by saying, I don't want a job, I'm signing on as a political gesture. I do not want to work in this country, I don't want to be part of this system – of course, not thinking about the fact that you get your money from the government. It was a thing that some people still

---

11  David Cook, in conversation with the author, November 2002.
12  Callum Sinclair, in conversation with the author, July 2002.

think, that you don't want to put your energy into working for somebody or something, that you wanted to put your energy into being a cultural worker, and the only way to do that is to sign on. You were quite skint but you could just about scrape by. I think now it would be quite difficult to just scrape by in Glasgow with nothing but your dole. During the Thatcher time people were much more opposed to being part of the system, it wasn't such a softly, softly approach – you were more aware."[13]

After several months of working on the new Transmission space with Anne Elliot, Billy Clark had put out an appeal to the membership for help with the move and making the new space ready. Douglas Gordon was back in Glasgow for the summer, and offered to help. He remembers, "Transmission was rebuilding in King Street, I got involved with banging up walls and sanding floors and all that stuff, and I painted the Transmission sign, so for me that was a really big important thing, so I had a kind of physical investment as well as a spiritual one."[14] Other local artists including Mike Ellen, Pete Gilmour, Anne Vance, Euan Sutherland, Martin Boyce and Dave Allen, architect Ian Brown and electrician Kenny Little were also drafted in to make the new space ready.[15]

That summer a group of male Environmental Art students had graduated from Glasgow School of Art who were specifically interested in how social history impacts upon leisure pursuits and the design of everyday objects: Roderick Buchanan (b.1965), Nathan Coley (b.1967) and Iain Kettles (b.1966). Roderick Buchanan quickly developed an interest in how identity could be asserted through affiliation with certain organisations such as gangs and football teams. Nathan Coley explored the points where architecture, art and design meet, and how the needs of individuals might be subsumed within existing systems, or expressed through self-built forms, for example, pigeon lofts. Curator Ulrich Loock later wrote of Coley's work, "The actual purpose of these constructions, though, is not made apparent

---

13  Cathy Wilkes, in conversation with the author, August 2001.
14  Douglas Gordon in conversation with Graham Fagen, *Transcript* Volume 03 Issue 03, School of Fine Art, Duncan of Jordanstone, 2001.
15  The committee for the new King Street gallery would eventually be comprised of Billy Clark, Dave Allen, Christine Borland, Mike Ellen, Pete Gilmour, Euan Sutherland, Anne Vance and Craig Richardson.

in the presentation: it is limited to general rhetoric concerning the proposed advantages, options, usefulness and status of the various models, all disguised as information."[16] Iain Kettles' work displayed a more pop influence and he was well-known on the local scene for his prodigious talent for building sculptures from a variety of unconventional materials, such as a corrugated cardboard shark and a sand sculpture of a couple embracing.

Several of these young graduates participated in the first show in the new Transmission space, The Fifth International Festival of Plagiarism: Slogans of Reversal/Reversal of Slogans in August 1989. This show of mixed media works, lectures and discussions included contributions from Nathan Coley, Ross Sinclair, Roderick Buchanan, Jayne Taylor and Billy Clark and local bands AC Acoustics and The Tape Beatles. A Xerox workshop by Jamie Reid, Anarchist/Situationist videos and a music and performance event entitled *Night of the Slack* completed the line-up. The exhibition poster, designed by Environmental Art student Ross Sinclair (b.1966) read "Now you can reach those with a disposable income BEFORE they dispose of their income." The gallery also hosted the degree show of the first MFA graduates including Jim Hamlyn, Craig Richardson, Julie Roberts, and two Northern Irish-born artists: Peter McCaughey from Omagh, and Edward Stewart from Belfast. Roderick Buchanan left for MA Studies at the University of Ulster, Belfast in October, maintaining the current link between the art scenes of Belfast and Glasgow established by Cathy Wilkes, Nicola White, Christine Borland, Peter McCaughey and Edward Stewart.

The new Transmission was a "white cube" gallery space with white walls and grey floorboards and, as Nicola White remembers, "Previously the gallery had deliberately positioned itself outside the cultural mainstream. In the early '90s Transmission became, not mainstream, but certainly more allied to the international art scene. Entering the clean-lined space, one could have been in any city in Europe. Alliances and exchanges were made with like-minded artists and galleries in such places as Belfast, London,

16  Ulrich Loock, "Mutual Contextualisation", Glasgow, Kunsthalle Berne, 1997.

Chicago and Cologne. The gallery became increasingly recognised outside of Scotland, and increasingly reviewed in the art press."[17]

Information, held in 1989 at Paisley Museum and Art Gallery, was a group show of work by artists including Roderick Buchanan, Ross Sinclair, Nathan Coley and Environmental Art undergraduate Jacqueline Donachie, providing an early grouping of the Glasgow-based neo-conceptualists in much the same way as Urban Life had prefigured later New Image painting exhibitions. The title of the show was a self-conscious allusion to the seminal 1970 exhibition of conceptual art at the Museum of Modern Art in New York,[18] indicating that the group were already aligning themselves with a particular artistic tradition. Linda Graham at the Collective Gallery in Edinburgh was also offering exhibition opportunities to young artists from both Edinburgh and Glasgow, such as Christine Borland and Callum Innes,[19] who both had their first solo exhibitions there in the late '80s and early '90s.

Nicola White recalls, "In 1989 The Smith Gallery in Stirling used to be quite go-ahead, when Andrew Guest was the curator, and they had this annual exhibition called the Stirling Smith Biennale. That year they asked myself, Linda Graham from the Collective in Edinburgh and Gary Fisher, a sculptor from Dundee to be the selectors. It was a great time to be looking at new work – there were a lot of people either on the MFA or recent graduates [in Glasgow] doing fantastic stuff, and we got very excited. We put together an exhibition, and there was a big prize which we split between four people – Douglas [Gordon], who had just graduated not so long ago, the Wilson twins, one of whom was studying in Dundee,[20] Julie Roberts, who was on the MFA and a guy called Steve Dilworth, who worked up in Harris, who was making very interesting work. A lot of the slightly older artists were absolutely up in arms about it. In fact, one of

---

17  Nicola White, "Perpetual Motion", unpublished essay on Transmission 1995.

18  The title of the original exhibition was derived from Sol LeWitt's statement that art should be "pure information."

19  Edinburgh-based painter Callum Innes (b.1962) studied at Gray's School of Art in Aberdeen, and graduated from a post-graduate course at Edinburgh College of Art in 1985. He then became involved in the Collective Gallery and, by extension, Transmission.

20  Between 1986 and 1989 Louise Wilson took her undergraduate degree at Duncan of Jordanstone College of Art in Dundee, while her twin sister Jane studied at Newcastle Polytechnic. From 1990–92 both Wilsons would undertake masters studies at Goldsmiths.

them wrote to the Stirling Smith and said that a 23 year old – meaning Douglas – should not get a prize when there were much more experienced artists there showing work. There was a sense of schism between the more figurative painters and the younger people who were emerging. The age difference wasn't even that big but the difference in terms of outlook was vast. I remember that it seemed like a point at which lots of things were changing, and not everyone liked those changes."[21]

In 1989, artist-run gallery City Racing was established in a former betting shop at the Oval, South London. Matt Hale of City Racing said, "We tried to make it as white-cube like as possible. There was no high principle behind it, just a desire to show … We were fed up of waiting to be offered a show, so we thought, 'show yourself'."[22] The artists involved with City Racing showed their own work, and future yBa stars including Gillian Wearing and Sarah Lucas, but also offered exhibition opportunities to several Glasgow-based artists over the 11 years of the gallery's existence, including Roderick Buchanan, Annette Heyer, Ross Sinclair, Richard Wright and Julie Roberts. During this period, Julie Roberts was making studies of the apparatus of institutions, notably paintings of medical equipment, including gynecological chairs and restraints. Roberts painted these detailed images of 'loaded' objects on a flat monotone background, creating a split between the charge of the associations and the coolness of the representation. As well as showing in the pristine new Transmission space that year, Roberts also stayed closely involved in events taking place at the newly established Women in Profile headquarters in Dalhousie Lane, Garnethill.

Adele Patrick remembers, "Rachael Harris had heard about this space but I wasn't at all sure about taking it on. It was a dive – a tiny little rat-infested space, with no natural light or heating. It was basically an old storage space with no proper walls or floor. We got a pittance to run it. On one particularly disgusting occasion we found that a rat had gotten into the space and eaten so much that it had become really bloated. It had then tried to get

21  Nicola White, in conversation with the author, November 2002.
22  Matt Hale, "Career Opportunities, the ones that never knock", *Variant* issue 5.

back down the toilet to get out and drowned itself, so we had to literally pull this dead rat out of the toilet again."[23] Despite such setbacks, the fledgling organisation persisted in organising various confidence-building events for local women artists, including slide evenings, where trained and amateur artists could compare notes on each others' work. However, a schism was opening between the local artists' ideas for the Women In Profile events and those of the university academics, including founder member and sociologist Barbara Littlewood. Patrick remembers, "They wanted to have a writing competition, whereas we wanted a writers' group that would carry on after 1990. They wanted to select an exhibition of art-works, whereas we wanted lots of participation, and for people to be able to add work as the exhibition went on. It was a baptism of fire on that level, I hadn't realised that there would be barriers between women relating to class, or the ways they wanted to work. Eventually though, we managed to meet in the middle on the plans for the International Conference."[24]

By now, Craig Tannock's Tower Studios, Tower Beat and Demo Disco gigs had acquired a following, and Tannock had branched out into promoting tours by groups such as Savage Republic from California and bands from the New Zealand label Flying Nun. In 1988, Tannock had been invited to attend the Independence Days conference organised by Network, Berlin, which proved to be something of a turning point. "The idea behind the conference was to forge links between small promoters and agents so that bands could arrange tours without going through the larger agencies. Hundreds of bands were playing there, including some Glasgow bands like The Fains and The Primevals. Independence Days was a real eye-opener for me and showed me an alternative to dealing with the majors. I had much more empathy with the people I met there."[25] On returning to Glasgow, Tannock teamed up with Stuart Cruikshank, cultural theorist Simon Frith[26]

23  Adele Patrick, in conversation with the author, August 2002.
24  Women Setting Agendas for Change, which took place in September 1990. Adele·Patrick, Ibid.
25  Craig Tannock, Ibid.
26  Simon Frith, the author of several books on popular music including *The Sociology of Rock* (Constable/Sage, 1978) and *Sound Effects* (Constable/Sage, 1983) taught sociology at the University of Warwick for fifteen years, before taking up the post of Professor of English Studies at the University of Strathclyde during the 1980s. He is now Professor of Film and Media at the University of Stirling, and chairs the panel of judges of the Mercury Music Prize.

and music journalist John Williamson,[27] to hammer out plans for a similar conference in Glasgow, to coincide with the Year of Culture. Glasgow City Council agreed to fund the venture, plus a trip to New York for the gang of four to launch the New Music World conference at the 1989 New Music Seminar.

By the late '80s Glasgow City Council's new focus on tourism and retail had begun to regenerate the city's public profile through developments like the £23 million luxury shopping centre Princes Square which opened in 1987. The Glasgow Garden Festival (1988) and the approaching European Year of Culture (1990) also played their role in re-establishing Glasgow's international profile as a viable tourist destination. A sizeable industry had also begun to grow up around the work of Charles Rennie Mackintosh, and his now celebrated Glasgow School of Art, Scotland Street School, Hill House at Helensburgh, and the Mackintosh House at Glasgow University's Hunterian Art Gallery. While the fortunes of the city seemed to slowly improve, so too did those of the young visual artists associated with Transmission. The kind of work being made and the techniques for getting the work seen were also changing, and in October 1989 the first Transmission international exchange took place with Oceaan in Arnhem. Dave Allen, Billy Clark, Louise Crawford, Steven Harty and Karen Vaughan travelled to the Netherlands to exhibit their work.


## DANCE AND PROTEST


1989 was a year of uprisings and political change in Eastern Europe and China. Television news footage of a lone student walking towards a tank became emblematic of the June massacre of students at a pro-democracy demonstration in Tiananmen Square, Beijing. In Eastern Europe, communist regimes were collapsing, in part due to Mikhail Gorbachev's[28]

27 John Williamson began writing for *The List* while a teenager in the mid-1980s, later writing for the *Glasgow Herald* and other publications. As well as his close involvement in various live music ventures including The Apollo, the 13th Note and Mono, he was for several years the manager of Glasgow band Bis.

28 Mikhail Gorbachev, the youngest member of the Poiltburo, had come to power in 1985 and quickly implemented a series of radical economic and political reforms, informed by a new commitment to glasnost (openness) and perestroika (restructuring).

sweeping reforms in the former Soviet Union. In September Hungary had opened her frontiers, followed by Czechoslovakia: in three days 12,000 East Germans crossed from these countries to the West. Then, in November, on the eve of the planned celebration of 40 years of socialism in the GDR, young East Berliners who had gathered to hear a music concert taking place on the West side of the wall became increasingly agitated and began attacking the wall. Once the wall had been breached, the Politburo agreed to completely demolish the remainder. Within a few days more than 9 million East Germans had visited West Berlin. Demands for free elections were made all over Eastern Europe, resulting in a new government in Poland, "The Velvet Revolution" ending communist control of Czechoslovakia, and the overthrow and execution of President Ceaucescu in Romania.

The collapse of communism had a particular resonance in Glasgow, as Glaswegian writer Angus Dixon recalled: "The Cold War was on my doorstep in the shape of large Trident submarines and naval families who were shipped in from other parts of the country. The gravy train had arrived a few years before and no-one liked the thought it might be upset by kids who wanted to hear pop bands. We were listening to the Stone Roses the night the wall came down, trying to drown out the noise of my parents fighting downstairs. Huddled in my bedroom smoking badly rolled joints, we watched the telly with the sound turned down. Dave put on side one and *I Wanna be Adored* played from the battered old stereo as young Germans took sledgehammers to the wall that had divided their city since they were born. The wall came down slowly at first."[29]

House music and "dance drug" ecstasy had also caught on in London clubs like Shoom and Future by '88, and by 1989 the sound of acid house and the new recreational drugs were attracting thousands of young people to raves across the country. Then in 1989, 16 year old Claire Leighton collapsed and died at the Hacienda after taking ecstasy. Factory Records' Hacienda, and 'Madchester' bands associated with the club, like New Order, The Stone Roses, The Happy Mondays and The Inspiral Carpets became the

---

29  Angus Dixon, 1989, published in *Swing*, Glasgow, September 1998.

focus of national media attention. In Scotland, clubs like Katch in Edinburgh, Splash 1 and Psycho Kandy in Glasgow and the Hype Club in nearby Paisley were promoting the music from Northern England, as well as home-grown bands like the Close Lobsters, who had released their third album, *Headache Rhetoric* that year. Besides The Pastels, Primal Scream and Close Lobsters, other local bands making an impression in the late '80s included the BMX Bandits, The Vaselines, The Soup Dragons, The Boy Hairdressers, The Groovy Little Numbers and Teenage Fanclub.

Despite the gradual facelift of the city centre shops and cafés, the overall economic profile of the city was still looking pretty grim. In 1989 17% of Glasgow's population was unemployed and 23% of men in the city were out of work. The collapse of communism in Eastern Europe had also left those Scots who had aligned themselves with communist thought in an ideological quandary. Alexander Moffat remembers, "The Cold War had lasted so long and everybody had been conditioned by it to a certain extent. Then there was just a period when everyone was regrouping and trying to imagine what would happen next."[30] Political unrest rose as Margaret Thatcher implemented the new "flat-rate" Community Charge or "Poll Tax" in Scotland a year ahead of the rest of the country. Scotland was already being used as a guinea pig for nuclear weapons storage and processing, and the new tax, which would leave many people in Scotland worse off, met with wide resistance. Under the new system, a young person on a low wage renting a flat in the same street as a home-owning professional would be charged the same rate in Community Charge, whereas before the introduction of the Poll Tax landlords had been responsible for paying rates on properties.

Militant[31] co-ordinated a non-payment campaign across Scotland, setting up Anti-Poll Tax Federations to provide advice and support, and coining the phrase "PAY NO POLL TAX". This slogan appeared on posters displayed in windows across Scotland. Militant advised those who were issued with a court summons to attend the hearing, knowing that the courts would not

---

30  Alexander Moffat, in conversation with the author, May 2002.
31  Militant has been known as The Socialist Party since 1997.

be able to cope with the volume of cases. Like the Glasgow Rent Strikes of 1915, the Poll Tax was a political issue that united whole communities in a spirit of resistance. Thatcher had famously stated that "there is no society", but the anti-poll tax campaigns in Scotland seemed to prove the reverse was true. As the *Evening Times* reported, "Using tactics modelled on the South African townships many areas have become no-go areas for sheriff officers, with literally hundreds of eyes on the lookout … While it is certain Militant has been involved in the campaign's organisation, go into one of the dozens of meetings that take place in the city every week and it's not loony lefties you'll find but housewives and kids … they're the backbone of a campaign which has undoubtedly put the uncollectable into the poll tax."[32]

In 1990, Glasgow's year as European City of Culture began. Glasgow's Glasgow, a multimedia exhibition of the city's history, attracted controversy when the £4 million budget was revealed (this represented 30% of the District's total cultural budget).[33] The city spent a further £32 million on cultural capital works: The Royal Concert Hall opened, and the King's Theatre, the Citizen's Theatre, the McLellan Galleries and Tramway were also refurbished as part of the City of Culture celebrations. The City of Culture events were opposed by many local left-wing groups, including the Workers City activist group who felt that many of the planned events were political window-dressing which cost a great deal of public funding but didn't improve the basic living situation of most Glaswegians. The Festival office allocated only 1% of Glasgow City Council's £15 million budget towards funding of local arts events. The majority of the Festival budget and all of the sponsors' money went towards supporting high-profile and often imported cultural events such as performances by the Bolshoi Ballet and Frank Sinatra.

Despite the controversy surrounding Glasgow's City of Culture celebrations, the successful nomination did bring some additional public funding for arts events such as Sites/Positions. This was the first event of

---

32   *Evening Times*, Glasgow, 1989.
33   The budget for the exhibition is reputed to have eventually reached circa £10 million.

Glasgow's Year of Culture and was organised by Malcolm Dickson and Ken Gill as an EventSpace project. The project comprised six different "art as intervention" public artworks by Euan Sutherland, Alison Marchant, Gillian Steel,[34] Christine Borland and Douglas Gordon. Douglas Gordon had participated in the inaugural Windfall exhibition held in Bremnen the previous year, and was now only a few months away from completing his Masters at the Slade. On his return to Glasgow, Gordon embarked on a series of new works, first making a site-specific wall painting at Glasgow Green Station on London Road. *Proof* commemorated the civil uprisings of 1787, 1812, 1820, 1916, 1922 and 1932 – but in a very different style from the murals Ken Currie had completed on a similar theme for the People's Palace a few years earlier. Besides the word mute written in large italics, Gordon had simply listed the dates of the uprisings. The work was an early instance of the ambigious and evocative word-play which would be developed in Gordon's later work.

In January, *Scottish Child*, The Free University, *Variant, Here & Now* and *The Edinburgh Review*[35] invited left-wing critic and author Noam Chomsky to speak at the Self-Determination and Power conference at the Pearce Institute in Govan. Malcolm Dickson felt that "The culmination of the '80s was Self-Determination and Power. Bringing together writers, artists, community workers, anarchists, socialists, nationalists (a few), Christians (fewer), tenants-group representatives, anti-racist campaigners, publishers, women's aid workers, teachers, such a phenomenal mix of people from different backgrounds."[36] A report on the conference in the *Times Higher Education Supplement* recorded that, "Professor Chomsky continued to duck the role of oracle, denying the need for oracles at all. There had been a sense, he recognised, that there was something deeply unsatisfying about general and abstract discussion which did not direct itself to concrete

---

34 Former Transmission committee member and Women in Profile founder member Gillian Steel made an animated film with girls from the deprived area of Springburn for the project.

35 In 1990 The Scotsman art critic Murdo MacDonald (b.1955) took over from Peter Kravitz as the editor of *The Edinburgh Review*. MacDonald, an art critic for the *Scotsman* between 1987 and 1992 and edited *The Edinburgh Review* until 1994, during which time he also taught at the University of Stirling. In 1997 he was appointed Professor of History of Scottish Art at the University of Dundee.

36 Malcolm Dickson, "Letter 6", *Justified Sinners*, Ibid.

discussion of oppression and justice. Somebody recalls Vaclav Havel's dictum that "truth and love will triumph over hatred and lies". Chomsky's response? "It's a nice thought". Yes, but is it true or false? "Neither. It could become true, to the extent that people struggle to make it come true".[37]

In January that year Women in Profile held an auction at the art school to raise money for their programme of events. Pavement portraits by Julie Roberts, Liz Lochhead books, babysitting for a week, bass guitar lessons and 'feet washing" by Jayne Taylor were all up for grabs. The auction raised £900 for the Women in Profile coffers. Transmission's first exhibition in the long-awaited Year of Culture was Installation Work by Dave Allen and Peter Gilmour which opened in February. The invitations for Installation Work were printed on pages torn from a catalogue from home improvement store B&Q, literally emphasising the "DIY" mentality of artists associated with the gallery. Martin Boyce remembers, "At that time Transmission seemed really central to not just the work but a complete attitude. It was kind of a central place socially and was a focus – it was the first port of call for friends coming up to visit. I remember being there invigilating before I was on the committee and people would come off the train from London and go straight there because they knew they could meet somebody there and go for a drink. No-one had studios so it was the place to go to hang out or to talk to someone."[38]

In 1990 Tramway also began a visual arts programme, with Nicola White as curator. For the next five years the converted tram depot would offer the largest visual arts exhibition space in Europe. She remembers, "It was the first time the building had been used for visual arts and it was a slightly odd post initially because the exhibitions had mostly been set up by Tessa Jackson in the 1990 office. David Mach[39] built these huge Roman pillars around the existing pillars out of tabloid newspapers – mostly copies of the

37  Olga Wojtas, "Report from Govan on a Conference on Self-Determination", *Times Higher Education Supplement*, 26th January, 1990, p15.

38  Martin Boyce, in conversation with the author, February 2002.

39  Here to Stay 5th March–29th April 1990.  David Mach (b.1956) made sculptural works out of everyday objects – typically those with a 'Scottish' association, such as Irn Bru bottles filled with forth Bridge paint or copies of local newspapers. A link can be drawn between his practice and that of another Scottish artist, Calum Colvin (b.1961) who makes construction and collage-based work that addresses stereotypical notions of national identity.

*Evening Times*. It made the space into a huge basilica, it was really simple but really beautiful. There was also a new French art show called Le Cinq.[40] Absalon filled the central space between the pillars with machine parts made of hardboard that you looked down on from the balcony. It felt very international and fresh and I remember Douglas [Gordon] saying, 'It doesn't feel like Glasgow anymore'. That was to do with being able to do things on a large scale, or in a speculative kind of way, bringing artists over from abroad. There was also an Italian sculpture show [Temperamenti: Contemporary Art from Northern Italy][41] which was amazing. There were large scale sculptures by Giuseppe Penone and Giovanni Anselmo, and most of the Arte Povera artists came over to install their work."[42]

In early 1990 the list of artists was announced for The British Art Show 1990.[43] One of the selectors of the exhibition was Andrew Nairne, who had replaced Nicola White as Exhibitions Co-ordinator at the Third Eye Centre, and the selection of Scottish artists in the show chimed closely with that of his exhibition, Scatter, held at the Third Eye Centre the previous year. Scatter had included the work of Callum Innes, Wendy McMurdo, Gareth Fisher, Linda Taylor and Kevin Henderson. Edinburgh-based artists Innes and Henderson then made the line-up for The British Art Show, along with four Glasgow-based artists – Matthew Dalziel, Brian W. Jenkins, Louise Scullion and Linda Taylor. In the catalogue's introductory essay, Joanna Drew, director of the Hayward commented, "The two 'tend-encies' amongst younger artists, which have been made most visible in Britain in the 1980s are an expressive kind of figurative painting, perceived as emanating from Scotland (summed up in The Vigorous Imagination, which took place during the 1987 Edinburgh Festival) and the 'New British Sculpture'. The 'New Sculptors' are a loose group of artists who have responded to aspects of Modernist sculpture and to the possibilities opened up by an associative and referential language."[44]


40  2nd July–26th August 1990.
41  11th October–18th November 1990.
42  Nicola White, Ibid.
43  The exhibition opened the newly renovated McLellan Galleries as the first major exhibition in the city's year as European City of Culture. The exhibition then toured to: Leeds City Art Gallery (30th March – 20th May) and the Hayward Gallery, London (14th June – 12th August).
44  *The British Art Show 1990*, Hayward Gallery Publishing, London, 1990, p12.

Although New British Sculptors Tony Cragg, Richard Deacon and Bill Woodrow had been showing internationally for several years at this point, their last notable exposure in Scotland had been in the early 1980s when all of the "Lisson sculptors" were shown together at The Fruitmarket in Edinburgh in an exhibition entitled Objects and Figures: New Sculpture in Britain. Richard Deacon had then had a solo show at The Fruitmarket in Edinburgh in 1984, which was followed by Bill Woodrow in 1986. However, the work of the Scottish artists in the exhibition did not correspond convincingly with either of the "tendencies" identified by Drew – being neither figurative painting nor New Sculpture. Callum Innes' minimalist paintings worked through erasing part of the painted surface, creating an interesting controlled adjunct to 1950s Abstract Expressionism. "The series of works from the early 1990s collectively referred to as the *Identified Forms* show the impact of turpentine on the immaculately painted surfaces of solid colour, the 'forms' referred to in the title being absences rather than presences. The outlines and eventual shapes of these forms are dictated simply by time – the time taken for the turpentine to move across the surface before it (quickly) evaporates, having stripped away the paint in its path."[45]

Like Callum Innes, Kevin Henderson (b.1963) graduated from Gray's Art School in Aberdeen. In common with several of his contemporaries, Henderson had originally been a painter, but began to work with objects in the early 1990s, commenting "I feel that I can work with any material. I'm not biased towards any one thing but if I moved from where I am living now, then the materials I use would undoubtedly change …"[46] Henderson's "ideas-based" practice chimed with that of other local artists, notably Christine Borland, Roderick Buchanan, Douglas Gordon and Craig Richardson, who would exhibit with him in Self-Conscious State at the Third Eye Centre later that year. Matthew Dalziel and Louise Scullion had graduated from separate courses at Glasgow School of Art in 1988, and exhibited separately in this exhibition, although they would begin to work

45  Katrina Brown, *Here + Now*, DCA, Dundee, 2001.
46  *British Art Show 1990*, Hayward Gallery Publishing, London,1990.

together collaboratively two years later. Environmental Art graduate Louise Scullion (b.1966) was concerned in these early works with how natural forms intersect with ideas about tactics in the "Military Landscaping" that surrounded her native town of Helensburgh. Matthew Dalziel (b.1957) had graduated from a Sculpture and Fine Art Photography masters, which fed into the duo's later collaborative film, video and sculptural works relating to the Scottish landscape.

Glasgow's growing reputation continued to attract students and artists from elsewhere, such as Simon Starling (b.1967), a graduate from Nottingham Polytechnic interested in the history of objects. Starling joined the MFA course at Glasgow School of Art in 1990, where his work contributed greatly to the dialogue emerging between the language of design and art. Starling was part of the group of predominantly male artists who emerged from the school in the late '80s and early '90s, who often made works that interrogated the process and history of physical design. Another artist who, like Starling, was also influenced by the Duchampian idea of the Readymade was Martin Boyce, who had graduated from the Environmental Art department in 1990. A sense of ambiguity was at play in much of the work made by these artists: their work set up questions about both functionality of the object and the mysterious qualities ascribed to art.

During this period, Andrew Miller (b. 1969) was nearing the end of a photography degree at the art school in 1990, and planning to proceed directly onto the MFA the next year. Following his early studies at technical college, Miller's work also dealt with the interface between design and art. "The piece of work that I am interested in presenting is ready, I just need to find it. Everyday items such as table frames, bicycle racks, kitchen units and building materials/structures have for some time now been the inspiration and starting point for my work."[47] A parallel between the practice of Nathan Coley, Simon Starling, Martin Boyce and Andrew Miller could be found in the work of London-based artist Simon Patterson, who had exhibited at the Third Eye Centre with Damien Hirst in 1989. In London, the artists

47  Andrew Miller, artist's statement, *New Art in Scotland catalogue*, CCA, Glasgow,1995.

associated with Goldsmiths were building an ever greater profile, aided by shows like Modern Medicine (March 1990), a show of eight young artists, curated by Damien Hirst, Billee Sellmann and Carl Freedman and held in Building One, a disused biscuit factory in Bermondsey. Later that year Carl Freedman would use the same venue to stage influential exhibitions such as Gambler, a group show in July, and Market, a solo show by Goldsmiths graduate Michael Landy in October. These exhibitions were distinguished from those usually staged by recent graduates not only by the slick appearance and installation of the artists' work. The professional approach of the organisers, who secured corporate sponsorship to fund the publication of exhibition catalogues and openly courted the attentions of both London gallerists and the media also marked a significant change in approach.

Although there may have been certain shared thematic concerns between artists working in Glasgow and London, Glasgow-based artists did not have access to a comparable infrastructure of commercial galleries and influential media contacts. Indeed, the key support to artists working in the city continued to be the Benefits Agency, a point emphasised by the exhibition Dependants, which opened at Transmission in April 1990. For the show, the five participating artists (Nathan Coley, Heather Allen, Iain Kettles, Evelyn Jardine and Susan Montford) were given thirty pounds each to make their work – at the time this amounted to more than a week's dole money. Unemployment benefit had been the unofficial mainstay of the arts scene in Glasgow from the sixties onwards and Dependants was one of the few events to pointedly draw attention to the fact. *The Glasgow Herald* commented, "this underlines the reality of inadequate help for most artists." Two of the artists in the show, Susan Montford and Northern Irish artist Heather Allen were also involved with Women in Profile. Montford was curating an exhibition on The History of Women's Aid in Glasgow, due to open in September that year, while Allen had volunteered to exhibit work in the Womanhouse tenement. Billy Clark points out that, "Transmission, Women in Profile, Worker's City and The Free University were all autonomous groups, but to a certain extent they operated in a similar way – a kind of cell-like structure."[48]

48  Billy Clark, Ibid.

Environmental Art graduate Claire Barclay (b.1968) was also working with Women in Profile and was involved in the scene around Transmission during this period. Barclay's work combined hard materials with a more craft-orientated approach. For example, in a Barclay installation, polished steel or glass might co-exist with machine-stitched fabric, or found "natural" objects. There were certain similarities between Claire Barclay and Christine Borland's conceptual strategies in this early period, notably in their use of soft fabrics and "feminine" handicrafts such as sewing, and their careful arrangement of objects. Curator Susan May wrote of this approach to materials, "The proliferation of modest handicraft in contemporary art may be connected to the period in which many of the artists grew up. By the 1970s, post-war tendencies towards a distinct division of labour between the genders was becoming diluted, due largely to the influence of a nascent feminist movement, which repudiated such stereotypes. With feminism's celebration of the significant and positive aspects of culture normally associated with women, the home being one of them, the appropriation of traditional handicraft – or "women's work" – for radical intentions was encouraged."[49] However, both Borland's and Barclay's works were crafted with a precision that effaced their own presence, to create a mechanical or scientific feeling – the feeling produced was more of anthropology than handicrafts.

Claire Barclay later commented, "For most people there is a mixture of desire and fear of being on the outside. That can turn into a suspicion of those who seek out solitude. That's why witches, or wise women became mistrusted. They were also considered to be closer to animals, nature and the supernatural."[50] Borland and Barclay were amongst the first Glasgow-based female artists to explore the (perceived) tension between intuitive, craft-based working and a "knowing" appropriation of systems ranging from architecture to medicine. Julie Roberts, Cathy Wilkes and Heather Allen were other artists working in and around Transmission during this period whose work dealt with gender issues, although it would be an over-

---

49  Susan May, *Here to Stay* catalogue, British Council, London, 1998.
50  Claire Barclay, Moderna Museet Projekt, 16th June–13th August 2000.

simplification to read the work of any of these artists as being exclusively concerned with ideas of femininity. Their work could be seen as symptomatic of a general post-conceptual approach to art in Scotland – a negotiation between the definition of art, and the definition of society.

In 1990 opposition to Margaret Thatcher increased as the Poll Tax was implemented in England. The non-payment campaign was quickly adopted in the south and by spring of 1990 there were 2,000 Anti-Poll Tax Federations and 20 million people had been summonsed to court for non-payment across the UK. The palpable sense of anti-Thatcher sentiment peaked on March 31st in a march of 200,000 anti-poll tax demonstrators on Trafalgar Square in London and a march of 50,000 demonstrators in Glasgow. This unified show of public dissent helped force Thatcher's resignation after 11 years in power. The Scottish electorate had never voted for the 'Iron Lady' and her departure was greeted with widespread jubilation. Four months after Thatcher's resignation cabinet minister Michael Heseltine announced, "We have therefore decided that from the earliest possible moment the Community Charge will be replaced by a new system of local taxation. *The Financial Times* called the Poll Tax debacle "the most expensive mistake in modern political history."

Thatcher was replaced by the allegedly bland John Major, who was only to quick to lend support to George Bush's mooted plans to go to war in the Gulf. However, despite the Conservatives remaining in power, the rescinding of the Poll Tax, the ousting of Thatcher and the release of ANC leader Nelson Mandela after 27 years in jail in South Africa combined to make 1990 a year of many significant political turning-points. There had been a long history of active anti-apartheid campaigning in Scotland, with Aberdeen imposing sanctions as early as 1964. However, Thatcher had long been reluctant to impose sanctions, an attitude that was shared by the Republican government in America. In 1986, The Comprehensive Anti-Apartheid Act was adopted by the US Congress against the wishes of the White House, and Thatcher had bowed to public pressure to follow suit, along with Japan and Israel. Although Mandela's release was a significant advance in the struggle against the apartheid regime, and was viewed as such, it would be another four years before apartheid would end in South Africa.

## SITE SPECIFIC

Evidence of the increasing profile of Glasgow on the international art map came in September 1990, with the Glasgow stage[51] of the Four Cities Touring South West Arts (TSWA) project. Work by Judith Barry, Stuart Brisley, Janette Emery and Kevin Rhowbotham, Peter Fischli and David Weiss, Cildo Meireles, Richard Wilson and Rosemarie Trockel was exhibited in various locations around the city until the end of October. Rosemarie Trockel devised a series of posters that subverted the language of advertising, on circular pillars under the green glass pyramid of the St. Enoch's Shopping Centre. Stuart Brisley's work was installed at Govan Graving Docks in "a huge sunken edifice like the internal space of an embedded sculptural pedestal, an inverted memorial." Brisley wrote, "There is a sense of fragility, especially when I realised that the vast space is kept dry by the use of a huge floodgate at one end. This is an essentially insecure place – at some time or another water pressure from the Clyde will overcome the floodgate installation."[52] In this location Brisley arranged a series of oversized white plaster casts of body parts based on Action Man – a "typical toy model" of what "a Western hero should look like." When the water level rose and flooded the dock, the white plaster body parts were displaced or submerged. Another work that referenced the changing fortunes of Glasgow was the permanent piece by Ian Hamilton Finlay that was installed on two of the eight existing pillars of the old bridge over the Clyde at the foot of Oswald Street. A text derived from Plato's *Republic* (ALL GREATNESS STANDS FIRM IN THE STORM) was inscribed on the pillars in English and the original Greek.

Another project that was commissioned for the Year of Culture was Force 10, an artist's flag project that Newcastle-based arts organisation

---

51  The other three cities involved were: Derry, Plymouth and Newcastle.
52  Stuart Brisley, *Govan Dock Proposal*, TSWA Four Cities Project, TSWA Ltd., Bristol, 1990.

Projects UK, run by Jon Bewley and Simon Herbert, worked on collaboratively with EventSpace. Both Herbert and Bewley were in close contact with the art scene in Glasgow throughout the early '90s, working on collaborative projects with Glasgow-based arts organisations, and contributing articles to and commissioning a 1990 video edition for *Variant*. For the flags project, Keith Piper produced multicultural reworkings of the Union Jack, incorporating pictures of Asian and Chinese people, that were hung at Kelvingrove Art Gallery and Museum. Conrad Atkinson produced a series of banners with American football players with political slogans on their shirts, that were positioned over the road at Kelvinhall Sports Arena. Graham Budget made eastern European flags with superimposed images from TV adverts, as a comment on the rise of consumerism after the fall of the Berlin Wall, which were installed at Watt Brothers department store on Sauchiehall Street. Part of the 1990 Edge events were co-ordinated in Glasgow by Nicola White, including works by Marina Abramovic, Cornelia Parker and Black Market International.[53] "Black Market arrived at Tramway in taxis, boiled some water outside, and put cardboard boxes on their heads, then drove away again," remembers Simon Herbert, "Cornelia Parker did a chalk work on the exterior of an old school room at the back of Tramway and Marina Abramovic did a performance piece with snakes at the Third Eye Centre."[54]

Nicola White says, "People remember Marina Abramovic's performance because we had to move it to the Third Eye Centre as snakes were involved. The performance entailed Marina sitting in a circle of ice and with five pythons draped over her and they were supposed to be contained by the circle of ice because snakes won't go over anything cold. It was really just her sitting there completely still while the snakes moved over her. One of them did make a bolt for freedom across the ice during the performance and escaped upstairs, and this missing python became one of the great

---

53 Formed in 1985, this loose artist's collective has included Boris Nieslony (Germany), Jurgen Fritz (Switzerland), Norbert Klassen (Germany), Tomas Ruller (former Czechoslovakia), Jacques van Poppel (Netherlands), Roi Vaara (Finland) and Zbigniew Warpechowski (Poland). The group meet intermittently to produce performative works, and have occasionally been joined by British artists Brian Catling, Nigel Rolf and Alisdair MacLennan.

54 Simon Herbert, in conversation with the author, July 2002.

stories about the Third Eye Centre. It disappeared into the floorboards for a year before re-emerging. Myself and Trevor Cromie, who was helping out with Edge, were sitting up at nights with an electric heater trying to get the python to come back out. It did turn up a year later, but I remember at the time thinking that you took so many risks putting up shows but the worst thing that could usually happen would be that the doors wouldn't open on time or the paintings would fall down. This time I thought, what's the worst that could happen – the snake could kill someone."[55]

## THE SECOND SUMMER OF LOVE

Glasgow's planned renaissance as a city of culture played out against a revisiting of the cultural idioms of the '60s in British fashion and music. 1990 was 'the second summer of love', when an unknown teenage model called Kate Moss was photographed for the cover of *The Face* by Corrine Day, wearing a feather head-dress, beads and a toothy smile. Indie favourites The Stone Roses played Spike Island that summer, in a move reminiscent of Jimi Hendrix and Pink Floyd's legendary Isle of Wight gigs of the '60s. By then, a new dance sound from Detroit had burst onto the Scottish club scene courtesy of Pure, which began in August 1990 at The Venue in Edinburgh. Resident DJs Twitch and Brainstorm played an eclectic mix of house and techno, and as Brainstorm remembers, "The club quickly changed the club scene in Edinburgh, arriving as it did as the Summer of Love exploded on the UK … stroboscopic flashes of scenes of crazy people in mad smoke-filled rooms stick in my mind … it had a freshness that came with the birth of a scene; before cynicism and wariness crept in. Pure was bringing the likes of Derrick May, Juan Atkins, Blake Baxter, Ritchie Hawtin, Orbital and Jeff Mills to play before the UK techno scene became fashionable."[56] The Pure DJs also organised a series of memorable outdoor raves, as their friend Sam Hayes remembers. "There was a party in 1990 organised by Brainstorm in a field in Fife on the rainiest day in 24 years. It

---

55  Nicola White, Ibid.
56  Excerpt from information on Pure, on the Renegade website, www.ren-com.com

rained all day, but 12 people held a tarpaulin over the decks while everyone else danced."[57]

Like Northern soul, the new music from America came from a source and sensibility that chimed with the frustrated creative energy in Scotland. "Techno as we know it descended from the Detroit region, which specialised in a stripped-down abrasive sound, maintaining some of the soulful elements of the Motown Records palette, over the innovations that hiphop's electro period had engendered. Techno also reflected the city's decline, as well as the advent of technology, and this tension was crucial to the dynamics of the sound. As [Inner City's] Kevin Saunderson recounts: "When we first started doing this music we were far ahead. But Detroit is still a very behind city when it comes to anything cultural."[58]

In Glasgow, Harri and Slam started Atlantis that year at the Sub Club, which would become one of the most popular and respected house music clubs in the UK. Queues around the block were usual at the Jamaica Street club, and the glamorous crowd was full of boys in Fred Perry poloshirts, and girls with false eyelashes and Vivienne Westwood corsets. The stylish basement interior featured low banquet seats around a sprung wooden dance floor, UV lights that made the gin and tonics glow, and the best sound system in the city. The reputation of the club and the "up for it" crowd soon attracted high profile guests, like Andy Weatherall, who launched Glasgow band Primal Scream onto the national consciousness with his remix of *Loaded* that summer.

Primal Scream had left behind their earlier C86 pop associations after Jim Beattie had left the band in 1988. The rest of the band had decamped to Brighton, were they had been busy immersing themselves in the local club culture. *Loaded* reflected their new direction: a fusion of their old '60s rock influences and the sound of house and techno. The record opened with a sample taken from the Roger Corman film *The Wild Angels* (1966), which had first been sampled by Genesis P.Orridge and Richard Norris' for their 1988 *Jack the Tab* album. The question "Just what is it that you want

---

57  Sam Hayes, in conversation with the author, May 1998.
58  Colin Larkin, *Dance Music*, Virgin Books, London, 1998, p335.

to do?" posed by a "square" to a Californian biker (played by Peter Fonda) elicits the reply, "We wanna be free … we wanna be free to do what we want to do, and we wanna get loaded, and we wanna have a good time. And that's what we're gonna do! We're gonna have a good time. We're gonna have a party!" Fonda's sampled speech was quickly adopted as a modus operandi by Glasgow clubbers.

Serving on the Transmission committee that summer were Dave Allen, Christine Borland, Billy Clark, Douglas Gordon and Craig Richardson, although Katrina Brown, Roderick Buchanan and Elsie Mitchell were beginning to get more closely involved. Billy Clark remembers, "What the gallery could do best was draw on all the people who were around. Windfall started around that time, and we also did the Saltoun Art Project. Everyone was functioning brilliantly."[59] The Saltoun Art Project in the summer of 1990 had begun when American property owner Martin Yudowitz had telephoned Transmission to ask if the gallery would be interested in putting on a show in his empty warehouse property. Steven Harty, Jacqueline Donachie, Ross Sinclair, Karen Vaughan, Kenny McKay and Stuart McGlinn all exhibited new works, with Vaughan also working on the building's electrics and Donachie organising the drinks for the opening.

Richard Wright remembers, "The way Transmission was at the beginning is very different to the way that it is now. I think initially there was a more idealistic attitude, a more left-wing political approach. In the early '90s what really changed, when Douglas Gordon, Christine Borland and Dave Allen were involved, was that there was a much more conscious attempt to engage with an existing art world. I think that people were still aware that Glasgow was outside, looking in, but there was a strong move towards empowerment, a strategic approach towards making something happen here – but also to make other people elsewhere aware of what was happening here. That was done in lots of different ways: by going places, often as a group, but also by getting people to come here. That was a really new thing, and I think the model of Transmission being an agent of

59  Billy Clark, Ibid.

attraction and a bridgehead into other situations is still in place."[60]

Artist and writer Thomas Lawson (b.1951) left Glasgow for New York in 1975, when the city was in the grip of widespread unemployment. Before moving to LA in 1989, Lawson had lived in New York, building a distinguished career as a painter, in addition to curating shows at experimental spaces like White Columns and PS1, writing for *Flash Art* and *Artforum* and running the highly acclaimed *Real Life* magazine (1978–1994) with his wife and collaborator Susan Morgan. Now Dean of the California Institute of the Arts, Lawson recalls his shock at the changes in his home town on a return visit in 1990 to exhibit paintings at the Third Eye Centre: "I still remember sitting in a pub that summer with Christine Borland, Douglas Gordon and Craig Richardson, utterly amazed that young artists who clearly had the ability and information to operate in a more cosmopolitan arena were not desperately saving up for their tickets out. I quickly realised that these three were ambitious for their work, it took longer to get that they were also ambitious for their hometown. But this was because I had not yet fully understood the vast change that Transmission had made to the psyche of Glasgow's younger artists."[61] In September that year Transmission sent Claire Barclay, Malcolm Dickson, Nathan Coley, Ross Sinclair and Martin Boyce to Norway, to show at the Hordaland Kunstnersentrum. A local publication commented, "There is a recognisable unity about the show, which bears witness to the exhibitors' familiarity with each other's artistic ideas and expressions."[62]

Also in September 1990, Women In Profile's Womanhouse opened at 39 Glenacre Quad, a disused tenement block in Castlemilk. Besides the four key organisers, Adele Patrick, Rachael Harris, Julie Roberts and Cathy Wilkes, several other local artists participated including Claire Barclay, Christine Borland, Lesley Burr, Louise Scullion, Heather Allen and Susan Montford. Earlier that year a public controversy had errupted when Elspeth King, the long-term curator at the People's Palace, had been overlooked for the newly created post of Keeper of Glasgow's Social History. By June,

---


60  Richard Wright, in conversation with the author, September 2001.
61  Thomas Lawson, "Three Datelines and a Postscript", unpublished essay on Transmission, 1995.
62  Bergens Tidende, October 1990.

3,000 people had signed a petition to protest at the council's decision, and at the comments of certain council employees, including Julian Spalding, who went on record as saying "there are no jobs for the girls." Women in Profile organisers Rachael Harris and Julie Roberts responded by making t-shirts emblazoned with the slogan "Jobs for the Girls". After successfully securing £35,000 of funding from Glasgow District Council, Scottish Office funding was also granted for a further 3 years to allow the Womanhouse to be run as a community resource beyond the 1990 Year of Culture.

Another key part of the Women in Profile events was Susan Montford's exhibition A Working History of Glasgow Women's Aid, which was held in a caretaker's office in a semi-derelict building near the art school. Adele Patrick remembers, "She used a series of really evocative sound recordings to make this very powerful installation. She was working with women whose histories had never been told."[63] Glasgow's Women's Aid Centre was one of 200 nationwide providers of advice and refuge for women and their children suffering from physical or emotional abuse. In Scotland alone, Women's Aid received 15,000 calls each year. Later in September, the Women Setting Agendas for Change conference went ahead with an impressive line-up of guest speakers including film theorist Annette Kuhn, poets Liz Lochhead and Gerry Fellowes, writers Agnes Owen and Jessie Kesson, and various local artists including Cathy Wilkes, Julie Roberts and Sam Ainsley. Christina McBride from the Photography department at the art school also curated Photoworks for the new exhibition space at Tramway. Photoworks was an exhibition by women artists working with photography and time-based media including Super 8, slide projection, installation and video, while at the art school a show called The Women's Own Annual exhibition was held in the Assembly Hall where the first major Women in Profile meeting had been held three years earlier.

In October, Self-Conscious State, curated by Andrew Nairne, opened at the Third Eye Centre. Nairne had already indicated his interest in the neo-conceptual work emerging in Scotland with his previous Third Eye Centre exhibition Scatter (1989) and his selection for The British Art Show

63  Adele Patrick, in conversation with the author, August 2002.

in 1990. Self-Conscious State served to consolidate the existing collaborative connections between Craig Richardson, Roderick Buchanan, Christine Borland and Douglas Gordon and also featured the work of Edinburgh-based artist Kevin Henderson. Christine Borland remembers that "… the exhibition tried to bring together our shared concerns of the body/individual/state and their (and our) co-dependence and conflicts."[64] A text piece on the floor by Craig Richardson spelt out the acronym GRIT from the words Group Range Indication Type of fire, and the exhibition also included Christine Borland's skeleton shadow work, *Supported*, marking her move closer into the thematics surrounding forensic science. *Supported* provided an early instance of Borland's abiding interest in the role that interpretation plays in medical and scientific investigations. Human bones were arranged on a glass shelf, dusted with powder and then removed, so that only an outline remained. Light shining through the glass then cast a distorted duplication of the skeletal outline onto the wall below. Self-Conscious State was also the first time that Douglas Gordon exhibited his *List of Names*, a vast text work that catalogued all of the people he could recall knowing. *List of Names* included 1,440 names and resembled a kind of memorial, although as with *Proof*, the site-specific text piece he had made earlier that year, a degree of ambiguity surrounded the work, as no indication was given as to the identity of the people listed, or the criterion for their selection.

"I remember when I first made that list of names it was as a result of some 'frustration', actually. I had just moved back to Glasgow, after two years in London, and was involved in the exhibition Self-Conscious State at the Third Eye Centre. Like a lot of other people, at that time, I was making works that were site-specific – usually in relation to a scant research visit's findings, or an architectural 'intervention', or a chanced upon piece of information at the site. At some point around 1990 I began to feel uncomfortable about this 'method' of working. Partly because I had learned how to 'do it' and more so because I had experienced many other artists flying into Glasgow and completely misjudging the site and the intimacies

64  Christine Borland, in response to questions sent by the author, June 2002.

that exist in unfamiliar places. A lot of the work produced seemed weak and lazy to me. These projects were like the Garden Festival, the TSWA installations, even some Transmission events and public art placements by Art in Partnership. In the midst of this I was trying to think my way through making something for the Third Eye show. I realised that I couldn't use 'the method' in my own city. A quick trip to the library, a wander through abandoned buildings, or a series of interviews with 'locals' was not going to do anything but make me realise I already knew too much. Eventually, this frustration with 'knowing too much' led me to try and examine what it was that I really did know about the place that I considered 'mine'. I thought that I knew people. More so, 'other' people seemed to be the very thing that made up my memories, stories, wishes, past and future of this 'knowledge'. I bought a blank book and started to write one name after another. Stream of consciousness. And so on. The names were not based on a city, a country, a nation, or whatever. It was a broad sweep of my experience, wherever that might be, or have been."[65]

65  Douglas Gordon, in response to questions sent by the author, May 2002.

CHAPTER 5

# SPEED
## (1991–1993)

"Unlike their contemporaries in London, artists who have deliberately chosen to base themselves in Scotland and the North of England particularly Glasgow and Manchester had first to establish and sustain a forum for their activities. This was only achieved through an international perspective and a genuine solidarity in the face of an uncertain future."[1]

In March 1991, Alan Johnston, the minimalist painter who had taught both Richard Wright and Callum Innes at Edinburgh College of Art in the 1980s, had a solo show at Transmission, with the Joycean title Silence Exile Cunning[2]. Johnston had continued to teach at Edinburgh Art College while maintaining numerous connections with artists and institutions outside Scotland. Ross Sinclair explained, "While Alan Johnston's reputation continues to grow in Europe, Japan and America he is rarely given the opportunity to exhibit at home."[3] Funding difficulties had begun to seriously affect several central belt art spaces during this period, and between 1990 and 1991 Edinburgh's Fruitmarket, 369 Gallery and Richard Demarco Gallery and Glasgow's Third Eye Centre had all closed. Despite this unpromising cultural climate, Alan Johnston had continued to maintain a successful career by maintaining a base in Scotland but looking

---

1    Rebecca Gordon Nesbitt, "Urban Myths", *Contemporary Visual Arts*, Feb 1996.

2    "Silence, exile and cunning" were the means by which Irish writer James Joyce planned to escape what he considered to be the oppressive atmosphere of his native land. In his 1916 novel *A Portrait of the Artist as a Young Man*, he wrote, "When the soul of a man is born in this country there are nets flung at it to hold it back from flight. You talk to me of nationality, language, religion. I shall try to fly by those nets."

3    Ross Sinclair, 1991, quoted in *Transmission*, Black Dog, 2002, p118.

outside his home country for work opportunities. In this regard, he would prove an inspirational figure to several young artists in Glasgow. Johnston also used his art-world influence generously, and would later arrange for Douglas Gordon and Craig Richardson to meet with American conceptual artist Lawrence Weiner at the ICA in London, as the first stage in arranging Weiner's solo show at Transmission.

That summer Women In Profile founder member Cathy Wilkes was working in a variety of media, including works on paper, film and video, as she prepared for her first solo show at Transmission in June. But while working from a high ladder on a large-scale drawing, Wilkes lost her balance and fell, breaking her arm. This accident delayed the opening of her show and left a blank space in the Transmission programme. As an alternative, the exhibition Speed was put together from submissions from the membership. Works from 36 artists were gathered in three weeks, including Dave Allen, Claire Barclay, Christine Borland, Martin Boyce, Roderick Buchanan, Douglas Gordon, Julie Roberts, and Cathy Wilkes' brother, Jonnie Wilkes. Speed was the first of several large group shows held at Transmission in the '90s which helped to build the gallery's reputation. Unlike Edinburgh's Collective gallery, which tended to offer artists solo or two-hander exhibitions, Transmission was becoming known for group shows that offered a sense of the breadth of work being made in the city. But the show that really put Transmission on the international art map that year took place outside the walls of the gallery.

Windfall was the banner under which a series of inter-European collaborations between artists took place. The first Windfall exhibition had been held in London's Hyde Park in 1988, the second in the docklands of Bremen, Germany in 1989. There were many people involved in organising Windfall, but David McMillan was the key instigator of the project in Glasgow.[4] McMillan had travelled through Europe the previous summer scouting for artists to include in the Glasgow leg of the project, and later organised much of the logistics of the exhibition back in Glasgow. Douglas

---

4    McMillan has been omitted from several accounts of the contemporary art scene in Glasgow, although he was instrumental in the Windfall exhibition, set up Glasgow artists' initiative Breathe, and was the Project Manager of Intermedia gallery when it opened in 1993.

Gordon also played a key role, as he had exhibited in the second exhibition in Bremen, and was to exhibit in the planned third stage, in Glasgow. Given that between Freeze and Windfall Gordon had completed a Masters at The Slade, and was obviously aware of events taking place in London, he has often been cast in the role of "the Damien Hirst of Glasgow". However, he has always vehemently refused the mantle of 'leader' of the Glasgow scene, insisting, "There's no central person – everyone who is involved in art in Glasgow has a role to play."[5]

The line-up of local artists invited to participate in Windfall included Dave Allen, Claire Barclay, Douglas Gordon, Craig Richardson, Julie Roberts, Nathan Coley, Roderick Buchanan and Martin Boyce, who were emerging as the city's most successful artists since the 1980s New Image painters. The Glasgow project included the work of 25 artists from six countries (UK, France, Germany, Spain, Eire and the Netherlands) and was held in the disused Seaman's Mission by the Clyde, itself an evocative starting point for the installation, time-based and performance work that filled the thirty exhibition spaces. However, this was considered to be the least loaded of the buildings offered to the organisers, who had rejected a warehouse space and a lawyer's offices as being unsuitable. As Nathan Coley explained, "The artists from abroad expected people to be making work that absolutely engaged with the fabric of the building. And that's not what happened. This has been our main topic of conversation in Glasgow for the past year or so; we feel that the term site-specific has become meaningless."[6] The Windfall exhibition is seen by many as the point at which the new energy in the local art scene visibly crystallised. Participating artist Roderick Buchanan later recalled, "Several things could be identified as our common, starting assumptions. We were all interested in side-stepping the gallery circuit, and as a result we were all accustomed to working in so-called 'dead' spaces. Beyond that we all felt strongly that an artist should be trusted to pursue his or her own ideas once invited to exhibit."[7]

<hr>

5   Douglas Gordon, *24 Hour Psycho: Douglas Gordon*, BBC Scotland 1996.
6   Nathan Coley, Matthew Slotover, "Northern Lights", *frieze*, issue 1, p.40.
7   "Guilt by Association", *Museum of Modern Art*, Dublin, 1993.

The press were invited for the opening in August. Windfall was warmly reviewed in the first issue of *frieze*[8] magazine, bringing the work of Glasgow's neo-conceptual artists to the attention of the international art community. Interestingly, the title of *frieze* editor Matthew Slotover's lead article was "Northern Lights", a title not dissimilar to that of *The Guardian* article which had heralded the arrival of the New Image painters some six years earlier ("The Glow that Came from Glasgow"). In both cases the article that followed the headline was overwhelmingly positive, but the implication remained that Glasgow was a "dark place". The favourable media coverage of the Glasgow leg of the Windfall exhibitions, and the growing confidence of artists associated with Transmission, translated into a "buzz" about Glasgow that quickly spread throughout the international art world. Artist Tom O'Sullivan (b.1967) moved to Glasgow to study on the MFA after completing an undergraduate degree at Leeds University and working in London. He says, "I came because I was living in London and working at the Serpentine Gallery. I wanted to do an MFA and it was just after 1990 and Windfall. The first issue of *frieze* had all this stuff about Windfall and everyone was talking about Glasgow. I was thinking of applying to a London college and everyone said don't bother with the Slade or Goldsmiths: Glasgow is the place to go."[9]

One of the most significant aspects of the Windfall exhibition was that a combination of private and public funding made possible the publication of a catalogue, giving the exhibition wider impact.[10] The Windfall catalogue included photographs of the installation at the Clyde Seaman's Mission, the finished works, and a group photograph of some of the 25 exhibiting artists, and friends including Katrina Brown, Heather Allen and Jacqueline Donachie. The catalogue also included essays by Glasgow-based artist Ross Sinclair and Italian artists and critics Gianni Piacentini[11] and Cassiro

---

8   *frieze* magazine of "contemporary art and culture" has been published bi-monthly in London since 1991 by Matthew Slotover and Amanda Sharp. *frieze* has offices in Berlin and New York and offers an international perspective on new contemporary art, published in the UK. Prior to *frieze*, Artscribe was the most contemporary art publication, while *Art Monthly* took a broader editorial stance, covering more traditional art forms as well as the burgeoning Brit-Art movement. *Artscribe* folded in 1992, a year after *frieze* began.
9   Tom O'Sullivan, in conversation with the author, January 2001.
10  *The Windfall* publication was produced by Tony Arefin, who was an important supporter of Scottish art publications.
11  In 1991 Gianni Piacentini lived in Glasgow for six months as part of the Pepiniere European residency programme.

Berdetti. Ross Sinclair wrote in his essay, "Energy is being harnessed and moulded into forms which proclaim an overwhelming attitude of just getting out there and getting on with it. In Glasgow at any rate, whingers get short shrift. What has finally been exorcised is a feeling evident in years gone by that coming from Glasgow or Belfast or any other city meant having a chip on your shoulder, feeling short-changed because you weren't born in New York or London."[12] However, the young London art scene had taken a massive leap forward in terms of public recognition that year with the publication of Andrew Renton's *Crème Anglaise: Current Trends in British Art*, the first of many publications to begin to mythologise the Goldsmiths' generation. However the dialogue between artists working in Scotland and those based in London continued when in August, a group show of paintings by Angus Hood, Thomas Walsh and London-based artist Simon Patterson opened at Transmission.

## SIDELINED OR EVEN IGNORED ALTOGETHER

On Saturday 21st of September, a former second-hand clothes shop on Hill Street reopened its doors as the newly established Glasgow Women's Library. The library had grown out of the preceding Women In Profile events and also encompassed the Scottish Women Artists and Writers Archive. "Despite all the fine phrases and all the money spent in the Year of Culture, we have not received a penny for this from the councils", said Women in Profile founder member Adele Patrick. "We are trying to embarrass the politicians into recognising that while millions are spent every year maintaining and encouraging a culture which has always been dominated by masculine values, the female side of our culture is still sidelined or even ignored altogether."[13]

At the beginning of October, Cathy Wilkes' delayed Transmission solo show, Like Moth took place, after which she moved back to Belfast, to study on the Masters course at the University of Ulster. The previous year,

12  Ross Sinclair, "Bad Smells But No Sign of the Corpse", *Windfall*, Glasgow, 1991.
13  *Glasgow Herald*, October 29th, 1991.

Transmission had hosted the Belfast MA show of the work of Roderick Buchanan and eight classmates, and now in 1991 Roderick Buchanan returned to Belfast, with Douglas Gordon, to present *Army* and London Road at the Orpheus Gallery, Belfast. *Army* was a large scale text piece based on a gable-end Salvation Army advertisement that Buchanan and Douglas had come across in Glasgow. Part of the sign had been boarded over, leaving only the emotive word "army" visible. Gordon later commented, "If a single word can mean many things, then anything can. It's very much about opening up meanings and not fixing them."[14] The long-running links between Glasgow and Belfast continued to make the news of the Troubles in the '80s and '90s seem very close to home. Scotland had never been targetted by the IRA, but continued bombing attacks elsewhere, such as the 1987 bombing of the Remembrance Day parade at Enniskillen had meant that there were frequent news reports relating to the Troubles (although since 1988 the Conservative government had banned Sinn Fein politician's voices from television and radio).

Graffiti and flyposters had long been a public means of expression for subcultural groups in most cities, Glasgow being no exception. Several local artists including Ross Sinclair were quick to see the possibilities of the form. Sinclair had pasted up pairs of posters reading "Capital of Culture" and "Culture of Capital" around town during the 1990 celebrations. The 1990–91 Bellgrove Station Billboard Project initiated by MFA student Alan Dunn also sited temporary artworks in "dead" spaces: there were 15 hand-painted posterworks and 17 contributors, including Pavel Buchler, Douglas Gordon, James Kelman, Thomas Lawson, Craig Richardson, Julie Roberts and Ross Sinclair. Ross Sinclair's work was of a Union Jack stripped of red, augmented with the word ache, while Douglas Gordon's simply read "walk a million miles". In addition to shows in "unloved" spaces, exhibitions in domestic settings would become increasingly important to sustaining artistic activity in Glasgow from the early '90s onwards. Elsewhere in the city, the Italian artist Gianni Piacentini, organised a show in his flat, The Living Room Project, where Christine Borland, Ross Sinclair and Jacqueline

14 Transmission Gallery, *The Late Show*, BBC Scotland, 2nd April 1994.

Donachie were among the participating artists.

In November, Lawrence Weiner exhibited at Transmission for the first time. Weiner, and his contemporaries Carl Andre and Sol Le Witt had greatly influenced the aesthetic strategies of the young artists involved with the gallery but he had not shown in Scotland since 1986, when he had concurrent exhibitions at Edinburgh's Fruitmarket and the Pier Arts Centre, Orkney. For his Transmission show, Weiner installed a band of black type around the inside of the gallery at eye-line height, which read "AN ARCH AFFORDED IN A WALL OF STONE WITH A KEYSTONE OF CHALK & IMPOSTS OF SLATE". A sticker designed by Weiner bearing the same text was circulated in the Transmission mail-out and within the pages of *Variant* to coincide with the exhibition. Interviewed by Douglas Gordon for an accompanying article, Weiner argued that the sticker had a subversive quality that the projects like the Bellgrove Station Billboard Project of the same year had lacked. "The sticker operates in this context where, economically and culturally, most people are feeling really rather under attack. This economic situation encourages the general attempt to put art back in its place … But when one talks about the billboard and so on – the billboard is a total imposition. That's a taking up of a public space, that's buying space, that is essentially paying for the dominant culture to let you put up what you feel is functioning as art at that moment."[15] Weiner's sentiments chimed with an intervention that had been carried out the previous year by Jonathan Monk, who was studying in the Environmental Art Department at the time. For *Cancelled* (1990) Monk had fly-posted cancellation strips across numerous billboard posters advertising concerts and other cultural events around the city.


## BACK TO BASICS

The fallout from the Falklands War and bombing raids on Libya were still relatively fresh in the public mind that year as Operation Desert Storm was launched in the Gulf. There were widespread public misgivings about Britain entering into yet another foreign conflict and, when the 1992

15 *Variant*, Winter 1991, pp36–41.

election came around, Scotland again voted overwhelmingly against the Conservative government. Yet again, due to the lack of proportional representation in the British electoral system, the votes cast by the Scottish electorate were not reflected in the election result, meaning that John Major was in charge for another term. In some respects the 1992 election can be regarded as a turning-point in Scottish politics, as many voters became increasingly disillusioned with the democratic process. Major had impressed few Scots with his "Back to Basics" keynote speeches which championed a traditional family unit that was no longer the norm. Statistics showed exactly how out of touch with reality Major's rhetoric was: households of single people were at their highest at any point in history, and marriage rates and birth rates were falling year on year.[16]

Despite growing critical interest in the artists associated with Windfall, no showcase exhibition along the lines of The Vigorous Imagination was forthcoming in a Scottish museum. Instead, the first major museum show by the Scottish neo-conceptual artists was in Ireland in 1992. Guilt by Association at the Irish Museum of Modern Art, Dublin, showcased the work of Christine Borland, Roderick Buchanan, Douglas Gordon, Kevin Henderson and Craig Richardson. Quoted in the catalogue for the exhibition, Douglas Gordon says, "The title of the show underlines the attitude of the group's working process; a recognition that meaning accrues through time and place(ment). One work informs another, and another…"[17] This exhibition, along with Information, Self Conscious State, Speed and Windfall emphasised that the working process of certain Glasgow-based artists was dependent on the conversations generated within a collaborative network of peers. The work made by many Environmental Art graduates in the late '80s was often concerned chiefly with language and ideas, with objects acting as a referent alone. The key element was the context, the social world that art could impact upon. Douglas Gordon, Craig Richardson and Christine Borland in particular used ideas about mortality, memory and identity that were highly evocative.

16  Recent media exposure of Major's extra-marital affair with junior minister Edwina Currie has further undermined his moral stance of the early '90s.

17  "Guilt by Association", Ibid.

Borland's *Small Objects That Save Lives* (1991–1993) is one such example. Borland asked various friends and associates to send in an item suggested by this title and the objects, which ranged from a condom to a photograph, were later displayed on trestle tables alongside the names of the contributor.

Douglas Gordon's works also often touched upon ideas of loss or regret, such as a 1992 wall text piece which spelt out the phrases, Those I do not know / Those I can not know / Those I would like to know / Those I would not like to know / Those I have forgotten but will remember / Those I have forgotten and will never remember. The idea of defining personal or collective identity in Borland and Gordon's work could find echoes in the practice of both Felix Gonzales-Torres and Christian Boltanski, who also utilised everyday language and ordinary objects to express concerns about responsibility and mortality. Despite the deeply resonant and affecting nature of Gordon's work, he resisted the notion provided by a 1995 interviewer that his work was either poetic and mysterious, joking that, "I would be hung, drawn and quartered in Glasgow if I said that my work was 'poetical' and 'mysterious' – it's not in our culture to make these claims for oneself".[18] However, it was during this period that Gordon began making his *Letter* and telephone *Instruction* works, which operated on the basis that they would unsettle the normal flow of the recipient's day. Gordon sent letters to various members of the art world (many of whom he did not know personally) from 1991 onwards containing messages such as "I am aware of who you are and what you do", and "I forgive you". The letters provoked a range of reactions: unease and anger from those suffering from a guilty conscience, to amusement from those who appreciated the gall of a relatively unknown artist sending such messages to powerful curators and high profile artists. The telephone *Instruction* works were initiated in response to an exhibition curated by Gianni Piacentini at a café in Rome in 1991, and were subsequently repeated for exhibitions by Gordon held in Bremnen, Connecticut, Copenhagen, Glasgow, Milan, Nice and Paris. Each day for the duration of the exhibition, the owner of the gallery or an assistant would make a telephone call to local café or bar, the proprietor of

18  Douglas Gordon in conversation with Jan Florizoone, Shift , De Appel, Amsterdam,1995.

which had agreed to participate in the project. The proprietor would then call a person in the bar or café, who they knew by name, to the telephone. The chosen customer would then receive the artwork as a spoken message, typically an enigmatic phrase such as "Don't hide your love away" or 'I believe in miracles" followed by a click as the caller hung up. These two cycles of work in particular demonstrated Gordon's interest in "constructing the unexpected" through his work, and in this sense his practice can indeed be read as poetic, but very much in the spirit of the Situationists' maxim "The poetry is in the streets".

A central characteristic of this neo-conceptual group was their practice of quoting from culture at large: from the history of the city around them, from art history and the history of film and popular music. And as the '90s progressed, their tendency to connect fine art practice more with broader cultural discourses manifested itself in various ways. In the early '90s, Bar 10 on Mitchell Lane, designed by Haçienda designer Ben Kelly, was the place to be. The bar combined 1950s ice cream parlour tiling and zinc counters with modern industrial styling – exposed vents and metal pipes threaded across the ceiling. The bar was a congregation point for clubbers en route to the Sub Club or the newly opened Arches on Midland Street. The Arches Theatre had opened in 1991 as a non-profit-making organisation under director Andy Arnold, who had recently returned to Scotland after a post as director of London's Bloomsbury Theatre. The huge stone-walled venue beneath Central Station began to stage experimental theatrical productions, but became better known amongst young people in the city for the club nights that ran there at the weekends, such as Café Loco. The Arches came into its own for large, multi-DJ dance events, as it had three enormous linked rooms that could be used for different types of music – typically the end room would feature a big name DJ from Chicago or Detroit such as Jeff Mills, the middle room would be the province of the resident DJs (often Slam or Pure) and the room nearest the exit would function as the chill-out room. Around the corner at the more intimate Sub Club, Slam were still playing to packed houses at Atlantis, while also organising the first series of legal all-night raves in the UK on the side. The Slam raves attracted crowds of up to 5,000, and soon McMillan and Meikle were able to set up their record label Soma, releasing their first 12 inch single, *Eterna* the same year. Other Glasgow dance music record labels followed throughout the '90s, including Glasgow Underground and Solemusic, which were sustained by local specialist record stores like 23rd Precinct, Bomba and Rub A Dub. In the summer of 1992 Glasgow band One Dove also attracted Andrew Weatherall's attention at a rave in Rimini, but he was unable to recreate the magic he'd worked on Primal Scream, who had raced up the album chart with their third album *Screamadelica* the previous year. With *Screamadelica* Weatherall had created a new genre of music: an infectious mix of the distinctive soul-inflected guitar sound so characteristic of many Glasgow bands with the beats found in the latest house and techno tracks.[19]

In September of 1991, Craig Tannock, Simon Frith, Stuart Cruikshank and John Williamson's New Music World five day conference had opened at various locations, including the Renfrew Ferry, Traders on Glassford Street and Tramway. The organisers had cannily managed to bring the whole event in for the £24,000 budget allowed by their council funding. Tannock remembers, "There was an international cast of music worthies there to talk shop, from all over Europe and America. We had Bill Drummond talking about manipulating the media, and a guy from [scally-rock band] The Farm and Tony Wilson from Factory – he was there to steal ideas for In the City, which took place later on in Manchester."[20] By 1992, Craig Tannock and business partner Calum McLean had begun running their own studio complex and live music venue, The Apollo, at Renfrew Court – a move prompted by the sudden doubling of their rent at Tower Studios. Tannock remembers, "Calum went to see a guy about a space across from the old Apollo theatre – it was a basement premises that had been opened up in '88 by an architect called Larry Diamond, who was Jim Diamond's brother."[21] The Shelter had incorporated a small venue and café bar with a rehearsal room, and an advice centre for bands but had failed to take off. Craig Tannock and McLean sublet the premises and opened up

19 Alex Paterson and Thrash from The Orb and Jah Wobble were amongst the contributors to the album.
20 Craig Tannock, in conversation with the author, August 2002.
21 Craig Tannock, Ibid.

their new venture on November 26th. They also recruited Gerry Coleman, the assistant manager from The Halt to help run the bar. Tannock remembers, "For the first few weeks at the Apollo we didn't have any money for bar staff, so Gerry and I were the bar staff, from early morning to early morning. John Williamson did the PR, and we also had a lot of people who were helping us, although no-one was getting paid at that point – Douglas Young, Ritchie Dempsie and Steven Nelson mainly, who had all been with us since Tower."[22]

Nicola White summed up part of the appeal of places like The Apollo when she later wrote, "Parties matter. They are part of the glue that holds any artistic community together, compensation for pursuing what is, at heart, a very solitary line of work."[23] Social interaction and music had always formed a valuable aspect of the arts scene in Glasgow, but as a background to the work, rather than a recognisable thematic strand. That now began to change. In the early 1990s a performative aspect appeared in the work of 1989–1991 Transmission committee member Dave Allen (b.1963), and recent Environmental art graduates Jonathan Monk (b.1969), David Shrigley (b.1968) and Jacqueline Donachie (b.1969). Leicester-born artist Jonathan Monk's work was often concerned with mischievously subverting the flow of everyday meaning. For example, one work placed him in a crowd at an airport arrival gate with a sign reading "Andy Warhol" as though greeting the legendary dead artist. In 1992 Dave Allen, Jacqueline Donachie and Jonathan Monk's work was presented together with work by Michael S. McGlinn, Colin Pettigrew and Derek Scanlan in a Transmission project held in Flanders entitled Really Saying Something, suggesting that links between their work were apparent even at this early point.

David Shrigley, who was born in Macclesfield, made interventions, sculptural works and drawings on paper, which often expressed a mordant humour similar to Jonathan Monk's. At one time he shared a flat in Bentinck street with Monk and Jacqueline Donachie, across the road from

22  Craig Tannock, Ibid.
23  Nicola White, "Perpetual Motion", unpublished essay on Transmission, 1995.

the former Hellfire Club and the Cava recording studios. Bentinck Street is locally nicknamed Beatnik Street due to the mixture of student flats, brothels and bed and breakfast accommodation located there, something Shrigley sent up with a red neon sign in his window that read "SLUM". During this period Shrigley had made some alterations to a disused public toilet on Woodlands Road to give the impression that it was a bar named The Ship. Shrigley also staged numerous memorable performances in the early '90s, including a piece where he sewed the skins back onto a bucket of peeled potatoes at Café Loco at The Arches. Another work was annotated with a reference to the drinking culture of his adopted city: "Charm is at an end – now we drink heavily."[24] Shrigley began publishing small print runs of his books of drawings in the early '90s, initially through Black Rose, and then through his own Armpit Press from 1994 onwards.[25] He would often give readings from new books at Transmission openings, such as the reading from *Merry Excema* he gave at the opening of Contact: 552 4813[26] in June 1992.

A connection can also be traced between Shrigley's work and that of Glaswegian poet and musician Ivor Cutler (b.1923). Cutler, author of such humorous texts as *Life in a Scotch Sitting Room* (1984) and *Glasgow Dreamer* (1990), first shot to fame when his absurdist monologues, poems and songs accompanied by pedal-driven harmonium were transmitted on BBC Radio's Home Service. He came from a Jewish middle class family, and grew up in Govanhill. After being dismissed from the army for "dreaminess" he worked for many years as a teacher, before branching into poetry and music. Both an agnostic and member of The Noise Abatement Society, the influence of Cutler's idiosyncratic books and recordings has been wide-

---

24  David Shrigley, Blank Page and Other Pages, the Modern Institute, 1998.

25  David Shrigley's publishing ventures took place within a wider context of small independent publishers in Scotland, of whom one of the best known is Alec Finlay, the son of Scotttish artist Iain Hamilton Finlay. Finlay has been instrumental in a number of Scottish arts publishing enterprises, including the Morning Star Folio (est. 1990), and more recently pocketbooks, which has recently ceased to publish after coming to the end of a three year period of SAC funding. Another notable independent publisher in Scotland was Polygon, where *The Edinburgh Review*'s Peter Kravitz worked as an editor between 1980–1990, and published James Kelman's *The Bus-Conductor Hines* (1984) and Janice Galloway's *The Trick is To Keep Breathing* (1990).

26  Contact: 552 4813 was another vast group show in the vein of Speed, with work from over 42 artists including Toby Webster, Adrian Wiszniewski, Kirsty Ogg, John Shankie, Richard Wright, Jonathan Monk, Christine Borland, Douglas Gordon, Roderick Buchanan, Kevin Henderson and Jacqueline Donachie.

ranging. We can read the work of Shrigley and Cutler as exposing the underlying absurdity of contemporary life. As Douglas Gordon once proposed, "You could say that it is the artists' job to construct the unexpected, to be provocative, in the academic sense."[27]

Edinburgh College of Art graduate Richard Wright had continued working as a figurative painter after moving to Glasgow in 1986, but by the end of the '80s he had become disillusioned with art and didn't make any further work for two years. After stints as a musician and training as a signwriter, he began making paintings on board, and later site-specific wall drawings. His new body of work dealt with ideas surrounding performance, expressed through the discipline of painting. He explains, "I did not think of myself as being an artist, I had no associations with artists. Sometimes I would go to this old warehouse where I had my little space and just fiddle about with things. If I didn't like them I would just turn them to the wall. I very much liked the idea that the work had this very fragile or unstable kind of existence. This was the sort of thinking that informed the first wall paintings that I made. Some time later, when I was asked to be in a group show at Transmission in the early 1990s, I remember feeling quite resistant, not to the invitation but to being drawn back into the idea of thinking about what I was doing as being connected to art. I had already made some temporary things in disused spaces (which had been seen by nobody) and it seemed very obvious to take this attitude into the gallery and try to make something with what I could remember and what I was able to do."[28] Thomas Lawson captured something of the mood of the new wave of work being made in the city when he wrote about Wright's wall paintings, "He wants his art to be alive, and a part of life. He does not want it to become part of a back catalogue of hallowed and therefore 'beautiful' objects to be revered but not touched. Instead, he delights in the more generous idea that making art is more akin to playing music, or having a conversation … "[29]

27 Douglas Gordon, *Kidnapping*, Stedelijk Van Abbemuseum, Eindhoven, 1998, p41.
28 Adam Szymzcyk, Conversation with Richard Wright, Richard Wright, *Kunstverein fur die Rheinlande und Westfalen*, Dusseldorf, 2002, pp56–58.
29 Thomas Lawson, Richard Wright, Locus+, Newcastle, 2000.

In 1990, some thirty years after Edinburgh's Gallery of Modern Art had been established, Glasgow City Council had begun to use interest from a £3 million investment fund to purchase work from living artists for the city's collection, and selected works by Bruce McLean, Alan Davie, John Bellany, Steven Campbell, Peter Howson and Ken Currie to add to the collection at Kelvingrove. Throughout the early '90s Transmission continued to bring new reference points to young artists in the city, by inviting artists of international stature to show at the gallery. However, while shows at Transmission by established non-local artists like Lawrence Weiner, Simon Patterson, Jo Spence and Alan Johnston were welcomed by some, Christine Borland remembers that they also resulted in "membership grumbles that we were out to make career advancing art-world contacts in the name of Transmission."[30] However, all subsequent committees have continued the practice of mixing exhibitions of established, international artists with less well-known, local practitioners. Douglas Gordon recalls that the intention was "to actually see real people from other places who were making things and thinking thoughts and talking about ideas. I mean, It's better to hear it from the horse's mouth, rather than just browse through *Artscribe*."[31]

In March 1992, the exhibition Outta Here took place at Transmission. The show "focussed on artists whose practice utilises elements related to a shared environment" including UK based artists Martin Creed, David Wilkinson, Willie Doherty and Jonnie Wilkes, Italian artist/critic Gianni Piacentini and Hamburg-born artist Annette Heyer (b.1960) who had moved to Glasgow in 1986. Heyer's subtle photographic and sculptural works were often concerned with the play between light and shade that exists in natural occurring forms such as plants and bodies of water. Willie Doherty's contribution to the exhibition was a screen-printed poster which referenced the ongoing problems in Northern Ireland. The poster, which was pasted around the streets of Glasgow during the run of the exhibition, combined the phrases "nowhere is the sky so blue/nowhere is the grass so green" with a phrase from a popular song, 'a nation once

30  Christine Borland, "Dear Green Place No More", unpublished essay on Transmission, 1995.
31  Douglas Gordon, Ping Pong, an unpublished conversation with Hans Ulrich Obrist, 1995.

again'.[32] This, the last show Christine Borland oversaw as a committee member, indicated the shift towards lens-based work, and artistic practice referencing music and popular culture. That year, ex-Transmission committee member Anne Vance and Paula Larkin set up New Visions[33] in Glasgow, a bi-annual platform for challenging contemporary work in video, experimental film, animation and digital imaging. New Visions was staged in collaboration with the GFVW, where the well-established monthly Café Flicker screening session had now shown work by Shaz Kerr, Martha McCulloch, Paul Cameron and Jim Rush.

In 1992 Czechoslovakian artist and writer Pavel Buchler (b.1952) took up his new post as Head of Fine Art at Glasgow School of Art. Buchler had formed the group KQN in Prague during the 1970s, whose aim was described as "a collective creative resistance to the degradation of cultural, political and social values in the aftermath of 1968."[34] By the late '70s his practice had shifted from street action to more ritualised "theatrical" performances, although he was also well known for his photographs and writings. Buchler was an influential figure in Glasgow in many ways, quickly involving himself in local initiatives including Transmission and *Variant*. However, probably the most significant contribution of his five-year stay at Glasgow School of Art was his establishment of The Friday Event, a series of public lectures staged at arthouse cinema Glasgow Film Theatre, in 1992. Buchler was able to draw upon a list of impressive art world contacts for the programme, and Stan Douglas, Terry Eagleton, Susan Hiller, John Baldessari, Jochen Gerz and Thomas Lawson were amongst the guest speakers in the first few years of the Event. Buchler wrote, "What emerged was a set of addresses that took up, departed from and returned to a number of common issues. We might call this common space 'our shared anxiety for sustaining work and belief' or, phrased more optimistically, the necessity

32  Like the work of Newcastle-born artists Jane and Louise Wilson, the work of Willie Doherty (b.1959, Derry) had particular resonance for certain Glasgow based artists, specifically those who would later work with video such as Smith/Stewart and Douglas Gordon.
33  New Visions folded due to lack of funding after a final event in 1996, which showcased work by Veit-Luip, Finn McAlinden, Beverley Hood, Smith/Stewart, Stephen Hurrell and Keith Stutter.
34  Pavel Buchler, Untitled Portraits, Third Eye Centre, Glasgow,1988.

to define starting points and contexts."[35]

Pavel Buchler also recruited sociology lecturer Nikos Papastergiadis from Manchester University to teach critical theory on the MFA for a week each term. Papastergiadis remembers, "It was a very productive and exciting time in my life. The art school became a real focal point for passionate discussions on artistic and cultural events. For the first time I saw evidence of an engaged art community. Many of the recent graduates who lived nearby would hang out with the current students, attend the Friday lectures, drink at the same pubs, play soccer, go clubbing – as well as supporting each other's openings. I became conscious of how the city was divided between the new generation of emerging artists, many of whom would have meteoric careers in the international art world, and the established fathers of the Glasgow artisan. Patrons of the school, with their fine appreciation of Art Deco, model trains and realist paintings, were conspicuously absent from the events that I witnessed over the years. Similarly the politicians in the Labour-run City Council, who were eager to promote Glasgow as a city of culture, consistently ignored the new generation."[36]

In August 1992 a fire had broken out in the artists studios above The Apollo, and the resultant water damage effectively destroyed the premises. Fortunately, Craig Tannock and John Williamson had taken out a lease on the ailing Traders on Glassford Street earlier that year, which they had been overseeing as a new Celtic themed bar under the unlikely name of The Boglestone. They now decided that The Boglestone should be changed into a bar like the one at The Apollo, and Williamson thought of a new name, inspired by an album out at the time by Galliano, called *In Pursuit of the 13th Note*. The 13th Note opened for business on the 1st December after relatively minimal alterations. A mish mash of furniture, including some old church pews, was dotted around the dark, low ceilinged bar. There was a stage at one end of the room where local bands played, and in the orange


35 Buchler & Papastergiadis eds., *Random Access*, Rivers Oram Press, London, 1995, pp1. *Random Access* was the first in a series of two anthologies that collected together the contributions from the School of Fine Art Friday Events from 1992–3 and 1993–5.

36 Nikos Papastergiadis, "Melbourne Glasgow Edinburgh", *Stills*, March/April 1999, pp30–33.

painted basement, where esoteric DJ night were held, there was a massive old fashioned space invader machine, squashy sofas and a bass heavy soundsystem. The activities at the new 13th Note were bolstered by the Glasgow Music Collective (GMC) which had been set up in 1991 to promote local bands and independent venues and record labels. The collective, which organised gigs by bands like AC Acoustics, Badgewearer and the Dog Faced Hermans, said "We are retaining some form of hands-on control of our own entertainment at a local level [ … ] the attempt to work outwith the established music business and the belief that it is probably the most corrupt industry in the UK make what we do political."[37]

In 1992 Young British Artists I was being held at the Saatchi Collection in London. The work featured in this exhibition, and the subsequent Young British Artists II, III and IV centred around a group that mainly emerged from Goldsmiths College – including Damien Hirst, Sarah Lucas and Gary Hume. Young British Artists I featured Damien Hirst's notorious *The Physical Impossibility of Death in the Mind of Someone Living*[38] which was treated in the national press in much the same way as the Tate's acquisition of a Carl Andre piece had been sixteen years earlier[39] proving that tabloid coverage of contemporary art had advanced little in the intervening years. The work of Hirst, and his contemporaries received vast amounts of media coverage, usually oscillating in tone from derision to outrage. Hirst in particular was adept at manipulating the attentions of the press, with one stunt involving a bag of chips placed near his "shark" exhibit to produce a "fish and chips" photo opportunity.


## LONDON CALLING


Later that same year, Graham Gussin curated the group show Love At First Sight for The Showroom in Bethnal Green, London, then run by Kim Sweet. Gussin invited several Glasgow-based artists including Dave Allen,

---

37  http://users.colloqium.co.uk/~Feebee/gmc/.htm.
38  The piece consists of a tiger shark suspended in a tank of formaldehyde.
39  In 1976 the *Daily Mirror* had expressed outrage over the acquisition of Andre's *Equivalent VIII* (1966) referring to the work as ì a pile of bricks.î

Martin Boyce, Nathan Coley, Douglas Gordon and Julie Roberts to participate in the exhibition, along with other UK artists including Padraig Timoney and Emma Rushton. "Around that time we were making friends with London-based artists so we felt more of a connection to the wider international scene", remembers Martin Boyce, "Being able to have a drink with people whose show announcements you'd seen in *frieze* – that was so significant at the time, you'd pore over these things."[40] Later in the same year, Douglas Gordon and Jonathan Monk were invited by Liam Gillick to show with yBas including Gary Hume, Michael Landy, Angela Bullock, Simon Patterson and Gillian Wearing, in the exhibition Il Misterio dei 100 Dollari Scomparsi (The Mysterious Case of the 100 Dollar Bill) at the Gio Marconi gallery in Milan. For the exhibition, all of the artists involved faxed instructions to Liam Gillick in Milan, who then made the works. Around this time a second exchange took place with London's City Racing, with concurrent shows by London based artists John Burgess, Keith Coventry, Matt Hale, Paul Noble and Peter Owen at Transmission, and four artists from Transmission showing at City Racing (Annette Heyer, Andrew Lockhart, Julie Roberts and Ross Sinclair) from September through October. The City Racing committee remember that they "were partly aware of the different aesthetics, attitudes and practices between us and Transmission" – the key difference being that artists working in and around Transmission had consciously decided to try to establish a workable art scene outside of London, while City Racing was of course London-based. Also, the political agenda of Transmission was considerably more overt than that of City Racing. However, the young London gallerists felt that their "extra-curricular activities" (squatting, playing in bands, protesting against road building, working collectively) "made Transmission's politicised aesthetics less alien."[41]

"Transmission had selected Annette Heyer, Andrew Lockhart, Ross Sinclair and Julie Roberts, who all came to City Racing to install their work. Ross installed a stack of canvases that were tightly painted black and white

<hr>

40  Martin Boyce, Ibid.
41  Matt Hale, Paul Noble, Pete Owen and John Burgess, *City Racing The life and times of an artist-run gallery*, Black Dog Publishing Ltd., 2002, p90.

161

versions of the state flags of America and a hand printed wall text. Julie showed one large painting of a wheelchair floating on a coloured background, and Annette had framed black and white photos of barely visible fragments of glass. Andrew showed a Marlboro packet and some fag ends glued to the floor, a neon pizza sign that read "Deep Pan" and a dead plant on a shelf. A large contingent of Transmission members and supporters turned up for the opening, some even became City Racing supporters and friends."[42] The first Transmission at City Racing exhibition opened up the dialogue between the two spaces so successfully that several other Glasgow based artists were invited to show at City Racing over the next few years, including Richard Wright in 1992, Dave Allen and Roderick Buchanan in 1994 and Jonathan Monk in 1996.

Galleries in Edinburgh continued to offer exhibition opportunities to Glasgow-based artists. Ross Sinclair's Fanclub was shown at new photography gallery, Stills in Cockburn Street in 1991. The exhibition invitation quoted London art duo Gilbert & George: "All my life you give me nothing and still you ask for more." Environmental Art graduate Sinclair was still combining his art practice with a sideline playing drums with Glasgow band The Soup Dragons, contributing to a strong musical strand in his practice. Sinclair was friends with Glasgow band Teenage Fanclub, which had been formed by Raymond McGinley, Gerard Love and Norman Blake after Blake had left the BMX Bandits. The Fannies, as they were affectionately known, had subsequently eclipsed BMX Bandits with their melodic "California-meets-Glasgow" songs on both their highly acclaimed 1990 debut *A Catholic Education* and 1991's *Bandwagonesque*. Besides his local musical connections, Ross Sinclair's approach to making work had also been influenced by a term on exchange at the Californian Institute of the Arts, in Los Angeles during 1992. The strong tradition of performance art in Los Angeles, and the influence of Cal Arts Dean Thomas Lawson resulted in Sinclair's increased confidence in socially engaged practice. Sinclair later said, "I want my art to be like meeting someone new in a bar, and they might be from a whole different situation and culture but

42  Matt Hale, Paul Noble, Pete Owen and John Burgess, *City Racing The life and times of an artist-run gallery*, Ibid, p92.

surely you have all these things in common, shared histories you never shared with anyone before. Sure you won't agree about everything but that's what makes life interesting, I guess it's called conversation."[43]

After recovering from the serious financial problems of the late '80s, The Fruitmarket had reopened in 1992 after a major refit courtesy of Richard Murphy architects. The Fruitmarket was now under the directorship of Graeme Murray, who was well known around the city for his eponymous private gallery, where he had shown work by artists including Alan Johnston, Sol LeWitt, Ian Hamilton Finlay and Richard Long. The new-look Fruitmarket, which included stairs styled like a New York fire escape, hosted a number of exhibitions by high profile international artists, as well as showcasing a mixture of Edinburgh and Glasgow-based artists. One such show was the Glasgow MFA graduation group show Invisible Cities (1992) which included the work of Glasgow-based artists Ross Sinclair, Andrew Miller, Claire Barclay, Lesley Punton and John Shankie.

In October Lux Europae, a three-month long installation of works made using outdoor light opened in Edinburgh, to mark the UK's Presidency of the European Community. 38 artists participated, from all 12 European community states, including established Scottish artists like Ian Hamilton Finlay, George Wyllie and Adrian Wiszniewski, younger Glasgow-based artists including Nathan Coley, Kenny Hunter, Stephen Hurrell and Louise Scullion and invited guests from further afield, such as Italian Vittorio Messina. Vittorio's installation *Spostamenti sulla banda del rosso* simply illuminated 24 windows around the city centre with red lights, but succeeded in being more thought provoking than some of the other works – perhaps the most obvious example being the neon phrase "LET'S TALK ABOUT ART … MAYBE" by Italian artist Maurizio Nannucci installed on the proscenium arch of the High Street's Bank Hotel. While Nannucci's text work was easily identified, and dismissed, as a rather self indulgent piece of art Vittorio's red lights, positioned in various prestigious buildings in the city centre addressed a social issue particulary relevant to his host city. Unlike Glasgow, Edinburgh has a system in place which partially safeguards the

43  Ross Sinclair, Shift, De Appel Foundation, Amsterdam 1995.

welfare of prostitutes working in the city. Prostitutes in Edinburgh may choose to work in a licenced sauna rather than walking the streets, where they are more vulnerable to violent attack.

Meanwhile in Glasgow, the Third Eye Centre had reopened as a new organisation: the Centre for Contemporary Arts (CCA), with a new director, Jo Beddoe. David Cook, the newly appointed director of WASPS, remembers, "CCA used to have brilliant parties. After an opening they would have a band playing and everyone would go. There was a real sense of community there, and in the bar at the Tron, these places that everyone hung out."[44] Tramway had been closed after the Year of Culture celebrations, as there was only a remit for the building to function as an art space for that year. But after several months of negotiations, Neil Wallace, who had been the deputy director of 1990 was given the post of theatre director at Tramway and invited Nicola White to return to curate the visual art programme. As one of her first exhibitions at Tramway, White invited Windfall organiser and artist David McMillan to mount a solo show, Hunger for Gold and another Glasgow-based artist, Matthew Dalziel, to make work for a concurrent solo show, which was titled Blue and White and opened at the beginning of May. Nicola White remembers, "That year we also did a big show with Tony Cragg,[45] which was his first big UK show he'd had since his solo at the Hayward ten years earlier. That show was the first time we collaborated with CCA – the two spaces had that natural affinity, although Tramway worked especially well with 3D work, with sculpture."[46] White also remembers that both CCA Exhibitions Co-ordinator Andrew Nairne and the new CCA director were easy to work with collaboratively. 'Jo's principle was, 'I'll take care of the politics and the finances and you get on with making the work look good'."

In October Read My Lips – New York Aids Polemic, which acted as a kind of epitaph to the successful work of ACT-UP [47] in publicising the Aids epidemic in America, opened at Tramway. The AIDS epidemic in Britain

---

44  David Cook, in conversation with the author, November 2002.
45  25th July–6th September 1992.
46  Nicola White, in conversation with the author, November 2002.
47  The AIDS Coalition to Unleash Power was formed in New York in 1987. ACT-UP organised numerous high profile protests, including stopping the traffic on Wall St., disrupting the New York Stock Exchange and staging 'die-ins' in front of pharmaceutical companies.

had recently started to receive more media attention as new statistics indicated that the largest growth area for HIV infection was amongst heterosexuals. Nicola White remembers, "Of the shows that we did at Tramway, one of my favourites was a big show about Art & Aids in New York called Read My Lips. There were Felix Gonzales-Torres billboards in the streets – it was the first time he had shown in Britain. We treated the Tramway space like an outdoor space and we built a gallery in the middle of it. The work that artists had made for galleries that was quite personal work about their own situation went in the gallery. So we had Keith Haring, Felix Gonzales-Torres and Jenny Holzer in the gallery setting and outside we had all the public art that had happened as billboards and fly-posters in the streets. It had been an incredible time in New York in '89–'90 where the idea of politics and art really fused. Those political issues around AIDS had come to be a subject for conceptual work, which had been quite cool up until then, and had become emotive. It was '92 and those kind of issues hadn't really been discussed here, the language and imagery used was not at all sophisticated – it was either doom-laden or it was cheerful cartoons of a man beside a palm tree saying, take condoms on holiday. It wasn't being dealt with as a Scottish problem, so we worked with Scottish Aids Monitor on that show, and it was a very good experience."[48]

In an interview with Ewan Morrison for *Variant*, British writer and AIDS activist Simon Watney commented, "Looking at the pathogenesis of the epidemic in the UK it is gay men who constitute the largest number already infected and by far the greatest number of new cases is still amongst men coming out, young men, old men, who haven't got the message properly. I think you have to target different groups. Prevention does work. Look at Scotland, five years ago 81% of new cases were amongst injecting drug users, this year it's 34%. This is because of the introduction of needle exchanges. The paradox of the British epidemic is that the government has done pretty well in introducing needle exchanges, and in targeting injecting drug users with advertising but has done very little for gay men. Prevention is still being prevented."[49]


48  Nicola White, Ibid.
49  "Read My Lips", Ewan Morrison, *Variant*, Issue 13, Winter/Spring, 1993, pp4–7.

However, the public profile of Glasgow's gay community increased dramatically the following year when David Peutherer founded Glasgay! which would become the UK's largest multi-arts festival for gay people, attracting performers including Annie Sprinkle, Split Britches, DV8 and hosting exhibitions by Pierre et Giles and Robert Mapplethorpe. There hadn't been a drop-in resource for gay people in the city since the Glasgow Gay Centre on Sauchiehall Street had closed at the end of the '70s, but the energy surrounding Glasgay! inspired Strathclyde Gay & Lesbian Switchboard to begin making plans to set up a dedicated Gay and Lesbian Centre in the city, which would open in March 1996.

Late in 1992 Tramway curator Nicola White had approached Douglas Gordon about producing a major new work for Tramway. She says, "I really liked Douglas' work and I'd known him for quite a long time. When I asked him, I half expected him to do something with text, and I knew that he could handle the space because he'd done a couple of large, outdoor text pieces before. I knew he had the confidence to do it but then when he went away and came back and said he wanted to make a video work we were both a bit uncertain. It took a long time to work out the practicalities of it: the display and the screen and how to slow the film down. But it was brilliant. I don't think you can beat it for a title, *24 Hour Psycho*, so it becomes an iconic thing that people don't forget, it triggers a remembrance. And I think that *Psycho* is such a shared subject matter, the same way that *The Searchers*[50] is. I knew it was very successful, it was fantastic in the space. It wasn't like anything anyone had done – it wasn't like anything that Douglas had done."[51]

For this landmark exhibition, Gordon drew on both his childhood experiences of watching films and the potential for image manipulation brought by video technology. Gordon "stretched" Hitchcock's *Psycho* (1960) to a running time of 24 hours, producing an effect that was half erotic, half grounded in film theory. He remembers, "Quite often, when I was younger, and I couldn't sleep at night, my parents would take me out of bed and I

---

50  A reference to a later Gordon piece, *5 Year Drive-By* (1995) which "stretched" John Ford's *The Searchers* to a viewing length of five years.

51  Nicola White, Ibid.

would sit with them and watch TV until I fell asleep. Most times I managed to stay awake until the end of the movie so I've grown up with quite a peculiar experience of cinema based on these childhood memories."[52] Gordon's interest in using found footage stemmed from the shared cultural resonance of certain films, but also from the common practice of watching certain scenes on slo-mo to maximise erotic pleasure or satisfy morbid curiosity. He commented, "We are the video generation. I always remember the statistics, doing modern studies and all this at school, that although the west of Scotland could be one of the most depressed areas in the world, the big example was always that Drumchapel had the highest number of video recorders per family in the world."[53] *24 Hour Psycho* had the curious double-effect of breaking and expanding the spell of Hitchcock's thriller. The cinematic mirror, in which we see our own desires reflected, "cracked from side to side" as the film was stretched to the length of a day and night, then projected in the cavernous tram depot. "The web flew out and floated wide", as visitors left the gallery and wandered into the city, knowing that behind them Norman Bates was talking to himself, or Janet Leigh was screaming.

*24 Hour Psycho* opened at Tramway in April 1993, and toured to Kunst-Werke in Berlin later that year, launching Gordon's international reputation and also putting Tramway on the international art map. The show caused something of a sensation in the art world, both for the audacious simplicity of the idea and the surprisingly complex effect of the work. *Art Monthly* reviewer Mark Sladen wrote, "This piece consists of Hitchcock's film slowed down to two frames a second, and when I entered the exhibition the very first scene of the movie was playing. In one long shot the camera first takes in a city skyline, then gradually zooms in on a window, enters a cheap hotel room, and shows us Janet Leigh and her hunk in post-coital abandon. I expected Gordon's intervention to rid the film of any dramatic tension but the reverse is true. I expected the piece to expose Hitchcock's manipulation of the viewer, but this is almost irrelevant. I kept revisiting the work and willing it to fail, but each time found myself

---

52  Douglas Gordon, *Kidnapping*, Stedelijk Van Abbemuseum, Eindhoven, 1998, p137.
53  Douglas Gordon in conversation with Graham Fagen, "The exact..vague..history", *Transcript*, Volume 03, Issue 03, School of Fine Art, Duncan of Jordanstone, Dundee, 2001.

recreating the shock of my first encounter with the original film."[54] *24 Hour Psycho* also resulted in some overdue local media attention for the neo-conceptual artists, as indicated by a BBC Scotland documentary made that year: *Out There: Conceptual Artists* featuring Christine Borland, Douglas Gordon and Craig Richardson.

In the spring of 1993, just after *24 Hour Psycho* opened, Nicola White decided to transfer back to CCA, explaining, "The reason I went back was that I think the Tramway space is very difficult, and it continues to be. A lot of the work that I was most interested in was very small scale, domestic sorts of work – new kinds of painting, work that was deliberately modest and unassuming. I just thought that I couldn't present that kind of work in Tramway – it's made for the Tony Craggs, for the *24 Hour Psycho*s. As I found myself thinking about the things I couldn't do there, I thought it would be good to go back to the kind of space where there are better proportions, and also, to be honest, a better audience.[55] Because it's really hard work when you work your guts out for what you believe to be a brilliant show and then about a dozen people a day come to see it. I missed the city centre, people coming and going and the debates you could have around that."[56]

Andrew Nairne moved from CCA to the Scottish Arts Council, where he took up the post of Head of Visual Arts, and Charles Esche was appointed Visual Arts Director of Tramway. Esche's tenure at Tramway would be distinguished by a series of shows of neo-conceptual art from local and international artists. Unfortunately, his vision was not shared by all members of the city council or the local press. Esche remembers, "We made mistakes, but there wasn't much encouragement to deal with the local situation. The mistake that we made was not thinking enough about local politics, that was true for all of us, not just Tramway. In 1993, if you said you were an artist from Glasgow it was difficult to get taken seriously, it was

---

54 "Spellbound: Art and Film", in *Art Monthly*, April, 1996. *24 Hour Psycho* was included in Spellbound, a 1996 group show at the Hayward in London, which exposed the work to a wider audience.
55 The CCA is located on Sauchiehall Street, one of Glasgow's main thoroughfares, whereas Tramway is on the south side of the city, with considerably less passing trade.
56 Nicola White, Ibid.

beginning to change but very slowly [ … ] there was no concept that you could have a career here, and if you did, it was as a painter, like Peter Howson or Ken Currie. An ideas-based art, which we were all interested in and that was coming out of Glasgow, was difficult to establish and so a lot of our energies went in that direction. In doing that we forgot to bring in people like the city council and the politicians. I guess as the one individual in all this directly employed by the council this was a bigger issue for me than anyone else.[57]

During this period, the projects taking place at Transmission, Tramway and CCA were very closely linked, with constant dialogue taking place between the three organisations. The closeness of the three organisations was also promoted by the CCA gallery manager at the time, Iain Irving and his wife, Judith Findlay, who regularly reviewed exhibitions by Glasgow-based artists at Tramway and Transmission for *Flash Art*. After the previous Tramway installations manager John Clarke had left to work in the computing industry, local artist Nathan Coley had moved into the post, heading up an installations team of artists including Richard Wright, David McMillan, Jamie Burroughs, Iain Kettles and Kenny McKay. Charles Esche says, "Transmission, CCA and Tramway was very much a three pronged attack, but I don't think we were ever in competition at all. We were really keen on saying to visitors: 'there are some really interesting things going on in Glasgow generally – go and see the other people and places here, it should be seen and shown elsewhere. We were concerned to 'internationalise' the whole situation. We knew we had to bring people here and to take what was happening here out to other cities especially in Europe."[58] Esche was committed to touring major Tramway shows by Glasgow-based artists abroad, while Transmission's forays overseas had continued after Transmission in Belfast with Transmission at Artemesia in Chicago.[59]

57  Charles Esche, in conversation with the author, July 2001.
58  Charles Esche, Ibid.
59  5th–27th November 1993. Oona Ball, Nathan Coley, Michael Ellis, Craig Richardson and Heather Allen took part in this gallery exchange project.

## THE FREEDOM TO TAKE CHANCES

The UK economy remained in a slump in 1993, with unemployment reaching 3 million for the first time since 1987. The arts infrastructure in the city was still relatively underdeveloped, meaning there were very few opportunities for young art school graduates in Glasgow. Patricia Fleming had graduated from Duncan of Jordanstone in 1990, and moved to Glasgow soon afterwards. She remembers, "I got a first class degree and then faced the depression of standing in a dole queue and feeling that the people there understood nothing about me. It was a really dark time, and I wanted to help other artists to avoid that situation."[60] Inspired by examples of studio provision schemes for artists operating in Europe, such as Les Ateliers in Amsterdam, Fleming approached the Glasgow Development Agency (GDA) and Unemployment Services in 1992 for backing to set up a project to offer artists free studio space, materials and exhibition opportunities.[61]

Fleming says, "I said to the GDA that artists were the city's natural resource and that they shouldn't abuse them, or they would leave. Fuse was partly motivated by a desire to stem that cultural brain-drain. I realised that what artists require is space and an environment conducive to the production of art and also being able to share information within a close-knit community."[62] There were 24 artists in the first Fuse project, which was located within WASPS Hanson Street premises, including Zoe Walker, Richard Wright, Anne Elliot, Colin McFarlane, Heather Allen, Ashley McCormack, Alan Frame, Donna Jamieson and Cath Whippey. Fleming then approached the Scottish Arts Council and the Foundation for Sport and the Arts for additional funding to put on annual Fuse exhibitions, the first of which opened at the Collins Gallery at the University of Strathclyde in January 1993.

Other facilities for making and showing work in the city were also

---

60  Patricia Fleming, in conversation with the author, December 2002.
61  This Employment Training Scheme was colloquially known as "Extra Tenner" because of the money for materials which artists received on top of their usual benefits.
62  Patricia Fleming, Ibid.

continuing to improve as, in 1993, the Glasgow Sculpture Studio moved from Dennistoun to new 5000 square foot premises at Maryhill, with improved specialist and industrial equipment for artists. Dave Shrigley, Andrew Miller and Kenny Hunter were among the 28 artists based there full time. In the same year, the Glasgow Film and Video Workshop began to offer broadcast-quality production facilities for film and video makers and artists, in addition to training courses. Intermedia, another new art space, opened that year in the Merchant City. The first Intermedia lasted for six months, and artists including Richard Wright, Nathan Coley, Jacqueline Donachie, Lesley Punton, Iain Kettles and Susie Hunter showed there during this time.

WASPS director David Cook remembers, "There was a woman called Fiona Mekie who was working at Scottish Enterprise, who had also been on WASPS board and she had got wind of cultural uses being given to empty premises in London and she phoned me up and asked if I knew about it. The project had been in West Soho and shops that had become vacant temporarily were given over to artists. She was keen to see Scottish Enterprise pursuing this idea and so we put together a small steering group that included myself, Tom Laurie and Andrew Nairne, who was then at CCA. We looked at the Cheesemarket and some other places and eventually settled on a former hairdresser's shop in Virginia Galleries, opposite Delmonica's. We knew of David McMillan's work on the Windfall project and also of his Breathe artist's initiative, and because we wanted someone in charge who understood what was cutting edge, we invited him to be the project manager. So Intermedia started on that premises on Virginia Street, and then when that premises was let it moved to King Street. To my knowledge the space is unique in Scotland in that artists are given a free rein and a small grant to mount exhibitions there. Since the beginning there has been quite experimental work shown there – sometimes you walk in and get knocked out, other times you're not so impressed. That's because people have the freedom to take chances."[63]

In early 1993, Streetlevel Photoworks moved from the High Street down to new premises next door to Transmission on King Street, and in June the

63  David Cook, Ibid.

country-wide Fotofeis photography exhibition, directed by Alisdair Foster, opened at venues in Glasgow, Edinburgh, Aderdeen and Inverness. In Glasgow, Womanhouse presented "a riotous photographic exploration of sex and stress", Streetlevel commissioned an exhibition of work from the Baltic States, and Transmission invited Vancouver-based artist Stan Douglas to present *Hors-champs* (1993), a video installation based on the work of four American musicians (George Lewis, Douglas Ewart, Kent Carter and Oliver Johnson) who had lived in France during the Free Jazz movement. The Transmission committee on which Christine Borland and Douglas Gordon served had been succeeded by Jacqueline Donachie, Katrina Brown, Martin Boyce, Kirsty Ogg and Simon Starling, who shared many of the previous committee's concerns. However, this committee was different from the preceding group in two crucial ways: Katrina Brown had studied modern languages at university, and was not a fine artist, and Kirsty Ogg and Simon Starling had trained at art schools outside Glasgow, respectively at Edinburgh College of Art and Nottingham Polytechnic. This gave the new committee a different approach that would be reflected in a very distinctive run of exhibitions.

By the summer of 1993 the Fuse project had moved three times: WASPS had proved too cold, while a second venue at Fox Street had been a temporary solution until a brighter space was found on Otago Street, beneath the Great Western Auction Rooms. By then the project had expanded to include 42 artists, including Douglas Gordon, Iain Kettles, Ross Sinclair, Simon Starling, Martin Boyce, Anne-Marie Copestake and Jonathan Monk, all of whom exhibited in the November Fuse show at Atlantic Quay on the Broomielaw. Clare Henry wrote in *The Herald*, "Patricia Fleming [ ... ] exhibits an apt rotorboard piece, *To Be This Good Takes Wages*, contrasting life as an artist and administrator. The "names" here in clude Douglas Gordon and Ross Sinclair, who fill a wall with *Let's Hang Out*: an exuberant display of text, t-shirts and photos. Much of the interesting work (Nichol, Starling, Neilson, Suttie) is conceptual and there's also video, and regular painting both abstract and figurative ... "[64]

64  Clare Henry, "Visual Arts", *The Herald*, 3rd December 1993.

Two of the UK's other post-industrial cities also continued to produce artists and organisations that were sympathetic to the aims of Glasgow's artist-led organisations. The link to the visual art scene in Northern Ireland maintained by Christine Borland, Cathy Wilkes, Douglas Gordon and Roderick Buchanan's studies and exhibitions there found further expression in 1993 when the artist-run gallery Catalyst Arts was established in Belfast. An exchange project took place between Catalyst and Transmission as the first show in the new gallery, when works by Gerard Byrne, Jacqueline Donachie, Anna Milsom, Emma Neilson and Richard Wright were installed in the disused shop unit. A review of the show in Irish art magazine *Circa* recorded that "Richard Wright's painting on the wall looks as though it should be an anamorphic image but isn't, and Jacqueline Donachie's sign-writing style phrase also directly put on the wall are if you like 'painting', rather than Painting [ … ] and Anna Milsom's vast map of Belfast, streets of powder stretching across the floor was to an even greater extent a quotation of the activity of painting."[65]

Also in 1993, Jon Bewley and Simon Herbert's Projects UK[66] evolved into artist-run commissioning agency Locus+ in Newcastle Upon Tyne. They wrote, "Locus+ is a visual arts facility that recognises the partial incompatibility and imbalance in the relationships between contemporary artists and the exhibition mainstream. As part of an established history within the northern region of the UK, Locus+ places the artist at the centre of production and provides logistical and financial support to those who wish to work in different contexts and/or across formats.[ … ] Locus+ is not an organisation that promotes the interests of one area of practice or the issues of a particular exhibition or production methodology. Rather, through collaborative relationships with artists and organisations, it seeks to create opportunities and frameworks that are in response to artists initiatives."[67] Both Catalyst and Locus+ would work on a variety of collaborative projects with Glasgow-based artists, and offer vital support to artists attempting to maintain a contemporary art practice outside London.

65  Hilary Robinson, "Artist-run", *Circa* No.66, Winter 1993, pp41–42.
66  Projects UK operated from 1982–1992.
67  Locus + 1993–1996, Locus+, Newcastle Upon Tyne, 1996, p5.

Meanwhile in London, Edinburgh University graduate Jay Jopling had made sufficient profit from selling '70s conceptual art on the secondary market to open White Cube, 'a temporary project space for contemporary art'. Although one of the smallest exhibition spaces in Europe, the gallery quickly became very influential, and boasted a roster bursting with yBas: Tracey Emin, Damien Hurst, Gavin Turk, Jake and Dinos Chapman, Gary Hume and Sam Taylor Wood. Around this time Glasgow-based artists begin to make more frequent trips to London to appear in exhibitions such as Christine Borland and Craig Richardson (1993) at The Chisenhale Gallery or Julie Roberts (1993) at Maureen Paley's Interim Art. However, Glasgow artists made their biggest impression on the London art scene with Wonderful Life (1993) at the Lisson Gallery, when Graham Fagen, Christine Borland, Roderick Buchanan and Douglas Gordon showed alongside yBas such as Sam Taylor Wood and Georgina Starr.[68]

The inclusion of Martin Boyce and Simon Starling in group exhibition Matter and Fact at The Collection Gallery, London, that year with Jake and Dinos Chapman and Hilary Lloyd only emphasised the growing interest in Glasgow artists. Boyce recalls, "The exchange projects with City Racing made a difference to our feelings of isolation, but the big leap was realising people like Simon Patterson were essentially the same as us. I remember seeing gallerists like Nicholas Logsdail for the first time at the Matter and Fact opening. At that show I sold a piece of work, the *Souvenir Placards*, to Saatchi. It felt as though things were possible, that they could happen in a way they couldn't in Glasgow."[69] Simon Starling's work was also included in another high profile show that year, BT New Contemporaries 1993–94, alongside London-based artists Gillian Wearing, Mike Nelson and Jane and Louise Wilson.[70] The idea of the artist as a social or historical researcher emerged as a theme in many of the works on display, including Wearing's

---

68  Christine Borland, Douglas Gordon, Roderick Buchanan and Jonathan Monk all joined the Lisson Gallery's roster during the 90s.

69  Martin Boyce, Ibid.

70  9th March 1993–23rd April 1994. This exhibition toured to five venues, the last of which was the CCA, Glasgow. The preceding four venues were in Manchester, Derry, Sheffield and Stoke-on-Trent.

*Signs That Say What You Want Them to Say (And Not What Someone Else Wants Them to Say)*. Starling's *Blue plaster cast of the bottom teeth of Frank Gilsen made on the 5th of May 1992 and found on the 10th May 1992 in the grounds of the Museum Haus Ester's, Krefeld, during an exhibition of the work of Lothar Baumgarten* provided an early example of his presentation of objects as narratives.

The 1993 Turner Prize was awarded to Rachel Whiteread, who was simultaneously named "the worst artist in Britain" by the K Foundation, who offered her a £40,000 award. They threatened to burn the money if she refused the award, which she accepted, giving £10,000 to the charity Shelter, and 11 grants of £2,400 to young artists. The K foundation had previously had numerous top 40 hits in the 1990s under names including JAMMs, The Timelords and KLF. They had heavily sampled other records on their first album, *What The Fuck Is Going On?* (1987) and they found the process of getting to number one with their Timelords single, *Doctorin' the Tardis*, so easy that they wrote a guidebook about how to top the charts. Their satirical attack on the Turner Prize was only the latest of a series of outrageous stunts, although they would later surpass themselves by burning £1 million on the Isle of Jura.

Throughout 1993 the Criminal Justice and Public Order Bill was being debated in parliament and the media.[71] The Bill outlawed public gatherings of more than three people and the playing of "repetitive beats": effectively targetting travellers, festivals and raves in the UK. The opposition of the government to the house and techno scene made it even even more alluring to most young people. For a youth increasingly disenfranchised from the prevailing party of government, floundering in a depressed social economy, the hedonistic world of the clubs offered a fleeting release. As cultural theorist Hillegonda Rietveld notes, "The participants of the party and club life surrounding the musical discourse of house music were empowered by the celebration of a sense of community, which shaped identities that were excluded from, or given less power by, the world in which they were administratively ruled by government and mass media.

---

71  The bill was passed and became law in 1994.

The very existence of the house scene as a space for the bonding of "alternative" identities was therefore a starting point for an opposing strategy."[72] Historically, the music scene in Glasgow had been associated with insubordination ever since the 19th century shebeens had been opposed by the city council and the temperance movement. The banning of public houses on the peripheral housing schemes in the '50s and '60s had also been seen by many as an attempt to dismantle the local folk scene and any political unrest it might foster. This latest attempt to curb the recreational behaviour of the city's young people met with spirited resistance, and outdoor raves and house parties continued to flourish alongside the numerous city centre clubs. Indeed, the government's opposition to the house and techno scene directly contributed to a conflation of the dance music scene with the activities of other groups, such as anti-nuclear protestors and other 'green' campaigners. In Glasgow, mobile sound units such as Breach of the Peace and Desert Storm would stage deliberately provocative dance events in public spaces, which can be understood as part of a general "party and protest" movement. 1993 was also the year that put Glasgow dance music label Soma on the map, with the release of Slam's *Positive Education*, the start of their weekly Friday night club at the Arches, and their infamous summer parties on the Renfrew Ferry. Terry and Jason of Pussypower were also central to the development of the house scene in Glasgow and were the first to book Cajmere, DJ Pierre, Evil Eddie Richards and Dajae to play at their Psyche and Hardwax parties. Meanwhile, at Glasgow School of Art, a Saturday night techno club called Knucklehead had been started up by Hamish McChlery and Environmental Art student Jonnie Wilkes.

The publication of Edinburgh-based writer Irvine Welsh's *Trainspotting* in 1993 put in writing for the first time the experience of the new dance clubs and recreational drugs. Welsh was hailed as "the poet laureate of the chemical generation" by *The Face*, for his graphic tales of highly sexed, drug-addicted youth. It wasn't just the stomach-churning accuracy of Welsh's

---

72 Hillegonda Rietveld, "The House Sound of Chicago", *The Club Cultures Reader: Readings in Cultural Studies*, Steve Redhead ed., Blacknell, Oxford, 1997.

book that made it a bestseller: it was also his acute ear for dialogue. Welsh had captured what people were saying at clubs and parties all over Scotland, right from the opening sentences, "The sweat wis lashing oafay Sick Boy; he wis trembling. Ah wis jist sitting thair, focusing oan the telly, trying no to notice the cunt. He wis bringin me doon."[73] After Alasdair Gray's *Guardian* Fiction Prize and Whitbread Prize winning *Poor Things* (1992), the attention of the literary establishment had turned to Scotland once more. The emergence of several younger Scottish writers, in addition to Welsh, including A.L. Kennedy, Iain Banks, Janice Galloway and Alan Warner no doubt added to the talk of a Scottish literary renaissance. In 1994, James Kelman would win the Booker Prize with *How Late It Was How Late*, and Edinburgh's Canongate imprint would be taken over by young publisher Jamie Byng. Byng (b.1969) had also run the Thursday night funk club Chocolate City at The Venue in the early nineties and would later develop his interest in Afro-American culture further with his Payback Press, which reprinted several neglected books including *Pimp* by Iceberg Slim. Canongate also republished Alasdair Gray's 1981 magnus opus *Lanark*, and encompassed Rebel Inc., the imprint associated with Irvine Welsh and the re-issue of "classic outsider texts" like Nelson Algren's *A Walk On the Wild Side* and Glaswegian author Alexander Trocchi's *Young Adam* (1954). Trocchi's literary reputation subsequently enjoyed a revival as he was hailed as a Scottish literary hero by Irvine Welsh, amongst others.

---

73  Irvine Welsh, *Trainspotting*, Minerva books, 1993, p1.

# CHAPTER 6

# Brilliant?
## (1994–1995)

"It's important to go elsewhere, in the sense that it lifts ambition."[1]

Towards the end of 1993, some of the most prominent neo-conceptual artists working in Glasgow began to suffer from accusations of careerism from other artists in the city. In the summer of 1993, Christine Borland and Julie Roberts had shown at the Aperto, XLV, Venice Biennale at the invitation of *frieze* co-editor Matthew Slotover. Slotover commented, "I certainly felt that there should be some artists from Glasgow in the selection to reflect the significance of the activity there."[2] One of the pieces Borland showed, a stack of coloured woollen blankets entitled *A Lifetime of Love*, attracted a great deal of attention. Unfortunately Borland's increasing profile brought with it some negative side effects, as she recalled, "Once a gallery has shown a few big-name artists or once some younger artists have shown in 'prestigious spaces', they quickly enter a new arena. It is perceived that they can no longer engage in the area of debate where previously they functioned so well. To make valid comment is only acceptable from a position of non-privilege. Trying to break down barriers, dispense with labels, be concerned with good work and good people, seemed obvious goals. The ensuing local politics, guilt hang-ups and possible rejection on the home front are possible side-effects."[3]

Thomas Lawson, interviewing Douglas Gordon for *frieze* that year,

---

1 Craig Richardson, Transmission Gallery, *The Late Show*, BBC Scotland, 2nd April 1994.
2 Transmission Gallery, *The Late Show*, Ibid.
3 Guilt by Association, Museum of Modern Art, Dublin, 1993.

observed "It seems to me that your work circles a kind of anxiety of influence. The questions it raises are about what is possible, about who might care."[4] Perhaps the "anxiety" and "guilt hang-ups" described by Borland and Lawson related to the their position within Glasgow as part of an alternative subculture. For Borland, inclusion in the Venice Biennale meant entry into a particular level of the art world's hierarchy, while Gordon too was showing increasingly in foreign museums as the '90s progressed. Both artists now often spent periods of time abroad, instead of in Glasgow, "on the ground". Mark Francis later wrote of Gordon, "He is torn between the sociable pleasures of football, or a bar in his home town of Glasgow, and the restless Ulyssean wandering in which he can make his mark in the world. From this tension arises the remembering ('forever') and forgetting ('remember me') that is at the heart of Douglas Gordon's work."[5]

Sam Ainsley's MFA course was also influencing the increasingly international outlook of the Glasgow art scene at this time, most significantly perhaps through the possibility it offered for students to go on exchange to the California Institute of the Arts, in Los Angeles. Ross Sinclair had been the first MFA student to spend a term at the acclaimed art school in 1991, followed by Dave Allen in 1993. The exchange programme was continued by Richard Wright's stay there in 1994. He recalls, "It was so stimulating to be exposed to other ideas in America. Also, you went to another place and realised that you were involved in an interesting scene in Glasgow, you saw it from another point of view."[6] The exposure to the specific culture of Los Angeles, and the particular architecture, design and contemporary art made there had a palpable effect upon the work of these three artists, which can be traced in their later practice. Perhaps most significant to Sinclair, Allen and Wright was their exposure to ideas of LA-based artists who worked in the realm of performance, such as Bruce Nauman, Bas Jan Ader, Chris Burden and Paul McCarthy, and artists who drew on the iconography of American mass culture such as Mike Kelley and Ed Ruscha.

4    Thomas Lawson, "Hello, It's Me", *frieze* Issue 9, March–April 1993.
5    Mark Francis, The Corsair, *Douglas Gordon Black Spot*, Tate Liverpool, 2000, p122.
6    Richard Wright, in conversation with Michael Wilkinson and Sarah Lowndes, extract from the forthcoming MFA book.

Martin Boyce's work also took on a new direction as a result of his study trip to Cal Arts, although his exchange came a few years later. However, his experience of the school chimed with that of his three friends in Glasgow. He says, "It changed everything completely. In my memory it was like I was there for a year but in fact it was four months. There was this Michael Asher critique class that Ross, Dave and Richard had all attended too. There were long days, often into the night, talking about just one or two people's work, really stripped down – looking at one slide for five hours and just talking about it. There was a rigour and a level of intelligence that we hadn't experienced before. You could spend all week in critical theory, or be in your studio: the school was just structured completely differently. I questioned my whole approach to art-making back in Glasgow. [ … ] On returning to Glasgow I started to bring the things I was interested in into my practice, and that stemmed from being able to be critical about the objects, rather than just being gooey-eyed in love with them."[7]

Nicola White felt that the time was right for a showcase exhibition of emerging artists, and invited Douglas Gordon and art historian and writer Jane Lee[8] to co-curate a linked series of three exhibitions, to "describe what is emerging at this time in contemporary art, to hazard a version, a selection of what is interesting and current."[9] New Art in Scotland I, II and III at the CCA featured 30 Glasgow-based artists including James Thornhill, Nathan Coley, Steve Hollingsworth, Tanya Leighton, Kirsty Ogg, Carol Rhodes, John Shankie, Stephanie Smith, Edward Stewart, James Thornhill, Clara Ursitti, David Shrigley, Richard Wright, Jacqueline Donachie, Victoria Morton and Louise Hopkins. Nicola White remembers, "That was a good time – the time when the tide had turned, and artists were coming to Glasgow rather than leaving the city. There was a really strong community of artists here, as well as things happening in Edinburgh. All of the openings were slightly wild – lots of people, density, lots of interest and debates."[10]

Recent MFA graduate Louise Hopkins (b.1965), was best known at this

7   Martin Boyce, in conversation with the author, February 2002.
8   Jane Lee was a lecturer at Glasgow School of Art between 1994 and 1997.
9   Nicola White, *New Art in Scotland*, CCA, Glasgow, 1994, p6.
10  Nicola White, in conversation with the author, November 2002.

point for her paintings on the reverse of floral furnishing fabrics, fusing ideas of romance with mechanical reproduction. Exhibition selector Jane Lee wrote, "Louise Hopkins' 'assisted chintz' paintings [ … ] demand a certain amount of contemplation. As the painted-over rose floats away from the painted-out interstices of the pattern, the buoyancy of the forms brings into play certain expectations of image-making. The viewers' desire to associate this buoyancy and this aerial blue with something else which will extend our understanding certainly 'conducts' us among signs. They are not in this case the abstract signs with which 'our reading and our knowledge' have peopled our minds but those which have come to us from our habits of looking at pictures. The roses are soon establishing themselves in the vast skies and floating apotheosis of the age of Tiepolo – the age, of course, of chintz fabric."[11]

Two of the exhibitors, Stephanie Smith and Edward Stewart, were moving towards a collaborative working partnership, and showed both solo works and a collaborative work in New Art in Scotland. Stephanie Smith (b.1968) was from Manchester, and had studied at The Slade, before completing Masters Studies at the Rijksakademie van Beeledende Kunsten, in Amsterdam, where she met Belfast-born artist Edward Stewart (b.1961), who had previously studied painting at Glasgow School of Art. In 1993 Smith and Stewart moved to Glasgow to work and live, and began working collaboratively on video installation works the following year. The influence of Marina Abramovic's collaborative work with Ulay could be seen in the work of several Glasgow-based artists, but it was perhaps most notable in Smith/Stewart's practice. Their work was characterised by shared interests in identity, language and the body, often focussing on the mouth. Mouths spitting, biting and breathing have formed the focus for a cycle of Smith/Stewart works which test the boundaries of trust and endurance. In the video installation *Sustain* (1995), for example, there is an extended sequence of Smith covering Stewart's torso in lovebites. Their works often destabilised gender roles, for example in another sequence that formed part of the same body of work, Smith "sustained" Stewart with her

11 Jane Lee, Ibid., pp16–17.

breath while he lay submerged in a bath of water for an hour.

In March, the Tramway programme included *Live Version* by David Allen, which revealed Allen's new direction, partly inspired by his exchange visit to Los Angeles. Music and performance now began to feature heavily in his work, in particular the relationship the amateur musician has with classic rock standards, such as Led Zeppelin's *Stairway to Heaven*. In the same month, Richard Wright had his first solo show of his site-specific wall paintings at Transmission. Using bright gouache, he painted a series of precise abstract designs that seemed to obliquely reference many different types of cultural insignia. "By applying patches of colour directly to the wall Richard Wright creates flat patterned forms that seem to defy their support (the architecture), creating their own sense of space. His work is perhaps an investigation/critique of the language of painting (its boundaries, its frame) proposed as a matter of experience rather than principle."[12] Wright arranged to borrow a set of six multi-coloured Eames chairs to place in the gallery for the duration of the exhibition – a direct reference to his own Californian exchange experience.

In April, three shows by Christian Boltanski that had been arranged by Nicola White opened simultaneously at Glasgow School of Art library, CCA and Tramway. Lost Property at Tramway engaged with the local culture through a simple yet trenchant strategy: all of the unclaimed lost property from Strathclyde Region's public transport was gathered, and laid out on grey Dexian shelves. The display showed something of the complexity of Glasgow's cultural life, with rosary beads and key rings featuring William of Orange lying side by side. Like Christine Borland's *Small Objects that Save Lives* (1993), the installation touched upon the evocative qualities of personal possessions. A schoolgirls' jotter, a shoe, all these lost things seemed to be breathing with life, and also haunted with the idea of dead people's effects. Boltanski's Dead Swiss, showing simultaneously at CCA, emphasised further the complexity that exists within the idea of national identity. The main gallery space at CCA was closely packed with towers made of square silver biscuit tins, each emblazoned with a small black and

12  From Transmission press release, March 1994.

white photograph of an anonymous "dead Swiss" person. The spectator's fear of accidentally knocking a pile of tins clattering to the floor became cognate with the complex issues of Switzerland's "neutrality" during World War II. Tramway's June exhibition, Part Edit by Jacqueline Donachie also explored the divergence between overarching narratives and individual experience. Donachie recorded herself retelling pieces of stories overhead on the streets of the city, sampled snippets of cars, footsteps, breathing and excerpts from various popular songs, including Louis Armstrong's *What A Wonderful World*, Bananarama's *Robert de Niro's Waiting* and Dolly Parton and Kenny Rodgers singing *Islands in the Stream*. The songs were played louder than the stories, enticing the listener to lean closer to hear the contingent "truths".

In April 1994 BBC Scotland commissioned a special edition of *The Late Show*, as Transmission clocked up over ten years of activity, which highlighted the conflicting opinions between figurative painter Ken Currie and the current committee. Currie had only exhibited at Transmission twice, in 1983's opening exhibition, Urban Life and in Winning Hearts and Minds (1984), and had then ceased to be closely involved. Unlike his New Image contemporaries, Steven Campbell and Adrian Wiszniewski, he had not donated any work to the 1987 auction which had prevented the gallery's closure. Despite his lack of active involvement in the gallery for over ten years, Currie was given the opportunity to discuss where he felt Transmission had gone wrong. In the programme hosted by ex-Hue and Cry singer Pat Kane, Currie claimed that a change in approach after the early years of the gallery (1983–1989) had offended some of the original members. He complained, "The current generation is obsessed with a crude kind of career-building at the expense of engagement with the political situation in Scotland and beyond."

Katrina Brown, who had left the gallery to work as a curator at Tramway with Charles Esche by the time the programme aired, was quoted as saying, "Transmission wouldn't be an exciting and dynamic place if we tried to fit in with established premises." Lawrence Weiner was interviewed in New York for the documentary and he offered the opinion: "If they weren't cliquey they wouldn't be doing their job. Their mandate is to show what they consider is the best art being made in their own times. They can't show everyone." While most people actively involved with Transmission considered the programme to be unrepresentative, it did emphasise that it was unrealistic to expect Transmission to cater for a wide audience. As former committee member Martin Boyce says, "Given the size of Transmission and the number of people running it, what it can do is limited. Those limitations are built in, because the committee will do what it wants to do. It will always leave some people feeling excluded, or that they haven't been represented."[13] The title of a show curated that year by Jonathan Monk for Galleri Campbells Occasionally, Copenhagen,[14] highlighted this side to the scene around Transmission. It was called Some of My Friends.

The Transmission constitution dictates that a committee member can serve no longer than two and a half years, and this ensures that no particular taste or style can become too entrenched at the gallery. And, as ex-committee member Katrina Brown comments, "This has undoubtedly been Transmission's strength over the years, keeping it bright and fresh with transfusions of young blood. Though it does seem to scare the hell out of funders and others who like to know the name of 'the man in charge'."[15] By 1994, arguments about the direction of the gallery had been brewing for some time, and continued to flare around instances of "bias" to either side of the approach (ie "political" and "local" vs "careerist" and "international").

The Scottish Arts Council funding for Malcolm Dickson's polemical *Variant* magazine had been withdrawn in February 1994, and the magazine folded soon afterwards. But *Variant*'s passing was not the only topic of conversation in the Glasgow art scene that spring. Talk in the city indicated that the newly appointed Director of the new Gallery of Modern Art (GoMA), Julian Spalding, was planning to snub the local neo-conceptual artists in favour of purchasing figurative works by the New Image painters for the new gallery's collection. In June, a massive group show opened at

13  Martin Boyce, in conversation with the author, February 2002.
14  Christine Borland, Dave Allen, Jacqueline Donachie, Andrew Miller, Kirsty Ogg, John Shankie, David Shrigley and James Thornhill showed in this exhibition.
15  Katrina Brown, "Never Being Boring", unpublished essay on Transmission, 1995.

Transmission. Modern Art was partly intended as a riposte to rumours concerning Spalding's planned "art for the people" collection at GoMA. The show's title stemmed from the disclosure at a council meeting that the new gallery had been called the Gallery of Modern Art (as opposed to the Gallery of Contemporary Art) because it fitted better on the building's facade. Like Speed and Contact: 552 4813, Modern Art provided a broad survey of the work being made in the city, and included work by 79 Glasgow-based artists including Simon Starling, Ross Sinclair, Christine Borland and David Shrigley, as well as up and coming artists like Victoria Morton, Anne-Marie Copestake and Eva Rothschild. The diverse variety of work being made in Glasgow was exposed to a wider audience in 1994 when artist, curator and writer Jeremy Millar invited Ross Sinclair, Simon Starling, Christine Borland, Roderick Buchanan, Douglas Gordon, Martin Boyce and Claire Barclay to participate in The Institute of Cultural Anxiety at the ICA in London. Millar reconfigured the usual structure of the building, removing the partition walls and dividers and providing a recording of a Jean-Michel Jarre theme instead of an acoustiguide. Millar's selection of artists was also somewhat idiosyncratic, combining works by Hieronymous Bosch, Hans Haacke and writer J.G. Ballard with pieces by younger artists from London and Glasgow.

In September, Claire Barclay's first solo show opened at Transmission. The exhibition featured works made from a variety of manmade and natural materials, such as steel or bone. Euan McArthur wrote in *Art Monthly* that, "The body is not far from her work although never figured within it. Use, however, seems close. Each work has the character of purposes not wholly or at all aesthetic, and some appear to be offered to the viewer to find or invent a use for them … The works uncover an unwillingness to identify with the organic world, the distancing and objectifying of bodily being."[16] The same month the Glasgow Women's Library which Barclay had helped support from its earliest inception moved to new premises behind King Street, at 109 Trongate. There was still no core funding for the library, but volunteers, donations from supporters and

16 *Art Monthly*, October 1994, pp29–30.

sporadic allocations of cash from the Scottish Office, City Council and charitable organisations kept the library running. Plans were immediately put in place to relocate the Lesbian Archive and Information Centre from London to the Glasgow Women's Library. However, after the many advances of the '70s, the late '80s and '90s saw the feminist movement splutter and stall, a situation that was emphasised by the closure of seminal feminist magazine *Spare Rib* in 1993 after twenty years in business. The Scottish literary magazine *Harpies & Quines* also closed, publishing a final issue in 1994 after just two years in circulation. A media backlash was taking place in reaction to the extremes of late '80s "political correctness" and feminism was increasingly being portrayed in the mass media as "a dirty word". The ideological territory was further muddied by post-feminist writers like Naomi Wolf and Camille Paglia, both of whom emphasised women's own complicity in their oppression.

Christine Borland had continued to explore ideas relating to gender issues in her work, using particular materials and techniques associated with "masculine" or "feminine" qualities in unexpected combinations to expose the inherent contradiction of gender related distinctions. Borland's stack of woollen blankets at the Venice Biennale (*A Lifetime of Love*, 1993) had been an early exposition of the idea that something comforting could also be suffocating, in both a physical and an ideological sense. In another series of works made between 1992 and 1993 Borland began using a gun to shoot various materials, including apples, shoes and panes of glass.[17] In the course of her research Borland discovered that a tightly packed roll of cotton wool could halt a bullet in its tracks. This juxtaposition of a soft, "maternal" material with the hard, "masculine" gun found further expression with *Blanket Used on Police Firing Range, Berlin: Repaired* (1993), where bullet holes in a blanket were laboriously repaired by hand by Borland. In addition to making a clear contrast between the ideas of damage and repair, this work also successfully conveyed an apparent difference in "masculine" and "feminine" ideas of time and efficiency: the

17  *Shot Apples* (1992), *Shoes with 9mm hole* (1992), *9mm Sig Sauer P6, 9mm Heckler and Koch MP5A37, 7.62 Natokaliber Heckler and Koch G3 (1993).*

instantaneous mechanised hole wrought by the bullet as opposed to the slow and careful darning. This exploration of the perceived divisions between masculine and feminine areas of knowledge and expertise were developed still further in Christine Borland's first major solo show, which opened at Tramway in October.

*From Life* attracted massive media attention, primarily because the work revolved around research into a female skeleton Borland had purchased through the internet. Borland worked with various experts to piece together the background of the skeleton, discovering among other details that the dead woman had had "at least one advanced pregnancy". The different branches of her investigation were laid out in portacabins around the yawning 1030 square metre space of Tramway 2. Charles Esche wrote, "Particular forms of her practice are, in their process and sometimes final presentation, a form of social archeology – a system of archeological investigation which emphasises interpretation over excavation. In common with her contemporaries in the academic world, the artist rejects the urge to dig simply to reveal, but absorbs herself in the context of the work being produced. Where the work differs from academic archeology is not so much in her choice of contemporary objects and contexts but in its final presentation. Unlike the archeologist, the artist has no need to recreate the position any object or individual occupies within a dominant social system. She does not have to say, for instance, 'A gun is used to commit acts of violence'. She can present it back to her society, where that interpretation is completely familiar, and leave herself free to excavate the hidden contexts."[18] Like *24 Hour Psycho, From Life* also later toured to Kunst-Werke, Berlin, and helped to establish Borland's international reputation as an artist with a highly sophisticated research-orientated practice.

In November, London-based artist Mike Nelson devised *Charity Shop*, a project for Transmission which investigated the role of the charitable organisation and recalled the 1988 Transmission jumble sale. While Glasgow's Buchanan Street precinct had become increasingly exclusive by the mid-'90s, the area of town around the gallery was as yet ungentrified,

18  Charles Esche, Christine Borland, Tramway/Kunst-Werke, 1994, p7.

populated by amusement arcades, shops selling fancy goods and leather clothes, and bordered by the Barras and Paddy's market. In many ways the street market tradition in Glasgow had informed the work being made at Transmission: Paddy's Market was only a stone's throw from the gallery, and the Barras a ten-minute walk away. Although the traditional fruit, vegetable and fish markets at Candleriggs had been moved to vacated industrial premises at Blochairn during the '60s and '70s, the street-market tradition was still thriving at the Barras, which was now the biggest enclosed market in Europe. Paddy's Market, a cornucopia of second-hand clothes and bric a brac set up in 1824 by Irish settlers, had been forced to move location eight times over the years but still showed no signs of closing down.

"Sometimes he would walk the whole length of the lane and find nothing, and the place would assail him with its dismal drabness. Then he would notice only the smells and dirt; nothing but old junk and stinking rags. Even the people would look bedraggled, pathetic, their faces brutalised and harsh. There were other times though, when the place had another quality altogether, when it seemed colourful and alive, when every stall might reveal some treasure and everything pulsed with a warm underlying humour."[19]

Paddy's Market could be seen as being analogous with the grassroots art scene in Glasgow, which has prospered in unwanted spaces. The Trongate had lost its position as the cultural centre of the city when Glasgow University had moved up to the West End in 1870, but a revival had been slowly building there through the 1980s as the relatively low rents in the area attracted artists' organisations like WASPS, the Print Studio, Transmission, Streetlevel and Intermedia. The aesthetics associated with the local fringe economy could also be traced in several of the younger artists associated with Transmission. Jonathan Monk's screenprinted replicas of hand drawn signs, Jonnie Wilkes' sculptures made from cabbage sacks, his

19  Alan Spence, "The Palace", *Its Colours They Are Fine*, William Collins Sons & Co Ltd, London, 1977, p142.

sister Cathy's use of scraps of fabric and Jim Lambie's masks made out of tinfoil shared a common style. Market stalls had a makeshift energy: of things that were a little bit broken, or about to go off. The work that drew on that atmosphere shared the same transitory glee.

Elsewhere in the city, artists were continuing to show work in "dead spaces"; one notable example being the 99 Gallery, in the premises where the short-lived Strip gallery had been held in the early '90s. Under the name Strip the building had been used for temporary exhibitions and per-formances and had also housed a number of "squatted" artists studios. The 99 Gallery opened in 1994, after renovations funded by the SAC had been carried out by artists. Early exhibitions included Unbuilding: a show by James Thornhill, Andrew Miller and Michael Gerkin and Difficult Relationships, a group show initiated by Will Bradley and Tim Cullen that included work by Martin Boyce and Kirsty Ogg. In the same year the Fringe Gallery opened in Castlemilk shopping arcade, with New Clothes by Alan Dunn and Alex Dempster, and an installation by Stella Tobias and Claire Barclay in the nearby stable block.

Patricia Fleming's Fuse project continued to provide a means for graduating artists to keep making work in a supported atmosphere. Will Bradley had moved to the city in 1992 to do a postgraduate degree in photography at the Art School and joined the project after graduating. "I can't speak highly enough of the Fuse project. Even though it was sometimes in strange buildings and strange parts of town I got more out of that than anything else. I started to meet some really nice people, like Eva Rothschild and Jonathan Monk, who were serious about what they were doing and I learnt a lot. You got a studio, and ten pounds extra a week on your dole for materials. It stopped a lot of people quitting – it gave you a sense of being an artist, even if you only had two shows a year. It was a really good support structure."[20]

By January 1995 the Transmission committee had recruited recent Glasgow School of Art graduates Toby Webster, Eva Rothschild, Kirsty Ogg, Will Bradley, and Tanya Leighton. One crucial change that became part of

20  Will Bradley, in conversation with the author, April 2001.

the gallery's policy around this time was that committee members were no longer allowed to exhibit in the gallery during their tenure. This change in policy demanded a more critically detached curatorial attitude from the committee members. The new committee continued to expand upon the gallery's remit to support artists within Glasgow, and to spread the news about their work in the UK and overseas. Glasgow-based artist Chris Evans set up the artist-run Three Month Gallery in Berry Street in Liverpool with Duncan Hamilton and Andy Small that year, adding to the growing number of regional art initiatives that collaborated with Transmission. The Three Month Gallery was initially intended as a one-off exhibition of Evans, Hamilton and Small's work with London based artist Erlend Williamson. They decided, however, to run a gallery inviting people whose work they were interested in mainly from Liverpool or Glasgow. Some of the artists associated with the gallery were Will Bradley, Tom O'Sullivan, Joanne Tatham, Caroline Woodley, Elizabeth Price, Mathew Thomson, Eva Rothschild and Padraig Timoney.

Later that January Roderick Buchanan's first solo show, Work in Progress opened at Tramway. The exhibition reflected Buchanan's grow-ing interest in the shared dream of football supporters. The exhibition featured a series of photos Buchanan had taken in Glasgow of men wearing AC Milan or Inter Milan shirts. All of the photographs had been taken against a blue background, with the men adopting the pose familiar from football annuals. The photographs were then arranged in rows as teams on white shelves, placing an emphasis on the uniformity of the players' clothing and stance. Judith Findlay reviewed the show for *Flash Art*, writing, "We all exchange messages and Buchanan uses foot-ball metaphorically to signify that exchange. I don't know that much about football. I don't need to. For I know here in this work it signifies dialectic and dialogue."[21] Although Buchanan used the language and rules of games as a device for asking questions about society, his work also had more local resonance than Findlay suggests.

Football had been eagerly adopted in Scotland in the late 19th century,

21  Judith Findlay, *Flash Art*, Summer 95, pp131–2.

both as a street game and a recreational pastime. A crowd of 40,000 watched Celtic in the first Scottish Cup Final, in 1892, and derby matches between Celtic and Rangers quickly became a focus for existing sectarian tensions. Football matches, like the first cinemas that opened up in the city, were an affordable and popular mass entertainment which offered a temporary respite from the pressures of everyday existence. In Work in Progress, Buchanan had also referenced the links between Italy and Glasgow that also inform part of the city's cultural identity. Football, and particularly Italian football, had a long-running association with excitement and recreation, with escape. On one level, Buchanan's work seemed to be about that dream of being a star football player, of displaying the skill that would set you apart from others, while in another sense it was about the desire to be accepted. In 1995 Buchanan had exhibited in London, Geneva, Belfast, Budapest and Saint Lazare, and on his travels he began to be struck by the ways in which people expressed their identity through affiliation with a particular team, either through donning a football shirt or a basketball cap.

When Buchanan's girlfriend, Jacqueline Donachie, won a Fulbright scholarship to study at Hunter College, New York between 1995 and 1996, Buchanan visited, and his exposure to American sports culture influenced later works such as the video work *Chasing One Thousand* (1996). *Chasing One Thousand* also dealt with the idea of aspiration, as he and artist friend Paul McGuire[22] headed a ball between them one thousand times without it touching the ground. Both McGuire and Buchanan were clad in basketball clothes and standing on a basketball court, although it was a football they were heading back and forth, emphasising that the idea of sport as an escape was equally prevalent in Scotland and America. The idea of a shared dream emerged again in a later work, *One in a Million* (1999), a compilation of slow circular panning shots filmed from the centreline of numerous football pitches.

---

22　Paul McGuire (b.1968) graduated from Glasgow School of Art in 1992, and later taught computing at Glasgow School of Art and the University of Plymouth. McGuire moved to London in 1997 and has subsequently won several prestigious awards for his website designs and interactive installations.

# TRUST THE WORK

In the spring of 1995, artist-organiser James Thornhill staged a series of group exhibitions in a dilapidated tenement on the corner of Wilton Street and Belmont Street, which included work by 15 Glasgow-based artists over the course of three weekend openings. Thornhill (b.1967) had moved to Glasgow in 1990 after studies in Bournemouth, and at the Frei Universitat fur Bildende Kunst in Hamburg. He had also been closely involved in renovating the 99 Gallery. Thornhill's work was concerned with ideas of urban waste, often using plastic, neon, metal and wooden letters taken from abandoned business premises, and reworking the signage into "letter-twocker" configurations such as *(un)bounded* and *wasteland*. The artists he invited to participate in the events at the former Belmont Hotel included Andrew Miller, Richard Wright, Jamie Burroughs,[23] Deirdre McCloskey, Edward Stewart, Stephanie Smith, Tom O'Sullivan, Cathy Wilkes, Heather Allen, Iain Kettles, Will Bradley and Hilary Stirling.

"Each weekend there was an opening, it was quite an event. The basement of the building had been a jazz club in the '70s and the top half, which we were using, had been a brothel. It created quite a strange dynamic in the street, people wondered what was happening and I had a neon work, which read 'Saturn' hanging on the front of the building, which had originally been called The Belmont Hotel. Every-one made work especially for the space, which was really run down. The last weekend, three days before, these guys came in and erected a scaffold in the stairwell, knocking a hole in the ceiling. Two days before the opening everyone was here, dismantling this scaffolding and tidying up so that we could have the opening. Then, after the opening, we had to put the scaffolding back up. It was a real community event, it was very involved and everyone had to muck in. It was hard work and quite mad."[24]

In 1995, Nicola White invited curator Hans Ulrich Obrist to present the

---

23  Glasgow-based artist Jamie Burroughs also played percussion in a band called Junk Culture with local architect Greg White, of Loci Design.

24  James Thornhill, in conversation with the author, August 2001.

group "instructions" exhibition Do it[25] at CCA, which featured the work of Christian Boltanski, Maria Eichhorn, Hans-Peter Feldman, Felix Gonzales-Torres, Mike Kelley and Rirkrit Tirivanija. Obrist had been influential over the Glasgow art scene in a number of ways. He was an articulate and internationally respected figure, given to statements such as "It is only through a movement through an unknown resonant space that a show can support art in its fight against clichés of opinion."[26] He was also actively supportive of artist-run initiatives and maintained that he was as interested in organising an exhibition in his kitchen as he was a major museum show. He was in close contact with the artists working around Transmission and provided a dynamic role model for artists who were interested in organisational or curatorial activities in Glasgow. Obrist's influence was also vital in building the international profile of Glasgow artists as he included their work in shows he curated, wrote about their work and discussed it with other artists and curators.

Obrist also brought the work of artists like Mike Kelley to Glasgow for the first time, which then influenced the work of emerging artists in the city. In a 1992 interview Kelley had explained his approach to using found ephemera. "I've always been interested in the particularity of the junk; how it became junk. Why is this junk and that not junk. I don't simply go to Pick and Save and get the lowest piece of shit and tape it to the wall ..."[27] Kelley's work had a particular resonance for artists including Jim Lambie, James Thornhill and Cathy Wilkes, who often constructed works out of material sourced from second-hand shops, street markets or skips. The inclusion of Rirkrit Tirivanija in Do It was also significant, as his work used the social rituals of eating and drinking in a way that struck a chord with artists/organisers like Toby Webster and Kirsty Ogg. Significantly, one of Obrist's most famous projects had been to stage an Art and Science conference, which featured all the informal chats, drinking and socialising that usually surround a conference but without the usual

---

25 The idea for Do it came from a discussion between Hans Ulrich Obrist and artists Christian Boltanski and Bertrand Lavier who were interested in observing how artists translate or interpret a set of intructions. Do it appeared in various incarnations in numerous contemporary art spaces including venues in Austria, Paris and Bangkok.
26 Hans Ulrich Obrist, quoted in Flash Art, Nov./Dec 1992.
27 Mike Kelley, Flash Art, Nov/Dec 1992.

seminars, workshops or speeches.

Over at Tramway, Charles Esche and curator Katrina Brown were meeting with resistance in a number of ways. Esche recalls, "Most of the people who worked at Tramway, apart from Nathan Coley and Katrina Brown, seemed to be opposed to what we were doing. It did feel as though we were in a defensive position, and people were constantly having a go. Nathan and Katrina never had proper contracts throughout the time they worked there. Katrina was on these ridiculous three month renewable contracts, and I had to go all the time to Bob Palmer, who was the Head of the Performing Arts, and plead with him to allow us to employ her for another three months. They said if you were employed for more than a year it was illegal, which was true but basically just a way of keeping control. There was always the money to give her a proper job."[28] Aside from the internal pressures of Tramway, Esche remembers the local press being far from sympathetic towards the programme of exhibitions he devised with Katrina Brown's assistance.

Strained relations between the new generation of Glasgow artists and the city's council and media reached breaking point when the international group show Trust opened at Tramway in May 1995. Trust was jointly curated by Charles Esche, Katrina Brown, and neo-conceptual artists Christine Borland, Douglas Gordon, Roderick Buchanan and Jacqueline Donachie. Esche explained, "Trust partly came out of a social opportunity: the curators had worked with all these artists in different ways and got on well with them. Between us we came up with the idea that we should do a group show which acknowledged the growing international network we were starting to have. We decided to make a show about that network and try to bring it back to Glasgow, to say, this is our city and we're proud of it and want to show it to you, also to show the artists that we thought were good to our audience. We used to talk about a network of trust that was building up. One of the rules we had was that one of us had to have met the artist, and to have had some sort of reasonable personal encounter with them: that trust should be there on a personal level. Also, the only way that

<hr>

28  Charles Esche, in conversation with the author, July 2001.

you can respond to the type of criticism that the council or [local journalist]
Clare Henry were coming out with, is to say to anyone interested: 'just trust
the work, and your own reaction to it, without listening to the negativity
that surrounds it'. I believed that if you saw some of the work in Trust and
just went with it, you would get something from it. So all of these ideas
went into the exhibition."[29]

Trust showcased the work of 22 internationally renowned artists
including Carsten Holler, Andrea Zittel, Marina Abramovic and Ulay, Stan
Douglas, Lawrence Weiner, Cady Noland, Rosemarie Trockel, Felix
Gonzales-Torres and Rirkrit Tirivanija. The curators hoped to promote
engagement between local audiences and international artists, but the
exhibition was immediately lambasted as being pretentious and inaccessible
by figurative painter Ken Currie and *The Herald's* Clare Henry, who had
been one of the selectors of The Vigorous Imagination in 1987. Trust's
curators, especially Esche, were accused of self-serving and elitist
intentions.[30] Clare Henry wrote a piece called "Don't Trust Tramway" in *The
Herald*, which prompted Scottish Television to pit Esche against Henry in a
studio debate. An article written by Currie condemning the exhibition was
printed in *Scotland on Sunday*, which claimed that Andrew Nairne [then
Head of Visual Art at the SAC], CCA Director of Exhibitions Nicola White
and Esche were "like the Mafia". Nicola White says, "I think Andrew Nairne
was so key to the success of Glasgow, outside Glasgow, by helping establish
the city's artists in the eyes of people elsewhere. Some people criticised him
unnecessarily because he was at the SAC and that was somehow seen as
being on the other side of the fence. But no-one worked harder or achieved
more than Andrew."[31]

In response to Henry and Currie's articles, Charles Esche called a well-
attended public debate at Tramway, which led to a particularly heated
exchange between Douglas Gordon and Ken Currie. The open forum,
entitled Can We Trust Tramway? drew 150 people. Sam Ainsley recalls,

---

29  Charles Esche, Ibid.
30  As curator and critic Neil Mulholland notes in "Onwards and Upwards" (*Art Monthly* May 1998) an article reviewing recent events
    in Glasgow's cultural life, "Esche was said to have used his tenure at Tramway to promote this gang of artists" – ie Douglas Gordon,
    Christine Borland, Jacqueline Donachie, Roderick Buchanan et al.
31  Nicola White, in conversation with the author, November 2002.

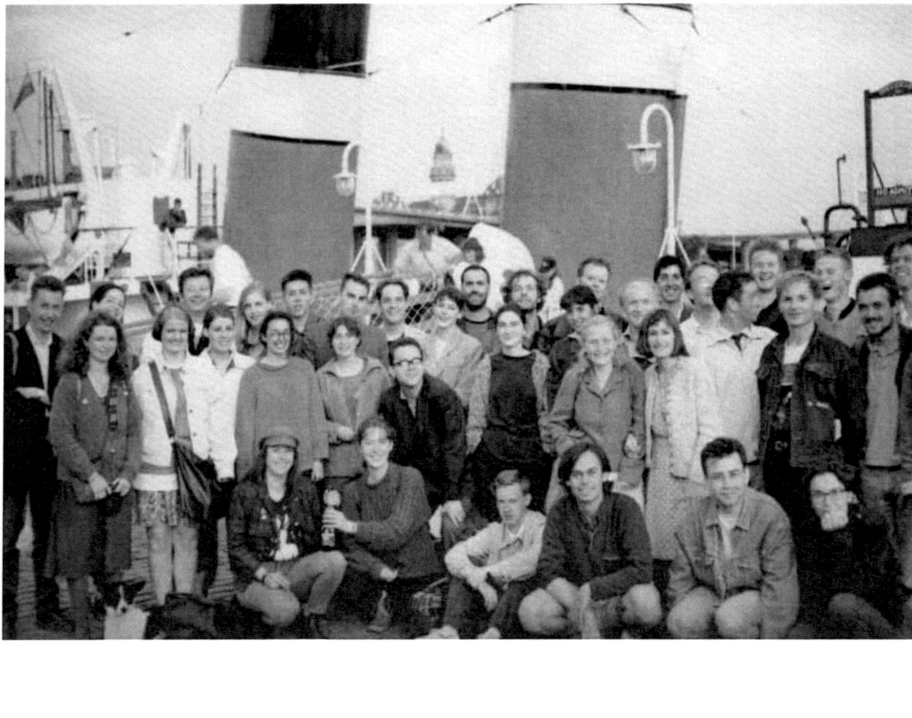

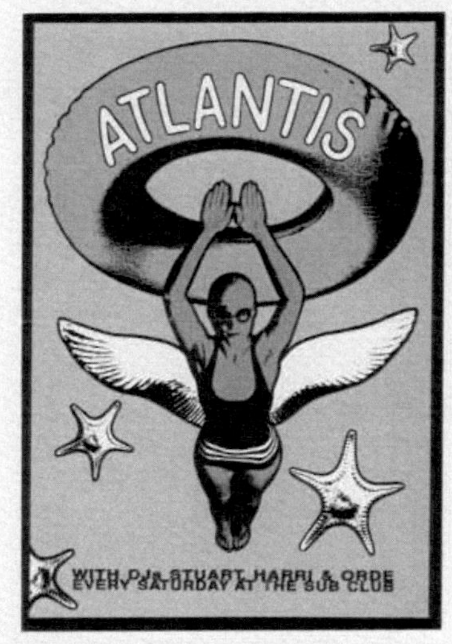


Photograph of artists participating in Windfall and friends, summer 1991. Group includes: Heather Allen, Katrina Brown, Susie Hunter, Dave Allen, Claire Barclay, Craig Richardson, Jacqueline Donachie, Iain Kettles, Julie Roberts, Roderick Buchanan, Douglas Gordon and Nathan Coley.
Atlantis flyer for residency at the Sub Club, circa 1991.

Lawrence Weiner, Transmission, November 1991. Weiner's text work reads: an arch afforded in a wall of stone with a keystone of chalk and imposts of slate.
MFA trip to Berlin, 1993. Second row from back, left to right: Jonnie Wilkes, Tom O'Sullivan, Satoshi Watanabe. Front row, left to right: Douglas Gordon, John Shankie, Leigh French, Richard Wright, Alan Currall.

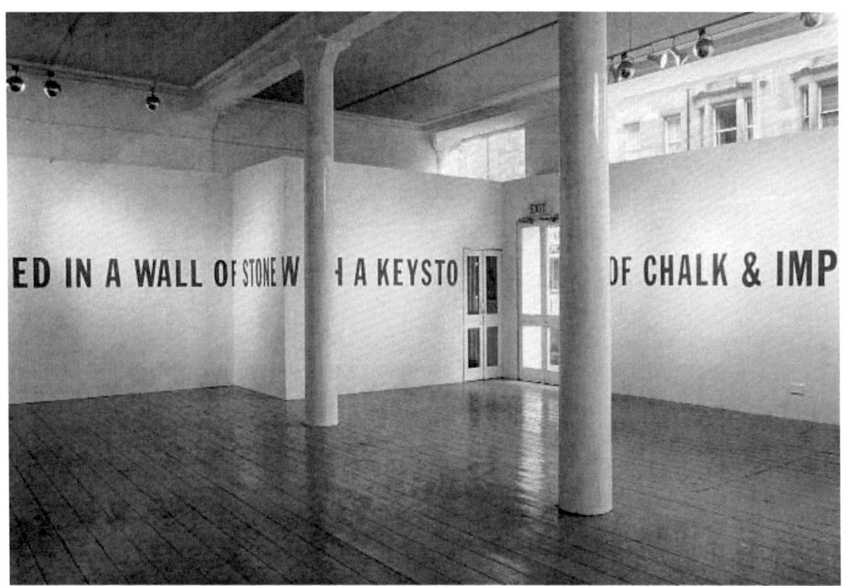


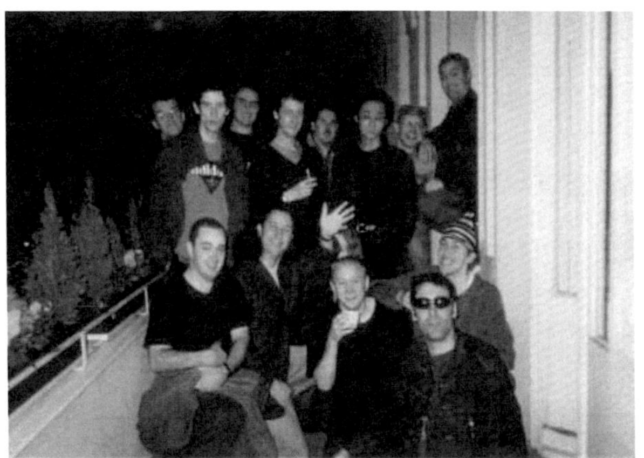

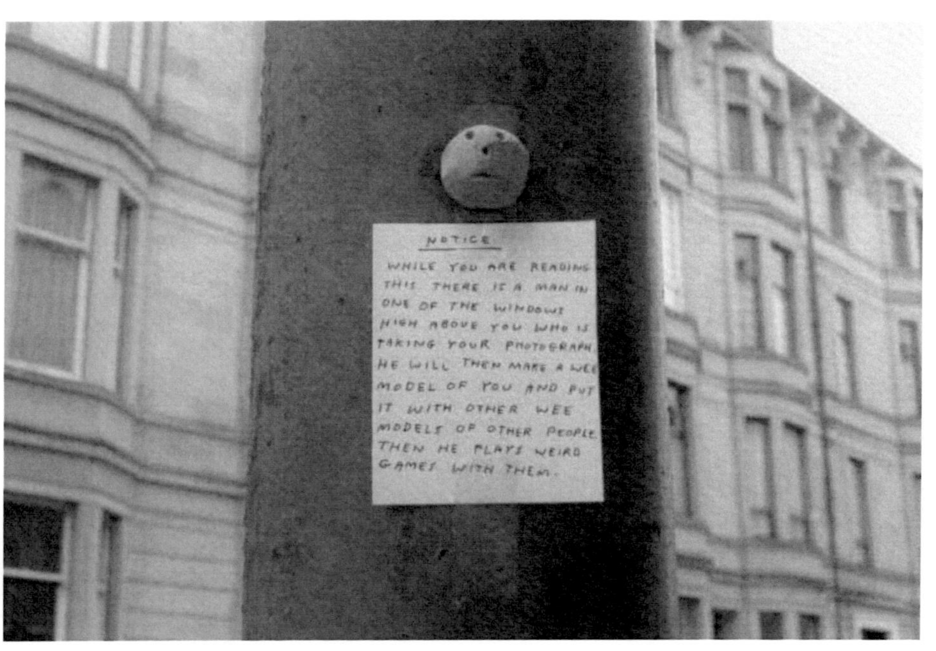


David Shrigley, *Notice*, 1996.

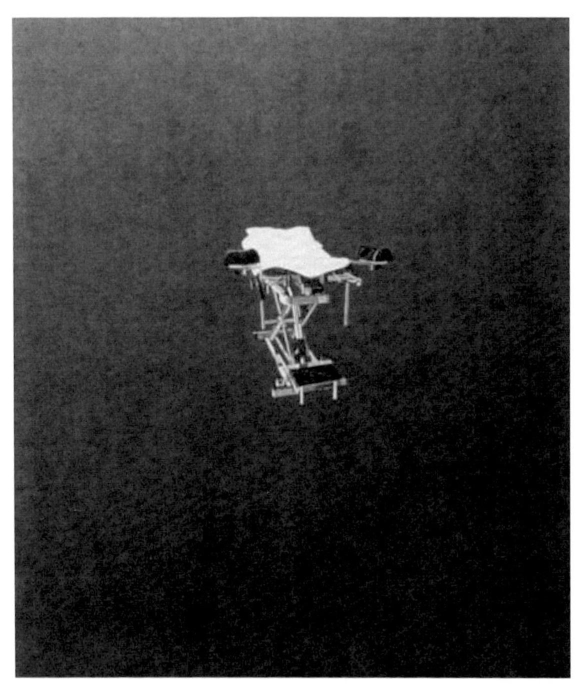

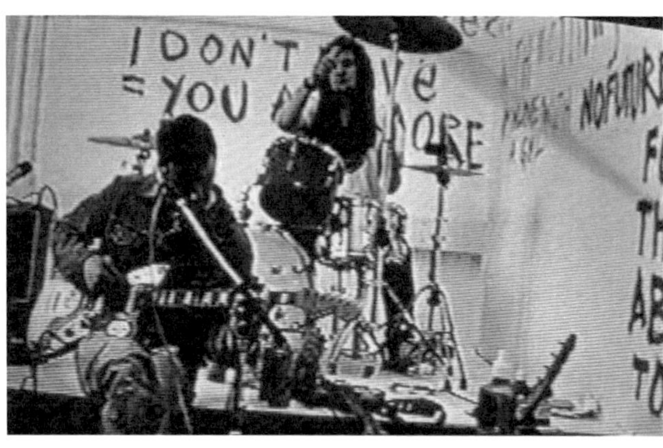


Julie Roberts, *Gynecological Couch*, 1993.
Dave Allen and Ross Sinclair, *For Those About To Rock*, 1994.

OPPOSITE
Douglas Gordon, *24 Hour Psycho*, Tramway, 1993.

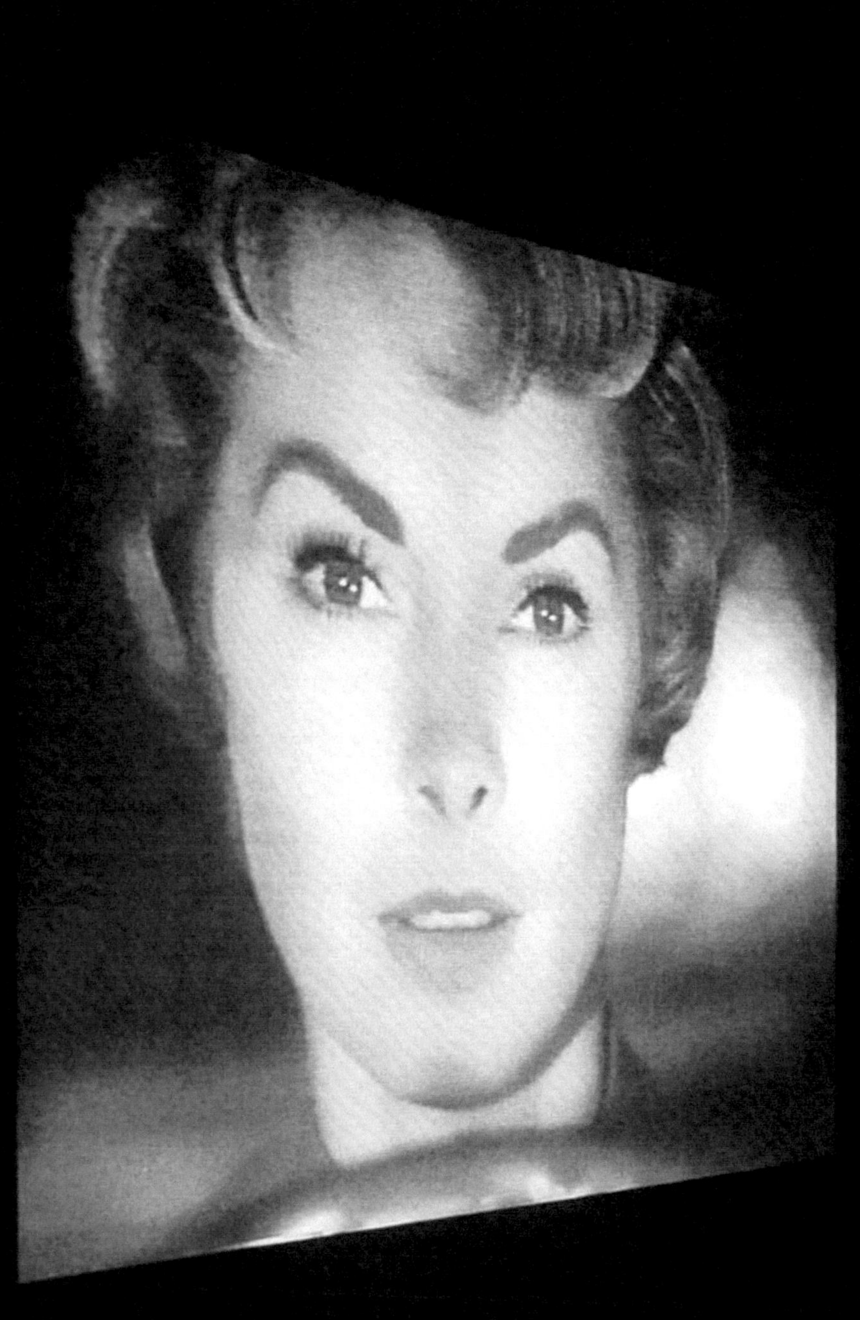

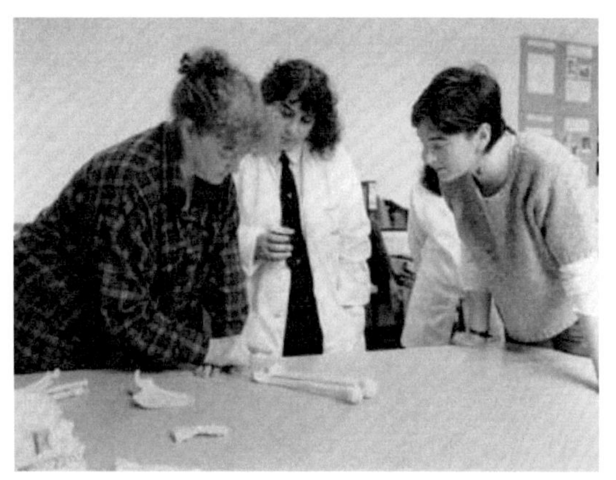

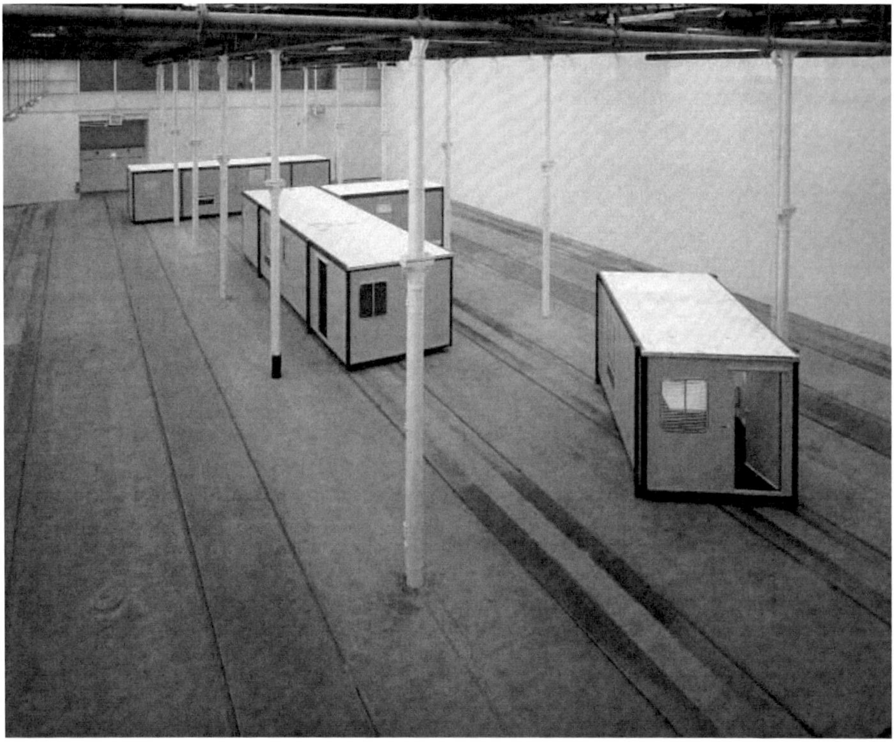

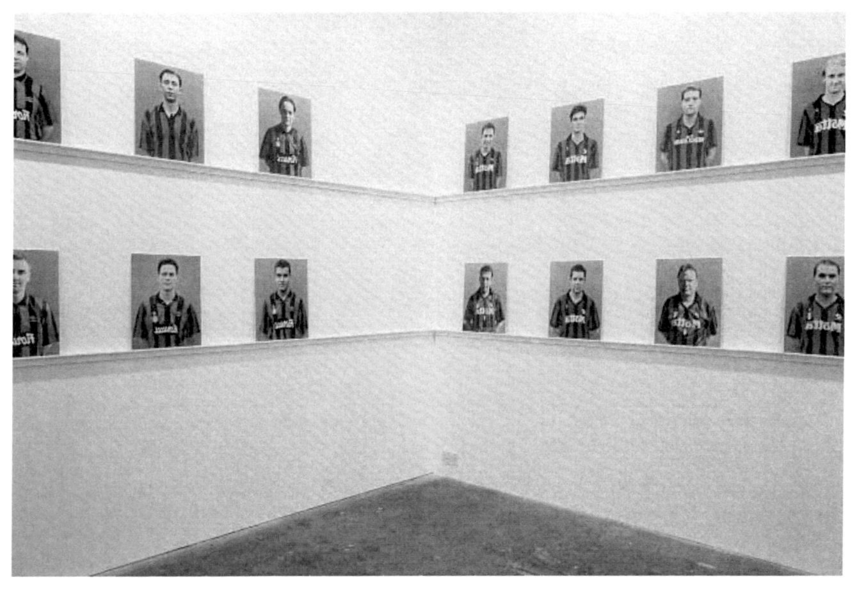

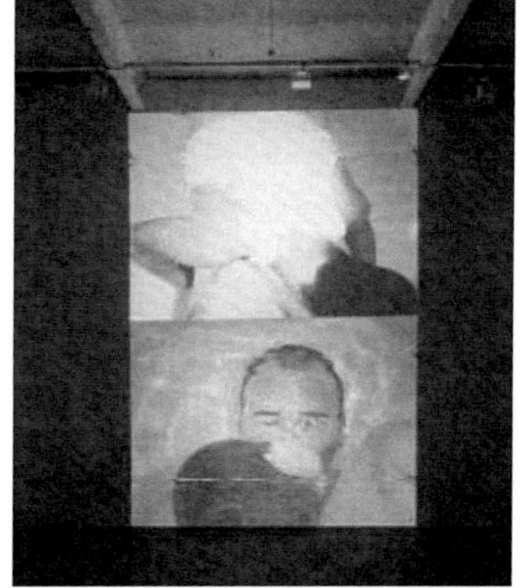

Roderick Buchanan, *Work in Progress*, Tramway, 1995.
Smith/Stewart, *Sustain*, Tramway, 1995.

OPPOSITE
Christine Borland researching *From Life*, 1994. Here
shown determining the basic characteristics of the
skeleton with Dr Susan Black.
Christine Borland, *From Life* (installation view),
Tramway, 1994.

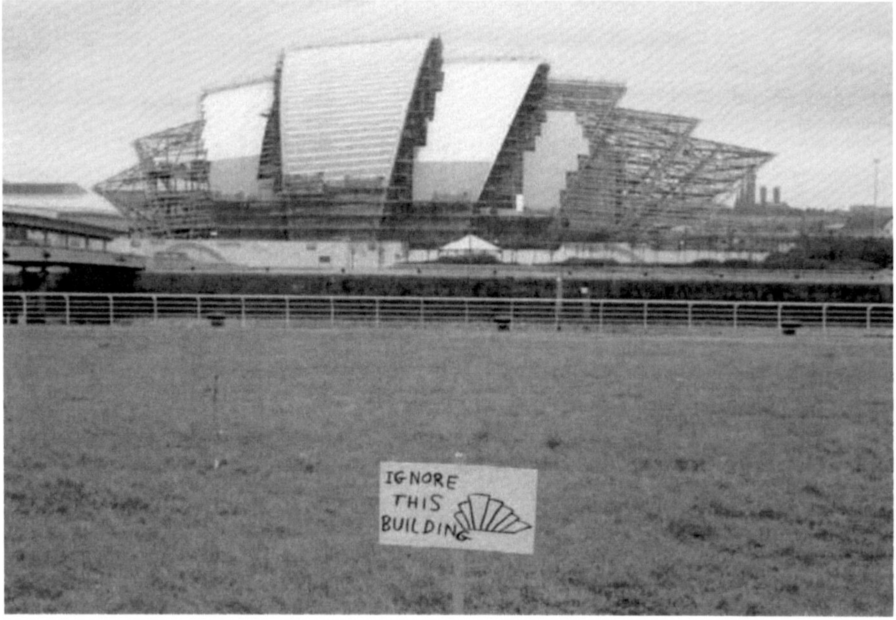

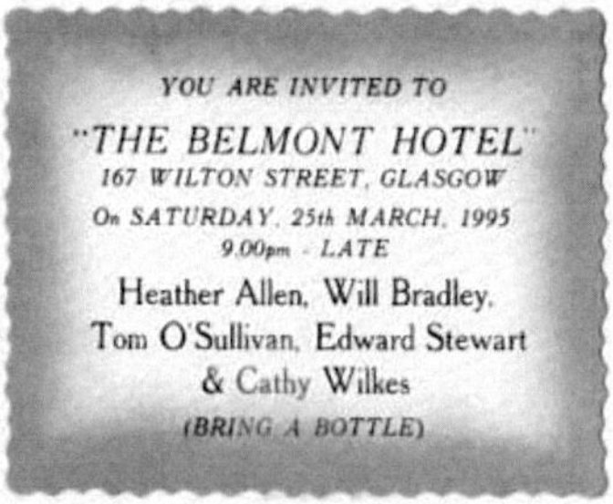

YOU ARE INVITED TO

## "THE BELMONT HOTEL"
167 WILTON STREET, GLASGOW
On SATURDAY, 25th MARCH, 1995
9.00pm - LATE

Heather Allen, Will Bradley,
Tom O'Sullivan, Edward Stewart
& Cathy Wilkes

(BRING A BOTTLE)

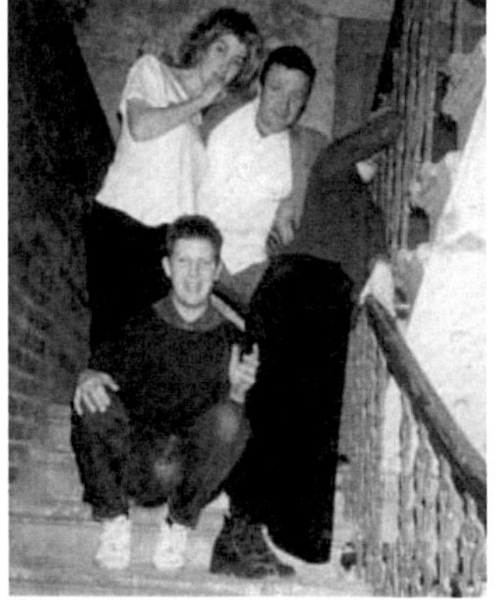

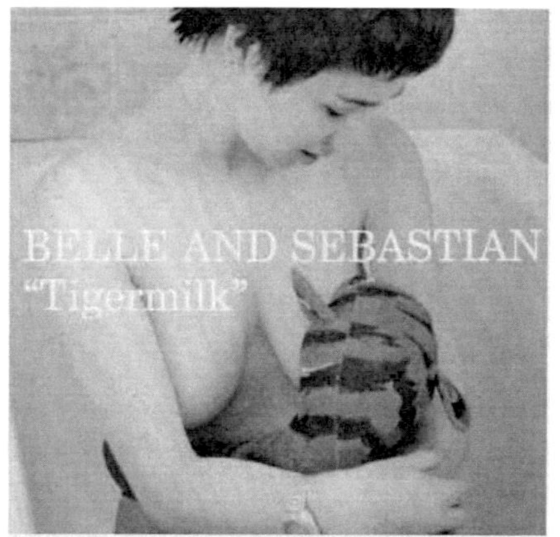

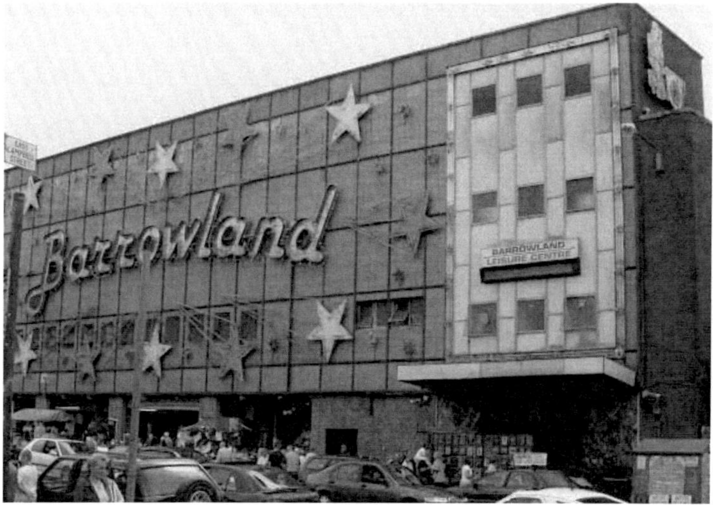


Belle & Sebastian's debut album, *Tigermilk*, 1996.
The legendary Barrowland Ballroom and Barras market in the East End of Glasgow. A major music venue, the Barrowland Ballroom has played host to numerous local and international bands over the years including Mogwai, ESG and David Bowie, while the Barras weekend market is now the largest indoor market in Europe.

OPPOSITE
David Shrigley, *Ignore This Building* (1996).
Invitation for an opening at The Belmont Hotel, 1995.
Opening at The Belmont Hotel, 1995. Clockwise from top left: Cathy Wilkes, Jamie Burroughs, Deirdre McCloskey and James Thornhill.

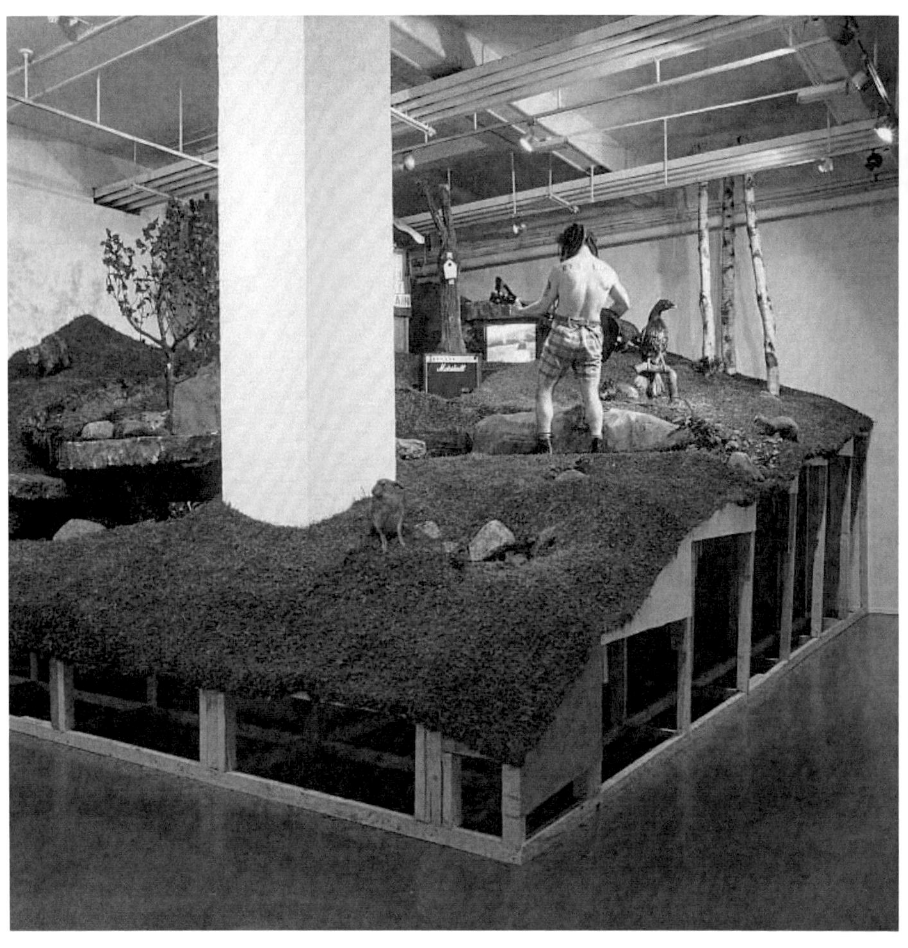

Ross Sinclair, *Real Life Rocky Mountain*, CCA, 1996.

OPPOSITE
*Art for People* (installation view), Transmission, May 1996.
Poster for *Art for People*, Transmission, May 1996.
Flyer for The Society for the Termination of Art performance at the Gallery of Modern Art opening, 1996.

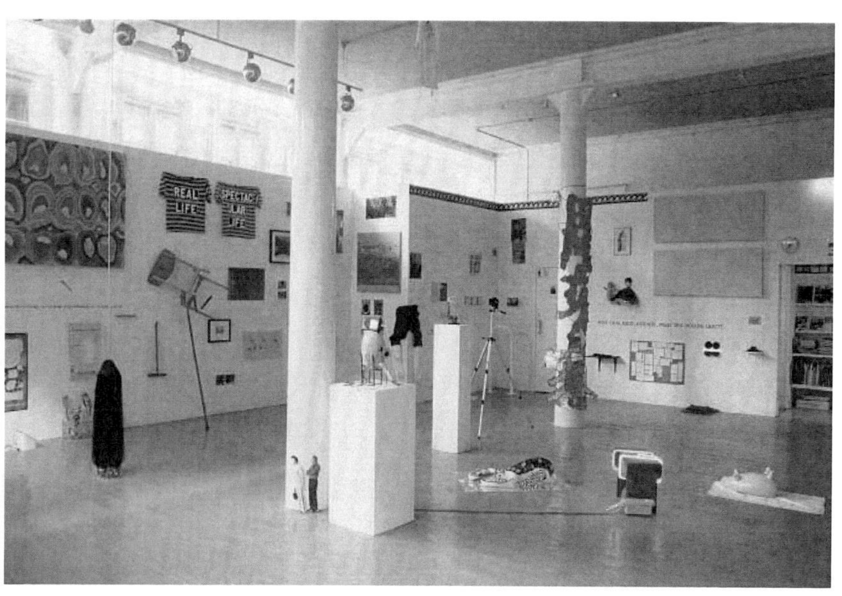

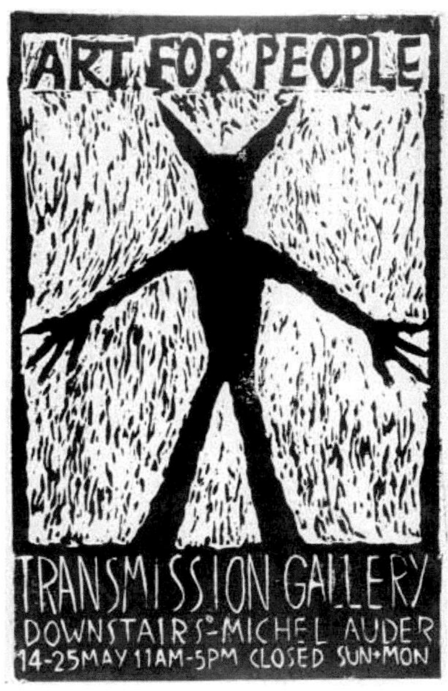

ART FOR PEOPLE
TRANSMISSION GALLERY
DOWNSTAIRS · MICHEL AUDER
14-25 MAY 11AM-5PM CLOSED SUN+MON


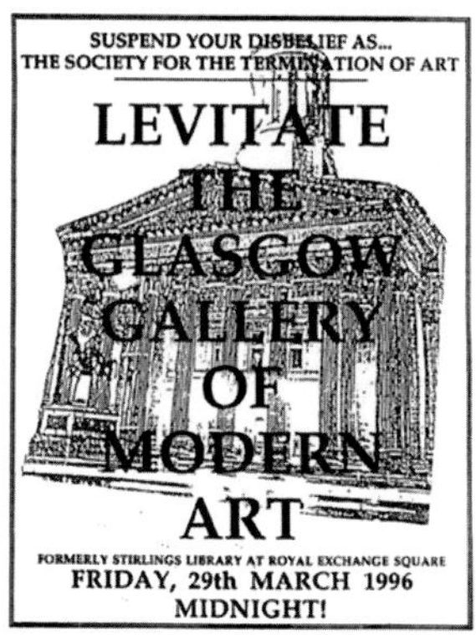

SUSPEND YOUR DISBELIEF AS...
THE SOCIETY FOR THE TERMINATION OF ART
LEVITATE
THE
GLASGOW
GALLERY
OF
MODERN
ART
FORMERLY STIRLINGS LIBRARY AT ROYAL EXCHANGE SQUARE
FRIDAY, 29th MARCH 1996
MIDNIGHT!

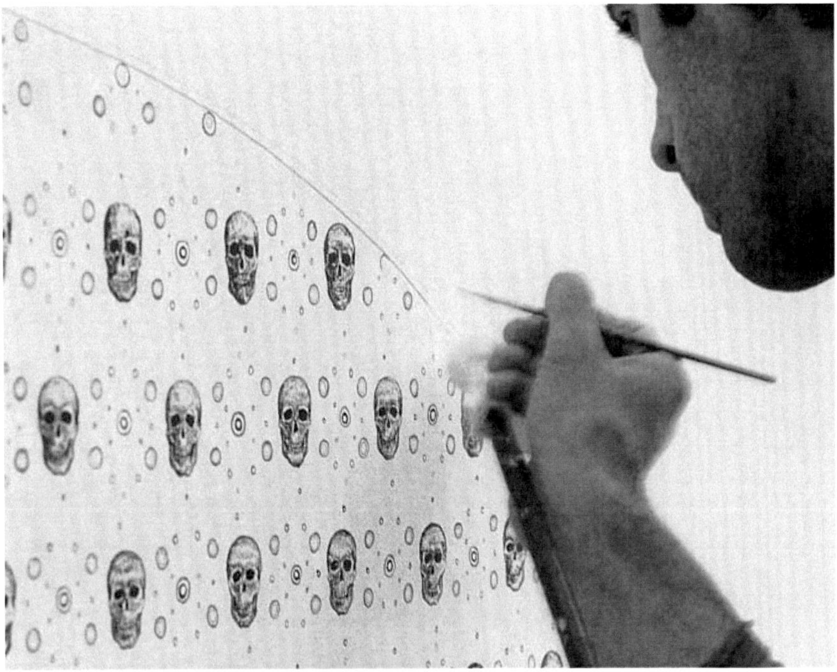

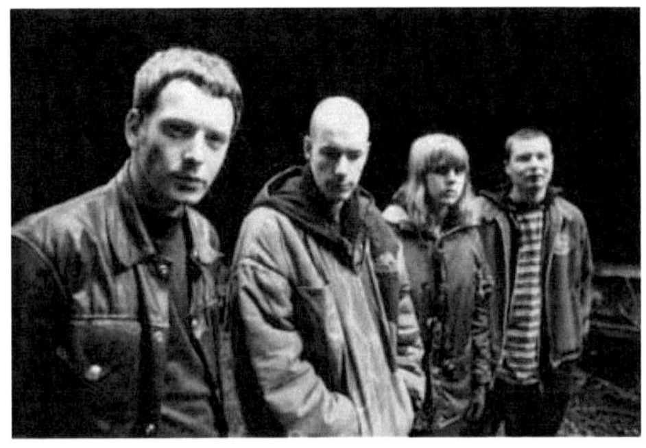

Richard Wright installing work for *Live/Life*, Paris, October 1996.
Ganger, circa 1996. Left to right: Graham Gavin, Stuart Henderson, Lucy McKenzie and James Young.

OPPOSITE
Wish You Were Here Too, exhibition at 83 Hill Street, 1996.
Nathan Coley, *Pigeon Lofts* (1997).

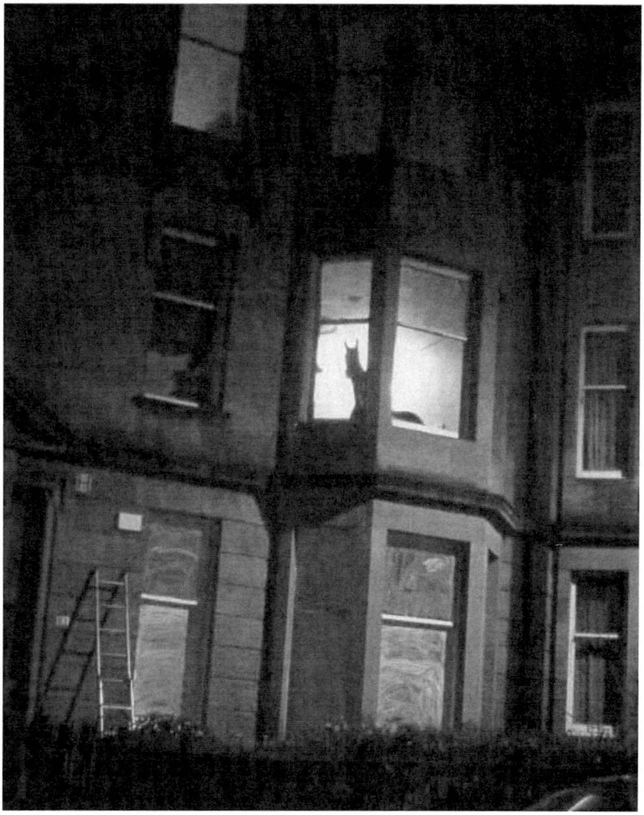

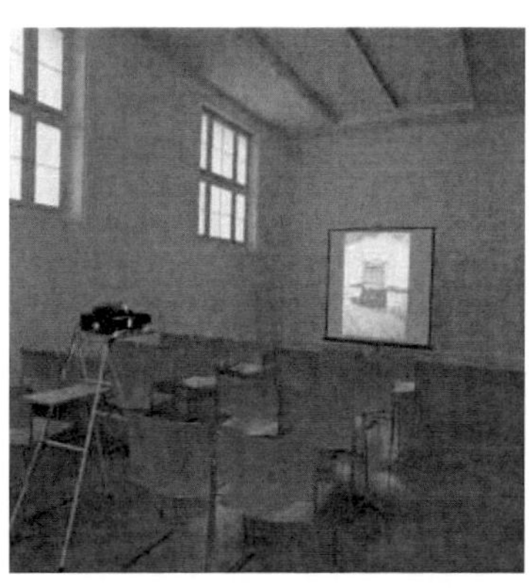

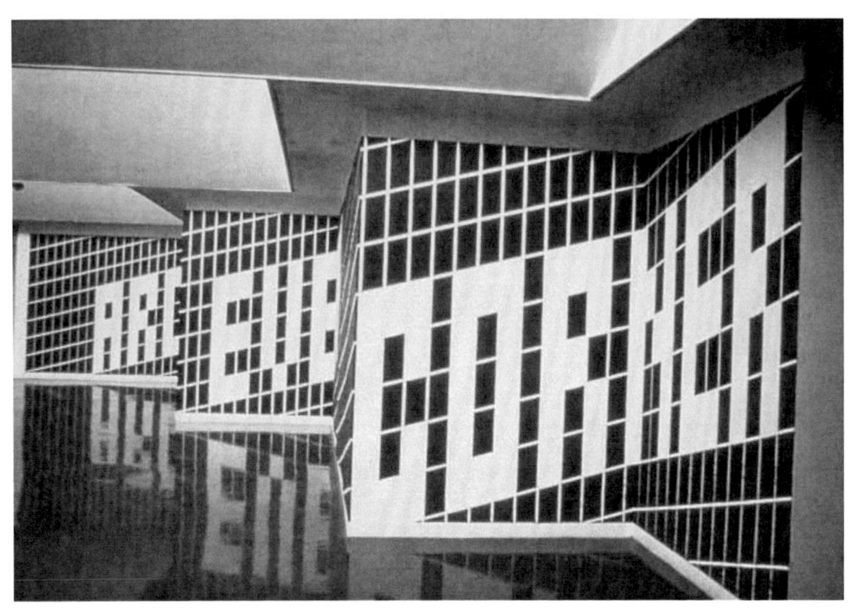


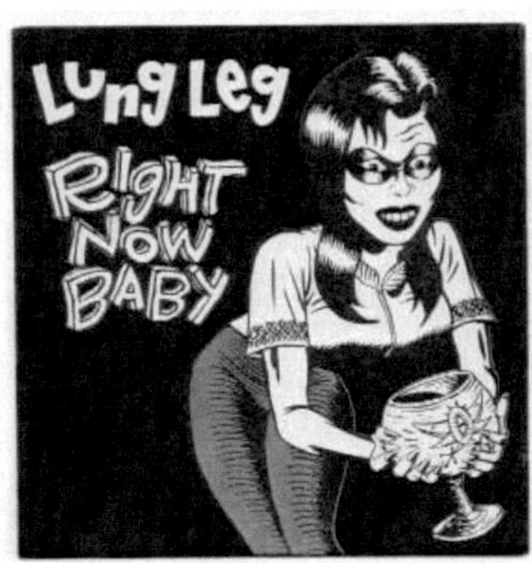


Martin Boyce, *Around Every Corner*, installation at the Loggia Gallery, Toronto, 1996.
Marc Baines' sleeve design for *Right Now Baby*, Lungleg, 1997.

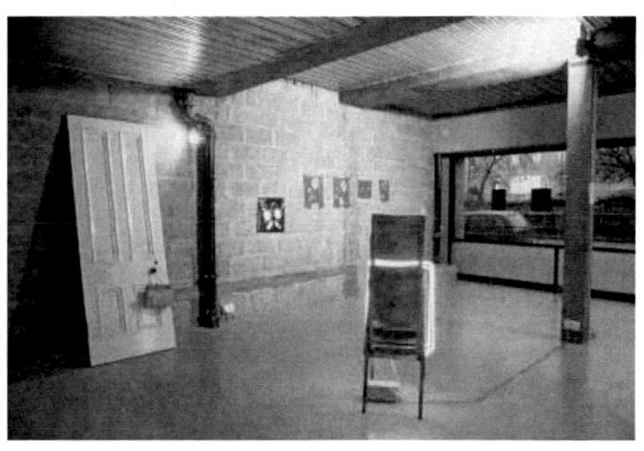

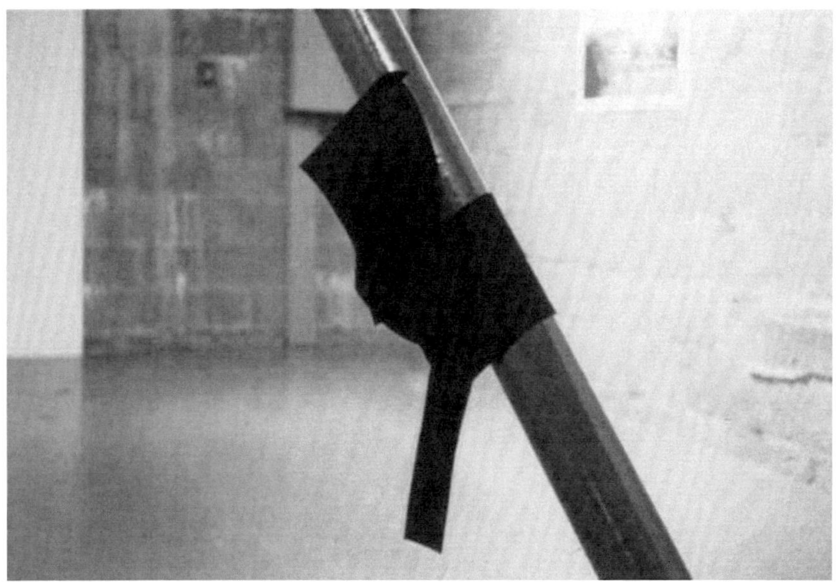

*Fly 3*, installation view of work by (left to right) James Thornhill, Cathy Wilkes and Steve Hollingsworth, Fly, 1997.
*The Social Life of Stuff*, installation detail of *Drop Berry* by Mary Redmond, exhibiting alongside Caroline Kirsop, Janice McNab, Hayley Tompkins, Sue Tompkins and Sarah Tripp, Fly, 1998.

OVERLEAF
Jim Lambie, *18 Carrots*, 1996

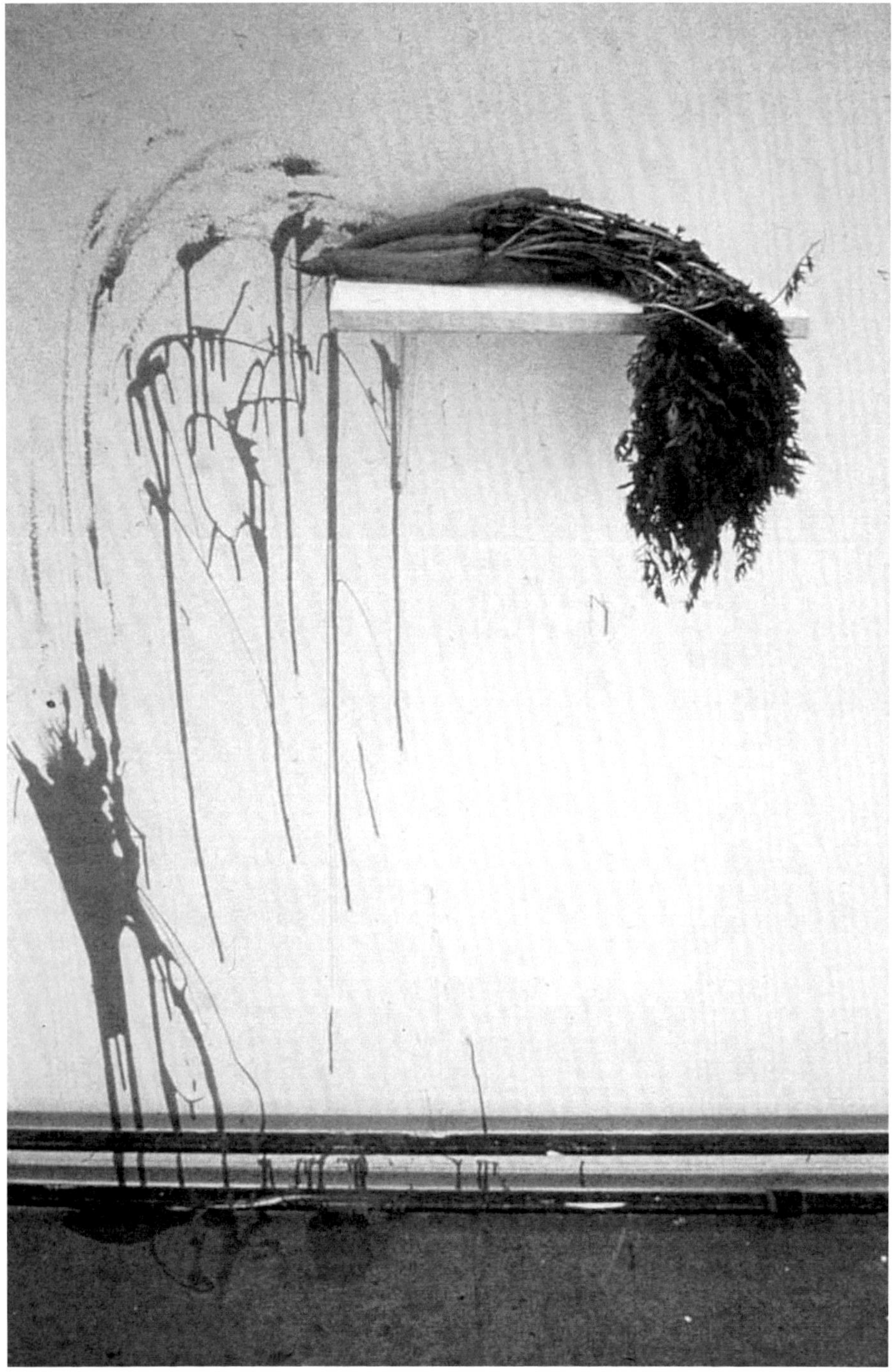

"The suggestion at the Trust meeting, by people like Ken Currie was that places like Tramway did not show painting, and the fact is it does show painting and had shown painting but not of the kind that were commercially saleable locally. Why should you support an artist who can make a fortune in another context and whose work is not seen to be challenging the status quo? I find this argument really frustrating: 'You're only interested in showing conceptual art'. The fact of the matter is that most of the interesting art that has come out of Glasgow, at least since the mid '80s, has been conceptually based. The suggestion that the figurative painters need support is ludicrous – there are hundreds of possibilities for them, and very few for people working in a different field."[32] At the end of the exhibition a weekend of discussions and social events was held, which 100 people attended, drinking cocktails mixed by Jacqueline Donachie and eating food prepared by Rirkrit Tirivanija inbetween lively discussions. During one such discussion Lawrence Weiner announced, "The job of the artist is to fuck up this society."[33]

## A BRACING DIET OF IRONY AND SCEPTICISM

By 1995 the yBa phenomenon was reaching its peak, and the selection for national touring exhibition The British Art Show 4 reflected the apparent explosion of Brit-art. The success of the Windfall generation was roughly concordant with that of the yBas,[34] and The British Art Show 4 featured Glasgow-based artists Christine Borland, Julie Roberts and Douglas Gordon alongside a host of Brit-art stars such as Damien Hirst, Gary Hume, Sam Taylor-Wood and Gillian Wearing. Thomas Lawson was one of the selectors for the exhibition, as was *The Times* art critic Richard Cork, who wrote about the featured artists, "Unencumbered by any thread-bare idealism, and spurning the visionary fervour that gave so many avant-


32  Sam Ainsley, in conversation with the author, May 2001.
33  Lawrence Weiner, from an informal talk by Lawrence Weiner in the Campsie Hills, as part of the Trust weekend, quoted in Charles Esche, "The Experience of Trust", *Kunst & Museum Journal*, Volume Six, Number Five, 1995.
34  Both Douglas Gordon and Dalziel & Scullion showed at the Venice Biennale in 1995, alongside Jake and Dinos Chapman, Sam Taylor-Wood and Tacita Dean in The British Council exhibition General Release.

garde artists a headlong impetus, they thrive instead on a bracing diet of irony and scepticism."[35] However, the three Glasgow-based artists in the exhibition were producing work that differed in certain key respects from the work of their London-based contemporaries. The yBas were already being accused in some quarters of merely recreating works by earlier conceptual artists, without substantially advancing the potential meanings of the earlier work.[36] Amongst several London-based artists there was also a tendency towards "one-liners", such as Hirst's dissected shark, sheep and cow works, which seemed quite different in intention from the complex, investigative nature of Borland's *A Place Where Nothing Has Happened* (1994)[37] or Gordon's *Something between my mouth and your ear* (1994).[38]

Although the three Glasgow-based artists included in the British Art Show 4 worked in very different ways, to a greater or lesser extent they were all concerned with questioning the accuracy of certain types of knowledge: specifically scientific and medical knowledge. In Borland and Gordon's case in particular, their work could also be seen as less readily consumable than that of their London-based contemporaries. Their work required the audience to spend time with it in order to fully absorb potential readings, and it did not always come in a stable or materialised form, for example, Borland's *Shot Apples* (1992) or Gordon's *Instructions works* (1992–).

When Damien Hirst won the Turner Prize that year, beating Mona Hatoum, Mark Wallinger and Edinburgh-based artist Callum Innes, the ascendancy of the yBas seemed complete. Hirst had by now added to the cult of his personality by opening his own London restaurant, Quo Vadis with "bad boy" chef Marco Pierre White. The relentless "lifestyle" coverage

---

35  Richard Cork, "Injury Time", The British Art Show 4, 1995, p32.

36  One often quoted example of this is Georgina Starr's recreation of Bas Jan Ader's seminal 1970 performance piece *I'm Too Sad to Tell You*.

37  Commissioned as part of the Tyne International in Newcastle, England in 1993. Borland selected an abandoned site near the centre of the city used variously as a carpark, a pedestrian short-cut to the main shopping area and a sheltering place for local homeless people, and worked with the local police to search the site for samples of a type that would be used in a criminal investigation. The resultant samples of crushed glass, tyre tread marks and litter were classified and laid out on trestle tables in a portacabin on site.

38  A work, commissioned by Bookworks, London, which involved the creation of a listening environment with blue walls, beanbags and a stereo playing music released between January and September 1966 (the period that Gordon's mother was pregnant with him).

of the yBas coupled with the Blur vs Oasis "controversy"[39] made London the colourful shock centre of British culture (at least as far as the mainstream press was concerned). But although the Glasgow neo-conceptualists were regularly appearing in international group shows with yBa artists, they managed to largely escape the media over-exposure visited upon their London-based contemporaries. Artists working in Manchester also escaped the notice of the mainstream media, and the selectors for the British Art Show 4 – there were no artists from the North-West of England included in the exhibition. In response, Manchester-based artists Nick Crowe and Martin Vincent curated ha!, the first high-profile warehouse show to take place in their home city. The momentum generated from this project continued into The Annual Programme, a "chain" exhibition co-ordinated by Crowe and Vincent which involved ten artists working as host/curators to a variety of projects held in domestic settings. This then led to links being forged with art-led initiatives in other cities, namely Transmission, London's City Racing and the Three Month Gallery in Liverpool, all of which were also intent on devising new strategies for making and showing work.

Storm clouds were gathering over the "swinging" London art scene as 1995 drew to a close, provoked in part by the catalogue for yBa showcase exhibition Brilliant! at the Walker Art Center in Minneapolis. Curator Richard Flood had given a pre-opening spiel to *frieze* in November in which he declared, "This group of artists – again, unlike any other group that I can think of – have an intentionally adversarial relationship with the gallery system."[40] Flood's bold assertion, and the catalogue cover, which featured a photo of a 1992 IRA bombing of London, proved a little hard for critics including Matthew Collings and Jeffrey Kastner to take. As they pointed out, most of the yBas had been taken into the protective embrace of gallery owners Charles Saatchi and Jay Jopling relatively early in their careers. Neville Wakefield's attempt to align the yBas with both the '70s punk scene and the Situationist International in his catalogue essay also did not quite

---

39  This could be interpreted as a somewhat cynical attempt to recreate the 1960s "rivalry" between The Beatles and The Rolling Stones which formed part of the mythology of "Swinging London".
40  *frieze*, November/December 1995, pp32–36.

square with the yBa's choice of patrons: Saatchi, the man who came up with Thatcher's ad campaigns and Jopling, the son of the Conservative MP for Westmoreland and Lonsdale. And in his review of the British Art Show 4 Robert Garnett wrote in *Art Monthly*, "There should be a moratorium on Hirst promotion until he comes up with something new and interesting himself. Like Hirst's, much of the work of the type that emerged at the turn of the century is starting to look a bit thin and tired."[41]

In an article published in *The Guardian* in 1995, Slade tutor Stuart Brisley wrote that contemporary art in London "has a particular energy because we have been moving from the welfare state to the free market. It doesn't suffer from the constraints of state patronage. There is an atmosphere of libertinism and a release from social responsibility."[42] For some London-based artists that release from social responsibility came courtesy of their entree into the gallery circuit and sales to private collectors. But in cities like Newcastle, Manchester, Belfast and Glasgow, artists who didn't meet the criteria of public funders often had no other means of financial support. The free market that Brisley refers to only really positively affected a few Glasgow-based artists who had gallery representation in London, America or Europe. The atmosphere of libertinism that he cites was definitely in the air though, as artists worked collaboratively on low budget self-funded projects. The prevalent attitude of non-compromise was summed up by artist and organiser Cathy Wilkes. "I think that it's really important if you want to do something just to get on with it. I don't think because you are an artist you should feel bad because it's not going to appeal to everyone."[43]

One way in which many Glasgow artists maintained their autonomy was to host shows in their flats. Although previously there had been isolated examples of these kind of shows in Glasgow such as Gianni Piacentini's 1991's Living Room Projec*t*, from 1994 onwards several artists started to show work in more domestic, non-gallery settings. A good example of this new strategy was Notell Hotel (1995) a group show with

41  Robert Garnett, "The British Art Show 4", *Art Monthly*, December 95/January 96, p28.
42  *The Guardian*, October 7th, 1995.
43  Cathy Wilkes, in conversation with the author, August 2001.

work by Graham Fagen,[44] Martin Boyce, James Thornhill, Richard Wright and Hilary Stirling that was held in a room at the Moathouse Hotel. This move to stage shows in spaces that weren't easily accessible to the general public was part of a general "turning in" of the local art community after the events surrounding Trust and the imminent opening of the Gallery of Modern Art. Notell Hotel was staged in association with Tramway – indicating the mood of Director Charles Esche post-Trust.

Jonathan Monk had previously made work in bars and for nightclubs, and in 1994 he invited some friends to make work for another unlikely location: his bathroom. He explained, "'My Little Toilet' was a show of about 35 artists in the bathroom of my flat. I like putting together small exhibitions and I think there are more artists in the city now who are doing that – such as Cathy Wilkes and James Thornhill. You have to make opportunities for yourself and I think that's why artist-run spaces get set up. If no one is offering you shows, you just may never get one unless you do it yourself! But projects like 'My Little Toilet' aren't strategic moves or anything. These things are for friends, because no-one really saw 'My Little Toilet' apart from the opening." Jonathan Monk had produced a series of thirteen video works for the CCA for a show named Almost Enough (1995). The videos featured Monk engaged in various surreal activities including making naked telephone calls and leaving a frozen chicken in the road.

For his September 1995 solo show A Brush With Death at Tramway, Monk sent up the myth of the Abstract Expressionist artist, creating two large scale black, grey and white paintings in the style of Jackson Pollock. Also displayed as part of the show were speakers blaring death metal by Slayer and Napalm Death, and a studio area, littered with empty bottles of Beck's beer and painting ephemera. In the corner there was a video playing which joined the dots between these elements: onscreen Monk was seen painting (dripping and flicking) the paint onto a canvas on the floor, and

44 Graham Fagen had graduated from the Sculpture Department at GSA in the late '80s but had subsequently moved to Kent to undertake Masters studies, and then to Birmingham, where he worked at Birmingham Institute of Art until 1995. In 1995, he returned to Glasgow to live, and began teaching at Duncan of Jordanstone College of Art in Dundee at this time.

drinking beer, as the extreme music played. Monk made a sly link between the mediated destruction that Slayer and Napalm Death scream about, and the mythologisation that surrounded Pollock's demise. Not that Monk was adverse to building his own drunken myths as his performance video works *Pissed (10 Pints)* (1994) and *Yard of Ale (Get Shirty)* (1994) demonstrated. While discussing these works with Douglas Gordon, Monk said, "The way I see it is if it is something that you enjoy, you should do it, why make things difficult. I guess it also has something to do with experimenting. Most people we know drink and maybe take drugs so it's just taking it and making art out of it."[45]

Monk's A Brush With Death also indicated the issues surrounding painting. Although performance-related work had played an important role in the practice of many Glasgow based artists throughout the '80s and '90s, painting had also continued to be an important medium. Towards the end of 1995, Nicola White opened an exhibition of contemporary painting at CCA with the controversial title The Persistence of Painting, which featured the work of Hayley Tompkins, Carol Rhodes, Julie Roberts, Richard Walker, Graeme Todd, Louise Hopkins and Richard Wright. Nicola White says, "Some people hated the title because they thought it suggested that painting was really embattled. The artists in the show were linked in my mind by a kind of modesty – it was the very opposite of the very grandiose gestural painting that you got in the '80s when every symbol and figure was flung at it. The restraint and self-consciousness and even a kind of awkwardness which was employed by nearly all of the artists in the show was really to do with knowledge, about where they were in the history of painting and what had gone before."[46]

45  Jonathan Monk, "Don't Get Shirty (with me)" in conversation with Douglas Gordon, September 1994, Jonathan Monk, Tramway/Frac Des Pays de la Loire, 1994. During their conversation Monk and Gordon identified various works by other artists relating to intoxication, including Andy Warhol, Gilbert & George, Graham Gussin and Jane and Louise Wilson.
46  Nicola White, Ibid.

CHAPTER 7

# SOMETHING LIKE POETRY
## (1995–1996)

"Douglas Gordon and Christine Borland's generation were all growing up around the time of the Miner's Strike, this point of great political change in Britain. There was still a strong awareness of the Labour movement in their work. The younger generation are not unaware of that, but they are less concerned with it; it's less a part of their identity and sense of being connected. The first new wave of artists in the early '90s was very Glasgow-based and they looked to people with similar political consciousness, but as Glasgow emerged more as a scene people have come here for different reasons and with different backgrounds. It's not just that they are younger, but their influences are different and that has seeped into a newer, different kind of work. There is a playful, pop element, but also a tactile element to the work, that has to do with a reinstatement of a concern with material and its poetry, still done in a stripped-down way. The influence of Environmental Art has stayed strong, but the work is now much more gentle and open."[1]

The pop element in much of the work emerging in the city in the mid-'90s could also be read as relating to the wealth of information that was now available, through the internet, computer games and dozens of cable TV channels. The idea of careful research into other discourses fell away as a more intuitive and personal way of working came to the fore. With so much media fantasy readily available, it seemed almost inevitable that

1   Richard Wright, in conversation with the author, September 2001.

203

there would be a hidden or semi-erotic feel to some of the work. Cathy Wilkes[2] encouraged the development of this new style by staging a series of exhibitions in the spare room of her flat in the Dalriada towerblock in Anderston. From 1995, Wilkes Gallery hosted eight shows over a two year period including the first exhibition in Britain by Claude Closky. That year a review in *Flash Art* noted, "Closky catalogues simple signs and obsessions. He's interested in the obvious: things one can have, do or be. He uses magazines, camera, scissors and computer to catalogue the reflections of a seemingly listless, heavily media-saturated surrogate self devoted entirely to daydreams and absurd preoccupations."[3]

'Daydreams and absurd preoccupations' could also be traced in other Wilkes Gallery exhibitions by Jonnie Wilkes and Jim Lambie, Hayley Tompkins, Sue Tompkins, Heather Allen and Victoria Morton. The work of the artists who showed at Wilkes Gallery could be broadly characterised as moving away from the fetishisation of the design object, and into constructing works that circled the history of sculpture, using materials such as old t-shirts, plastic bags and electrical tape. Well-known works by Meret Oppenheim, John Armleder and David Hammons were often 'knowingly' referenced by this contingent of artists. Although Jonnie Wilkes (b.1967), Jim Lambie (b.1964) and another artist associated with this group, Mary Redmond (b.1971) were all recent graduates from the Environmental Art Department, twin sisters Hayley Tompkins and Sue Tompkins (b.1971) and Victoria Morton (b.1971) were graduates of the Painting Department, and worked with drawings and paintings as well making sculptural objects.

The work of Cathy Wilkes and her collaborators had a distinctively feminine style, which often touched upon the domestic, upon fashion, and ideas of personal relationships. Angela Rosenburg, writing recently about Wilkes' work in *Flash Art* said that, "With a logic of her own, scepticism, and minimal means, her sculptures consist of found, throw-away and neglected objects, furniture, from which she produces her own poetic and

---

2   Wilkes had returned to Glasgow after completing her MFA at the University of Ulster in 1992.
3   Jeff Ryan, *Flash Art*, Nov./Dec 1995.

ambiguous narratives ... Cryptic, but with their own impoverished 'povera' – charm oddly timeless, the single pieces assume the characters in a complex narrative of individuals and relationships."[4] The influence of Eva Hesse and Lygia Clark could also be detected in the sculptural works made by several members of the group. The everyday materials they selected were imbued with potential meanings beyond their original purpose, and often bore traces of careful labour: stitching, folding and rubbing. Often in their work the arrangement of objects was also as important as any other factor, with a dialogue opening between a saucer, a skein of gold sequins, a painting. Hayley Tompkins remembers, "The first time I saw Cathy's flat it was almost like a beach – things were perfect. There was something ... 'as it was', as though things were untouched but at the same time there was a precision, a sense of arrangement."[5]

Will Bradley found the relative lightness of the work around Wilkes Gallery a refreshing change. He says, "I remember seeing a piece of Jonnie Wilkes' work called *The Only Features Visible Were a Haze*: it was a torn piece of blue nylon gaffa taped to the wall. It was so close to nothing, so casual, but at the same time completely framed and intentional – almost camp. It's really performative to be so self-consciously devil-may-care. It expressed an idea about the history of culture. He used those conventions in order to discuss them, making a piece of art to talk about art, to talk about the role of art, and what art means."[6] Jonnie Wilkes, like David Shrigley and Jonathan Monk, seemed to enjoy confounding expectations of what art should be about, or where it should belong. Present in all these artists' work was also a kind of physicality, a delight in the particular properties of materials. In both these senses we can also reconnect this work to the tradition of Glasgow-born musician and poet Ivor Cutler, in particular the relish with which Cutler describes a childhood memory of tearing a pair of blue rubber pants: "The rubber smell was new and exciting/my hands sought out the hemless edge. To my delight/the rubber tore, soft and quiet. A deep

4    Angela Rosenburg, *Flash Art*, May/June 2001.
5    Hayley Tompkins, in conversation with the author, October 2000.
6    Will Bradley, in conversation with the author, April 2001.

satisfied peace/entered me."[7]

Jim Lambie, who had shared a flat with members of Primal Scream in the late 1980s, was making work that was increasingly influenced by the iconography and attitude of rock'n'roll. This direction in his work was encouraged by his friendship with various local DJs and musicians, in particular Joe McAlinden, the lead singer of Superstar, who knew Jim Lambie from his stint playing in the BMX Bandits offshoot band The Boy Hairdressers. Their friendship resulted in Lambie designing a series of album covers for the band, featuring his own work, and occasionally that of other artists, such as Hayley Tompkins. Lambie's work often turned on a visual or linguistic gag, as in one-liners like *18 Carrots*: a bunch of carrots dipped in orange paint and displayed on a shelf. The loose and intuitive connections he drew gave the work a realness, and alluded to his record collection, the Barras market, and the conversations that went on in the Variety Bar[8] on a Thursday night. Close Lobsters lead singer Andrew Burnett had once said, "My lyrics are entirely influenced by Page 1 and 2 of Henry Miller's *Tropic of Cancer* and talking to my mum on her days off work",[9] and Lambie's work shared a similar insouciance.

Victoria Morton's highly colourful paintings took cues from dance music, fashion, design and high art, using a variety of mark-making techniques: oils, magic markers and spray were all used to build up her highly textured and evocative works. Her earlier works used earthy, Rothko-esque colours in simple blocks and stripes, but by the mid-1990s Morton's work owed more of a debt to Arshile Gorky, and employed a multi-coloured palette and a huge vocabulary of mark-making techniques to inscribe vague planets, swirls and loops. At this time, Hayley Tompkins was making delicate watercolours that were neither paintings nor drawings. She

---

7    Ivor Cutler, "Blue Rubber Pants", *Glasgow Dreamer*, Methuen and Reed Consumer Books Ltd.,1990.

8    The original Variety Bar was located in Cowcaddens Street until the 1960s, and took its name from the surrounding theatres and music halls.  The art deco signage was augmented with images of a ballet dancer, a Scottish piper and a jester.  In the early 1980s a new Variety Bar opened on Sauchiehall Street, replacing the former Norsk bar, across from the former Beresford Hotel. The 1920s exterior and interior of the earlier bar were replicated in the new premises, although the figures of entertainers were not featured on the new sign. In recent years the bar has been a popular haunt of students from the nearby art school, and hosts popular DJ nights, including a dub reggae night and, until recently, Knucklehead/My Machines DJs Hamish McChlery and Jonnie Wilkes in the Thursday night slot.

9    Andrew Burnett, quoted in *Do It For Fun*, Issue # 2.

remembers, "I started to do things with fingerprints, finger print paintings – I think I was reacting against the meticulous paintings I'd done previously, so they probably looked really primitive – 'she can't be bothered'. But at the same time it was about seeing yourself, but also being a completely open self: my fingerprint looking like everyone else's."[10] Her twin sister, Sue Tompkins often worked with pages torn from magazines, incorporating fragments of text and cuttings into her works on paper. Her free association prose was influenced by the Beats and by allusive references to songs, literature and conversation. For example, she might take Bob Dylan's *One of us Must Know* and filter it through those personal interests. "... keep it coming back piano up piano up keep it up piano I didn't mean it sooner or later do d albums do d albums I really did try to get close to you I couldn't see I couldn't see piano up your mouth romansos de romansos de piano up I couldn't see I couldn't see in my ear in my ear in my ear romansos de agua de agua de boca de agua de boca in the aguain the agua I really did try to get close to you ..."[11]

Eva Rothschild (b.1972) was a Transmission committee member between 1994 and 1996 and her work shared some concerns with this group of artists, particularly in her interest in reworking images and styles associated with the 1960s and '70s. This recent description of Rothschild's work by *frieze* critic Jennifer Higgie could apply equally to many of her Glasgow-based peers: "There's something present that refuses to state its business – perhaps an intimation of the restless, often fickle way our tastes and interests shift with age. That we fling things aside to make way for new things may be how our culture works, but it's not necessarily the best way. Rothschild's recycling, not only of materials but of memories, is like trying to recall, and so to understand, that which we assume we can easily forget. As a result – as with all recycling – the original is woven into the heart of what it has now become, haunting the heart of it."[12]

What the work of these artists has in common is their "dematerialisation of the art object" as described by Lucy R. Lippard. For example, Jim

10  Hayley Tompkins, Ibid.
11  *British Mythic*, No 3, November 1998.
12  Jennifer Higgie, "Paint It Black", *frieze*, November/December 2000, pp78–79.

Lambie's *Ultralow*[13] film, which showed the artist smoking cigarettes in a darkened room, the glowing tips tracing light in the blackness, or Sue and Hayley Tompkins' *Lo Religion* (1998), made from magazine pages stuffed into a gap between a wall and floorboards. Artist Richard Wright also became associated with this group, having studied on the MFA at Glasgow School of Art with Jonnie Wilkes and Victoria Morton between 1993 and 1995. Wright worked collaboratively with Jonnie Wilkes on some early works, and also wrote a review of the Wilkes/Lambie show at Wilkes Gallery for Irish art magazine *Circa*. Jonathan Monk and Jonnie Wilkes had also collaborated on a few projects, such as Monk's *Holiday* paintings, which were first exhibited at Wilkes' club night Simting at Reds on Sauchiehall Street. Monk recalled, "Initially I was asked to make some paintings for a club, a night-club in the city quite close to the gallery. So, I made some paintings of advertisements for holidays; the type of places where people might go for a rave or whatever. Places like Ibiza or the south of Italy. The idea was that the painting represented the idea of the holiday, the idea of an escape – and this could be bought for the same price as the experience itself."[14]

Another characteristic of this scene was the Fluxus-like blurring of the boundary between the exhibitions and the after-parties. Both Heather Allen and Sue Tompkins gave live spoken-word performances at Wilkes Gallery. There was also a spontaneous, private quality to the events that lent them an extra edge. Cathy Wilkes says, "I really wanted to do more shows than I did, but I couldn't because I was funding them myself. I really didn't want to get money from the SAC or anywhere else. So basically I was working in a bar, saving up the money and doing the exhibitions. It made highly bad business sense, because I was saying, 'I'm paying for the invitations', but I had no money. In a way I'm glad I didn't apply for money because I didn't have to tell anybody what was going to happen, or when it was going to happen. If possible I tried to have a live event happening on the opening night that would never happen again. It was so packed, and

13  Exhibited in the basement of Transmission as "the b-side" of the exhibition Voidoid, 1999.
14  Jonathan Monk, "Don't Get Shirty (with me)" in conversation with Douglas Gordon, Jonathan Monk, September 1994, Tramway/Frac Des Pays de la Loire, 1994.

really memorable, but there are no slides or video of it, there are two snaps. It wasn't about getting a good picture of it though, it was about saying you were there. That in itself was quite an old fashioned kind of a cabaret idea – that you could say you were there on the night that this happened."[15]

A parallel could be found between Glasgow's artist-run projects and the independent record labels that were also starting up around the city, such as Douglas McIntyre's Creeping Bent label, which he set up in 1994 "due to complete boredom." In the early 1980s McIntyre had played in the new wave band Article 58 but had subsequently moved into music promotion. He said, "My intention was to create a sustainable platform for groups, artists, mavericks, weirdos...to unleash their bile upon the world. I borrowed some money and launched Creeping Bent with 'A Leap into the Void', a live event at Glasgow's Tramway in December 1994. This was followed by our first record release in April 1995, the 10" *Milkmetal* EP by sonic terrorists, Spacehopper. I feel that one of our greatest achievements to date has been to remain solvent without jumping into bed with a major record or publishing company. We're a totally independent, artist-orientated label, and as such, have had to develop largely without the support of the mainstream press or radio."[16] In 1995, another independent local organisation, the Glasgow Film and Video workshop consolidated its early work by becoming a limited company and moving into permanent premises in Albion Street, just off the Trongate.

Further connections between different art, design and musical organisations in the city were demonstrated by the group show New Rose Hotel, which opened at Transmission in April 1995. The show featured a refreshment area, seating and a soundtrack mixed by Knucklehead DJs Jonnie Wilkes and Hamish McChlery, and work by Allford Hall Monaghan Morris Architects, Victoria Morton, Julian Opie, Linn Electronics, Phillipe Starck, Toby Webster, Andrew Miller, Dene Happell, Steven Harty and hip clothing store Dr. Jives. Will Bradley remembers, "There were a couple of shows that I thought were really terrible, but it's good to have the freedom

15  Cathy Wilkes, in conversation with the author, August 2001.
16  From Creeping Bent's *5 Year Plan*, 2000, www.creepingbent.org.

to fail. We had a couple of blockbusters where we broke the 1000 attendance. With New Rose Hotel we got a bit scared one Saturday because
people kept coming in and coming in and the people that were in wouldn't
go out again."[17] During his committee tenure Toby Webster (b. 1968)
attempted to explain the enduring effective Transmission rationale, saying,
"Transmission does things differently. We can show people who aren't very
well known with people who are. New Rose Hotel included people who are
still at college with artists like Julian Opie. We say that all these things are
valid and worth seeing. Although a person might not be famous, he or she
should still be shown if the work is good. It is a real feeling in Glasgow (and
it is actually quite a big deal) that your work is actually worth something,
and that it is acceptable to leave college and be an artist. I don't mean that
it's financially acceptable, but that as a role in the community it is a viable
option – you can be an artist and show your work."[18]

In July, the exhibition In Stereo opened in the gallery, with work by Jim
Lambie, Robert Montgomery, Mary Redmond and James Thornhill, and
accompanied by a new film work by Heather Allen. Jim Lambie showed a
piece called *Roadie*, made of three deluxe gold amplifier cases, such as rock
bands take on tour. In Stereo was launched by the event *Guitar Amp Action*,
was a "crazy punk rock party" with local alternative rock bands Hello
Skinny, Lungleg,[19] Superstar and Par Cark, a band formed by Richard
Wright, Will Bradley and David Shrigley. Wright says, "Par Cark was a kind
of surreal pop band – we had no real songs, and would improvise around
certain ideas. We played a version of Jonathan Richman's *Roadrunner* and
we had something else called *A Song About Jazz*, which took the piss out of
jazz. It was a call and response number, where Dave would say, 'You come
to me in my sleep' and we would respond, 'Jazz'. He would ask, 'And what
did you say to me?' and we would say, 'Jazz.' And so on."[20]

Late in 1994 local band The Delgados had set up their own independent


17  Will Bradley, in conversation with the author, April 2001.
18  Toby Webster, interviewed in *Flash Art* May/June 1996.
19  Lungleg were one of several Glasgow based bands, including Cylinder, The Yummy Fur and Ganger who released records on
    Vesuvius, a Glasgow-based independent label established by Marc Baines, Pat Crook and Brian McDougall in 1993. Vesuvius
    also released recordings by Jad Fair, Sally Skull and The Makeup before folding in 1998.
20  Richard Wright, in conversation with the author, February 2003.

label, Chemikal Underground, from their kitchen table. The first release on the label was The Delgados' *Monica Webster/Brand New Car*, which was released in February 1995 and was acclaimed some six months later as *Melody Maker* Single of the Week. Chemikal Underground's next two releases were by Glasgow disco/guitar outfit Bis and were *Disco Nation 45* and *The Secret Vampire Soundtrack* EP, featuring the irritatingly infectious *Kandypop*. Brothers Sci-Fi Steven and John Disco and school friend Manda-Rin made history when they were invited to appear on Top of the Pops, the first "unsigned" act to ever appear on the show with a song which hadn't yet been released. *Kandypop* went on to hit number 25 in the UK singles chart and created massive media interest around the teenage band, with keyboard player and singer Manda-Rin's high pitched shouty vocals singled out for particular attention. Music journalist John Williamson, who had worked with Craig Tannock on setting up The Apollo and the 13th Note, was also managing the young band. He remembers, "From no-one being interested in the band, suddenly lots of people were interested. The Bis situation was quite unique because quite a lot happened so quickly. The first time I went to America with Bis all the record companies were trying to sign them. It was funny – they were 16 or 18 and limos were being sent to take them to fancy hotels. You knew next time they would be touring in a clapped-out transit van."[21]

Sci-Fi Steven from Bis also moonlighted as a drummer for another Glasgow band, Ganger, who modelled their sound on German bands like Can, Kraftwerk and Neu. Ganger's distinctive sound came partly from the inclusion of two bass guitarists, Stuart Henderson and Graham Gavin and two drummers, Sci-Fi Steven and James Young. On keyboard, guitar and clarinet was young artist Lucy McKenzie, who had written a series of articles for local magazine *Harpies & Quines* and was also well-known for her rubber stage outfits. She remembers, "I started playing music when I was about 14, things just came together at the right time. I read in the newspapers about this thing called riot grrrl and I just liked the music – it was saying to me just do it, just go and do it. I met people from local bands like Lungleg and the Yummy Fur, and then later joined Ganger. The most important thing was the confidence it gave me."[22] As with the big Northern English bands of the late 1980s, John Peel had already picked up on the post-rock scene in Glasgow and was giving regular airplay to new bands like Ganger and the Delgados. Another Glasgow band racking up media accolades in 1995 was Teenage Fanclub, who had just released their fourth album *Grand Prix*. After a bit of a fall from grace with their subdued third album, *Thirteen*, their latest album was described as "a creative zenith, a gloriously sullen record buoyed by the group's distinctive three-part harmonies. The 13 songs – any of which would have made a great hit single – are a recording milestone of their label, Creation."[23]

In September, Dave Shrigley was offered his first Transmission solo show, Map of the Sewer, and exhibited a series of plasticine sculptural works, photographs of his public interventions and a selection of his esoteric and hilarious books. The gallery said, "Shrigley's unique sculpture, drawings, cartoons and public works are very, very funny. Absurd, satirical, full of random acts of violence and a fascination with the soiled and disfigured, they document a breakdown at the margins of culture as we know it."[24] Shrigley's work was also gaining fans outside the city, and in December he made the front cover of *frieze*. The *frieze* critic Michael Bracewell wrote, "With the acuity of a moral philosopher, Shrigley externalises the doubts and fears of the human condition in comic scenes and objects, the sincerity of which is reinforced by the seemingly painful amateurism of their author's style. Unlike the professionalism and apparent erudition of much contemporary art, Shrigley's dominant aesthetic is the crude vernacular of graffiti, doggerel, doodles and vandalism. The humour in his work conceals a vision of humanity which is derived from religious allegory and the deep absurdities which accompany notions of moral edification and social conditioning."[25]

Shrigley's interest in absurdity was shared by several other Glasgow-

22  Lucy McKenzie, in conversation with the author, October 2000.
23  Buhan Wazir, "Long to rain over us", *The Observer Review*, 17 September 2000.
24  Transmission press release, September 1995.
25  Michael Bracewell, "Jesus Doesn't Want Me for a Sunbeam", *frieze*, Nov/Dec 1995, pp50–51.

based artists, such as Alan Currall (b.1964) who graduated from the MFA in 1995, where he had refined his tragi-comic video works with titles like *Lying About Myself in Order to Appear More Interesting*. His work often humourously explored how systems designed to help us navigate modern life can be alienating. Currall, who is originally from Stoke on Trent, created his own informal systems based on advice from friends and family, or on ludicrous exchanges. In *Wordprocessing* (1995) he instructed a microchip, that was sitting on a desk, immobile and silent like a tiny black beetle. "Right then", Currall began, "Now, what I want you to do is: every time I press down on the keyboard, on one of the letters on the keyboard, I want you to put that letter up on the screen in front of me. OK? Now, every time I press down on one of the numbers on the keyboard I want you to do the same with that …"

Thomas Lawson continued to be an important influence on the Glasgow art scene throughout the 1990s, not least through the conferences he had at Cal Arts with exchange students Ross Sinclair, Dave Allen, Richard Wright and Martin Boyce. Lawson's politically engaged practice, insider knowledge of the New York and LA art scenes, and insightful critical writing made him a kind of mentor for several Glasgow-based artists. Ross Sinclair in particular was deeply affected by Lawson's ideas, explaining, "Tom gave me a couple of old issues [of *Real Life*] in the early 1990s. One night in Edinburgh I told Tom that I was thinking of getting a 'Real Life' tattoo put on my back, and he said that if he could use it on the cover of the magazine, they would pay for having it done. So that's what we did. It featured on the very last issue [*Real Life* Issue 23, 1994], along with an essay I had written about Glasgow. In a sense I like to think that I took hold of the baton. As the magazine rolled to its natural conclusion, it kind of jumped onto my back and I ran with it."[26]

Port cities tend to have numerous tattooists, and Glasgow is no exception. In fact, one of the city's longest established tattoo parlours, Terry's Tattoos, was located next door to the first Transmission space in Chisholm Street. Because tattoos exist only as long as the mortal body of

---

26 Nancy Hynes, *Real is a Four Letter Word*, Untitled, summer,1999.

the carrier, the medium had an attractive quality for some Glasgow-based neo-conceptual artists, notably Douglas Gordon and Ross Sinclair. Gordon made a number of tattoo works in the nineties, both on his own body and on the bodies of others. In 1994, he had the top of his arm tattooed with the words "trust me" – which can be read both as an open request and as something more sinister. His *Tattoo for Reflection* (1997), inscribed on his shoulder blade, says "guilty" in mirror writing. The mirror and the mark of evil are constant figures in Gordon's work, and re-emerge in numerous ways. The permanent tattoo to some extent thwarts the attempt to maintain a fluid identity, but it is also only readable through a mirror (a doorway, the other side of the coin). Sinclair's *REAL LIFE* tattoo throws up some of the same issues, namely relating to how the phrase is read. Artists are often accused of not living in the real world, of being interested in ideas that are unconnected to everyday actualities. In this sense, tattoos can be also be understood as being connected to the idea of otherness.

"Two reactions seem possible in persons who see a tattoo on someone. One is complete fascination, a feeling that here is the ultimate stud, the great macho, the sexual satyr, the Marlboro man, the far-travelling sailor, the incomparable sadistic master, the Genet prisoner just released from prison. The other is complete revulsion: the tattoo represents the epitome of sleaze, of low-class background, of cheap vulgarity and bad taste, everything that intelligence and sophistication have conditioned you to despise."[27]

For Sinclair, other works revolving around his tattooed phrase followed, including *Studio Real Life* (1995) and *Real Life Rocky Mountain* (1996). For *Studio Real Life*, Sinclair wrote and played songs, made videos, painted a slogan on a t-shirt every day; a continuous performance that engaged with the idea of culture and how it is represented, but also with the idea of "real life" pleasures like playing rock 'n' roll and drinking beer. "Coinciding nicely

---

27  Samuel M. Steward, *Bad Boys and Tough Tattoos: A Social History of the Tattoo With Gangs, Sailors and Street-Corner Punks 1950–1965*, reprinted Harrington Park Press, New York, 2001.

with the *Braveheart*[28] sweep at the Academy Awards, *Real Life Rocky Mountain* is a meditation on Scottish identity that acknowledges the enduring impact of popular legend and historical consciousness. If the idyllic setting mimics the Hollywood version, Sinclair positions himself – a real Scot of the '90s – against the whole of the tourist-seeking stereotype that literally surrounds him",[29] wrote London-based critic Melissa Feldman in the pages of *Art Monthly*.

Ross Sinclair and Dave Allen collaborated on several performance related video works in the mid 1990s, exhibited as part of Studio Real Life (1995), while Jonathan Monk, Dave Allen and Douglas Gordon made collaborative video works called *Stooges Burn-out* and *Dance Practice* (both 1996). Sinclair's experience of drumming for The Soup Dragons and the local scene that centred around live music venues like the 13th Note and Nice 'n' Sleazy's[30] may have influenced these works, although Dan Graham's *Rock My Religion*[31] was another obvious reference point. Dave Allen's work during this time was still concerned with musical performance, often transcribing popular songs into handwritten scores in works such as *Stairway to Heaven/Highway to Hell* (1997). Another example of Allen's personal re-interpretatation of modernist and rock'n'roll music would be his rewriting of Debussy's seminal composition *Interpretation of Prelude to an Afternoon of a Faun* for simple one-handed piano. Allen's reinterpretation of "classic" musical pieces played with the idea of the burden of history, and also with his own amateurish-ness. A more recent exhibition at The Showroom, London consisted of a recording of silence made in the Berlin

---

28  *Braveheart* (1995), was a somewhat overblown and historically inaccurate feature film, directed by and starring Australian actor Mel Gibson as 13th century Scottish hero figure William Wallace. If Braveheart had reinforced the "tourist-seeking stereotype" that many Scots failed to identify with, two other films released during 1995 could be said to do the reverse: *Trainspotting*, the film adaptation of Irvine Welsh's cult novel and *Small Faces*, Gillies and Bill MacKinnon's coming of age drama set in Easterhouse in the late 1960s. *Small Faces* brilliantly depicted the city's dancehalls and razor gangs, which the tourist board had been trying, with varying degrees of success, to erase from public memory. *Trainspotting*, which was set in Edinburgh but largely filmed in Glasgow, showcased an array of good-looking young Scottish actors, including Ewan McGregor, Ewan Bremner, Robert Carlyle, Kevin McKidd and Kelly McDonald and was a world-wide smash. However, the film was also derided by several pundits for allegedly glamourising heroin addiction.

29  Melissa Feldman, Ross Sinclair, *Art Monthly*, June 1996, pp196–7.

30  Nice 'n' Sleazy's in Sauchiehall Street was just a few doors down from the Variety Bar, and hosted regular gigs in the dark and smoky basement space.  In the retro-styled upstairs bar the jukebox was full of recordings by local bands besides those of Stateside bands like Nirvana and The Beastie Boys.

31  Both Graham's video work, *Rock My Religion* (1982–4) and his book, *Rock My Religion: Writing & Art Projects* 1965–1990, The Mit Press, Cambridge, MA, 1993.

recording studio where David Bowie had recorded his seminal album, *Low*.

While Sinclair, Monk, Gordon and Allen tapped into the more "masculine" side of performance, Jacqueline Donachie's work could be seen to reflect on the nostalgic and emotive properties of music. This was partly because recorded music provided a backdrop for Donachie's storytelling, and partly because of the kind of music Donachie used: more often Country and Western than the rock'n'roll favoured by her contemporaries. Donachie explained her attraction to this genre as stemming from Glasgow's numerous Elvis Presley fan clubs and country and western dancing clubs, like the Grand Ol' Opry. She said, "I read Tammy Wynette's autobiography *Stand By Your Man*, and you know, she was married with three kids by the time she was about twenty, before she ever did anything musically. Loretta Lynn's the same. They literally sang their way out of the miserable futures they had ahead of them. That's what I like about them the most, I think. All these women are tough as fuck; there's no messing with them. [ … ]And I like that their music is like storytelling."[32] Part Edit (Tramway, 1994) had drawn upon the emotive properties of popular songs, while for *Bar and Lounge* (1996) Donachie hired a singer to perform country and western torch songs such as *Crazy* and *I Fall to Pieces* in a gallery setting. In Donachie's work too, the presence of alcohol provided a social lubricant: for *Advice Bar* (1997) people seeking her advice were given free gin and cigarettes in return.

However, there is another aspect to Country and Western music, aside from the emphasis on drowning your sorrows and bad luck in love, that makes it particularly resonant in Glasgow. It is the idea of the miraculous. The idea of redemption is strong in the work of several Glasgow based artists, perhaps most notably Douglas Gordon, Roderick Buchanan and Jacqueline Donachie. In country and western music it is often the path of the God-fearing man that leads to redemption, as this excerpt from the biography of Dolly Parton's sister, Willadeene suggests: "Randy was healed at church. Mother wasn't there that night, he came running into the house and cried, 'Mama, I got healed!' She asked, 'How do you know, Randy?' He

32  Jacqueline Donachie, in *Sawn Off*, Enkehuset, Stockholm, 1996.

said, 'It felt like fire going through my chest when they prayed for me.' 'What kind of fire?' Randy announced, 'A warm fire, Mama.' Later when the doctor examined Randy he confirmed that the valve was repaired, just like he'd had open-heart surgery. Yes, we believe …"[33]

## RESISTING THE SYSTEM

In November 1995 an exchange show took place at artist-run space Free Parking in Canada by five artists from Transmission, featuring the work of Alan Currall, Martin Boyce, Sue Tompkins and James Thornhill, plus photography graduate Tanya Leighton. The show featured a range of media and styles, from Boyce's silkscreen poster describing a drive-by shooting in a supermarket carpark to Tompkins' *Breathless Gear* installation made from sheets of silver foil and deflating balloons. Exchanges like this continued to build the sense that the projects supported by Transmission had appeal not only amongst a certain audience in Glasgow, but across the UK, Europe and America. Richard Wright wrote in the exhibition catalogue, "I recall Lyotard going on about the fighting for the incommunicable as a strategy for resisting the system. Which can only process information and knowledge of a very limited type. It's a kind of refusal of conventional reality, but there is a way of doing it (a subterfuge); it is called something like poetry but not that word: how about useless."[34]

Transmission continued to provide an inspiring model to other artist-run organisations, such as Catalyst in Belfast (est. 1993) and Generator in Dundee (est. 1996).[35] Generator followed the same mould as Transmission, in that it was run by a voluntary committee of artists which changed at regular intervals. The gallery was set up by a group of Duncan of Jordanstone graduates "who got together in response to the lack of opportunities for young, unestablished artists to work, exhibit and meet together in the

33 Willadeene Parton, *Smokey Mountain Memories*, Rutledge Hill Press, 1996.
34 Richard Wright, in *Forget Brown Spot Save the World* catalogue, Transmission, Glasgow/Free Parking, Canada, 1996.
35 Aberdeen's artist-run gallery Limousine Bull was established two years later, in 1998.

city."[36] In addition to providing a missing link in Dundee's art venue infrastructure, Generator became another organisation that worked collaboratively with Transmission, frequently hosting exhibitions of work by young Glasgow artists associated with the gallery. Other artist-run spaces also opened in the more immediate environs of Transmission throughout the 1990s, including The Glasgow Project Room (est. 1995) in Osbourne Street, a space within the Independent Studios complex where local artists could hold exhibitions. The Osbourne Street venue was run by a voluntary committee of five, who oversaw studio provision for 30 artists and a variety of solo and group exhibitions in the gallery space. Each exhibition was usually open for one week only, making for a busy schedule, but one which was programmed no more than three months in advance. This rapid turn around of shows meant that the Project Room was even more accessible than Transmission, and it quickly became a popular venue for young artists. Another change in the Trongate art spaces was that Malcolm Dickson became director of Streetlevel photoworks in King Street in September 1995, while still maintaining his interest in the New Visions video festival and various other organisations he had instigated and supported.

Early in 1996, MFA graduate Leigh French and ex-Transmission treasurer Billy Clark had decided to resurrect Malcolm Dickson's dormant magazine, *Variant* which made a comeback as a black and white tabloid-sized newspaper later that year. Continuing in the spirit of the earlier publication, the new *Variant* attempted to challenge what Leigh French described as "the benign culture of entertainment. This imagined utopia, this Disneyland without the rides, is a product of the repressive prioritisation of public funds which has become social Darwinism run mad."[37] *Variant* continued to question to what extent the Scottish Art's Council could be considered to be "at arm's length" from the directives of the Scottish Executive. Discussion of locally engaged issues identified the magazine as Scottish, although both editors also made deliberate efforts to connect with international cultural and political debates. Billy Clark says,

---

36 Generator information leaflet, summer 2001.
37 "Glasgow Goes Conceptual", *Newsweek*, Oct. 1997.

"My position is that we are Scottish but we're as good as anyone else. Language is an expression of consciousness – if you're not allowed to talk in your own language there's certain things you can't talk about. That's at the heart of the antipathy towards *Variant*. The nascent, indigenous things are the culture: they [cultural funders] think they're not, that culture is something you ship in."[38]

In February 1996 21 Days of Darkness, a group show with Douglas Gordon, Christine Borland, Simon Periton, Art Club 2000 and photographers Weegee and Lee Miller opened at Transmission. Melissa E. Feldman wrote in *Art Monthly*, "The five curators painted the gallery black 'like we painted our bedrooms when we were 15', and this teenage sense of radicalism lingers like incense. Occasionally, their collaborative quest for the freakish turns wayward, as in such selections as Art Club 2000's photograph of themselves posing in '70s 'Goth' style complete with Kiss hair-dos, foul attitude and perched crows, or Neil Miller's *Winterland 1* featuring a naively modelled, giant head of a creature resembling ET sitting in a snow drift of salt and intoning 'come with me' through mini speakers. The show's genuine inventiveness and art-world sophistication, however, greatly outweigh such youthful indiscretions."[39]

Although Douglas Gordon was still showing at Transmission and closely involved in other local arts initiatives, his international reputation had now grown to such an extent that he received a nomination for the 1996 Turner Prize.[40] Gordon's international standing had been consolidated in the mid-'90s by a series of powerful text works like *From God to Nothing* (1996) and *30 Seconds Text* (1996) and works using appropriated film footage such as *5 Year Drive-By* (1995) and *Confessions of A Justified Sinner* (1995/6). However, he had continued to suffer from numerous accusations of charlatanism from various members of the Scottish media over the years. After Gordon was nominated for the Turner Prize, BBC Scotland commissioned a documentary, *Douglas Gordon: 24 Hour Psycho* to "get to the bottom" of his work. Douglas' *Instruction* and *Letter* works were held up as

---

38  Billy Clark, in conversation with the author, June 2002.
39  Melissa E. Feldman, "21 Days of Darkness", *Art Monthly*, April 1996, pp38–40.
40  The other nominees were Craigie Horsfield, Gary Hume and Simon Patterson.

examples of his perplexing approach to making art. In the documentary, Gordon is painted as an enigmatic and elusive figure who is constantly on the move and who never returns phone calls or keeps arrangements with the hapless BBC interviewer. On the occasions when the interviewer is able to catch up with Gordon, he repeatedly asks him to offer an explanation of what his work means. Finally Gordon responds, "If I wanted to say one single thing that everyone could understand I'd probably be a church minister or a politician – I'd be a newscaster. I'm an artist and ambiguity is what it's all about as far as I'm concerned."[41]

At Tramway, Charles Esche was curating a series of new exhibitions, the first of which was Sugar Hiccup with Elisabeth Ballet, Sam Samore and Richard Wright. Samore's photographs, and Wright's site-specific wall paintings co-existed with Elizabeth Ballet's sculptural forms and floor covering of salt, which gradually took on the footprints of visitors. Pavel Buchler wrote that, "Salt becomes snow not by visual analogy but by an imaginary spatial and temporal shift of perspective. This also makes it possible for us to recover in our experience of the work's here and now a sense of that which we 'had not seen for such a long time' and which, in those rare moments when the wandering metaphor stumbles upon the determination of precise form, can be suddenly glanced as if for the first time right under our feet."[42] In his introduction to the catalogue Charles Esche commented that "Tramway is a space to think and respond rather than passively consume."

As the opening of Glasgow's new Gallery of Modern Art (GoMA) approached, the controversy that had been growing ever since Director Julian Spalding's "populist" collecting procedure had become known began to peak. Spalding had decided against including any work by the Glaswegian neo-conceptual artists in his collection, although in the same year that the gallery opened, news came that Douglas Gordon had won the Turner Prize. As Robert Johnston later wrote, "GoMA … was a pathetic, embarrassing joke at the expense of one of the most vibrant art scenes in

41  *Ex-S*, BBC Scotland, 1996.
42  Pavel Buchler, Sugar Hiccup, Tramway, 1996.

Europe."[43] Barry Barker, then a director at London's Lisson Gallery commented, "Douglas Gordon has an international reputation based upon the quality of his work. Unfortunately, many galleries, including the new Gallery of Modern Art, have not picked up on the vitality of the Glasgow art scene at the moment."[44]

In his introduction to the text, *The Gallery of Modern Art: The First Few Years*, Julian Spalding wrote, "Glasgow's collections contain a great deal of traditional art, particularly painting, which has developed strongly in Scotland over the last few years simply because it can still say more than modern media, and will, I believe, have more to say in the future. The idea that a painting may have something to say has become unfashionable, odd though this may seem to anyone outside the art world. If you ask anyone what a work of art is about, you are likely to be thought naive. Art, it is often asserted, is not about anything; it just is. [ ... ] Art that is about something still has to be art, otherwise, it would remain just a statement, an instruction or a direction, something that you might just as well think, and that there is no need to paint. Statements are not art because they lack feeling."[45]

Nicola White says, "So much money was spent on the refurbishment, and the collection that had nothing to do with the international things that were going on. Julian [Spalding] especially, as this sort of patriarchal figure who lived in Edinburgh, had very little respect for anyone in Glasgow. The whole ethos of the museum was art that ordinary people could enjoy is art that you don't need to think about. It just reeked of such paternalism, it was horrible."[46]

On the night of the opening in March 1996, The Society for the Termination of Art, led by the artist and Glasgow School of Art lecturer Ross Birrell (b.1969), demonstrated outside the gallery with the hope of "levitating the Glasgow Gallery of Modern Art", Birrell remembers, "A group of us all met up at Nice'n'Sleazy's, to read out various manifestos and

---

43  Robert Johnston, "Don't Mention the Book", unpublished essay on Transmission, 1998.
44  Lisson gallery press release, 1996.
45  Julian Spalding, *Gallery of Modern Art Glasgow: The First Years*, Scala Books, London 1996.
46  Nicola White, in conversation with the author, November 2002.

writings on performance art. We got really tanked up and then got down to the Gallery of Modern Art a bit later than planned. We had this idea that the Gallery of Modern Art was on a Presbyterian leyline – you need five points on a trajectory to make a leyline and we'd plotted a leyline that stretched from the statue of John Knox at the Necropolis, to the cathedral, the city chambers, GoMA and then on to Ibrox [Rangers'] stadium. We decided to realign the energy of the Gallery of Modern Art by standing in a triangle formation outside and raising our hands towards the building while making a symbol of a triangle. Several of the people who turned up, including some journalists, pointed out that our attempt had failed – to which we replied that we had managed to lift the building, and the force of it coming back down to earth had caused the terrible mess which could be seen inside."[47]

Charles Esche was not surprised by the approach taken by Julian Spalding, given his own experiences at Tramway. He said, "The idea that you can't create a puzzle, a way of discovering something by thinking it through – that meaning has got to be made instantly available … it was something we just couldn't get past. It just went round and round in circles. When Douglas Gordon won the Turner prize I remember going into the office and saying, isn't it brilliant, our boy won the Turner Prize, and they just looked at me blankly and said, oh yeah, we read it somewhere. At this point they'd pushed Katrina out so it was just me and Nathan left, wondering what we were still doing there. I had endless discussions with people about whether I should leave or not for about a year before I did, because it was getting increasingly difficult."[48]

Typical amongst the media reaction to GoMA was that of *The Guardian*'s Adrian Searle, who wrote that the new gallery was: "A travesty, a mockery, quite the worst arranged collection of dire purchases that I have ever seen."[49] The collection included works by Scottish artists John Bellany, John Byrne, Ken Currie and Peter Howson plus works by Andy Goldsworthy, Beryl Cook and Bridget Riley. Spalding defended his collection by drawing


47  Ross Birrell, in conversation with the author, August 2002.
48  Charles Esche, in conversation with the author, July 2001.
49  *The Guardian*, March 1996.

attention to the visitor numbers at the end of GoMA's first year. The gallery had exceeded its target visitor numbers of 300,000 by 100%, leading many to defend the collection as being truly populist. However, with no comparable display of conceptual works in the city, the collection in GoMA could not really be described as the preferred art of the people.

Charles Esche says, "All GoMA did was make flesh an argument that existed anyway. In a way it dissipated the argument because there was somewhere that represented what I think is pretty poor work and there was a home for it. Ken Currie did have his paintings on show in Glasgow [ … ] but then what became annoying for him was that it wasn't taken seriously. People were very critical of the Gallery of Modern Art."[50] Douglas Gordon reacted with disappointment at the wasted opportunity he felt was represented by the new gallery. He said of Julian Spalding, "I think it's a supreme arrogance for anybody to set themselves up as a spokesman for the intellectual capability of a city."[51] One of the most damaging effects of the ongoing argument between the city's young artists and the council was that many of those artists increasingly chose to expend their future energies elsewhere, by concentrating on shows and projects abroad, where their works had been well-received for some years.[52]


## THAT'S ENTERTAINMENT

In March, a group show of paintings and photographs by all-male artist collective Filthy Swan took place at Transmission. With Love Filthy Swan featured the work of Glasgow School of Art graduates Toby Paterson, Gary Rough, Robert Johnston, Douglas Payne, Scott Waugh and Iain Dickinson. The group's working methods included painting (Paterson, Waugh and Dickinson), photography and sculpture (Johnston, Payne and Rough), and their works could be broadly described as being nostalgic, optimistic or romantic in tone, such as a photograph by Johnston which showed a

50  Charles Esche, Ibid.
51  *Transcript*, Vol. 03, Issue 03, School of Fine Art, Duncan of Jordanstone, Dundee, 2001.
52  By 1996 several artists had also left the city – including Craig Richardson who relocated to London, and Dave Allen and Jonathan Monk, who both moved to Berlin.

suburban bungalow with the number 1977 on the wrought iron gate. Paterson's early paintings were bright, precise depictions of grain elevators, while Rough often worked in a variety of forms, such as his t-shirt printed with the words, "If only I could tell you". Toby Paterson says, "Filthy Swan was a group of friends who thought they had a few ideas about how to do things when they were at art school. They were half right …" After the group's exhibition at Transmission, Toby Paterson was invited to join the gallery's committee.

An exhibition of all-female artists, Grapefruit in the World of Park, curated by Cathy Wilkes, followed the Filthy Swan show. Wilkes remembers, "Kirsty Ogg asked me to curate an all female show because they hadn't had one for a while. I had this idea about role models, of a show with quite well-known artists. The friends that I was working with were girls and women who weren't that well-known, and I liked the idea of bringing work to Glasgow by women with established careers."[53] Wilkes selected works by Judith Dean and Tracey Emin from London, and Mary Heillmann and Yoko Ono from New York – Ono's *A Cross to Hammer a Nail Into* was recreated under instruction for the exhibition. Kirsty Ogg (b.1967) was keen to promote female artists at the gallery, which made for a particularly supportive atmosphere at this time. Hayley Tompkins recalls, "I remember Heather Allen doing a performance in the Transmission basement in 1996 or 1997. It was the first time that I'd seen a woman leading the whole room like that – she read out a Virginia Woolf short story, 'A Room of One's Own' and there was a projection of Paul Weller and then she played *That's Entertainment* really loud afterwards. It really threw up the idea of people being at an opening and talking about everything except personal things. The piece of writing was really 'guts' and it slightly embarrassed the whole crowd – it turned the tone of the night. People weren't sobbing but it was emotional and brave and exciting."[54]

During late 1996, Cathy Wilkes, Hayley Tompkins, Sue Tompkins, Victoria Morton and Sarah Tripp began discussing forming an all-female

53 Cathy Wilkes, in conversation with the author, August 2001.
54 Hayley Tompkins, in conversation with the author, October 2000.

artist's group. Early in 1997, Elizabeth Go exhibited together for the first time. The collective "came about through common interests", explains Hayley Tompkins. "We were each into what the other ones were doing. We saw things in each other's work that we thought could enhance more when we worked together. It was also a response, although not a strong reaction, to what was going on with male artists."[55] The group would produce mixed media and sculptural works, spoken word/musical performances and Super 8 films. Cathy Wilkes says, "Elizabeth Go has been really confidence-building for all of us. We always have a good time and don't worry. We're not anxious. Everybody has said that they do things they just wouldn't do if they were by themselves. The music and the film were the two things that we felt wouldn't be taken apart, no one person had to be performing the same role all the way through, you could change from editor to camera person or from lyricist to singer and no-one needed to know."[56]

The possibilities of cross-disciplinary practice were reinforced for several Glasgow-based artists when Californian artist Raymond Pettibon, well-known outside of art circles for his sleeve design for Sonic Youth's *Goo*, showed a selection of his graphic ink drawings in April at Tramway. Pettibon had influenced a number of younger Glasgow-based artists, particularly those with an interest in the iconography of record sleeves and comic book art. Glasgow had numerous comic book stores including Futureshock, Forbidden Planet and A-1 Comics, and also a number of talented young artists whose work linked with the comic book tradition. Marc Baines, who set up local independent record label Vesuvius with Pat Crook and Brian McDougall in 1993, was one of the the best known and most talented of the local graphic artists. In addition to publishing his own imprint Beechnut comic books, he also designed the record sleeves of several Vesuvius releases including the *In Spelunca* compilation and Lungleg single *Maid to Minx*, and created memorable sleeves for Pete Shelley's Smells Like … Records label. There were also many other interesting graphic artists active on the local scene, including Glasgow School of Art

55  Hayley Tompkins, Ibid.
56  Cathy Wilkes, in conversation with the author, August 2001.

graduate Lorna Miller, best known for her *Witch* series, *Strange Weather Lately* authors Metaphrog, *Honeypears* author Heather Middleton and *Dead Trees* creators Graham Johnstone and Kevin Hobbs.

In May, Art for People, the first open submission show of gallery members' work took place at Transmission. As curator Rob Tufnell relates in his essay, "Recent History of Artist's Initiatives in Scotland", "An important inclusion to the gallery's programme has been the open Members Show which was started in 1996 with Art for People. This first open was made in response to Glasgow City Council's Gallery of Modern Art which opened in the same year."[57] In the summer of 1996 Dave Allen, Christine Borland, Nathan Coley, Jacqueline Donachie, Douglas Gordon and Julie Roberts were invited to participate in the Sawn Off project in Stockholm, curated by Maria Lind. Lind remembered, "I had seen Julie Roberts' paintings on a couple of occasions and remembered Christine Borland's bedclothes from 1993 Aperto at the Venice Biennale. I had come across Douglas Gordon's work in art magazines. But that was enough to draw me further, to Glasgow – via the Victorian resort of Llandudno[58] – and to Dave Allen, Nathan Coley and Jacqueline Donachie. At roughly the same time Galleri Enkehuset asked me if I wanted to curate a show at their space, preferably an international one. Interested in and impressed by the personal, contextually aware and socially sensitive conceptualism – it has been called 'lyrical conceptualism' – which lies at the root of all these artistic practices, the choice was simple for me."[59]

The artists showed their works in six locations around the city, including the Kulturhuset, a kind of prototype Pompidou Centre (Dave Allen), a house containing the collection of the painter Olle Olsson (Julie Roberts) and the Enkehuset, or Widow's House (Christine Borland). In a review of the project published in *Art Monthly*, Katrina Brown wrote, "It is important to note that, at the time of the exhibition, 'Glasgow-based' had become

---

57  Rob Tufnell, "A Recent History of Artists' Initiatives in Scotland, catalogue essay for Open Country", Musee cantonal des Beaux-Arts, Lausanne, 2001.

58  A reference to group show Riviera, held at Oriel Mostyn, Wales in 1994, which included the work of Dave Allen, Christine Borland, Roderick Buchanan, Nathan Coley, Jacqueline Donachie and Julie Roberts.

59  Maria Lind, Sawn Off, Galleri Enkehuset, Stockholm, 1996.

'Glasgow-affiliated', with four of the six artists involved being based in either Berlin, New York or Rome. The time and distances which separate Sawn Off from [Maria Lind's] first trip to Glasgow in late 1994 have seen a lot of changes, in practices and situations."[60]

60  Maria Lind, Sawn Off, Galleri Enkehuset, Stockholm, 1996.

# CHAPTER 8

# Slow Burning
## (1996–1998)

"So many record companies were stung for large amounts of money by Scottish bands in the late '80s – the unsuccessful ones – that there was a period from about 1990 to 1994 when, from my memory, there was hardly a Scottish band signed. I think that, during that period, people became more resourceful, and that was when new labels started emerging."[1]

A government training course for the unemployed at Stow College was the unlikely starting point for the eclectic and prolific Glasgow band Belle & Sebastian in early 1996. Stuart Murdoch and Stuart David met on the Beatbox course run by the college, and began writing and recording songs with the help of friends Isobel Campbell, Richard Colburn, Mick Cooke, Chris Geddes, Stevie Jackson and Sarah Martin. The band's demo tape was selected by the college for their annual recording project, resulting in their debut album, *Tigermilk*. The album was recorded in three days on a budget of £400, and only a thousand copies were pressed. These quickly started changing hands for inflated amounts when Radio 1 DJ Mark Radcliffe began enthusing about the melodic uptempo arrangements of Murdoch and David. Belle & Sebastian's sound had a local antecedent in the "shambling" sound of The Pastels, but also nodded to easy listening stars like Burt Bacharach and Astrud Gilberto, and the wise-cracking lyrics of Morrissey. They released a second album, *If You're Feeling Sinister*, on Jeepster later that year which brought their sound to a wider audience,

---

1   John Williamson, interviewed by Alastair Mabbot, "Right Here Right Now", *Caledonia*, March 2002.

although even at this early point the band were reluctant to do promotional interviews, and their record covers tended to feature photographs of their friends.

During 1995, Glasgow band Glass Onion had managed to negotiate a rent-free practice room above the Horseshoe Bar,[2] off Renfield Street, and had recorded their first demo tape with a loan from frontman Fran Healey's mother. The tape then fell into the hands of Neil Young producer Niko Bolas, who helped the band refine their sound and produced their debut album, *Good Feeling* (1996) under the new name of Travis for Independiente. The resultant album of playful rock numbers was well received, and drew comparisons to other Glasgow bands like Teenage Fanclub and Superstar. Before long the band had caught the attention of Noel Gallagher and won a support slot on Oasis' tour the following year, which made for a kind of neat symmetry as the Manchester band had been "discovered" in Glasgow by Alan McGee.[3]

Meanwhile, Chemikal Underground had received a rough demo tape from a band from Falkirk named after a device for boosting flagging male erectile function. Arab Strap had started making music together after a strained first encounter. "I was in a club with a girl, and I went to buy her a drink, and she left with Malc," remembers singer Aidan Moffat, "so that was how we met, through our shared affection for this young girl."[4] Moffat and Malcolm Middleton signed to Chemikal Underground, which released their first single, *The First Big Weekend*, in the summer of 1996. *The First Big Weekend* was a series of queasy recollections of a lost summer weekend on ecstasy, which Radio 1's Steve Lamacq called "the best record of the decade". The single still holds the record for the most continuous plays on Radio 1's Evening Session, and was later used, sans lyrics, for a 1998 Guinness advert.

---

2   The Horseshoe Bar (1880) one of Glasgow's most ornate public houses, boasts a huge horseshoe shaped bar, reputed to be the longest bar in Europe.

3   In May 1993, King Tut's Wah Wah Hut on St. Vincents' Street secured its place in the annals of '90s rock folklore when The Verve, the then-unknown Oasis and Radiohead, who had scored a massive sleeper hit with "*Creep*" that year all took to the small stage in a two week period. For Oasis, the King Tut's gig proved particularly memorable because Creation Records impressario Alan McGee was in the audience and signed the Manchester band on the spot.

4   Aidan Moffat, in conversation with the author, October 2000.

Moffat's lyrics occupied a ground that was somewhere between James Kelman and Irvine Welsh, described by the NME as "compellingly horrible." In the world that Moffat's lyrics described, getting up on Monday to go to work was shunned in favour of a lifestyle of drinking and recreational drug-taking interspersed with dysfunctional sexual liaisons. Moffat says, "Being in a band is much better than having a real job, and that was always part of the plan. I worked in a record shop and all the records people bought were shite. I've always had a difficulty in dealing with the public so I decided to make my own records instead."[5] Like Belle & Sebastian's *Tigermilk*, Arab Strap's debut album, *The Week Never Starts Around Here*, was recorded in just three days on a shoestring budget.

Glasgow-based artist Cathy Wilkes thinks that, "It takes a great deal of force and effort, within one system to create a whole other system. Artists working within Glasgow manage to create a whole other system, that is not like the one they are working within i.e. the city council, GoMA, etcetera. There are idealists and they are people really wanting to stay underground. Especially people doing work that isn't object-based, that is music or film or live work, that isn't necessarily going to be jumped on by a buyer. There are events and clubs that spring up and last for a while, and they are part of that economy that works on a different basis from exchange economy, because people don't make money out of them, and they just do it for the love of it. Because they want to be with people who they think they can have a special time with, and make something happen."[6]

Music and performance were still high on the agenda at Transmission that summer, and the summer show was a disco installation by New Yorker Karen Kilimnik, which paid homage to The Beatles. Me and the Boys was initiated by Kirsty Ogg, who had been a long-standing fan of Kilimnik's kitsch, "girly" work. Girly work of another kind took place in the gallery that July when Graham Bell, also known as Jackie Derrida, took over the basement for his *24 Hour TV* event. Bell specialised in a deliberately unconvincing form of transvestitism, with loopy make up and improbable

5   Aidan Moffat, Ibid.
6   Cathy Wilkes, in conversation with the author, August 2001.

outfits, which he often showcased at the city's West End festival. On another memorable occasion he became the focal point of a party with an impromptu song, performed with a vacuum cleaner wrapped around his neck while standing in a sink of dirty dishes.

In October, Glasgow-based artist Victoria Morton had her first solo show at Transmission, which was marked with the publication of a pamphlet, *Red Eyes*, which featured a conversation between Morton and her friend Cathy Wilkes. Morton said, "I've narrowed down the way I'm painting to such an extent that I'm only working with four or five ways of putting the paint on. I mean I did something weird on that painting [*Happiness*, 1996]. I think I took a marker pen and drew all over it with all circles. Then I did something else. Why shouldn't I be able to paint hoops all over? [ … ]Although I work practically on one thing at a time, in a sense there is that kind of flitting from one thing to another and the ideas are minute. I mean they're just like – what would it be like if I put pink on top of this?"[7]

In early autumn of 1996 an exhibition was held at the Old Fruitmarket in Glasgow to celebrate 10 years of the Environmental Art department at Glasgow School of Art. 49 artists participated in Girls High including Claire Barclay, Christine Borland, Martin Boyce, Roderick Buchanan, Nathan Coley, Jacqueline Donachie, Douglas Gordon, Iain Kettles, Jim Lambie, Jonathan Monk, Mary Redmond, David Shrigley, Ross Sinclair, Toby Webster and Jonnie Wilkes. After Environmental Art Head David Harding discussed the project with Rebecca Gordon Nesbitt, she had taken on the organisation of the show and catalogue. In her introduction to the catalogue she wrote, "Specifically unconfined to a particular media, the course has attracted an eclectic mix of students. The eluctable relationship with the department now persists in the memory like an old love affair; some artists have made a clean break and begun lives elsewhere, with others remaining 'just good friends' – the exhibition is symbolic of this (re)union." The striking assemblage of exhibits included an enormous smashed mirror on the floor (Jonathan Monk's *Whatever Will Be*), Claire Barclay's sculptural work made from white leather, a black feather boa and

---

7   Victoria Morton in conversation with Cathy Wilkes, Red Eyes, 1996.

machined aluminum, Jim Lambie's *Psychedelic Laughing Buddha* made from a black pudding, paint and a laughing buddha ornament and Toby Webster's *Heel Browser* – a parked red BMW with steamed up windows and bass heavy music blasting from the stereo. Elsewhere in the city, Glasgow-based artists Peter McCaughey (b.1964) and Stephen Skrynka (b.1962) were implementing a public art project that alleviated the dark autumn evenings on West end streets and around the city centre. *Borrowed Light* illuminated the grids of glass blocks at pavement level which filter light to the basement area below, using multicoloured lights, inset with bubbling pots of water and coloured images.

In Paris in October 1996 the Hans Ulrich Obrist curated exhibition Life/Live opened at the Musee d'Art Moderne de Paris. The exhibition represented the diversity of artist-run spaces and projects in the UK, and featured representative groups from BANK, Cubitt, Independent Art Space, Matthew Higg's *Imprint 93*, City Racing, Locus+ and Transmission.[8] Some critics questioned how 'socially engaged' the work in the exhibition really was, while others criticized Suzanne Page's catalogue essay, which reiterated Neville Wakefield's earlier link between the new British art and the Paris-based Situationists in the '60s and '70s. Michael Finch wrote in *Contemporary Visual Arts* that "Political radicalism can be located on the left or right, but Debord states that any vanguard using spectacular forms may find that its best intentions are 'offset by the reactionary element present in all spectacles'. This reactionary element is most certainly present in the British scene shown by Life/Live – the apolitical or anarchic gloss of the scene does little to conceal this fact."[9] However, "the British scene" that Finch describes could perhaps more accurately be described as 'the London scene' as the artists his review refers to were almost all London-based.

The different educational, cultural and economic influences at work in London and Glasgow had created work that was identifiably different in approach. For example, Heather Allen, one of the artists from Transmission whose work was included in the show, had a history of making work with

---

8   Participating Glasgow based artists included Richard Wright, Martin Boyce, Christine Borland, Douglas Gordon, Sue Tompkins, Heather Allen and Roderick Buchanan. The exhibition toured to Lisbon the following year.

9   Michael Finch, "Life/Live", *Contemporary Visual Arts*, issue 14, 1997, pp13–19.

a feminist and/or political slant. Previously she had made work that dealt with domestic violence, and in Life/Live she painted ambiguous words onto wooden signs that were like protest placards gone wrong. Richard Wright's labour intensive yet ephemeral wall paintings provided another example of work from Glasgow that had more than an "anarchic gloss". Douglas Gordon's installation *Something between my mouth and your ear* invited visitors to listen to a compilation of records he may have heard while in his mother's womb. The comparative lack of mainstream media exposure, or a network of dealers, collectors and art organisations in Glasgow meant that most artists working in the city were never faced with the accusations of toadying to the establishment now being regularly levelled at the yBas. In fact, many of the Glasgow-based artists who were now well-known internationally had a negative profile in their home city. Hans Ulrich Obrist said "There is a very small art world in Glasgow yet a very small number of people have made an unbelievable impact. But it's as if in Scotland, people … are not aware of it."[10]

However, Ross Sinclair recalls being distinctly unimpressed with talk of 'the Glasgow Miracle' at a talk at the Tate Gallery concerning that year's Turner Prize. "On the panel were the contemporary top dogs of young(ish) Euro-curators: Hans Ulrich Obrist, Uta Meta Bauer, John Roberts, Charles Esche (the then director of Tramway) etcetera etcetera. Anyway, Hans Ulrich Obrist started going on about this idea 'The Glasgow Miracle', I'm still not sure exactly what he meant, but back then in '96 I really thought it sounded odd. I think he was asking, or maybe reflecting, or perhaps proposing – how could it be that so many interesting artists develop in a place which was so bereft of culture with no history of, or relation to, modern art? How could this city be hosting and generating so many important exhibitions and conferences, writers, artists etc. when there was not even a system of private galleries for the commissioning, buying and selling of contemporary art. No infrastructure, no rules, the Wild West, I guess he was thinking. So. After everyone on the podium had waxed lyrical on this point for 20 minutes I felt compelled to make an observation from

---

10  *The Scotsman*, 24th June 1996.

the floor (a little intimidating in a room holding a couple of hundred of the most righteous London cognoscenti). So, anyway, I get up and say that, amazing as it all seems, the dynamic of Glasgow was, in fact, a very tenuous proposition, a castle built on sand, if you like. A ghost – a spectre – a phantom. I tell them all that the main gallery spaces, Tramway, CCA, Transmission etc. etc., were effectively being kept going by a tiny group of individuals who put their heart and soul into carving out a space for these galleries in a very unforgiving civic climate. There was no provision within the structure of these spaces for the success to be consolidated in a longer term way – it was all about the individuals and their ambition and passion for art."[11]

Later that year hybrid art organisation Salon 3, which aimed to maintain a dialogue with artists outside the capital, was set up in the Elephant and Castle shopping centre in London by Rebecca Gordon Nesbitt, Maria Lind and Hans Ulrich Obrist. The first Salon 3 was located upstairs from a run-down bar, but large crowds attending the gallery openings soon caused a rift with the bar owner, and Salon 3 was forced to move to second location, a former electrical goods shop still within the shopping centre. Rebecca Gordon Nesbitt had recently completed her Masters thesis *When Bad Men Conspire, Good Men Should Associate, Transmission Gallery 1983–1995* at London's Courtauld Institute, and organised the Girls High Environmental Art retrospective, while both Maria Lind and Hans Ulrich Obrist had also worked closely with Glasgow-based artists previously on various projects including Sawn Off and Life/Live. This powerful triumvirate of curators would continue to promote the work of Glasgow-based artists throughout the 1990s.

Other young curators with a marked interest in Glasgow art were also emerging, such as Kirsty Ogg. After leaving the Transmission committee, she had moved to Norwich to work as assistant curator at the Norwich School of Art & Design. Projects that Ogg curated there included Single Screen, an exhibition of video works by Alan Currall, Douglas Gordon,

---

11  Ross Sinclair, *The Glasgow Miracle vs. Utopian modernism done by Third World peasants*, Circles, ZKM, Karlsruhe, 2003, pp193–199.

Rodney Graham, Rachel Lowe, Mabel Palacin, Liza May Post and Smith/Stewart and group drawing show Slight, which included work by Rita Ackermann, Russell Crotty, Tracey Emin, Graham Gussin, Karen Kilimnik, David Shrigley, Thomas Schütte and Hayley Tompkins, which later toured to the Collective Gallery in Edinburgh. Kirsty Ogg remembers, "While I was there I also put together some shows in my flat at 7 Alexandra Mansions, to try and widen the context for showing work beyond the scene that existed when I arrived. In 1997 that programme included Cultural Tourists with Keith Blakeway, Will Bradley, Simon Starling and Toby Webster and This is My Home … These are Friends with Claire Barclay, Paul Kuzemczak and Jim Lambie."[12]

Kirsty Ogg, Toby Webster, Will Bradley and Tanya Leighton had all emerged from their experiences on the 1994–1996 Transmission committee as curators. Indeed, that particular committee spawned more curators than any committee before or since. A new breed of young curators like Matthew Higgs, Charles Esche and Rebecca Gordon Nesbitt[13] were increasingly challenging the dominance of the traditional art historian curator through their ability to work more closely with artists, and in a variety of settings. Although emerging curators like Webster, Bradley, Ogg and Leighton had trained as artists themselves, often they found critical ideas around production of work and curating exhibitions and events more rewarding and less isolating than working as an artist. The "cross-over" projects the four had organised while on the Transmission committee, like New Rose Hotel, had successfully united the elements they found interesting in the art world, with the disciplines of design, music and fashion. These young Glasgow-based curators were influenced by antecedent projects by conceptual artists like Gordon Matta-Clark's *Food* (1971) and Dan Graham's pavilions, but also by more recent projects, like Rirkrit Tirivanija's studios and other social projects. The cross-disciplinary projects of the Beastie Boys and Sonic Youth in New York, encompassing publications, curation, filmmaking, recording music and fashion design, may also have been influential.

---

12  Kirsty Ogg, in response to questions sent by the author, November 2002.
13  Matthew Higgs was an art school graduate, Charles Esche had studied medieval history and Rebecca Gordon Nesbitt had a degree in biochemistry.

Toby Webster curated a number of projects outside Transmission during this period that either linked different disciplines together, or were staged in non-gallery settings, or both. In the late summer of 1996, Webster and his girlfriend April Crichton, a designer for Paris fashion house Sonia Rykiel, hosted the show World of Ponce at their West-end flat. Friends including Toby Paterson, Simon Starling, Sarah Tripp, Will Bradley, Victoria Morton and Jonnie Wilkes installed their works in the open-plan living-room, where an evening opening party with fancy drinks and food was held. Later that year, Webster made a show connecting the aesthetics of skateboarding with the work of his artist friends, which opened at Glasgow's Concrete Skates, before touring to Cubitt in London. The show's title, Insanestupidphatfuctpervert, was an amalgam of the names of five skateboard clothing labels, and the show was a collection of boards that had been customised by Victoria Morton, Cathy Wilkes, Toby Paterson, Jim Lambie, Jonnie Wilkes, Jeremy Deller, Jonathan Monk, Martin Boyce, Toby Webster, Richard Wright and David Shrigley.

Perhaps typically, David Shrigley was the only artist of the twelve to decorate the grip tape side of the board. Shrigley's work had been included in the last major show curated by Charles Esche at Tramway, The Unbelievable Truth, which opened in November 1996, and also featured AP Komen & Karen Murphy, Jop Koelewijn, Fanni Niemi-Junkola and Barbara Visser.[14] Shrigley had recently published his seventh book of drawings, and commented, "I just do what I do. My absurdist drawings have hairy bones and invisible socks – but I seem to have come into vogue this year. You can't grumble about success."[15] He had a series of solo shows throughout the year, at CCA in Glasgow, Francesca Pia in Bern, The Photographer's Gallery, London, Stephen Friedman Gallery, London and Galleri Nicolai Wallner, Copenhagen.

The new Transmission committee now included Toby Paterson, Judith Weik, Caroline Kirsop, Sarah Tripp and Lucy Skaer. The gallery's autumn programme in 1996 included Stay On Your Own For Slightly Longer, which

---

14  This exhibition later toured to Stedelijk Museum Bureau in Amsterdam.
15  Visual Arts, *The Glasgow Herald*, 27th December 1996.

was one of four exhibitions by Swedish artists curated by Maria Lind. Lotta Antonssonn, Henrik Hakansson, Annike Hausswolff and Anders Widoff showed at the gallery from October through November. Henrik Hakannson installed a work called *War of the Worlds (Sipyloidea sipylus)*, made of ten blackberry bushes and a community of stick insects at the gallery. He explained, "To study insects as a scientist has in a way always been the big dream and something untouchable, a dream too big. I never went to university, instead I tried hard to be a rock star, in the end I failed both (I still try). I accidentally became an artist which helps me with my own studies, with the help of the public eye, and I certainly learn a lot. There's always some things that matter more than others and for me this has been a deep interest in insects. What I'm saying is that insects came before art in my life and I wish they had stayed there."[16] The next show at the gallery was called SEETHROUGHBRAIN and featured artists from Italy, Japan, Australia, Canada, Ireland, Scotland and England, again representing the spread of international connections forged by the gallery.

What Transmission often continued to do best was draw on reserves of local talent, as in group show Hong Kong Island, which invited various generations of Glasgow artists, from Billy Clark to Claire Barclay to Alan Currall, to show work relating to unrealisable projects in January 1997. In March, Transmission also participated in Young Parents, an exhibition in Manchester of artists and artist-run spaces with London's City Racing and Liverpool's Three Month Gallery. After Andy Small left the Three Month Gallery in 1997, curators such as Godfrey Burke and Rebecca Gordon Nesbitt were invited to stage shows in new premises on Wolstenholme Square before the gallery evolved into All Horizons Club – an organisation hosting exhibitions in public premises such as Unemployment Benefit Offices (Crystal State 1998) and Village Halls (The Village Hall Roadshow 2002). Transmission's contribution to Young Parents was curated by Tom O'Sullivan and Joanne Tatham and featured work by Jamie Burroughs, Steve Hollingsworth, Eva Rothschild, Toby Webster, Beáta Veszely and Caroline Woodley. In between shows, some changes of personnel were

16  *I Am Curious*, The Beacon Press, Sussex, 1996.

happening again, as first Caroline Kirsop and then Judith Weik left the committee. Sarah Tripp left Transmission after only six months, and Robert Johnston, Ewan Imrie, Julian Kildear, Sophie MacPherson and Rose Thomas joined Toby Paterson and Lucy Skaer as replacement committee members. This new committee was characterised by interests in alternative music and underground culture, as in New York Cable Access Experience (March 1997) which consisted of hundreds of hours of clips from New York's public access cable TV stations organised by Alex Bag, Patterson Beckwith and Sam Soghor.

Changes were also afoot at Tramway, where Charles Esche had now tendered his resignation. Esche finally left his post in April 1997 to pursue other opportunities, such as curating Intelligence: New British Art at Tate Britain, and setting up The Modern Institute in Glasgow with Will Bradley and Toby Webster. Before leaving Glasgow, Esche held a show in the flat he shared with artists David Wilkinson and Beáta Veszely at 83 Hill Street. Wish You Were Here Too was held in memoriam of London-based artist Erlend Williamson, who had recently died in a climbing accident. The occupants and artists including Martin Boyce, Nathan Coley, Tanya Leighton, Richard Wright, Douglas Gordon, Christine Borland and Julie Roberts installed various works in the first floor tenement flat. Notable works included Beáta Veszely's life-size fibre glass horse which looked down onto the street below, David Wilkinson's *Fake Christian* wallpaper in the hall and Tanya Leighton's handful of coins submerged in the bathtub.

After Esche's departure, a curatorium of advisors including Douglas Gordon, Sam Ainsley, Judith Findlay, Amanda Crabtree, Cath McCornick and Thomas Lawson was formed to lobby for the future curatorial direction of Tramway. At CCA, Nicola White had also tendered her resignation. She says, "I felt that the rot had set in. There was a new director, Penny Rae, and I felt that she didn't really understand the strengths of the organisation and how it worked. I felt that she was interested in change for its own sake, rather than change which made the organisation stronger. Before the previous director Jo Beddoe had left we had initiated a funding application to make the galleries larger. At that time CCA was seen as a place where the core strength was the visual art programme and the galleries had always been a bit limited and falling down, with leaking roofs. Under Penny this became a giant lottery funded application.[17]

By 1997 both the performance director, Mark Wadell and the talks director, Margaret Ritchie had left and I was offered the job of running the whole of the artistic programme but with very little support. Penny was advocating that I be more administrative and that people come in to curate short-term. We already did that, and had invited Toby Webster, Kirsty Ogg and Francis McKee[18] to curate shows – but what I was being asked to do seemed like a worse job than the one I was doing already, so I decided to leave. I did also get tired of all the grant applications and all the effort you had to put into just keeping the gallery going, and building bridges to the public and usually getting quite a lot of flak for the decisions that you made. There would literally be comments slips saying Nicola White should be taken out and shot."[19]

Charles Esche says, "I was disinterested in, maybe even fearful, of playing a political game and I think that's why in the end Tramway was lost for a time. I would say now that we did lose. If you look at the CCA and Tramway now I think there is a different kind of atmosphere to them – they have been brought to heel a bit and behave themselves a bit more. That was partly because we couldn't be bothered to fight those political battles that hard, but actually we wanted to get on with showing some good art."[20]

## THINGS CAN ONLY GET BETTER?

Finally, on May 1st 1997, Tony Blair led Labour to election victory, with the party's highest ever number of Parliamentary seats. Blair was the

17  In 1995 the National Lottery had been launched, and 5 million people had rushed to buy tickets, encouraged by the slogan, 'It Could Be You!' The Lottery provided many new funding opportunities for charitable causes, including the arts, which had brought changes to the visual art scene in the city, specifically in the level of public art commissions and in the redevelopment of contemporary art spaces.

18  Northern Irish academic Francis McKee had read for a PhD in the history of medicine, before becoming more closely involved in the arts. Since the early '90s McKee had been a close colleague of both Douglas Gordon and Christine Borland. He also worked in a curatorial capacity at CCA, taught on the MFA at Glasgow School of Art. and contributed to many publications, including frieze and Untitled. In 2002 he joined Kay Pallister as one of the two selectors for the first Scottish Pavilion at the Venice Biennale.

19  Nicola White, in conversation with the author, November 2002.

20  Charles Esche, in conversation with the author, July 2001.

youngest British Prime Minister since 1812, and the election had returned unprecedented numbers of female, black and Asian candidates. Blair's campaign song was the rave-lite anthem *Things Can Only Get Better*, by D:Ream. However, it soon became clear that Blair was not exactly the socialist leader that many Scots had hoped for. The first Labour government for eighteen years did not reverse the privatisation of public companies that had begun under the Tories, and also took the highly unpopular decision to do away with student grants. In addition to abolishing student grants, Blair introduced tuition fees of £1000 a year, which soon led to a fall in university applications and a dramatic rise in drop-out rates.

Blair's speeches studiously avoided the use of the word 'socialism' and his 'Third Way' politics would soon be attacked by commentators who thought he pandered too much to the traditionally Conservative-voting Home Counties. However, the new Prime Minister also implemented some welcome changes, by filling several posts in his cabinet with women, and initiating parliamentary reform in Scotland and Wales. A few months later, a referendum was held on devolution for Scotland and Wales, which demonstrated public support for devolved parliaments in both countries. The issue that had toppled the last Labour administration became one of the key strengths of Blair's government, which rather took the wind out of the Scottish National Party's sails. Since the 1979 referendum and election, the SNP had built its support on Scottish voters' dissatisfaction with Westminster, but now that the government was responding to the popular desire for devolution the political map was less clearly defined.

Sarah Munro, Director of Edinburgh's Collective Gallery[21] was alert to the possibilities that the new government might bring for artists living and working in Scotland. In an essay she wrote that year Munro observed, "to adopt a policy of cultural isolationism would smack of stupidity and racism. However, there does at least in Edinburgh, Glasgow and to some degree Dundee and Aberdeen exist the opportunity and potential of developing an infrastructure in the respective arts communities capable of germinating

---

21 The Collective operates differently from Transmission, in that it has a paid staff in addition to a voluntary committee, but it shares the Transmission ethos of showing work by local artists.

and sustaining a more independent self-perpetuating entity. There are more artists practising in Scotland than ever before and with the unprecedented availability of Lottery funding there are exciting and potentially greater opportunities for new artist-initiated projects. Coupled with this, the election of a new government with options towards devolution (and a hopefully forward-looking Ministry of Culture as opposed to a reactionary Heritage dept.) and we have a situation that, if developed strategically, could create a real opportunity for artists to structure their own agenda, an agenda aimed at creating a more vital artistic community."[22]

Since the mid '90s Munro had staged several shows at The Collective by Glasgow-based artists such as Tatham & O'Sullivan's *Blow Your Mind* (1997) and touring drawing show *Slight* (1997), curated by Kirsty Ogg. Across the road, Glasgow-based artist Nathan Coley was working on a commission for Stills photography gallery, based around the idea of urban sanctuary. Coley investigated the various permutations of this idea through conversations with a professor of theology, an artist, a Feng Shui expert, a policeman and Edinburgh tourist office. The results of his investigations were collected together in a book, although as Coley admitted, "My motivation is very rarely to come up with answers for the world, or even answers for my world. Perhaps I'm more interested in identifying the situation we find ourselves in, you know 'this is of interest to me, what do you think?' "[23] Interestingly, the Feng Shui consultant recommended that a space in which people might hope to find sanctuary should have high windows, to allow plenty of light to enter the space, but to prevent a view of the outside world from intruding – exactly describing Transmission.

In the summer of 1997, the first all-female list of Turner Prize nominees was announced, and Christine Borland made the list with Angela Bullock, Cornelia Parker and Gillian Wearing. Adrian Searle wrote in *The Guardian*, "Parker and Borland's [ … ] works involve an almost forensic approach to objects, and both depend on ideas of context, playing with the conventions

22  Sarah Munro, "Go Left at the Lights", STOPSTOP, Glasgow, 1997, pp53–54.
23  Nathan Coley, *Urban Sanctuary*, The Armpit Press, Glasgow, 1997, p7.

of museum display and taxonomy. Furthermore, both are artists whose sensibilities touch on life's mutability and its miseries, commemorating losses and falsifications. Both, too, are highly dependent on labelling, inscriptions, and the histories of the items they work with."[24] Although Borland lost to Gillian Wearing, the inclusion of a Glasgow artist on the Turner shortlist for two years running focussed international attention more closely on Glasgow, an effect that was heightened by Douglas Gordon winning the Premio 2000 Award at that year's Venice Biennale.

Young Glasgow painter Victoria Morton was in London that summer, hanging her first London solo show, Dirty Burning at the Andrew Mummery Gallery. Elizabeth Peyton, Rita Ackermann, Chantal Joffe, Gary Hume and Damien Hirst's "spot" and "spin" paintings had created a fashion for colourful paintings that referenced celebrity, music and fashion. Although Morton's work was not really similar to these other artists, there were certain superficial similarities in terms of her vibrant trademark colours: acid yellows, pink, and orange. The key painting in Morton's show, *Dirty Burning* featured areas of densely worked coloured patterns, with looser, more expressive areas. Morton had worked on the painting for over a year, as she tried to find a way of expressing the repetitive compositional patterns of music through her painting. The title was partly inspired by the 1992 Sonic Youth album *Dirty*, and also by the flickering flame-like colours of the finished canvas. This painting marked a stylistic departure in Morton's practice, as her work took on greater contrast and depth, and a more "worked" feel.

In September that year the most well attended British exhibition of all time opened at the Royal Academy in London. Sensation: Young British Artists from the Saatchi Collection showcased work by several of the most prominent yBas, including Tracey Emin, Chris Ofili, Jake and Dinos Chapman and Sam Taylor-Wood , and nine of the artists who had exhibited in Freeze – Richard and Simon Patterson, Mat Collishaw, Ian Davenport, Damien Hirst, Angela Bullock, Michael Landy, Sarah Lucas and Gary Hume. Tabloid outrage was sparked by the inclusion of Marcus Harvey's

24  Adrian Searle, "May the best woman win", *The Guardian*, October 29, 1997.

portrait of "Moors murderer" Myra Hindley, made up of children's handprints. The work had ink and eggs thrown at it in two separate attacks. The exhibition also included Jake and Dinos Chapman's conjoined child mannequins with genitals attached to their faces *Zygotic acceleration, biogenetic, de-subliminated libidinal model (enlarged x 1000)*, Richard Billingham's bleak photographs of his parents' towerblock existence and Tracey Emin's infamous appliqued "tent" piece, *Everyone I Have Ever Slept With 1963–1995*.

In addition to securing acres of media coverage, Sensation also succeeded in capturing a young audience: 80% of the visitors to the exhibition were under 30.[25] In his introductory essay, Norman Rosenthal compared the artists in Sensation to "enterprising" 19th Century French artists including Courbet, Manet and The Impressionists, who produced "work that the public for art neither wanted nor expected, but were forced to swallow because it raised issues of modernity that could not be avoided." He con-tinued that "a visitor to this exhibition with a clear mind and well developed antennae for life and art will perceive an uncommonly clear mirror of contemporary problems and obsessions from a perspective of youth. Presented with both seriousness and humour (often black), and in extraordinary diversity of materials and approaches, both traditional and unexpected, these works serve as memorable metaphors of our times."[26] The hype about the yBas made excellent fodder for London-based style mags like *Vogue* and *Vanity Fair*, who devoted pages to "the rebirth of swinging London". On one memorable *Vanity Fair* cover that year actress Patsy Kensit snuggled under a Union Jack duvet with her husband, Oasis frontman Liam Gallagher. The strapline read "Cool Brittania", a phrase that Tony Blair's spin-doctors were also pushing. The desire to prove the new government was more "with it" than the last prompted Downing Street to invite Noel Gallagher round for drinks, and offer consultancy posts to several music industry figures including Alan McGee of Creation Records and James Palumbo of London superclub The Ministry of Sound. However,

---

25  *Young British Art, The Saatchi Decade*, edited by Timms, Bradley and Hayward, London 1998.
26  Norman Rosenthal, "The Blood Must Flow", *Sensation*, The Royal Academy, 1997, pp8–11.

the government's plans to enforce stricter drug controls, abolish grants and introduce tuition fees for students and to coerce the unemployment into 'New Deal' employment training schemes met with criticism from many artists and musicians, notably Alan McGee, Damon Albarn of Blur and Bobby Gillespie from Primal Scream.

Events in London, in particular the new vogue for Union Jack clothing, seemed curiously distant, as Glasgow's fashions and music scene were entirely different. For example, jungle and garage music failed to find a secure foothold in Glasgow, although that was the music of choice in many London clubs. Glasgow band Belle & Sebastian released a stream of eps that summer which hovered on the outer reaches of the Top 40: *Dog On Wheels*, *Lazy Line Painter Jane* and *3..6..9 Seconds of Light*. Several Belle & Sebastian members also played in other local bands, including V-Twin, The Karelia, Hefner, Camera Obscura, The Gentle Waves, Future Pilot AKA, Looper and Salako. The band continued to shun the attentions of the mainstream media, although their network of associations in their home city was widespread. Belle & Sebastian bandmember Chris 'Beans' Geddes played Northern soul at Divine,[27] held on Saturday nights in the basement of the Vic at the art school, while the bass rumble of Knucklehead went on upstairs. Other Belle & Sebastian members might be found chatting in the record department of John Smiths bookshop on Byres Road, where their friends Stephen Pastel and Jason Macphail from V Twin worked. Although The Pastels had been releasing records since the early 1980s, they made their biggest impact with two albums released on Domino records during this period, *Mobile Safari* (1995) and *Illuminations* (1997). Bis were also doing well at this time, having secured a deal with Wiija Records in the UK and the Beastie Boys' Grand Royal label in the US to release their debut album, *The New Transistor Heroes* (1997). As had happened with Teenage Fanclub, the British music press which had built the band up now started to knock them down, which did little to deter the group's fans, especially in

---

27  Divine was established in 1990 by Geddes and Andrew Symington – it is now Glasgow's longest running club. A similar kind of music (Northern Soul, Hammond jazz, Latin soul and reggae) is played by DJ Chris Barron at another of the city's most popular clubs, Goodfoot/Uptight, which is now entering its eleventh year. Another popular non-electronic club is run on Fridays at the Buff Club in Sauchiehall Street by DJ Mark Robb.

Japan where they were something of a sensation.

Arab Strap's *The Girls of Summer* EP, released in 1997, was named single of the week by both *NME* and *Melody Maker*. However, it was the band's second album, *Philophobia* (fear of falling in love), which caught the attention of supermodel Helena Christensen, who interviewed the band for *The Face*. The record opened with the memorable lyric "It was the biggest cock you'd ever seen/But you've no idea where that cock has been." Belle & Sebastian's Chris Geddes and Stuart Murdoch collaborated on this album, although Murdoch would later criticize Moffat's "lewd and lascivious boasts" on the 1998 Belle & Sebastian top 20 album *The Boy With the Arab Strap*. *Philophobia* also provided an unusual commission for Glasgow School of Art student Marianne Greated, who painted the nude portraits of Moffat and his girlfriend that featured on the record sleeve.

Greated remembers, "I was in art school one day and out of the blue Sandy Moffat said that some band wanted to use one of my paintings. What had actually happened was Aidan and Adam Piggot – their graphics man – had been wandering around looking for a potential artist or image. They had told Sandy that they wanted to use one of my paintings but by the time I was told this, some three weeks later, I had painted over what they had seen. I ended up meeting up with them, to show them some slides and they asked me to produce new paintings for them. Since I was painting new work I discussed who should be in them – the original image was me and my boyfriend at the time – and I suggested they model. Aidan was up for it and a couple of weeks later him and Laura, his girlfriend were in my bedroom naked … hmmm, this sounds very seedy. I basically did the paintings and handed them over, but then there were lots of issues about the nudity – black dots on posters, problems releasing it in the US etcetera…"[28] The live album *Mad for Sadness* followed, recorded at the Queen Elizabeth Hall, with bassist Gary Miller, drummer David Gow, trumpeter Alan Wylie, cellist Cora Bisset and vocalist Adele Bethal. Moffat later said that part of the motivation for recording *Mad for Sadness* was to quell critics who said the band were terrible live. As Arab Strap's profile

28  Marianne Greated, in response to questions sent by the author, September 2001.

grew, they were lured to London record label Go! Beat for the release of their third album, *Elephant Shoe.*

Around this time another Chemikal Underground band, Mogwai, was starting to gather increasing attention. Mogwai's sound was influenced by British bands including Joy Division, The Jesus and Mary Chain and Spaceman 3, but they were more often compared to American bands like Slint and Tortoise. Their early records were characterised by subtle instrumental passages, that built to crescendos of white noise, often interspersed with snippets from telephone calls or film soundtracks. Their first LP release, *Ten Rapid,* was an atmospheric compilation of early tracks, and was followed by their first major album, *Mogwai Young Team,* released in November 1997 on Chemikal Underground. Colin Hardie, who managed the band between 1996 and 2002, says, "You start managing a band because you believe in them and think you can achieve great things. You tend to work as a team, because you were there at the beginning, driving them to gigs and lifting guitar amps. But the band never thought they'd play Barrowlands or headline at Glastonbury."[29]


## YOUNG DESIGNERS

A distinctive Glasgow design style was also emerging in the work of the young architecture and design consultancies established in the city in the late 1980s and 1990s. Zoo Architects, Timorous Beasties, One Foot Taller and Graven Images' work was appearing in a range of highly visible local contexts, ranging from style bars and hotels to major public institutions. Timorous Beastie's decadent printed velvet furnishings for the Arthouse Hotel, Graven Images' isobar mural and clustered lighting for Queen Street Style bar Strata and Zoo architects' wood and chrome sushi restaurant Oko were a few of the more notable examples of the work of these young companies. The fascination with architecture and design had also remained a constant theme in the work of many of Glasgow's young male artists, in

---

29  Colin Hardie, in conversation with the author, October 2000.

parallel with artists working elsewhere like Londoners Julian Opie and Liam Gillick and California-based artist Jorge Pardo. An interest in the history of design remained central to the work of Glasgow based artists Andrew Miller, Simon Starling and Martin Boyce, all of whom were now well-established and exhibiting internationally.

Simon Starling's first Transmission solo show, *Blue Boat Black*, opened in September 1997, and was later reviewed by committee member Julian Kildear in the pages of local art fanzine *British Mythic*. He wrote, "I was informed that the charred remains in the gallery began life as a redundant display case from Scotland's National Museum in Edinburgh. It was then transported to Marseilles, deconstructed, reconstructed as a fishing boat, used to catch fish, and then returned to Scotland to be shown at Transmission." Kildear went on to suggest that the exhibition was overloaded with visuals and information to convince the viewer of the "truth" of Starling's project, which Ross Sinclair had described in an earlier review of the same show as "an open opportunity to join him [Starling] in the realms of the unbridled imagination."[30] This was the first of many works by Starling which involved him undertaking a physical journey, and reconfiguring or transforming objects as part of that journey. Starling's work was realised enroute from one place to the next, and exhibitions representing his journeys became depositories for the artefacts he sent back (transformed objects, photographs and other documentary evidence). Although there was a romantic idea of exploration and alchemy inherent in his practice, Starling's methods also questioned both what the audience was prepared to believe, and what they expected from the gallery/museum.

Starling's contemporary Martin Boyce had begun to reference the language of Hollywood suspense films in his work, in particular the Saul Bass title sequence from Hitchcock's *North By Northwest* (1959) that utilised the associative potential of the grid. This archetypal modernist motif would begin to appear frequently in Boyce's installations, the wall paintings *Around Every Corner* (1996) and *Fear View* (2000) graphically expressing the physical and intellectual claustrophobia of city living. Boyce also began to

30  Ross Sinclair, "Blue Boat Black", *frieze*, issue 38, 1998.

work with distorted grids, and shapes like spiderwebs that broke apart over thresholds, or broken windows: the darkness of the city night seemed to peer over the shoulder of the viewer. In one work he quoted a sinister Houseblessing (1999): "bless each door that opens wide, to stranger as to kin." The figure of Robert Mitchum in *Night of the Hunter* or John Wayne in *The Man Who Shot Liberty Valance* seemed to be evoked, unknowable strangers cloaked in religion and the law – illusionary grids imposed in the wilderness.

In the later 1990s Miller, Starling and Boyce's interest in the history and implications of design found echoes in the work of several GSA graduates, including Steve Hollingsworth (b.1967), Dene Happel (b.1970) and Toby Paterson (b.1974). Hollingsworth was experimenting with the properties of neon, fixing neon to bicycle wheels, constructing chairs from neon tubing, and making a sculpture from the crushed mass of his car.[31] Dene Happell had exhibited in crossover show New Rose Hotel at Transmission in 1995, and had since set up his own consultancy, working on the design of style bars such as Air Organic (1998) and Groucho St. Judes (1999).

Toby Paterson's wall paintings, paintings on perspex, reliefs and sculptures re-examined the work of Modernist architects such as Le Corbusier and Mies van der Rohe. Although Paterson often chose "failed" post-war architecture as his source material, his bright, precise compositions re-endowed the structures with the optimism of the original plans. This approach may have stemmed from his enthusiasm for skate-boarding, which had lent him a different take on buildings dismissed as ugly or beyond repair. For example, the no longer extant Angel Lites skate park, set up in Glasgow in the late 1980s in a disused church, and the new town of Livingston, often derided as a planning disaster, were two locations which had long been a mecca for central belt skaters. Even Glasgow's real skate shops (as opposed to the city centre skater fashion boutiques) flourished in out-of-the-way spots where rents were relatively low – Clan in Hyndland Street in Partick, and MBC in Elderslie Street, Finnieston.

By 1997 Simon Starling and Martin Boyce's former Transmission

---

31 These works exhibited at The Fruitmarket, Edinburgh, 2000 as part of the Visions for the Future series.

colleague Kirsty Ogg had left her post in Norwich for a new position as curator of London's Showroom Gallery. As Craig Richardson wrote in a recent essay, "Kirsty Ogg escaped from Norwich, set up shop at The Showroom Gallery near my local in London's East End, and exhibited the latest work of Jim Lambie, David Allen, Claire Barclay and others. When I visited the exhibitions I believed I may have been seeing the first real Transmission Gallery 'franchise'."[32] After leaving the Transmission committee Toby Webster had begun curating exhibitions at the CCA. His trio of 1997 shows: Lovecraft, Slipstream and Waves In … Particles Out marked out his interest in the places where music, art, fashion and design met. Webster also continued the "mix and match" Transmission tactic of placing local artists in shows with established art names, for example including Cathy Wilkes alongside Tom of Finland and Simon Periton in Lovecraft.[33]

Webster co-curated Lovecraft with Martin McGeowan of London's Cabinet gallery, and the exhibition later toured to the South London Gallery and Spacex in Essex. The exhibition featured *The Uses of Literacy* (1997), a work by London-based artist Jeremy Deller that compiled art-works and memorabilia collected from Manic Street Preachers fans. Duncan of Jordanstone student Lucy McKenzie wrote, "When I saw the piece *The Uses of Literacy*, the re-presentation of the fanatical grassroots fandom cult surrounding the Manic Street Preachers, the work discomfitted me on a personal level. But only because it related directly to experiences with somebody real and not imagined. It is a difficult thing to look at, and nothing is more difficult than heartfelt, pubescent outpourings."[34]

Toby Webster also suggested that the CCA should commission Jeremy Deller to stage one of his acclaimed *Acid Brass* concerts in Glasgow. Deller (b.1966) had worked on several previous projects that dealt with popular culture. Deller's *My Booze Hell* t-shirts had become notorious after ex-Take


32  Craig Richardson, Letter 8, *Justified Sinners*, Pocketbooks, Edinburgh, 2002.
33  The influence of writer H.P. Lovecraft was strong during this period in the central belt arts scene, as Cumbernauld-born painter Graeme Todd (b.1962) also produced a work entitled *Lovecraft*, followed two years later by Mike Nelson's installation at the Collective Gallery, Edinburgh entitled *To The Memory of H.P. Lovecraft*.
34  *Accelerated Learning catalogue*, edited by Luke Fowler, Duncan of Jordanstone, Dundee, 1999.

That singer Robbie Williams appeared in one, and his *I love joyriding* bumper stickers also hit the headlines after they were installed on the bumpers of police cars in Middlesborough, the UK's joy-riding capital. Deller saw *Acid Brass* as a way of uniting what he considered to be the two most important social phenomenons since the early 1980s: the Miners' Strike and the Acid House explosion. CCA Director Penny Rae liked the idea, and Webster's suggestion that the concert be staged on the grassy slopes of the Botanical gardens. One sunny afternoon in late June the concert went ahead, and the Stockport's Williams Fairley Band played uptempo renditions of a selection of club classics including a Guy Called Gerard's *Voodoo Ray* to an assembled crowd of artists and bemused pensioners.

In Slipstream, the second exhibition Webster curated for CCA, works by former Glasgow-based artist Heather Allen, who was now living in Northern Ireland again, and Duncan of Jordanstone graduate Alan Michael were included with those of Raymond Pettibon, Ed Ruscha and Jim Shaw. In an essay published to accompany the exhibition Will Bradley wrote, "It's the return of the repressed, society's subconscious coming out in group therapy. Comic collections, adolescent scribbling on a schoolbag, building a private world when the one out there doesn't meet specifications. And it means improvisation, working with the stuff that comes to hand, old videos, posters, pencil and paper, because let's face it, when you're way out there, nobody's going to let you fiddle around with the expensive equipment … "[35]

In October, the third and final exhibition curated by Webster for the CCA opened with Martin Creed's band Owada playing on Piotr Uklanski's flashing multicoloured disco floor. Waves In … Particles Out was described in the press materials as "a show that falls between collusion and accident, highlighting the area where the onlooker becomes involved in the piece of work or situation created by the artist." Glasgow-based artists Mary Redmond and Diane Main's work was shown with pieces by Piotr Uklanski, Jonathan Monk and Henrik Hakansson, and electronic act Pansonic, local

35  Will Bradley, Slipstream, CCA, 1997.

artists Hayley and Sue Tompkins, and musicians Vodershow (Jonnie Wilkes, Hamish McChlery, James Seenan and Keith McIvor) made use of an in-gallery studio during the run of the show.

Keith McIvor was well-known locally for establishing independent record label Pi, seminal house and techno club Pure in Edinburgh, and ambient Sunday night club Sonora at the 13th Note in Glassford Street.[36] McIvor had also staged several experimental music events at Shakespeare Street community centre in Maryhill, remembering that "One event we held there was a bit of a triumph. It was a Saturday night and we managed to get 400 people to come and sit down and listen to experimental music – there were no beats. Mix Master Morris played and M.P. Lancaster did a live set."[37] Prior to forming Vodershow, Keith McIvor had known Wilkes and McChlery from their Saturday night art school club, Knucklehead, and he had previously released a record by The Painkillers (James Seenan and Frances McKee) on Pi. Vodershow's fusion of disparate musical elements (techno, house, electronica, rock'n'roll … ) resulted in a series of tracks with staccato beats underpinned by a dub sensibility, captured on the 12" single released to coincide with the exhibition, Evurb 001 (1997).

The pub and club culture of Glasgow had fed the vibrant art and music scenes for years, although various set-backs were now affecting these venues, including the implementation in the late '90s of limited licensing hours for bars and strict curfews for nightclubs, and new legislation which classified street drinking as a criminal offence. The new restrictions placed upon bars and clubs were introduced in an attempt to curb the violence that often errupts in the city centre, particularly on Saturday night, which remains the big night out in Glasgow. However, the restrictions also negatively affected more innocent activities such as club-hopping and drinking beer in the park on (rare) sunny days. Like the 1994 Criminal Justice and Public Order Act, the new regulations seemed designed to curb the party-loving tendencies of young Glaswegians, and were met with

36  Several other experimental club nights operated at the 13th Note at this time, including Boudoir, an easy listening club with arcade games and Scaletrix, and Lube, a drum and bass night.
37  Keith McIvor, in conversation with the author, October 2000.

some resistance. Another blow came in 1997 when Mayfest folded in debt after council funding was withdrawn. The annual Glasgow arts festival, which had been founded in 1982 to celebrate Glasgow's cultural renaissance, had also brought later opening hours and more relaxed curfews for a few weeks in the year.

The fusion of art and music in the city often found best expression not in galleries but in the nightclubs that kept running throughout the '90s. In the autumn of 1997 Pure DJ Keith McIvor asked his Vodershow collaborator, Jonnie Wilkes to join him in running a new Sunday night club, Optimo, at the Sub Club, which would break the deadlock that house and techno music had over the local scene. A text that was projected across the dancefloor made their intentions clear: "house music is my life/house music must die." McIvor's template was Larry Levan's legendary decadent New York club The Paradise Garage, which had run from 1976–1987 in a former garage in Soho. Levan mixed up anything that took his fancy, from reggae to rock, to the orgasmic moans of Donna Summer's *I Feel Love*, to gospel vocals and Manuel Gottsching's epic 1976 electronic classic *E2:E4*. McIvor explained that, "The name [Optimo] came from a song by Liquid Liquid which summed up how the core of the night should sound – raw, percussive, out-there sleaze funk and a return to the ideals of early '80s New York where lots of different scenes (hiphop, punk, no wave, disco, gay, straight, art, photography, anything goes) briefly collided into one of the most important creative moments in the history of art, music and clubbing."[38]

However, the influence of late 1990s Berlin became at least as important to the music sound of Optimo's playlist as early '80s New York, as the club forged a link with Berlin nightclub WMF in late 1998, through mutual friend Toby Webster. This relationship strengthened the links between Berlin and Glasgow already established by migrant Glasgow-based artists Jonathan Monk and Dave Allen and exhibitions held there by Glasgow artists such as Korrespondenzen (1997), held at both the Berlinische Galerie and the Gallery of Modern Art, Edinburgh. Korrespondenzen co-curator[39]

---

38  Source: www.optimo.co.uk
39  Keith Hartley, senior curator at the Scottish National Gallery of Modern Art in Edinburgh curated the exhibition in collaboration with Ursula Prinz.

Ursula Prinz wrote that, "In Berlin the scene is changing almost daily, particularly with the influx of artists and galleries from elsewhere. Since the Wall came down and Berlin has been chosen as the new capital of Germany the city's powers of attraction have increased. The wastelands left in Berlin both by the War and the Wall provide extensive opportunities for re-building."[40] Like Detroit and Glasgow, the relatively barren cultural scene in Berlin had created a fertile ground for musical and artistic experimentation. The music of German acts like Chicks on Speed, Miss Kittin & The Hacker and Pole provided a fresh injection of skewed electronica to Glasgow's house and techno scene, inspiring local acts like Mount Florida, Creme de Menthe, Mendel, Pro Forma and Bis, all of whom went on to perform at Optimo.

In 1998 all of the members of Vodershow collaborated on the 12" single *Majik Moment*, released on Frances McKee's new independent label Left Hand Recordings. McKee had set up the label with royalties received from American grunge super group Nirvana, who had covered songs she had written for The Vaselines on their *Nirvana Unplugged* and *Incesticide* albums, perhaps most notably, *Jesus Wants Me For a Sunbeam*. *Majik Moment* also featured vocals from McKee and her sister Marie on reworkings of The Silver Apples' *Lovefingers* and *Lost in Space* by The Painkillers. McKee was also working with her former Painkillers collaborator James Seenan on a new folk-influenced project, which would become known as Suckle, while McIvor was collaborating with local experimental musician M.P. Lancaster under the name Mount Florida, inspired by the Glasgow suburb where Lancaster lived.

Elsewhere in the city, other dance clubs like Club 69, Tangent, Off the Hook, Mystec/Spanner and Disco X also built the popularity of the new European electro sound in low-key locations and through word of mouth. Club 69 had operated from the basement of an Indian restaurant in Paisley since the early '90s. Run by Martin Mackay, Wilba and Barry, the people

---

40  Ursula Prinz, "Letter from Berlin", *Korrespondenzen*, Berlinische Galerie/Scottish National Gallery of Modern Art, 1997, p16. The exhibition featured the work of Glasgow-based artists Nathan Coley, Jacqueline Donachie, Smith/Stewart, Kerry Stewart and Richard Wright, and Berlin based artists Nina Fischer/Maraon el Sani, Gunda Forster, Johannes Kahrs, Veronika Kellndorfer and Christine Kramer.

behind Glasgow's specialist Rub a Dub record store, the Saturday night club remained a haven for underground dance music, and high calibre guests like Underground Resistance were not at all unusual. However, a poster or flyer for Club 69 was a rare sight, and the club's location so obscure that it would be almost impossible for the uninitiated to find. Resident Club 69 DJ Martin Mackay says, "It is truly an underground club, as it's in the basement, and the music we play could probably be classed as underground, but really we're just a music club with a passion for things a bit different. I have absolutely no interest in trends, and I have no notion of what is in the charts."[41] Techno/trance club Tangent, which was run at Glasgow venues including The Arena and the Sub Club for many years by DJs A-Man and Panic, also staged special one-off parties on boats, trains and even in an underground bunker. Newer club Disco X has continued in this fine tradition at the Soundhaus, a concrete industrial complex by the side of a dual carriageway, while another club, The Unit, moves around from week to week to various secret Southside locations. Recent posters for warehouse parties run by acid house club Shake the Disease offer no clue to their whereabouts, only the crytic message "You know where to go."

The "outsider" status of many of Glasgow's clubs and bands was brought home in 1998 when Belle & Sebastian, who had continued to shun the usual modes of generating publicity for the group, beat Steps to the Brit Award for Best Newcomer. *The Sun* claimed that the result was a fix, brought about by block e-mail votes from Belle & Sebastian fans. Belle & Sebastian manager Neil Robertson says, "'The non-marketing' of Belle & Sebastian was never contrived, but they did stick to that idea as they became more successful. The Brit Award probably was rigged in a way – one of the fansites organised a big movement to vote. But then there's this other poll called the charts that Steps win every week, hands down: we've only been shortlisted once. But Belle & Sebastian have had a top 50 album so it wasn't like we were some guy who does karaoke down the pub."[42]

Another Glasgow band, Mogwai, made no attempt to conceal their

41  From an interview with the author, published in Metro, Glasgow, 2000.
42  Neil Robertson, in conversation with the author, October 2002.

fondness for Glasgow's pub culture, even if it did occasionally impair their performance. Mogwai's lead singer Stuart Braithewaite said, "There is an aesthetic to the lifestyle here. A lot of the music in Glasgow has a melancholy side to it, maybe because getting really drunk has always been inherent in Scots culture. There's a lot of hedonism in Glasgow and it's really unhealthy [ … ] The first time we had a sell-out show in London we got really drunk. It was that Scottish mentality – we never thought we'd get this big, so just before the gig, we decided to get totally fucked. You can't play really well when you're really drunk. The thing is though, one time out of ten you'll play well. Then you'll think, I can play drunk now, and that's when it all goes to fuck. The motto for that tour was 'tipsy for soundcheck'."[43] After the success of *Young Team*, the band enlisted the services of Mercury Rev bassist and producer Dave Fridmann for their second album, *Come On Die Young*, which was released on Chemikal Underground in March 1998. That summer South Lanarkshire council had imposed a curfew on school-age kids being out later than 9pm, which Mogwai responded to with a "fuck the curfew" sticker campaign, and an EP entitled *No Education = No Future (Fuck the Curfew)*. Steve Malkmus of American indie *uber-group* Pavement fanned the flames of the band's growing reputation by calling them "the best band of the 21st century".

43  Stuart Braithewaite, in conversation with the author, October 2000.

CHAPTER 9

# WHEN NO-ONE'S WATCHING
## (1998–1999)

Enthusiasm for obscure ideas, non-profit making schemes and obsessive interest in small details characterise the activities of numerous DJs, musicians and artists working in Glasgow. That approach may well be the reason for the scene's originality and longevity, as Rebecca Gordon Nesbitt recently observed. "In terms of the kind of work being produced, the tendency toward post-conceptual work that is slow-burning and well-considered has persisted, at the expense of London and the yBa phenomenon, which provides a solid artistic framework for younger artists. It's my impression that this basis allows both for a continuation of the same kind of work or a radical departure from it."[1]

In the late '90s young British artists were notable by their absence in international group exhibitions such as Manifesta 2, Documenta X and the 1999 Venice Biennale. However, as artist and curator Matthew Higgs pointed out in his essay for the British Art Show 5 catalogue, Glasgow-based artists were largely exempt from the backlash, and in some ways benefited, as curators looked for an alternative to the brash London-based art. Maria Lind, now the curator of Stockholm's Moderna Museet, commented "I find the art coming out of Scotland generally more interesting than that from London. Artists like Christine Borland, Simon Starling, Claire Barclay, Nathan Coley, Jacqueline Donachie and Richard Wright produce work that is more complex and investigative, direct and multifaceted, and therefore more difficult to "consume". It takes more time

1   Rebecca Gordon Nesbitt, in response to questions sent by the author, August 2001.

and commitment to enter this work, and consequently it has not received as much attention as that of the yBas. Significantly, these artists have gone "international" without first having a presence in London."[2]

In 1998, Richard Wright and Christine Borland were the only two British artists included in international group show Manifesta 2 at Luxembourg, while in America, Douglas Gordon scooped the country's biggest contemporary art prize, the Hugo Boss prize, becoming the only artist to achieve the hat-trick of the Turner, Premio 2000 and Hugo Boss prizes. Ross Sinclair and Richard Wright received the £30,000 Paul Hamlyn Foundation Award to Artists in this year, Graham Fagen had his first solo London show at Matt's Gallery, and Simon Starling had a major solo show at the Camden Arts Centre. The international reputation of Glasgow artists also continued to be confirmed by group exhibitions throughout the late nineties such as Shift (1995),[3] Glasgow (1997)[4] and Nettverk – Glasgow (1998)[5] which took place respectively, in the Netherlands, Switzerland and Norway.

The furore caused by GoMA Director Julian Spalding's collecting decisions and public statements had not abated, and in 1998 the city council "restructured", abolishing his post of Director of Museums. In his place came Mark O'Neill, Head of Museums and Galleries, who admits, "I do agree that visitors to the city are disappointed [not to be able to see Douglas Gordon's work on display] although those kind of visitors may have seen his work elsewhere. But Glaswegians do not have an opportunity. That's a bigger failure than just disappointing visitors from elsewhere who expect to see his work, it's the fact we failed the local audience. Even if they dislike it, they have a right to see it first and make up their own minds."[6]

In the end, Julian Spalding's actions had specific impact upon council policy, as O'Neill explains, "Julian Spalding reported directly to a council

2   Cream, Phaidon, London, 1998.
3   Group show at De Appel Foundation, Amsterdam which included the work of Jacqueline Donachie, Douglas Gordon and Ross Sinclair.
4   Group show at the Kunsthalle Bern, with work by Nathan Coley, Louise Hopkins, Fanni Niemi-Junkola, Ross Sinclair, Simon Starling and Smith/Stewart.
5   Group show at the Museet for Samtidskunst, Oslo with Richard Wright, Ross Sinclair, Julie Roberts, Louise Hopkins, Douglas Gordon, Nathan Coley, Roderick Buchanan, Martin Boyce, Christine Borland and Claire Barclay.
6   Mark O'Neill, in conversation with the author, July 2001.

committee, whereas now I report to my boss, Bridget McConnell, who reports directly to a council committee. It might sound bureaucratic but it's about a change in policy from the kind of Director Julian was, who made very much his own decisions and was very much an individual, to a more accountable post like mine."[7] Despite this welcome change, the unfortunate legacy of Spalding's tenure is the unrepresentative GoMA collection of locally produced art. Sam Ainsley says, "People come from other countries and they say, where can we see Ross Sinclair or Christine Borland's work, and there isn't any anywhere. There is no public collection even of the really established people, let alone succeeding generations. I think it's scandalous."[8]

However, the 1995 introduction of Lottery funding with an emphasis on "making the arts available to those who have had few or no opportunities to experience them"[9] had created new resources for commissioning public artworks in Scotland. Edinburgh-based public art commissioning agency Art in Partnership was partly responsible for the increased number of local artists working for public commissions, siting a highly visible series of artworks including Patricia Leighton's *Sawtooth Ramps* (1993), Dalziel & Scullion's *The Horn* (1997) and David Mach's *Big Heids* (1998) beside the M8 Motorway during the '90s. A similar organisation, Visual Art Projects had been set up in Glasgow in 1992 by Julia Radcliffe, who had then been joined in 1997 by MFA graduate Lucy Byatt. From small beginnings, renting office space from Graven Images, Visual Art Projects had established itself in an office on King Street and had realised a wide range of projects, including the redevelopment of The Tron Theatre, and Claire Barclay's Govanhill and David Shrigley's Possilpark projects. David Shrigley explained that "the designs on the concrete [in the play area] are meant to resemble pages of a children's encyclopaedia. I naively hoped by placing this information on the ground that after months and years of wandering over it and writing on it they might absorb some of it and become better spellers or be able to calculate the area of a triangle."[10] Other local artists who have worked on commissions for

7   Mark O'Neill, Ibid.
8   Sam Ainsley, in conversation with the author, May 2001.
9   Strategy: The Distribution of Arts National Lottery Funding in Scotland, Scottish Arts Council, 2000.
10  From an interview broadcast on BBC Knowledge, 27th October 2000.

Visual Art Projects include Nathan Coley, Jim Hamlyn, Kenny Hunter, Andy Miller, Tracey McKenna, Lucy Skaer and Douglas Gordon.

The Douglas Gordon project, *Empire* (1998), was particularly meaningful because it meant that a work by the Turner Prize winner was now on show in Glasgow, despite Julian Spalding's efforts to the contrary. Lucy Byatt remembers, "I started talking to the Merchant City Civic Society chaired by Ross Hunter, who co-directs Graven Images, about the idea of inviting Douglas to do the *Empire* piece. What I was really interested in as part of my own practice was fellowship, research and understanding artists roles within that as being very public, as having a conversation with someone else. Do we regard that as public art? Just asking, what is this very contested thing we call public art in a city where the galleries don't function, where they don't buy the work [of local artists], where they're not interested. How can we hit all these buttons, how can we make sure that the lottery money comes through to artists? How can we see public practice as being something that interesting artists want to do? How do we see it away from the idea of stuff on the roundabout, stuff you trip over?"[11]

Douglas Gordon recalls, "I'd been approached by Lucy Byatt and Visual Arts Projects in Glasgow, who wanted a work for Brunswick Street, just at the Mitre, and I'd always wanted to do something there, always loved the idea that it was almost like a wee cinematic atmosphere in the lane, you could be right in the centre of the city but outside the city at the same time… "[12] Gordon produced a work that was a mirror image replica of part of a neon sign glimpsed in a scene from Hitchcock's *Vertigo*. The word 'Empire' was particularly loaded in the context of Glasgow's Merchant City, but as always, Gordon intended the work to be read in numerous ways.


## THE ART COMES OUT OF DISCUSSION

While the success of several Glasgow-based artists had brought an atmosphere of generally increased confidence in the city, a more specific

11  Lucy Byatt, in conversation with the author, April 2001.
12  *The Scotsman*, 24th June 1996.

way in which these artists had made a difference to the local situation was through teaching. When Borland received her Turner prize nomination in 1997, she was still teaching three days a week at Glasgow School of Art. While studying on the MFA, Anne-Marie Copestake was taught by both Borland and Gordon and recalls: "At art school, conversations with Douglas Gordon and Christine Borland were particularly encouraging for me personally and in my practice, because they both refused to spoon feed and give cheap stock answers. Douglas was like a miner digging and digging deep."[13] Toby Paterson is another artist who graduated post-Windfall who feels that the success of Gordon, Borland et al has had a positive effect on Glasgow's art scene. He says, "Of course that generation has had a positive effect. They showed that it is possible to base yourself outside London and not be compromised, either in terms of your work or your career. Although these artists increasingly don't need to be viewed as a chronological step, their active support and advice has greatly aided the scene in Glasgow in general and individual artists in particular."[14] Hayley Tompkins agrees, 'I think Glasgow is generational – there were influences that suggested to me how I could live and work here [as an artist]."[15]

Forming artist's collectives is another strategy successfully utilised by the Glasgow-based artists to avoid the professional pitfalls of jealousy and isolation. Although artists' collectives such as BANK do exist in London, they are often considered to be willfully refusing to conform to the demands of the London art scene, which prefers single identifiable "art stars", such as Damien Hirst or Tracey Emin. BANK had shown a rotating programme of videos produced in London and Manchester in the basement of Transmission in September of 1996, and would return to show in Glasgow twice more by the end of the decade. Although the aesthetic approach of BANK was not widely imitated by Glasgow artists, their collective strategies found numerous parallels in the city.

Glasgow-based art collectives include Filthy Swan, Elizabeth Go and Henry VIII's Wives (Rachel Dagnall, Jonas Eggen, Bob Grieve, Simon Polli,

---

13  Anne Marie Copestake, in response to questions sent by the author, January 2001.
14  Toby Paterson, in response to questions sent by the author, April 2001.
15  Hayley Tompkins, in conversation with the author, October 2000.

Lucy Skaer and Per Saunder)[16] and art making duos in the city have been even more numerous. Complecity (Neil Bickerton and Lorna Macintyre), A Love Laboratory (James Thornhill and Michelle Naismith), Iain Kettles and Susie Hunter, Smith/Stewart, Jess Worrall and Rob Kennedy, Joanne Tatham and Tom O'Sullivan, Charisma (Lucy McKenzie and Keith Farquhar), Tayto and Mr. Tayto (Alex Pollard and Neil Mulholland[17]) and Beagles & Ramsay[18] are just a few of the current collaborative ventures. Tom O'Sullivan, who has worked collaboratively with Joanne Tatham since 1995, says, "The whole reason we started working together is that its just too demoralising being an artist on your own. The art comes out of a discussion between two people."[19] O'Sullivan's comment echoes Douglas Gordon's often quoted statement "making art is really just an excuse for a conversation."

Another benefit that arises from collaboration is the opportunity to play with notions of the "genius artist". Lucy McKenzie says of her Charisma collaborator Keith Farquhar "There are similarities between what we do, there are overlaps in what we think and do. We play around with ownership and authorship – we have synchronicity. I rip him off. He rips me off, it doesn't matter."[20] Often collaborations take place as the extension of a romantic relationship. As Sam Ainsley writes in a recent essay, "Artists in Glasgow don't just work and show together; they meet each other all the time; in pubs, clubs, at openings and other events. They talk a lot, discuss, argue, fall out, make up and sometimes fall in and out of love."[21] James Thornhill, who works collaboratively with Michelle Naismith, says, "A very intense thing happened between us and partly that was to do with work, we recognised something: we realised that we were very excited about the same things. One of the natural ways of expressing that is to work together, so we did."[22]

16  Since the late 1990s Sirko Knupfer has replaced Jonas Eggen in the group.
17  Neil Mulholland has worked collaboratively with both Keith Farquhar and Lucy McKenzie, and taught in the Historical and Critical Studies Department at Glasgow School of Art between 1996 and 1998 while completing his PhD on British Art since 1975 at Glasgow University. He now teaches at Edinburgh College of Art.
18  MFA graduates John Beagles and Graham Ramsay have been producing collaborative art projects since the mid 1990s and have also curated numerous projects, including Be Er Monsta, a touring exhibition of video works by 25 artists, and Angel Dust, an exhibition to be viewed by torchlight, at Intermedia in Glasgow.
19  Tom O'Sullivan, in conversation with the author, January 2001.
20  Lucy McKenzie, in conversation with the author, October 2000.
21  Sam Ainsley, "Falling in and Out of Love", introductory essay to 2001 Haiku publication, GSA, 2001.
22  James Thornhill, in conversation with the author, August 2001.

In 1996, Rebecca Gordon Nesbitt had written that, "Outside London, the paucity of commercial galleries has forced a sometimes lengthy gestation period on certain artists, during which they have given thorough consideration to their artistic practice."[23] That paucity of commercial galleries also meant that the majority of the city's young artists were living on low incomes. The 1998 SAC Survey *A Socio Economics of Artists in Scotland* found that over 70% of artists in Scotland had an income of £10,000 or less a year. Most young artists continued to find the transition from art school student to professional artist a painful process. Many sustained themselves by claiming benefits, and/or working at an unrelated and often low-status, low-pay job, most often bar and shop work. Sam Ainsley says, "There aren't any of the opportunities at all that you have in London with commercial galleries or sales but somehow people seem to manage to keep their interest and their involvement in art going. It's often because they are invited to take part in shows in other countries. They are probably less well-known here than they are in Europe and the USA. People have managed to stay afloat because they get an interested response to their work here, although there isn't much financial reward for most of them."[24]

By early 1998, Charles Esche had formed The Modern Institute with Will Bradley and Toby Webster, with a view to promoting Glasgow artists in ways that extended beyond the remit of the city's existing museum and galleries system. Will Bradley recalls, "Toby Webster, Chas Esche and myself had all been thinking of starting something. Toby and I had been at Transmission, and Chas had left Tramway. It's partly you get into a habit of doing things and you want to keep doing them – but it came about really from having experience of what's going on outside Glasgow. Also a lot of artists who were working here were starting to become quite successful – the artists that we knew were starting to get involved, and showing abroad.

23  Rebecca Gordon Nesbitt, "Urban Myths", *Contemporary Visual Arts*, 1996.
24  Sam Ainsley, in conversation with the author, May 2001.

We got a real sense something like [a commercial gallery] could work in Glasgow, and wanted to give it a try. We wanted to be everything: a record company, a publishing company, organising exhibitions and representing artists. We'd be all singing, all dancing. We tried to keep the definition of The Modern Institute loose: we called ourselves a research organisation and production company rather than a 'gallery'."[25]

Charles Esche remembers, "Toby had been working at CCA and one obvious thing would have been for him to have taken over there, he could've done it but there was real antagonism there, after what had happened with Richard Wright and Dave Allen.[26] We all shared a feeling that the CCA wasn't going to go anywhere with someone like Graham McKenzie in charge,[27] and Tramway was closed and it didn't seem like it could do the job that it had done before. So we said we should do something. Basically, The Modern Institute came about from sitting around a table in a pub and talking about what we wanted to do. We talked about the artists we wanted to work with, and trying to be commercial in the sense of commissioning editions and selling them. The idea of representation came up quite naturally afterwards. We also wanted to produce events like the Rirkrit Tirivanija cinema project and to try to work with bodies like the Year of Architecture and Design, the SAC and the city council."[28]

The initial group of artists represented by The Modern Institute were Martin Boyce, Jim Lambie, Victoria Morton, Toby Paterson, Mary Redmond, Eva Rothschild, Simon Starling, Hayley Tompkins, Joanne Tatham and Tom O'Sullivan, Cathy Wilkes, Jonnie Wilkes and Richard Wright. The work of The Modern Institute included releasing recordings and publications, organising artists' projects in their own premises, or in other venues in various locations (such as Sadie Coles HQ, London and Kiasma, Helsinki), dealing with overseas collectors and curators, and exhibiting at

---


25  Will Bradley, in conversation with the author, April 2001.

26  A planned collaborative project by Richard Wright and Dave Allen was abandoned due to the CCA scheduling building works in the gallery during the installation period, failing to secure the materials the artists required or to pay agreed artists' fees.

27  Graham McKenzie, a former social worker, freelance writer and Glasgow City Council Principle Arts Officer for South East Glasgow, replaced Penny Rae as Director of CCA in late 1997.

28  Charles Esche, in conversation with the author, July 2001

art fairs in European centres such as Cologne and Basel. The Modern Institute held a launch party in April for three limited editions by local artists: *Blank Page and Other Pages* by David Shrigley, a Vodershow record with a silkscreen print by Jonnie Wilkes, and from Christine Borland, a recording of an adolescent boy reading The Monster's Monologue from Mary Shelley's *Frankenstein*.[29] The newly formed company then invited each of the artists they represented to stage a three-day exhibition in the Robertson Street gallery.

Anne-Marie Copestake remembers, "I was struck by the series of one person, three day exhibitions at The Modern Institute. The space was a commercial venture and had lots of short project shows – that was something that you could find in London but it was the first time I saw it in Glasgow."[30] For many Glasgow-based artists there was little or no expectation of selling their work and The Modern Institute changed that situation to some extent. Transmission exhibited at international art fairs, but the gallery was more concerned with securing overseas exhibitions and exchanges for Glasgow artists and raising awareness of the art scene in Glasgow, than selling works to collectors. Will Bradley says, "Transmission is great but also self-limiting in that it's never going to become something that can operate at the next level, where it deals with institutions like a commercial gallery. That is something Transmission should never have to do."[31]

Two other former Transmission committee members had already been invited by Nicola White to curate shows at CCA in 1998, the first of which was Tanya Leighton's When Worlds Collide, including work by Pierre Huyghe, John Waters and the first Scottish showing of Johan Grimonprez's *Dial H-I-S-T-O-R-Y*. Later in the year, Kirsty Ogg curated Henry VIII's Wives' Green Stick Fracture, followed by High Red Centre with work by Christine Borland, Eva Rothschild, Kendall Geers, Gregory Green, Phillipe Meste and original Hi Red Centre artist, photographer Tomatsu Shomei, who had

---

29  Two Glasgow based writers had previously reworked ideas drawn from Shelley's novel: Liz Lochhead in her 1984 collection of poems, *Dreaming Frankenstein* and Alasdair Gray in his 1992 novel *Poor Things*.
30  Anne-Marie Copestake, Ibid.
31  Will Bradley, Ibid.

documented the student riots that took place in Tokyo in 1968. Ogg explained, "The show explores ideas of rebellion and how far you can rebel within any structure, how far it's appropriate for artists to rebel before it becomes a futile statement. Rather than looking at highly politicised or issue-based work, we're looking at approaches to making work by artists – in this case, a very self-determined, direct stance. I'm not convinced how successfully art deals with politics. Artworks can be highly political, but in quite a covert way, rather than in your face, saying 'this is the issue we're going to beat you over the head with'. I just don't think that works, there's no kind of subtlety, it doesn't leave anything to take away and think about later."[32]

Alexia Holt, who had previously worked at Glasgow School of Art, was formally appointed Visual Art Officer at Tramway during 1998. She recalls, "In the interim of Charles leaving and there not seeming to be a commitment to reinstate that post, you can imagine there was quite a lot of concern in the city. Sam Ainsley had this idea to set up a curatorium, a network of people internationally who were keyed into what Tramway was doing and were supportive of that. This idea was developed as an interim measure, and Sam was the chair. I was brought in to assist on organising the Ulay/Abramovic show[33] which came here as a touring show, recurated by Sam for Tramway. My contract initially was on a three month term, and then it was extended for another three months and made permanent at the end of that 6 months."[34]

In the spring of 1998 the Tramway program included Host, a vast group show curated by Peter Lewis, featuring contributions from Filthy Swan, STOPSTOP, Elizabeth Go, Jim Lambie, Mary Redmond, Evol Urbain, Will Bradley, Toby Webster, Jacqueline Donachie, Henry VIII's Wives, Tatham & O'Sullivan, Erlend Williamson, Jonathan Monk, Roderick Buchanan and Ross Birrell, as well as London-based artists' initiatives such as BANK and Sarah Staton's Supastore. Local band Superstar played at the opening, and a stall serving hotdogs filled the space with a fairground smell. Host

32  Kirsty Ogg, in Elizabeth Mahoney, "Another Story", *Untitled*, Spring 1997.
33  Ulay/Abramovic: Performances 1976–1988, 14th February – 14th March 1998.
34  Alexia Holt, in conversation with the author, July 2001.

captured several of the strengths of the Glasgow scene: the support drawn from the music scene, the "strength in numbers" strategy of the artist collective, and the sheer diversity of approaches going on. Elizabeth Go's installation was a case in point: it featured a photograph, a small abstract painting, a sculptural piece and a sound work. Transmission committee member Robert Johnston impersonated Low-period David Bowie at the opening, while Gary Rough and Ross Birrell showed matching tombstones indicating that they had both already died.

A few weeks earlier, it had been announced that the CCA had been successful in its bid for a £7.5m Capital development lottery grant. Tramway now learnt it was to receive a £2.3m SAC Lottery grant, and closed for refurbishment a few months later. The CCA leased the McLellan Galleries to host temporary exhibitions, and Alexia Holt planned a series of Tramway projects in alternative venues around the city. However, the simultaneous closure of both Tramway and CCA for Lottery funded renovations in 1998/9 left the previously vaunted "contemporary art triangle" of Tramway, CCA and Transmission looking severely depleted. Sam Ainsley remembers: "CCA and Tramway were meant to close at different times but the Lottery group put so many impositions on what was happening at Tramway that the renovation process was delayed and delayed, and eventually the closure ended up coinciding with that of the CCA. It was very bad for the city and for morale."[35]

However, the relocation of the 13th Note alternative music venue and café from Glassford Street to King Street in 1998 helped to forge closer links between the art and music communities in the city. During the spring of 1998 Transmission capitalised on the new proximity of the heartland of alternative music in the city, by staging Something Aaah! Nothing, an exhibition that turned the gallery into a live music venue. The 13th Note donated their old stage from the Glassford Street premises for the occasion. The name of the show was explained by a gallery press release, "In the mid '80s four drunken US dysfunctionals formed Drunks With Guns and made slow, simple and loud hardcore when similar bands were getting faster and

---

35  Sam Ainsley, Ibid.

faster. In *Zombie* the words 'SOMETHING NOTHING' are growled alternately against a backdrop of two highly distorted guitar chords. A sound born of anger and substance abuse stumbles into the territory of some sort of conceptual art text thing. The crossover of art ideals and uncompromising sound creating a powerful musical force."

Something Aaah! Nothing featured live performances by Fukuyama, The James Orr Complex, and Cylinder. Cylinder were the longest established of the bands, and had been releasing records on local independent label Vesuvius for a few years. Guitarist Martin Young and bass guitarist Tony Swain were also well known as artists, and were familiar faces on the Transmission scene. Singer and songwriter duo Fukuyama had just released their first EP on independent record label Wurlitzer Jukebox. Natasha Noramly and Craig Beaton had met while studying at Glasgow University, and their music combined elements of the Red House Painters and Mark Eitzel with influences drawn from experimental bands like Tortoise and Directions in Music. Noramly explained, "It's really close music. If you really listen to it it's right there in your head, you can't distance yourself from it. But we also use weird samples … there's humour there."[36] The James Orr Complex was the solo project of Glaswegian musician Christopher Mack, who also played with local alt-rock band Eska. Mack combined a fingerpicking acoustic guitar style with enigmatic lyrics to create a uniquely warm and involving sound. He claimed to be inspired by "changes in atmospheric pressure, all possible escape routes, chewing tobacco, evil inclinations, Dr. Pepper, new salty waves, the noise wars of 42, and the theory of spasmodic light."[37] For the next three years, fans of Mack's evocative acoustics songs would have to attend live performances to hear them, as no recordings were yet available.

The roots of the performance movement in Glasgow were still very much intact, as Streetworks, a four day international festival of interventionist live

---

36 From an interview published in *Swing*, self-published, Glasgow, February, 1998. Craig B and his Fukuyama collaborator Natasha Noramly had been recruited to join Ganger in late 1997 by original drummer James Young. With original bassist Stuart Henderson, they had gone on to record the album Hammock Style (1998), although Beaton then left the band to concentrate on Aereogramme the following year.
37 From an interview published in *Swing*, self-published, Glasgow, May 1998.

art, organised by Ross Birrell, and held around Streetlevel, proved. Birrell had established his reputation as a performer locally with actions like *Working Class Hero b.1969*, which involved standing on a plinth in George Square for several hours, with the intention of redressing the class ratio of the statues there.[38] Birrell invited artists from Europe, South America, USA and Russia to participate in the festival of site-specific live art, and recalls his "important discussions with Malcolm [Dickson] regarding the contradictions of counterculture, public funding of critical art, and the urge to document and preserve the temporary condition of live art. To record these actions seemed to run counter to the very urgency that gave rise to their existence."[39] The festival included performances by Tara Babel, Andre Stitt and Julie Laffin, which were interrupted by Strathclyde Police, and an intervention by Alistair MacLennan which was brought to a halt completely by the local constabulary.

In 1998 another contemporary art space, Fly gallery in Dennistoun, had been opened in Glasgow by Fuse-founder Patricia Fleming, with the help of local artists Jamie Burroughs and Colin McFarlane. She remembers, "The funding for Fuse had changed and we couldn't be selective anymore about the artists in the project, so I felt I needed a different project to work on. I had been involved with community work in the East End for several years, and when some empty shop units became available in Duke Street, we took three of them on. One was an artist-in-residency studio, which Torsten Lauschmann and Michael Wilkinson worked in, and the other two we used as our new gallery space. Jamie Burroughs was integral to the project, he was great for bouncing ideas off, and he used to do a lot of the building work, as well as co-programming the exhibitions. Colin McFarlane had been on the Fuse scheme for several years, I kept bringing him back because he was such a great sounding block, and by now he was also closely involved in the running of the Glasgow Project Room. Other people who were very supportive included Will Bradley and Caroline Woodley – it really did feel like a group effort, you

---

38  The centrepont of George Square is a column supporting a statue of Sir Walter Scott, best known for his novels about Edinburgh.

39  Ross Birrell, Letter 1, *Justified Sinners*, Pocketbooks, Edinburgh, 2002.

believed in the people you were working with."[40]

Exhibitions staged at Fly in the first year of the gallery included The Social Life of Stuff, curated by Caroline Woodley and featuring work by Caroline Kirsop, Janice McNab, Sarah Tripp, Mary Redmond, Hayley and Sue Tompkins. The exhibition featured several collaborative works, such as Hayley Tompkins, Mary Redmond and Sue Tompkins' *Stola*, produced on site, which local curator and academic Francis McKee described in his review for *Untitled*. "A Helmut Lang cloak is painted on the wall beside two cut-out felt silhouettes and a small painted paper bag of flour on the ground. The cloak is a sci-fi self-contained garment, ballooning around the torso with a cavernous, all-enveloping hood. The accompanying felt silhouettes lie protectively on top of one another – a non-committal beige flap hiding a blazing red beneath. The combined materials of the work – felt, flour, paper and paint – not only recall Beuys and Robert Morris, they draw out the implicit desire for safety and retreat in Helmut Lang's design."[41]

Michael Wilkinson and Torsten Lauschmann made a collaborative work at Fly called *What Is Is, What Ain't Ain't Nothing* which was based on the kind of small bars and nightclubs that spring up and disappear in Berlin. The project marked the beginning of Wilkinson and Lauschmann's Ideal Home music/installation collaboration. Wilkinson and Lauschmann are in many ways representative of the way in which the Glasgow art scene has continued to attract artists from elsewhere. Wilkinson is originally from Liverpool, while Lauschmann was born in Bad Soden, Germany. After studying at Glasgow School of Art, they have both remained living and working in the city. At that time photography graduate Lauschmann's work touched upon how meaning is constructed and/or directed, for example his *Places of Exposure* series from 1997/1998 focussed on the wallpaper around paintings and the carpet beneath display cases in museums.

Michael Wilkinson made works that revolved around the idea of a built environment, such as the structure he built for The Janus Programme at

40  Patricia Fleming, in conversation with the author, December 2002.
41  Francis McKee, "The Social Life of Stuff", *Untitled*, 1998, p27.

Transmission in November 1998. The gallery invited a group of eight artists to make works for the gallery for a one week show, at the end of which the works would be rearranged according to the principles of Feng Shui. Wilkinson's piece was rebuilt outside the gallery, creating a second entrance. This same concern with utopian built environments was explored in two other shows in the city that year, including How to Build A Universe That Doesn't Fall Apart Two Days Later at Fly, which was curated by Will Bradley and featured Toby Paterson's *Idyllic Chalet* painting, Lindsey Orr's miniature model of the Kon-tiki, and assorted other works by Duncan Hamilton, Eva Rothschild, Denise Allison/Clifford Scullion, John Marshall, Rick Guidice/Nasa and Mike Nelson's proposal to recreate the Hanging Gardens of Babylon. Earlier that year, Alex Frost had exhibited a geodesic dome in the style of Buckminster Fuller in Transmission, which fellow artist Alan Michael reviewed: "The dome looked close to having production values or at least aspiring to them in a way that didn't seem unfeasible. I took this as a sign that the dome was meant to be itself and about itself simultaneously."[42]

Art fanzine *British Mythic*, edited by Joanne Tatham and Tom O'Sullivan, was launched in 1998, and over five subsequent issues featured contributions from several local artists including Alan Michael, Julian Kildear, Ewan Imrie, Kevin Hutcheson, Alex Frost, Rose Thomas, Sue and Hayley Tompkins and Anne-Marie Copestake. Transmission committee member Ewan Imrie and artist Alex Frost were also closely involved in compiling the fanzine. The publication was produced using the photocopying facilities at Transmission, and distributed free of charge. O'Sullivan says, "The title and format is quite tight, but within that you could let something go. I felt like giving something back to the art community. It's like an imaginative space … different from our own work because that's got a more specific agenda."[43] O'Sullivan suggested that the variety of approaches emerging in the Glasgow scene in the mid 1990s stemmed from a new approach to making work. He says, "I think the

42  Alan Michael, 1998, quoted in press release for Frost's Transmission project.
43  Tom O'Sullivan, in conversation with the author, January 2001

Glasgow art scene has really opened up now. The neo-conceptual way of working wasn't quite so diverse, as a certain amount of attitudes or preconceptions went with that."[44]

Glasgow's neo-conceptual artists found young pretenders biting at their heels as the Millennium approached. In 1998, Transmission committee member Robert Johnston complained of a lack of visceral, discordant energy in the practice of Gordon, Borland et al in the pages of *Art Monthly*. Johnston remembers, "There was a lot of pressure on the gallery to be an ambassador organisation for the Miracle. I think this worked to the detriment of artists 'on the ground' and left the gallery ripe for change."[45] The key neo-conceptual artists were not unaware of these issues, as Douglas Gordon demonstrated in a published conversation with his contemporary, Graham Fagen. He said, "Glasgow's got a lot of good people working in it, but because it's a small city there's a bottleneck situation where there's a few people who are doing very well, and could be seen to be jamming up the bottleneck, not by anything deliberate, just by the fact that they're there. And if I'm one of those people then my leaving might release the thing a bit. If people come to Glasgow who specifically wanted to see me, if I'm not around then they'll have to see someone else, that's a fact."[46]

Cathy Wilkes observes, "There is a certain amount of success with a certain group of artists in Glasgow but there will always be those who are less successful in terms of their career or finances. That creates divisiveness and makes people feel that they can select the good and the bad which I don't necessarily think is a good thing. But in order for some people to be well known, other people have to be less well known. The art world is totally linked up with fashion and always has been. Some people have taken the initiative to do things that have been responsible for helping people grow in confidence and achieve success, but as a spin-off of that they've become taste-setters. I don't think you can just say 'that's not a good thing' but it does have other effects."[47]

---


44  Tom O'Sullivan, Ibid.
45  Robert Johnston, "Don't Mention the Book" unpublished essay on Transmission, 1999.
46  *Transcript* Volume 03 Issue 03, School of Fine Art, Duncan of Jordanstone, Dundee, 2001.
47  Cathy Wilkes, Ibid.

Graduates from Dundee's Duncan of Jordanstone have made a noticeable impact on the Glasgow art scene in recent years: often these graduates have been taught by Glasgow-based artists and part-time Duncan of Jordanstone lecturers Cathy Wilkes, Victoria Morton[48] and Graham Fagen. *Transcript* magazine, first published by Duncan of Jordanstone in 1994, offered intelligent coverage of contemporary art in Scotland although since the untimely death of co-founder Alan Woods in 1999 the magazine has lain dormant. The presence of active artists on the teaching staff at Duncan of Jordanstone has had a definite influence on the work of the students, as former student Luke Fowler attests: "Dundee's only exception to other provincial cities – i.e. boredom plus frustration equal creativity – which I suppose make it special is that it has a great art school with some exceptional equipment and open-minded tutors."[49] Other graduates have identified Dundee's comparatively low-key pub and club scene as an unexpected advantage, allowing for a more concentrated and sustained practice.

For Lucy McKenzie (b.1977), studying in Dundee provided the necessary distance for her to synthesise all of her accumulated cultural reference points into a sustained approach. She says, "When I went to art college I already had an idea of what I was interested in. So I couldn't just do something really distant like paint a still life – I wanted to reference the life I had, what I was really interested in. The fanzine I had made shaped the way I made work – instead of plucking abstract things out of my head it was about fitting together these different cultural plates, creating new meanings by dusting them off and giving them some kind of new life."[50] McKenzie's existing disparate interests encompassed fanzine culture, the ideas surrounding riot grrrl and 1970s cultural icons including child gymnast Olga Korbut. Her paintings collaged together these ideas, together with heroic poses and imagery derived partially from Socialist Realism and partly from the work of older Glasgow-based artists like Alasdair Gray.

48  Victoria Morton stopped teaching at Duncan of Jordanstone in 2000, while Cathy Wilkes has been on a leave of absence since 2002.
49  Luke Fowler, in conversation with the author, March 2001.
50  Lucy McKenzie, Ibid.

However, the interest from commercial London galleries that surrounded the interest from commercial London galleries that surrounded McKenzie's show at EAST International a few weeks later ended in harsh criticism from some of her peers, who intended to stay in Dundee and build the scene around Generator. Like Glasgow School of Art alumna Jenny Saville, McKenzie sold some of her work to notorious art impresario Charles Saatchi soon after graduating from art school. She says, "I sold to Saatchi at a point when I had no money and no-one was interested in my work. I just thought, right, I need the cash. The whole debate about Saatchi has quite dubious moral overtones both ways – people want to sell to Saatchi because they think it furthers their careers, and others refuse to sell to Saatchi because they are in a certain position – a moral high ground. I have quite a cynical attitude towards making work – I know that I enjoy it, I love it but I know that it's just as much a commodity and as kitsch as anything else – and I don't think that's a high thing and I don't think of myself as a more serious artist than someone who is doing anything else. Art is treated as this hallowed pastime, given this kudos that it maybe doesn't deserve. Art is part of a commodity culture, like fashion."[51]

Connections between art and fashion are by no means a new alliance, but in the 1980s and '90s the hybridity was propagated by new London-based style magazines like *The Face, i-D, Dazed and Confused, Sleaze Nation* and French publications *Purple* and *Self Service.* Photographers associated with these magazines like Corrine Day, Juergen Teller, Elaine Constantine and Wolfgang Tillmans and artists including Rita Ackermann, Sylvie Fleury and Berlin-Paris based collaborators Bless further blurred the distinctions between fine art and fashion. Croydon-born supermodel Kate Moss consistently graced the pages of the style magazines throughout the 1990s, but also acted as muse to several yBa artists including Gary Hume and Marc Quinn. The process worked in reverse too, as German designer Helmut Lang proved when he signed up Louise Bourgeois for an ad campaign. There were also several stores that were halfway between gallery and boutique, like Sarah Lucas and Tracey Emin's shortlived The

<hr>

51  Lucy McKenzie, Ibid.

Shop (1993), Colette in Paris and London's The Pineal Eye, not to mention young British designers whose work had distinctively sculptural qualities, such as Hussein Chalayan, Alexander McQueen and Robert Carey Evans.

To a certain extent, Lucy Mckenzie's work fitted well with the London fashion/art scene, especially given that she had modelled for artist/pornographer Richard Kern. Although she was keen to leave Dundee, a move to London was never on the cards for McKenzie. Instead, she headed back to Glasgow in 1999, to reconnect with the social scene there, which had fed much of her early works. She said, "I know if I'd stayed in Dundee [after graduating] I would have kept painting a lot and working hard. I'd made quite a good life for myself in Dundee – I was really healthy and I didn't go out too much, I painted a lot and read a lot. I knew when I moved to Glasgow things would really change, that I would go out a lot more and drink a lot more, but then I knew I'd be too lonely if I stayed in Dundee. Dundee is fine if you're within the support system of the art school but outwith that it's too isolating."[52]

In Glasgow, former Duncan of Jordanstone graduates including Alan Michael, Ewan Imrie, Clare Stephenson and Anna McLauchlan were already active in the scene around Transmission.[53] McKenzie joined them there, as her work continued to attract widely spread acclaim, particularly in Germany, where her new figurative style chimed with that of young German painters like Neo Rausch and Kai Althoff. She continued to initiate projects within Glasgow, such as the Flourish showcase[54] and worked with Edinburgh-based artist Keith Farquhar on their collaborative venture, Charisma, while exhibiting widely in the UK and overseas.[55] Another Duncan of Jordanstone graduate, Scott Myles remembers, "Alan Michael, Ewan Imrie and Clare


52  Lucy McKenzie, Ibid.

53  Ewan Imrie served on the 1997–1999 Transmission committee, Alan Michael from1999–2001, and Anna McLauchlan and Clare Stephenson were members of the 2000–2002 committee.

54  A series of events held at the Flourish studio at Robertson Street by the artists working there, beginning in 1999. Artists participating in the first series of talks and screenings included Steven Sutcliffe, Joanne Tatham and Tom O'Sullivan, Sophie MacPherson, Fred Pedersen, Oliver Payne and Nick Relph. The name of the studio and events series derived from the city motto 'Let Glasgow Flourish'.

55  Lucy McKenzie is represented by Cabinet gallery, London and Daniel Bucholz, Cologne. In 2000 she was selected for inclusion in the British Art Show 5 and Beck's Futures competition with older peers including Cathy Wilkes, Roderick Buchanan, David Shrigley and Martin Boyce, while in 2001 she appeared in international group show Painting At the Edge of the World, at the Walker Art Center, Minneapolis.

Stephenson were all in the year above me – they all moved to Glasgow. At the time Dundee Contemporary Arts didn't exist and Generator hadn't yet found a permanent location, so when you left college there weren't actually that many opportunities. I came to Glasgow and found that it's a good place to make art, there is a lot going on here. That was the first time I thought that I could remain living in Scotland for a longer period of time."[56]

The new ideas that these Duncan of Jordanstone graduates brought to the Glasgow scene connected with the work of Glasgow-based artists who were exploring different areas of practice. Robert Johnston (b.1973) had recently made a number of works that related to music, and he began working in 1998 on a collaborative project entitled Punish with fellow committee member Ewan Imrie. Punish had its roots in an event entitled *Nausea*, which took place in June 1998, as part of Radar, an exhibition held by artist-run initiative Generator in a Dundee warehouse. The DJs were Graeme Esson, Mark Vernon, Lucy McKenzie and Ewan Imrie. The five-hour event was attended by around fifty people, twenty of whom faced the 2K PA for most of the night, as tracks by renegade musos like Throbbing Gristle, Captain Beefheart, Faust, Black Flag and the Meat Puppets blasted out. Imrie remembers, "Music was played at a volume in an improvised club environment to form a barrage of sound, sometimes unpleasant, difficult, noisy – designed to take people to an almost sickening level of saturation. The idea – that you can find some sort of gratification, and perhaps a sense of freedom, by testing the thresholds of pleasure and endurance."[57]

Once Ewan Imrie moved to Glasgow, he enlisted the services of Robert Johnston in organising Punish events at Lucy McKenzie's Robertson Street studio and the 13th Note club in Clyde Street. Johnston says, "I think we wanted it to represent ideas about radicalism and resistance in general, by many different means – playing an apparently disorganised selection of music really loudly, developing a signature design style based around radical and/or ignored cultures, circulating esoteric literature, etcetera, etcetera."[58] Often the only light source at Punish events was an orange bar-heater type

56  Scott Myles, in conversation with the author, September 2000.
57  Ewan Imrie, *British Mythic*, No. 2, July 1998, p1.
58  Robert Johnston, in response to questions sent by the author, January 2001.

lamp on the bare floor. Imrie and Johnston later toured their Punish project to Galleri Wang in Oslo, which produced a limited edition of photographs of the orange light and projected inscriptions from run-out grooves on records. Most of the source records were released by Factory Records or Underground Resistance, which included inscriptions such as "experimenting for the future of our existence" from UR013.5-B. Robert Johnston explained, "I'm interested in anything that's sort of submerged in culture – like the collection of run-out groove inscriptions Ewan Imrie and I did for Punish – or doesn't have mass recognition. I just like that there's more actually going on in the world than there seems to be, and that some of it doesn't actually mind being a hidden, minority thing – in fact it values that status. That's a lot to do with ideas about freedom I think. When no-one's watching, you have a lot of freedom."[59]

59  Robert Johnston, Ibid.

# CHAPTER 10

# HIGH, LOW, MEDIUM, SLOW
# (1999)

At the end of 1998, London-based artist-run gallery City Racing had closed after ten years of activity. The gallery run by Peter Owen, Matt Hale, Paul Noble, John Burgess and Keith Coventry, had staged 51 shows over a ten year period, and the exhibition City Racing 1988–1998 a partial account was held at the ICA to commemorate its passing. Fiona Banner, who had her first solo show at City Racing, said "They showed people who they liked, although they might contest that point now. There were no 'careers' involved, it wasn't that kind of endeavour. It's different to the situation now where you'll turn up at a private view and the curator's showing off about how he just sold a ton of work to Saatchi before the gallery has even opened. There doesn't seem to be an equivalent place these days."[1]

But in Glasgow, there were still numerous City Racing equivalents, the most notable example of which was still Transmission. In January, the committee invited Jim Lambie to do his first solo show at the gallery, who came up with the simple but brilliant idea for *Voidoid*. Lambie's father ran a signwriting company that produced vinyl lettering, and Lambie had been thinking for a while about using vinyl tape to make a work. He struck upon the idea of sticking one colour of tape around the edge of the room, then another colour inside that, and so on until the centre of the room, creating a psychedelic minimalist carpet that echoed and amplified the dimensions of the space. He said, "For me something like the floor piece, it's creating so

---

1   *Untitled*, Spring 2001, p15.

many edges that they all dissolve. Is the room expanding or contracting? With the record decks, covering them in glitter pulls all those edges into one idea, it centres them all … Covering an object somehow evaporates the hard edge off the thing, and pulls you towards more of a dreamscape. The hard, day to day living edge disappears."[2] Irish art magazine *Circa* was the first one to pick up on the potential of the piece and put it on their cover in spring 1999. Soon several other art magazines, including *frieze*, commissioned articles on Lambie, and soon curators everywhere were clamouring for their own Lambie floor, not to mention fashion stylists, including style doyenne Isabella Blow.

*Voidoid* had been a very palpable hit, and the follow up, Tobias Rehberger's Standard Rad, was another coup for Transmission. The exhibition was "an environmental portrait" of Rehberger's friends Standard Rad (a design company based in London and Frankfurt). The floor of the gallery was painted scarlet, and low groupings of Japanese style tables and seating were arranged around the space. Overhead, a cluster of white paper lanterns on strings pulsed on and off, leaving an impression of redness behind the eyes as the darkness fell. Behind pink, red and orange partitions films that had scared the Standard Rad designers as children (*The Incredible Shrinking Man*, *A Man Called Horse*, *Soldier Blue* and *The Invasion of the Body Snatchers*) played on video monitors.

In January 1999, James Thornhill followed up his previous curatorial projects such as The Belmont Hotel (1995) by turning the living room of his East End flat into a gallery space called Ready Steady Made. Nine artists including Michelle Naismith, Annette Heyer, Will Bradley, David Bellingham, Jim Hamlyn, Nina Lehrfreund, Andrew McNiven, Douglas Gibb and Richard Wright were invited to stage projects. Thornhill recalls, "It was quite hard giving up that amount of space in our flat. It was a very different experience from The Belmont Hotel, which was very involved. We had less of a social grouping, partly because we were living in Dennis-toun. I don't know if it was a successful run of shows. Many of the shows I didn't like myself, but that was okay. In a sense I was the patron in this

2   Jim Lambie, interviewed by Andrea Tarsia, Early One Morning, The Whitechapel Gallery, London, 2002.

scenario – I didn't apply for any SAC funding, it was just done on a really low budget. I was giving people the opportunity to do something and fail within this space, and I think that's quite good. It was quite a modest undertaking."[3]

The following month, temporary exhibitions organisation Switchspace was set up by Glasgow School of Art graduates Sorcha Dallas and Marianne Greated, in the spare room of Dallas' West-end flat. Switchspace was partially inspired by a talk given at the art school by Cathy Wilkes about her own flat gallery initiative. Marianne Greated says, "At our Professional Practice Conference in fourth year Cathy Wilkes had talked to us about having exhibitions in any available spaces like your own home, and this certainly set off ideas which led to Switchspace. At this conference I also had an interesting talk with Vicky Morton. Sorcha and I also had an appointment with Christine Borland to ask her advice on setting up exhibition spaces. She was very helpful. Some of the tutors, especially Richard Wright, gave me an idea of how things could be done in alternative ways and introduced us to concepts, people, organisations which otherwise I may not have heard about."[4]

Switchspace showed GSA graduates including Maria McCavana, David Sherry, Mick Peter, Stuart Gurden, Marianne Greated, Anne Walton, Sorcha Dallas and Anne Bjerge Hansen in the initial one-year period, although there were certain difficulties involved in showing work in a domestic setting. Marianne Greated remembers, "The shows in the flat went very well, and they were well attended with on average 70–80 people attending each one. This was actually quite a lot of people considering we could not advertise publicly and many attended through word of mouth. We couldn't make it completely public because it was Sorcha's home … she also had very awkward neighbours so openings had to be strictly finished at 9pm to avoid problems."[5] Despite these restrictions, Switchspace hosted a number of memorable works, including Anne Bjerge Hansen's traditional Danish bakery, Stuart Gurden's enormous spiky sculpture made from cable

3   James Thornhill, in conversation with the author, August 2001.
4   Marianne Greated, in response to questions sent by the author, September 2001.
5   Marianne Greated, Ibid.

ties found on lamp posts and Anne Walton's highly flammable floor of peat briquettes and a 'rug' made from red-tipped matches.

In April the first leg of the exchange project with Malmö's Pineapple gallery took place, with six artists from Malmö showing at the gallery, and a performance, by Lena Mattson, taking place in the Mitre bar on the opening night. A few months later, Hayley Tompkins, Sue Tompkins, Scott Myles, Anne-Marie Copestake, Sarah Tripp and Duncan Campbell would travel to Malmö to show in a disused cinema for the return leg of the project, in a show called Fields and Rays and Green Numbers. These artists' work was characterised by an interest in the language of popular culture, often manifested in the appropriation of song lyrics and references to both fanzine culture and high fashion magazines. Anne-Marie Copestake's 1998 book *Take Hold Tightly Let Go Lightly*, featured lyrics from popular songs, and she later developed her interest in performance with her on-line Trigger tonic video archive, which showcased Glasgow based artists interviewing interesting visitors to town, sometimes writers or artists, but often musicians. The archive includes footage of Victoria Morton interviewing Chicks on Speed and Scott Myles interviewing Le Tigre front-woman Kathleen Hanna, formerly of riot grrrl band Bikini Kill.

Belfast-born artist Duncan Campbell (b.1972) was in the final year of his MFA, and was making sculptural and video works incorporating elements from fashion magazines, club flyers, posters and plastic bags. A 1999 video work was comprised of a collage of pages taken from "lifestyle" magazines like *Loaded, Wallpaper, Dazed & Confused, FHM* and *Arena*. Campbell edited together excerpts from accompanying articles about fashion and celebrity, and put them through the Apple "spell and speak" programme. The clipped computerised speech and the flow of disconnected ideas and images made a subtle challenge to the channel-hopping culture that now seemed ordinary. While this work was seductive to listen to and watch, the realisation was never far from being nonsensical: a slippery jumble of limbs and make-up techniques, famous lives and sexual yearnings. Campbell also reworked flyers and posters from local clubs such as Optimo and Hi Karate, making them into origami animals, or knitted wall hangings.

In May, twin sisters Hayley and Sue Tompkins presented a collaborative solo exhibition Sounds of Grass at Transmission. For the show, the white cube of the gallery was reworked with a diagonal chipboard partition hung with loosely draped squares of hessian sackcloth. Elsewhere, there were a number of colourful and exact wall paintings, a display of painted eggs and a hanging group of magazine pages that had been crumpled in the palm of the hand until they took on a soft and shiny form, like leaves. The gallery floor was painted black but dust had been left unswept in a corner, and disturbed by footprints. On the floor, like a picnic blanket, was a hessian square stitched with a neon pink seam and a glass of orange liquid, either paint water or summer orangeade.[6]

In June, a shop/gallery called Echo Park[7] opened on St. George's Road in Glasgow, selling limited edition artist's books, independent label records, crockery, oddments, and clothes, jewellery and accessories made by artists including Claire Barclay, Sarah Tripp, Sue and Hayley Tompkins, Luke Fowler and Toby Webster. Echo Park also showed the work of local artists including Kirsty Anderson, Martin Clark, Hanneline Visnes and Diane Main and hosted launch events for local fanzines like *British Mythic*. The shop was influenced by Paris boutique Colette and London's Pineal Eye, but also had a local antecedent in the work of Lapland, which had been set up by Hugh Pizey and Patrick Macklin in 1994. Lapland staged temporary exhibitions of limited edition works made by artists in a variety of locations, including a shop on Byres Road, the window of modish hairdresser's DLC[8] and some allotments on the south side of the city.

That summer, Sue Tompkins, Hayley Tompkins, and Duncan of Jordan-stone graduates Alan Michael and Scott Myles set up another self-funded flat gallery at 78 Roselea Drive in Dennistoun. Myles had previously staged a group exhibition in an empty property in Dundee in his final year at art school, which had been reviewed by Judith Findlay for *Flash Art*. He was making works that addressed his interests in transformation and travel,

6   Adapted from a review by the author published in The List, 13–27 May, 1999, p73.
7   Echo Park was established and run by the author for a period of six months.
8   DLC stands for the first names of the founder members: Derek, Leigh and Cath. Leigh Ferguson in particular was a stalwart supporter of the local arts scene, sponsoring various clubs including Paul Cawley's Audio Psy-Phi and Jonnie Wilkes and Keith McIvor's Optimo. More recently Ferguson has formed a band, 5 Piece Horse Family, with local artists Victoria Morton and Anne-Marie Copestake.

such as a pair of photographs showing the artist posing in front of Monument Valley. Closer inspection revealed the first photograph to have been taken in Dundee, in front of a Marlboro advertising hoarding, whereas the second photograph, from 1998, showed Myles smiling beside the genuine landmark. Myles staged a number of exhibitions at his new flat in Glasgow, including White Bear zz with Alan Michael, and Hayley & Sue Tompkins, new works by David Thorpe and Film Club, a screening of Super 8 films shot by Glasgow artists. He says, "Hayley Tompkins, Sue Tompkins and Alan Michael were talking about doing a show using this disused room in the flat. So we did a show with the four of us and then kept it going from there – asking David Thorpe to come up to Scotland – he was pretty receptive although he was doing well commercially. We also showed Raydale Dower and the final show was Film Club, which I had to get some money for. For the other shows I'd got things like paint and David Thorpe's train fare out of my own pocket. So for Film Club I persuaded Transmission and the Glasgow Music Collective to give me half the money each to buy 11 super 8 films. I wanted to ask a few groups of artists to make films – I asked Punish and Elizabeth Go and I asked The Cocktail Party, which was Fred Pedersen and Thomas Seest. I asked Habitat to give us some beanbags and Douglas Gordon also helped us out with beanbags and equipment. Although he's  pretty busy he still helped out for this one night, grassroots event. About 100 people came and we had to do two showings because it was so packed."[9]

## EDUCATION IN REVERSE

Chris Evans, Duncan Hamilton and Padraig Timoney of All Horizon's Club[10] had been touring their Free Tutorials project around art colleges in the UK throughout January and February of 1999. The three of them with

---

9   Scott Myles, in conversation with the author, September 2000.

10  All Horizons Club had evolved out of the activities of the Liverpool-based Three Month Gallery early in 1999. The new organisation worked without a gallery or fixed base on a variety of projects: publishing, online artworks, event-based projects, conferences and exhibitions.

a changing group of invited artists[11] travelled in a minibus, visiting art colleges and offering free tutorials at each institution.[12] No prior arrangements were made with the art colleges on the route, with the aim of giving students the opportunity to talk freely about their work outwith the structure of their course and their usual tutor's expectations. At a conference held to discuss the outcome of their project at the CCA in Glasgow in February, Pavel Büchler, former Head of Fine Art at Glasgow School of Art and artists Jacqueline Donachie and Sarah Tripp were invited to speak.

Sarah Tripp was in the process of developing her Education in Reverse project, by inviting proposals for ideas for educational events in spaces that weren't already being used for that purpose through the Transmission mail out, and direct mailings to art galleries, universities and art colleges in Scotland. She said, "Firstly, it is an attempt to redefine what an educational experience might be, or even to redefine studenthood. I think the ideas we have of students and studenthood at the moment are quite impoverished. Secondly, I am interested in a concept used by sociologists in the Seventies called The Hidden Curriculum. This idea states that while you are at college or at school, learning skills or learning about a particular subject, at the same time you are also learning about social control, about how authority works and about how to behave in social situations. However, having some kind of an educational experience which isn't part of an institution might be a way of unlearning some of those assumptions. Thirdly, I believe there should be more open access. In other words there is an open access system for applications for colleges (although applications are based on qualifications) but there isn't a system of open access for people who want to present information at colleges. I think that is one of the things Free Tutorials has gone some of the way toward equalising [ ... ]. There just aren't enough alternative influences within colleges, or ways of venturing

---

11  The participating artists were: Olof Bjornsdottir, Damien Duffy, Chris Evans, Alex Frost, Kate Gray, Duncan Hamilton, Ewan Imrie, David Mackintosh, Tom O'Sullivan, Joanne Tatham, Elizabeth Price, Andrew Small, Padraig Timoney, Sarah Tripp, David Wilkinson and Caroline Woodley.

12  Edinburgh College of Art, University of Northumbria – Newcastle, Manchester's Metropolitan University, John Moores University – Liverpool, Central St. Martins – London and Kingston University – Surrey.

in to be part of an educational experience."[13]

In April, another project relating to education took place, this time at Transmission. Although Ewan Imrie had by now left the committee, he was responsible for instigating the Philosophical Enquiry season at the gallery. Two groups of a dozen Transmission members met up in the gallery on Wednesdays for ten weeks, to "reason from their own thoughts" on ideas, concepts and statements raised during the meetings, without citing the work or theories of others. A gallery press release stated, "Transmission believes that Philosophical Enquiry could fulfill a significant role in promoting dialogue in an art context with practising artists [ … ]. These confrontations with other people's opinions will provide a useful test for ideas and encourage a healthy dialogue free of assumptions and received, second-hand ideas." In October 1999 Sarah Tripp's Education in Reverse, a week-long series of free educational and conversational events took place in and around Glasgow. London-based artist Alan Kane's Education in Reverse talk took participants on a flaneur-like "drift" across the city, while Hayley and Sue Tompkins presented an idiosyncratic spoken-word *A-Z* in the luxurious surroundings of The Corinthian Bar on Ingram Street. Jacqueline Donachie held her event in less salubrious but no less enjoyable surroundings, at Shawfield greyhound racing track.


## DEMOCRACY FOR SCOTLAND?

On the 6th of May, 1999 elections were held for Scotland and Wales' new, devolved parliaments. Turn out for the elections for the new Scottish Parliament was just 56%, while just over 46% of the Welsh electorate went to the polls for the first ever Welsh Assembly. This low turnout was surprising, as the establishment of a devolved Scottish parliament had been campaigned for by increasing numbers of people since the failed devolution referendum of 1979. However, this low turnout at the polls was part of a countrywide pattern, with a survey of 700 key local

13 Transcript from Free Tutorials conference, CCA Glasgow / Tate Liverpool published by All Horizons Club, 1999.

authority wards indicating that voter turnout was down eight points on the same wards in 1995. Labour's position had weakened, with the Labour share of the vote falling in many working-class constituencies, and 'New Labour' failing to secure an overall majority in either Scotland or Wales.

Although Glasgow had lost out to Edinburgh as the site of the Scottish Parliament, the city had been named City of Architecture and Design 1999, enabling a series of projects to commence, such as the Homes for the Future complex at Glasgow Green, and the opening of The Lighthouse Centre for Design and Architecture on Mitchell Lane, in Charles Rennie Mackintosh's former *Evening Times* and *Glasgow Herald* building. All of the new buildings weren't confined to Glasgow, however. Dundee Contemporary Arts was also under construction, with ex-SAC Head of Visual Art, Andrew Nairne in place as director, and former Transmission committee member Katrina Brown returning from Tate Liverpool to take up the post of curator.

From its opening night, DCA displayed a commitment both to connecting with existing artistic traditions in Scotland and to showing the work of younger generations of Scottish artists. Joseph Beuys' *Three Pots for the Poorhouse – Action Object* (1974) was borrowed from the Scottish National Gallery of Modern Art in Edinburgh for the opening exhibition, Prime. This "action object" was the physical evidence that remained of Beuys' 1974 performance at the Poorhouse in the Forrest Hill area of Edinburgh, for Richard Demarco's Edinburgh Arts summer school. The Beuys connection continued with an opening night performance by Glasgow-based artist George Wyllie, who had assisted Beuys on his 1981 *Poorhouse Doors* project in Edinburgh. Wyllie was well-known for his Beuysian public sculptures and "pataphysical performances", notably his *Straw Locomotive* (1987), *Paper Boat* works and the spires he had erected in various international sites. For the DCA opening he performed an action entitled *A Bucket of Ice*. He explained, "The inability of solid to always remain in that state suggests that it might appreciate occasional conversion, and so I chucked some of the ice out of my bucket, and left some in it. By this simple device we should be able to see what happens to the freed ice and the captured ice. It's like trying to harpoon a moving target – a cloud for example. It seems a good way to talk about art."[14]

Prime also featured work by numerous younger Scottish artists, including Callum Innes, Douglas Gordon, Simon Starling, Louise Hopkins, Callum Innes and Christine Borland, a combination of London-based artists of various ages (Tony Cragg, Anish Kapoor, Anya Gallachio and Catherine Yass), plus works by Andy Warhol and Rebecca Horn. For the opening, Cathy Wilkes was commissioned to produce a series of limited edition commemorative flags. She said, "The idea that the souvenir should incorporate an existing universal symbol was an important, initial response to the project, and that this be a really recognisable symbol of unity and individuality. Ears, sheaves and fields of golden wheat – planted, ripened, harvested – are political and religious symbols of community, survival and the cycle of life."[15] Ideas relating to cycles of life also informed another important commission that Katrina Brown had already set in place for DCA's autumn programme – Christine Borland's first solo show in Scotland since *From Life* in 1994. Borland was undertaking a residency in the Biochemistry department at Dundee University which would inform the exhibition What makes for the fullness and perfection of life, for beauty and happiness, is good. What makes for death, disease, imperfection, suffering, is bad. The centrepiece of the exhibition would be the video projection Aether Sea, which focussed on the luminous jellyfish whose luminous structure enables the visualisation of DNA.


## MUSIC AND T-SHIRTS


In May, Victoria Morton presented Decapoda, a solo exhibition of paintings, drawings and sculptures at Stirling's Changing Room gallery.[16]

14  George Wyllie, Dundee Contemporary Arts 1999, Dundee, 1999.
15  Cathy Wilkes, Dundee Contemporary Arts 1999, Dundee, 1999.
16  The Changing Room, Stirling's contemporary art space, was established on the second floor of a Victorian shopping arcade in 1997. The gallery is funded by Stirling Council's Heritage and Cultural Services and is managed by the Council's Visual Arts Development Officer (currently Kirsteen McDonald) and a staff of volunteers. Previous Changing Room exhibitions include Deep in this Custard (2000) with Torsten Lauschmann, Marcus Mitchell, Fred Pedersen and Michael Wilkinson (2000), Avalon (2000) with Sue Tompkins, Hayley Tompkins, Joanne Tatham and Tom O'Sullivan and Ladies Rock (2003) with Katy Dove, Raydale Dower, Keith Farquhar and Mary Redmond.

The exhibition included a large and elaborate work entitled *Winter Painting After: All Friends Together the Friends Turn Into Flowers*, which looked a little like a Clyfford Still, a little like a 1970s textile design, and a little like a garden, but a garden of faces and gestures. Her friend and Elizabeth Go collaborator Sarah Tripp wrote in the catalogue essay, "All these buoyant forms, rituals, clothes, places and scenarios which lend their color and shape to any ideal and anyone, are gathered together by us and become our self-image. These wishful images and accessories help us define our aims and describe the roles we want to play, they are inspired by the world we live in and are built by our imaginations. Between books and beaches, music and T-shirts, friends and flowers there is the potential to reveal through the inter-images born out of change something about ourselves which is in the process of becoming – something which isn't recognised yet, because it is personal and new."[17] The influences and materials that Tripp cites, especially fashion and music, were becoming increasingly familiar in the work of young artists in Glasgow, often expressed through collaborative ventures.

New Glasgow band Life Without Buildings had played their first gig in London in June 1999, which guitarist Robert Johnston described as "Terrifying! I've never been so scared in my life. Even the soundcheck was terrifying. I don't think any of us enjoyed it much because we were so scared and we had to concentrate so hard on remembering our three songs."[18] Johnston and lead singer Sue Tompkins, bassist Chris Evans, and drummer Will Bradley had all known each other for years, from the art school and their involvement in Transmission. The band described their influences as encompassing Sonic Youth, Joy Division, Television, The Slits, The Raincoats and Galaxie 500, although Will Bradley insisted that the key influence on their sound was 'under rehearsal'.[19] Despite their modesty, the band managed to secure a recording deal with London's Tugboat record label, although they were still reluctant to play on home turf. Evans explained, "There's no venue big enough for the laser show."[20]

<hr>

17  Sarah Tripp, essay from Victoria Morton's Decapoda exhibition catalogue, The Changing Room, Stirling, 1999.
18  Excerpt from an interview with the author, originally published in Swing, autumn 1999.
19  Excerpt from an interview with the author, Ibid.
20  Excerpt from an interview with the author, Ibid.

Another group of local artists, who had just graduated from the MFA at Glasgow School of Art, were also working on a music-related project that summer. Alex Frost remembers, "It was the summer after graduat-ing, and Duncan Campbell had come up with an idea, which he spoke to me about. I was living with Mark Vernon at the time, who was into experimental music. The three of us came up with the idea of facilitating all the people around us who were making art in the form of sound. That just came out of the fact that it was fairly apparent that there were a lot of people around who were into art, but who also made music, or people who were in bands but also made art: there was a bit of cross-over happening. We decided the best way of broadening that out was to ask people who we thought were generally quite interesting to do something that would push them into that sound arena. There was a discussion element to it – they could record their own composition, or even just a mix of records – we kept it quite wide. The first four Radio Tuesday broadcasts were on four consecutive Tuesdays in June."[21] The first  broadcasts were collected onto a cassette release supported by New Media Scotland, The Modern Institute and All Horizons Club, which featured a wide range of contributions, from artist and Cylinder musician Tony Swain's composition *He Flips, Twists, Blinks, Lying Still, Flies Again Then Stops*, to Hayley and Sue Tompkins' free verse, to Lucy McKenzie's *Socialismus* DJ mix.

Duncan Campbell and Alex Frost were also continuing to make their own artworks, which, especially in the case of Campbell, incorporated elements drawn from the language of popular culture. Alex Frost's earlier work had included building a Buckminster Fuller Geodesic Dome for his 1998 Theme Show at Transmission, which he lived inside for a week at the gallery, and replicating an architectural scale model of new town Cumbernauld, for another sculptural work, *Model for the ice town centre* (1998). His interest in utopian ideals and how they might translate or be mistranslated into built environments[22] fed into the activities of Radio Tuesday, which got off to an explosive start. "The first one we did from a

---

21  Alex Frost, Ibid.
22  Around this period Frost also started to make smaller, more decorative works, composed of tiny bugle beads and worked metal, that resembled miniature skeletons of churches, or 1970s childrens' climbing frames.

hillside", remembers Frost, "and we powered the transmitter off a car battery and strapped the aerial to a fence. There was this great view of Glasgow, and then a puff of smoke as the transmitter caught fire. It was just a small part of the circuit fortunately … "[23]

The playlists of all the mainstream radio stations that summer were dominated by three hit songs by Glasgow band Travis. Their second album, *The Man Who …* had become a sleeper hit, crammed with one top 40 hit after another. *Writing to Reach You, Driftwood* and *Why Does It Always Rain On Me* were playing on every car radio and in most clothes shops around town. By the end of the year, the Horseshoe Bar in Drury Street where the band had rehearsed as unknowns had become the custodian of several gold discs. Along the road at Jamaica Street, things were going well at the Sub Club. Saturday night club Subculture had remained constantly popular throughout the 1990s, as resident DJ Harri released a number of soulful dance records on various labels, including *Calling All Dancers* on Paper Recordings, plus various tracks on Limbo, Bomba, Glasgow Underground, Tronic Sole, Disco Sole and his own Tax Disc Records. In 1998, under the guise of Daddy's Favourite, he had scored his first Top 20 hit, with the infectious *I Feel Good Things for You*. Sunday night club Optimo's unique brand of 'sleaze funk for freaks' had recently gone from being something of a well-kept secret to being the hottest ticket in town. Devotees regularly had their ears assaulted by a crazy melange of Soft Cell, The Stooges, ESG, Dub Narcotic, Devo, Joy Division, Alec Empire and Chicks On Speed. Resident DJ Keith McIvor said, "As a DJ I hope [dance music] moves into ever more uncharted waters – more risks, more experimentation and much more variety. I'd say a club like Optimo is maybe 20% there, but it could go much further – there is the whole of recorded 20th century dance music to explore and that's a lot of music that can be danced to. Are people ready for it? Am I ready for it? I guess we'll have to see. Tibetan thigh bone trance anyone?"[24]

23  Alex Frost, Ibid.
24  Excerpt from an interview with the author, published in Swing, autumn 1999.

Charles Esche left The Modern Institute in 1999 in order to take up his new post as Director of the Rooseum, in Malmö, and to attend to his numerous other roles: co-editor of the journal *Afterall*,[25] research fellow at Edinburgh College of Art, and instigator of the Edinburgh-based research and exhibition body the protoacademy. The protoacademy, a meeting point and discussion forum, operated in association with Edinburgh Art College, aimed "to draw together students, graduates and emerging artists from academic institutions across Europe."[26]

The Modern Institute had begun hosting exhibitions by local and foreign artists in their Robertson Street premises in 1998, supplemented by projects that they initiated outside the gallery. The most ambitious of these projects was Rirkrit Tirivanija's *Cinema for A Quiet Intersection (against Oldenberg)* – which for one evening in late September 1999 transformed a quiet Partick street into an open air cinema, screening four films selected by local residents. *Casablanca*, *It's a Wonderful Life*, *A Bug's Life* and *The Jungle Book* played simultaneously on a cube of fifteen by twenty foot cinema screens at the intersection of Gardener Street and Partickhill Road. Partickhill is one of the city's steepest drumlins, creating a spectacular aspect for crowds walking down towards the intersection. Many people had brought deck chairs, rugs and picnics and settled down to enjoy the show, while others wandered, taking in the scene, and snippets from the films: the chorus of "The Bare Necessities", Ingrid Bergman's tearfilled eyes. With the assistance of a group of local artists, Tirivanija cooked up Thai food in a nearby community centre, which was given away to the crowds of residents and visitors. A light rain started to fall after about an hour, but even then most of the audience stayed to watch the credits roll.

The red sandstone building in Robertson Street that housed The Modern Institute, the studios of various artists, a pro-life organisation, socialist MSP

---

25  Since mid 2002, *Afterall*, originally published solely by Central Saint Martin's, London, has been published in association with the California Institute of the Arts, where Thomas Lawson is Dean.
26  Source: www.protocademy.org

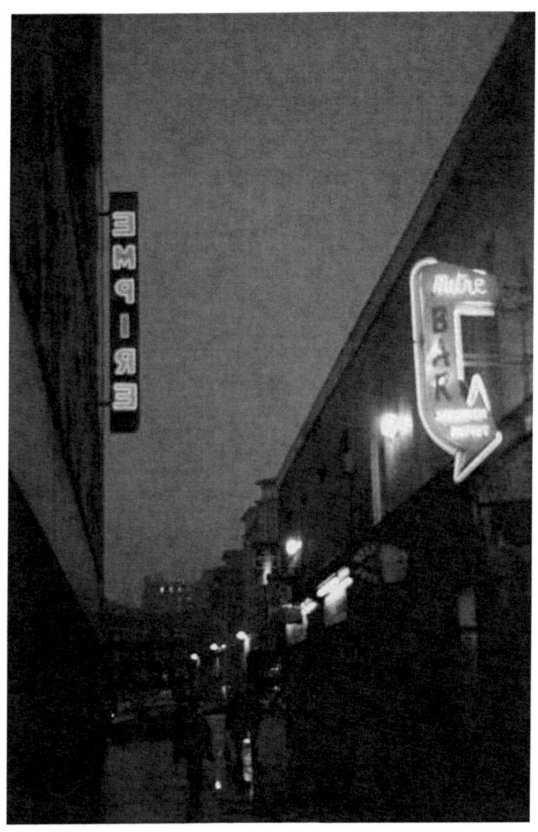

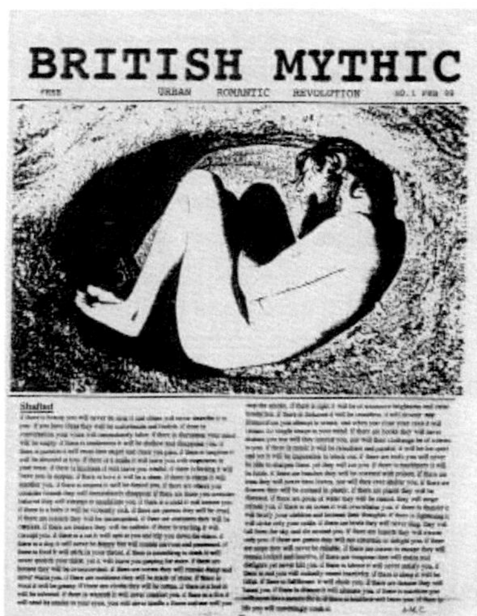


Douglas Gordon, *Empire*, 1998, the first public art commission by Visual Art Projects.

*British Mythic*, Issue no.1, 1998.

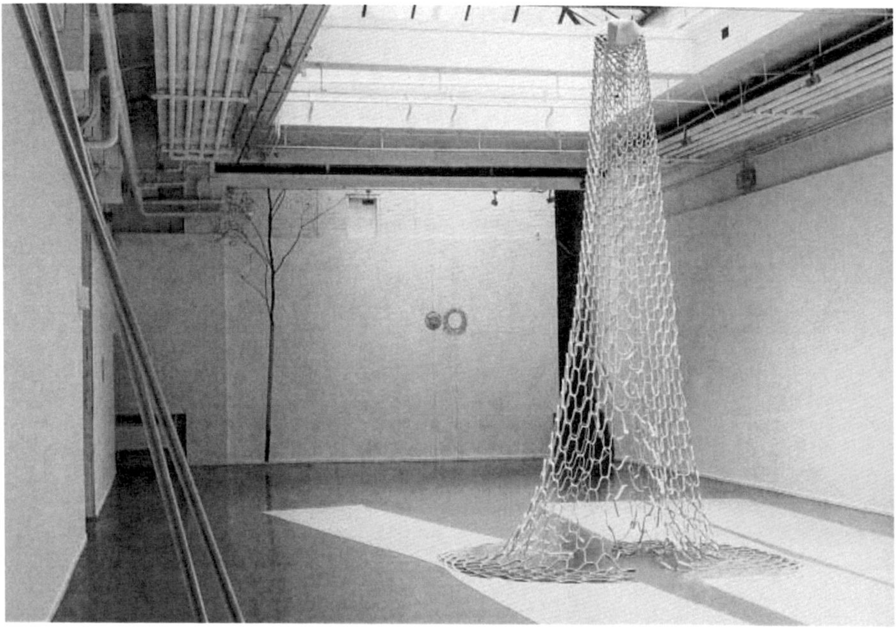

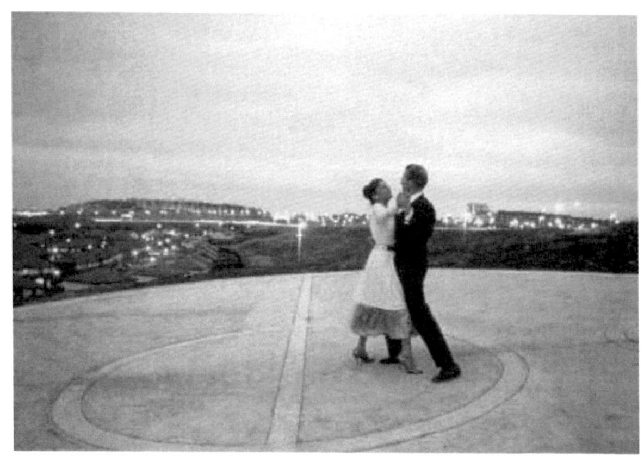

Claire Barclay, *Out of the Woods*, CCA, 1997.
Jacqueline Donachie, *The Trees, The Book and The Disc*, Darnley, managed by Visual Arts Projects, Glasgow between April 1998 to March 1999.

Marianne Greated, sleeve illustration for
*Philophobia*, Arab Strap, 1998.
Victoria Morton, *Dirty Burning*, 1997.

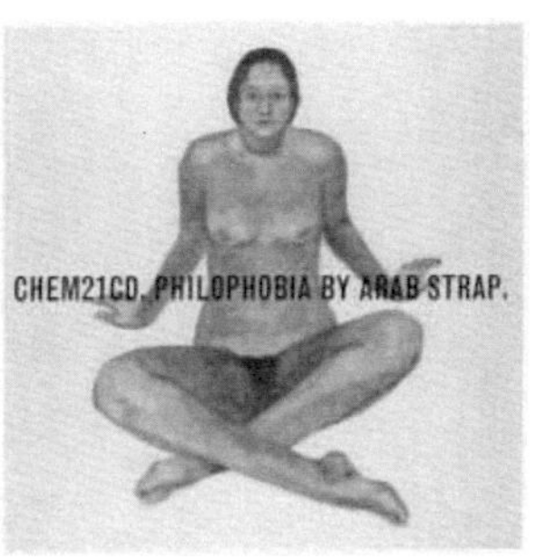

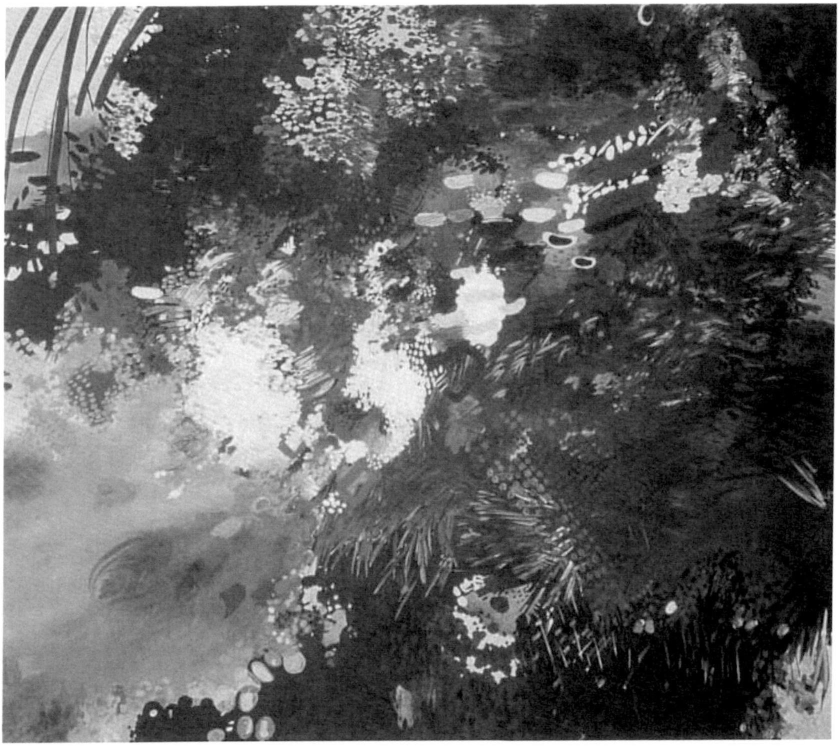

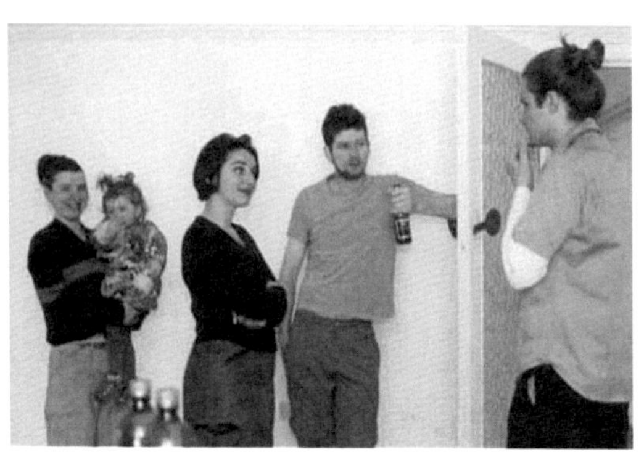

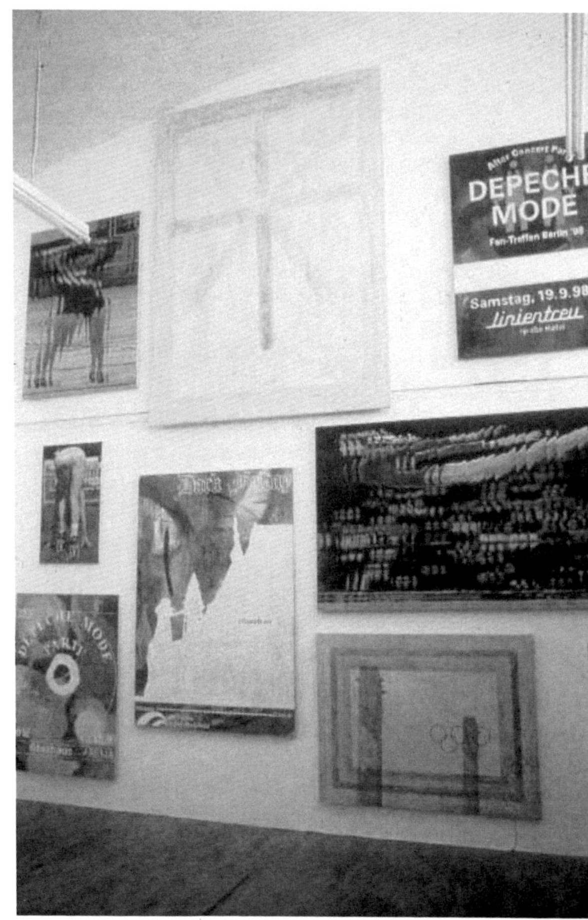
After Concert Party
DEPECHE
MODE
Fan-Treffen Berlin '98
Samstag, 19. 9. 98
linientreu
DEPECHE MODE
PARTY

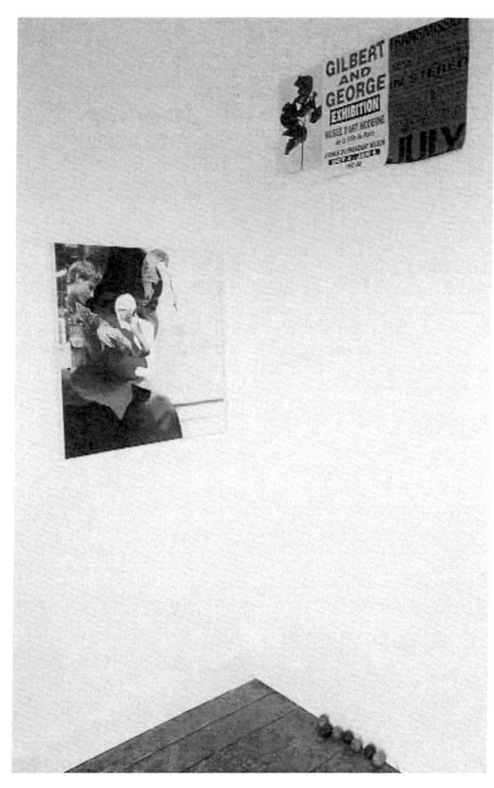

White Bear zz, exhibition at 78 Roslea Drive, 1999. Installation of work (l-r) Alan Michael, Sue Tompkins.
Film Club screening at 78 Roslea Drive, 1999. Left to right: Neal Beggs, Rob Kennedy, Jess Worrall, Caroline Kirsop, Scott Myles. Seated: Ewan Imrie.

OPPOSITE
Opening party for The Modern Institute, April 1998. Left to right: Diane Main, Coco Kay Main, Rebecca Gordon Nesbitt, Jonnie Wilkes and Toby Webster.
Lucy McKenzie, degree show at Duncan of Jordanstone College of Art and Design (1999).

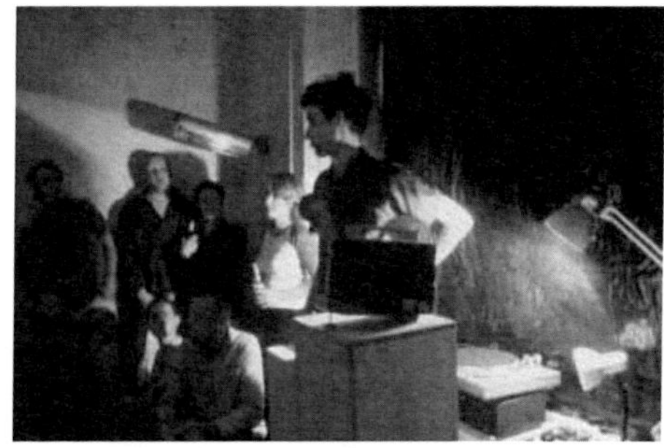

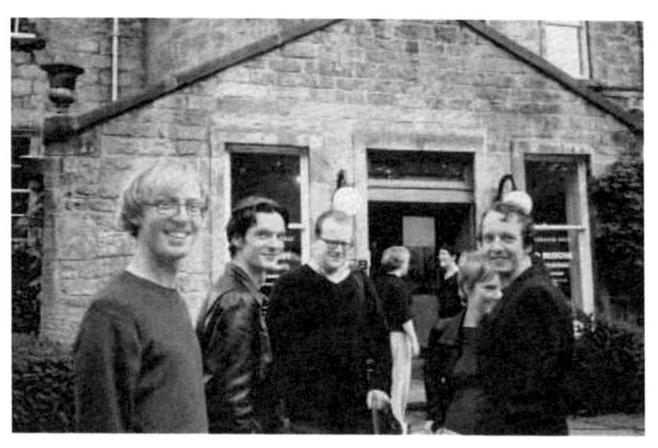

Ed Ruscha opening at Inverleith House, Edinburgh, August 2001. Left to right: Toby Paterson, Robert Johnston, Matthew Higgs, Camilla Low and Will Bradley.
Flyer for Optimo, Sub Club, 1999.

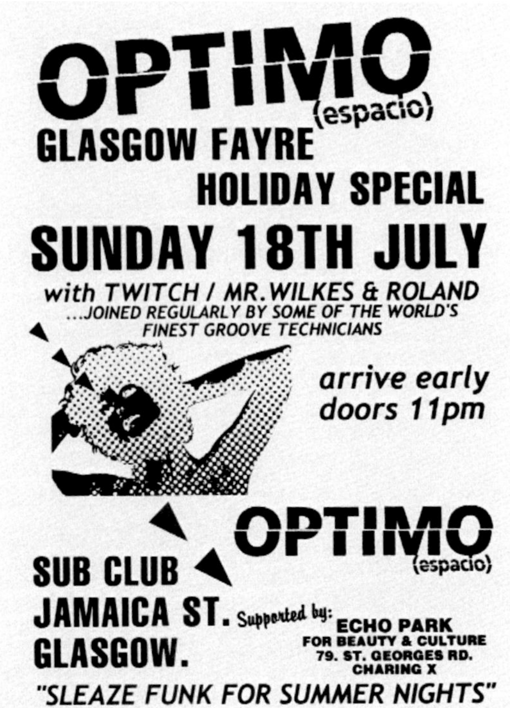

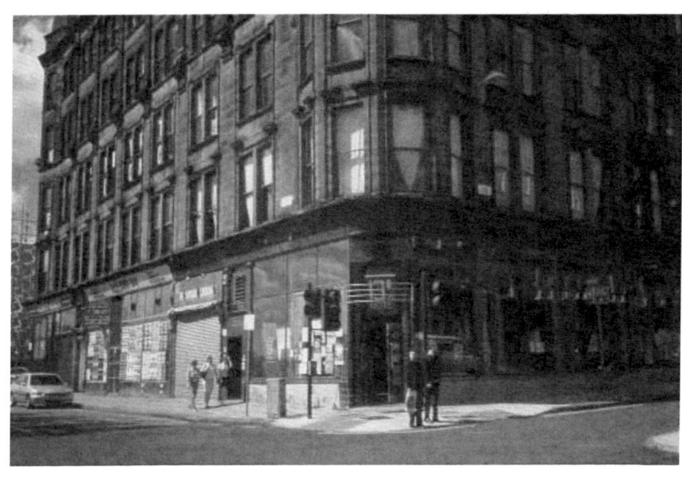

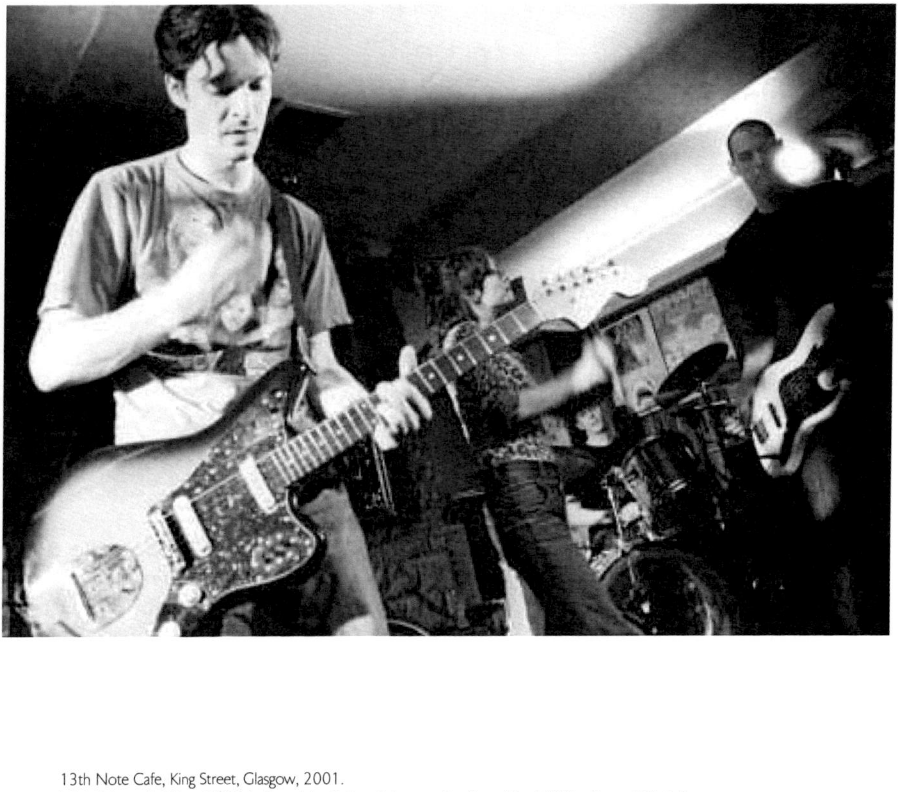

13th Note Cafe, King Street, Glasgow, 2001.
Life Without Buildings, 2000. Left to right: Robert Johnston, Sue Tompkins, Will Bradley and Chris Evans.

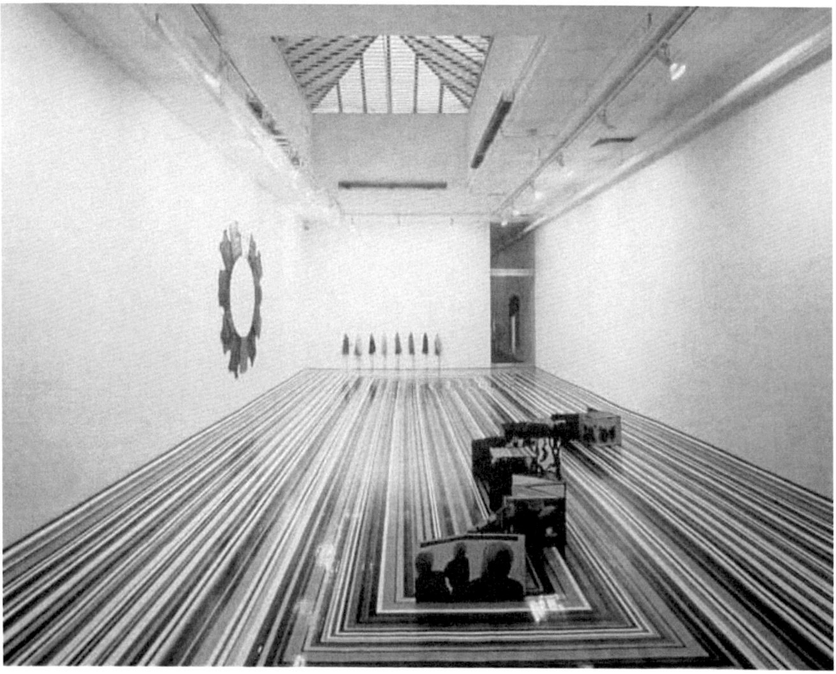

Jim Lambie, *Black Glass*, Anton Kern, New York, 2000.
Joanne Tatham and Tom O'Sullivan, *The Glamour*, Transmission, 2000.

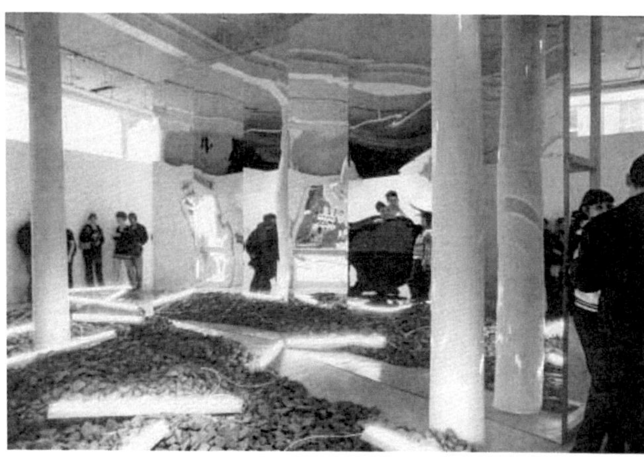

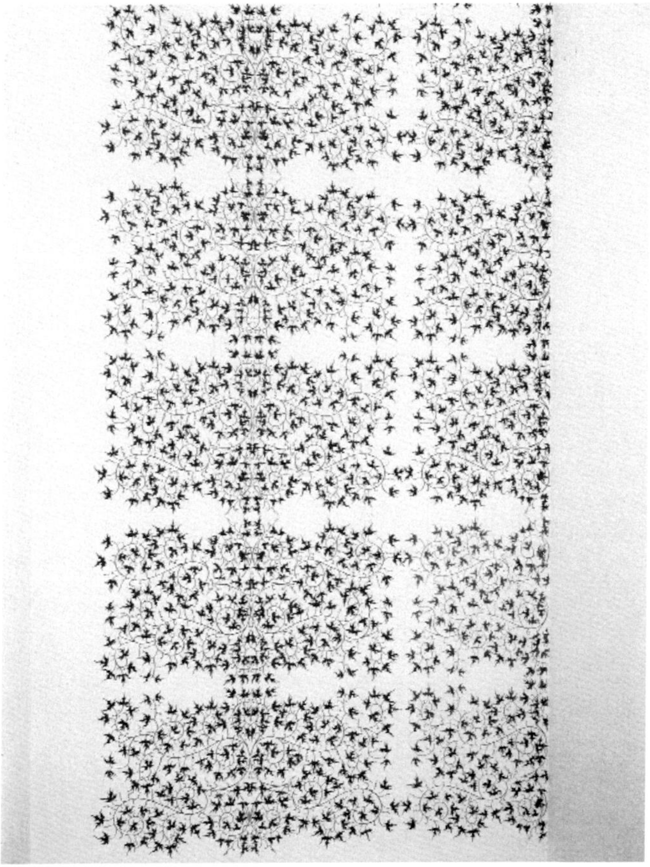

Richard Wright (installation detail), Gagosian Gallery, New York, 2000.
Pyramids of Mars, The Fruitmarket Gallery, Edinburgh, 2000. Left to right: Luke Fowler, El Hombre Trajeado bass player Stevie Jones and Chris Mack of Eska and The James Orr Complex.

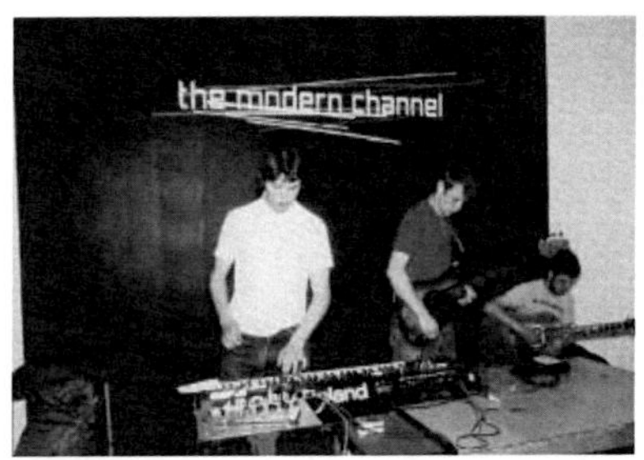

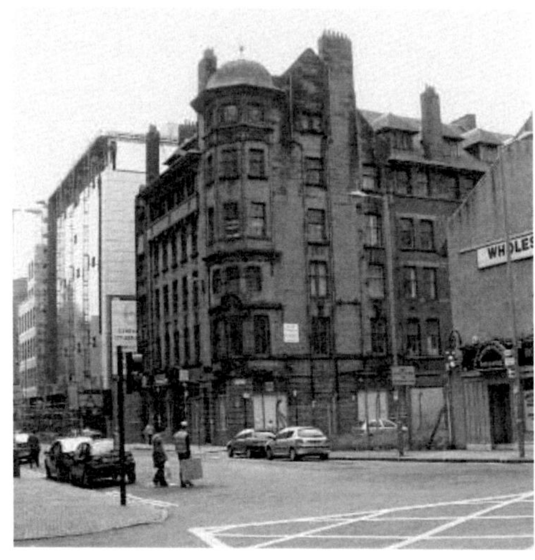

73 Robertson Street, the building that in the 1990s and '00s housed Flourish Studios, The Centre and The Modern Institute amongst other organisations.
Rirkrit Tiravanija, Community Cinema for a Quiet Intersection, 1999.

OPPOSITE
Simon Starling, *Rescued Rhododendrons*, 2000.
Graham Fagen, *Royston Road Trees* (as part of The Royston Road Project), 2001.

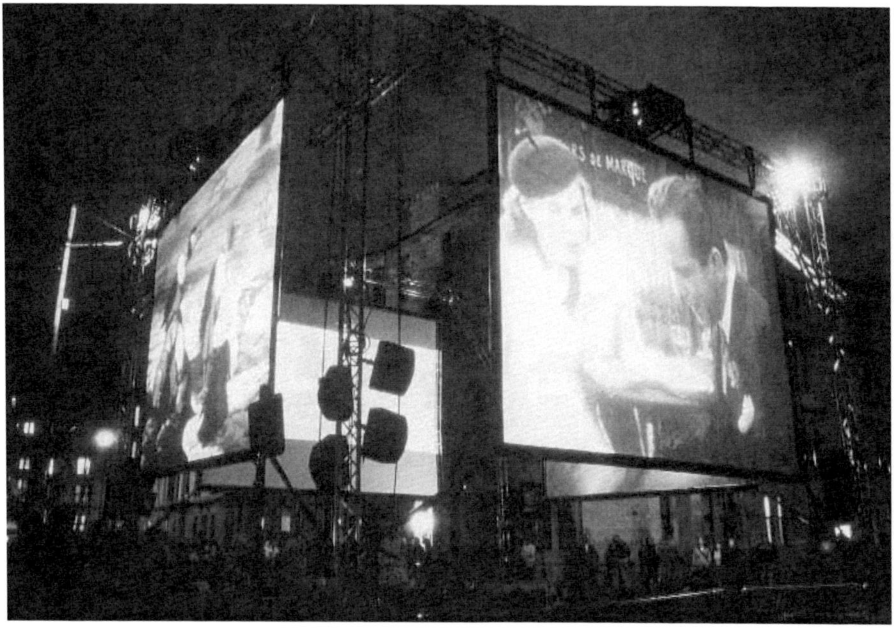

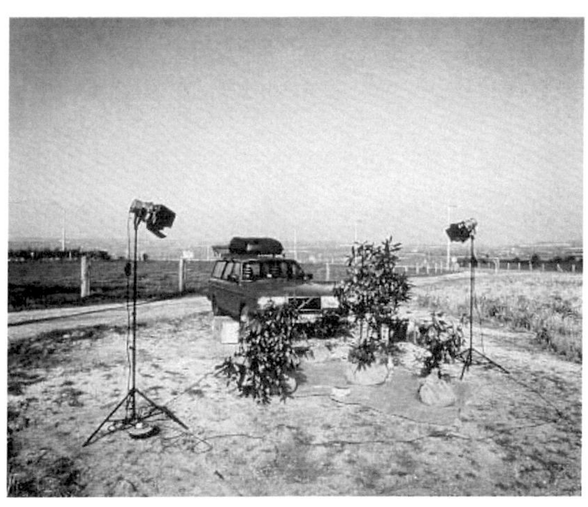

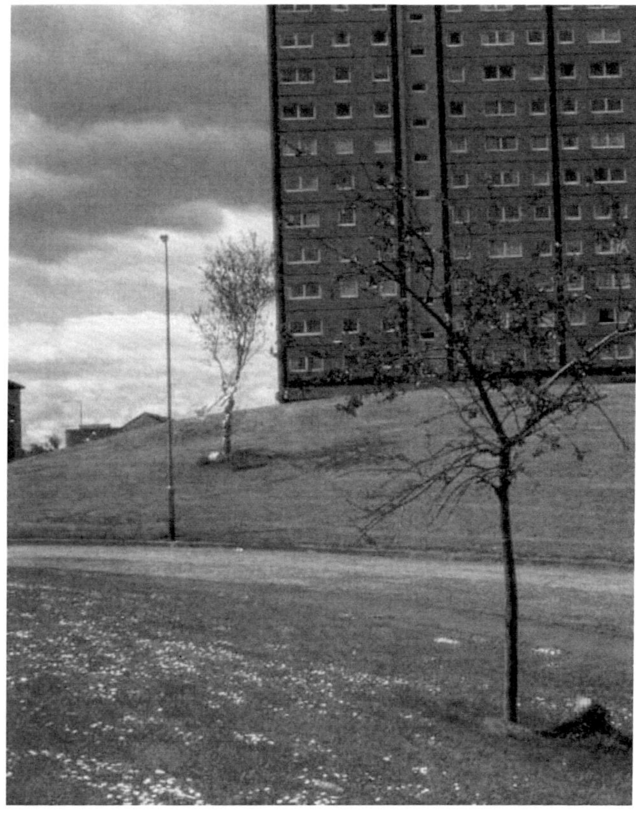

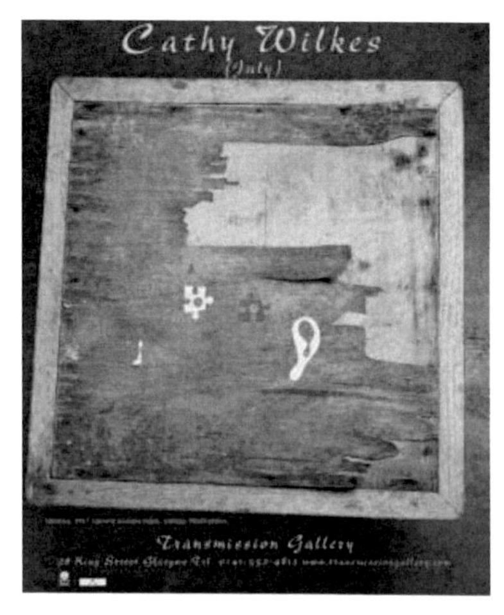

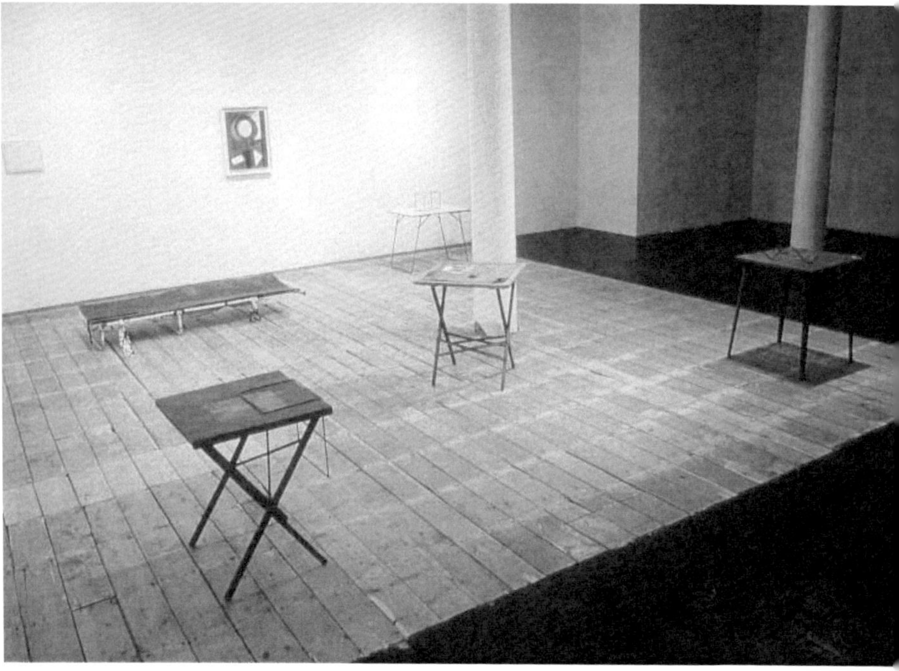

Cathy Wilkes, exhibition poster, Our Misfortune, Transmission, Glasgow, 2001.
Cathy Wilkes, Our Misfortune, Transmission, 2001.

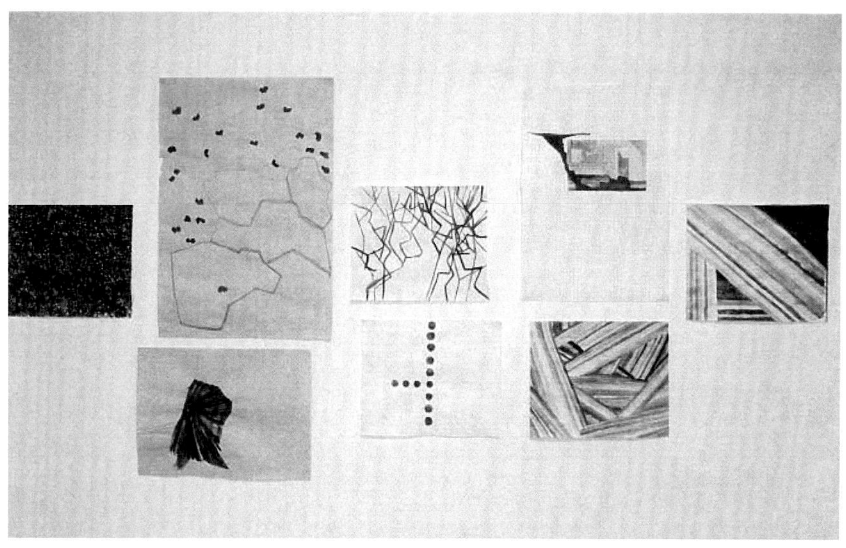

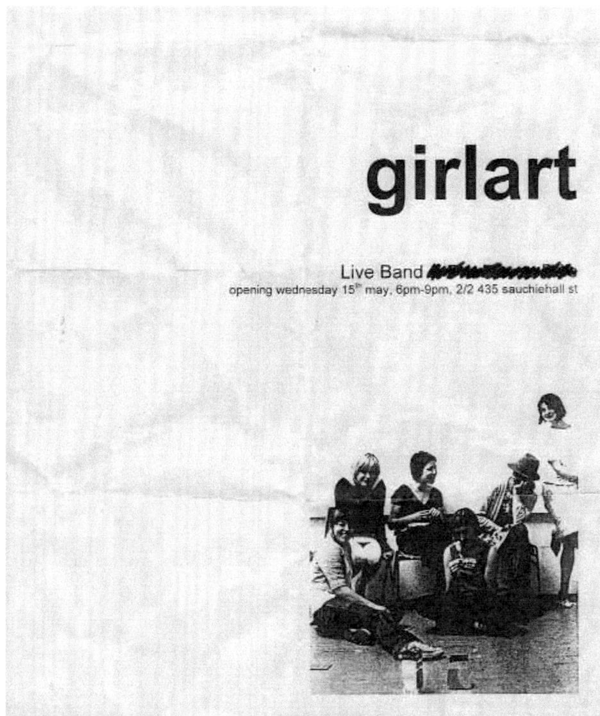


Hayley Tompkins (installation detail), Jack Hanley, San Francisco, 2001.
Poster for Girl Art exhibition by Hannah Robinson, Harriet Tritton, Sara Barker, Jo Robertson, Celia Hempton and Aleana Egan, May 2002.

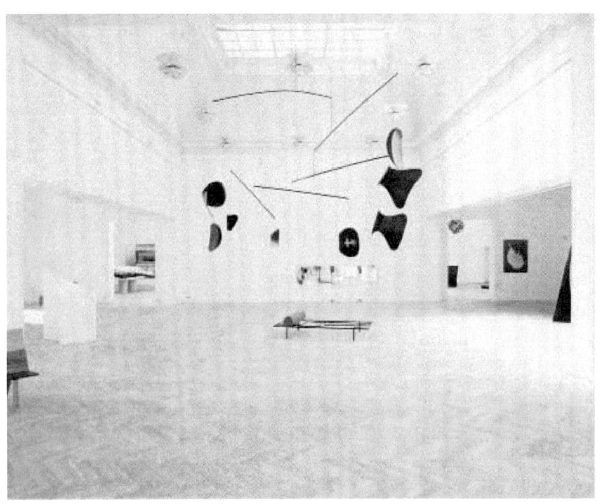

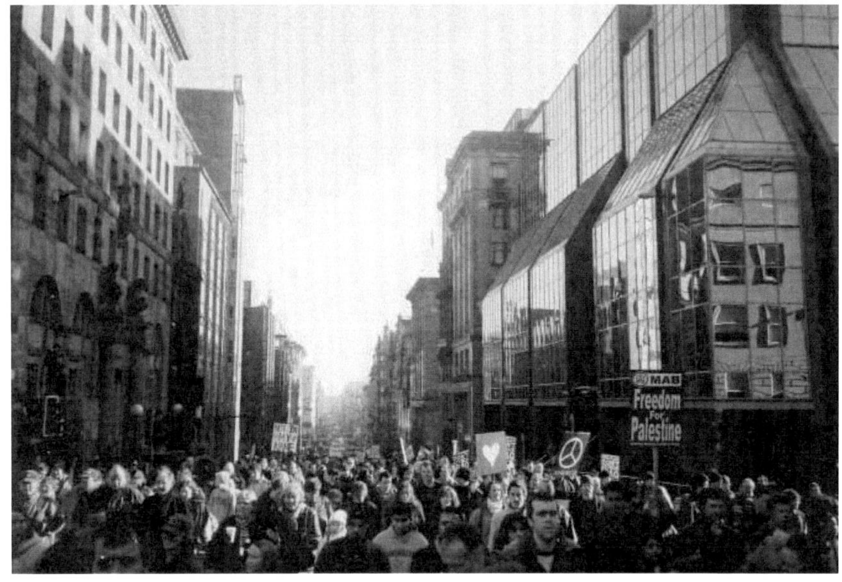


Installation view of *My Head Is On Fire But My Heart Is Full Of Love*, Charlottensburg Exhibition Hall, Copenhagen (2002).
Anti Iraq war demonstration, Glasgow, 2003.

OPPOSITE
Toby Paterson, *New Facade* (installation view), CCA, Glasgow, 2003.
Jim Lambie, installation view, *Zenomap*, Scottish Pavilion, Venice Biennale, 2003.

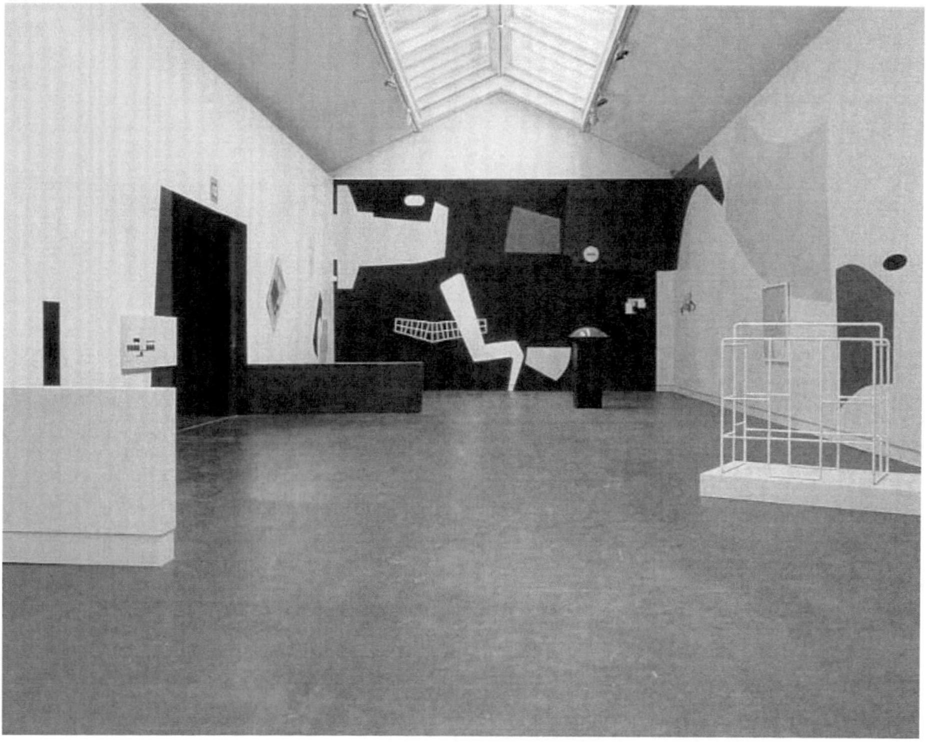

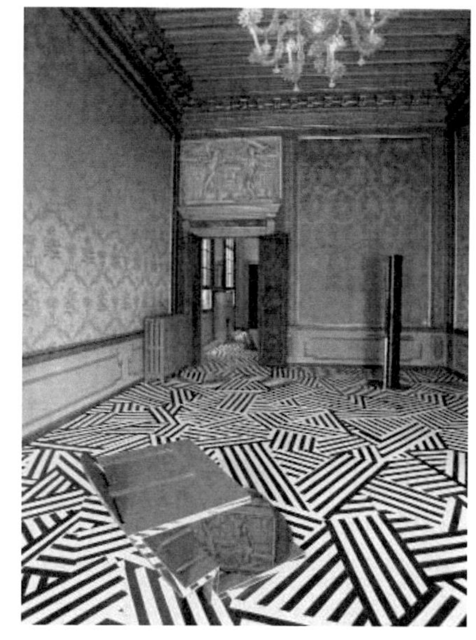

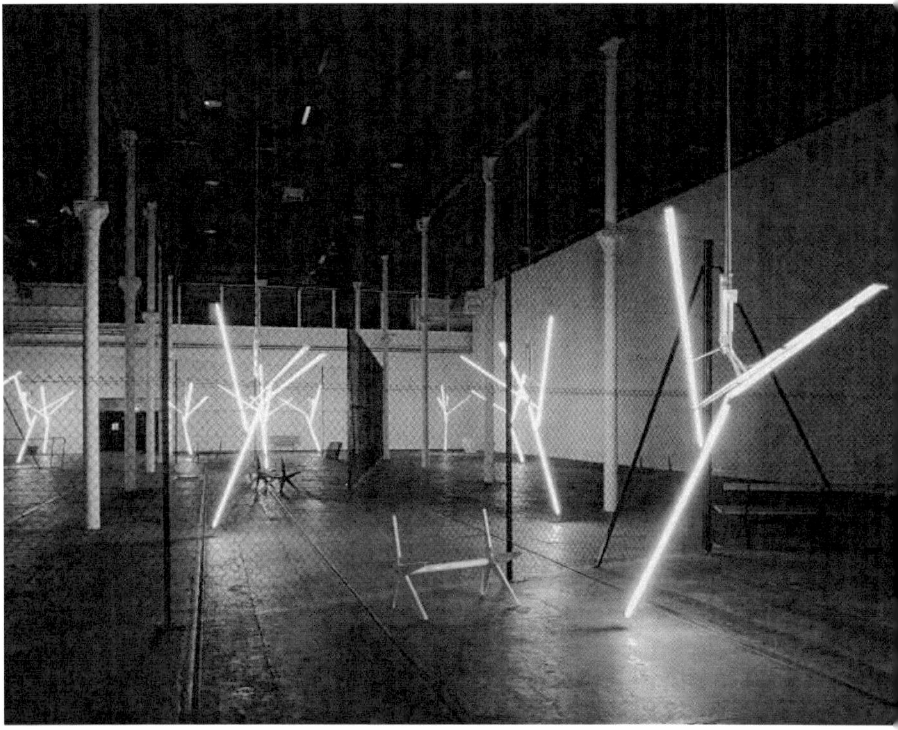

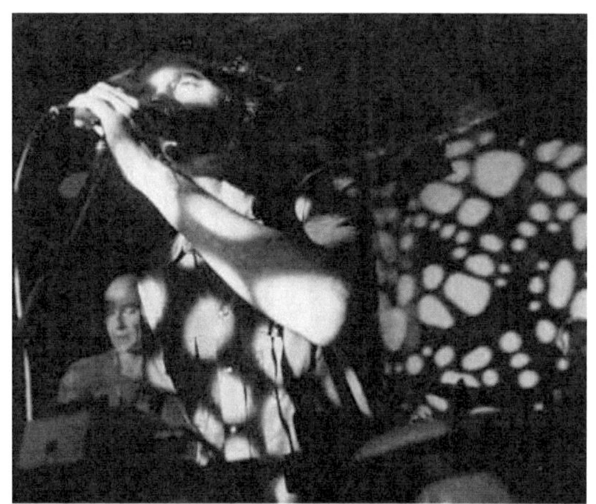

Martin Boyce, *Our Love is Like the Flowers, the Rain, the Sea and the Hours* (installation view), Tramway, 2002.
Liquid Liquid performing live at Optimo, Sub Club, 2003.

Tommy Sheridan's office, a detective agency, a bookbinder, an invisible mender and a maker of masonic regalia, also welcomed a new tenant that year. Lucy Byatt had left Visual Art Projects to found her own organisation, The Centre. Byatt had already worked on numerous important public art commissions in Glasgow, including Douglas Gordon's *Empire* sign, that had set the high-water mark in terms of other projects underway elsewhere. At The Centre she planned to continue to work with local artists on projects within Scotland, connecting local artists with park planners and architects, and setting up commissioned projects whereby artists designed new physical landscapes. She quickly began to work on a number of projects, including publishing Thomas Lawson's research on late 18th-century political pamphleteer Thomas Muir, commissioning artists (including Simon Starling and Mary Redmond) to make site-specific works for the National Park Project at Loch Lomond, and developing two linked community park projects at Royston Road, designed by Graham Fagen and Toby Paterson, in collaboration with architect Greg White, director of Loci Design.[27]

Toby Paterson says, "What I didn't anticipate was the effect the parks project would have when reflected back on my own work. I suppose the community consultation and issues around the politics and dynamics of public space that arose have left my other work with more of a political or social edge to it than before. Maybe it has become less about only pleasing myself … The hidden status of Glasgow's art scene is a result of various factors, both internal and external. I don't think this really changes too much during the process of consultation because, no matter how successful the dialogue is, you're just another funny looking head bussed in from outside the local community. However if the ground work has been done

27  The Royston Road project began in 1997 when the local community banded together to save the Townhead Spire from demolition, helped by artist George Wyllie, who burnt a cross in front of the spire, generating some television news coverage. The Royston Road Project company that formed from two local community groups (The Roystonhill Spire Group and the Molendinar Community Council) approached Liz Gardiner from Fablevision, an arts company involved in regeneration projects and working with communities for advice on realising their ambitions for the area. Fablevision facilitated the development of the Royston Road Project as a company, working to devise and deliver a funding strategy and managing the £1.7 million initiative. Funding was secured from Community Fund, the Scottish Arts Council, European Regional Development Fund, Esmee Fairbairn Trust, Glasgow City Council and The Wise Group. The Centre established the design team and commissioning process and commissioned eight artist's projects by Paul Carter, Steven Healy, Jenny Brownrigg, Radio Tuesday, Eddie Ladd, Scott Myles, Toby Paterson and Graham Fagen.

and people are aware of the ideas and motivations behind the work – and feel involved in its creation, I think it can make a difference to how they view the role of art, and its place in the world."[28]

In the East End of the city, another new space opened in 1999 in an old funeral parlour on the High Street. Bulkhead was established by artist and organiser Nicola Atkinson-Griffith, who invited local artists to display work in the 24-hour viewing window and to enter the annual Bulkhead prize.[29] The Bulkhead Prize offered £1000 development funds to three short-listed artists to realise artworks sited within the City of Glasgow boundary, which were accessible to the general public. The winner received an addition £3000 prize, which in the inaugural year went to Glasgow-based artist Lisa Gallacher (b.1974) for *Sewing Machine*, a vast installation made from polypropylene rope and a huge stainless steel needle.

Although Tramway's Albert Drive premises were closed from 1998 until 2000, curator Alexia Holt kept the organisation's profile high during this period by staging a series of Tramway projects at other venues in the city such as inviting local artists Iain Kettles and Susie Hunter (b.1967) to make one of their trademark colourful inflatable sculptures. Environmental Art graduate Kettles and Silversmithing and Jewellery graduate Hunter had worked together since 1993, producing meticulously crafted pieces from ripstop nylon in luminous colours, such as *It's a Girl* (1998), an oversized version of a pink bunny helium balloon. *Space Invader*, which they installed in the space between the carpark and office buildings at Union Place, was a complex arrangement of orange and red inflated spheres and grids.

Glasgow-based artist Stephen Hurrell (b.1965) drew upon the historical resonance of the city for his soundwork *Zones: an audiology of the river Clyde*, while artist and Environmental Art tutor Peter McCaughey continued his investigation into film projection in disused spaces with *Arc*, held at the disused ABC cinema in Sauchiehall Street. McCaughey directed his audience through the side entrance of the cinema, along various underground passages, and out into an auditorium without seats, where an aerial film of

28 Toby Paterson, in response to questions sent by the author, April 2001.
29 Both the gallery and the Bulkhead Prize closed in 2002 after an initial three year period of funding came to an end.

the cinema played on the 70mm projector and the sounds of Wagner and other clips from the soundtrack to *Apocalypse Now* filtered through the quadrophonic sound system. The effect of this was disconcerting, as Ross Sinclair wrote in his *frieze* review, "Walking around this strange non-space conjured up feelings of watching a movie during a wartime emergency – the audience were not present to see a film but to be with other people, even if words were never exchanged."[30]

Most of these projects drew upon the unique social fabric of Glasgow, but this was especially true of *Glaschu* by Anya Gallaccio at the Old Court House.[31] Gallachio's project referenced the city's gaelic name which had given rise to the city's nickname, the dear green place. Gallachio was born in Paisley, near Glasgow, to Scottish parents of Italian and Polish descent and her family history partly informed her installation on the floor of the former Virginia tobacco mansion. The property had also served as a bank and the city's High Court before finally being earmarked for renovation into a bar and restaurant.[32] She explained, "We have made a new floor for the room, using a tiny part of a pattern taken from a carpet in the Templeton factory archive. The pattern is from around 1840, the same time as the building. It is blown up to such a scale that the source is not recognisable, but as you walk across the floor you can determine large leaf and flower forms. The floor is concrete with a living green line cutting through the surface planted with fairly common green plants, things we take for granted but that are not indigenous – which all came from far away."[33]

Around this time, Glasgow-based artist Simon Starling was also developing a work that dealt with how non-indigenous plants might be used as a metaphor for ideas relating to identity. Starling decided to repatriate a number of rhododendrons that were about to be destroyed in Aberdeenshire, back to their native Spain. He says, "I took the plants on a road trip to Spain and planted them back with their ancestors. In its

---

30  Ross Sinclair, Peter McCaughey, *frieze*, May 2000, p105.
31  This Tramway project was managed in association with Locus + Newcastle.
32  The property had been earmarked for conversion by entrepreneur Stefan King, who had previously converted several other large merchant city buildings into lavish theme bar/restaurants, such as The Corinthian and Arta.
33  Chasing Rainbows, Anya Gallacchio, Tramway/Locus +, 1999, pp59-60.

simplest form, the piece inverts a historical trajectory, but Scotland is a place where people's cultural identity is linked to the landscape. It's interesting to think about how that has come about. The rhododendron is such a standard part of Scotland's countryside now, yet it isn't indigenous. Perhaps, in a sense, this has greater significance in relation to all the issues of emigrating peoples, refugees and Scottish nationalism. That in a way, is obliquely linked to notions of purity. On a more lighthearted note, the work deals with things that are quite central to the way that people think about culture. And maybe even to me, as an artist who's actually from England, thinking about being a weed in Scotland."[34] Both *Rescued Rhododendrons* and Gallachio's *Glaschu* had a particular resonance within the city partially because of the increased number of refugees entering Glasgow in the late 1990s, and the various tensions that this had brought in deprived areas such as Sighthill, Barmulloch and Royston.[35]

## MOVING THE CCA

Patricia Fleming left artists' training scheme Fuse and East End gallery Fly to work as exhibitions organiser at CCA in December 1999. Fly closed for a few months before re-opening under the name Market with new funding and organisers Luci Ransome and Nicola Cooper. Fuse was then located in purpose-built studios at Bridgeton, with a computing suite, two project supervisors and an administrator. But just four months later, the funding manager who had dealt with Fuse for several years left. Patricia Fleming says, "There was no-one there to fight for it. I felt it needed new blood but nobody felt ready to take it over, so in the end I had to wind the company down."[36] Fleming's new post brought certain challenges, as both she and CCA director Graham McKenzie found that temporary relocation

---

34  *Scotland On Sunday*, 16th September, 2001, p13.

35  Between 1999 and 2001, four thousand asylum seekers from more than 35 countries moved to housing estates at Sighthill, Royston and Red Road. The tensions between existing tenants and asylum seekers in Glasgow were brought to national media attention by the murder of Turkish immigrant Kurd Firsat Dag in Sighthill in August 2001. The Scottish Refugee Council estimates that there have been 70 racial attacks, seven of which were serious, in Glasgow since January 2001.

36  Patricia Fleming, in conversation with the author, December 2002.

of the CCA to the dauntingly ornate surroundings of McLellan Galleries had created an unusual environment for showing contemporary art. The Sauchiehall Street gallery had first opened in 1856, when the sweeping marble staircases and copious chandeliers had provided an ideal background for Salon-style painting exhibitions. CCA director Graham McKenzie says, "At the McLellan galleries we did some good exhibitions and live events but a lot of what we did was trying things out, dipping our toes in the water. The McLellan was a difficult space to put the kind of work we present into."[37]

Sarah Tripp's CCA film commission *Anti-Prophet* was premiered at the temporary CCA in October. The documentary followed Tripp around Glasgow as she asked various people, "What do you believe in?" The question was invariably interpreted in a religious sense, and each participant directed Tripp onwards to someone they felt might be able to answer her better. This daisy-chain of enquiry took Tripp to the Glasgow Buddhist Centre, and to an order of Carmelite nuns, as well as to a school, and into various living rooms and kitchens around town. Ex-Vaselines and Painkillers singer Frances McKee appeared, and answered, "I believe in me", while the nuns at first only smiled and said nothing at all. Robert Johnston wrote in a review for *Untitled*, "Taken at face value, [Tripp's] reluctance to really quiz the speakers makes for bad documentary and there often seems to be little to grab hold of. But, in true Taoist style, the film's fragility is a strength. In the end, *Anti-Prophet* seems to want to become something quite other than what we're used to calling 'documentary film'."[38]

One definite success of the temporary CCA was the well attended Baustelle German electronic music festival in September, which drew large audiences to see experimental dance music acts including Pole, Kriedler, To Rococo Rot and Tarwater. The appearance by Berlin-based act Pole in particular was especially eagerly anticipated, as Stefan Betke's crackly dub sound was the popular choice for warm-up sets at local clubs like Club 69

37  Graham McKenzie, in conversation with the author, July 2001.
38  Robert Johnston, *Untitled*, Autumn 1999, p31.

and Optimo. Betke utilised a defective freeware computer filter that emitted a sound similar to radio interference or the hiss of well-played vinyl. Although his music was electronic, it lacked the claustrophobic repetitiveness of much modern techno and drew inspiration from dub masters like Lee 'Scratch' Perry, Augustus Pablo and The Mad Professor. And, as in the case of the Roland TB 303 bass machine that had created the unique squelchy sound of Acid House, the equipment used by Pole could be easily acquired by other musicians keen to emulate the sound. Local electronic acts like Mount Florida, Vodershow and Mendel were all using Pole-esque filters on their recordings around this period, and they all turned out to see Betke in action.

In the autumn of 1999 the 13th Note Cafe in King Street was still the place to go after Transmission openings, or on almost any other night. Graphic artist and Vesuvius-founder Marc Baines teamed up with Anne from local band Lungleg to present a night called Salty Cellar, with themed film clips and an eclectic soundtrack. All female DJ night Stiletto[39] also began at the cafe, moving to the 13th Note club the following year. Stiletto's playlist encompassed various genres, raging from new wave to hiphop and indie to punk, and local artists Anne Marie Copestake and Diane Main were drafted in to help with the decorations: slide projections, black and white animations, clouds of tulle, glitterballs, mobile sculptures, tea lights, incense. *Sleaze Nation* wrote, "Sadie and Anna J continue to espouse the beauty of Punk, Hip-Hop, '80s Rock and their overall love of a guitar. Real proper art video walls, Billy Idol/Missy Elliot soundclash mixing and strictly no male geeks behind the decks."[40] Stiletto, and spin-off events Seven Sisters and Give the DJ a Break, cast many of the city's artists and musicians in the role of guest DJ, including Cathy Wilkes, Robert Johnston, Scott Myles, Isobel Campbell, Anne-Marie Copestake, Hayley and Sue Tompkins, Lucy McKenzie, Clare Stephenson, Sarah Tripp, Stevie Jones, Luke Fowler and Toby Paterson.

In October, Optimo DJ Keith McIvor and his musical collaborator M.P

---

39 Set up by the author, Anna Johnston and Lynne Watson, although Lynne Watson left the collective in 2000.
40 *Sleaze Nation*, November 2000.

Lancaster released their first 12" single, *Storm*, on American label Matador, home of numerous experimental bands including Solex, Matmos, Bardot Pond and Yo La Tengo. McIvor said, "A lot of Scottish bands are on Matador in America – they put out Mogwai, Belle & Sebastian and Arab Strap – they just always said working with Scottish bands was a joy. They have a fondness for a spirit and attitude they see here – so maybe when they saw our unsolicited demo CD came from Glasgow, that went in our favour."[41] Mount Florida's sound is somewhat hard to define – it could reference the feel of film soundtracks, or be buoyantly dub inflected, and featured the talents of an array of local musicians, including Frances McKee, local chanteuse Madeleine, jazz singer Martin MacDonald, Craig B from Aereogramme and Natasha Noramly of Ganger. "We are most definitely not a dance act – although feel free to try", said McIvor. "We sound like the sum of our influences which are extremely varied and are not just musical. Key adjectives would be rhythmic, percussive, spatial, abrasive, melodic, intense, frivolous and self-indulgent."[42]

In November disaster struck the Sub Club when a fire started in an adjacent building, forcing the temporary closure of the world-famous venue. Optimo, Subculture, Tangent and Test were forced to relocate, with varying degrees of success. Optimo moved first to the 13th Note club, before settling at Planet Peach in Queen Street, where Harri and Domenic's Subculture soon joined them. Sub manager Mike Grieve said, "Because Planet Peach is a basement club it has that similar underground feel, and we're sure we're going to have some great parties in here."[43] Although Sub regulars were glad to be able to hear their favourite DJs again, most people agreed that Planet Peach, with its terrible air conditioning and confusing warren of rooms, was no match for the much-mourned Sub Club.


41  Keith McIvor, in conversation with the author, October 1999.
42  From an interview with the author, originally printed in Swing #5, autumn 1999.
43  From an interview with the author, originally published in Metro, February 2000.

# CHAPTER 11

# Survival of the Fittest
## (2000–2001)

In March 2000, Mark Vernon, Alex Frost and Duncan Campbell's Radio Tuesday collective were invited to undertake a project at Transmission. For the fortnight-long exhibition, E.g. Sometime Instant, the gallery was turned into a makeshift rehearsal room/studio/performance space with on-line live streaming of events. The busy schedule of events included performances by art bands Life Without Buildings and Cylinder, a choral performance orchestrated by local artist Ian Balch, and public debates, including a discussion on the DIY music scene, with speakers from local independent record labels Flotsam and Jetsam, Chemikal Underground and Creeping Bent. Radio Tuesday co-organiser Alex Frost said, "When Life Without Buildings played in Transmission it made a lot of sense – they are so affiliated to the gallery that it was like a homecoming."[1] Life Without Buildings guitarist Robert Johnston said, "Music is so much more fun and so much more immediately rewarding [than art]. Writing and playing songs is the best fun I've had in years. I always find making art quite hard. It's difficult, solitary and quite often boring and few people get much out of it in the way of financial or critical reward. The reward is being part of the community, which I still value a great deal … "[2]

Transmission offered a place where ideas could be tried and developed, without the performer fearing ridicule. When local artist Danny Saunders, who had previously written songs for local band Lungleg, replaced Sophie

---

1    Alex Frost, in conversation with the author, April 2001.
2    Robert Johnston, in conversation with the author, January 2001.

MacPherson on the committee, the gallery's receptivity to the local music scene increased still further. The importance of Transmission as a secure environment for nurturing new talent can be measured by how many artists/musicians from the city have gone on to more "mainstream" success, for example Elizabeth Go members Victoria Morton and Sue Tompkins. Victoria Morton now played bass guitar for Chemikal Underground signing Suckle, while Sue Tompkins was lead vocalist in Life Without Buildings. Suckle was fronted by ex-Vaselines and Painkillers singer songwriter Frances McKee and her sister Marie, plus ex-Long Fin Killie member Kenny McEwan on drums, flautist and keyboardist Elanor Taylor[3] and Brian McEwan on guitar. The band's folk-tinged multi-instrumental compositions and the McKee sisters' hypnotic, deadpan singing style lent some credence to comparisons that were drawn with Venus In Furs-era Velvet Underground. McKee laughed at the suggestion, saying, "It's a huge compliment but I could never hope to achieve anything as great as them." There was a folk element to the music, but "some people get put off on hearing that we have a folk-influenced sound, but that's just because so much folk music is crap. Our sound is quite dark and modern because of the keyboards."[4] Their well received debut album, *Against Nurture* was released in May 2000, followed by their ep *The Sun is God* which featured Cornershop's Ben Ayres, Peter Bangry and Anthony Saffery.

Another Glasgow band which signed to Chemikal Underground around the same time as Suckle was Aereogramme, fronted by ex-Fukuyama and Ganger guitarist Craig B (Beaton), ably supported by Campbell McNeil, known sound engineer around town on bass, Martin Scott on drums and Iain Cook on guitar and programming. Although Beaton had previously been known for gentle Mark Eitzel style compositions, his new band had a considerably harder and louder sound – however, as nu-rock bible *Kerrang* reported, the band was still "avant-garde and enigmatic". The band released two singles on their own Babi-Yaga label before signing to Chemikal Underground. Aereogramme's debut album, released on Chemikal, was

---

3   Taylor later left the band and was replaced by cellist and guitarist Janis Murray.
4   Excerpt from an interview with the author, published in Metro, 31 March 2000.

called *A Story in White* (2001) and became *Rocksound's* Album of the Month, while *Metal Hammer* said the band were "writing better songs than anyone in UK rock music today." Radio 1 DJ John Peel was quick to take the band under his wing, offering them a much-coveted Peel Session and an invitation to the Eurosonic festival in the Netherlands.

Arab Strap's relationship with Go! Beat had proved to be unsuccessful and the band happily re-signed to Chemikal Underground in 2000, sealing the deal with a trip to the nearby Tennant's brewery. Their highly acclaimed fifth album, *The Red Thread,* followed soon after. Lead singer Aidan Moffat explains, "Go! Beat ruined the release of our record [*Elephant Shoe*] by not paying any attention to us and how we wanted our record marketed – they had no respect for independent markets and outlets. We've got a maternal bond with Chemikal Underground – we would never have got a record out without them. The achievement of doing something outside of London is really important – in that respect Chemikal Underground is similar to Factory Records in Manchester."[5]

Mogwai had by now left Chemikal Underground to sign with major label Southpaw. Their new label had more money to spend on production, meaning that the band could once again call upon the services of producer Dave Fridmann, but this time travel to upstate New York, and the studio used by The Flaming Lips, to record their new album *Rock Action.* The Delgados, the band that runs Chemikal Underground, had also used the services of Friedman for their album *The Great Eastern* (2000), which won them a nomination for the Mercury Music Prize. Besides Suckle and Aereogramme, Chemikal Underground's roster also now included Norwich-based Magoo, Australian/American group Cha Cha Cohen and The Radar Brothers from Los Angeles, who all released records on the label throughout the late '90s.

During this period the work of Environmental Art graduate Michael Wilkinson (b.1965) began to reference the "trainspotting" mentality of the avid record collectors who trawled the racks of local independent vinyl stockists like Missing, Fopp and Rub A Dub. Wilkinson's ongoing *Record*

5   Aidan Moffat, in conversation with the author, October 2000.

*Collection* (2000–) is a series of paintings on board that reference each record that comes into his own collection. Wilkinson's minimal reworkings of classic sleeves includes such seminal recordings as The Smith's *Hatful of Hollow* (1984), reducing the elements of the design to a blue background, with a dark box and a white line. "I'm interested in how little information can actually carry a meaning", he says, "Ultimately, it's not about music, but about the relationship between an individual and an object, between a fan and the object they're a fan of."[6]

Wilkinson's musical collaborator, Torsten Lauschmann had begun to use digital software to manipulate and/or animate images, altering the meaning(s) of found material. For example, he digitally enlarged photographs from celebrity magazines such as *Hello!* in order to focus on incidental details. Liz Hurley and Hugh Grant were edged out of the frame, with the focus of the photograph becoming a manhole on the road behind them. His film *Berlichtungen* (2000) took classic images from the history of photography, by Eugene Atget and Lee Friedlander and added a soundtrack of recordings made on the streets of Glasgow, and a visual overlay of flickering light and scratches. Eerily, the still images started to seem as though they were moving.


## GLITTERING PRIZE

The profile of the Glasgow art scene was continuing to grow, as increasing numbers of Glasgow-based artists were selected for The Turner Prize or Beck's Futures, or showcase exhibitions such as Bloomberg New Contemporaries or The British Art Show as the 1990s progressed. The solidarity of the "Scotia Nostra" was necessary for the continued advance of the Glasgow art scene, but it still aggravated those who felt excluded from the circle. *Guardian* journalist Jonathan Jones had an adverse reaction to Douglas Gordon's famous *List of Names*, when reviewing his solo show, Sheep and Goats at the Musee National d'Art Moderne in Paris in March

6    *Scotland on Sunday*, 25th March 2001, p25.

that year. "The most uncomfortable thing in the show is a brightly lit space in which are written the names of all the people Gordon acknowledges knowing. The list is alienating, irritating, frightening. He does not know you. You are cast out."[7] Jones' review neglects to mention that this work has been constantly updated and expanded since it was first shown in 1990, to accommodate the names of new friends and acquaintances – by now it could well include his name.

With combined prize funds of £65,000 Beck's Futures was now the UK's richest art prize, outstripping The Turner Prize. The inaugural year of the exhibition, which opened at the ICA in March, featured five Glasgow-based artists: Lucy McKenzie, Cathy Wilkes, Martin Boyce, David Shrigley and Roderick Buchanan, plus Perth-born artist Liz Arnold, who all received £4000. Roderick Buchanan then won a further £20,000 for his short film *Gobstopper*, which recorded a group of small children attempting to hold their breath as they were driven through the Clyde Tunnel in a camper van. Francis McKee wrote, "the unrehearsed observation of the children playing catches a game in its early moments before it becomes standardised. At this point we can see that the activity is an informal kind of education. Not an intellectual exercise, but a sensual education where children learn to measure their own stamina, their competitiveness, and their willingness to push themselves through their physical performance. This self-discovery is as important as anything gained in a classroom."[8]

Beck's Brand Director Maurice Breen wrote in the exhibition catalogue, "From commissioning Rachel Whiteread's *House*, in partnership with Artangel, to sponsoring Gilbert & George's first major British exhibition […] Beck's has played a pivotal role and was a constant presence in warehouses, galleries, museums and other unique spaces through the late eighties and early nineties, helping young and upcoming artists. It was hard to go to a new show anywhere across Britain without finding Beck's sponsoring it."[9] However, not all artists were convinced that this is a good thing. Cathy Wilkes, one of the artists shortlisted for the 2000 Beck's Futures exhibition

---

7   Jonathan Jones, *The Guardian*, March 16th 2000.
8   Circular Breathing, Francis McKee, Beck's Futures, ICA, London, 2000, p20.
9   Beck's Futures , ICA, London, 2000, p6.

said, "Unless you have a really wonderful curator with a bit of vision – it tends to be the sponsor who gets the most out of these kind of exhibitions"[10] Wilkes may well be right. Beck's had first been imported into Britain as a little-known pilsner in 1984, but thanks to Anthony Fawcett's ingenious arts sponsorship strategy, it was now one of the top three bottled beers in the UK. But as another shortlist candidate, Lucy McKenzie, says "Artists are still finding their feet around this whole corporate sponsorship idea, but if someone is going to wave four thousand pounds at you you're not going to say no."[11]

The inaugural year of Absolut Open at Inverleith House that summer was also dominated by Glasgow-based artists including Ian Balch, Chris Evans, Marianne Greated, Claudine Hartzel, Steve Hollingsworth, Louise Hopkins, Andrew Kerr, Sally Osborn, Alex Pollard, and overall winner, Ross Birrell, who showed several works including pencil wall drawings based on psychometric tests, a children's encyclopaedia of the cell that had been put through a mincer and a text piece that suggested "imagine Yoko Ono does not exist". For Birrell's prize commission he persuaded a Zurich bank to allow him to place a bottle of Absolut vodka and an envelope with undisclosed contents in their vault for 30 years.

Some of the artists involved in the show still had some reservations about their inclusion, including Switchspace founder Marianne Greated, who said, "I think singling out artists, often on individual pieces of work, and putting them on a pedestal isn't ideal and in many ways it just reflects our sad consumer society. The result can set people up without the background or indeed the backing or support they may need in the fickle art world, and can leave people with a long way to fall if indeed they do. On the other hand these shows do give many less established artists fantastic opportunities to be shown in often extremely prestigious spaces, very much in the public eye and for many artists it is shows like these that can really set off their career. I was very appreciative of the opportunity to have work in Inverleith House. My main problem with competitive

10  Cathy Wilkes, in conversation with the author, August 2001.
11  Lucy McKenzie, in conversation with the author, October 2000.

exhibitions is the fact that they are judged and of course do set a precedent for what is 'in' – what is good art and what isn't. And of course those judging will often have their own remits for what they want to support or promote. They are also very biased by current scenes and for what are supposedly 'open' or all-encompassing shows they often seem to represent what the 'art world' is all about rather than concentrating on interesting work."[12]

When survey show The British Art Show 5 opened in Edinburgh in April 2000 it featured 50 artists, ranging in age from 20 to over 60. The survey exhibition also included the greatest number of Glasgow-based artists in the exhibition's history: Martin Boyce, Graham Fagen, Jim Lambie, Lucy McKenzie, Carol Rhodes, David Shrigley, Simon Starling and Richard Wright were included in the exhibition, in addition to Edinburgh-based artist Chad McCail. Artist and curator Matthew Higgs said of his selection, "I wanted this show to be inclusive and to reflect, both geographically and in terms of cultural practice, a spread of interests. Although we know that artists gravitate towards the metropolitan centres for many obvious reasons, the idea was to reflect a more complex and less centrally-located story. This is especially important at the end of the 1990s, following the phenomenal interest throughout the earlier part of the decade in young British art. There is definitely a different kind of approach to thinking about and making art that this British Art Show has to reflect."[13]

In London, Jay Jopling opened White Cube 2 in the newly fashionable area of Hoxton Square. In comparison to the flagship gallery, the second space was vast. Gilbert & George had recently "defected" to White Cube from Anthony d'Offay, who had represented them for twenty years. Anthony Gormley and Mona Hatoum had also joined Jopling's roster in the '90s, lending some weight to his rather yBa populated gallery. With Jopling's new space his position in the pecking order of the London art scene seemed secure. The same summer, the Tate Gallery at Millbank was renamed Tate Britain and the eagerly awaited £134m Tate Modern designed by Herzog

12  Marianne Greated, in response to questions sent by the author, September 2001.
13  The British Art Show 5, Hayward Gallery, London, 2000.

Demoron opened. Tate Modern was located in a converted power station on Bankside, and the new national museum of modern art opened in May under the guidance of director Nicholas Serota. In July, Tate Britain hosted Intelligence: New British Art curated by Charles Esche and Virginia Button and featuring work by twenty two artists including Martin Creed, Sarah Lucas, Liam Gillick, Tacita Dean, Susan Hiller, Michael Craig-Martin, Graham Gussin, Julian Opie, Alan Johnston, Douglas Gordon and Richard Wright.

The exhibition launched New British Art, a series of exhibitions of contemporary art to be held at three year intervals at Tate Britain. In their introductory essay to the exhibition catalogue Virginia Button and Charles Esche drew an analogy between the artist and the investigator, writing, "The artwork itself is subject to the processes of its production by the artists only as the beginning of a journey towards meaning and significance. Its interpretation is determined just as much through the processes of insight and translation in the eyes and mind of the viewer. It is this negotiation that lies at the heart of an apparent uncertainty or ambiguity in much contemporary work. Perhaps this does not suit a broad cultural expectation of confident certainties built on the approach of politicians, economists or media celebrities, but it is the basis for a thoughtful, self-critical society. For art to encourage this would seem to be one of its primary aspirations."[14]


## AMBIENT SURFACE TENSION


Lucy McKenzie had her first solo London show in the summer of 2000 – Decemberism, at Martin McGeowan and Andrew Wheatley's Cabinet Gallery. The press release proposed that, "Erasure and Depeche Mode's names should be as interchangeable as Sigmund Freud and Wilhelm Reich's (Freud literally meaning "Joy", Reich meaning "Empire". They should have swapped, at least when it came to their sex policies). "Erasure" is a word reminiscent of the Soviet desire to rebuild on the rubble of the

<hr>

14  Virginia Button and Charles Esche, "Intelligence is the Great Aphrodisiac", *Intelligence*, Tate Britain, 2000, p11.

past, "Depeche Mode" ("Fast Fashion") pure consumerism. DM's bash at Totalitarian gimmicks was so endearingly pathetic; and Erasure's rally cry is Pure Love." Cabinet gallery had been set up by McGeowan and Wheatley in a Brixton flat in 1992 because "We wanted to provide a showcase for art that has no place in the present system. The debased, profane, indefensible – all those things that recent art has chosen to ignore, but which obsess the rest of society."[15] Later Cabinet secured premises at Coldharbour Lane and then at Northburgh Street, where they worked with various artists including Lily Van der Stokker, Jeremy Deller, Rob Pruitt and Tom of Finland. Cabinet was one of several smaller exhibition spaces which opened in London in the 1990s, including Cubitt (est.1994) and Sadie Coles HQ, which was estabished in 1997 by former Anthony D'Offays director Sadie Coles in a small space at the end of Heddon Street. It was at Sadie Coles HQ that Jim Lambie had a high-profile London solo show that summer, exposing his brand of low-tech, high octane sculptural installation to the London art audience. Lambie was now producing a series of works which combined everyday pop culture materials with a shamanistic sensibility – for example, his *Psychedelic Soul Sticks* were wooden staffs wrapped in countless layers of multicoloured thread. Objects like sunglasses and punk lapel badges were concealed beneath the tightly bound layers. Later in the year, Lambie followed in the footsteps of Ross Sinclair, Simon Starling and Richard Wright by winning one of the annual £30,000 Paul Hamlyn Foundation Awards to artists – the largest individual award made to artists in the UK.

In Glasgow complaints were being made in some quarters about the dominance of a particular generation of artists. In April, the group show If I Ruled The World, curated by Bryndis Snaebjornsdottir and Ross Sinclair and featuring Roderick Buchanan, Claire Barclay, Martin Boyce, Simon Starling, Clara Ursutti, Rose Thomas, Ross Sinclair and Bryndis Snaebjorns-dottir opened at the CCA. Commenting on some of the apparent misgivings raised by this exhibition GSA lecturer John Calcutt said, "I suppose there is a feeling that a standard history is beginning to emerge now with standard

15  Moving Targets 2, Louisa Buck, Tate Gallery Publishing, London, 2000, p177.

candidates. When curators come over here looking for artists for international shows, they tend to be directed to the same people. These are undoubtedly important artists but it would be fantastic if visiting curators also got introduced to an alternative roster of artists – because with shows featuring 'Glasgow artists' you pretty much know who is going to be in them. Paradoxically, one of the potential weaknesses [of the art scene in Glasgow] is the extraordinary success of the so called neo-conceptualists. There is a danger it could become a bit suffocating and stagnant, particularly because many of those individuals are not doing that much here these days – simply because they've got flourishing international careers. So I think unless there is more encouragement of 'the next generation', we could end up with a kind of 'new academy' installed by default – and I don't suppose anybody wants that."[16]

Equally though, some of the neo-conceptual artists had reservations about the new work emerging from the studios of Jim Lambie, Lucy McKenzie and other "young pretenders". Ross Sinclair wrote in a recent catalogue essay that, "Most recently it's all gone international style; it's all about a feeling of ambient surface tension stripes – glitter brand soul Olympics – the empathetic Eamesism experience (are you experienced?) – no meaning (in a good way), wallpaper (in a good way) – don't worry – be happy (any way) a dynamic and beautiful void, (cut out or painted over, it doesn't matter) – head nodding recognition of utopian modernism done by African villagers kind of thing 'architecture as emotion' 'design as dogma' the best quality for most people at the cheapest prices turned into the exclusive Masonic lodge of recognition of the feel good relics of the modernist saints. Old dogs like me (35 years) should maybe keep quiet about a passionate feeling that art is often working well when it's talking about ideas and is about something rather than nothing (which has become vogueish, too), if you know what I mean. Above all else I think I should keep quiet about retaining an embattled ideal that art can still change people, begin a dialogue which can alter perception, CHANGE THE WORLD."[17]

16  John Calcutt, in conversation with the author, 18th April 2001.
17  Ross Sinclair, "What's in a Decade The Glasgow Miracle vs. Utopian modernism done by Third World peasants", *Circles*, ZKM, Karlsruhe, 2003, pp193–199.

Ross Sinclair's contemporary Claire Barclay[18] was increasingly exploring the tension between the search for spiritual enlightenment and how New Age ideologies are packaged by lifestyle magazines and outdoor and health food stores in her work. Using natural materials like mud and clay, beside colourful ripstop nylon and polished steel, Barclay's work explored the new fashion for spirituality and environmental issues. She said in a recent interview, "You go into a craft shop and it's full of mass produced things, like, for example, some sort of product, say a dream catcher kit for kids. I'm quite interested in how new age culture is becoming commodified, and amalgamated with craft."[19] The work of former Transmission member Eva Rothschild, who had lived in London since the late '90s, also forced a comparison of how the new hippies compare to the peace movements of the '60s. A characteristic work is the sculpture *Disappearer* (1999), which is comprised of multicoloured joss sticks, jutting in a spiky sphere from the wall, burning and filling the air with fragrant smoke.

The appeal of the Scottish Highlands as a place to escape, or to heal, had become complicated by the various abuses it had been subjected to in recent years, mainly environmental (nuclear dumping, landfill sites, tourism, oil spillages). The "Caring '90s" refocussed attention on alternative lifestyles and complementary therapies, as practiced in communities founded in the '60s like the Findhorn Community in northeast Scotland. In 1988 Hamish Henderson and Margaret Bennett had supported Angus Farquhar of Test Department in re-initiating the Beltane Fire Festival on Edinburgh's Calton Hill, and the continued popularity of the April pagan festival, as well as Farquhar's later NVA projects, like The Path (1999) seemed to attest to a growing interest in the dramatic possibilities of the natural environment. The Path was an open-air sound and light installation, interspersed with tableaux that those following the route came upon such as Tibetan monks brewing tea. The route was followed at night time, and participants were

18  For *If I Ruled the World* Claire Barclay had collaborated with Toronto-born artist Clara Ursitti (b.1968) to examine the myth that female pheromones work to the advantage of female fishers. Ursutti graduated from the MFA at GSA in 1995, and had been working with biochemist George Dodd on the artificial reconstruction of naturally occurring perfumes since 1993. For previous works, Ursitti had recreated the smell of her own body, The Sub Club, August 8, 1998 and Judy Garland (*The Smell of Fear: Part One and Two: Judy Garland*).
19  Interview by Iwona Blazwick, Early One Morning, Whitechapel Gallery, London, 2002.

asked to walk slowly and quietly, in order to take in the waterfalls, the trees, the whispered soundtracks and chiming of bells. NVA's highly evocative countryside installations required an enormous amount of planning, technical expertise and highly choreographed performances, but when they worked, they gave the audience an impression of a magically heightened world.

## ANOTHER PLACE

Tramway reopened in June, with group show Another Place, which featured the work of Alan Currall, Mike Nelson, Joachim Koester, Sean Synder and Tacita Dean. London-based artist Mike Nelson was a research fellow at Edinburgh College of Art, and his previous shows at Transmission and the Collective had established a loyal local audience for his work. His installation at Tramway was called *The Resurrection of Captain Mission*, a title taken from the William Burroughs novel, *Cities of the Red Night*. Nelson had constructed an abandoned military nightclub, perfect in all its sleazy details. There was no-one behind the cracked glass of the cashier's window; only a fan whirling round, trailing a tiny confederate flag. Across the threshold, there was a bar without glasses or drink, and an abandoned drumkit and a grimy glitterball. Backstage, an abandoned T-shirt and half-full bottle of water had been left behind by a visiting rocker before twenty years of dust descended.

Tramway's Dark Lights Commissions continued to provide a platform for emerging talent in the city, including Environmental Art graduate Sally Osborn (b.1963) who had been attracted to study at Glasgow partly because of the influence of Christine Borland. Osborn's work was also closely engaged with the interstices of the manmade and the natural, for her solo project at Tramway she built a bulky and amateurish "hide" to observe birds and animals inhabiting the wasteland behind the converted tram depot. Like other Glasgow-based artists Callum Sinclair, Justin Carter, Jenny Brownrigg, Katy Dove and Graham Fagen, Osborn had also been able to develop her ideas further during an artist's residency at Grizedale Forest.[20]

Another Glasgow-based artist making work that engaged with the onflict between modern "progress" and the natural environment was Justin Carter. After a residency at Cove Park, near Loch Long, he had made a series of works that referenced the nearby naval bases of Faslane and Coulport and the Faslane Peace Camp, which were shown at Tramway in September 2000. His show at Tramway featured a temporary living structure, emblazoned with phrases like "For Life" and "Conservation". A link could be drawn between these works and Martin Boyce's *Souvenir Placards* of the early 1990s (Coal Not Dole, Free South Africa, etc.) or Ross Sinclair's *Real Life Rocky Mountain* (1996). The contrast that the natural wilderness of Scotland offers to the pollution of inner city Glasgow had also previously informed works by Dalziel & Scullion, Claire Barclay and others.

Conversely, Joanne Tatham and Tom O'Sullivan's solo show The Glamour, which had opened at Transmission in June 2000, represented a clash between the ideas of Robert Smithson and Dan Flavin. The main installation used pink neon lights, rubble and mirrored panels to create a theatrical and archly allusive work. O'Sullivan said, "There always seemed to be something really boring about having a style, and what it can stop you doing. What we wanted was a framework of practice that allows you to explore different things, and different looks as part of your theme." Tatham & O'Sullivan had previously made works that circled "natural" concerns (poetry about woodlands, tie-dyed cloth, unfashionable ceramics) and harder, more "artificial" works (an installation of body prints shown with a relentless, looped techno soundtrack). This exhibition seemed to link these dual concerns, and as O'Sullivan pointed out, "The rocks, scattered neon lights and mirrors are generic art things, but they can still be somehow mysterious and interesting."[21]

In July, Keith Farquhar and Lucy McKenzie (Charisma) curated a show called It may be a year of Thirteen Moons but it's still the Year of Culture at

20  Artists residencies have been offered at Grizedale since 1977. Grizedale has the largest collection of site-specific work in the UK, including works by Andy Goldsworthy and Richard Harris and continues to expand its network of provision for artists under current director Adam Sutherland.

21  Tom O'Sullivan, in conversation with the author, November, 2000.

Transmission, which explored the young artist/curators' interest in things that exist on the periphery of good taste. To this end, McKenzie and Farquhar invited New Image painter Steven Campbell to show at Transmission for the first time, an invitation he responded to with two earthy folk-themed paintings, *To the North With Good Luck* and *Man with Spiral Tree*. Charisma also decide to eschew any curatorial objectivity, by including their own work in the show. Elsewhere in the show, London and Berlin-based painter Merlin Carpenter showed a couple of his paintings of fast cars and sketched-in female bodies, while Farquhar went for an installation of vitamin containers and a cream carpet with red wine spilt on it in the shape of the feminist symbol for woman entitled *Sex in Scotland*. Edinburgh College of Art lecturer Neil Mulholland wrote in his *Untitled* review, "Inscrutable historical exegesis takes us to Ken Currie's painting, *Sex in Scotland*, which hangs in the Glasgow Museum of Modern Art."[22] The inclusion of works by Campbell and a reference to Currie (who had frequently derided earlier members of the Transmission committee and Tramway curator Charles Esche) was in many ways characteristic of Charisma's provocative approach. Lucy McKenzie's contribution was an installation of 'Mockintosh' doors, *Force the Hand of Change*, which addressed what she called "the desensitised aesthetic" of ubiquitous Mackintosh-style tourist industry tat. She said, "The work is also utilitarian, as you have to walk through it, making the paintings used and scuffed. I'm totally against art being thought of as pristine and untouchable."[23]

By now Rose Thomas had left the Transmission committee, and Alan Michael's two-year stint was also drawing to an end. For Michael, leaving the committee meant more time to spend on his paintings, which collaged together disparate cultural reference points ranging from "high" art to imagery sourced from record sleeves or street posters. Michael was known for his skilfull appropriation of motifs from works by twentieth century artists including Amedeo Modigliani, Barbara Hepworth, Lucien Freud and Georgia O'Keeffe. His work was informed by an interest in cultural

22  Neil Mulholland, "Nasal and Facial Hair Reactions to Various Heritage Disasters", *Untitled*, Autumn/Winter, 2000, p34.
23  Excerpt from an interview with the author, July, 2000.

repression, specifically with how the use of certain kinds of imagery might be connected with a liberal political outlook. This interest underpinned his replication of the Franco-approved alternative cover of the Rolling Stones 1971 album *Sticky Fingers* and his improbable reconfigurations of Philip Pearlstein nudes.

The artists replacing Thomas and Michael on the Transmission committee were Clare Stephenson (b.1972) and Alex Pollard (b. 1977), who were both painters. Duncan of Jordanstone graduate Clare Stephenson made delicate works on paper using stencils and sprayed ink, combined with small sculptural works, while Pollard was experimenting with paintings using coffee and nail varnish. Pollard had also collaborated on a satirical newsletter, *Mainstream,* since 1997 with fellow GSA painting graduate Ian Hetherington (b.1978). Hetherington and Pollard used *Mainsteam* to take pot shots at various targets, including Tracey Emin, Glasgow City Council and pseudo-Marxist rhetoric. Imaginary reader's letters detailing "tragic" events, special offers for 'Free Profundity Pills (£5.44)' and Shrigley-esque drawings made *Mainstream* a lively addition to local fanzine culture.

In August, Lawrence Weiner returned to Transmission to present a new video work, *Hearts and Helicopters.* On the closing day, a series of short films was shown including *Trailer Plowmans Lunch* (1982), *Do You Believe In Water?* (1976), *Passage to the North* (1981) and *Altered to Suit* (1979). DCA's assistant curator Rob Tufnell rose to the challenge of interviewing Weiner at the gallery before an audience of local artists that included Douglas Gordon and Cathy Wilkes. Asked about his support of small independent galleries like Foksal Gallery in Warsaw and Transmission, Weiner retorted, "It's not any kind of a gracious gesture, it's done because the people themselves are doing something that interests me. If they're not then it's not very interesting."[24]


## CROSSING OVER


In November, Vivre Sa Vie, a season of talks, exhibitions and workshops revolving around contemporary French art, curated by Tanya Leighton,

24 *Untitled*, Autumn/Winter 2000, pp4–6.

opened at several venues across the city, including the Glasgow Project Room, Tramway and Transmission.[25] After leaving the Transmission committee, Leighton had worked at Dundee Contemporary Arts, and at Manchester Metropolitan University as a research fellow, alongside Research Professor Pavel Buchler. After a stint as an intern at the Whitney in New York, she had returned to Glasgow a few months before Vivre Sa Vie opened. She said, "I'm interested in art and projects which are about the whole social fabric, which cross over into music, fashion and film. This work is very much engaged in the social. Take Matthieu Laurette, for example, an artist who tours his mobile exhibition space around the country. Or Thomas Hirschhorn."[26] Hirschhorn's altar to the writer Raymond Carver, made out of pieces of rubbish (left-over paper, rough cuts of wood, an old umbrella) was assembled against the wall of a Gorbals towerblock during the exhibition. Over at Transmission, Paris/Berlin-based design duo Bless presented a selection of their art/fashion pieces including leather boot socks and fur wigs alongside the dreamy posterworks of Laurent Fetis in Ideas About A Place.

In November, Transmission sent Duncan Campbell, Chris Evans, Luke Fowler, Michael Fullerton, Andrew Kerr, Michelle Naismith, Clare Stephenson and Cathy Wilkes to Athens to participate in the exhibition Me We at Project Space. A wide range of approaches were taken by the artists within the group, as Rob Tufnell's catalogue essay reflected. "Michael Fullerton's idiosyncratic practice has included photographs of anti-nuclear protestors (taken whilst he was under the influence of LSD), 'paintings' which consisted of human hair on canvas and pictures constructed from blank audiotape arranged under glass. Andrew Kerr produces roughly crafted objects from found materials such as polystyrene and card. These works can appear as bathetic representations of the monumental 'public artworks' produced by a previous generation of artists. Michelle Naismith's work is made in the performance art and video tradition pioneered in the late 1960s and '70s. Faintly familiar explorations of sexuality, violence and

25  Vivre Sa Vie came soon after another European showcase exhibition – in September Plano XII, a cross-city event curated by Antonio Rego, to survey art production in Portugal had taken place in Glasgow.
26  John Calcutt, "Tanya Takes Paris", *Scotland On Sunday*, 19 November, 2000, pp14–17.

myth that we associate with the black and white era of Sony's Portapack are now reinvented with the self-focussing digital video camera."[27] For Luke Fowler, the exhibition created an opportunity to collate and release some of the new electronic music being made by his friends and associates in Glasgow. He says, "I'd come from an art background, not a musical one, and was just experimenting with generating music on my PC. With the availability of inexpensive technology, suddenly there were so many people around me making exciting music."[28] Fowler put together a CD compilation and an accompanying fanzine entitled *Shadazz: The Scottish Demo Collective*, which he distributed in bars and clubs around Athens.

Duncan of Jordanstone graduate Fowler had relocated to Glasgow during 2000, where he developed his interests in art and music in a number of ways. In February 2000 he staged The Social Engineer at Transmission, recording interviews between a series of invited participants, and commissioning local artists working in sound to "re-mix" the interviews for a limited-edition CD. The project also included contributions from Chad McCail, London based electronic musician Scanner and Jakob Kolding. Copenhagen-based artist Jakob Kolding's work used collages of found images and text to call to mind questions on how post 1960s town planning could be seen to affect the behaviour of residents, while the drawing by Chad McCail included in the exhibition referenced Stanley Milgram's notorious 1961 "Obedience to Authority" experiment. Fowler's work was also influenced by other sociological and psychological theory, in particular, the work of Glaswegian psychologist RD Laing. The influence of Laing can also be traced in the work of several other contemporary Glasgow-based artists, including Douglas Gordon, who titled a 1996 video work *The Divided Self*, and Joanne Tatham and Tom O'Sullivan, who had used the graphics from the cover of a paperback edition of one of his books as the basis for their sculpture *You've got to get into it to get out of it* (1999).

Earlier that year, Luke Fowler had been recruited by The Modern Institute to work as a researcher on their forthcoming exhibition Electric

27  Transmission at Project Space, Athens, 2000.
28  Brian Beadie, "Shadazz: Evil Eye is Source", *Untitled*, Summer 2002, pp44–45.

City. Fowler was also working on his own art/music projects including releasing the first *Shadazz* compilation by local electronic musicians, booking guests for electronic club Off the Hook[29] and his own foray into composition, Rude Pravo with El Hombre Trajeado's Stevie Jones. He said, "The crossover between music and art is a very significant and interesting phenomenon, though I wouldn't say it was a recent one or a particularly happy marriage … I guess both are perceived as outsiders with a lot of time on their hands"[30] Electric City aimed to give an overview of the Glasgow music scene of the last 25 years, from Johnny and the Self Abusers to Belle & Sebastian. The exhibition, which opened in November 2000, included a vinyl floor installation by Jim Lambie, commissioned interviews, memorabilia and performances by local and foreign bands and DJs, including Peaches from New York and DJ Manou Krause from Berlin. Perhaps unsurprisingly, the exhibition was widely criticised by those either who felt it was unrepresentative of the diversity of the local music scene or that it should not have been held in the somewhat conventional environs of The Lighthouse.

## THE CULTURAL STRATEGY

Late in 2000, *Creating Our Future … Minding Our Past Scotland's National Cultural Strategy* was published by the Scottish Executive. The Cultural Strategy recommended the establishment of A National Theatre for Scotland and backed the provision of more funding for local film makers. Promotion of the visual arts was not high on the list of stated priorities, but the launch of The Creative Scotland Awards (14 awards of £25,000 to be awarded annually to leading Scottish creative workers) would provide a major boost to the careers of a few Scottish artists. The Scottish Arts Council *Lottery Funding Strategy*, published the same year, identified eight strategic priorities, five of which were concerned with education, social inclusion, and developing art activity in outlying and disadvantaged areas. Of the eight strategies, only two[31] could be said to benefit artist-run organisations such as Transmission.

29  Guests included DonAtellA, the musical project of Mark Leckey, the artist who made the acclaimed art documentary *Fiorucci Made Me Hardcore*.
30  Luke Fowler, in conversation with the author, March 2001.
31  Helping arts organisations achieve lasting positive change and developing the creative and technical skills of those who work in the arts.

At the end of the year, Magnus Linklater, SAC chairman for five years, stood down to be replaced by James Boyle, former head of BBC Radio Scotland and Radio 4. Shortly afterwards, SAC Director Tessa Jackson resigned, and was replaced by the former Head of Finance. Fears circulated that these changes would lead to more funding for "populist" cultural projects and less for more challenging proposals. The SAC announced it would spend £54.9 million on arts in 2001, an increase of £4.4 million on the previous year. The 2001 Creative Scotland Awards were announced, and artists Steven Campbell, Nathan Coley and Roderick Buchanan were all awarded £25,000 to realise new works. 2001 was also International Year of the Artist, and 100 residencies in non-gallery settings were undertaken by artists including Ross Birrell, Nathalie de Briey and Nathan Coley.

Ross Birrell proposed to "occupy" the Scottish Parliament for the period of one year, staging a seven week "Night Class in Utopia" open to all those who work in the parliament in the General Debating Chamber. He also proposed that the same room be taken over for a series of televised concerts by young Scottish bands such as Teenage Fanclub, Primal Scream, the Pastels, Belle & Sebastian, Mogwai, Life Without Buildings, the Beta Band and Travis. He wrote, "This would bring popular youth culture right to the heart of a political environment which is often viewed as alienating and distant by young people." Birrell's proposal was rejected as being "outwith the scope of the SPCB, its staff and accommodation."[32] Nathan Coley, who proposed to undertake a research trip to the site of the Lockerbie trial in the Netherlands, was more successful, and eventually negotiated the use of the witness stand for use in a future exhibition.


## A SWING TO THE RIGHT

On January 20th 2001 Republican candidate George W. Bush was inaugurated as the new president of the United States after a controversial and very close-run election, leaving most left-wing critics in despair. The

---

32  Letters replicated in *Justified Sinners*, Pocketbooks, Edinburgh, 2002.

new president was criticised for his lack of knowledge about the world outside America, after admitting that he did not know the name of the Chinese premier, and until relatively recently had not possessed a passport. There was also a revisionist aspect to this swing to the right, with Bush's father's presidency, and the Gulf War he had pursued, still a fresh memory for many. Clinton had been an important ally for Blair, and instrumental in brokering the Good Friday agreement in Northern Ireland. It seemed unlikely that Bush would possess similarly moderate views or diplomacy, especially given that many commentators believed that Bush Snr. would probably attempt to use his son's presidency to settle old scores in the Middle East.

In February Lucy McKenzie, Jim Lambie and Richard Wright were installing their work for the international group show, Painting at the Edge of the World, at the Walker Art Center, Minneapolis alongside the work of other artists including Paul Thek, Helio Oiticica, Franz Ackermann, Michael Raedecker and Thomas Schutte. The international stature of Glasgow-based artists was further emphasised by two group shows: G3NY13[33] at Casey Caplan, New York and Circles at ZKM Karlsruhe.[34] Meanwhile, in London, the Brit-Art bubble seemed to well and truly burst as Apocalypse: Beauty and Horror in Contemporary Art opened at the Royal Academy in March. Andrew Gellaty wrote in *frieze*, "Apocalypse: Beauty and Horror in Contemporary Art was a misbegotten exhibition created by an institution still tripping on the impact of its till-ringing 'Sensation' in 1997. I half expected to find David Foster Wallace-style footnotes tagged to absolutes such as 'beauty' and 'horror', but the bathos here was pretty much intact, unsalvaged and unenjoyable."[35] Elsewhere in the capital, Michael Landy began his *Breakdown* project which entailed systematically destroying everything he owned, including artworks by himself and yBa friends such as Gary Hume and Gillian Wearing.

---

33  With Gary Rough, Martin Boyce, Ross Sinclair, Jim Lambie, Graham Fagen, Mary Redmond, Toby Paterson, Douglas Gordon, Christine Borland, Jonathan Monk, Simon Starling, Richard Wright and Claire Barclay.

34  Dave Allen, Claire Barclay, Christine Borland, Martin Boyce, Roderick Buchanan, Nathan Coley, Jacqueline Donachie, Douglas Gordon, Jim Lambie, Lucy McKenzie, Jonathan Monk, Elizabeth Go, Toby Paterson, Craig Richardson, Julie Roberts, Eva Rothschild, David Shrigley, Ross Sinclair, Simon Starling, Jonnie Wilkes and Michael Wilkinson participated.

35  Andrew Gellaty, "Apocalypse", *frieze*, March 2001.

As the summer approached, the Transmission committee evolved once more. Danny Saunders, Alex Pollard, Anna McLauchlan and Clare Stephenson, were joined by new additions Lawrence Figgis and Lorna Macintyre, as photography graduate Fred Pedersen stood down. Pedersen continued to work on photographing surreal situations, such as "found" groupings of cars of the same colour parked together, or the participants /audience at a viking festival and a heavy rock concert. In addition to her Complecity projects with Neil Bickerton,[36] Lorna Macintyre (b.1977) also made solo works using a variety of materials including silk thread, paint, drilled holes and map pins to create decorative and representational effects. In March, John Beagles and Graham Ramsay curated a show of art making double acts, Dub'l-Introoder at the gallery, which was launched with a performance by Bob & Roberta Smith and David Burrows which lampooned Beuys' "coyote" performance, *I Like America and America Likes Me*. Elizabeth Mahoney wrote in *The Guardian*, "In Transmission gallery's manic tribute to duality and plurality, John Beagles and Graham Ramsay's miniature industrial unit dominates the proceedings. Orderly from the outside, inside it is a deviant house of fun, crammed full of demented wind-up toys, newspaper cuttings, two dummies of drone workers and a severed hand with a fried egg."[37]

## SOME KIND OF BREAKTHROUGH

By the late '90s, most of the artists who had first collaborated together in Cathy Wilkes' towerblock flat project in Glasgow had established a significant international reputation. In December 2000, Richard Wright was in New York, installing his first solo project in the city at Gagosian Gallery, New York. Wright painted a delicate filigree pattern of red and blue foliage in the light recess high above the gallery assistants' desks. He told critic Neville Wakefield, "I wanted to get to the work by the shortest possible

---

36 Glasgow School of Art graduates Lorna MacIntyre and Neil Bickerton have worked collaboratively under the name Complecity since autumn of 1998. For their eleventh project together, at Transmission in January 2000, the duo decided to make an enormous multicoloured sculpture out of elastic bands.

37 *The Guardian*, March 2001.

route. By doing away with the object, I can concentrate on the action of painting. [ … ] It's what you do live that really matters, that creates the tension between elements you know and control and those you cannot."[38] The following month group show Open Country Contemporary Scottish Artists opened at the Musee Cantonal des Beaux-Arts, Lausanne, with David Shrigley, Martin Boyce, Simon Starling, Callum Innes, Smith/Stewart, Roderick Buchanan, Alan Currall, Douglas Gordon and Louise Hopkins.

Also in December 2000, Victoria Morton became the second Modern Institute artist to have a solo show at Sadie Coles HQ in London. Artist and writer Polly Staple wrote for *Make* about the changes she saw in Morton's painting style. "*Plus and Minus* is an epic canvas and although the grand specularity is a little overbearing, this painting seems to signal some kind of breakthrough. The easy organic reference points have gone and any hint of decoration has been eliminated, leaving you temporarily bereft of reference points. Large pockets of smudgy black and ochre provide the backdrop to a more turbulent arrangement of merging colours and varied brushstrokes; the trademark turquoises and oranges lead your eye around the canvas, strung together by scratchy lines of mauve and green – a valley, a boulder, a wing, a pool of colour, a mark. *Plus and Minus* is a really weird thing to behold but I like the beautiful strangeness and the pleasure derived from the suggestion of things only partially forgotten, of incomprehensible terror and brilliant ecstasy, the detached consideration of Francis Picabia's compositional energy and the sublimity of a Turner sunset; from how you might even begin to make a painting to what colour you should paint your eyelids and whether glitter is necessary."[39]

In the spring of 2001, Jim Lambie had travelled to New York for his first solo show there, at Anton Kern's gallery. Lambie installed his trademark vinyl tape floor, and hung a series of coloured polythene carrier bags filled with different shades of paint, then punched holes in the bags so that the paint oozed down onto the striped floor below. The show, which also included

38  Neville Wakefield, "The Painting is on the Wall", *Elle Decor*, April 2001, pp98–102.
39  Polly Staple, Victoria Morton, *Make*, issue 91, March–May 2001, p33.

one sculpture made from leather blousons and another made from gatefold record sleeves, brought Lambie's work to the attention of the American critics, curators and collectors. *Flash Art* correspondent Sylvia Chivaratanoud enthused, "Lambie's world is controlled yet naughty, conceptual and trashy. In his balancing act, he challenges the hidden meanings and obsessions with our mass consumption of music, religion and Modernism."[40]

In July 2001 Cathy Wilkes' second solo show at Transmission opened, ten years after her first. Our Misfortune was a graceful meditation on complex ideas of family, artistic antecedents and the inexorable effects of time. For the exhibition, a corner section of Transmission's floor was turned over, revealing the numerous drillings and sawings that fourteen years of exhibitions had inflicted upon the boards. In this space Wilkes arranged four dilapidated card tables, all splinters and precarious legs, dressed with penciled texts, scraps of fabric made to look like a disembodied face, and delicate wooden sculptures made from slender lengths of wood. Completing this group of strangely animated tables was an ancient sun lounger, which trailed a Picasso-influenced necktie like a tongue. A group of four white canvases hung around the periphery of the tables, traced with compass-point circles and changing configurations of letters. Wilkes also included a bold painting in the cubist style by her father, George Wilkes. Describing an earlier piece in the same cycle of works, Will Bradley wrote, "*Beautiful Human Body* is a still life, a portrait and a landscape all at once, just as it's representational, allegorical and factual simultaneously. It's as though Wilkes doesn't want to let go of any of the possibilities that the work allows, and a big part of her aesthetic is finding this precarious balance. Perhaps this is what she means when she says she wants her work to be 'unstable'. On the face of it that's an odd quality to ascribe to things that seem so still, so mannered, but if you – I mean I – spend some time with them in the right mood, then the tension between the different potential states of the work causes it to shift, to flicker like the fluorescent tube in the adapted display cabinet *Stag*."[41]

40  Sylvia Chivaratanoud, Jim Lambie, *Flash Art*, May June 2001, p141.
41  Will Bradley, "Quiet Radical", *Untitled* Summer 2001, pp4–6.

# DEPRIVATION

In April 2002, 15,000 marchers took part in an anti-drugs demonstration in central Glasgow, the climax of a campaign run by the country's biggest-selling tabloid newspaper, *The Daily Record*. The demonstration was led by Mothers Against Drugs, an organisation set up in Cranhill after 13 year-old Allan Harper died from a massive heroin overdose. It was the largest public demonstration since anti-Thatcher demonstrations of the 1980s, and highlighted the severe health problems affecting the city's underclass.[42] Greater Glasgow Health Board estimated that there were as many as 10,000 injecting drug users in the city, and as a recent report by the Social Inclusion Committee attests, "Problem drug use in Scotland is inextricably linked with other extreme forms of social exclusion, notably homelessness, persistent offending and street prostitution."[43]

Street prostitution is particularly common in Glasgow, with over 1,140 women registering with Base 75, a city centre health and social care provider since 1990. 92% of these women are known to be injecting drugs. 6,500 people in Glasgow have experience of street homelessness every year: 2,500 are newly homeless, the rest have continuing or repeat experience of homelessness.[44] The Office for National Statistics found in a recent study that 84% of 25–34 year old homeless people in Glasgow were dependent on drugs, had a hazardous pattern of drinking, or both.[45] Unsurprisingly, the prevalence of drug and alcohol abuse, prostitution and homelessness, and mental health problems was found to be far higher in deprived areas. People living in a deprived area, such as Shettleston, were 2.7 times more likely to be admitted to hospital for depression, 3 times more likely to commit suicide, 4.5 times more likely to be admitted for self-poisoning, 6 times more likely to be admitted with schizophrenia, 10 times more likely to be admitted for an alcohol-related problem and 33 times more likely to

---

42  The term underclass was first used by Ball and Lapeyre, 1997, in reference to certain groups, who are increasingly occupying the lowest paid, least secure and most unpleasant occupations.
43  Report by the Social Inclusion Committee of the Scottish Executive, 2nd Dec 2000.
44  Report of the Glasgow Street Homelessness Review Team, Scottish Executive, 14th March 2002.
45  Substance Misuse and Mental Disorder amongst Homeless People in Glasgow, Office for National Statistics, March 2000.

be admitted for a drug misuse-related problem, than those residing in an affluent area such as North Kelvinside.[46] Social realist filmmaker Ken Loach has focussed on these issues in his recent films *My Name is Joe* (1999) and *Sweet Sixteen* (2002), set in Glasgow and nearby Greenock, and scripted by Glaswegian screenwriter Paul Laverty.

In November 2001, Joanne Tatham and Tom O'Sullivan's *HK* opened at Tramway. The focal point of the exhibition was a series of enormous 3D black letters spelling out the 1980s anti-drugs campaign slogan HEROIN KILLS.[47] The show split opinions in the city's artistic community in a way that hadn't been seen in some time. Edinburgh-based lecturer and critic Neil Mulholland supported the work, writing in *Flash Art*, "In the present world of polite bourgeois *No Logo* mores, heroin remains more than a PR dilemma, particularly in Glasgow, which has more addicts than the rest of Great Britain put together. Nevertheless, confronted by Scottish tabloid newspapers that hysterically encourage mob witch-hunts of evil dealers, *HK* conscientiously acknowledges heroin's continuing resistance to representation and easy solutions (the letters are too large to view from a single perspective, the texts take time to deliberate)."[48] On the other side of the debate was the contention that the work did not engage with the locally significant issue of heroin addiction in any serious way, and was in fact driven by an ironic sensibility that was bordering on offensive. A heated discussion of these issues later took place at Tramway, which did little to resolve the tensions surrounding the work, but at least confirmed that the whole 'social engagement vs. elitism in art' argument was far from dead.

On June 7th, only 59% of those eligible to vote in the general election did so, echoing the low turn out at the elections for the Scottish Parliament. Only 39% of 18–24 year olds voted[49] in the election that returned Tony Blair to government for a second term. One explanation for this could have been that many people felt alienated from the political process – after Blair's initial "Cool Brittania" PR splash it became clear that he was just as

---

46  NHS Executive Summary of a Report on Mental Health Issues in Greater Glasgow, 11th December 2001.
47  The font used for the letters was designed by Robert Johnston under the auspices of his Pause Button Edit design company.
48  Neil Mulholland, *Flash Art*, March/April 2002, p106.
49  *The Observer*, 28th April 2002.

disinterested in young people as John Major had been. Another explanation for the low turn out was that registering to vote now equated with paying council tax, which was set in bands for areas. Although the Poll Tax had long since been replaced by council tax, the responsibility for paying the tax continued to fall on tenants, unless they could avoid being registered as living there, or claim unemployment benefit, rendering them ineligible to pay council tax.

"Although I am working again at the moment, sometimes I have to sign on. Often I bump into other artists I know. It's generally better to keep chat to a minimum in this situation. I feel defiant when I fill in what job I'm looking for, although you know they don't have a clue what you mean. At least it's a recognised job in their system now. A couple of years ago it was artiste or monumental stone carver – I can't remember which one I opted for."[50]

At the present time, as in the past, the main financial support system for many of Glasgow's artists comes from unemployment and housing benefit. This situation had been addressed by a number of exhibitions organised by Glasgow-based artists, notably Dependants (Transmission, 1990) and Crystal State (Three Month Gallery, 1998).[51] Although the current level of those benefits is clearly set to discourage long-term benefit claimants, for many artists it remains their most viable option. No other means of income allows enough time off to sustain an art practice. However, the level at which housing benefit and Jobseeker's Allowance payments are set leaves a considerable shortfall between incomings and outgoings, meaning that a "cash in hand" job is often essential to make up the difference.[52] This kind of situation, where benefits are supplemented with a casual job, can seem like

---

50  *Dole Story*, printed in British Mythic, February 1998.
51  For artranspennine98 the Three Month Gallery in Liverpool proposed a project to take place in 14 Benefit Agencies across the region inviting artists that had previously been involved in exhibitions and events at the gallery, including Alan Michael, Eva Rothschild, Robert Johnston and Padraig Timoney. The project was originally called "3 Million People Can't Be Wrong" though following discussions with the DHSS was renamed with the more opaque title of 'Crystal State'. From the outset the project recognized the double-life of many that 'sign on' acknowledging the undercurrent workforce that claim benefits as a wage in order to make art, music, write etc.
52  In 2001 housing benefit in central Glasgow was set at £167 a month, despite the fact that a room in an average flat in this area costs £200–£250 a month to rent.

a better option than earning a time-consuming full-time wage, which is then eaten into by taxes, National Insurance contributions, Student Loan repayments and of course, monthly council tax payments. The "benefit trap" situation then arises, where claimants are reluctant to try to find full-time work in case they become worse off, or dislike the job but can't leave it because that would then affect future benefit claims.

Recent Scottish Executive reports suggest that in future it will be possible for young artists and musicians to state their true career aspirations in New Deal training for work interviews, thus avoiding the "lying to the dole" that has been the bane of many artist's lives. Fuse and Fly-founder Patricia Fleming joined the steering group for the New Deal and Creative Industry to help develop a new strategy for dealing with unemployed artists and musicians. Scottish Industry Minister Brian Wilson announced in July 2001, "My aim has been to accommodate the raw energy of young creative artists within the New Deal. The advice and support which the New Deal provides for unemployed people will now also enable Scotland's budding creative talent to flourish in a way which benefits the whole community. It makes sense for the New Deal to be flexible enough to encourage young unemployed musicians and others who wish to pursue creative careers, as this not only helps the individual but impacts positively on the wider community."[53]

However, once a claimant reaches the "gateway" period of their New Deal – after six months of signing on – they are often pressurised by the Benefits Office to undertake a Training for Work scheme, to take an unrelated job or to re-enter higher education. Training for Work schemes can lead to surprisingly successful outcomes – as we have seen in the case of Glasgow band Belle & Sebastian and the many artists who participated in Fuse. However, the threat of benefit withdrawal to encourage claimants to move through their "gateway" and off the Benefit Agency's books means that Scotland is poles apart from countries like Ireland and the Netherlands, which actively subsidise emerging artists.

Ireland's system of tax breaks and free artist's flights has meant that in

53  Source: The Scottish Executive website, www.scotland.gov.uk, 17th July 2001.

recent years several films set in Scotland, including *Braveheart,* were filmed on location in Ireland. In a recent SAC Report, Ruth Wishart writes, "It was the Irish that pioneered the system now being contemplated in England and Wales [ ... ] their tax structure has been encouraging to inward investment by the creative industries. Some people would argue that this has been an expensive way to bring jobs, but there is no question that the Department has raised the country's cultural profile at home and abroad and helped place artistic development centre-stage."[54] Other examples of countries with buoyant creative industries include Norway and Sweden, where the governments see themselves as the employer of the artist. However, the situation here may breed resilience in young artists, believes Lucy McKenzie. She says, "There is a very different situation here than there is in Holland, where artists are really supported by the state: there is cheap studio provision and welfare subsidy available. But the amount of bad art that gets made there is unbelievable. Survival of the fittest is a really capitalist view but in Glasgow there is a real sense of people doing something out of the love of it."[55]

Glasgow-based painter Toby Paterson agrees. "Not to come over as too Darwinian, but I really believe that where there's a will there's a way. Personally speaking my hiatus from making art was valuable, and not just because I worked at Transmission throughout that period. If I'd had public funding thrown at me during that period I wouldn't have known what to do with it, would have been embarrassed and felt guilty about it. Call me a Calvinist, but I think a relatively uncertain and barren outlook at such a time promotes vigorous decision making and sets one's resolve! I think commitment to your practice as an artist is vital and sometimes it takes a while to realise this."[56]

54  Ruth Wishart, *Scottish Arts in the 21st Century,* SAC Report 2000.
55  Lucy McKenzie, in conversation with the author, October 2000.
56  Toby Paterson, in response to questions sent by the author, April 2001.

CHAPTER 12

# Craftless Tat
## (2001–2002)

By 2001 Glasgow's economy had become stronger than it had been for 20 years, buoyed by strong high street spending, the financial sector and new economic companies. Although unemployment at 4.5% was higher than the national average, the city had achieved economic growth of 3.6% over the past three years, ahead of the Scottish average of 2%. £25 million had been spent on streetscaping in central Glasgow during the 1990s, contributing to the increasingly affluent atmosphere in the city centre, especially in the Buchanan Street precinct, which is now punctuated with saplings, polished stone benches and blue floodlights. The new Buchanan Galleries shopping development has contributed to the £7.5 billion netted annually by the city's retailers, meaning Glasgow is still the UK's biggest shopping centre after London.

"I think Glasgow has become much more 'spectacularised' recently with the facelift of Buchanan Street – there are different kinds of shops, different kinds of bars, different kinds of restaurants. It's become much more self-consciously stylish … particularly in terms of bars. Sometimes you say the name of a bar to a taxi driver and he doesn't know it so you say, well it used to be such and such, and if he still doesn't know it you say, well before that it was called this … This constant building, that is inseparable for me from the rise of Douglas Gordon and Christine Borland. The city has become inseparably connected with those things too."[1]

---

1   John Calcutt, in conversation with the author, April 2001.

The deification of tourist industry "patron saint" Charles Rennie Mackintosh, had proceeded apace in the 1990s with the opening of the renovated Lighthouse in Mitchell Lane and The House for an Art Lover (1996) at Bellahouston Park, built to unrealised plans made by Mackintosh almost a hundred years earlier. Although much of Glasgow's most impressive architecture has been razed over the years, new developments such as the Glasgow Science Centre have also helped bolster the city's visitor attractions in recent years. In the spring of 2002, Glasgow City Council leader Charles Gordon announced a £1bn plan to redevelop the Clyde with a combination of landscaping, modern business, leisure resources and luxury flats, which aims to rival similar developments in Newcastle and Liverpool. This announcement has been followed by the unveiling of plans for a £250 million financial district to be developed off the Broomielaw, which runs along the north bank of the Clyde.

Ironically, the recent gentrification of Glasgow, which the city's artists helped support, has recently brought the current location of Transmission and other Merchant City arts organisation under threat. The City Council has decided to sell off some of its Merchant city properties for development as bars, eateries and luxury flats although, it has recently been announced that the council has committed itself to keeping the North block of King Street as a dedicated arts building. It seems likely that Transmission will stay in its current location, although Project Ability and the Glasgow Media Acess Centre will be moved from Albion Street into King Street, and that the Independent Studios and The Glasgow Project Room will probably also be forced to move from their current Osbourne Street venue. This will result in most of the arts organisations in the Trongate area being consolidated into a single "one-stop" location, something many local artists are uneasy about.

The Mitre Bar is another Merchant City property set to disappear, as the area of land has been bought by property developers and is set for demolition in the near future to make way for a £25 million Selfridges department store. The lane outside the bar is the site of Douglas Gordon's *Empire* sign, and is where numerous Transmission's artists' talks and parties have been held, including Jonathan Monk's *Yard of Ale (Get Shirty)* performance of 1994. Although the Mitre is just one small venue, it is representative of the few sympathetic places that have been so important to building Glasgow's art community. In other areas of town, several long-established haunts of the city's student and bohemian population have been squeezed out by developers, notably Café Equi on Sauchiehall Street, a favourite haunt of actors, musicians and artists, and the Grosvenor Café in Ashton Lane, frequented by students and academics from the nearby Glasgow University. Many bars and shops that had retained the same signage and interior since the 1950s are now replacing their hoardings with modern vinyl signs and refurbishing, or else closing down completely. There is a definite sense that the Glasgow that remained relatively static in terms of city centre redevelopment between the 1960s and the early 1990s is now being rapidly erased. In addition to the city's new status as a major shopping centre, in recent years Glasgow has also become one of the UK's 'conference capitals' with numerous new hotels springing up around town[2] to meet the demand. Local artist James Thornhill, who has previously staged exhibitions in a semi-derelict former hotel and in a room in the city's Moathouse Hotel, comments, "The city has changed a lot – it's become a lot cleaner. There are many more hotels, too. I hate it when derelict buildings get knocked down and they build these really nasty, cheaply fabricated buildings in their places. Places you go disappear, or the architecture becomes really ugly."[3]

According to their budget for 2002/2003, the Scottish Arts Council has spent almost £55m in support of the arts in 2002, with £35m coming from the Scottish Executive, and £20m from the National Lottery Fund. This £0.1m increase from 2001 resulted in reduced support for most projects and schemes. As *Art Monthly* commented, "This state of affairs is worrying indeed: that in a period of 20 years in which Scottish artists have developed high profiles and reputations internationally, SAC's support for contemporary art (as for other artforms) is slowly diminishing. At a time when organisations should be building on their reputations they are having

---

2   New hotels that have opened in the city centre of Glasgow in the last two years include Langs, Ibis, Bewley's Hotel, Holiday Inn and Novotel.
3   James Thornhill, in conversation with the author, August 2001.

to tighten their belts and hold their breaths."[4] Although most arts organisations which depend on SAC funding will be forced to implement a budget which is effectively the same as last year's or less, the funding for drama will increase by £3.5 m over the year, in line with the calls for a National Theatre made during the consultation process for 2000's *National Cultural Strategy*. Although the comparatively low funding levels for visual arts have often been linked to its alleged inaccessibility of the visual arts, the national arts companies Scottish Ballet, Scottish Opera and Scottish National Orchestra, attended mainly by those from "AB" social groups, continue to receive a substantially higher chunk of the SAC budget each year.

Glasgow City Council is another source of possible funding for local artists, although council restructuring, which recently led to the provision for visual arts coming under the jurisdiction of the new department of Culture and Leisure Services, has swallowed up a lot of time and resources. "From 1982/3 to 1992/3 local authority funding for the arts rose by around 125% and underpinned a cultural regeneration. Unfortunately, local government re-organisation and public sector constraints reversed this pattern, with a reduction of over 30% in the last five years. These significant reductions in funding for the arts have caused, and continue to cause, problems for the arts and cultural delivery."[5] However, a major boost to subsidised studio provision for artists working in the city recently came about in the form of the new purpose-built WASPS studio and events complex at Hanson Street in the East End, which opened in April 2002. The complex, supported by the SAC and Glasgow City Council, contains provision for over 300 artists, and significantly bolsters the existing network of shared artist's facilities and exhibition spaces around the city. WASPS have also recently secured the use of the disused Briggait complex, and plan to move from their smaller King Street premises into the nearby Briggait in the next two years, along with the Glasgow Sculpture Studios, who have already given up their Maryhill base in favour of this new, more central location.

---

4   Artnotes, *Art Monthly*, March 2002.
5   The Scottish Art's Council's Response to the Consultation on the National Cultural Strategy, February 2000.

The lottery capital funds[6] that have funded the renovation of arts centres such as Tramway and CCA, as well as theatres with "cafe/gallery" spaces such as The Tron and the Arches, have done little to improve the staffing levels for visual arts projects and programming within these institutions. Former CCA Director of Exhibitions Nicola White says, "The whole lottery process is something a lot of organisations have gone through and ended up as completely different organisations at the other end, which I think is a real pity because what you end up with are these quite complex, expensive to run buildings without any heart or staff left, because the building has mopped up all the lifeblood."[7]

As DCA curator Katrina Brown says, "There is a problem in that the two main "venues" for visual art in Glasgow are funded and run, in SAC terminology, as combined arts centres – there is no major dedicated visual arts space or institution in a city that has such an amazing reputation internationally. I think there's a real challenge to keep up in the face of that."[8] Glasgow now has to compete with several other post-industrial cities throughout the UK that have recently re-invented themselves as "cities of culture". Although arts organisations like Waygood and Locus+ have been operating in Newcastle for many years, the profile of the Newcastle-Gateshead area was significantly boosted when Anthony Gormley's imposing 20-metre-high *Angel of the North* sculpture was unveiled in 1997. The sculpture, which overlooks the A1 motorway, and the Baltic Gateshead "art factory" which opened in June 2002 on the Tyneside Harbour under Swedish director Sune Nordgren, have also greatly increased Newcastle's international profile. Other cities weren't far behind – notably Liverpool, which has enjoyed an increased profile as an art centre due to the combination of the artstranspennine98 projects[9] the launch of the Liverpool Biennal in 1999[10]

6   Since 1995 the Scottish Arts Council has distributed a total of 151 million in National Lottery funds to 1,296 projects. Of the total, 103 million has gone to 593 different capital projects, including both buildings and equipment. Source: SAC Latest News, "Arts Buildings Boom Thanks to SAC Funding", 17th July 2001, www.sac.org.uk

7   Nicola White, in conversation with the author, November 2002.

8   Katrina Brown, in response to questions sent by the author, September 2001.

9   artstranspennine98 was a multi-site exhibition of international contemporary art shown in venues across the north of England. Tracy McKenna, Christine Borland, Bernd and Hilla Becker and Anya Gallaccio were amongst the participating artists.

10   The second Liverpool Biennal was delayed until 2002 in order to take advantage of Liverpool's new Foundation for Art and Creative Technology centre and the newly refurbished Walker Art Gallery.

and the high profile exhibition programme at Tate Liverpool.

In Glasgow, budgeting restrictions continue to limit the programme of several of the city's leading art spaces. Tramway post-redevelopment runs on a smaller staff and similar budget than before the building's closure in 1998. Tramway curator Alexia Holt explains, "There used to be a travel budget for programmers at Tramway and that budget isn't really in existence anymore.[ … ] I think the international reputation of Tramway slipped after Charles Esche left because there was no-one going around waving the flag at events and going to all the art fairs, we just didn't have that possibility anymore. We also need to be able to tour shows – at the moment we don't have the amount of administration and resources needed to tour shows. The Pipilotti Rist (2001) show, for example, could have toured to some amazing venues but we just couldn't afford to do it. We've got three additional spaces and stables studio spaces that could be used for additional programming during summer but we're on the same budget as before and have even less staff than before the building closed. I think the people who devised the Lottery awards have realised that now and the criteria and the type of grants you can apply for are changing, but it is a huge problem – which I'm sure CCA will suffer from too."[11] The National Executive has advised the SAC to make a shift from capital to non-capital (activities-based) spending,[12] but tangible results of that shift are not yet apparent.

However, Tramway has recently received a major boost when it was announced that arts production company NVA had received £500,000 of National Lottery funding from the SAC to transform the 5000 square metres of derelict land behind Tramway into Hidden Gardens, "a contemplative open space featuring a series of artworks including land sculpture, installation, poetry and story telling, herbs and fruiting trees." In 2002, Holt was able to commission two major new works by Glasgow-based artists, with artists' collective Henry VIII's Wives' Light Without Shadow opening in April and Martin Boyce's Our Love is Like the Flowers, the Rain, the Sea and the Hours in November. Henry VIII's Wives, in their

11  Alexia Holt, in conversation with the author, July 2001.
12  Appendix: Govt. Policy Directions, in Strategy, The Distribution of Arts National Lottery Funding in Scotland.

most ambitious project to date, made two new film works featuring blind people and acting students, which were shown within a 1:1 scale model of neolithic settlement Skara Brae. In recent years the group have made several works that linked together disparate elements – such as a portrait of Che Guevara rendered in coffee beans, and a group photograph of people of different religious denominations gathered in a disused flight control tower. However their installation at Tramway marked a significant development in the group's practice and posed questions about how knowledge and identity are constructed – both in terms of the physical experience of negotiating the exhibition, and through the disjointed narratives presented in the film works.

Martin Boyce turned Tramway 2 into a twilit concrete playground, with neon trees that phased on and off, and an eerie looped soundtrack. The space was punctuated with stylised waste paper bins and benches based on a design by Jean Prouve, making this a learned environment – an idea of a playground filtered through remembered design allusions. Accompanying the looped soundtrack was an animation of a flickering grid, which spelt the phrase, "this place is dreaming" on the bricks of the wall before fading away.

Glasgow's Centre for Contemporary Arts reopened in October 2001 in a gush of champagne and publicity, accompanied by a lot of grumbling from local artists and curators. The new CCA buildings had now expanded into various surrounding properties including the former Mandor's fabric shop and the Cotton Club nightclub on Scott Street but, curiously, the main café bar now seemed larger than the main gallery space. Director Graham McKenzie had also laid plans to invest in other art forms including new media, literature, electronic music, children's events, dance and live art, and only planned to host a minimum of four visual art exhibitions a year. He defended these decisions by saying, "The organisation had to become more outgoing and recognise its responsibilities to the cultural life of the city and not have the slightly isolated, introverted stance that it had in the past. It had to look to its responsibilities not just to the artistic community but to look at what part we play in the economic life of the city, such as tourism and corporate business."[13]

13 Graham McKenzie, in conversation with the author, July 2001.

Local architects Page and Park had designed the new CCA building, while international art star Jorge Pardo had been commissioned to design a mural, lighting and furniture for the bar. Many thought it seemed odd not to offer the commission to one of the numerous local visual artists working with design. McKenzie explained, "Jorge's name kept coming to the top of the list. I was very impressed with his work at the Dia Centre in New York, and the Pier project he did in Holland. We have demonstrated that we have confidence in local artists by showing them here and abroad, but I don't think that it's a good thing for those artists, for CCA or Glasgow or Scotland to be too parochial. We're an international organisation, we work with a network of international artists and institutions."[14]

Another of the changes at CCA included Vivienne Gaskin, former head of Live Art at the ICA, being appointed as Head of Artistic Programme and Education, while Francis McKee was given the part-time post of Head of Digital and New Media. Throughout the renovation period, Patricia Fleming had been planning a visual arts programme for the new building that included a joint show by Jim Lambie and Lothar Hempel, a film commission for Cathy Wilkes, a residency for Cologne-based gallery BQ and installing a Ugo Rondinone rainbow piece with the phrase "Hell yes" on the M8 motorway approach from the airport into the city. Fleming had already held detailed discussions with all of the artists concerned when she was informed there wasn't sufficient funding for both her post and that of Vivienne Gaskin, and that she was being made redundant. After discussing her position with her union Unison, Fleming was reinstated, but as Gaskin's assistant. All of Fleming's proposed visual projects were cancelled in favour of a programme devised by Gaskin, featuring a number of club culture orientated events, featuring London-based clubs like Sonic Mook Experiment, Batmacumba and Future World Funk. Francis McKee curated the opening exhibition, Words and Things, featuring Glasgow based artist Simon Starling, alongside Mark Dion, Cheryl Donegan and cyber artists JODI.

14 Graham McKenzie, Ibid.

The CCA's decision to make Patricia Fleming's post as visual arts officer redundant basically meant that the CCA did not employ somebody with sole responsibility for the visual arts. Many people felt that the CCA would no longer be able to function as a major league venue without a dedicated full time visual arts programmer. Graham McKenzie refused to be drawn on the subject, stating that "We hadn't contracted to anything, so we haven't cancelled any contracts."[15] In August, a few months before the new CCA opened, Patricia Fleming resigned. She subsequently produced a series of documentaries on six contemporary Scottish artists for Channel 4[16] and was later appointed the curator of the Welsh Pavilion for the 2003 Venice Biennale. A few months after the opening, CCA made the news-papers when it was announced that the new look arts centre had failed to meet target budgets, with the new restaurant and bar failing to attract the projected levels of trade. Vivienne Gaskin curated several new shows in 2002, notably Rod Dickinson's The Tenth Level, which included a re-enactment of Stanley Milgram's 1961 electro-shock *Obedience to Authority* experiment. However, she recently resigned her post at CCA and returned to London, to work at the ICA again. Since then, Glasgow School of Art lecturer John Calcutt, Tim Nunn and Ele Carpenter have been appointed as part time associate curators at CCA alongside Head of Digital & New Media, Francis McKee.

## SOCIAL INCLUSION

Glasgow City Council continued to place great emphasis on audience development and education at Kelvingrove, GoMA, Tramway and CCA, a direction in-keeping with Scottish Executive guidelines. As Ruth Wishart wrote after 2000's National Consultation on the Arts, "To borrow a soundbite from the current UK government, the consultation threw up one central imperative: education, education, education [ … ] there was a clear belief that ways had to be found to embed the arts in the educational

15  Graham McKenzie, Ibid.
16  The artists were: Victoria Morton, Chad McCail, Nathan Coley, Wendy McMurdo, Iain Kettles and Susie Hunter.

experience."[17] However, the emphasis on social inclusion in publicly funded arts has led to a frustrating situation for some of those working in visual arts in Glasgow. Even Graham McKenzie, who is an enthusiastic supporter of 'less introverted' arts programmes feels that the City Council and Arts Council place too many restrictions on the institutions they fund. He says, "The starting point has to be something that excites you: that's how everyone gets involved in art. There's one moment when they go to something and go, wow. That's what's missing at the moment. I do feel that things are weighed too much towards social inclusion. [ … ] I'm very committed to removing the barriers between so called high arts and community arts but that has to be through a meaningful dialogue, not because people don't have the confidence to fund art for art's sake."[18]

Ruth Wishart wrote in the section of her SAC report entitled *Facing the Future*, "Conceptual artists in particular often feel aggrieved at their work carrying explanatory labels as if gallery visitors were uniquely gifted in the process of mind reading"[19] In some ways this statement seems typical of the existing relationship between funding bodies and the visual art community in Glasgow – an explanation of the work must be offered in exchange for public funding. However, the compulsion to close off the potential meanings of a piece of art by spoon-feeding a single interpretation to the public could also be seen as a dis-service to both the artist and the viewer. Tramway curator Alexia Holt says, "Quality has almost become a dirty word – the merit of producing work for its own sake. A lot of the kind of work we show here has as much focus on process as on final product, and it's very difficult to fit that into the equation and into the outcomes that organisations now want to see."[20]

Glasgow-based artist Martin Boyce says, "Art is not about being understood, it's about being interpreted and read in an open way. I don't

---

17  Ruth Wishart, Scottish Arts in the 21st Century, SAC Report, 2000. On the 4th of October Education Secretary Estelle Morris had announced that the government was bowing to student protests and reinstating grants for higher education, although they would now come with a "graduate tax" attached. Morris said that the government had accepted that fear of debt was deterring poorer students from applying to university.
18  Graham McKenzie, in conversation with the author, July 2001.
19  Ruth Wishart, Scottish Arts in the 21st Century, SAC Report, 2000.
20  Alexia Holt, in conversation with the author, July 2001.

understand a lot of things but they are still part of my life. I don't understand exactly how a computer works but I use one every day. If you were asked if you 'understood' Shakespeare , you would probably say no – that doesn't mean that you haven't read it and got something from that reading."[21]

In some respects, the arguments that are regularly trotted out against conceptual art have advanced little since the Tate was "conned" into buying Carl Andre's *Equivalent VIII* in 1976. This old argument was still rumbling on in 2002, when Ivan Massow, millionaire chairman of the ICA, wrote an article in *The New Statesman* that compared the "tyranny of conceptual art" to Soviet-era socialist realism, and dismissed much of the work championed by the Turner Prize and the Tate as "craftless tat".[22] This followed widespread media outrage sparked when Martin Creed won the Turner Prize with his neo-conceptual work, *The Lights Going On and Off*. Creed (b.1968, Wakefield) was brought up in Scotland, and exhibited at both Transmission and the Modern Institute during the 1990s. He is best known for works made of insubstantial materials such as blu-tak, crumpled balls of paper and balloons, such as *Work No. 201 Half the Air in a Given Space* (1998), for which he fills a gallery with multi-coloured 11 inch balloons. Creed takes the instruction works associated with '70s conceptual art as the departure point for his work, but his practice is also infused with a dead-pan humour, seen in his neon work, *Everything is Going to be Alright*, and the minimal recordings of his band, Owada. Creed is also known for his refusal to make ambitious claims relating to his work, and has often been quoted as saying it is "about nothing in particular." At the Turner Prize press conference Creed refused to defend his work, saying, "People can make of it what they like. I don't think it is for me to explain it."

Creed's comment recalled the argument advanced by Virginia Button

21  Martin Boyce, in conversation with the author, February 2002.

22  The New Statesman, January 18th, 2002. Massow's comments were echoed a few months later by Culture minister Kim Howells, who described the latest Turner Prize exhibit as "cold, mechanical conceptual bullshit", going on to tell *The Independent*, 'If this is the best the British art establishment can come up with, then God help us. It consists entirely of conceptual bullshit. And the final insult was to walk through a room of Francis Bacons and Henry Moore that exuded artistic ability and humanity.' Source: *The Independent*, Thursday 31st October, 2002, p1.

and Charles Esche in support of their exhibition Intelligence at Tate Britain in 2000. Esche and Button wrote that the interpretation of a given artwork does not rest solely with the artist but "is determined just as much through the processes of insight and translation in the eyes and mind of the viewer." Obviously this kind of dialogue between artist and audience is only possible if a receptive audience exists. In Glasgow it still feels as if there is resistance in many places to work that is not object-based, or which pushes the boundaries of art practice in other ways. As local artist Toby Paterson says, "In terms of public support, Glasgow's artistic community would benefit from some kind of unified and trustworthy policy in terms of galleries and museum spaces. The fact that the city's population and government is, in general, oblivious to or disinterested in the fervent activity going on under its nose can be a little disheartening."[23]

It is an unfortunate fact that much of the work of the most high profile Glasgow-based artists is in collections overseas, notably in the collection assembled by Ami Barak at FRAC Languedoc, Marseilles and the Van Abbemuseum at Eindhoven. However, since the early 1990s Aberdeen Art Gallery and the Scottish National Gallery of Modern Art in Edinburgh have also acquired several significant works by Douglas Gordon, Christine Borland and other Glasgow-based artists.[24] However, in Glasgow the collection of recent art by Glasgow-based artists remains marked by certain notable absences. Head of Museums and Galleries Mark O'Neill says, "I think it would only be honest to say that we've missed out on a whole generation of Glasgow artists because of the narrow collecting policy up to 1998. We're slowly changing that and since August 2001 we have been implementing a different way of collecting. We haven't been very active in collecting because we had to think through what a new direction might be. We honestly admit that we missed an opportunity, and it is too late, because we now cannot afford to purchase work by that generation of artists."[25]

23  Toby Paterson, in conversation with the author April 2001.
24  SNGMA now owns, amongst many other works by young Scottish artists, Christine Borland's *Spirit Collection: Hippocrates* (1999), Douglas Gordon's *List of Names* (Random) (1990–ongoing), Roderick Buchanan's *Work in Progress* (1995), a Jim Lambie floor from the Zobop series (1999) and Victoria Morton's *Dirty Burning* (1997).
25  Mark O'Neill, in conversation with the author, July 2001.

These changes in collecting policy included setting up a collecting panel with two council members, two experts (one of whom is Francis McKee) and one curator from GoMA, to decide on purchases, plus a proposed plan to involve the public in purchasing art twice yearly. Mark O'Neill says, "We hope to collect more systematically and to relate the collection more to our temporary exhibitions, because it doesn't relate at the moment. Just now the gallery can look like a bunch of unrelated pieces, there is a lack of coherence and we hope to redress that."[26] The Scottish Art Council's Head of Visual Arts Amanda Catto confirms that "Collecting by museums and galleries looks set to increase, although it will take some time for Scotland to recover a sound collecting base given the years of under-investment in this area."[27] However, despite the lingering resentment that some members of the visual art community have towards the city council, there are other members of the community who appreciate the limitations placed upon public funding bodies. Will Bradley says, "When you are dealing with funders you have to all the time address the question, what is art for? You learn about the political ideology around state funded art. There has to be an ecology of places and approaches. It's very hard for the Arts Council or City Council – a lot of their staff have a really good understanding [of visual arts] but then they also have policy and will be judged on that."[28]

Another angle on this debate would be to look at ways in which the lack of local recognition and/or funding has forced Glasgow-based artists to seek ever cheaper ways of getting their work seen, and making connections with other artists working elsewhere. Over the course of the summer of 2001 Glasgow-based polemical magazine *Variant* had once again been stirring up the hornets' nest surrounding the public funding of art. By autumn of 2001, *Variant*'s SAC funding was withdrawn for the second time in the magazine's history, after an SAC report on *Variant 13* (which contained the work of James Kelman, *The Edinburgh Review*'s editor Peter Kravitz and playwright Harold Pinter) concluded, "The consensus of feedback on the quality of *Variant* has been that it has declined ... The content is very

26  Mark O'Neill, Ibid.
27  Amanda Catto, in response to questions sent by the author, September 2001.
28  Will Bradley, in conversation with the author, April 2001.

often biased or inaccurate ... we cannot agree that you meet your stated objectives as a broadly accessible magazine; the language, editorial stance and quality mitigate against this."[29] Also in issue 13 was an article written by Billy Clark[30] which lambasted the decision-making processes of SAC, which would not have gone in the magazine's favour. Despite this setback, *Variant* continued to operate on the basis of funding from Glasgow City Council and money raised from advertising revenue, and now has in excess of 14,000 e-mail subscribers in addition to the same number reached by the circulation of the magazine's print version.

In their 1996 essay Artist-run Spaces Laurence Bosse and Hans-Ulrich Obrist noted, "As sites of independence and transgression, artist-run spaces effect a permanent critique of the traditional operation of art galleries and institutions, refusing any predeterminism ... "[31] One of the most important ways in which Transmission has facilitated the flow of information between artists and artist-run groups has been to allow members to use the gallery's photocopier, to "piggy-back" the gallery mail-out with flyers, and by providing a 'care of' address for fanzines, magazines and various groups. Although some ex-committee members may feel Transmission has shifted from its socialist roots, it seems the gallery still poses an ideological threat to the status quo. Transmission was recently forced to clarify its "care of" service so that the city council could defend their position as funders.

The gallery's September 2001 newsletter reported, 'Some of you may have been shocked to learn that your true-blue Transmission is "being investigated by council bosses over its links with Scottish anarchist groups'. These allegations appeared at the end of July in the *Scotland on Sunday*, which was clumsily trying to get a local angle on the anti-capitalist riots in Genoa. The council were 'concerned' when someone contacted them some months ago, complaining about an article written in the politics/culture magazine *Here and Now*. The address for the magazine was care of Transmission. During its earlier years, Transmission had a more radical agenda and this was evident in the programme of exhibitions and public

29  Printed in *Variant* 15, Summer 2002.
30  The Tainted Word, *Variant*, Summer 2001.
31  "Artist-run Spaces", essay by Laurence Bosse and Hans-Ulrich Obrist From Life/Live catalogue, 1996.

debates involving groups of radical thinkers/writers such as the Free University and Workers City."[32]

The question of how successfully art can deal with politics had become increasingly complicated in the late 1990s. Exhibitions like Life/Live (Musee d'Art Moderne de Paris, 1996), Hi Red Center (CCA, Glasgow, 1998) and Fundamentalisms (Charlottensburg Exhibition Hall, Copenhagen, 2002) had appeared to suggest that art could no longer be used politically as it had been in the 1970s and '80s. The role of the artist as a disrupter of meaning was still valid, but the strategies used by most contemporary artists seemed to be more covert and perhaps spoke more to a specialised audience. However, the global political situation had been becoming increasingly unstable since the Al Qua'ida attacks on the twin towers of the World Trade Centre in New York and Washington's Pentagon on September 11th 2001. As public feeling ran high in America, George W. Bush had appeared on television to announce that he intended to capture Osama Bin Laden "dead or alive".

Bush's Wild West parlance, combined with the dramatic televised coverage of the planes hitting the towers and office workers leaping from the buildings, gave an almost unreal quality to the situation. Bush was quick to authorise military repercussions in Afghanistan, where Bin Laden was rumoured to be in hiding, resulting in the loss of many civilian lives in an already impoverished nation. However, these anonymous deaths were quickly eclipsed in news coverage as the long-running tensions between Israel and Palestine began to escalate once more. After attempts to capture Bin Laden failed, Bush took the opportunity to re-launch his father's military campaign against Iraq, in an attempt to oust dictator Saddam Hussein. Bush's overheated hyperbole conflated the ideology of Bin Laden and Hussein, and posed America's intervention as a "moral war" on terrorism. Biased American media coverage of the unfolding crisis in the Middle East began to generate considerable concern in left-wing circles in America, prompting numerous actors, writers and artists to place advertisements in American newspapers to register their opposition to

32 *Transmission Newsletter*, September 2001.

Bush's tactics. In the UK, the protests of American cultural figures like Arthur Miller, Susan Sontag and Kurt Vonnegurt were supported by many people[33] who had major misgivings about Tony Blair's uncritical support of Bush's position.


## A GLASGOW ATTITUDE


Transmission remains closely connected to the local music scene, and in May 2002, Luke Fowler's[34] *Shadazz* compilation of music videos made by local artists for local bands, *Evil Eye is Source*, was premiered at the gallery. The compilation featured ten videos including Katy Dove's psychedelic animated work for James Seenan's new project Devotone, and G.F.M.'s mix of film and animation for the music of Hasslehound (formed by Cylinder's Tony Swain, Radio Tuesday's Mark Vernon and David Fulford). Torsten Lauschmann made a video for local band Pro Forma's track *Passion Prefix* that reworked found images from porn films into swirling "chaos theory" patterns while Anne Marie Copestake and Fred Pedersen produced a montage of live performance footage and found images for Life Without Building's *PS Exclusive*. Fowler says, "Personally my relationship between the two worlds [of music and art] is, I hope, pretty blurred. I loathe the terms 'curator' and 'sound artist' and the associations they both conjure. I love dancing and discovering new music, and new ways to listen and think about sound. Though for me music is primarily a visceral experience, not a conceptual one, concept albums as we know are frightening things."[35]

Transmission is still a good place to check out emerging talent in the city, a standard kept intact by the bi-annual committee reshuffle. In 2002, Glasgow School of Art graduates Kate Davis, Gregor Wright, Jane Topping and Nick Evans have joined the committee as Anna McLauchlan, Danny Saunders, Alex Pollard, Clare Stephenson and Lorna Macintyre have

---

33 On the 15th of February 2003, 100,000 protestors marched in Glasgow to protest against the Gulf War. Across the UK 2 million people marched, with a further 8 million attending anti-war rallies worldwide, making this the biggest peace rally ever held. Euan Ferguson, "One million. And still they came", *The Observer*, Sunday February 16, 2003, p1.

34 Soon afterwards it was announced that Duncan of Jordanstone graduate Fowler had been selected for inclusion in Manifesta 4.

35 Brian Beadie, "Shadazz: Evil Eye is Source", *Untitled* Summer 2002, pp44–45.

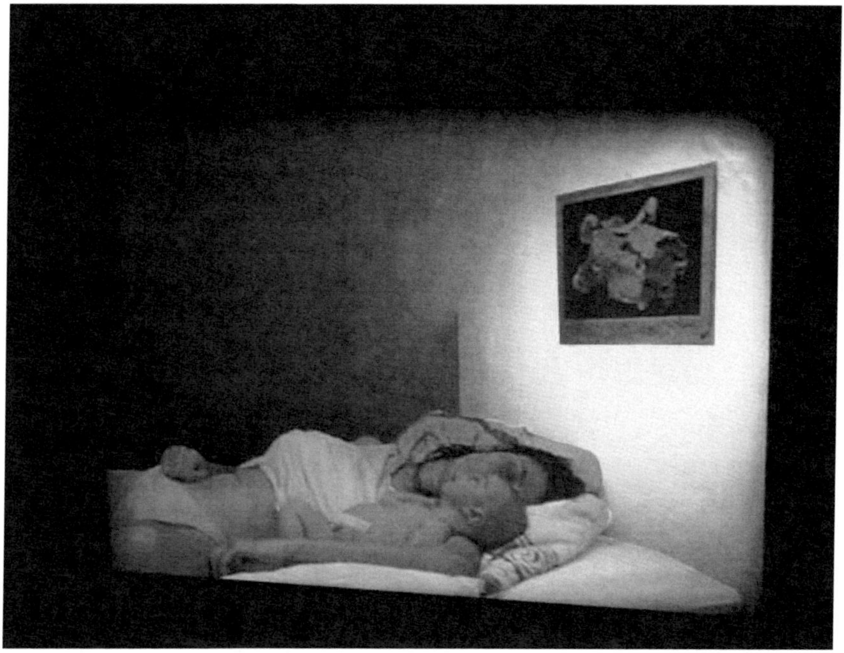

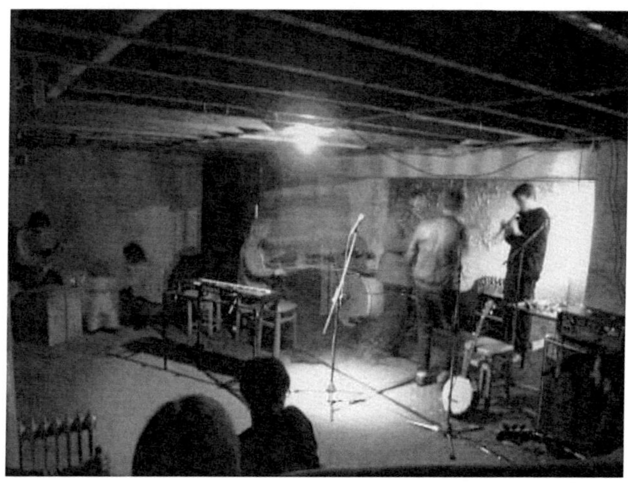

Torsten Lauschmann, *Mother and Child* (2004)
Torsten Lauschmann, *Wunst* performance, Transmission (2004)

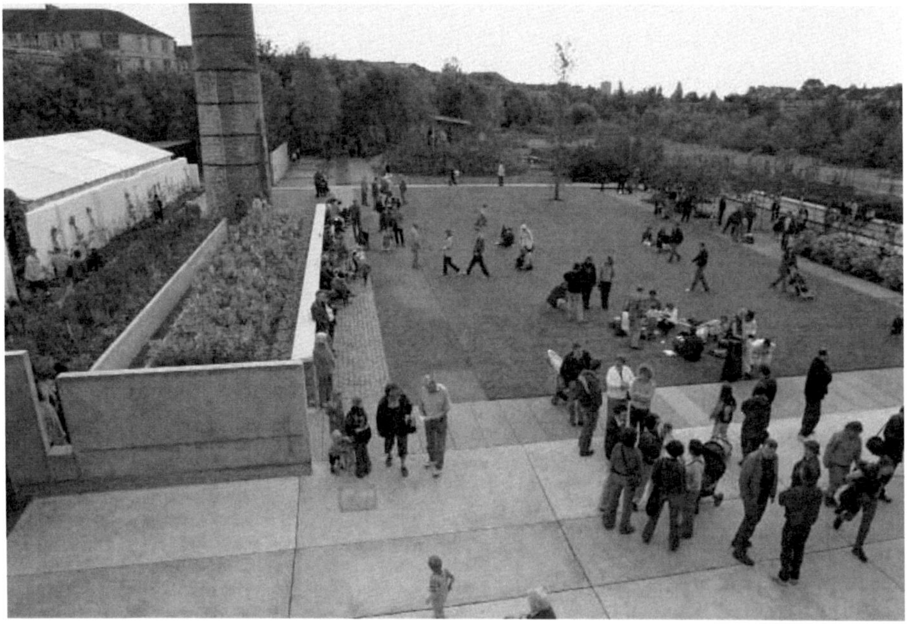

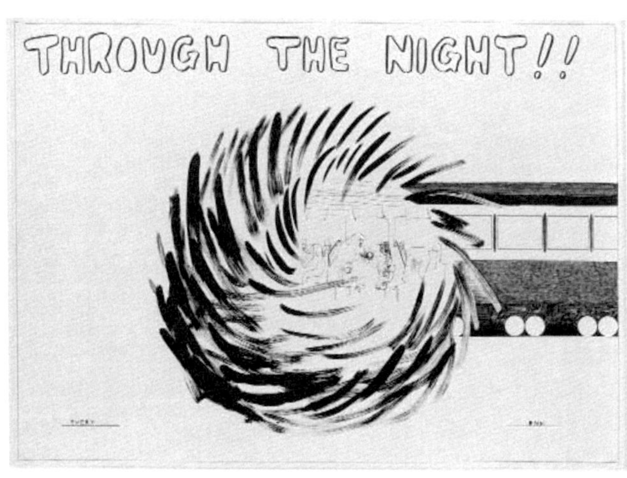


Saturday afternoon at The Hidden Gardens, Tramway (2005)
Rob Churm, *Untitled* (*Through the Night*) (2005)

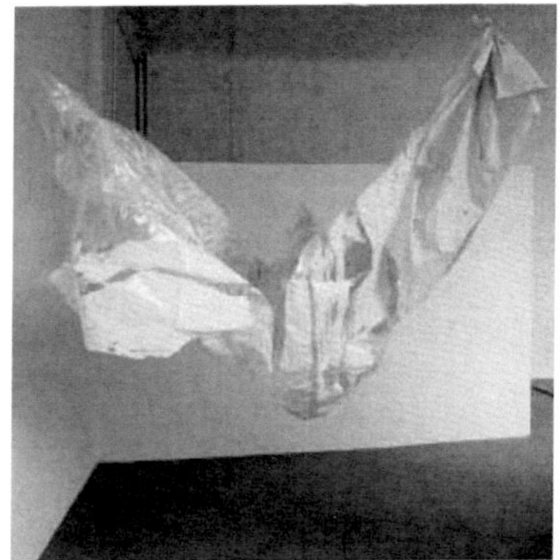

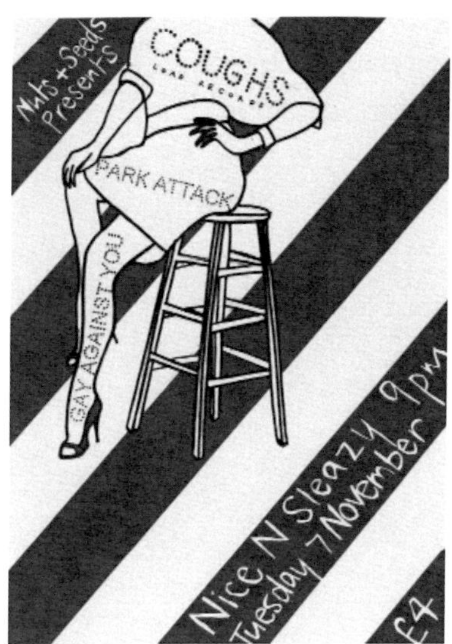


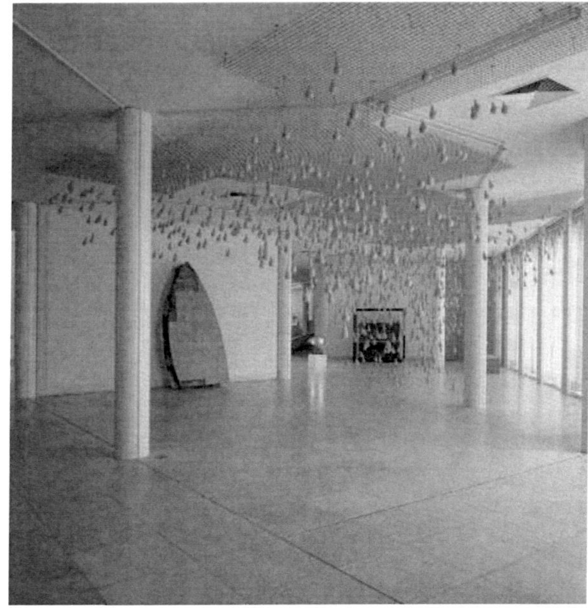

Karla Black, *Opportunities for Girls*, Mary Mary (2006)
Poster for Nuts and Seeds show by Coughs, Park Attack and Gay against You, designed by Louise Shelley (2006).
Installation view of *Strange, I've Seen that Face Before*, Museum Abteiberg, Moenchengladbach (2006).

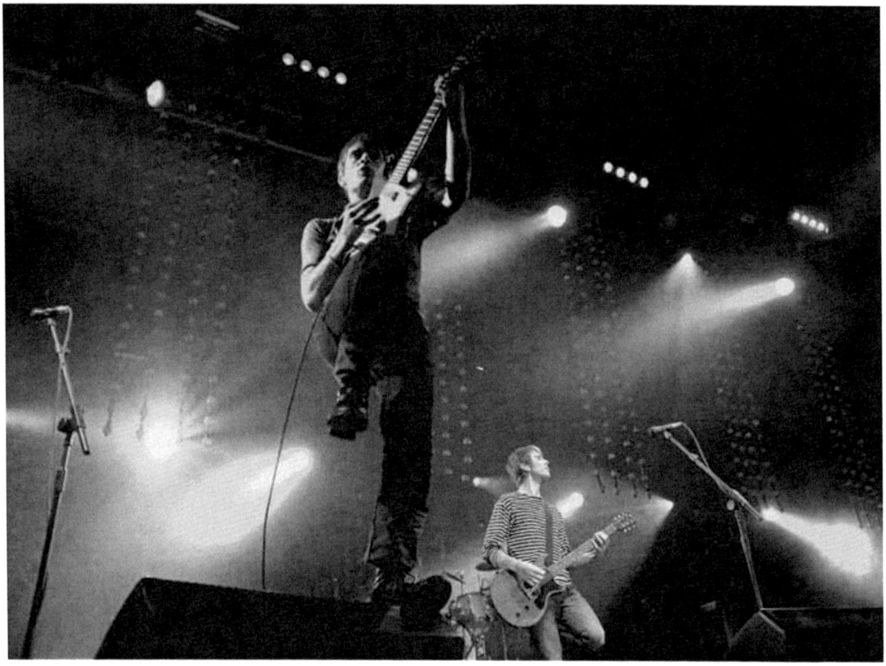

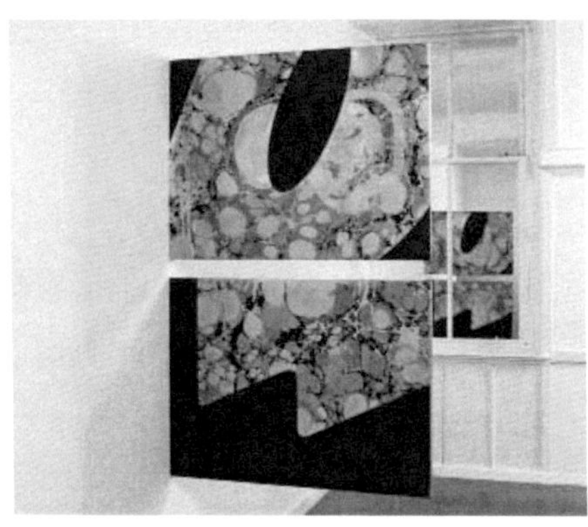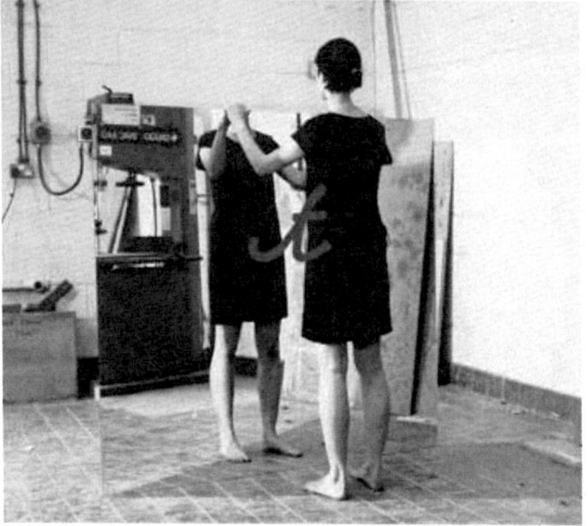

Franz Ferdinand, live in Dundee, 2006.
Installation view, Scott Myles, ASKIT, The Modern Institute, 2007.
Kate Davis, *The Clear Stark Vision is Getting Lost Again* (2007)

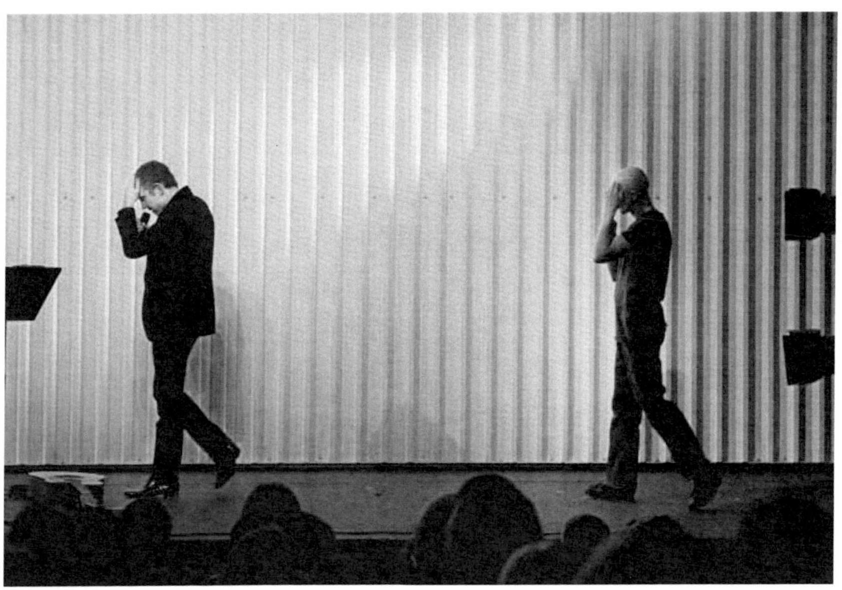

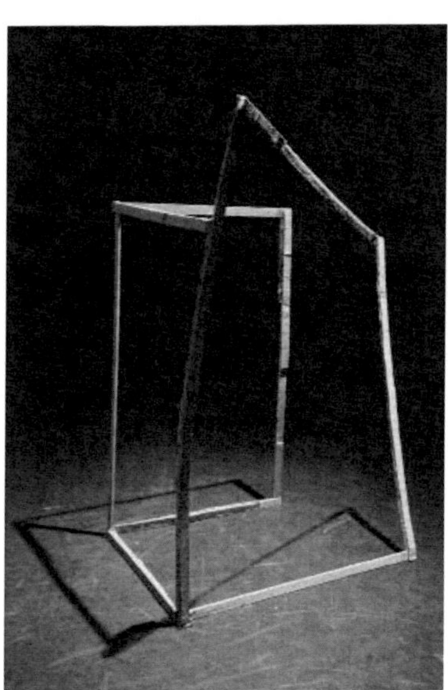

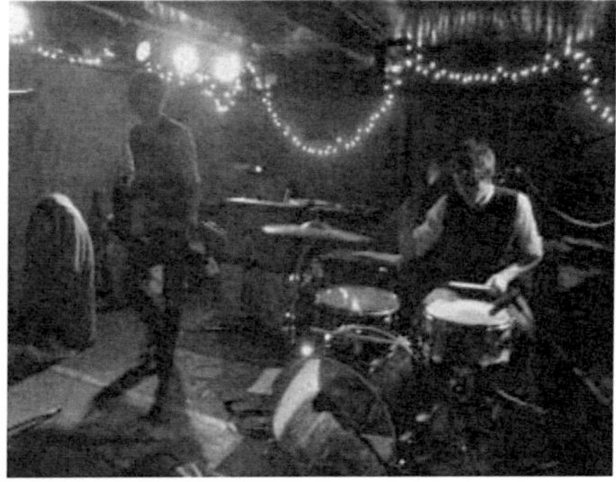

Martin Creed, Words and Music, Royal Scottish Academy of Music and Drama, Glasgow (2007).
Sara Barker, *Variations on my own* (2008)
Triple School (l-r: Giles Bailey, Tom Varley) play The Hot Club, Nice 'N' Sleazy's (2008).

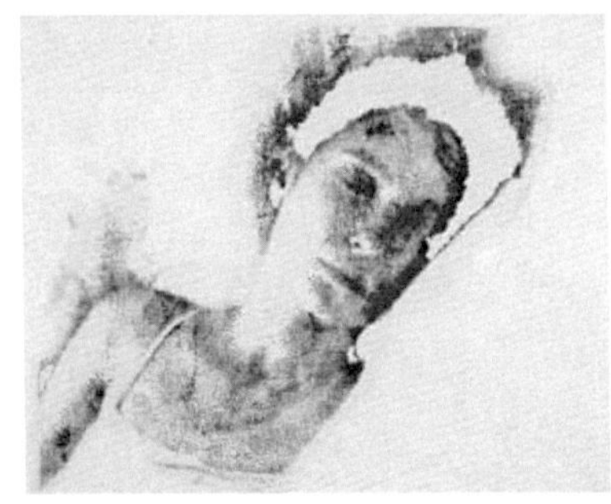

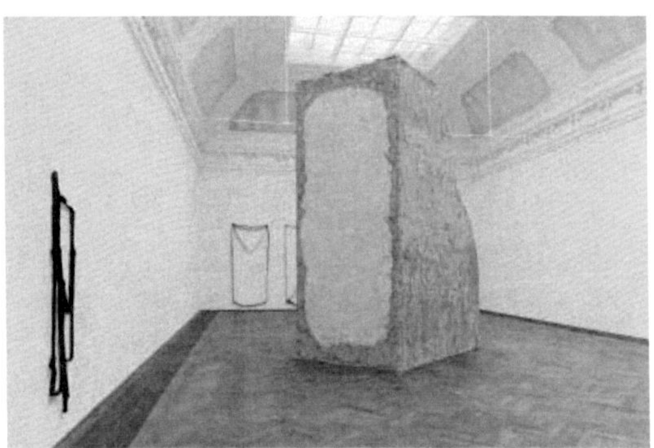

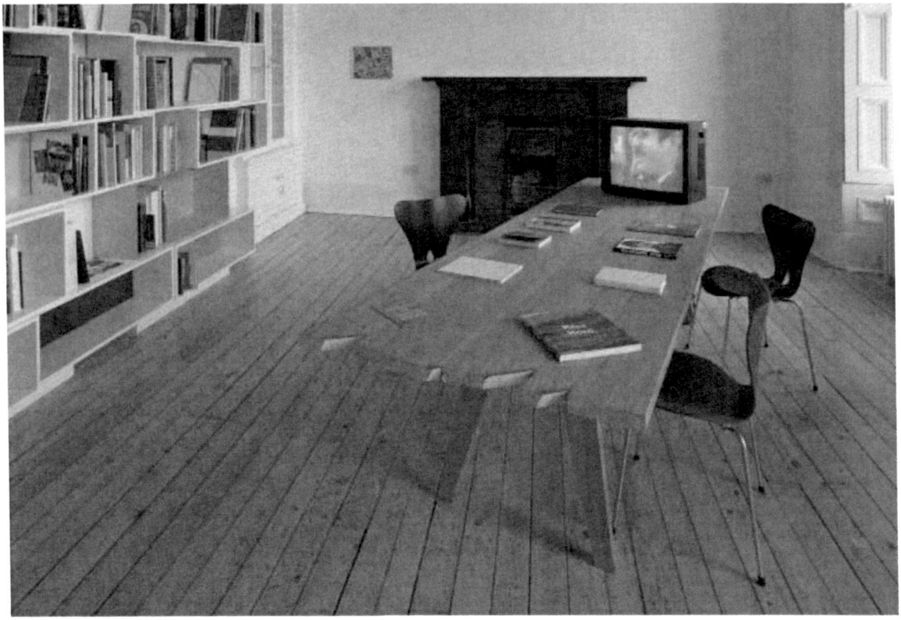

Alex Frost, *Blind Drawing (Ruth Sleeping, 2)*, (2008)
Aleana Egan, *We Sat Down Where We Had Sat Before*, (2008)
Andrew Miller, *Library* (2001) seen at the opening of Always Begins By Degrees, the The Common Guild's first exhibition held at Douglas Gordon's home in Woodlands Terrace, Glasgow (2008).

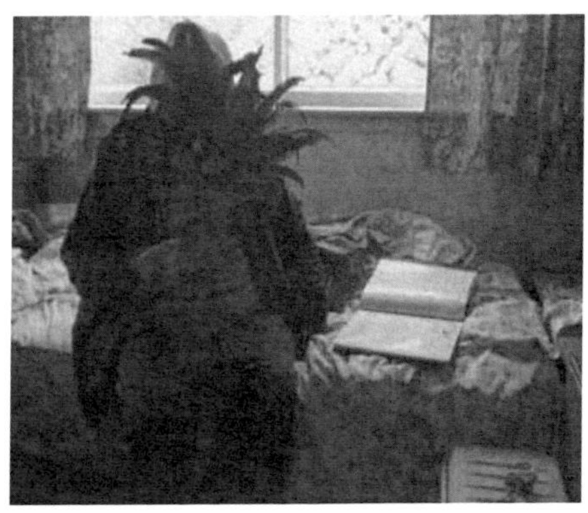

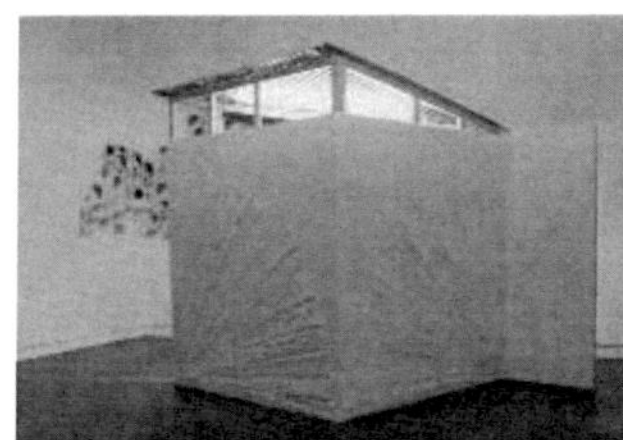

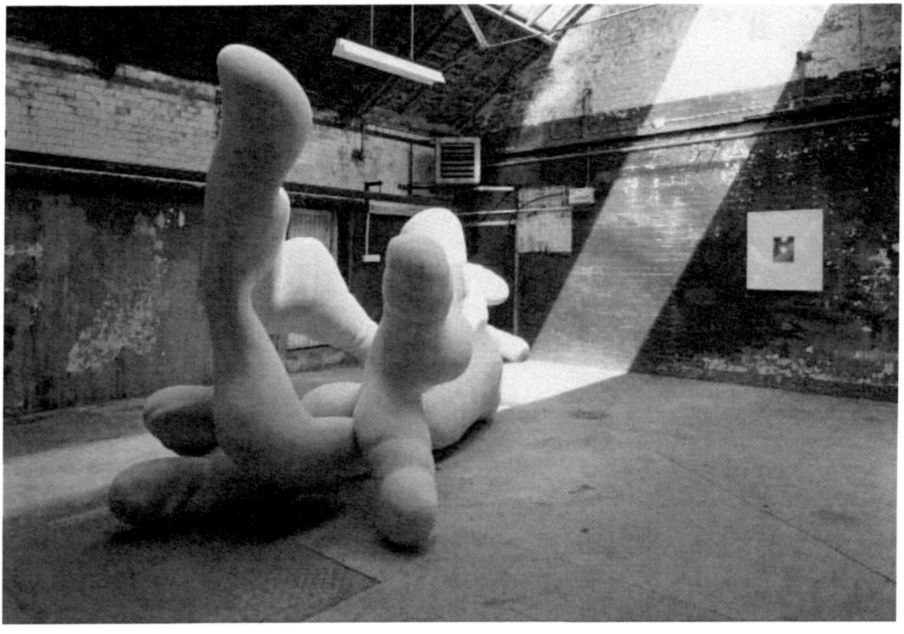

Still from Luke Fowler's *Bogman Palmjaguar* (2008)
Sophie Macpherson, *Cutting Station* (2008).
Simon Starling, *Project for a Public Sculpture (After Thomas Annan)*, The Modern Institute/Toby Webster Ltd (offsite), Glasgow International, 2008.

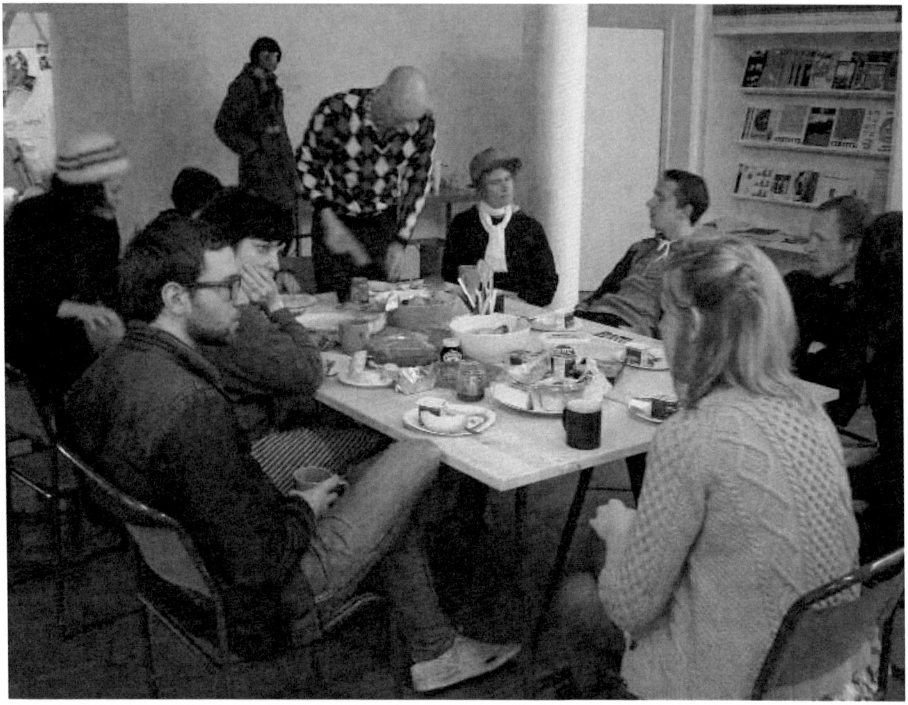

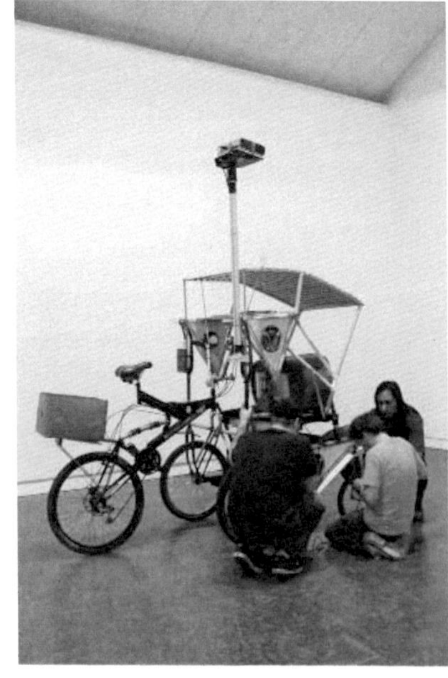

*Moot Points*, Transmission, 2008. Seen in foreground: Laura Aldridge
and Darren Rhymes in conversation with Kathryn Elkin.
Abraham Cruzvillegas, Autoconstrucción, Centre for Contemporary
Arts, Glasgow (2008). CCA staff Michael Joyce and Alan Keane help
Abraham Cruzvillegas make adjustments to his mobile sound system.

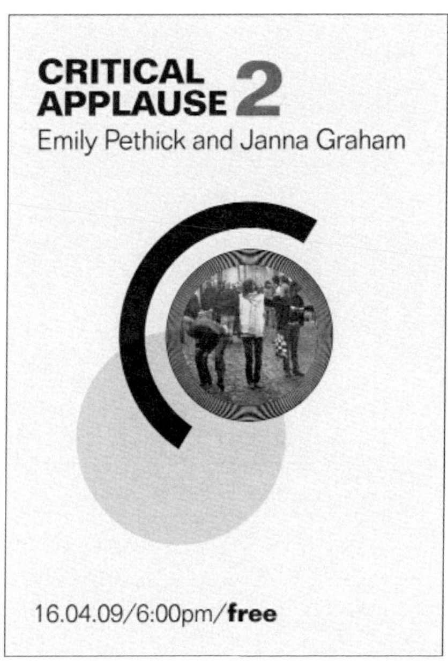


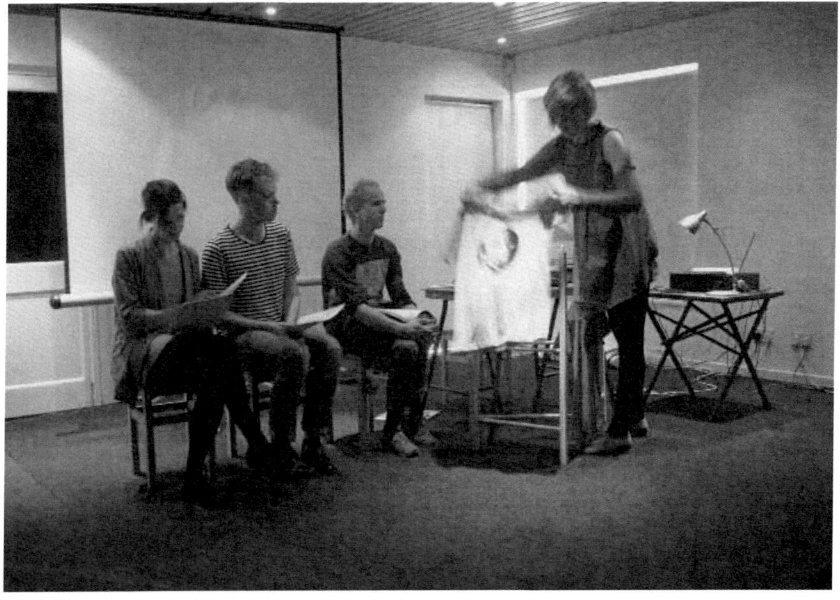

Flyer for Emily Pethick and Janna Graham's Critical Applause talk, Centre for Contemporary Art, Glasgow (2009).
Louise Shelley, Conal McStravick, Jens Strandberg and Kathryn Elkin perform part of Elkin's "Dead Hands" series at Cove Park, May 2009.

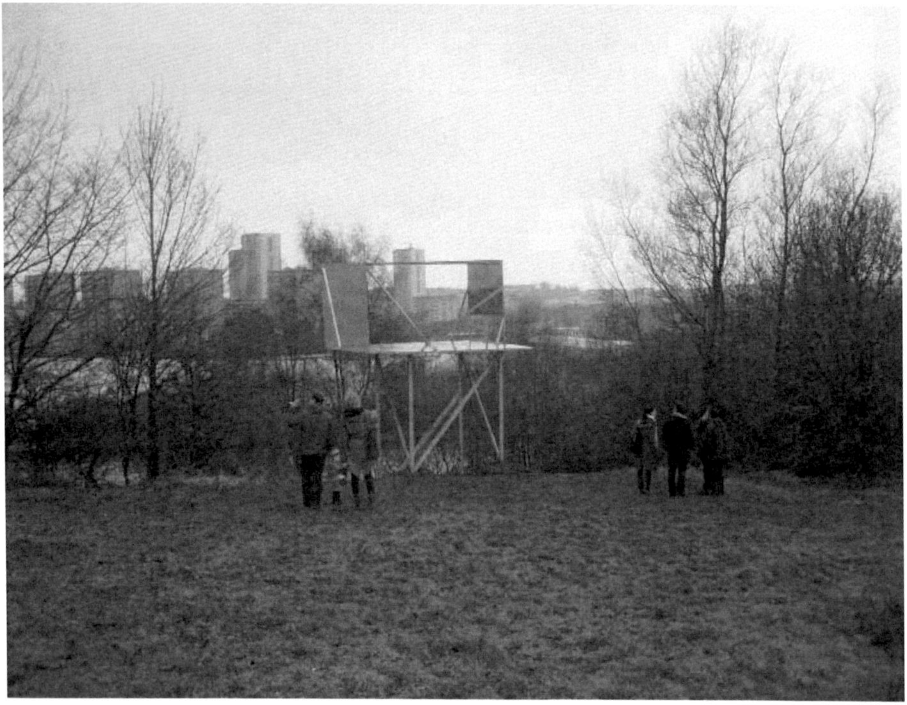

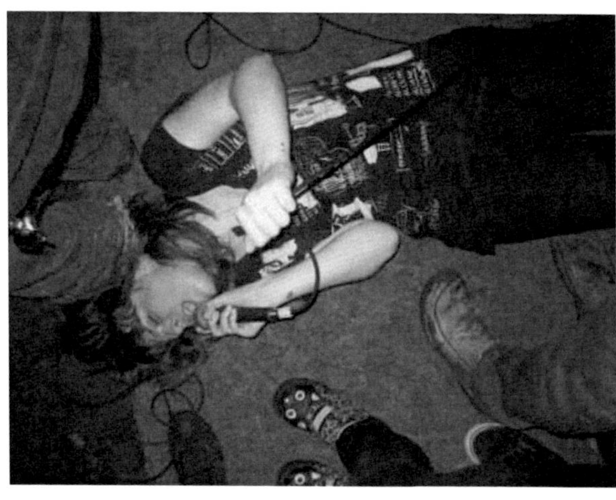

Alex Gross, *Swamp Thing*, Transmission (offsite), Ruchill Golf Course Annex, 2009.
Divorce singer Sinead Young, on tour in England, 2009.

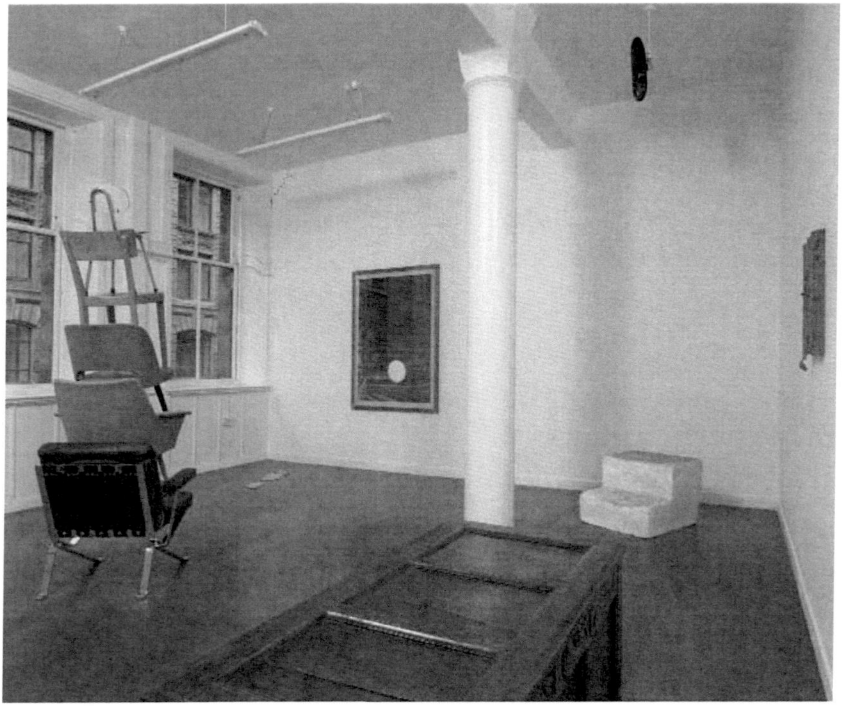

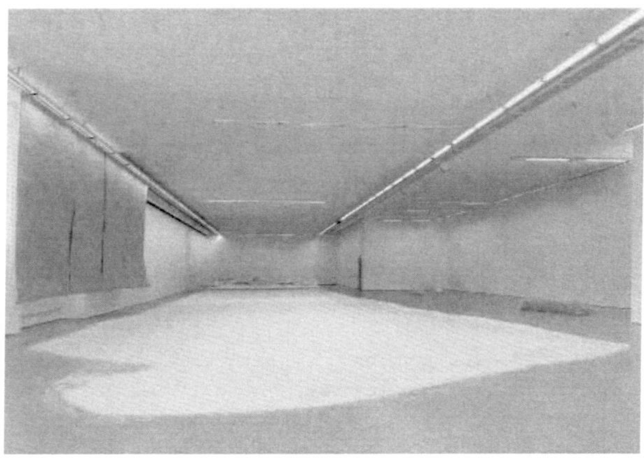

Installation view of the group show TONITE, The Modern Institute (2009)
Karla Black, installation view, Migros Museum, Zurich (2009)

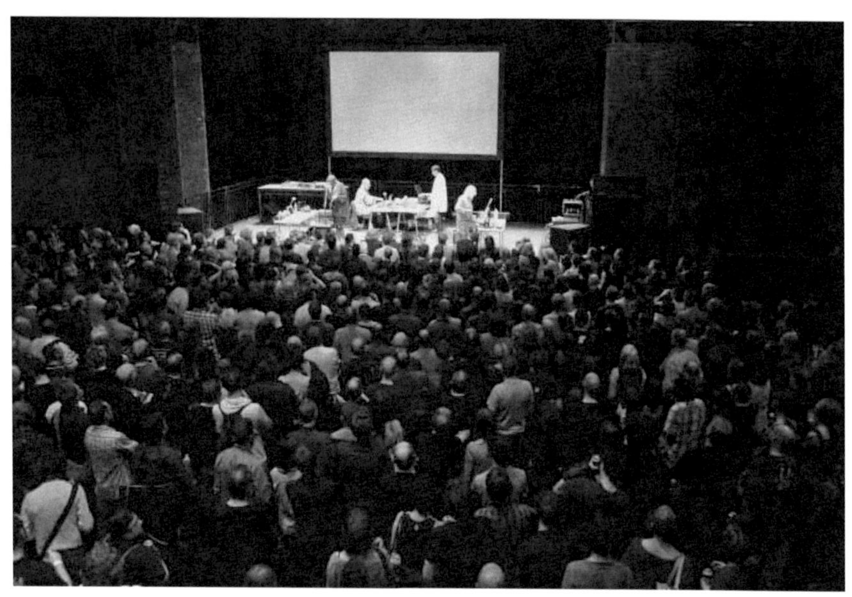

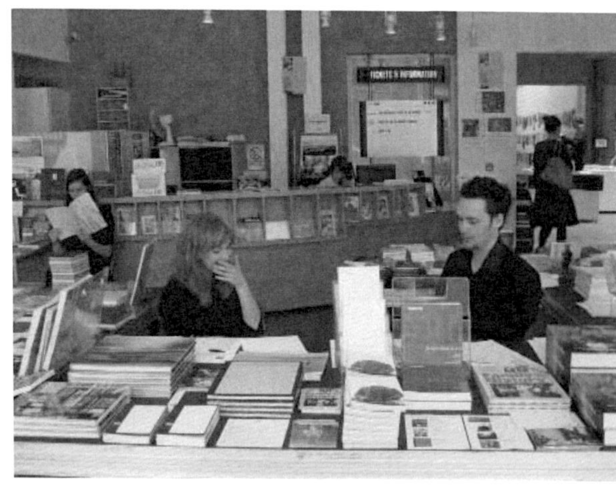

Throbbing Gristle performing Apparition Foretold, Tramway (2009).
Book fair at the Centre for Contemporary Arts, Glasgow, 2009.

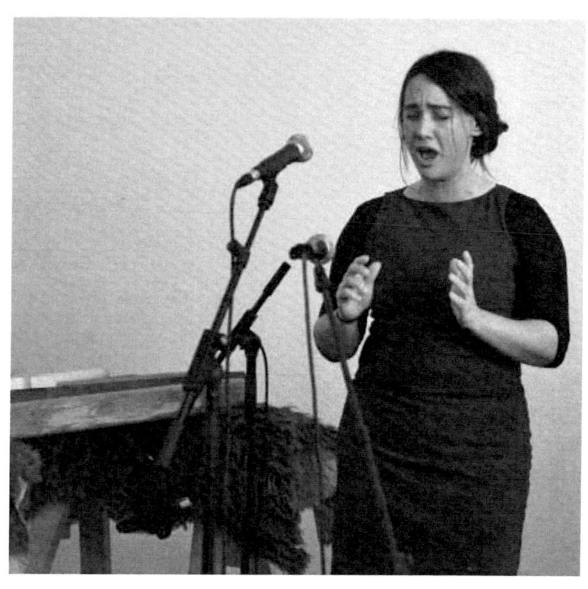

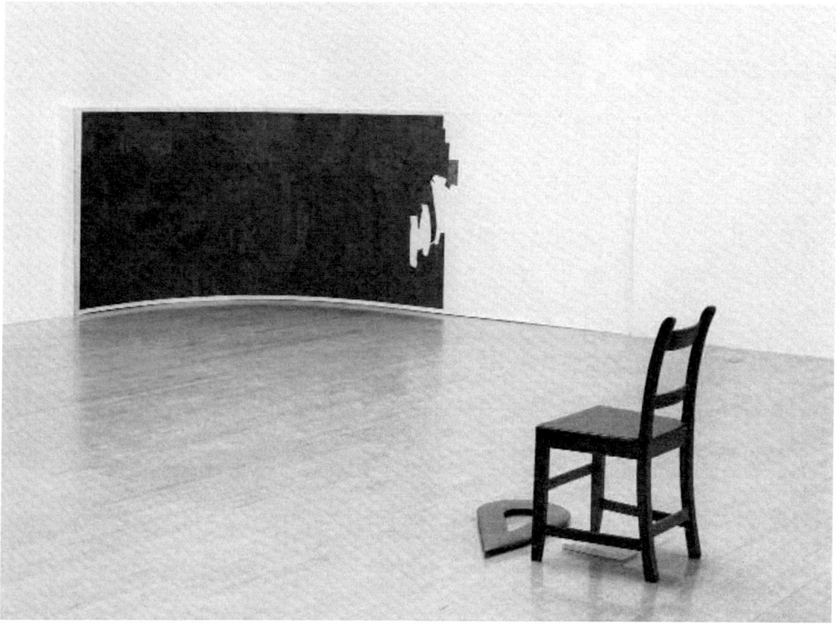

Nerea Bello performing at the opening of Votive, Centre for Contemporary Arts, Glasgow, 2009.
Lucy Skaer, *Thames and Hudson*, Turner Prize exhibition, Tate Britain (2009). Courtesy of the artist and doggerfisher, Edinburgh.

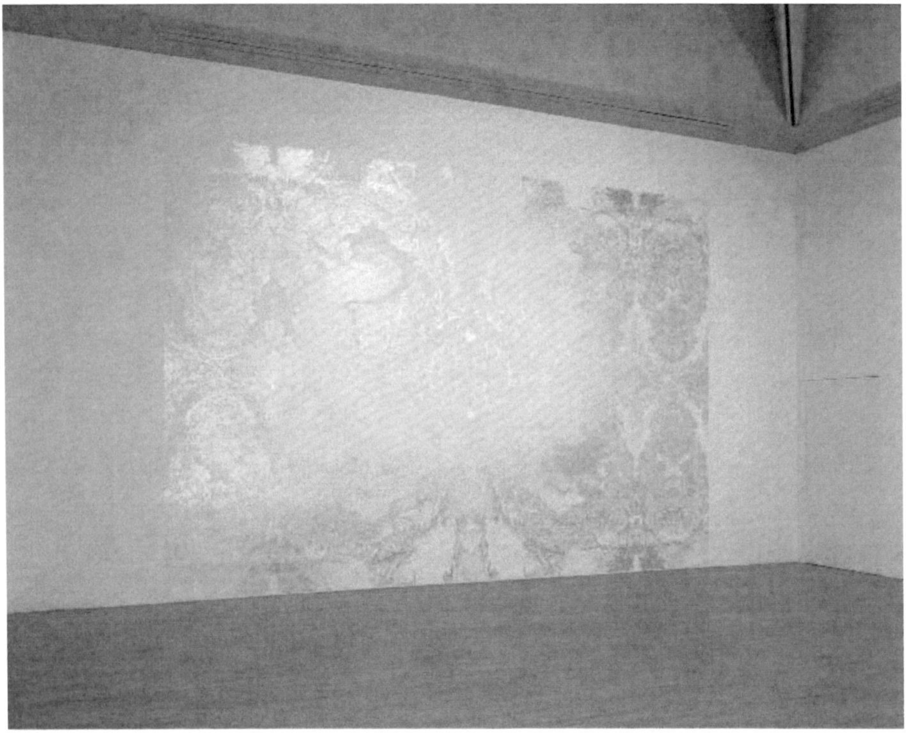

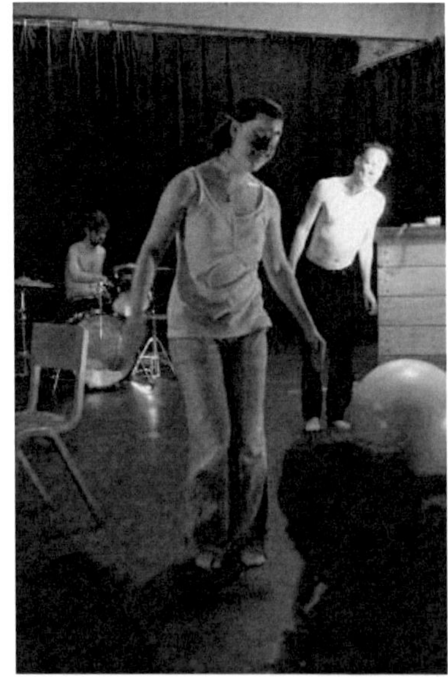

Richard Wright, *No Title* (2009), Turner Prize, Tate Britain, London, 2009.
Shelly Nadashi, Cliff Laine and Laurie Pitt perform "Ambush in Wedding" at SGW3, Glasgow, 2010.

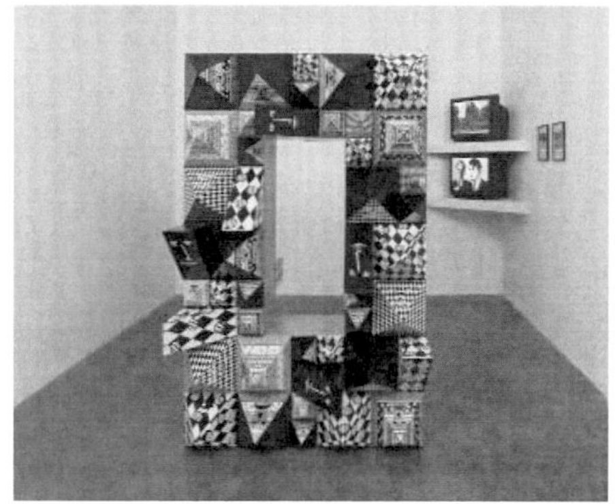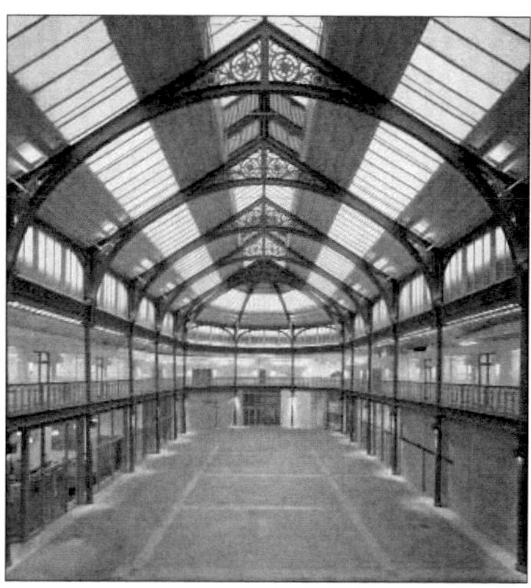

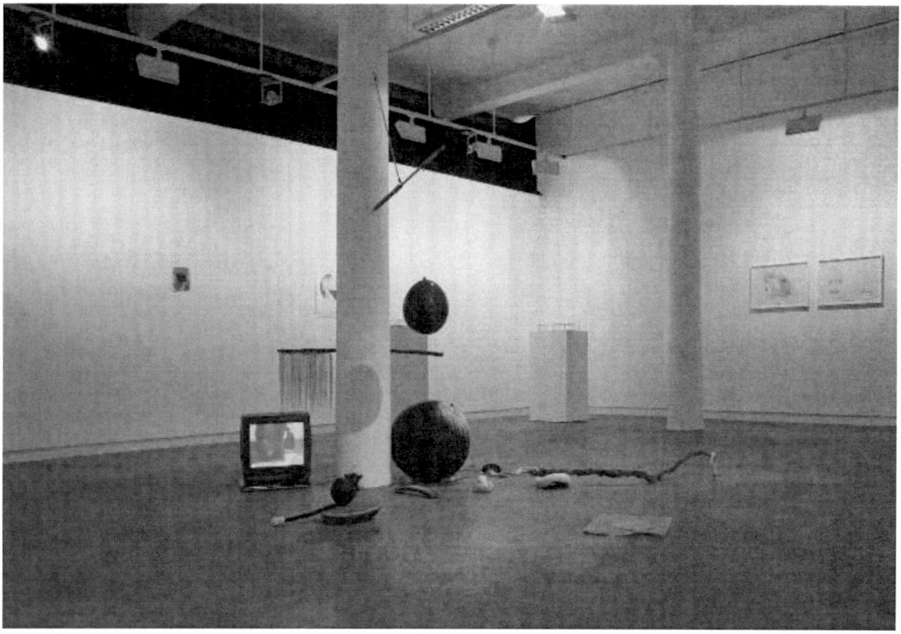

Installation view, Love, Sorcha Dallas, Glasgow, 2010. L-R, Tom O'Sullivan and Joanne Tatham, *This has reached the limit conditions of its own rhetoric* (2008), Gilbert & George, *A Portrait of The Artists as Young Men* (1972 and *In the Bush* (1972).
New WASPS studio complex at The Briggait, 2010.
Carolyn Barrett and Harriet Tritton, Guest, Transmission, 2010.

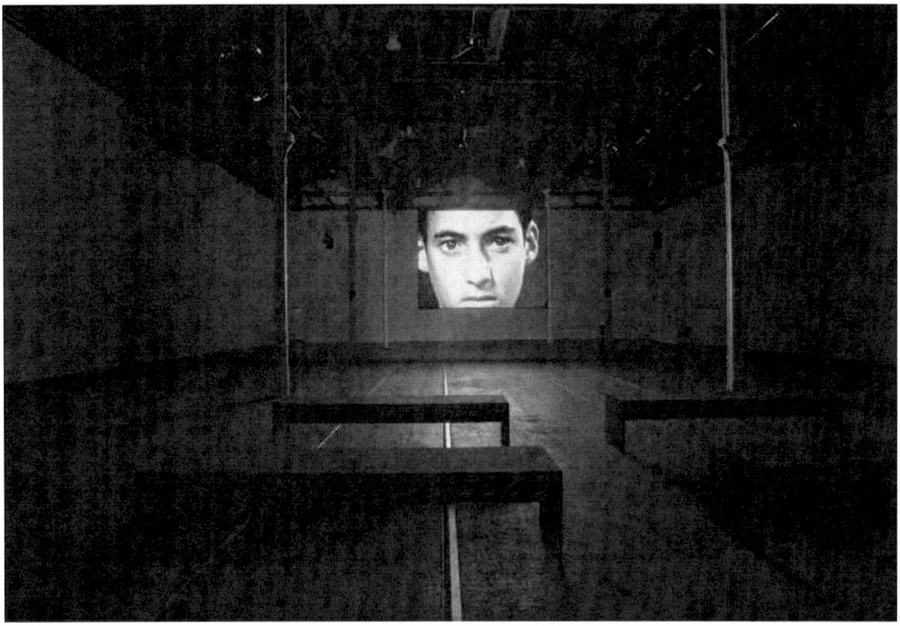

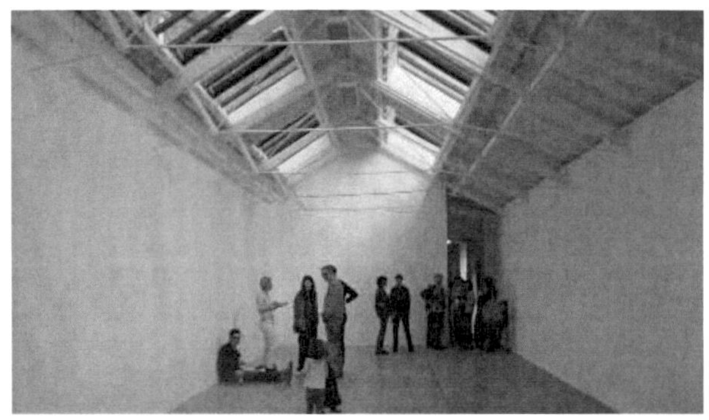

Duncan Campbell, Make It New, John, Tramway (2010).
Friends and family opening of The Modern Institute's Osborne Street gallery, March 2010.

departed. The programme at the gallery remains as contentious as ever, and the committee still suffers from periodic accusations of cliquey-ness. One thing most people agree on is that Transmission throws good parties. Before the gallery closed for the summer recess, there was a closing party where former committee member Danny Saunders performed his punky songs solo. He was followed by new band Son of Kong, formed by cellist/guitarist Janis Murray and bassist Victoria Morton after Frances McKee disbanded Suckle and mutant disco outfit Pro Forma, fronted by keyboardist and guitarist Simon Henderson, who had previously run the 803 independent record store.

A recent article in *The Guardian* surveying the UK music scene focussed on the success of Glasgow club Optimo, and the club's series of highly acclaimed OSCARR singles releases by local acts Creme de Menthe, Bis and Pro Forma. *The Guardian* journalist seemed puzzled by the combination of eclectic playlist, Sunday night slot and jampacked dancefloor, as in addition to being held on the quietest night of the week, Optimo has moved location four times in as many years and has also used an "anti-marketing" strategy, with posters claiming that the club "isn't as good as it used to be." The article said, "This combination of high-minded artiness and 'difficult' music should, by rights, attract a crowd of bearded, chin-stroking Wire magazine subscribers. Instead, by 1am, Optimo's dancefloor is rammed with beautiful girls in stiletto heels and short skirts, floppy-fringed indie kids, trendies apparently decked out from a 1983 edition of the Freeman's catalogue and boozy young lads on the pull. It is, as club vernacular would have it, going right off, and what's more it's going right off on the least sociable night of the week, to the sort of music most people would consider unlistenable. Shouldn't they all be in bed? 'I don't think there's a Glasgow sound, but there's definitely a Glasgow attitude,' explains DJ Keith McIvor. Which is? 'This,' he grins, raising his middle finger'."[36]

The 13th Note Cafe and club went into receivership at the end of 2001, largely due to debts the company was still carrying from the fire at The

---

36  Alexis Petridis, *The Guardian*, May 3rd, 2002.

Apollo in 1992. Fortunately, 13th Note founder Craig Tannock quickly established a new premises, West 13th,[37] on Kelvinhaugh Street in Finneston, where all the essential ingredients of his philosophy (live bands, reasonably priced drinks, vegan food) remain intact. Tannock was also busy planning a city centre venue encompassing a bar/restaurant, record store and fair trade grocery shop. In November 2002 (the same month that the Sub Club finally reopened its doors at its spiritual home in Jamaica Street) Craig Tannock's Mono opened in King's Court. Besides a vegan bar and restaurant, microbrewery and a fair trade shop, Mono also boasts a mural by Lucy McKenzie and an independent record store, Monorail, with an esoteric stock of experimental British, European and American music.[38] Sadly, the Glasgow Music Collective disbanded in May 2002, releasing a statement that said, "The events over the last two or three years leading to this demise have totally destroyed my faith in the sustainability of an alternative music-based community, human nature itself and by implication, in the possibility of living in a better world." The GMC had staged numerous excellent gigs over the previous few years including shows by Glasgow bands The PH Family, Eska, Hernanadez plus experimental American bands including The Black Heart Procession, US Maple, and perhaps most memorably, DC rockers Fugazi, who played Glasgow School of Art in May of 1999. The GMC was a vital force that supported local bands and brought excellent foreign bands to Glasgow, and will be greatly missed.

The Modern Institute has continued to change in various ways, most notably when Will Bradley began to work in a consultative capacity for the organisation in 2001, leaving Toby Webster as sole director. The initial group of 13 Modern Institute artists had now been joined by Glasgow-based artists Andrew Kerr, Scott Myles and Michael Wilkinson, London-based Jeremy Deller, Katja Strunz (Berlin) and Henrik Håkansson (Denmark). This roster of artists shares a loosely identifiable style, although there is a wide range of approaches within the group. The Modern Institute

---

37  In December 2002 West 13th was renamed Stereo.
38  Since the John Smith's on Byres Road closed during 2000, there has been a decided gap in Glasgow's range of independent record shops, which Monorail has now successfully filled.

does not claim to represent the full scope of the Glasgow art scene, but it has succeeded in significantly raising the international profile of its Glasgow-based artists. The organisation continues to represents a pro-active spirit in the city, creating new opportunities and situations without drawing greatly on public funding.[39]

In 2002 the Modern Institute participated in art fairs in Milan, Basel, Cologne, Berlin and Miami but decided against participating in the Glasgow Art Fair, which had been the least successful of the fairs attended by the company in the last two years.[40] The Glasgow Art Fair (est. 1996) is the largest contemporary art fair in the UK outwith London, but galleries such as Transmission and The Modern Institute struggle to make sales there, in contrast to more traditional commercial art galleries such as Cyril Gerber. The Modern Institute concentrated instead on projects such as screening a series of films by the late LA-based artist Jack Goldstein[41] at their Robertson Street premises and curating the large group show My Head Is On Fire But My Heart Is Full of Love, organised around Robert Smithson's concept of "psychedelic minimalism". The show, held at the Charlottensburg Exhibition Hall in Copenhagen, included works by 41 artists including Paul Thek, Andy Warhol, Robert Smithson and local heroes including Martin Boyce, Jim Lambie and Victoria Morton. Will Bradley, who co-curated the exhibition with Toby Webster and Henriette Breton-Meyer, wrote that "A radical aesthetic isn't necessarily a convulsive revolution, an assault on convention or a dive into obscurity. It's anything that can lead you into a reassessment of formal language, a refusal to accept orthodoxy."[42]

The refusal to accept orthodoxy had been a key idea associated with most of the artist-run galleries and musicians' collectives in the city since the early 1980s. Drawing on that local atmosphere, The Modern Institute had built a distinctive identity as a young gallery that was also part

---

39  In 1999/2000 The Modern Institute received £6000 from Glasgow City Council, in comparison to Streetlevel, which received £39,500 or CCA which received £110,400. Source: Best Value Review Glasgow City Council January 2001.

40  Because of the lack of collectors of contemporary art in Glasgow, art fairs provide a crucial means for The Modern Institute to generate interest and sales for their roster of artists.

41  In cooperation with Cologne gallerist Daniel Bucholz.

42  Will Bradley, "Exploits", *My Head Is On Fire But My Heart is Full of Love*, Charlottensburg Udstillingsbyngning, 2002, pp13–18.

publisher, part record company. Bradley and Webster had reassessed the formal language of art exhibitions with their art/music cross-over projects like Can 303s Heal? (Helsinki, 1999), Electric City (2000) and Pyramids of Mars (2000/2001), but that approach had also brought the gallery and the artists it represented a higher public profile than ever before. The work being made by several of these artists had developed in a supportive but relatively uncommercial environment. Now the artists associated with these initiatives, including Cathy Wilkes, Victoria Morton, Jim Lambie, Hayley Tompkins and Richard Wright all had secondary gallerists in London, New York, Berlin or Cologne, and were showing regularly at high-profile international venues.

In June 2002 Toby Webster established new gallery Roma Roma Roma in Rome, in collaboration with Turin gallerist Franco Noero and New York gallerist Gavin Brown. In the same month, The Modern Institute was invited to graduate from the Liste young art fair at Basel to the main fair, where the gallery received the prize for the best stand, featuring the work of Cathy Wilkes. However, within Scotland, The Modern Institute still operates in a comparative isolation, preventing the kind of "over-heating" of artists sometimes seen in London or New York. Also, having worked in relative obscurity for years, Glasgow-based artists may have a more sanguine approach to 'fame' than their contemporaries working in major art centres. Cathy Wilkes comments, "Sometimes you get ignored and sometimes you don't get ignored. It's nothing to do with the work. A lot of reviews are just adverts. [ … ] If something is advertised enough sometimes people buy it. I'm quite cynical about it – I think it's more important just to do your work."[43]

In early summer 2002, The Centre announced that its Director, Lucy Byatt would be moving to Bristol's Spike Island to take up the post of Director that autumn. The Centre's board, which consists of Byatt, architect Steven Spier, quantity surveyor David Neilson, artist Tom O'Sullivan, DCA assistant curator Rob Tufnell and CCA's former education officer, Rebecca Shatwell, continue to oversee the operation of the organisation, while

43  Cathy Wilkes, in conversation with the author, August 2001.

Project Manager Jenny Crowe is developing a series of new artists residencies across the Highland region. Other plans include developing a series of projects for artists who want to extend their practice within Glasgow in an organisational context. Lucy Byatt says, "The thing about this city is that none of the artists are working here, they are all working in other places. So, the idea of these projects is to provide a series of bursaries to allow artists to work with the city's infrastructure, as they have been rejected by the galleries and museums."[44] Although The Centre will continue to operate, Byatt's departure remains a serious blow to the city's existing arts infrastructure. Unfortunately, it seems that Ross Sinclair's 1996 description of the local arts infrastructure ("a very tenuous proposition, a castle built on sand, if you like. A ghost – a specter – a phantom")[45] remains as apt six years later. It is still the case that there is little provision for the success of artist-run initiatives like The Centre to be consolidated in a longer term way, beyond the hard work of certain determined individuals.

However, the Glasgow art scene has continued to foster new artist-led initiatives, such as Pearl Union, a series of talks launched in April 2002 by former Transmission committee member Rose Thomas, at the Mitchell Library in Glasgow. Working closely with DCA assistant curator Rob Tufnell and Transmission committee member Kate Davis, Thomas programmed a series of free lectures and events which began with New York filmmaker Leslie Singer talking about Laura Cottingham's *Not For Sale: Feminism and Art in the USA during the '70s*, which she had co-produced.[46] Another important aspect of the project was the intention to revitalise existing research resources at the Mitchell Library (itself the biggest reference library in Europe). Thomas invited a list of contributors from a range of disciplines, including Le Tigre frontwoman Kathleen Hanna, to select books and videos which were then made available within the library. Lucy McKenzie's Flourish events showcase, held at her Robertson Street Studio, has also

---

44  Lucy Byatt, in conversation with the author, June 2002.
45  Ross Sinclair, The Glasgow Miracle vs. Utopian modernism done by Third World peasants, "Circles", *ZKM*, Karlsruhe, 2003, pp193–199.
46  The series continued with a talk by American female cartoonist Trina Robbins, a free concert by acoustic guitarist and songwriter Bert Jansch and a lecture by Russel A. Potter on Vernacular Technologies: Folk Music in the Age of Digital Reproduction.

continued to provide another lively gathering place for local and visiting artists and Glasgow bands including Franz Ferdinand, Park Attack and the Mars Hotel. Local artists collective GFM have also been responsible for a number of interesting music/art cross-over projects in recent months including an exhibition recreating some of the history and social settings of Jamaican dub reggae, held in Intermedia.

Sorcha Dallas and Marianne Greated's temporary exhibitions organisation Switchspace was granted charitable status in spring 2001, and they have subsequently secured some funding from Glasgow City Council and the use of newly renovated properties in the Dennistoun area, to "support young artists by providing them with a free and independent space."[47] Property developer Susan White offered them the temporary use of certain properties after reading about their Switchspace activities in *AN* magazine. Dallas said, "For us it was incredible as we had been finding it hard, and costly, to try and acquire alternative spaces. We felt it would be a really appropriate development and very much in keeping with our philosophy, not only in terms of using a domestic setting but the transient nature of the spaces we would be able to use."[48] In November 2002, both Greated and Dallas joined forces with Robb Mitchell from Free gallery and musicians from local "kraut disco" band Franz Ferdinand to open The Chateau, a new visual art and music venue located in an old warehouse on Bridge Street. On the opening night there was an exhibition by Neil Bickerton and Lorna Macintyre, Karla Black, Paul Embleton, Alex Frost, Lotte Gertz, Emily Richardson and Hayley Tompkins. There was a live performance by artists Kim Coleman and Susie Green, and local bands Franz Ferdinand, Uncle John & Whitelock, Park Attack and experimental jazz collective Scatter performed. The local constabulary brought the evening to a premature end, but this was seen by many as a sign of the launch party's success.

Glasgow School of Art graduates Katie Exley and Karla Black have also emerged as proactive artists and organisers, often linking their activities to

<hr>

47 Switchspace letter to supporters, 2001.
48 Sorcha Dallas, in response to questions sent by the author, November 2001.

the Glasgow Project Room, where until recently Exley served as a committee member. In October 2001 the duo organised an ambitious project which built upon the strength of the artist-run initiative in Glasgow. They explained, "October presented the work of 31 Glasgow-based artists in the city centre location of St. Vincent Street. Each artist was assigned one day of the month of October 2001 in which they could make and show a work in any site along the street: bars, cafes, banks, offices, wasteground, churches, pavements, walls … Presenting public art in this way allowed the artists the freedom to bring their practice into the public realm without the constraints of producing a permanent work."[49] The range of works made by the artists included in October indicates the proliferation of different styles of work in the city, from Toby Paterson's steel text piece, derived from a Joy Division song, *Avenues All Lined with Trees*, to Karla Black's intervention with a pile of 2,000 Alka Seltzer outside a former council building, to David Sherry's performance *Advancement into Retreat*. Sherry dressed as an eccentric elderly lady and spent the day smiling benignly at passersby from the threshold of a portable doorway. Belfast born Sherry, who graduated from the MFA at Glasgow School of Art in 2000, makes video works, drawings and recordings about absurd and/or disturbing happenings. His previous projects include a film of the artist sitting in a swing park in his underpants on a frosty morning, and an attempt to canvas the general public's opinions of Tom Cruise's hairstyle. However Sherry's interest in disrupting the everyday is perhaps best seen in one of his simplest works, which involved taking a bucket of water everywhere he went for a week.

In Glasgow, as elsewhere, there have been numerous examples of artists utilising the internet to show their work, such as VisionOn, a virtual gallery set up in 2001 by Karla Black, which showcases the work of three different Glasgow artists every month: participating artists so far include Hayley and Sue Tompkins, Duncan McQuarrie, James McLardy, Katie Exley and Tayto & Mr. Tayto. Glasgow-based arts agency New Media Scotland also run an

49  http://www.october.org.uk

online gallery, named Host, which has so far displayed specially commissioned works by Gair Dunlop and Claude Closky. As Steve Dietz, the founding director of New Media Initiatives at the Walker Art Center in Minneapolis says, "For me, there are all sorts of parallels between artists getting on-line and doing their sites and the self publishing movement in photography in the '60s and '70s."[50] Glasgow School of Art lecturer and CCA Head of Digital Media, Francis McKee has also taken advantage of the possibilities of self-publishing on the internet, after he tried unsuccessfully to raise funding for a Glasgow-based arts imprint through the art school and the SAC. His eponymous website provides links to other related sites and he also regularly invites other artists to host guest pages. Recently McKee has received support from the Helsinki-based Nordic Institute for Contemporary Art (NIFCA)[51] to set up his publishing imprint, Diamond Heart, which has so far collaborated with NIFCA on publications on Icelandic artist Salla Tykka and the work of artist's collective The Icelandic Love Corporation.

Within Scotland, Dundee Contemporary Arts has continued to provide exhibition opportunities for Glasgow-based artists in exhibitions such as Simon Starling's recent solo show Djungel (2002) and group exhibition Beyond (2000) which showcased the talents of Duncan of Jordanstone graduates Luke Fowler and Clare Stephenson and GSA graduate, Toby Paterson. Perhaps Katrina Brown and then assistant curator Rob Tufnell's most significant collaborative contribution to the contemporary art scene in Scotland was their large-scale group exhibition Here + Now: Scottish Art 1990–2001, which ran at five venues in Aberdeen and Dundee from September to November 2001.[52] Here + Now was the first large scale survey show of contemporary Scottish art held in Scotland since New Art in

50  Quoted in *Flash Art*, January/February 2000.
51  Until recently Rebecca Gordon Nesbitt was a curator at NIFCA , an organisation which has successfully forged many links between Scotland and Nordic countries, partially through a series of NIFCA research residencies, funded as part of Network North a Nordic Council of Ministers Initiative for 2002. A number of Glasgow-based artists and writers were awarded NIFCA research residencies in 2002, including Luke Fowler, Will Bradley, Chris Evans, John Shankie, Ilana Halperin, Justin Carter, Jim Harold , Shauna McMullan, Sophie MacPherson, Camilla Løw and Anne Bjerge-Hansen, who were based in various locations including Helsinki, Inari in Lapland, Stockholm and Gothenburg.
52  A total of 63 Scottish artists were included in the linked exhibitions at DCA, Generator and McManus Gallery, Dundee and Peacock Visual Arts and Aberdeen Art Gallery, Aberdeen.

Scotland at the CCA six years earlier. The exhibition's press release stated, "With some of Scotland's artists winning important national and international art awards – Douglas Gordon's Turner Prize in 1996, Callum Innes' NatWest Prize in 1998 and Roderick Buchanan's Beck's Futures Prize in 2000 – the past decade has been one of extraordinary vitality. Here + Now is an invaluable opportunity for so much of this remarkable work to be considered on home ground."[53]

Edinburgh's Collective Gallery has also continued to support Glasgow-based artists, for example in the annual New Work Scotland seasons, which have included work by Mick Peter, Katy Dove and James Thornhill and Michelle Naismith's A Love Laboratory. Henry VIII's Wives Fear of Death (2001), Ian Hetherington (2002) and Mick Peter's Deceberator (2002) provide further evidence of Director Sarah Munro's continuing engagement with work being made West of the capital. More recently, the gallery has announced an intention to represent artists commercially, bringing the Collective closer to The Modern Institute model than to that of Transmission. The second stage of showcase exhibition Evolution Isn't Over Yet (1999) initiated by Sarah Munro and Fruitmarket Director Graeme Murray, entitled Presence (2002) took place recently at the Fruitmarket in Edinburgh, with works by Glasgow-based artists Alex Pollard, Kevin Hutcheson, Alex Frost, Fred Pedersen, Michelle Naismith and Scott Myles. The recent appointment of former Tate Liverpool and Hayward Gallery curator Fiona Bradley to replace Graeme Murray as director of the Fruitmarket has also been widely welcomed within the Scottish art scene.

Inverleith House curator Paul Nesbitt also frequently includes work by Glasgow-based artists in his programme – presenting major exhibitions by Richard Wright (1999), Lucy Mckenzie (in collaboration with Paulina Olowska) (2001), Cathy Wilkes (2002) and Jim Lambie (2003) – in addition to high profile solo shows by Carl Andre, Lawrence Weiner and Ed Ruscha. Elsewhere in the capital city, photography gallery Stills, and newer venues like Sleeper, Out of the Blue arts centre and gallery/agency

53  DCA Press Release August 2001

doggerfisher[54] also offer new exhibition opportunities for aspiring artists from both coasts.

## THE BUZZ OF THE FUTURE

In early May 2002, Glasgow based artist Toby Paterson became the second Scot in three years to win the £24,000 Beck's Futures Prize, fuelling a deluge of local art coverage not seen since Douglas Gordon and Christine Borland's back-to-back Turner nominations in 1996 and 1997. Paterson's work continued to look at the ways in which Brutalist post-war design could still be considered beautiful or even spiritual. On recent travels through Europe and America, he had tracked the work of the architects who rebuilt the post-war cities, and then traced how the ideas of Le Courbusier and Mies van der Rohe were translated by paler imitators in Britain. "I have a sort of morbid curiosity about the origins of these forms," he explains, "Le Courbusier introduced the doctrine that architecture directly affects behaviour, and then that was co-opted by other architects in a way that changed people's lives negatively. I am gripped by this kind of architecture because of the terrible results of Le Courbusier influenced '60s and '70s architecture in Scotland."

Examples of failed modernist architecture were not difficult for Paterson to find in his home town, from Basil Spence's intractably damp Hutcheson flats, that were finally demolished in 1993, to the abandoned Anderston complex near Glasgow city centre which formed the basis of his latest work. "It was built by Colonel Richard Siefert, who was also responsible for Centrepoint in London", says Paterson, "I've always been interested in Anderston because it was never really successful. At one time there was a bus station beneath it, and there was the idea of total lifestyle, that your flat, shops and transport were all connected. But it didn't work because people don't want to live in little pods." For the Glasgow leg of the Beck's Future's tour, which opened on the 3rd of August at CCA, he made a wall painting

---

54 Established by *The List*'s former Art Editor Susanna Beaumont in 2000.

based on a concrete and reinforced glass stairwell from Siefert's doomed development.[55]

Paterson had thought it was unlikely that he would win Beck's Futures given fellow Glaswegian Roderick Buchanan's win in the inaugural year of the competition. He said, "It was all a bit of a whirlwind when we got to the ICA – it was still a shock to hear my name read out – and up I went to stand beside Björk. She was really friendly, the photographers were all shouting, 'where did you get your dress, love?' and she told them, 'This is about art, not my dress'. 'It's nice of you to say that', I said, but I think it might really be about your dress'."[56] ICA director Philip Dodd was on hand, and exclaimed, "The Glasgow art scene is the buzz of the future and it's bypassing London."[57] Most of the artists who live in the city enjoyed a brief guffaw at Dodd's far from prescient comments before returning to work, including Paterson. Ten days after his unexpected win he was quoted as saying, "At the end of it I just looked at everyone and thought, 'Right, I'm back now. What's next?'"[58] Twelve months after Paterson a third GSA graduate, Rosalind Nashashibi, won Beck's Futures in the fourth year of the competition. Nashashibi, who graduated from the MFA in 2000, exhibited several cinema verite style documentary shorts.

Further high profile media coverage of Scottish arts activity accompanied the launch of Zenomap, the first nationally supported presentation of art from Scotland at the Venice Biennale in May 2003. Despite the increasing profile and influence of Scottish, and specifically Glasgow-based, artists over the last ten years, they have been notable by their absence from The British Pavilion at the Biennale. The new Scottish Pavilion was supported by the British Council and the Scottish Arts Council and the presentation was curated in its inaugural year by Kay Pallister[59] and Francis McKee. Former Transmission committee members Simon Starling and Claire Barclay and Glasgow-based artist Jim Lambie were chosen to present a

---

55  Quotes from Toby Paterson taken from interview with the author in July 2002, previously published in *The List* magazine.
56  *Scotland On Sunday*, 19th May, 2002.
57  Quoted in *The Guardian*, May 8th, 2002, p5.
58  *Scotland On Sunday*, Ibid.
59  Kay Pallister has worked in both non-profit organisations and commercial galleries, notably Gagosian Gallery in London and New York, and as contents curator for arts database Axis in the UK.

series of specially commissioned sculptural works on the piano nobile of a 17th century palazzo. 2003 was also the first year that Wales presented a pavilion at the Biennale – a selection that was curated in the inaugural year by Patricia Fleming. Although Zenomap received extremely positive coverage in *frieze* and other art magazines, the new national pavilions were also not without their critics. Former GSA Head of Fine Art Pavel Buchler commented, "I do not see the inauguration of the Scottish or Welsh Pavilions as a splitting up of the British Pavilion. I see it as a declaration of provincialism; the Scottish Pavilion represents in the first place the interests of the Scottish Arts Council. For national representation we should read institutional representation."[60]


## WHERE DOES IT GO FROM HERE?


Since the mid-1980s, Glasgow School of Art's Alexander Moffat, Sam Ainsley and David Harding have done much to propagate an atmosphere where students felt free to experiment. The strength of the Glasgow art scene owes in no small measure a debt to these influential teachers, yet in 2001 David Harding retired as head of Environmental Art,[61] and Sam Ainsley admits, "I've been doing this for so many years that I want to hand on the baton to the next generation."[62] The Art School that these teachers have done so much to invigorate has become a magnet for students from outside Glasgow, especially outside the UK. Sam Ainsley comments, "there is a much greater cultural mix amongst students on the MFA now: it's probably 50% UK students and 50% from other countries."[63] Curator Rebecca Gordon Nesbitt, who has recently moved from Helsinki to live in Glasgow, says, "In the mid–1990s, the generation of artists that includes Douglas Gordon, Christine Borland, Roderick Buchanan et al. was making

---

60  The Manchester Pavilion, Pavel Buchler interviewed by David Bellingham, *Matters* Issue 17, Summer 2003, p18–19.

61  Australian artist and lecturer Tanya Eccleston was appointed as the new Head of Environmental Art. Glasgow based artists Justin Carter and Clara Ursitti have also recently joined the teaching staff in the Environmental Art Department.

62  Sam Ainsley, in conversation with the author, May 2001. Ainsley is particularly active in the art scene outwith the arts school – she is a member of the Tramway International Curatorium and the Chair of the SAC's Visual Arts Committee.

63  Sam Ainsley, Ibid.

a contribution to the Glasgow infrastructure through a deliberate decision to stay in or return to Glasgow. This infrastructure keeps getting stronger, which is evident in the number of young artists from all over Europe and beyond who want to come to Glasgow to live and study. I can only imagine that this will continue." Unfortunately, there are also larger year groups and less funding for teaching at Glasgow School of Art, as budget cuts squeeze the school's resources. Since 1999 the percentage increase in funds from SHEFC has been lower than the annual pay award for the school, which has recently resulted in staff at the school being asked to take voluntary redundancy. Former Scottish Arts Council director Seona Reid took over as Director of the school in 1999, and has introduced a series of changes, aimed at streamlining the running of the school (for example Painting and Printmaking have been made into a single department, as have Environmental Art and Sculpture). However, a new Head of Fine Art, Klaus Jung, has recently been appointed, the first externally appointed candidate in this post since Pavel Buchler's departure in 1997.[64]

DCA curator Katrina Brown has also noticed the growing influx of artists moving to Glasgow in search of a "scene". She says, "I think an interesting factor is the extent to which artists, post-graduation, now move to Glasgow in expectation of there being some kind of supportive, engaged scene, which is of course quite a different prospect from people choosing to remain there and creating that scene in the first place. I guess that's very much to do with moving on to the next stage, having carved out some space – where does it go from there? Expectations have undoubtedly been raised as to likely opportunities and levels of success and I think the next few years will be interesting, to see how that keeps moving."[65]

Charles Esche, who is now based in Copenhagen and Malmö, co-ordinated a showcase of artist-run initiatives, including the protoacademy and Transmission, for the 2002 Gwangju Biennale in Korea. He believes

64 Sam Ainsley, Alexander Moffat and Thomas Joshua Cooper have taken turns as Acting Head of Fine Art since 1997. Jung trained at the Dusseldorf's Kunstakademie and the Royal College of Art, before moving to Norway to take up the post of Head of the Kunatakademiet in Trondheim, then the Kusthogskolen in Bergen. In 2009 Jung left GSA to become Rector of the Academy of Media Arts Cologne – his successor at GSA was Professor Roger Wilson.
65 Katrina Brown, in response to questions sent by the author, September 2001.

that Transmission's "two years in, then out" structure keeps the turnover of ideas and energy around the local art scene constant. "The uniqueness of Transmission follows through, and the reason it does that is because of the two year structure, because so many people have been really committed for that short period of time. You do the absolute best that you can for two years, and then pass it on. That's really special, I don't know if it's unique but it's certainly rare. That working structure has carried on through all the ups and downs of the CCA and Tramway – because these institutions pivot around a particular individual or a particular group of people. When they leave, the energy drains out: but Transmission just goes on and that's really special."[66]

66 Charles Esche, in conversation with the author, July 2001. In September 2003 Glasgow City Council announced to its staff at Tramway that, pending the outcome of a capital lottery application to the Scottish Arts Council, Scottish Ballet would relocate its entire operation to Tramway. This would mean that large-scale exhibition space Tramway 2 (where 24 Hour Psycho, From Life and other groundbreaking exhibitions were staged) would close in order to provide Scottish Ballet with a space for constructing stage sets. After this news was leaked to the local press, Tramway visual arts officer Alexia Holt was suspended from her post, and a series of protests were organised by local artists. However, when in October a delegation from the visual arts community met with Chris Barron, chief executive of Scottish Ballet, he explained that the public outcry in response to the lottery bid had not been anticipated and that his company was committed to reaching a mutually agreeable solution. At the time of going to press, the future use of Tramway remained unclear.

# CHAPTER 13

# FROM EMERGENT TO ESTABLISHED (2003–2010)

It is February 2010, and Toby Webster, director of the Modern Institute, is looking out of the window of his office at Robertson Street, where his organisation has been based for the last twelve years. In that time the surrounding neighbourhood has been gentrified with new office buildings and smart hotels, although the pawnbroker on the corner still does a brisk trade. Webster says, "We're moving to a new purpose-built premises at Osborne Street, and that's a major step for us – we've loved this building and it's really worked for us but the building's being developed now and we needed a bigger gallery space. We've been working out of a domestic gallery space for a long time and it's been really difficult to show certain pieces and to develop when we were renting our offices on short leases. We will still have studios for artists but not in the same building. The new gallery and office space is in a good situation, in the Trongate area, which everyone knows the artistic community has been investing in for a long time but now it is really noticeably becoming more developed."[1]

The building where the Modern Institute's new gallery and offices are located is a former semi-derelict former public baths and washhouse in the Saltmarket, which was used for The Modern Institute's presentation of a new work by Simon Starling, *Project for a Public Sculpture (After Thomas Annan)*, as part of the 2008 Glasgow International Festival of Visual Art. Starling scanned silver particles from a reprinted 1866 Annan photograph of a Glasgow slum and built a virtual model of their form – resulting in a large,

---

1   Toby Webster, in conversation with the author, February 11th, 2010.

amorphous pale grey sculpture, like an unpainted Franz West. However, Starling's work also described how technology and gentrification have erased a complex history of communal domesticity.[2] There is a connection between the communal activity of the washhouse and recent artistic practices in Glasgow, which might crystallise in the image of the "jawbox", a slang expression which was used historically to describe a communal sink – jaw meaning both "conversation" and "to pour". The Glasgow art scene is predicated upon a combination of social co-operation and an interest in process-based practices, as for example in the work of artists such as Cathy Wilkes and Richard Wright, whose work is concerned with material and its poetry, and grounded in "actual bodies and social sites".[3] There is a pleasing piece of symmetry in The Modern Institute completely renovating this building, which had been earmarked for demolition: the new gallery will open to the public with Metal Urbain, an exhibition of new works by Glasgow-based artist Jim Lambie, during Glasgow International in April 2010.[4]

When the first edition of *Social Sculpture* was published in 2003, The Modern Institute represented 19 artists, a mixture of the original Glasgow-based peer group of artists such as Martin Boyce, Jim Lambie, Cathy Wilkes and Richard Wright, and artists from other cities that Will Bradley and Toby Webster had met and worked with over the years. In 2010, Toby Webster has been sole director of the Modern Institute for nine years and the gallery now represents thirty-seven artists,[5] many of whom have enjoyed critical and commercial success in the last few years, such as Turner Prize winners Jeremy Deller (2004), Simon Starling (2005) and Richard Wright (2010),

---

2    This description of Starling's work originally appeared in: Sarah Lowndes, "Glasgow International". *Artforum*, September 2008, pp.474–5.

3    This terminology is derived from Hal Foster, who writes in his book *The Return of the Real* that since the end of the '80s there has been "an emphatic turn to the bodily and the social, to the abject and the site-specific." Hal Foster, *The Return of the Real* (Cambridge, Massachusetts: The MIT Press, 1996), p.124.

4    Some of my observations in this paragraph also appear in an essay I wrote for Public Art Scotland (PAR +RS), entitled "I Am the Space Where I Am" (2010).

5    The artists represented by The Modern Institute are: Dirk Bell, Martin Boyce, Björn Dahlem, Walter Dahn, Jeremy Deller, Alex Dordoy, Urs Fisher, Luke Fowler, Henrik Håkansson, Mark Handforth, Thomas Houseago, Richard Hughes, Chris Johanson, Andrew Kerr, Jim Lambie, Duncan Macquarrie, Victoria Morton, Scott Myles, Toby Paterson, Simon Periton, Manfred Pernice, Mary Redmond, Anselm Reyle, Eva Rothschild, Monika Sosnowska, Simon Starling, Katja Strunz, Tony Swain, Spencer Sweeney, Joanne Tatham & Tom O'Sullivan, Pádraig Timoney, Hayley Tompkins, Sue Tompkins, Cathy Wilkes, Michael Wilkinson, Gregor Wright and Richard Wright. Andrew Hamilton was made a director in 2009.

Turner Prize nominees Jim Lambie (2005) and Cathy Wilkes (2008), Beck's Futures winner Toby Paterson (2002) and Jarman Prize winner Luke Fowler (2008). Webster says that he is not surprised by the success of the artists he represents, saying, "I knew when I thought of the idea in 1996 that the artists [in Glasgow] were on the same level as great artists I had seen around the world and that was it. I never doubted it. I think those artists deserve to be amongst the best artists in the world – that's the way I see them. If I didn't believe that, why would I be doing this? There's something very special about the artists – they are not about public relations – their work has never been about the relentless promotion of art through the media. It's really real and it's quite a challenge to get it out there. I think the mechanism that's slowly working is that people realise that there's been no compromise in the art that these people are making – it's a gradual understanding of what people are doing. It's not like, 'Yeah, I get it' and then it's gone. It's gradually building. Sometimes it takes a while for culture to spin around and recognise something, but it will – culture bends round to the artist's way of looking rather than the artist making work for culture."[6]

In 2001, the curator and writer Will Bradley had left his role as co-director of The Modern Institute, leaving Toby Webster as the sole director of the organisation, although in 2002 he co-curated with Webster and Henriette Breton Meyer the exhibition My Head Is On Fire But My Heart is Full of Love, for Charlottensburg Exhibition Hall in Copenhagen. The exhibition was organised around Robert Smithson's idea of "psychedelic minimalism" and gave an indication of Bradley's future career trajectory, which would include curating the exhibition Radical Software at the CCA Wattis Institute for Contemporary Art, San Francisco (2006), and co-editing the anthology *Art and Social Change: A Reader* (2007) together with Charles Esche.[7] For Toby Webster, too, My Head Is On Fire… was an important exhibition, as for him, "the exhibition expressed the critical reason why The Modern Institute existed. It wasn't just about representation of the artists,

6  Toby Webster, in conversation with the author, February 11th, 2010.
7  Will Bradley continues to work as a curator and critic, but now lives and works in Oslo, Norway, where he intends to open a non-profit exhibition space in September 2010.

it was very much about, 'what critical point are you trying to make?' A lot of people had the mistaken impression that we had called ourselves The Modern Institute because we wanted to discuss modernism, but in fact we were interested in much more complex ideas about radical aesthetics, and those were the kind of things we were really interested in. Between 1998 when we founded The Modern Institute and 2002 when My Head Is On Fire… opened, there was a period when everything became much more conservative. We were going to lots of art fairs, and many more collectors and curators were coming to visit us, and this meant that we were no longer just with the critical group of people we started the organisation with – instead we had become a much more public organisation."[8] Indeed, as a recent interview with Bradley confirms, it was the more conservative direction that The Modern Institute appeared to be taking between 1998 and 2001 that led to his departure: "as the commercial side of The Modern Institute's activities had became more important, Bradley had found himself increasingly unsuited to the role of art dealer and opted out."[9]

Toby Webster says, "Although we do commercial shows and we show at art fairs we've always done something on the stand that's actually quite challenging for people, such as Cathy Wilkes's stand at the Basel art fair in 2002 [which won the prize for best stand]. Critically her work is a very interesting way of looking at the figure, this dispersal of form and the mixture of the soul and the emotion in the space with the physical sculpture, and that really hit a distinctive note because it was different from other things being shown at that level. We've gone through quite a conservative period in the last ten years, which the art fairs have partly created – one big shift that occurred was the understanding that you can make art and it goes into an auction straight away, the most obvious example of this being Damien Hirst [and his auction of 200 new works in 2008, just before the market collapsed]. The art fairs created this big beast of the auction houses – some dealers started wanting to start building a new secondary market through artists who were still alive and making

8    Toby Webster, in conversation with the author, February 11th 2010.
9    Interview with Will Bradley, Kopenhagen, 31st March, 2010, http://www.kopenhagen.dk/interviews/interviews/interviews_2010/interview_will_bradley/

paintings. Ridiculous prices were conjured up because they needed to make that much money to support this huge network and they got greedy and the thing just became bigger and bigger. This destroyed the essence of what art can be – but since [the art market collapsed] there has been a kick back against all that and a growing interest in less obviously commercial work by artists like Cathy Wilkes and Richard Wright – work that people experience as a great release because they can approach it in a different way, and don't only have to think about how much it costs."[10]

Richard Wright's work, which has attracted a great deal of critical attention since he won the Turner Prize in December 2009, attracted the attention of audiences partly because the work relies upon the movement of the viewer in the space. Wright's vast (seven metres by four metres) gold-leaf wall painting for the 2009 Turner Prize exhibition needed to be walked past, under, and around in order to reveal the way it changed at different hours of the day and under altering light conditions. The work was not only on the wall, but also in the air all around, amplifying the existing architecture and disclosing the invisible history and atmosphere of the room. The painting was partially inspired by the apocalyptic skies of certain works held in the Tate Collection, such as Turner's *The Deluge* (exhibited 1805), John Martin's *The Great Day of His Wrath* (1851–53), and the Tate's sizeable holdings of works by mystic, poet, and painter William Blake. The work struck a chord with many commentators, who saw within this "rippling field of delicately gilded patterns [...] allusions to Tiepolo, Blake, Turner",[11] "old engravings, baroque abstraction, clouds, a sun whose rays strike through a boiling mass of curlicues",[12] and "resemblances to a Chinese garden, dragons, the vertebrae of a spinal column, sunbursts, rivers".[13] The painting took about five weeks to realise, including two site visits to Tate Britain, a week spent making preparatory drawings in Glasgow, and three weeks installing the work in the gallery, and then was painted out after the exhibition closed. Many commentators observed that the work appeared as

10  Toby Webster, in conversation with the author, February 11th, 2010.
11  Rachel Campbell-Johnston, "Turner Prize: Thought Provoking, Not Shocking", *The Times*, 6 October 2009.
12  Adrian Searle, "The Turner Prize Trinity", *The Guardian*, 5 October 2009.
13  Martin Gayford, "The Turner Prize Startles", *Bloomberg*, 6 October 2009.

a flood of dazzling light, impossible to see completely: "Wherever you stand, parts of the fugitive image are swallowed in glare."[14] The ephemeral quality of gold leaf as a material is a literal reflection of the predestination of the work, which, to quote the performance theorist Peggy Phelan, "becomes itself through disappearance".[15]

Wright's win, following the year after Cathy Wilkes's 2008 nomination for the Turner Prize, has served to focus the attention of the art world on Glasgow even more intently than before. Hannah Robinson, director of one of Glasgow's three commercial galleries, says, "Artists from Glasgow being nominated for and winning the Turner Prize and other prizes makes people look more towards the city – it makes people think there must be something in the water. However, a lot of the strength of the local scene has to do with the art school – that makes for a community, and people staying here. For a lot of people who live here, although they might be showing internationally, the shows they do here are the most important in terms of the feedback they get from their peers. You do hear people having very serious conversations about one another's work – they will discuss it in quite a critical way. That keeps people on their toes, as does the fact that there isn't a big commercial scene here, different motivations are at work."[16]

Toby Webster agrees, saying "It's good for Glasgow that there's an artistic community that has various support networks. It's become quite strong. Tramway is suddenly doing really well under Sarah Munro, as is CCA under Francis McKee, then there's Sorcha Dallas, Mary Mary and SWG3. The Trongate 103 development and the new WASPS studio development at the Briggait also show that there's a real strength – it does almost feel like where we were twenty years ago [around the time of the 1991 Windfall exhibition] but now it's real. It's all kind of grown up and it's based on need. The Modern Institute is definitely based in Glasgow – I'm interested in Glasgow and investing in that. I did Roma Roma Roma [a gallery Webster founded in Rome in June 2002 in co-operation with New York gallerist

---

14  Searle, "The Turner Prize Trinity", *The Guardian*, 5 October 2009.

15  Peggy Phelan, "The Ontology of Performance: Representation without Reproduction", in *Unmarked: The Politics of Performance* (London: Routledge, 1993), p. 146. The section of this chapter pertaining to Richard Wright is adapted from, Sarah Lowndes, "Learned By Heart: The Paintings of Richard Wright", published in *Richard Wright*, (New York: Rizzoli, 2010).

16  Hannah Robinson, in conversation with the author, January 27th, 2010.

Gavin Brown and Turin-based gallerist Franco Noero] as part of The Modern Institute between 2002 and 2005 – but it came to a natural end because I couldn't afford the time and I didn't want to be away from here. It ended in 2005, which was the year that Jim Lambie and Simon Starling were both nominated for the Turner Prize and The Modern Institute really started to become established. The Modern Institute in many ways has a big turnover, but in a lot of ways that goes back into the community, whether that's through production, through an artist or through us employing different people, it gives back to the city. We have freelance people, people building stuff for us, making space – it benefits us and it benefits them."[17]

## SORCHA DALLAS, THREE BLOWS AND THE CARAVAN CLUB

In December 2004 Sorcha Dallas and Marianne Greated drew their temporary exhibitions project Switchspace to a close after five years of activity – their final show was an exhibition of new works, Moons by Cathy Wilkes, which was held in a disused flat in Sword Street, Dennistoun. Wilkes's installation used found objects associated with domesticity such as a pushchair and a bathroom sink. A few years later, in *I Give You All My Money* (2008), a short documentary made by her partner Torsten Lauschmann to accompany her Turner Prize exhibition, Wilkes would explain that she used readymade objects as a way to think through lived experiences, "I contemplate over and over again events that have happened – physical experiences of objects and bodies – to reassess what really happened."[18] Wilkes had inspired Dallas and Greated to start Switchspace in the first place, when as final year students at GSA in 1998 they had attended a lecture in which she had described how she had opened her flat gallery in the spare room of her flat in Anderston's Dalriada towerblock. Looking back over Switchspace's five year history, Sorcha Dallas said, "The highlight for me was the final show with Cathy Wilkes, which was also a succinct way to tie the entire project up as Cathy was such an inspiration

17  Toby Webster, in conversation with the author, February 11th, 2010.
18  Cathy Wilkes, "I Give You All My Money" (London: Tate Britain, 2008).

in establishing the project in the beginning."[19] The night after Wilkes's exhibition closed, Switchspace held a closing party and a book launch for the publication at the Woodside Social Club, with local DJs Andrew Symington (Divine) and Stiletto playing records. White balloons printed with Switchspace's trademark light switch logo were kicked around the dance floor at the first party of the Christmas season, an occasion with an unusually festive ambience, given it was to mark the end of a project that had done so much to bolster the local scene.

For both Dallas and Greated new opportunities were already on the horizon – Greated wanted to concentrate on her painting career and a new collaborative science and art project at Edinburgh University – the following year she would take up a position as lecturer in the Painting and Printmaking Department at Glasgow School of Art. Dallas had opened her eponymous gallery in the Saltmarket's St. Margaret's Place a few months earlier. She says, "From the outset Switchspace was never meant to be permanent, hence its nomadic existence and we saw other artist-run spaces starting to happen and felt it was only natural that Switchspace ended in order for new projects to develop. Also it had become clear to me over the final few years of running Switchspace that I wanted to set up a permanent gallery space, partly inspired by some of the great artists I managed to work with such as Alex Frost and Craig Mulholland. I decided to establish my own permanent commercial gallery to offer a sustainable support structure for a new generation of emerging artists based in the city. The gallery initially began with five artists, three of whom I had worked with during Switchspace, namely Henry Coombes, Alex Frost and Craig Mulholland, with Kate Davis and Clare Stephenson making up the initial five. The gallery is now entering its sixth year and represents fourteen artists[20] in creating commissioning, exhibiting and purchasing opportunities for them on a local, national and international level."[21]

Sorcha Dallas opened her new gallery with a solo show by Frost (b.1972)

19  Sorcha Dallas, in response to questions sent by the author, February 2010.
20  The artists represented by Sorcha Dallas are: Rob Churm, Henry Coombes, Raphael Danke, Kate Davis, Alex Frost, Alasdair Gray, Charlie Hammond, Linder, Sophie Macpherson, Craig Mulholland, Alex Pollard, Gary Rough, Clare Stephenson and Michael Stumpf.
21  Sorcha Dallas, in response to questions sent by the author, February 2010.

in which he exhibited two works that drew on his intensive, systematic working method and by his interest in a kind of compromised Minimalism. Frost's cycles of work have included prototype Buckminster Fuller domes (1998), Gaudí-esque tiled sculptures (2000) and a series of works from 2002 made after Robert Morris' *Untitled (L-Beams)* (1965–7). One of the works in the exhibition, *Untitled (Ear and Coat)* (2004) was one of a series of pencil drawings of himself and friends completed over the last year. These graph paper portraits emerged out of a complex system of pixelated squares, circles and dashes. Frost's system is derived from two sources: a computer programme that pixelates photographic images and the method of denotation commonly found in knitting patterns. The hours of meditative drawing, folding and fixing that characterise Frost's practice have given him an understanding of how systems affect the body, and of how bodies affect systems. Ideas relating to rationalisation and the body also informed the second work in the show, a sculptural piece entitled *Everyday* (2004). The work comprised numerous sloppy copies of Ryvita boxes, rendered in offset lithograph, ink, paint and varnish on paper and red pine, which had been messily soldered into a formation somewhat like a barbecue using grab-and-fill adhesive. Frost's choice of Ryvita, the cardboard-tasting snack beloved of dieters, gestures again to the tension in his work between a masculine Minimalist tradition of modular repetition and a more 'impure' corporeality – his work can be seen as a kind of monument to rationalism usurped by the very blobbiness of its construction.[22]

Several of the other artists on Dallas's roster also made works dealing with the collision of art and social reality, as for example Kate Davis (b.1977) who complicated her 2004 exhibition of drawings in the gallery by introducing a stage which occupied most of the floor space into the small gallery. This platform had previously belonged to local live music venue the 13th Note, before passing into the hands of Transmission Gallery, where Davis previously served as a committee member. In borrowing it for her exhibition, she was also appropriating the object's history of bodily impact, something emphasised by coating the wood in a fleshy pink paint. On the

---

22  This description of Frost's work originally appeared in Sarah Lowndes, "Alex Frost", *Frieze* Issue 84, June-August 2004.

opening night it seemed from outside that some unusually tall people were in attendance, surrounded by crowds of more diminutive guests. Entering the haze of smoke and noise, visitors tripped over the edge of the stage and thus realised the changed contours of the room.[23]

The continuing cross-over between musicians and artists, art galleries and live music venues in Glasgow was highlighted in the work of another artist represented by Dallas, Rob Churm (b.1979). Churm was the front man for Glasgow "what wave" band Park Attack, now plays in the band Gummy Stumps, and is the designer of numerous posters, flyers and T-shirts. It could be said that the play of mess against neatness in his drawings finds an aural corollary in his music. Certainly many of the influences that may be detected in his work seem to emanate from illicit places and borderline states of mind – his characteristic use of harlequin checks around the edges of his compositions, for instance, brings to mind Stanley Mouse and Alton Kelley's poster designs for the Grateful Dead. Something of the restless energy of Raymond Pettibon can also be found in the artist's work – although the frequent inclusion of Tippex in Churm's lists of materials seems to point to his attraction to controlled chaos. Yet even the more easily decipherable of these drawings have the inexplicable quality of strangeness that Jacques Lacan called *l'objet petit a* (object little a); something that is like us and yet unfamiliar is conveyed via Churm's pictorial language of robots, skeletons, cartoon animal faces, shadows, stripes, waves and clouds. These forms, and their attendant shadows of black scrawl, orientate the viewer towards the world, which slides away the moment we jolt awake.[24]

In the summer of 2008, together with the producer Katie Nicoll, I curated a weekend-long event, Three Blows[25], at Scotland's oldest purpose-built concert hall, St. Cecilia's Hall in Edinburgh, to showcase the new music being made by Glasgow-based artists/musicians including the painters Tony Swain and Richard Wright, the filmmaker Luke Fowler and the sculptor Sarah Kenchington. During the event, the participants performed music

---

23  This description of Davis's work originally appeared in Sarah Lowndes, "Kate Davis", *Frieze*, Issue 91, May 2005.
24  This section pertaining to Rob Churm is based upon Sarah Lowndes, "Rob Churm", *Frieze*, Issue 107, May 2007.
25  Three Blows is a not for profit association founded in 2007 by curator Sarah Lowndes and producer Katie Nicoll to develop and produce innovative projects and events with unique performance context, both in terms of venue and programme.

composed specifically for this architecturally and acoustically unique environment, including unaccompanied singing, non-amplified improvisation and interactive mechanical music contraptions – they were also joined by two experimental music pioneers from further afield, Mayo Thompson (The Red Krayola) and Keith Rowe (AMM). Many of the musicians who participated in Three Blows had parallel careers as artists, such as Correcto frontman Danny Saunders, who is an artist in his own right but has also worked for many years as Jim Lambie's assistant.

Saunders describes his band Correcto as "a bit of a revolving door" – as since they formed in Glasgow in 2003 the line-up has included curator Will Bradley, Franz Ferdinand's Paul Thomson, and Patrick Doyle (The Royal We), Jake Lovatt (Uncle John & Whitelock) and Colin Kearney (Bricolage). However, since the outset the two constants in the band's spiky new-wave sound have been songwriter, singer and guitarist Saunders and guitarist Richard Wright. The name of the band comes from a crude Spanish translation of Wright's name (Ricardo Correcto) and he designed the sleeves of their two single releases, *Joni* and *Do It Better*, and their eponymous debut album, all of which were released on Domino during 2007 and 2008. While Wright was well known for his dazzling and often vast site-specific wall paintings, made using "the most direct and simple means possible" – brushes and paint, Saunders maintained his close involvement in the local art scene but said, "I think music is the most exciting art form out there."[26]

Another artist associated with The Modern Institute who participated in Three Blows was artist and musician Tony Swain (b.1967). Swain had studied at Liverpool Art School and at Glasgow School of Art, and in recent years has attracted critical acclaim for his atmospheric paintings, rendered on pages of *The Guardian* newspaper. The pages of newsprint are painted over with considered delicacy, distorting perspectives and entwining abstract motifs with the landscapes and figures of the original print, creating surreal landscapes or a depiction of an intimate, but unrecognisable object. Swain had combined his mutual interest in music and art over many years, firstly in his band Cylinder, and since 2005, by playing in Dreghorn with his former

26  Danny Saunders, Three Blows programme notes, (Edinburgh, July, 2008).

Cylinder collaborator Chris Wallace and Torsten Lauschmann (Slender Whiteman). He is also one third of the critically acclaimed band, Hassle Hound, who released their second LP on Staubgold Records in 2007.

The third artist from The Modern Institute's roster who appeared at Three Blows was Luke Fowler (b.1978), the artist, filmmaker and musician, acclaimed for his experimental documentaries on enigmatic radical figures such as RD Laing, Homosexuals frontman Xentos Jones and the English composer Cornelius Cardew. Fowler had previously released a number of projects on his SHADAZZ label, including *Evil Eye Is Source* (2001), a VHS compilation of music videos for local bands made by Glasgow artists, and for Three Blows he performed as experimental band Rude Pravo with friend and collaborator Stevie Jones. Rude Pravo was formed by Jones and Fowler in 1998, and their occasional collaborators have included the Belgian artist and singer Lucile Desamory, Parsonage creator Janis Murray and the artist Cara Tolmie. Jones is well-known as the bass guitarist of post-rock bands including Maxton Grainger and Peel-favourites El Hombre Trajeado, and also plays guitar, piano and double bass with Malcolm Middleton, Alisdair Roberts, Bill Wells, Norman Blake and Aidan Moffat among others. Rude Pravo's debut release, *The Dust is Flying* (2004) was released on Fowler's SHADAZZ label, as had been *Gold* (2004), the debut 7" single by Correcto's Danny Saunders. One of the aims of the Three Blows project was to illustrate not only the musical outcomes of the Glasgow art scene, but also to show the spirit of co-operation and collaboration that exists between the artists, as they share instruments, knowledge and record and distribute one another's music.[27]

One of the most striking performances of the weekend was by Sarah Kenchington, a musician and sculptor who makes interactive mechanical music contraptions, such as *The Bel Tower*, a metal tower garlanded in crystal glasses which is played using metal ball bearings dispatched down tubes that strike the glasses. She adopts a sculptural approach to music: her instruments are constantly evolving, and the ongoing tinkering and

---

27 Similar intentions underpinned Three Blows most recent project, "Urlibido" (2010), a one-night performance event at Sloans Grand Ballroom, Glasgow by Kim Coleman & Jenny Hogarth, Susie Green, Shelly Nadashi, Kimberley O'Neill, Morag Ross and Cara Tolmie.

adjustment process spills over into her live performances. Kenchington explains that she often deliberately "plays too many, barely controllable, machines at once, creating a complex and dishevelled mix of patterns and sound. It is not so much about the craft of music or instrument making, but a means of gatecrashing the worlds of music and science, in order to obtain a new perspective on human limitations."[28] Kenchington also performs with experimental folk band The Book of Beasts, with Daniel Padden (Volcano the Bear, The One Ensemble) and Shane Connolly (Tattie Toes). In 2006 she established with her partner, Belinda Gilbert Scott, and artist Katy Dove, The Caravan Club, a self-funded residency programme for artists and musicians located in Balfron, on the edge of a dairy farm situated between the Campsie Hills and Loch Lomond. The scheme started with one caravan and has gradually expanded to four, plus additional studio spaces. Kenchington created her mechanical orchestra in a converted pigsty there while Gilbert Scott has a painting studio in an adjacent cowshed. Katy Dove maintains a home in Glasgow but is a regular resident at a caravan on the site where she develops her experimental animations and musical compositions. The twelve artists[29] invited to take part in the residency by Kenchington, Gilbert Scott and Dove used their time to work on scripts, devise impromptu performances, and also (under Kenchington's tutelage) learnt welding, chain-sawing and how to make and play an assortment of musical instruments. Since it began, The Caravan Club has been very significant in developing skills and alliances between artists and musicians in Glasgow, which has led to new collaborative ventures such as the eight-piece Glasgow-based band, Muscles of Joy, who often use improvisation, unconventional musical techniques and self-made instruments and four of whose members are former residents of The Caravan Club: Anne-Marie Copestake, Katy Dove, Leigh Ferguson and Sophie Macpherson.[30]

28  Sarah Kenchington, Three Blows programme notes, (Edinburgh, July, 2008).

29  The artists were: Ann-Marie Copestake, Anna McLauchlan, Barry Burns, Ben Craven, Christopher Deans, Dick Gilbert Scott, Hayley Tompkins, Kate Davis, Leigh Ferguson, Luke Fowler, Mark Vernon and Sophie Macpherson.

30  In November 2008, the work of the artists associated with The Caravan Club was highlighted in an exhibition called Open Field at Glasgow's CCA. Open Field, 22nd November 2008–17th January 2009. http://www.cca-glasgow.com/index.cfm?page=236B7D10-868E-4F86-A306909B378E5655&eventid=161C8422-93FF-1183-8A95171A930BACFF

"A door breaks space in two, splits it, prevents osmosis, imposes a partition. On one side, me and my place, the private, the domestic (a space overfilled with my possessions: my bed, my carpet, my table, my typewriter, my books, my odd copies of the *Nouvelle Revue Française*); on the other side, other people, the world, the public, politics", writes Georges Perec in Species of Spaces and Other Pieces (1974). His words have particular resonance for Mary Mary, a gallery which began in domestic surroundings before opening as a more conventional gallery space in 2006. The gallery has since retained a sense of privacy and interiority, located on the top floor of a winding staircase in a street near the River Clyde, and representing several artists who make understated, process-orientated works, reflecting director Hannah Robinson's interest in artists who employ "a system of remaking and recontextualising which is then left as a trace, a gesture or remnant".[31]

"Although both the project space and the commercial gallery have the same name, in my mind they are very separate entities", says Hannah Robinson of her gallery, which began in a bedroom in a tenement flat eight years ago and now represents thirteen artists from across Europe.[32] Mary Mary began as flat gallery up a close in Bath Street, a five minute walk from Glasgow School of Art. Robinson remembers, "Initially Mary Mary came out of something that we always did at art school – our group of friends always used to hire the Newbery Gallery at the school, or put on group shows in our flats when we were in second and third year at art school. It was always a tradition that if you made something, you made a show, or if your friend made something, you would put their work in a show. Our group of friends included Aleana Egan, Sara Barker, Harriet Tritton, Celia Hempton and Jo Robertson – all of them are still working as artists, and two of them I work with now. There was a really important dialogue between

31  This section pertaining to Mary Mary is adapted from Sarah Lowndes, "Arrival Inside", *Frieze*, Issue 125, September 2009.
32  Hannah Robinson in conversation with the author, 27th January 2010. The gallery artists are: Sara Barker, Karla Black, Ernst Caramelle, Aleana Egan, Nick Evans, Lotte Gertz, Iain Hetherington, Torsten Lauschmann, Lorna Macintyre, Lili Reynaud Dewar, Gerda Scheepers, Alexis Marguerite Teplin and Maximilian Zentz Zlomovitz.

us about our work, which set the scene for wanting to continue that when I left art school. One of the first things that we had done when we were at art school was to put on a group exhibition called Girl Art that included my work, and the work of Harriet Tritton, Sara Barker, Jo Robertson, Celia Hempton and Aleana Egan. I find the title slightly embarrassing now, but at the time it felt quite powerful. I remember us doing this poster for the show with a photo of the six of us on it, and people were writing things on the posters – like we put one up in the lift in the Mackintosh building, and someone wrote on it, 'you're not famous yet, girls'. The exhibition was in Celia's flat on Sauchiehall Street, and for the opening we asked a new local band, Franz Ferdinand, who were friends of ours, to play in one room of the flat while we had the exhibition in the other room, this was in May 2002."[33]

Franz Ferdinand played a set of five songs, including the songs that would be their first two singles, *Darts of Pleasure* and *Take Me Out.* By 2004 Franz Ferdinand would have achieved international acclaim, but Robinson remembers, "at the time they just seemed like another local band, like The Karelia or The Yummy Fur, especially as most of the people in Franz Ferdinand had played in several other bands before. It just seemed like 'oh, it's those guys doing something again.'"[34] What distinguished Franz Ferdinand from the other bands which lead singer Alex Kapranos and drummer Paul Thomson had played in previously was their close connection to the local art scene. Robinson says, "They had very particular links to the art world, in that Bob had been at the Glasgow School of Art. I think Alex and every-one knew it was an important link to have, because you automatically got an audience, and that audience understood the aesthetic idea of what they were doing – it wasn't just a music group, it was a cross-over thing, which was really important."[35] Following their May debut at the Girl Art exhibition, the band then played shows at a number of art events in 2002, appearing at one of Lucy McKenzie's Flourish events in Glasgow, playing at the opening of an flat show called Magnifitat in Edinburgh, and at the opening of the new visual art and music venue The Chateau in Glasgow in

33  Hannah Robinson in conversation with the author, 27th January 2010.
34  Hannah Robinson in conversation with the author, 27th January 2010.
35  Hannah Robinson, in conversation with the author, 27th January 2010.

November that year. On this last occasion Franz Ferdinand had chosen to illuminate their performance with multiple sun beds propped up against the walls – a memorable piece of stagecraft for a band whose suave shirts and ties, narrow strides, pointy boots and neatly combed hair were already inspiring armies of imitators. The following year the band would make their connections to the art world explicit in their 2005 hit *Do You Want To* with the lines, "Well here we are at the Transmission party / I love your friends they're all so arty, oh yeah…"

Transmission's summer and Christmas parties may have been a high point in the social calendar, but for recent graduates the prospect of getting a show in the city's oldest artist-run gallery was something of a remote prospect. Hannah Robinson recalled, "When we graduated [in 2003], at that point Transmission still felt quite far away, felt like a step that was a little bit too far for us when we'd just graduated. Then it became something that we had to do ourselves. Harriet Tritton, Sara Barker and I knew we had this really great flat and we began doing exhibitions there, through a really organic process. It was just the people we knew around us and as it grew over the couple of years we did it, it became a much more curated process, asking people that we didn't know, or having a much more specific idea of what was going to be shown. The exhibitions were held in Harriet's bedroom – there was always a week's install, the Sunday before we would move all of Harriet's stuff – which slowly depleted as the years went on, because she had no room. We'd pack her things away into the other rooms and then we would paint it, put lights in, clear out the hallway and then hold the show that weekend, from the opening on the Friday night until the show closed on Sunday."[36] They called the gallery Mary Mary after feminist pioneer Mary Wollstonecraft and her daughter, the writer Mary Shelley, and in the first year (from 2003 until 2004), Tritton, Barker and Robinson hosted joint shows by Sara Barker and Lotte Gertz, Martin Clark and Rob Churm and Aleana Egan and Lee O'Connor and a solo exhibition by Karla Black.

By 2004, Karla Black had begun to attract critical attention for her

---

36 Hannah Robinson, in conversation with the author, 27th January 2010.

process-based sculptural pieces, often made using familiar domestic materials such as face cream, clothing and flour. Both her "ingredients" and her method – intensive periods spent meticulously creating abstract tableaux – inevitably evoked "feminine" occupations such as baking and nursing. In this exhibition there were two works, the first of which was a large floor piece, *Push Push* (2004), consisting of layers of cardboard, newspaper, paint, water and polythene, shaped into an enormous low-sided tray. It had been built up as if from carefully wound bandages, creating a tactile surface very suggestive of skin. Within this imaginary landscape lay a few emptied-out tubes of steroid ointment. The smears of medicinal cream combined with the painted surface, deliberately spoiling its perfect whiteness. Although previously Black had made public performances, her work now existed as an installation artefact, or as a kind of indirect self-portrait. Black's art was not only concerned with the body; it also spoke to and of the surrounding space. This exhibition, for example, reflected and amplified its setting, in the tenement bedroom that doubled as Mary Mary's gallery space. Walls with painted-over cracks and holes paved with Polyfilla reappeared in the texture of Black's work. In the days she had spent in the space the artist had created images not only of herself but also of the atmosphere of the room.[37]

Apart from the emphasis on process-based work shown by the gallery, such as Black's site-specific and laboriously constructed sculptures and Rob Churm's prolific and mainly monochromatic drawings, one of the most striking things about the new gallery was their hand-drawn posters – rendered on sugar paper with coloured pencils. Robinson remembers, "We did this for the whole first year – me, Harriet and Sara would sit around the table and draw and colour about a hundred posters by hand. We would always pick three colours of pencil and then just sit there for a day and make the posters together. We wanted to make something a bit more distinctive than the photocopied 'DIY' posters and flyers that you saw everywhere, and also this approach made sense with the kind of work we all made, which was process-based and very time-consuming. We all had

37 The section relating to Karla Black's exhibition at Mary Mary is adapted from Sarah Lowndes, "Karla Black", *Frieze*, Issue 89, March 2005.

very different roles and reasons for doing the gallery, but when we made the posters that brought us together and made it more of a creative process, like an extension of making our own work."[38] The elegant hand drawn posters also had a personal quality that seemed to befit an invitation to come to an exhibition in a private home. Refusing the usual cut and paste aesthetic associated with DIY was just one of the ways in which Mary Mary distinguished themselves from more punk-influenced activity – the three founders also went to great lengths to convert their home as much as possible into a neutral, gallery-like setting, with the hallway completely emptied, aside from a visitors' book to record comments, the exhibition space painted white and the bathroom left devoid of all personal effects. Robinson says, "Part of our decision to start running the gallery was to try to offer an alternative to either doing a show in a really rough place, basically in someone's room where they hadn't made any difference to it but there happened to be a work in it – or if you were very lucky you got a show at Transmission. It felt like there was room for another possibility in between those two options. I think we were really keen on the idea that even though you were twenty-one and hadn't had a show before, you could still have a relatively professional environment in which to work. That desire to be professional was really important in all the aspects of what we did, including writing the press release and the hand out for each exhibition. It was much more about the artists than it was about us – it was about creating an environment for them. It wasn't our front room any more – it was their room and their space."[39]

In December 2004 Hannah Robinson opened a new incarnation of Mary Mary in a flat in the East End neighbourhood of Dennistoun, where rents were considerable cheaper than in the city centre and the West End. Robinson remembers, "I deliberately looked for a space that would be similar to Bath Street but larger, because it became really hard moving everything out all the time and living like that. We were having shows every four weeks and it was becoming a bit much. I think also, I had stopped

38  Hannah Robinson, in conversation with the author, 27th January 2010.
39  Hannah Robinson, in conversation with the author, 27th January 2010.

making work at this point, so I knew that this was what I wanted to do, so finding new premises was also about me taking the gallery into my own space. Harry [Harriet Tritton] had left at this point, so it was me and Sara – and Sara was working a lot on her own work [after Mary Mary had been in the new space about six months, Sara Barker would stand aside to concentrate on her own practice.] The decision to move to a flat with a spare room meant that we could have the shows open for a week instead of just a weekend and have more of a specific setting for the work."[40] Robinson shared the flat with art school friend and Franz Ferdinand bass guitarist Bob Hardy, who was away on tour much of the time and so had few objections to Mary Mary-related activity in the flat. One of the first exhibitions was Aleana Egan's *Doldrums* (2005), an installation that used the blue bedroom of the apartment as a space to respond to the writings of the British psycho-analyst DW Winnicott, who had written that the doldrums is a phase in which adolescents "feel futile and in which they have not yet found them-selves."[41] Egan had curtained the window with muslin, overlaid with dyed blue velvet, from which the silhouette of a girl had been cut. Spectators were asked to remain on the threshold of the room, looking in at a room that expressed the mental and physical condition of being in an in-between state.

During that year, Hannah Robinson had been working as an assistant at The Modern Institute, an experience that had developed her interest in translating Mary Mary into a commercial gallery. She remembers, "It had got to the point where the relationships I was having, with the people I work with now, like Karla Black, Aleana Egan, Sara Barker, Nick Evans, were almost like a transient, temporary part of their practice and their life, and then that exchange disappeared and you'd work with someone else. There was never a continuing relationship, no cumulative effect for them or for me either. I'd had really great experiences working with these people, and I thought, there's only so much you can do in a flat, when you only have a show on for a week and you don't work with them. It felt like lot of work for something that ended up feeling a bit empty – you'd close the

40  Hannah Robinson, in conversation with the author, 27th January 2010.
41  DW Winnicott, *The Family and Individual Development* (1968), Routledge Classics, London and New York, 2006, p.122.

door and that was it. By this point, Karla had been in a group show, Like It Matters at CCA (2005) and we had a lot of conversations – it was the first time I started to be involved in what she was doing. Eventually Karla and some of the other artists I'd worked with before said, 'if you start a gallery we will work with you.' I had to relinquish the small amount of SAC funding I'd been receiving in order to set up as a commercial company, but I got two business grants and borrowed money from my mum and dad. I looked for the space for a long time and found somewhere relatively inexpensive to rent. At that beginning stage we just did things really, really cheaply – you paid £10 out, you got £10 back in, it was sort of like that for quite a while. We opened the gallery in April 2006 with a show by Karla Black for Glasgow International, and we also started going to art fairs, which straight away made a big difference to our profile. We couldn't afford to go to any of these fairs at all, but we had to do it. I only sold two or three things, but the majority of what happened the next year happened because of contacts made at those art fairs."[42] Mary Mary now represented the next generation of artists to have emerged in the wake of the Modern Institute and Switchspace founder Sorcha Dallas's eponymous gallery, which she had established in 2004. "Toby Webster gave me some really useful advice at the beginning, and so did Sorcha Dallas", remembers Robinson, "It would be crazy not to have mutally respectful relationships – especially as we are essentially three different generations of people working three different galleries – that is mutually beneficial for everyone and we aren't treading on each other's toes."[43]

One of the first exhibitions at Robinson's new space in Dixon Street was by Torsten Lauschmann (b.1970), the German-born, Glasgow-based artist who had originally trained as a photographer, but who also performed as a VJ and solar-powered busker known as Slender Whiteman, designed software and websites, and had made an elegiac film about the phenomenological investigation of the street lamp's function in consumer society (*Misshapen Pearl*, 2003). His Internet campaign *World Jump Day* (2005),

42  Hannah Robinson, in conversation with the author, 27th January 2010.
43  Hannah Robinson, in conversation with the author, 27th January 2010.

conducted under the moniker Professor Hans Peter Niesward from the Institute for Gravitational Physics in Munich, was an attempt to reverse global warming through a synchronised single jump across the globe. The scope of his work could also telescope from the global to the domestic – most poignantly in *Mother and Child* (2004), the extremely intimate film he made of his partner (the artist Cathy Wilkes) and their infant son while they slept.[44] A more recent work, Digital Clock (Growing Zeros) (2010) consisted of a looped 24 hour projection of a digital clock, the display of which matched "correct time" to within a two minute margin, although the red numerals were changed manually by visible hands. Lauschmann's clock recast the inexorable march of time as a process of altering and adjusting the component parts of the numbers hundreds of times: time was no longer automatic and relentless but rendered contingent and adjustable.

## SWG3, GLASGOW SCULPTURE STUDIOS AND LOWSALT

Besides Mary Mary, one of the other artist-run spaces that was starting to happen in 2004 was Studio Warehouse Glasgow (SWG3), a complex of music and art studios, a gallery and a nightclub space located at the end of Eastvale Place in the West End neighbourhood of Finnieston. Muttley, the director of SWG3 remembers, "The project began in 2003 when the opportunity arose to take on the first and second floors of the building at 100 Eastvale Place. The first floor had been running as an illegal party venue every Friday and Saturday night for a few years. It was now well on the police radar and regularly got shut down by the authorities. I started the project with George Matheson, who is a sound engineer and source of PA for many of the underground parties throughout Glasgow and beyond – his PA was already in the building and we wanted to develop an alternative space for artists and musicians to produce new work, exhibit and perform. Music was always as important as visual art and although we are now more advanced with our artist studios and gallery program there have always been rehearsal studios, live music nights and parties here. George remembers

---

44  The section pertaining to Torsten Lauschmann was adapted from Sarah Lowndes, "Torsten Lauschmann", *Frieze*, Issue 103, November–December 2006.

there was one infamous fancy dress party where nobody believed it was the 'real police' and the decision was made by the officers that it would be more trouble than it was worth to try and clear the building."[45]

He continues, "Before moving into the building I was organising small exhibitions and events, as I realised at art school I was far more interested in supporting the work of other artists than developing my own practice. By doing so I quickly realised there was demand for more studios and different studios in different parts of the city. I was obviously aware of the Chateau and the energy around it was very exciting but I wanted to develop a business at the same time as creating space and opportunities. The space developed slowly and organically, usually with some kind of party to punctuate the development stages. I lost count of how many skip parties we had in the first year but we filled fifteen forty-yard skips with rubbish. There were electricity parties for about a year and a half as that's how long it took to pay the bills, but for the most part everyone volunteered happily. By this stage Gary Mackay and Matthew Thomas had also become very involved with the project. I think eight artists moved into the 'studios' in February 2004 after a graffiti event was held on the studio walls, the wood was donated by Norbord. There were between 4 and 8 buckets in each studio collecting drips from a neglected flat roof. That summer we re-felted the 15,000 sq ft roof and continued building more studios and a photography studio. I set up Clydeside Initiative for Arts Ltd as a vehicle to run the building in 2005, by which time there were about twenty artists and a couple of bands based there and the building was being used for lifestyle/fashion shoots, music videos and a variety of other interesting projects. In 2005 we received funding from Scotland UnLtd that enabled us to buy a lot of the raw materials for building the studios. Their ability to support projects at an early stage in development was so refreshing compared to the signals we received from so many other public sector bodies."[46]

The emergence of SWG3 has been accompanied by a number of other

45  Muttley, in response to questions sent by the author, February 2006.
46  Muttley, in response to questions sent by the author, February 2006.

interesting projects that have regenerated the Finnieston area – such as Craig Tannock's vegan bar The 78 (formerly known as Stereo) on Kelvinhaugh Street[47], *The Wire* contributor David Keenan and singer Heather Leigh Murray's Volcanic Tongue record shop just off Argyle Street, and the arrival of Glasgow Sculpture Studios (GSS), which moved from its base at The Briggait to 145 Kelvinhaugh Street in 2008. GSS has subsequently become a centre for research, production, and presentation, which offers various residencies, including research and production residencies, beneficiaries of which have so far included AHM (Sam Ainsley, David Harding, Sandy Moffat) and the American sculptor, essayist and poet Jimmie Durham. In March 2009, after hosting many successful nomadic exhibitions, the contemporary art gallery Washington Garcia, which is run by artist-organiser Kendall Koppe, announced that they too were moving to "the up and coming Eastvale district of the city, cementing the area's reputation as the home of cutting edge contemporary art in Glasgow."[48]

Another significant addition to the local grassroots scene in the G3 postcode is Lowsalt gallery, which began operations in a shuttered garage space off Renfrew Street in 2006, but has perhaps become better known for their imaginative offsite projects, such as Lowsalt Presents: *The Secret Agent* by Raydale Dower & Judd Brucke (2008), a series of experimental street performances based on a vintage anarchist plot. Combining visual art, puppetry, projections and a musical score, a "chorus" of artists led the audience on a walking tour through alleyways and into private derelict grounds; beginning at Mr Verloc's shop on Renfield Lane and ending in Glasgow's oldest bar and restaurant, Sloans. Lowsalt is a non-profit organisation and artist-run gallery, run by Krisdy Shindler and Rebecca Anson and "positioned at the crossing of DIY gallery culture and institutional networks in Glasgow. Lowsalt provides a platform whereby a multitude of contemporary artists can collaborate, produce and exhibit their work in unique and alternative environments."[49] For Glasgow

---

47  Since the first edition of *Social Sculpture* was published, Tannock has opened another two live music venues in Glasgow: Stereo on Renfield Lane and The Flying Duck, on the site of his former recording studio/bar premises, The Apollo.
48  http://www.washingtongarciagallery.com/news.html
49  http://www.lowsalt.org.uk/

International 2010, Lowsalt gallery have transformed half an acre of scrubland in the Finneston area of the city into a temporary archaic sculpture park for Glasgow International Festival of Visual Art 2010. The gothic wrought-iron gates to the park, *Serifs in Rust* (2010) were designed by Judd Brucke and lead to a half-wilderness inhabited with "sculptural life forms inspired by the pre-Darwin evolutionary essay 'Vestiges of the Natural History of Creation' (1844) including 'Pilzexperimentalar chitektur', a metal structure supporting a sprouting outcrop of live shitake and lion-mane fungi propagated by artist Alex Gross."

## THE COMMON GUILD

In 2006, The Modern Institute took the decision to relinquish the moderate amount of public funding it was receiving, and to channel that funding into a new non-profit project in Glasgow, which would be helmed by Katrina Brown, who was then curator and deputy director of Dundee Contemporary Arts. During her nine years as curator of DCA, Brown's approach had been characterised by ambitious projects such as the first UK solo shows by Christopher Wool and Miroslaw Balka and major solo exhibitions by Scotland-based artists including Christine Borland, Roderick Buchanan, Simon Starling, Claire Barclay and Richard Wright.[50]

Katrina Brown says, "The Common Guild really grew out of one of the original intentions of The Modern Institute – to effect high quality, international programming in Glasgow. As TMI became increasingly successful in and focused on its role as a commercial entity, the scope for something new to fill that gap became available and The Common Guild came into being. The guiding principle was to establish something where programme would take precedence over premises: allowing the organisation to work in and with different spaces and locations as suited artists' projects. I started working on it at the very end of 2006 and started in earnest, full-time when I finally left DCA in February 2007."[51] The Common Guild (TCG) originally set up shop in an office in Robertson Street, which was "lent to us from The

50  Brown's successor at Dundee Contemporary Art was Judith Winter, former curator at MiMA, Middlesbrough, with assistant curator Graham Domke, formerly of Edinburgh's Inverleith House.
51  Katrina Brown, in response to questions sent by the author, February 2010.

Modern Institute, which was a fantastic help in getting started. Our first bit of programming was Martin Creed's 'Words and Music' show which we presented at the Royal Scottish Academy of Music and Drama (RSAMD) in March 2007."[52] Quite early on Brown had articulated the desire to have a "three-pronged" approach to each of the artists The Common Guild worked with: for example, to work with them on an exhibition, a live event and a publication. She says, "It seemed to me that if we escaped the 'filling a building' model of programming to pursue this idea of programme first – and a range that we have since begun to summarise as 'projects/events/ exhibitions' – that we might work with the same artist in different ways over a period of time. Martin Creed's a good example of this – we did the stage show in early 2007 and then in 2010 we have made a focused gallery exhibition at [TCG's current exhibition space] Woodlands Terrace, so covering both sides of his practice. This way of working seemed appropriate and desirable to be honest, partly to give audiences a better chance of really getting an artist's practice than that offered by the 'one hit' and partly a reflection of the extent to which so many artists do not simply stick to one format or outlet for their work now: working on public projects alongside autonomous sculptures or films or events."[53]

At the same time the organisation had other adjunct events, such as the regular talks given to accompany The Common Guild's exhibition programme, by Glasgow University's Dr. Dominic Paterson, and another series of talks, entitled Detours, "introducing views from elsewhere by leaders in the visual arts. Speakers discuss the relationship between practice and context: how institutions and professional practice develop in response to specific situations, both geographic and cultural."[54] Speakers so far have included Jenni Lomax, Director of the Camden Art Centre, Vasif Kortun, director of Platform Garanti Contemporary Art Center in Istanbul, Nicolaus Schafhausen, Director of the Witte de With Center for Contemporary Art in Rotterdam and Richard Flood, Chief Curator at the recently re-opened New Museum in New York, amongst others. Brown says, "The 'Detours'

---

52  Katrina Brown, in response to questions sent by the author, February 2010.
53  Katrina Brown, in response to questions sent by the author, February 2010.
54  http://www.thecommonguild.org.uk/category/events/

project was devised really to run in parallel with our development – to fuel awareness of and appreciation of the possibilities for an art institution now. What shape might it take? How might it be structured? How might its programme relate to its context? These are the kind of questions we have asked speakers to address. We try to do talks with all of the exhibitions now – it seems really important to hold on to the thinking around the shows as much as the shows themselves and these talks are one way to do that."[55]

In late 2007, Brown's thoughts turned to finding a space for programming exhibitions in Glasgow. She remembers, "I think it was late 2007 and Douglas [Gordon, an old friend and one-time flatmate of Brown's] and I were out one night and talking about life and work and all, and at one point I was saying that I hoped to find a space where The Common Guild might do some shows and Douglas simply suggested using part of his building at Woodlands Terrace, which was largely unused. When Douglas and I talked about The Common Guild making use of his building – we saw that it was in almost every respect just like all those definitive "let's put the show on in the barn' self-initiated projects in Glasgow – by James Thornhill and Cathy Wilkes' great "Dalriada" project, for example – but just that now it's on a different scale. Still independent. Still trying to talk about ideas. Still fundamentally internationalist but totally rooted in Glasgow. Initially we saw it as a one-year project, but we didn't really have the resources immediately to put together a back-to-back programme so we decided to play it by ear and see how it worked. Fortunately it did. The first show we put together for the space was a group show called Always Begins By Degrees – a title borrowed from a work by Roni Horn (borrowed in turn from Emily Dickinson) which was included in the show. It was kind of an agenda-setting show in a modest way, around text, or word and image, which included a video of a performance by Marcel Broodthaers. Since then we've concentrated on solo shows and have really enjoyed seeing how each artist in turn (Adel Abdessemed, Spencer Finch, Roni Horn, Mircea Cantor, Martin Creed) has taken on and relished the very specific nature of the space."[56]

55  Katrina Brown, in response to questions sent by the author, February 2010.
56  Katrina Brown, in response to questions sent by the author, February 2010.

The space in question is a vast Victorian townhouse overlooking Kelvingrove Park, with silver backed mirrors, wooden floors, original fireplaces and a beautiful winding central staircase. The view, from the first floor sitting room of this temporary gallery, as Moira Jeffrey has written, "is a vision of a tiered and transforming Glasgow from the peak of its Victorian mercantile past."[57] The building even boasts a real library, custom designed by Glasgow-based artist Andrew Miller to house some of Gordon's books, which visitors to The Common Guild can browse alongside artist catalogues and exhibition information. Katrina Brown says, "We eventually moved the office from Robertson Street to Woodlands Terrace in April 2009, after we had decided that we would run the exhibition programme there for more than the year originally envisaged. As the staff team grew to three [Brown, Caroline Kirsop and Kitty Anderson] – we had outgrown the room at Robertson Street and it just made sense form every point of view to be closer to our exhibitions."[58]

Brown has also been mentoring Ben Harman, curator at the Gallery of Modern Art, with regards to a series of new GoMA acquisitions. Brown explains, "The Art Fund announced its Art Fund International scheme in 2007 and invited museums based outwith London or Edinburgh to bid for one of 5 pots of £1million to develop contemporary international collecting. They had devised it really to address what they saw as a dearth of international collecting outwith the capitals. Each applicant museum was obliged by the Art Fund to seek and secure an independent, curatorial partner on the bid and GoMA approached The Common Guild. Our bid was successful and it was announced in November 2007. The scheme will run for five years until the end of 2012.

"The partnerships were also encouraged to devise a specific focus for their collection – a 'theme' if you like. We resisted the idea of a 'theme' but instead suggested that the collection could be seen to help build an international context for the work of Glasgow-based artists that GoMA had begun to acquire. Over and above this, our focus is broadly on works that

57  Moira Jeffrey, "Home is where the art is", *Scotland on Sunday*, 9th March 2008, http://scotlandonsunday.scotsman.com/sos-review/Home-is-where-the-art.3857093.jp
58  Katrina Brown, in response to questions sent by the author, February 2010.

employ 'documentary media' in the broadest sense – film, video and photography, but also drawing and text. The timing of the scheme means it has benefitted from the 'slowing down' in the art market since 2008, with much better deals to be had. To date we have acquired works by Lothar Baumgarten – who showed at Transmission in Glasgow in 1994 – Matthew Buckingham, Peter Hujar, Emily Jacir, Jenny Holzer, Roni Horn and Fiona Tan. The works become part of the Glasgow Museums collection but are paid for entirely by the Art Fund."[59]

## TRAMWAY

Some of the most notable recent developments in the Glasgow art scene of the last seven years have taken place south of the river. When the first edition of *Social Sculpture* was published in 2003, the future of one of the city's most important visual art spaces, Tramway, was in doubt. During that year city council plans to close the venue's visual art space and transfer it to Scottish Ballet as part of their capital Lottery-funded relocation to the building reached the press. After these proposals were brought to public attention, Tramway visual arts officer Alexia Holt was suspended from her post and members of the local visual art community, including Professor Klaus Jung, head of Fine Art at the Glasgow School of Art, Richard Calvocoressi, director of the National Gallery of Modern Art, DCA curator Katrina Brown, CCA Director Graham McKenzie and Toby Webster, director of The Modern Institute called for a "genuine, in depth consultation process" into the future of the visual arts in the city and condemned Holt's continuing suspension as "unjustified".[60] Subsequently the plans to transfer the entire building to Scottish Ballet were revised to allow Tramway and Scottish Ballet to co-exist within the same building. Holt moved on to become director of Cove Park[61] and Tramway appointed Lorraine Wilson,

---

59  Katrina Brown, in response to questions sent by the author, February 2010.

60  Phil Miller, "Altered Tramway plan 'not a solution'", *The Herald*, 19th November, 2003.

61  Cove Park is an international centre based on Scotland's Rosneath peninsula (about an hour away from Glasgow) which offers an annual programme of residencies for the arts and creative industries. Founded in 1999 by Eileen and Peter Jacobs, Cove Park's annual programme of residencies enables national and international artists, working in all art forms, to undertake research and develop new projects. The residencies enable research and the development of new work in a supportive environment and are complemented by a programme of discussions and events. Previous residents include: Will Bradley, Luke Collins, Kate Davis, Graham Gussin, Ilana Halperin, Dan Kidner, Anja Kirschner, Michael Marriott, Duncan Marquiss, Olivia Plender, Mark Sladen, Polly Staple and Simon Starling. http://www.covepark.org/

former co-ordinator at Glasgow Sculpture Studios, as their new Visual Arts Officer.

Despite the turbulent events surrounding the threat of closure, 2003 was also the year in which Tramway began to move in a new and inspiring direction, when in June that year Glasgow-based environmental arts charity NVA's The Hidden Gardens opened at the rear of the building, on what had once been a debris field of bricks and rubble left from the partial demolition of the building in 1987–88. '"Scotland's first sanctuary garden dedicated to peace"[62] began as a Tramway open commission to NVA, and was developed through a collaborative design process that involved landscape architects City Design Co-operative, a team of international artists (including Gerry Loose, Alec Finlay, Stephen Skrynka, Julie Brook and Divya Bhatia) and the local community in Pollokshields.[63] Since opening, The Hidden Gardens has attracted more than 70,000 visitors and has also expanded its remit by opening a community resource, The Boilerhouse, within the gardens to extend its ongoing community activities programme. Despite this positive addition to Tramway's portfolio of activity, the visual arts programme had lost much of the momentum and profile associated with the venue's early '90s heyday, when exhibitions such as Douglas Gordon's 24 Hour Psycho (1993) had animated the largest exhibition space in Europe.

In 2008 Sarah Munro, who had been Director of Edinburgh's Collective Gallery since 1995, was appointed as Tramway's new General Manager.[64] At the Collective, Munro had commissioned a number of highly acclaimed projects including Mike Nelson's "shredded room", In Memory Of HP Lovecraft (1999) and implemented a number of important schemes, including New Work Scotland, which she established in 1999 as a platform for emergent artists and the One Mile project, which began in 2006, and was a three-year programme of public engagement and participation focused on

---

62  http://www.nva.org.uk/past-projects/the+hidden+gardens/
63  http://www.thehiddengardens.org.uk/
64  Munro's successor at The Collective Gallery was Kate Gray, who was the lead artist on the One Mile project from 2006–2009. Gray has worked since her appointment to increase the opportunities that the gallery offers to emergent curators (through the New Work Scotland programme) and to support off-site projects Rosamund West, "Happy Birthday New Work Scotland", The Skinny, 3rd December 2009, http://www.theskinny.co.uk/article/98152-happy-birthday-new-work-scotland

the communities living within a mile of The Collective's city centre location, described as "agenda setting" by the Paul Hamlyn Foundation.[65] Since her appointment, Munro has provided the leadership that the venue had lacked since the departure of Charles Esche, working together with Lorraine Wilson and performance programmer Claire Jackson to deliver a series of ambitious and critically acclaimed exhibitions and events including the European premiere of Cerith Wyn Evans and Throbbing Gristle's collaborative exhibition A=P=P=A=R=I=T=I=O=N (2009) and Throbbing Gristle's first ever live appearance in Scotland, Apparition Foretold, which took place on the hot summer night of the MFA degree show, at Tramway on 17th June 2009. Munro's other coups include staging Glasgow-based artist and 2008 Jarman Prize nominee Duncan Campbell's first major solo show in Scotland, Make It New, John (2010), which charted the (mis)-fortunes of the Delorean motor company in Northern Ireland, and hosting the European premiere of Phil Collins' exploration of globalisation through karaoke, The World Won't Listen (2009).

Munro said in an interview with Moira Jeffrey, published shortly after taking up the post, "I'm very passionate about public space and the public sphere; what you have here is one of the largest public spaces in Glasgow. [...] You're a custodian in this job, everybody has their own memories of the place, and often it's about the earliest days and works. My job is to take these strengths and start asking about the next twenty years, looking at what the role of an arts centre might be in the 21st century. We need to look at who we make work for, and how we engage with them. I'm not simply talking about adding on audience development or education, we need to really drill down into what we do and why. How do we make this a place for the public?"[66] Since joining Tramway in 2008, Munro has led the organisation through difficult times while re-visioning the visual arts programme and placing the relationship and engagement with the public

---

65  "One Mile is a series of collaborations between artists and groups of people who live or work within the one mile radius of the Collective Gallery. From t-shirt design to performance art, the work has involved groups from the women's circle at the local mosque, to Scottish Widows PLC, to recent Polish immigrants at the Cowgate Centre. In essence perhaps, One Mile suggests strategies to map how different communities and ideas exist within the same space and time within a given area of a city." Ruth Barker, "Between The Lines Of Maps: Wonders, Dragons, And The Philosophy Of One Mile", The Collective Gallery, *One Mile Newspaper*, Issue 2, 2007.

66  Moira Jeffrey, "All aboard the Tramway – Sarah Munro interview", *Scotland on Sunday*, 25th May 2008.

at the centre of the organisation's thinking. This strategy resulted in an increase in audience figures of nearly 150%.[67]

## CCA

The last five years have seen some equally tumultuous events unfold at one of Glasgow's other main public visual art venues, the Centre for Contemporary Art on Sauchiehall Street. When the first edition of *Social Sculpture* was published in 2003, there was a feeling locally that CCA had lost its way – then-director Graham McKenzie had decided that following the £7.5 million Lottery Capital development funded refurbishment of the building, there should be only four visual art exhibitions a year at CCA, and that the organisation should refocus on "tourism and corporate business".[68] Besides complaints from members of the local visual arts community regarding the new café being larger than the exhibition space, there had also been a number of issues around the visual art programming at CCA, with visual arts officer Patricia Fleming being made redundant in 2000. The refurbished building re-opened in October 2001, with Vivienne Gaskin being appointed as Head of Artistic Programme, and Fleming reinstated (following union negotiations) as her assistant. Fleming resigned in 2002, followed by Gaskin's resignation in 2003. It was widely reported in the local press that the building was failing to bring in the projected profits from tourism and corporate business.

The curator and writer Francis McKee had held the post of Head of Programme at CCA between 1997 and 1999, but returned in 2001 in the part-time post of Head of Digital and New Media. Throughout 2002, McKee had been touring Scotland with curator Kay Pallister, making studio visits to artists whose work they were considering for inclusion in the first ever Scottish Pavilion, to be launched at the 2003 Venice Biennale with the group show Zenomap, which showcased new works by Glasgow-based artists Claire Barclay, Jim Lambie and Simon Starling. Zenomap was the

---

67 "Women to Watch", Cultural Leadership Programme, http://www.culturalleadership.org.uk/women-to-watch/w2w/sarah-munro/
68 Graham McKenzie, in conversation with the author, July 2001.

first installment of (to date) four exhibitions in Venice, each curated by a different team, which have boosted the international reputation of artists from Scotland.[69]

When Graham McKenzie resigned at the end of 2005, to run Huddersfield Contemporary Music Festival, McKee was asked to take over running the building in the run up to Ross Sinclair's exhibition Real Life Painting, due in open in April 2006 as part of the second year of the Glasgow International Art Festival (GI), which McKee was also directing for the second year. Glasgow International had grown out of Real Art Weekend (RAW), the contemporary wing of the Glasgow Art Fair. McKee remembers, "I was the first director – I think no-one else wanted it. This often happens to me [laughs]. I know other people were approached before me and they said no, and part of the reason for their refusal was because it was connected to this Real Art Weekend, which ran during April to showcase more contemporary and innovative art, as an offshoot from the Glasgow Art Fair.[70] Glasgow International was originally discussed as an extension of this RAW weekend – which sounds horrible, doesn't it? A lot of chafing going on [laughs]. Being a bit ruthless, I felt that we would never establish a credible festival if it was connected to the Art Fair – for example we spoke to The Modern Institute and they weren't interested in being involved in it if it was just an extension of the Art Fair. So we distanced ourselves from it entirely and became a separate entity and we had separate advertising and separate marketing. This change in direction didn't necessarily go down that well [with certain people] but the city supported it. The first year there was very little money, £40,000, and the second year

---

69  Zenomap was followed by exhibitions curated by different individuals every two years: Selective Memory (2005) featured the work of Cathy Wilkes, Alex Pollard, Joanne Tatham and Tom O'Sullivan; Scotland & Venice (2007) included works by Charles Avery, Henry Coombes, Louise Hopkins, Rosalind Nashashibi, Lucy Skaer and Tony Swain; and in 2009 Martin Boyce was invited to make a solo exhibition, No Reflections (2009) which was presented at that year's biennale and then travelled subsequently to Dundee Contemporary Arts in winter that year.

70  The Glasgow Art Fair was established in 1996, and describes itself as "the most prestigious contemporary art fair in the UK outside London", but it promotes more traditional Scottish commercial art galleries like Cyril Gerber Fine Art & Compass Gallery and Roger Billcliffe Gallery – the younger commercal galleries in the city, The Modern Institute, Sorcha Dallas and Mary Mary, do not show at the art fair, which was part of the reasoning for starting the RAW weekend, as a means of involving these more cutting edge contemporary art organisations in the Glasgow Art Fair. On April 5th, 2010 The Herald and The Scotsman both reported that Pete Irvine, the director of the Glasgow Art Fair had stepped down, saying he would stand aside after fifteen years of being involved at the event. Both newspapers reported that Irvine's departure came amid concerns of a decline in quality at the festival.

was slightly bigger with a budget of £70,000, so everybody was working from goodwill.

"There was no team – the first year it was just me, and the second year there was just me and Claire Jackson working for three months in the lead up to it. I remember on the opening day of the first GI I was running furiously down the street trying to find a taxi to go and pick up plastic tops for cases from the Print Studio, because there was no-one else who could get them and the whole thing was going to open in two hours time. Really it worked upon the basis that there were people doing interesting projects in Glasgow all year round, so we used the festival to bring everyone together. Maybe the one thing that people didn't have at that time was a sense of overview – so the festival helped to build connections between organisations like the Collins Gallery and Transmission and the Hunterian Art Gallery, who perhaps hadn't been that aware of each other's activities up until that point."[71]

In the meantime, McKee was also trying to get to grips with his new role running the CCA. He remembers, "Initially I thought I was just coming in to look after Ross Sinclair's show, while they were advertising the post. In the time leading up to Graham McKenzie's departure there had been a gradual decline in terms of budget and a curatorial decline, and also the new building had had an impact in that several people had moved on to other posts during the renovations and the period immediately after we re-opened, including Patricia Fleming, Vivienne Gaskin, Caroline Woodley, Caroline Kirsop [who had been the Gallery Manager], and Rebecca Shatwell [who had been the Education Programmer] – so there was a general exodus from the building. Following Vivienne Gaskin's departure in 2003, we had assembled a committee of curators which comprised John Calcutt, Ele Carpenter, Tim Nunn and myself, but it was more a question of recommending shows – there were people saying 'I've seen a good show here', or 'How about showing that artist?'. It was makeshift and had no coherence because there was no overall curator, and there was no artistic director. However, there were some good shows – Ele Carpenter's RISK:

71  Francis McKee, in conversation with the author, March 2010.

Creative Action in Political Culture (2005)[72] was the best example of that, but there was no coherence to the programme and we all felt that."

Curatorial issues were not the greatest challenges facing CCA, as McKee was soon to discover. He explains, "What had happened with the budget, was that we had been running many different strands of programme but there wasn't enough money to do this. CCA was always borrowing ahead all the time from future grants, and building up greater and greater debts. So when I came in, there seemed to be little awareness of that but there was a great deal of debt, a great set of creditors hounding at the door, and most people had left or were on the verge of leaving. I then went to the city and the arts council and said, this place is bankrupt. And we talked to the bank manager and the bank manager knew the true situation. The board was dissolved. The arts council and the city put one member each on a new board, Richard Holloway, chair of SAC at that time became chair of our board during this transition and Bill English, who was ex-Head of Finance at Glasgow City Council, now retired, also joined. In a sense there were two representatives, one from the city and one from the arts council to say, this is our building, we support this. Graham Berry, who was the head of the arts council, also joined our board to support the organisation through this period. He had a really positive attitude, citing the original Third Eye Centre and early CCA as models, acknowledging that an adventurous spirit was part of the mission. The reconstituting work was done by people like SAC's Head of Visual Art, Amanda Catto, who became my direct line manager. We became a wholly owned subsidiary of the arts council, and we still are, although SAC have kept a deliberate distance in order to allow an arm's length situation to operate. The first two years, from 2006–2008, the arts council took us under their wing because that protected us from bankruptcy and gave us the opportunity to stabilise. Even our finance people had left, so with the arts council we were able to go through all the

---

72  Over 30 artists working across art and activism took part in RISK including: Aisling O'Beirn, The Atlas Group, Doug Aubrey, Ross Birrell, Jota Castro, Ruth Catlow, Clandestine Insurgent Rebel Clown Army, Critical Art Ensemble, Andrea Crociani, Ghazel, Gregory Green, Jordan and Hewitt, ICOLS, Martin Krenn, Torsten Lauschmann, Maris, Harold Offeh, Josh On, Platform, Jai Redman, Oliver Ressler and David Thorne, Kate Rich, Jackie Salloum, UHC, Yes Men, Vacuum Cleaner and *Variant*. http://crumb.sunderland.ac.uk/~ele/risk/riskwebsitenov06/risk.htm Francis McKee, in conversation with the author, March 2010.

bank statements and figure out what the real situation was and start rectifying that by paying creditors and working off the debt. I was on weekly budgets for the first 6 months and gradually we got to 3 month budgets and then up to 6 months. The initial discussions were very stark: 'Should we just shut this building because it isn't really working?' From that we decided to keep the building open for GI for Ross Sinclair's show and then see what we could do with it later.

"Before that it had been so precious, because it was a Lottery building and had cost £7.5million. Afterwards, the arts council said, we may have to shut the building anyway, so do what you want with it, experiment – if it's not working, and if various rooms aren't working, you can change it, we've nothing to lose. Part of the reason why the CCA wasn't working was that there was too much 'posh' empty space like the café, and the one thing that people really hated about the new CCA was that there wasn't enough space for art. After the renovations the galleries had grown smaller, art seemed to have taken a back seat to everything else – so we converted half of the upstairs offices into new art space for the Creative Lab programme, which offers twelve residencies a year, mostly for live art but for visual art as well. We also took on Intermedia gallery in 2006, offering them space within the building but on the understanding it would be programmed separately from us. Intermedia shows last for two weeks, so that brought a constant stream of young artists and their friends into the building – we hoped that they would start to feel some ownership of CCA. Inviting Intermedia in was also about breaking up the curatorship, so there wasn't one sole voice saying, 'everything here is chosen by me'. Instead there was a whole multitude of voices and different routes into the building and its associated programmes. So we agreed that if we were going to keep the building open, and spend public money on the building, then momentum had to be the criteria. Previously there was this Lottery business plan in which the building would make loads of money, and it would have all the income streams from the café and the cinema – but the cinema has never made a penny and the café, if it made enough, just made enough to cover itself.

"There was a separate commercial company that was running the café and haemorrhaging money, which was affecting the rest of the organisation

– so within the first two weeks we got the city's catering company, Encore (now Cordia) to take over the café – they came in overnight and kept the menus and the staff. Actually that turned out to be a great working relationship because they were developing the new café at Kelvingrove Art Gallery and Museum[73], and they said, we can learn from you – and the new café at Kelvingrove was modelled on CCA café. They also took over the bar – it had possibly been a contentious decision to appoint Jorge Pardo to design the bar in the first place, and as it got more run down over the years, that animosity grew. We kept emailing Jorge Pardo's studio about renovating the bar but they never replied, and the furniture was getting trashed and people were beginning to hate it – so in the end we took a decision to renovate it to make the place look plain, modern and fresh.

"At the time, I was working on research about Open Source, and ideologies rooted in the hippy idea of giving things away for free. One of things that killed the old CCA was saying, we have a cinema but if you want to use it we'll charge you £600 a night. That didn't work in Glasgow because people didn't have £600 to rent a cinema for the night to screen something where they would make a loss if only seven people turned up. So we offered the use of the cinema for free to groups like The Magic Lantern and Camcorder Guerillas, who began to host once a month events. They had a good sense of public programming and where to get the material they wanted to show, and they had their own audiences, so we were getting programme and audience, and also moving towards a more communal and less egotistical way of doing things, by facilitating their programme."[74] In 2008 McKee offered independent publishers Martin Vincent and Sapna Agarwal the opportunity to operate a rent-free outlet with paid utilities for their Aye-Aye Bookshop[75] in the foyer of CCA, a move

73  Kelvingrove Art Gallery and Museum was closed for a complete restoration of the building and radical redisplay of objects between spring 2003 and summer 2006. The £35million renovation project created thousands of square metres of new display space through the removal of offices and workshops, the opening up of the basement, and the use of off-site storage facilities and increased the number of objects on display by 50%. Kelvingrove was already the most popular museum outside London, but in the year following the renovations, the building had over three million visitors.

74  Francis McKee, in conversation with the author, March 2010.

75  In 2006 Martin Vincent moved to Glasgow from Manchester, where he had been co-director of the International 3 gallery and i3 Publications. In collaboration with Sapna Agarwal he opened Aye-Aye Book Depot – a year-long independent bookshop/project space at Glasgow Sculpture Studios (2006–2007) which they ran alongside the Aye-Aye Sorting Office at Islington Mill, Salford, to sell and publish books by David Mackintosh, Rachel Goodyear, Edwina fitzPatrick and Esther Shalev-Gerz.

that "gave the CCA a bookshop, made the place feel more human, and supported the work of people who might otherwise have struggled to make a profit."[76] Of the many interesting projects that were unfolding in CCA around this period, McKee remembers that, "Abraham Cruzvillegas's exhibition Autoconstrucción (2008) was important because he consolidated so many of the changes that had taken place in CCA and his work went right across so many disciplines. His show came out of a six-month Henry Moore Fellowship at Cove Park to enable the production of a new body of work."[77]

At a talk concerning his exhibition Autoconstrucción (Autoconstruction) at CCA, the Mexican artist Abraham Cruzvillegas played a recording of Woody Guthrie's song "This Land is Your Land" (1940). Its closing lines describe how exclusion and poverty can be reconsidered as an opportunity: "As I went walking, I saw a sign there / And on the sign there, It said 'Private Property' / But on the other side, it didn't say nothing! / That side was made for you and me." The relevance of Guthrie's words to Cruzvillegas' life and work was made apparent in the exhibition, which he explains "was inspired by my parents' house in Mexico City, an improvised and almost useless place made without budget, ideas or plans: chaotic, ugly and definitely unfinished". Cruzvillegas was brought up in a neighbourhood called Ajusco. Built on volcanic rock, the area was previously believed to be too difficult to inhabit. It was settled by rural immigrants from the south, who constructed their homes gradually and in collaboration with neighbours. This background informed Cruzvillegas' new works, made over a period of six months in Scotland, while the artist alternated between the rural setting of the Cove Park arts residency programme and the city-centre terrain surrounding Glasgow's Centre for Contemporary Arts. On the walls of CCA's largest gallery Cruzvillegas had handwritten the lyrics of eighteen songs he wrote while in Scotland about his formative experiences in Ajusco. Eighteen electronic, post-rock, folk and punk versions of these songs by

76 Francis McKee, in conversation with the author, March 2010.
77 Francis McKee, in conversation with the author, March 2010. This relationship between CCA and Cove Park continued in October 2009, when Dutch artists Liesbeth Bik and Jos van der Pol's exhibition opened at CCA, the culmination of a two-month residency at Cove Park.

Glasgow bands were broadcast by Cruzvillegas through the streets and squares of the city during his stay, using a mobile sound system inspired by those of Mexico and Jamaica. AC Mobile (2008) was made in collaboration with John O'Hara of The Common Wheel project, which provides bicycle repair work for people suffering from mental illness in Glasgow. This mobile sculpture chimed with the history of do-it-yourself activity in Glasgow, as did Big Heat's version of Cruzvillegas' song, "Aprons", which quoted Mexican revolutionary Emiliano Zapata: "It is better to die on your feet than to live on your knees".[78]

McKee remembers that behind the scenes, there were ongoing discussions with the city and with SAC about giving the space away for free – "initially there was some resistance and questions about why we weren't trying to increase profitability, but then gradually it was recognised that as long as we weren't losing money, and we were gaining momentum they were willing to run with that, accept it and enshrine it in policy. That was a big moment, I think, as they began to see it as a different kind of model – it had to be proven but they were very open and let it happen. The new board really helped too – we advertised publicly for new board members, we were one of the first public arts organisations to do that, and we got people who we would never have found otherwise – they include a lawyer, a curator and writer, a businessman, an English professor and someone who works in the NHS, all of whom are very hands on and there for a purpose."[79]

The second year of Glasgow International in 2006 had seen an increase in the level of public funding for the festival and with it, increased ambition and commissioning opportunities. Of the people who attended the 2006 festival, 27% came from outside Glasgow but within Scotland, 20% came from the "rest of the UK" and a further 7% came from overseas, generating £549,000 of economic benefit for Glasgow. Many of the 2006 exhibitions had been specifically commissioned for Glasgow International while others highlighted works that were being shown for the first time in Scotland. Some of the highlights of that year's festival included an exhibition of drawings

---

78  The section pertaining to Abraham Cruzvillegas is adapted from Sarah Lowndes, "Abraham Cruzvillegas", *Frieze*, Issue 120, Jan–Feb 2009.
79  Francis McKee, in conversation with the author, March 2010.

and a live performance by Patti Smith at The Mitchell Library, curated by Ben Harman, a show of new works by Gary Rough at Sorcha Dallas and a new site-specific large scale sculpture commissioned by The Modern Institute by Miami-based artist Mark Handforth. In a statement released around the time of the second GI, Francis McKee announced, "As a curated Festival, this mixture of commissioning and selection is vital. These emerging years of Glasgow International have proven that there is a role for the Festival and as it grows, there is then a need for more time for research and for the commissioning of more ambitious exhibitions. For these reasons, Glasgow International will become a biennial event with the next Festival taking place in 2008. We are confident that extending the period of development will enable us to respond to the growth and momentum that Glasgow International is stimulating."[80]

Francis McKee remembers, "By the third year of Glasgow International it was becoming evident that it was growing and it was a good platform, and people began being more ambitious. But also there was an interesting economic survey that the city carried out after the second year of the festival in 2006, that showed the economic benefits that the festival brought to the city – the survey found that for every £1 spent, £9 came back and that transformed the festival. It wasn't that the city didn't like contemporary art – but once they saw the economic benefit it became clear that Glasgow International was working for the economy of the city. The budget went up from £70,000 in 2006 to £400,000 in 2008, and consequently the third Glasgow International felt like a noticeable upsurge. There was more marketing, and there was a team working on the festival, as opposed to it just being me on my own, as it was in the first year, or me and Claire Jackson as it was in 2006. There was also a two-year lead time to make the commissions which made a huge difference. Before that you were finding exhibitions that people hadn't seen before in Britain – such as the William Kentridge show that had been in Venice and was very generously given to us.[81] By 2008 you could actually go to Wilhelm Sasnal

80  http://www.scottisharts.org.uk/1/artsinscotland/visualarts/projects/projectsarchive/glasgowinternational2006.aspx
81  Kentridge's first UK exhibition for ten years was held at Glasgow School of Art and included *7 Fragments for Georges Melies* (2003), a series of short films inspired by the early work of Bruce Nauman and the films of artist Georges Melies.

and say, here's some money, do you want to make a new work – you've got two years. That hadn't happened in the festival before."[82]

## 2HB, CRITICAL APPLAUSE, NUTS AND SEEDS AND DRAW OR DIE

CCA Programmer Louise Shelley (b.1982) came to the organisation after working for doggerfisher in Edinburgh while still a student at Glasgow School of Art, and then working for Mary Mary. She remembers, "I knew about Mary Mary from its first days as an exhibition programme in a flat which seemed very exciting and interesting. Mary Mary felt like a different opportunity, a very new commercial gallery, younger artists, a new permanent gallery space and Hannah [Robinson] was fun and interesting to work with, it felt like there was more space and involvement to be had."[83] Following this, Shelley moved to CCA, where she has contributed significantly to the repositioning of the organisation over the last few years, notably through co-editing a new creative writing journal, *2HB*, with Francis McKee.

She remembers, "The beginnings of *2HB* came out of organising the book fairs at CCA. Through doing this I found out about so many interesting publications and journals, *Dot Dot Dot, Fr David* are two that still stand out for me – they seemed to occupy a space in contemporary art that I wasn't that aware of, an experimental space for curating and presenting work. In 2008 I invited the Publish and be Damned archive to be a part of the book fair, which again was another fantastic opportunity to see a real wealth of self-published and interesting material, all very independent and providing different platforms for contemporary art and a more discursive space for work. This interest led to discussions with Francis, his writing practice often crosses over into these more creative areas, at the time he was involved in a Dexter Sinister writing project where a group of artists and writers produced a novel called *Philip*, another interesting publishing project. Along with Francis there were a few other things I had seen by artists in Glasgow, for example a text written by Fiona Jardine for Laura Aldridge's show at GSS that seemed to exist in this vein of creative writing in contemporary art. Also

82  Francis McKee, in conversation with the author, March 2010.
83  Louise Shelley, in response to questions sent by the author, February 2009.

important to *2HB* starting were discussions with Sarah Tripp, both in terms of her interest in writing and design. *2HB* in many ways is quite accidental in its final form, as it is open to submissions and grouped loosely, the editorial control is pretty slight really, but it has been a fantastic project, we have received so many amazing submissions and it feels like it has been really successful in providing a platform for this other vein of practice in contemporary art. It is now stocked in great places like Printed Matter and Dexter Sinister which were places that informed it at the beginning."[84]

As part of his drive towards opening up the building and giving emergent practitioners a platform, following on from the discussions that had come out of *2HB* and the CCA book fairs, around 2008 Francis McKee also invited Louise Shelley and Events Manager Kathryn Elkin (b.1983) to put on live music events at CCA under the aegis of the Nuts and Seeds DIY music collective and to curate a series of artists' talks for CCA, which came to be called Critical Applause. The talks and events organised by Elkin and Shelley, both of whom had graduated from Glasgow School of Art in 2005, had the aspiration of encouraging new approaches towards the model of the "artist's talk" and invited artists including Ryan Gander, Will Holder, Emily Pethick and Olivia Plender "to stage their contribution in a dynamic and spontaneous manner, eschewing any inherited notion of what an artist's talk might be, by focusing on a specific body of research or staging a performance."[85] Louise Shelley remembers, "Critical Applause came out of various discussions with Francis McKee, he suggested that we programme a series of talks at the CCA and was quite open as to how we interpreted this."[86] Kathryn Elkin says, "I think Louise and I had been to a lot of artists' talks over the years, and a lot of them were not very good. […] With Critical Applause, Louise and I had this feeling that there was something odd in the logic of an artist presenting slides of their work in chronological order to an audience who were in all likelihood already pretty familiar with said artist's practice, having elected to attend their talk. Neither did we like the strategy of making an immaculate intellectual support structure that

---

84 Louise Shelley, in response to questions sent by the author, February 2009.
85 "Critical Applause", http://www.cca-glasgow.com/
86 Louise Shelley, in response to questions sent by the author, February 2010.

rationalised everything they had ever done. [...] We wanted to play with the expectations one might have of an artist's talk – to look at the impossibility of an artist talking about their work totally rationally, totally honestly, in the first person etc. It is always a bit of a performance obviously! Ryan Gander, for example, gave a performance/talk about all the lies he has ever told as an artist – or so he says…"[87]

Since they had been students at Glasgow School of Art, both Elkin and Shelley had been involved, along with other local artist/organisers including Giles Bailey, Jens Strandberg, Thomas Sander, Duncan Robertson and Susan Berridge in running the non-profit independent music promotion organisation Nuts and Seeds. Nuts and Seeds began putting on gigs in Glasgow for bands touring the UK in 2002, when founder Giles Bailey (b.1981) was in first year at Glasgow School of Art. The ethos of the organisation was key: "The door prices are kept affordable and the bands are paid well in order to support a sustainable and ethical network for live music. Costs are kept low and bands are fed, paid and given a decent place to sleep. All the money made on the door goes to covering costs and paying the bands and consequently there are no guest lists. Every effort is made to keep music inclusive, cheap, anti-elitist and fun. Nuts and Seeds frown upon the following: Attempts to enter gigs without paying the door fee (rarely in excess of 4 pounds) because you work for music press/a record label/music publishing organisation etc. Deluded aspirations to major label stardom leaving the magnanimous and good willed trampled in your wake. Taking down our posters. Nuts and Seeds will not take down your posters."[88]

Louise Shelley says, "Giles [Bailey] and I came to Glasgow in 2002 – we moved from Leeds where there is a really great DIY music scene, Giles had been much more involved in this than me, I had been more of an audience member really. Giles had already started putting out records on an independent label in Leeds with a few other people called Obscene Baby Auction and various friends were doing the same. Then coming to Glasgow we would see a lot of bands playing here through professional promoters,

87  Kathryn Elkin, in response to questions sent by the author, February 2010.
88  http://www.myspace.com/nutsseeds.

when in Leeds they would play for half the door price in a much more exciting setting and line up. We had heard of the Glasgow Music Collective (GMC) and it seemed like a real shame nothing like this was happening anymore considering the amount of great music happening. Then bands that were playing DIY shows in Leeds would contact Giles when on tour or to pass on touring band contact details so he started booking the odd show in Glasgow. This grew into Nuts and Seeds and a few more of us got involved in things like cooking for the bands and making posters. After graduating N&S seemed to solidify more into a group with Kathryn [Elkin] and Tom Sander being involved, we ran a club night, Meowmix at [Nice 'n'] Sleazy's for while which meant we had a fund to put out some split seven inches which was really exciting. Being at art school and just after graduating was the perfect time for this really, we had plenty of spare time and were keen on entering into as much creative activity as possible, and particularly in working as a collective – meeting to talk over everything, and screenprinting the 7" records, T-shirts and bags we sold at our gigs. It was really rewarding being able to put bands on that maybe wouldn't otherwise play or maybe would but with a commercial promoter like PCL[89] usually meaning a higher door price and an unexciting line up."[90] Kathryn Elkin remembers, "Giles was running Nuts and Seeds himself for a number of years. The rest of us became involved slowly, just lending a hand at first, and then I think Giles was the one to conceive of this circumstance as a 'collective'. What I found most enjoyable about Nuts and Seeds was seeing bands that you liked and feeling that you had helped a gig to happen that might not have otherwise. If we were inundated with requests for gigs, we tended to go with the option that was the most interesting to us, rather than think about how well it may or may not go down."[91]

Nuts and Seeds founder Giles Bailey had joined the Transmission committee the year after graduating from the Environmental Art department at Glasgow School of Art in 2005. While at art school, his many

---

89  PCL promote mainstream bands such as Arcade Fire, Scissor Sisters, Katy Perry, Animal Collective, The White Stripes, Franz Ferdinand, The Fratellis, Foo Fighters and Green Day amongst others, and own the Captain's Rest in Glasgow and Sneaky Pete's in Edinburgh.
90  Louise Shelley, in response to questions sent by the author, February 2010.
91  Kathryn Elkin, in response to questions sent by the author, February 2010.

extra-curricular activities included running Nuts and Seeds, being frontman in local band Dananananaykroyd and subsequently in the band Triple School, with fellow GSA graduate Tom Varley (b.1985). Varley remembers, "I can't remember *exactly* how Triple School started, but Giles and I knew each other through a mutual friend and were often at the same gigs and exhibitions. We'd talked about playing music together for a while before we actually did. The first practice was in summer 2007 (I remember that quite distinctly because I dropped a bag of cymbals on my foot as we were walking to the rehearsal room: I bled without really realising throughout the entire practice and later had to go to hospital). Giles had recently quit Dananananaykroyd and my previous band The Beatles had ground to a halt. We practiced very irregularly (and quite unsuccessfully) for a long time before we played any shows – I think our first gig wasn't until March 2008 – this was partly because that I was in fourth year at art school and Giles was busy with Transmission [where he was a committee member] but the main reason was that we didn't really seem to 'get on' with any of the rehearsal studios we tried. Things started to come together really quickly when we realised we could practice in my living room (I can't believe no one has ever complained). Our first gig was with Plaaydoh at a free party in a disused space in the Barras. Plaaydoh became something like a 'partner band' – we played lots of gigs with them, toured with them, released a split single with them, Chris Plaaydoh did all our recording and Rob Plaaydoh released our EP through his website winningspermparty.com. That first gig didn't go well but the second – with Gummy Stumps at Nice'n'Sleazy – was soon afterwards and went much better. The name came from the Gay Against You song 'Triple Schiphol', which Giles misread as Triple School. I think our most memorable gig was at the Hot Club's first birthday party (27th Sept 2008). It was a Saturday night and there had been an opening at Transmission earlier that evening (Michael Kent, Kendall Koppe, Ariki Porteous, Darren Rhymes and Michael Roy). We weren't on until about 1am and Sleazy's was absolutely packed."[92]

Giles Bailey was also part of the group of drawing enthusiasts, Draw or

92  Tom Varley, in response to questions sent by the author, February 2010.

Die, which arranged drawing-events, "with an intention to increase an interest in drawing. Through arranging unconventional drawing events, where the act of drawing is more emphasised than the result, have Draw or Die tried reaching an audience which normally would not draw."[93] Jens Strandberg (b.1980), who also graduated from the Environmental Art department in 2005, says, "I set up this thing called Draw or Die, which tried to organise drawing events of various kinds around Glasgow – Giles got involved by coming to different drawing events, and I got to know him through that. There were a few different manifestations – there was the Glasgow Drawing Club, which was just meeting up with friends in cafés like The 78 in Kelvinhaugh Street to draw. Then there were drawing battles called Death Draw, and that happened in various venues, including Lowsalt gallery in Glasgow and the Collective Gallery in Edinburgh. It was set up as a breakdance battle, where you would draw on overhead projectors to music for a minute and then the audience had to decide who was the winner was by screaming which drawing they liked the most."[94] Strandberg also became involved in helping to run Nuts and Seeds, explaining, "This was more sustainable than Giles doing it on his own and also gave us all an excuse to hang out together and have fun. It was all about making music accessible for all, instead of making a profit or wanting it to function in the usual realm of promoting music, just trying to find alternative ways to do that."[95] Strandberg subsequently joined the Transmission committee in 2008, explaining "all of my work is about collaboration and collective working methods, in some way – Transmission was a great opportunity to think about how an art practice can fit in with programming a space."[96]

In 2008 Transmission invited Kathryn Elkin to curate a project for Transmission. The resultant month-long project, *Moot Points: Exercises in Self-Organisation, Discourse and Collaboration* (2008) reconsidered how an artist-run gallery should function. One of the outcomes of this project was that Elkin tabled a proposed change to Transmission's constitution at the gallery's

---

93  http://1200m.org/drawordieweb/glasgowdc/ddindex.html
94  Jens Strandberg, in conversation with the author, February 2010.
95  Jens Strandberg, in conversation with the author, February 2010.
96  Jens Strandberg, in conversation with the author, February 2010.

2009 AGM, proposing that 50% of the work shown there should be by women, a proposal that was not carried forth. Elkin explained, "A key point for me was to look at how Transmission had originated, and then reconsider how an artist-run gallery does or should function in the context of contemporary Glasgow. I was interested in finding examples within contemporary art practice and amongst other organisations that might reflect an attitude of opposition or independence or of attempted independence from commercial practices, or a strategic control over any dalliances with this side of things. I was interested in alternative discourses around art and culture more broadly, and that's how *Variant* and Dexter Sinister (who also make *Dot Dot Dot*) came to be involved. We had an independent art school – Salford Art Academy – do a week's residency in the gallery, we had a series of screenings from the Feminist Film Archive Cinnenova presented and selected by a variety of practitioners as well as Glasgow Women's Library, we published two books – one with Olivia Plender, one with Dexter Sinister, we had Resonance FM do a week's residency in the gallery, and had a work from the Faculty of Invisibility installed in the gallery."[97] The following year, 2010, Elkin and Shelley again tried to raise their proposed amendment to make Transmission gender-neutral at the gallery's AGM, with Shelley explaining, "The proposed constitution amendment seemed like a really exciting proposal to Transmission, both Kathryn and I have been very much involved with the gallery for a while and it is a really great space and feels like it is able to work and change very quickly and independently, as amendments are put to the whole membership it felt like a great opportunity to propose the change in a discursive environment. We also thought that if Transmission did this it would set a great precedent for other spaces too."[98] However, the amendment was again overruled on a legal technicality, with both Elkin and Shelley expressing the wish to continue the proposal forward to the 2011 Transmission AGM.

97  Kathryn Elkin, in response to questions sent by the author, February 2010.
98  Louise Shelley, in response to questions sent by the author, February 2010.

Meanwhile, other artist-run spaces continued to form around the city, such as Southside Studios, which provide studios, support and exhibition space for Glasgow-based artists at Westmoreland Street. The studios were set up in early 2006 by Olivia Gurtler and JR Ewen and are the first of their kind on the Southside of Glasgow, where there is a lack of available inexpensive studio provision. The exhibition programme at Southside Gallery has begun to attract considerable attention over the last two years – particularly as the exhibitions often combine works by established local artists with those of emergent artists, as was the case with the exhibition Unfinished Plan for a New and Better Tomorrow (2009), in which David Shrigley's work was shown alongside the work of two younger artists, the sculptor Billy Teasdale, who graduated from Glasgow School of Art in 2004 and the painter and Tiny Little Hearts bassist Alan Stanners, who graduated from GSA in 2007.

One of the most interesting artist-run spaces to emerge in the last few years is Dias, established by Michael Kent, Graham Kelly and Tom Varley in 2008, with assistance from Thom Walker and Rebecca Wilcox. Varley recalls, "We were keenly aware of a long and rich tradition of flat exhibitions in Glasgow when we established Dias. While the grassroots scene at the time was certainly vibrant, we felt something was missing that had perhaps existed in the past. We wanted to create an informal atmosphere but provide an exhibition space that didn't compromise or restrict artists' work in any way. We wanted the focus to be absolutely on the art and provide a setting where the work shown did not need to be site specific. It was important to us that previews did not feel like parties and that the space provided a context for work as close to a conventional gallery as possible: the space was properly lit, emptied of all furniture, the walls were white. We tidied up, turned the stereo off and used Helvetica… We wanted to demonstrate that DIY, self-organised projects don't necessarily need to have this crusty/punky aesthetic and, conversely, that self-organised projects which provide a gallery-like ('*neutral*') environment do not necessarily aspire to become anything *more* than a no-budget, DIY organisation. Dais was a reaction to exhibitions in nightclubs and in carpeted flats where artists' work coexists with the furniture, but equally a reaction to projects like Mary Mary and Switchspace *going commercial*."[99] To date there have been eight shows, featuring work by Thom Walker, Gavin Maitland, Sophie Mackfall, Rob Churm, Lauren Gault, and Tom Varley, Giles Bailey and Jens Strandberg, Rhianna Turnbull, Alistair Frazer and a joint show by Rebecca Wilcox and Graham Kelly that took up two floors of a vacant shop space on Dumbarton Road near Victoria Park.

On the 25th February 2010 Nuts and Seeds staged their final gig at 13th Note Cafe, with Phat Trophies, Vom and US Girls. Louise Shelley says, "I guess we always hoped that if the band is booking a show through us it is because they believe and support the DIY ethic but occasionally it feels like we're just good for putting the show on and it feels very one-sided. On a very cynical note occasionally it felt like DIY was being co-opted in a fashionable way or as an early career move. […] There are a lot more DIY promoters in Glasgow now so things will progress and carry on very well without us. It is certainly not the devastating crash that seemed to happen to GMC – I am still a firm believer in DIY activity and in an independent music scene in Glasgow, but I think often collectives have a limited period of activity and ours has come to a natural end really."[100] Kathryn Elkin concurs, "When Giles started putting gigs on under the title of Nuts and Seeds there wasn't really anyone else doing DIY gigs in the city. There had been lots of this happening in the past in Glasgow (GMC etc), but things had slowed down by the time we all moved here. Now there are several other DIY promoters in the city who we have a couple of years on. If the sort of gigs we want to see are happening, then we are happy to show our support by attending gigs put on by people like Cry Parrot, Psychic Dancehall and Winning Sperm Party rather than organising them."[101] However, both Elkin and Shelley will relocate to London in the summer of 2010.

Another sad ending was announced at the beginning of March, when Optimo DJs Jonnie Wilkes and Keith McIvor broke the hearts of countless club-goers in Glasgow and beyond when they announced on their website,

---

99    Tom Varley, in response to questions sent by the author, February 2010.
100   Louise Shelley, in response to questions sent by the author, February 2010.
101   Kathryn Elkin, in response to questions sent by the author, February 2010.

"After 12 and a half years (or around 650 Optimos), we have, after a huge amount of consideration and many sleepless nights decided that Sunday April 25th will be the LAST EVER night of Optimo (Espacio) at The Sub Club."[102] The response to this news was perhaps put most compellingly by one of the Glasgow bands that McIvor and Wilkes had championed in recent times, Divorce, who wrote on their website, "Today is the day that we know would eventually come but wouldn't admit to ourselves: OPTIMO (ESPACIO) IS GOING TO END. Like they explain, it's been a good run; 12 years, over 600 nights and a list of guest bands and artists who have graced their stage that reads like a who's-who of pioneering, envelope-pushing music from the last 30 years. When Optimo started NOBODY was doing what they did, nobody merged the blood-and-guts visceral thrill of seeing a genuinely intimidating/engrossing/breathtaking live performance within a 100% legitimate club format. It's a template that's been duplicated countless times all over the world, but back then the very thought was anathema. Even placing it in such simplistic terms does it a disservice. Ultimately what Twitch & Wilkes did was burn the schematics and simply PLEASE THEMSELVES – nothing was out the question, if it floated their boat then it went in. This breath of fresh air was exactly was the club scene needed and their 'anti-agenda' resonated with people not just in Glasgow, or Britain, but worldwide."[103] Yet even Optimo's demise will not affect the ability of Glasgow's young musicians to get their work heard. As Sinead Young, artist and lead singer of Glasgow noise band Divorce avers, "It's so much easier now to share MP3s, through Myspace, blogs and other sites… there's a sense in which other people give you permission to put your own work out there, even if it is a bit rough."[104] In contrast to 1980s Glasgow art school bands like Strawberry Switchblade (who formed as teenagers in 1981 but didn't release any records until 1983), members of emerging Glasgow bands such as Divorce and Ultimate Thush who are still students at the city's art school have already made their music accessible on their MySpace pages and available to download via the Glasgow-based music file-sharing website Winning Sperm Party.

102  http://www.optimo.co.uk/echationew/viewtopic.php?t=2917
103  http://divorcetheband.blogspot.com/2010/03/end-of-optimo.html
104  Sinead Young, in conversation with the author, Glasgow, February 2010.

Some of the implications of these new approaches are evident in the practice of the Israeli-born Glasgow-based artist Shelly Nadashi (b.1981), who has recently been commissioned by Public Art Scotland (PAR+RS) editor Ruth Barker to devise and present public projects, including a blog and a number of short filmed performances "broadcast" through the PAR+RS website. The relationship between "the individual situation and the social situation"[105] is an important aspect of Nadashi's multi-disciplinary practice, which includes video making, live performances, sound design, puppetry and written texts. The implications that accompany telepresence (a term derived from virtual reality, describing the sensation of feeling in a different place or time afforded by certain technologies) as opposed to the actual presence associated with live performance have interesting implications for Nadashi, whose work calls into question the nature of biography.

Nadashi's recent collaborative performance *Ambush in Wedding*, staged at SWG3 (in collaboration with Ultimate Thrush drummer Laurie Pitt and performance artist Cliff Laine) was "a complicated exploration of the relationships between public and private histories and spaces, and hinged around a powerful autobiographical re-telling of an urban public landscape."[106] The work dissembled the artist's experience of a misfired romantic liaison in Berlin, a process Nadashi describes as: "constructing a performative narrative that helps me to understand the reality of my life better. I find it interesting that this is something that requires the public – as if I need the public's live participation in order to contextualise my own individual emotions."[107] She ended her *Ambush in Wedding* performance by describing why she had revisited the events described in the performance: "I wanted to break this story. I am the one to decide how my biography is going to look. There are so many things that we can do that can change so many things that other people will ever do. This is the street, this is the staircase, this is the door. Break the story."[108] In her retellings of personal experiences, especially as reconfigured through internet-broadcast videos

<hr>

105   Shelly Nadashi, in response to questions sent by the author, January 2010.
106   Blogs +, Schloss Brollin What Are You, http://www.publicartscotland.com/blogs/21-Schloss-Br-llin-What-Are-You
107   Shelly Nadashi, in response to questions sent by the author, January 2010.
108   Shelly Nadashi, *Ambush in Wedding*, (self-published, Glasgow, 2010).

of her performances, Nadashi's home page and blog, allow the artist as subject to be "progressively erased, redefined and reinscribed as a persona/performer within the proscenium arch of the computer monitor."[109] However, as Nadashi herself has pointed out, her work relies upon "the public's live participation", as indeed do gigs by Glasgow bands like Divorce and Ultimate Thrush. It is not a question, as Miwon Kwon puts it, of choosing "between digital interfaces and the handshake. Rather, we need to be able to think the range of seeming contradictions and our contradictory desires for them together; to understand, in other words, seeming oppositions as sustaining relations."[110]

The potential of new technologies to facilitate the documentation of events and the circulation of information and to stimulate debate around current art practices is especially important in Glasgow, in order to render visible the exclusions and forgotten traces that constitute the secret history of the city. A New Path, a project developed in partnership by Sorcha Dallas Projects and Jenny Crowe Commissions has grown from first-hand experience and discussions around the commissioning of permanent and temporary artworks within Scotland, and "aims to reinvigorate and herald a new way (or path) for the commissioning of permanent artworks within the city".[111] Sorcha Dallas explains that, "I think we both feel that there is no real strategy in terms of how artworks are and were commissioned in the city so therefore there is a range of projects, with varying levels of success, failure and quality. As Glasgow has such a strong reputation for visual art being produced in the city we feel this is often at odds with how work has been represented within the public realm."[112]

For their first A New Path project, to be presented at Glasgow International 2010, Crowe and Dallas have selected six public artworks in Glasgow city centre, aiming to highlight the commissioning history and background behind the following public art projects: Niki de Saint Phalle at the Gallery of Modern Art; Graham Fagen's *Royston Rose Project*; Douglas

---

109 Steve Dixon, *Digital Performance* (Cambridge, Massachusetts: The MIT Press, 2007), p.4.
110 Miwon Kwon, *One Place After Another: Site Specific Art and Locational Identity* (Cambridge, Massachusetts: The MIT Press, 2004), p.166.
111 Sorcha Dallas, in response to questions sent by the author, March 17th 2010.
112 Sorcha Dallas, in response to questions sent by the author, March 17th 2010.

Gordon's *Empire*; Ian Hamilton Finlay at George IV Bridge; Christine Borland at Glasgow University; and Toby Paterson at the BBC. Crowe and Dallas have created a website containing their research on the history of each project, with accompanying images, and newly commissioned reappraisal texts on each work. They are hoping to encourage visitors to pay closer attention to these existing works while en route to other aspects of the festival, and have asked the Glasgow-based artist Graham Fagen to lead a public tour that connects Ian Hamilton Finlay's piece on George IV Bridge with Douglas Gordon's *Empire* in the Merchant City. Dallas explains that the next phase of the project is "to start to create temporary and permanent commissions by local and international artists and to create a blueprint for how future commissions can happen in the city. We are aiming to produce some temporary commissions and events in 2011 with the first permanent commission being in place for the next GI in 2012. We have been looking at cities like New York and Chicago and the exciting way they commission and make public art a priority within the urban environment."[113]

Crowe and Dallas's concerns chime with some of those expressed by Adele Patrick, Lifelong Learning Co-ordinator at Glasgow Women's Library (GWL), who has had a long and vested interest in the vexed question of the under-representation of women in public space. At the *Subject in Process: Feminism and Art* symposium which I co-organised (with Kathryn Elkin and Louise Shelley) at Glasgow's CCA in 2009, Patrick presented a paper entitled "Making space for women" in which she described how, "Glasgow Women's Library has been variously critiqued as not a real library, not a real artwork or artspace, as not living in the real world (principally for focusing on women and not men). What I hope to illustrate is that despite or because of this liminal, unsettling and indeterminate status GWL has been open to and uniquely positioned to develop work that responds to the heterogeneity of women's experiences from different worlds often using the agency of art and artists."[114] Since 1991, when GWL opened their doors in a former second hand clothes shop on Hill Street, the library has moved twice

113 Sorcha Dallas, in response to questions sent by the author, March 17th 2010.

114 Adele Patrick, "Making space for women: a review of the work of Women in Profile and Glasgow Women's Library, 1988–2009", http://www.womenslibrary.org.uk/2009/10/subject-in-process/

– to 109 Trongate (a premises they vacated during the Trongate 103 renovations) and then to Parnie Street (a premises they have recently been asked to vacate to make way for a new Workshop and Artists' Studio Provision Scotland Ltd (WASPS) studio complex). However, in 2010 Glasgow Women's Library will relocate to a permanent, independent base within the Mitchell Library – a move that has given Patrick and her colleagues pause to reflect even more closely on the specific significance of a "women's library" in the civic, cultural and historical landscape of Glasgow.

Patrick pointed out in her presentation that, "Working with communities is an antidote to both the endemic global homogenisation of the regenerated city and locally the perpetual modelling and remodelling of masculinised incarnations of Glasgow. [...] In the library space and in the other locations we have worked with women who have spoken about: not seeing themselves reflected in the city, confronting male violence in the streets and at home, that they are not heard or consulted and that they feel inadequately served or respected as citizens."[115] One of the most surprising statistics revealed during Patrick's paper was that there are only three statues of women in Glasgow – and of these, only one is Glaswegian and she paid for the monument herself. GWL have subsequently recruited the Glasgow-based artists Nicky Bird and Shauna McMullan, and Project Co-ordinator and Adviser Fiona Dean to work with GWL staff, volunteers, library users and learners on the first phase of an SAC funded Public Art project "Making Space" which will culminate in a brief for a new public artwork marking women's history and lives outside the Women's Library's new premises at the Mitchell Library.

Another fascinating yet unmarked site in Glasgow's cultural landscape is the decrepit house that sits on the corner at 27 Bank Street in Glasgow, recently described in *The Guardian* as "possibly" being the rooming house once run by the family of iconoclastic Glaswegian author Alexander Trocchi. Trocchi's statement, in his polemical essay, "The Invisible Insurrection of a Million Minds" (1963) that, "There is in fact no such permanence anywhere. There is only becoming." is an important one in terms of thinking both

---

115 Adele Patrick, "Making space for women: a review of the work of Women in Profile and Glasgow Women's Library, 1988–2009", http://www.womenslibrary.org.uk/2009/10/subject-in-process/

about apparitions (the action of becoming) and reactivating forgotten or dormant histories. Linear time moves onwards ("the time of being") on the horizontal axis, meanwhile events unroll vertically ("the time of becoming").[116] It feels as though the time has now arrived for Glasgow's artists and activists to step out of the corners and to begin to shape the city.[117]

It is apparent that the last seven years in the Glasgow art scene and the city as a whole have been characterised by ambitious growth and rapid change, a process that looks set to continue as the profile of Glasgow International increases, new funding schemes such as Creative Scotland's Vital Spark support practitioners in the creative industries and the 2014 Commonwealth Games brings economic and social benefits to the city over the next decade. Since the '90s, the Glasgow art scene has shifted from a marginal to a central position within the landscape of the city, becoming a valued and important part of Glasgow's identity and overall economy. Francis McKee says, "Whenever you go to New York or wherever, people will say, yeah, Glasgow, it's a great place for contemporary art – it's true and internally recognised as such, and now the Glasgow art scene is producing economic benefit for the city. Conceptual art was frowned on all through the '90s and the Gallery of Modern Art (GoMA) wasn't touching it. It took a bit of a mental turn somewhere in the city council – which I think was down to Mark O'Neill [who was appointed Head of Culture and Sport Glasgow in 1998]. To his credit, although he was sometimes sceptical, he really paid attention and learnt and also realised that even if he didn't like it, that wasn't his job. His job was to support the local contemporary art scene – and then he did, which was a really enlightened moment. The city became really sophisticated, and [Senior Arts Officer] Claire Simpson gave this new approach a structure, and money began to be invested – perhaps the most tangible evidence of this can be seen in the Trongate 103 development."[118]

116 CJ Isham and KN Savvidou, "Time and Modern Physics", in Katinka Ridderbos (ed.), *Time*, Cambridge University Press, 2002, p.9.
117 Some of the material in this closing section is adapted from Sarah Lowndes, "I Am the Space Where I Am", Public Art Scotland (PAR +RS), (2010).
118 Francis McKee, in conversation with the author, March 2010.

Toby Webster agrees that there has been a significant shift over the last decade. He says, "The Modern Institute is based in Glasgow but we're involved in the international art scene. That's what really changed, that The Modern Institute, and other galleries that emerged around the same time as us, like the Foksal Foundation from Poland or Kurimanzutto from Mexico, are rooted in particular places but we're working everywhere else – and that's because of the artists. Historically they might have lived here, but their gallery was in London. That's changed now – there's a good network and Glasgow is very much part of an international scene – it always was part of it but now it is a centre because of the people who stay here, and hopefully that will continue. I think that what will happen is that all of the galleries will only get stronger – there's doggerfisher and the Ingleby Gallery in Edinburgh, and Sorcha Dallas and Mary Mary here, and all of them have great artists."[119]

Sorcha Dallas says, "For me the development of a commercial scene has been really key – there are now three commercial galleries in the city and I am sure it's only a matter of time before there are more. This is a welcome development but on the grassroots level there is no collector base to support this development, this seems to be a greater issue to tackle and one that feeds into education and culture as a whole. Over the last eight years the scene has really developed from Transmission being the lynchpin and the main space to see cutting edge international work, this has become much more widely represented, not only in the other artist-run spaces but by the commercial and museum gallery programmes. It has been great to witness recently the improved programme at CCA and Tramway and experiencing really exciting, blockbuster shows there, as I remember it being when I was a student in the '90s."[120]

Katrina Brown says, "I think that a lot's changed in twenty years – unsurprisingly. I think that energy that marked the beginning of the decade 'Here + Now' looked at has become more substantial by sheer force of that collected experience: The Modern Institute is over ten years old now, for example; Tramway's re-discovering its form under Sarah Munro. There's

119  Toby Webster, in conversation with the author, February 11th, 2010.
120  Sorcha Dallas, in response to questions sent by the author, February 2010.

far *more* activity for one: more people coming to study, live, work here from elsewhere than back then. If you look at the committees at Transmission from the early '90s we were almost all born or at least educated in Glasgow. And of course the single biggest difference is that there are now commercial galleries in the city taking artists from Glasgow to fairs – and therefore collectors and collections – all over the world. It's entirely possible to be based here, have a successful, international career and a market for your work. What's exciting about now is I suppose that the next step seems possible – with so many people with such amazing collected experience in the city. There's undoubtedly a certain maturity at work – and I'm not just talking about myself! – that was not the case in the early 1990s. Artists travelling all over the world making shows of course come back here with expectations altered – so the infrastructure has to shift to accommodate those expectations, is one example. With the growth that's happened, the 'scene' is not just about recent graduates or only emerging practice, but looks likely to now be sustained over generations: it's proving to be not just the 'flash in the pan' that it could so easily have been. The two things we need to look for next are a kind of breaking through to broader public awareness of the reality of contemporary art, making really good major exhibitions available to people here; and a ramping up of critical discourse to keep the production side of things healthy."[121]

In the spring of 2010 these ideas are very much at the forefront of Brown's mind, as this year she has taken the role of director of Glasgow International for the first time. In a recent article she wrote, "For this outing of the Glasgow International, my first as director, we have been working around the theme of 'past, present, future'. This was in part suggested by prevalent trends in contemporary art practice of recent years, and in part by 2010 being the 20th anniversary of Glasgow's reign as European Capital of Culture, a fact which offers an interesting moment to look back, and, we hope, forward."[122] One of Brown's most striking choices was to invite Glasgow-based artist David Shrigley, in his first show in the city for a

121  Katrina Brown, in response to questions sent by the author, 2010.
122  Katrina Brown, "Glasgow International", *The Map*, Monday, 08 February 2010. http://www.mapmagazine.co.uk/index.cfm?page=96DF72AB-F328-CB28-B755B636C0C4F75F&bulletinid=C160F18D-107D-848B-FBFF8EC42D2048D2

decade, to show a group of new sculptures in a specially commissioned installation in the vitrines of Kelvingrove Art Gallery & Museum. This is the first time that the Glasgow International programme has penetrated the city's most famous museum, and as Brown rightly points out, "Working with Kelvingrove is a huge step and a really important one: I, like so many Glaswegians, grew up in there, with my father dragging me round his beloved Flemish paintings. It's a hugely important place. When I was thinking about what the Festival could be it seemed to me that Kelvingrove is like the first port of call for anyone from or in the city who wants to look at art – and so it was obvious that we should be there."[123] Shrigley and Brown, both of whom have been at the forefront of what Hans Ulrich Obrist called "the Glasgow miracle", reinvigorating the collections of Kelvingrove is a reflection of how far the city's predominantly self-organised and autonomous arts infrastructure has come. Kelvingrove opened in the days when Glasgow was known as "the workshop of the world" – it could be said that the city's innovative and highly acclaimed artists and musicians have made their city a workshop of the world once again.

Shrigley's intervention into twenty-one of the vitrines, drawers and cases of Kelvingrove Art Gallery and Museum was full of surprises, including a drawer filled with different kinds of varieties of crackers, from Ryvita to Jacobs cream, and another containing a dead rat lying on its side. A case containing a suit of armour was given the addition of several pairs of shiny black Wellingtons made of painted clay, in case the knight felt like a change of footwear. One of the most striking works, though, was a glass case containing two large white spheres, one on top of each other. Each sphere was inscribed with the words "the world". My daughter decoded the legend and turned to ask, smiling uncertainly, "But…isn't there only one world?"

Strong evidence of the existence of "another world" can be found all over Glasgow – in galleries, theatres, studios, bars, clubs, up stairwells and down side streets. The combination of social co-operation and interest in process-based practices that characterise the Glasgow art scene helped to shield the city's artists from the collapse of the art market in autumn 2008, and may

123   Katrina Brown, in response to questions sent by the author, February 2010.

well do so again during any downturn that may be wrought by the recent change in governments. Many of the city's artists have sustained their practice over many years without any expectation of making money from their work. It seems to me that the most striking exhibitions and events of the 2010 Glasgow International were those that took the essential thriftiness, imagination and goodwill of the local scene and amplified it.

Take for instance, Vestiges Park, half an acre of scrubland re-imagined as a temporary archaic sculpture park, realised in a three-week blaze of imagination and industry by Lowsalt's Rebecca Anson and Krisdy Shindler and their friends. Or the sprawling twenty-eight artist show Kiss of Life organised by the FINN Collective at The Glue Factory, perhaps the most talked about show of the festival, but located in a semi-collapsed building in Maryhill Industrial Estate and put together it seemed with more love than money. Or Glasgow-based environmental arts charity NVA's *White Bicycles*, a re-enactment of the 1960s Dutch anarchist project *Witte Fietsenplan*, launched by the Provos group on the streets of Amsterdam in July 1965. Across Glasgow, the sight of the white bicycles, whether temporarily chained outside a gallery or speeding through the traffic towards another festival site, was an uplifting and heartening display of how the public space of the city could be re-imagined.[124] Projects such as these are tangible demonstrations that another world is indeed possible. All of these projects were realised through the commitment and energy of the Glasgow visual arts community and through funders including Glasgow City Council, Culture and Sport Glasgow and the Scottish Arts Council. The growth of the art scene in Glasgow from "emergent to established" is as a result of the relationships that have formed over time between artists, musicians, curators, organisers, critics and funders. This is a story not only of individuals and families but also of society.

---

124 These observations relating to Glasgow International 2010 appear in a modified version in an essay I wrote for Axis's *Dialogue* webzine entitled "Another World is Possible: Glasgow International 2010" May 2010.

# TOWARDS A CONCLUSION

"…it is important to remember that in programmes of political resistance the relation of cause and effect is convoluted and often indirect. All struggle, all resistance is – must be – concrete. And all struggle has a global resonance. If not here, then there. If not now, then soon: elsewhere as well as here."[1]

Throughout this book I have tried to draw a link between the growth of class politics and political resistance and the development of an identifiable aesthetic tradition in Glasgow. The recent transition the Glasgow art scene has made, from "emergent" in the '80s and '90s to "established" as it has been for the last decade, could be viewed as proof that the struggles of the '80s and '90s have indeed brought effects. Certainly what I have remained most interested in while revising and updating this book is how ideas persist in the face of opposition – and how people can generate significant results through being together, talking and exchanging ideas.

The title for the book came from Joseph Beuys' idea of "social sculpture", which also chimed closely with Sol LeWitt's proposal that "all ideas need not be made physical…the words of one artist to another may induce an idea chain, if they share the same concept."[2] Both Beuys and the conceptual artists associated with LeWitt have had a significant influence on the development of performance related and post-conceptual practice in Glasgow from the early '70s onwards, reflected in the emphasis on non-object based

1 Susan Sontag, "The Power of Principle", *The Guardian Review*, 26th April 2003, pp4–6.
2 Sol LeWitt, quoted in Lucy R. Lippard, *Six Years: The Dematerialization of the art object*, Praeger, New York, 1973, pp xvii.

work in this book. The growth of activist groups and collectives in the city formed the key theme of my research, resulting in "a social history". The grassroots art and music scene in Glasgow came about largely as a result of an evolving conversation between many people. This idea of the accumulative effect of resistance to culturally prescribed ideas is one that appeals to me very much, now as much as ever.

Although in Scotland the Conservative Party won only one seat in the 2010 General Election, they commanded 36.1% of the vote across the UK, enabling Conservative leader David Cameron to form a coalition with the Liberal Democrats (who had taken 23% of the vote across the country), and become the first Conservative Prime Minister in the United Kingdom for thirteen years. In Scotland, (as in every election since 1979) the electorate voted in support of the Labour Party, with Labour taking 41 seats out of a possible 59, but the first-past-the-post electoral system delivered a result very similar to those of the elections of 1979, 1983, 1987 and 1992, when the Scottish electorate was forced to accept a Prime Minister who had not won their vote. Since 1997, Labour Prime Ministers Tony Blair and Gordon Brown had introduced record levels of investment in public services, improving healthcare and education and introducing schemes to benefit the less privileged such as Sure Start, Tax Credits and the National Minimum Wage. David Cameron has announced he will implement £6bn of public spending cuts in the next year – a move reminiscent of Margaret Thatcher's first term of office in 1979.

Looking at Glasgow, and specifically the political history of Glasgow, the power of public protest has been asserted in ever increasing numbers in the last century. From the early days of class politics (the rent strikes of 1915, Red Clydeside in 1919 and the General Strike of 1926) through to more recent protests, such the UCS Work-in of 1972, the anti-nuclear and anti-Thatcher demonstrations of the '80s and the more recent anti-Gulf War demonstrations, Glasgow has been a focus for political protest in Scotland. In the spaces of the city where people have traditionally gathered to demonstrate – Glasgow Green and George Square – there is a palpable sense of the power that can be generated by people standing together. What can be achieved by people coming together in a common cause is at the heart of

Glasgow's recent history, and I hope, at the heart of this book. Obviously there are many problems associated with conflating the artistic and the political, but since the '70s much of the independent artistic activity in Glasgow has addressed itself to political issues – ranging from theatrical companies like 7:84, polemical journals like *Variant*, to public art interventions. The next few years may see many more inspiring examples of politicised artistic activity in Glasgow.

Much of the activity I have documented in this book has been performances, openings, gigs and parties that have no "value" as commodities. Their value is in how they have, as LeWitt said, started "an idea chain", inspiring others to set up a gallery in their flat, start a band or write a fanzine. Despite the many changes in Glasgow in recent years, and in particular the recent gentrification process that has taken place as the city has reinvented itself as a retail and tourist centre, the resonance of the city's recent political and artistic history remains. Although many of the places where the city's artists and musicians used to congregate have closed down or been "redeveloped", although many of their projects may have lasted only a few weeks or months, the combined effect of the times people spend together is harder to erase.

This book is an attempt to express something of the feeling I have experienced in Glasgow in the company of like-minded people, whether demonstrating on Glasgow Green in the rain, listening to an artist's talk in the Mitre Bar or watching a band play at Stereo. That feeling has always been something that went beyond words, and the attempt to pin it down has been marked by predictable frustrations. Terry Eagleton says that "We are free, when like artists, we produce without the goad of physical necessity".[3] Until recently, artists and musicians based in Glasgow have not been able to rely upon either a surplus of public subsidy, the consistent support of public galleries or the local media. Rather, the grassroots scene has largely endured on small funds and the relentless enthusiasm of certain determined individuals. The outlook of these individuals has been informed less by an absence of financial constraints, than by a refusal to let those

---

3  Terry Eagleton, *Marx and Freedom*, Phoenix, London, 1997, pp27.

constraints limit their ambitions. To me, Glasgow has always been a place where I felt a kind of freedom, and where I got involved with doing things for the love of it rather than for more conventional gains. I hope that I have managed to capture something of the city and the people who have meant so much to me.

Sarah Lowndes
May 2010

# IMAGE CREDITS



Joseph Beuys performs *Celtic (Kinloch Rannoch)* – the Scottish Symphony. Edinburgh, August 1970. Photograph: Richard Demarco, reproduced courtesy of The Demarco Archive.
Ian Hamilton Finlay welcomes Edinburgh Arts to Stonypath. Summer 1972. Photograph: Richard Demarco, reproduced courtesy of The Demarco Archive.
The 1972 New 57 committee outside the gallery's premises at Rose Street, Edinburgh. Left to right: Alexander Moffat, Michael Doherty, Iain Patterson, Ian McLeod, Ian Paterson, Roger Askham, Kirkland Main and Jim Fairgrieve. Image lent by Alexander Moffat.
Nice Style, 1971–1974, reproduced courtesy of Bruce McLean.
David Harding and Alan Bold, Poetry Path, Glenrothes, 1977. Photograph: Copyright of David Harding, reproduced courtesy of David Harding and Glasgow School of Art Archive.
Ivor Cutler photographed by son Jeremy c.1988. Reproduced courtesy of Jeremy Cutler.
Invitation for Urban Life, inaugural exhibition at Transmission's Chisholm Street space. December 1983. Reproduced courtesy of Transmission.
Alexander Moffat, *Poet's Pub* (1980). Copyright: Alexander Moffat. Collection of the Scottish National Portrait Gallery, Edinburgh. Reproduced courtesy of Alexander Moffat.
Alasdair Gray, *Lanark*, Third Eye Centre launch (1981). Reproduced courtesy of the artist and Sorcha Dallas, Glasgow.
First *Variant* cover, 1984. Image courtesy of Malcolm Dickson, lent by Transmission. Reproduced courtesy of Transmission.
Adrian Wiszniewski, *Po-et* (1985). Photograph: John Gilmour, lent by Alexander Moffat. Reproduced courtesy of Adrian Wiszniewski and Alexander Moffat.
*Slow Dazzle*, issue No. 5, 1984. Cover features an early line-up of The Pastels. Image lent by John Williamson, reproduced courtesy of John Williamson.
Strawberry Switchblade, London, 1984. Photograph: Peter McArthur, reproduced courtesy of Peter McArthur.
Transmission Goes Verbal, February 1986. James Kelman and Tom Leonard at the gallery. Image reproduced courtesy of Transmission.
Event Space at Transmission – largest festival of film, installation and performance in Scotland for ten years. February 1986. Image reproduced courtesy of Transmission.
Blackhill mural project (1987) by 3rd Year Environmental Art students Nathan Coley, Alan Dunn and Meg McLucas, directed by David Harding. Photograph: Copyright of David Harding, reproduced courtesy of David Harding and Glasgow School of Art Archive.
Exterior of the Mackintosh Building, Glasgow School of Art. Photograph: Richard Wright, reproduced courtesy of Richard Wright.
Sam Ainsley, *Circle of Strength*, Third Eye Centre, Glasgow, 1987. Reproduced courtesy of Sam Ainsley.
Flyer for Tower Beat event at Fury Murry's, 1988. Reproduced courtesy of John Williamson.
The Puberty Institution (Douglas Gordon and Craig Richardson) present aNTEHYPERAESTHESIa at Transmission in December 1987. Photograph: Copyright of David Harding, reproduced courtesy of David Harding and Glasgow School of Art Archive.
Free University Flyer, circa 1987. Lent by Transmission, reproduced courtesy of Transmission.
*Desire in Ruins* installation at Transmission, May 1987. Installation and related events by Ed Baxter, Andy Hopton, Simon Dickason, Karen Elliot, Stefan Szczelkun, Glyn Banks and Hannah Vowles. Reproduced courtesy of Transmission.
Renovations at Transmission's new King Street premises, summer of 1989. Reproduced courtesy of Transmission.
Renovations at Transmission's new King Street premises, summer of 1989. Reproduced courtesy of Transmission.
Transmission's King Street premises, 1989. Reproduced courtesy of Transmission.
Jumble Sale at Transmission, October 1988. Reproduced courtesy of Transmission.
Women in Profile headquarters, Dalhousie Lane, 1989. Reproduced courtesy of The Women's Library.
Anti-Poll Tax demonstration, Queen Street Station, 1989. Reproduced courtesy of the Scottish Socialist Party.
Poster for Womanhouse, Castlemilk, 1990. Reproduced courtesy of Glasgow Women's Library.

David Mach installation at Tramway, February 1990. Reproduced courtesy of Tramway.
Steven Campbell, On Form and Fiction, The Third Eye Centre, 1990. Reproduced courtesy of Centre for Contemporary Art, Glasgow.
Jonathan Monk, *Cancelled* (1990). Photograph: Copyright of David Harding, reproduced courtesy of David Harding and Glasgow School of Art Archive.
Slam flyer for event at The Sub Club, circa 1990. Reproduced courtesy of The Sub Club, lent by ISO, www.isodesign.co.uk

SECTION II

Photograph of artists participating in Windfall and some friends, summer 1991. Group includes: Heather Allen, Katrina Brown, Suzie Hunter, Dave Allen, Claire Barclay, Craig Richardson, Jacqueline Donachie, Iain Kettles, Julie Roberts, Roderick Buchanan, Douglas Gordon and Nathan Coley, reproduced courtesy of Transmission.
Atlantis flyer for residency at The Sub Club, circa 1991. Reproduced courtesy of The Sub Club, lent by ISO, www.isodesign.co.uk
Lawrence Weiner solo show at Transmission, November 1991. Reproduced courtesy of Transmission.
1993 MFA trip to Berlin. Reproduced courtesy of the MFA Archive/Sam Ainsley.
David Shrigley, *Notice,* (1996). Reproduced courtesy of David Shrigley.
Julie Roberts, *Gynecological Couch* (1993). Reproduced courtesy of Julie Roberts and Sean Kelly Gallery, image lent by the MFA Archive/Sam Ainsley.
Dave Allen and Ross Sinclair, *For Those About to Rock*, 1994. Reproduced courtesy of MFA Archive/Sam Ainsley.
Douglas Gordon, 24 Hour Psycho (1993). Installation at Tramway. Reproduced courtesy of the artist and Gagosian Gallery, London.
Christine Borland researching *From Life* (1994), reproduced courtesy of Tramway.
Christine Borland, From Life (1994), reproduced courtesy of Tramway.
Roderick Buchanan, *Work in Progress* (1995). Installation at Tramway, reproduced courtesy of Tramway.
Smith/Stewart, Sustain (1995). Installation at Tramway, reproduced courtesy of Tramway.
David Shrigley, *Ignore This Building* (1996), courtesy of David Shrigley.
Invitation for an opening at The Belmont Hotel, March 1995. Courtesy of James Thornhill.
Opening at The Belmont Hotel, 1995. Clockwise from top left: Cathy Wilkes, Jamie Burroughs, Deirdre McCloskey and James Thornhill. Reproduced courtesy of James Thornhill.
Belle & Sebastian's debut album, *Tigermilk* (1996). Reproduced courtesy of Belle and Sebastian.
Barrowland Ballroom, 1999. Photograph: Richard Wright. Reproduced courtesy of Richard Wright.
Ross Sinclair, *Real Life Rocky Mountain* (1996). Installation at the CCA. Reproduced courtesy of Ross Sinclair.
*Art for People* installation at Transmission, May 1996. Courtesy of Transmission.
Poster for *Art for People*, Transmission, May 1996, reproduced courtesy of Transmission.
Flyer for The Society for the Termination of Art performance at the Gallery of Modern Art opening, 1996. Courtesy of Ross Birrell.
Richard Wright installing work for *Live/Life*, Paris, October 1996. Reproduced courtesy of Transmission.
Ganger, circa 1996. Left to right: Graham Gavin, Stuart Henderson, Lucy McKenzie and James Young. Lent by Marc Baines, reproduced courtesy of Marc Baines.
Wish You Were Here Too, 83 Hill Street, 1996. Reproduced courtesy of Beata Veszely.
Nathan Coley, *Pigeon Lofts* (1997). Reproduced courtesy of the artist and doggerfisher, Edinburgh.
Martin Boyce, *Around Every Corner* (1996). Installation at the Loggia Gallery, Toronto. Photograph: John Massier. Reproduced courtesy of The Modern Institute/Toby Webster Ltd.
Marc Baines' sleeve design for the Lungleg single *Right Now Baby* (1997). Reproduced courtesy of Marc Baines.
*Fly 3* installation of work by (l-r) James Thornhill, Cathy Wilkes and Steve Hollingworth (1997). Reproduced courtesy of Patricia Fleming Projects.
The Social Life of Stuff, Fly 1998. Reproduced courtesy of Patricia Fleming Projects.
Jim Lambie, *18 Carrots* (1996). Reproduced courtesy of The Modern Institute/Toby Webster Ltd.

SECTION III

Douglas Gordon, *Empire* (1998). Reproduced courtesy of the artist and Gagosian Gallery, London.
*British Mythic,* Issue No. 1, 1998. Reproduced courtesy of British Mythic.
Claire Barclay, *Out of the Woods* (1997). Installation at the Centre for Contemporary Arts, Glasgow, reproduced courtesy of the Centre for Contemporary Arts, Glasgow.
Jacqueline Donachie, *The Trees, The Book and the Disc,* Darnley, 1999. Photograph: Alan Dimmick, reproduced courtesy of Julia Radcliffe, Visual Art Projects.
Marianne Greated's sleeve design for the Arab Strap album *Philophobia* (1998). Graphics by Adam Pigott. Reproduced courtesy of Marianne Greated.
Victoria Morton, *Dirty Burning* (1997). Reproduced courtesy of The Modern Institute/Toby Webster Ltd.
Opening party for The Modern Institute, April 1998. Reproduced courtesy of The Modern Institute/Toby Webster Ltd.
Lucy McKenzie installation view at Duncan of Jordanstone College of Art and Design (1999). Photograph: Lucy McKenzie, reproduced courtesy of Lucy McKenzie.

White Bear zz, exhibition at 78 Roslea Drive, 1999. Installation of work (l-r) Alan Michael, Sue Tompkins. Reproduced courtesy of Scott Myles.

Film Club screening at 78 Roslea Drive, 1999. Left to right: Neal Beggs, Rob Kennedy, Jess Worrall, Caroline Kirsop, Scott Myles. Seated: Ewan Imrie. Reproduced courtesy of Scott Myles.

Ed Ruscha opening at Inverleith House, August 2001. Left to right: Toby Paterson, Robert Johnston, Matthew Higgs, Camilla Low and Will Bradley. Photograph: Sarah Lowndes, reproduced courtesy of Sarah Lowndes.

Flyer for Optimo at The Sub Club, July 1999. Reproduced courtesy of Keith McIvor/Jonnie Wilkes.

13th Note Café, King Street, Glasgow, 2001. Photograph: Sarah Lowndes, reproduced courtesy of Sarah Lowndes.

Life without Buildings, 2000. Reproduced courtesy of Robert Dallas Gray.

Jim Lambie, *Black Gloss* at Anton Kern, New York (2000). Reproduced courtesy of The Modern Institute/Toby Webster Ltd.

Tom O'Sullivan and Joanne Tatham, *The Glamour* at Transmission (2000). Reproduced courtesy of Transmission.

Richard Wright at Gagosian Gallery in Chelsea, New York (2000). Reproduced courtesy of Gagosian Gallery, New York.

Pyramids of Mars at The Fruitmarket, Edinburgh (2000). Left to right: Luke Fowler, El Hombre Trajeado bass player Stevie Jones and Chris Mack of Eska and The James Orr Complex. Reproduced courtesy of The Modern Institute/Toby Webster Ltd.

73 Robertson Street, 1999. Photograph: Richard Wright, reproduced courtesy of Richard Wright.

Rirkrit Tirivanija, Community Cinema for a Quiet Intersection, September 1999. Photograph: Andrew Lee. Reproduced courtesy of The Modern Institute/Toby Webster Ltd.

Simon Starling, *Rescued Rhododendrons* (2000). Reproduced courtesy of The Modern Institute/Toby Webster Ltd.

Graham Fagen, *Royston Road Trees* (as part of Royston Road Project), 2001. Reproduced courtesy of Lucy Byatt, The Cathy Centre

Wilkes exhibition poster, Our Misfortune, Transmission (2001). Reproduced courtesy of The Modern Institute/Toby Webster Ltd.

Cathy Wilkes, Our Misfortune at Transmission (2001). Reproduced courtesy of The Modern Institute/Toby Webster Ltd.

Hayley Tompkins installation at Jack Hanley, San Francisco (2001). Reproduced courtesy of The Modern Institute/Toby Webster Ltd.

Poster for Girl Art exhibition by Hannah Robinson, Harriet Tritton, Sara Barker, Jo Robertson, Celia Hempton and Aleana Egan, May 2002. Reproduced courtesy of Hannah Robinson.

Installation view of *My Head Is On Fire But My Heart Is Full Of Love*, Charlottensburg Exhibition Hall, Copenhagen (2002). Reproduced courtesy of The Modern Institute/Toby Webster Ltd.

Anti-Iraq War demonstration, Glasgow, 2003. Photograph: Fred Pedersen, reproduced courtesy of Fred Pedersen.

Toby Paterson, *New Façade* (installation view), CCA, 2003. Reproduced courtesy of the Centre for Contemporary Art, Glasgow.

Jim Lambie, installation view, *Zenomap*, Scottish Pavilion, Venice Biennale, 2003. Reproduced courtesy of The Modern Institute/Toby Webster Ltd.

Martin Boyce, *Our Love is Like the Flowers, the Rain, The Sea and the Hours*, Tramway, 2002. Reproduced courtesy of Tramway.

Liquid Liquid performing live at Optimo, Sub Club, 2003. Photograph: Gary Jamieson, reproduced courtesy of Keith McIvor/Jonnie Wilkes.


SECTION IV


Torsten Lauschmann, *Mother and Child* (2004). Photograph: Torsten Lauschmann, reproduced courtesy of Mary Mary, Glasgow.

Torsten Lauschmann, *Wunst* performance, Transmission (2004). Photograph: Torsten Lauschmann, reproduced courtesy of Mary Mary, Glasgow.

Saturday afternoon at The Hidden Gardens, Tramway (2005). Photograph: Alan McAteer, reproduced courtesy of The Hidden Gardens Trust.

Rob Churm, *Untitled (Through the Night)* (2005), reproduced courtesy of the artist and Sorcha Dallas, Glasgow.

Karla Black, *Opportunities for Girls*, Mary Mary, Glasgow (2006). Photograph: Olivier Bartenschlager, reproduced courtesy of Mary Mary.

Installation view of *Strange, I've Seen that Face Before*, Museum Abteiberg, Moenchengladbach (2006). Reproduced courtesy of The Modern Institute/Toby Webster Ltd.

Poster for Nuts and Seeds show by Coughs, Park Attack and Gay Against You, designed by Louise Shelley (2006). Reproduced courtesy of Nuts and Seeds.

Franz Ferdinand, live in Dundee, 2006. Photograph: Shoko Ishikawa, reproduced courtesy of Shoko Ishikawa.

Kate Davis, *The Clear Stark Vision is Getting Lost Again* (2007). Reproduced courtesy of the artist and Sorcha Dallas, Glasgow.

Installation view, Scott Myles, ASKIT, The Modern Institute, 2007. Reproduced courtesy of The Modern Institute/Toby Webster Ltd.

Martin Creed, Words and Music, Royal Scottish Academy of Music and Drama, Glasgow (2007). Reproduced courtesy of The Common Guild.

Sara Barker, *Variations on my own* (2008). Photograph: Alan Dimmick, reproduced courtesy of Mary Mary, Glasgow.

Triple School (l-r: Giles Bailey, Tom Varley) play The Hot Club, Nice 'N' Sleazy's (2008). Reproduced courtesy of Tom Varley.

Alex Frost, *Blind Drawing (Ruth Sleeping, 2)*, (2008). Reproduced courtesy of the artist and Sorcha Dallas, Glasgow.

Aleana Egan, We Sat Down Where We Had Sat Before, (2008). Photograph: Serge Hasenbohler, reproduced courtesy of Mary Mary, Glasgow.

Andrew Miller, *Library* (2001) seen at the opening of Always Begins By Degrees, the The Common Guild's first exhibition held at Douglas Gordon's home in Woodlands Terrace, Glasgow (2008). Reproduced courtesy of The Common Guild.

Sophie Macpherson, *Cutting Station* (2008). Reproduced courtesy of the artist and Sorcha Dallas, Glasgow.

Still from Luke Fowler's *Bogman Palmjaguar* (2008). Reproduced courtesy of The Modern Institute/Toby Webster Ltd.

Simon Starling, *Project for a Public Sculpture (After Thomas Annan)*, The Modern Institute/Toby Webster Ltd (offsite), Glasgow International, 2008. Reproduced courtesy of The Modern Institute/Toby Webster Ltd.

*Moot Points*, Transmission, 2008. Seen in foreground: Laura Aldridge and Darren Rhymes in conversation with Kathryn Elkin. Reproduced courtesy of Transmission.

Abraham Cruzvillegas, Autoconstrucción, Centre for Contemporary Arts, Glasgow (2008). Reproduced courtesy of the Centre for Contemporary Arts, Glasgow.

Flyer for Emily Pethick and Janna Graham's Critical Applause talk, Centre for Contemporary Art, Glasgow (2009). Reproduced courtesy of the Centre for Contemporary Arts, Glasgow.

Louise Shelley, Conal McStravick, Jens Strandberg and Kathryn Elkin perform part of Elkin's "Dead Hands" series at Cove Park, May 2009. Reproduced courtesy of Kathryn Elkin.

Alex Gross, *Swamp Thing*, Transmission (offsite), Ruchill Golf Course Annex, 2009. Reproduced courtesy of Transmission.

Divorce singer Sinead Young, on tour in England, 2009. Reproduced courtesy of Sinead Young.

Installation view of the group show TONITE, The Modern Institute (2009). Reproduced courtesy of The Modern Institute/Toby Webster Ltd.

Karla Black, installation view, Migros Museum, Zurich (2009). Photograph: A. Burger, reproduced courtesy of the artist and Mary Mary, Glasgow.

Throbbing Gristle performing Apparition Foretold, Tramway (2009). Reproduced courtesy of Tramway.

Book fair at the Centre for Contemporary Arts, Glasgow, 2009. Reproduced courtesy of the Centre for Contemporary Arts, Glasgow.

Nerea Bello performing at the opening of Votive, Centre for Contemporary Arts, Glasgow, 2009. Photograph: Alan Dimmick, reproduced courtesy of the Centre for Contemporary Art, Glasgow.

Lucy Skaer, *Thames and Hudson*, Turner Prize exhibition, Tate Britain (2009). Courtesy of the artist and doggerfisher, Edinburgh.

Richard Wright, *No Title* (2009), Turner Prize, Tate Britain, London, 2009. Reproduced courtesy of The Modern Institute/Toby Webster Ltd.

Shelly Nadashi, Cliff Laine and Laurie Pitt perform "Ambush in Wedding" at SGW3, Glasgow, 2010. Photograph: Kate V Robinson, reproduced courtesy of Shelly Nadashi.

Installation view, Love, Sorcha Dallas, Glasgow, 2010. L-R, Tom O'Sullivan and Joanne Tatham, Gilbert & George. Reproduced courtesy of the artists and Sorcha Dallas, Glasgow.

New WASPS studio complex at The Briggait, 2010. Photograph: Andrew Lee, reproduced courtesy of Andrew Lee and WASPS.

Carolyn Barrett and Harriet Tritton, Guest, Transmission, 2010. Reproduced courtesy of Transmission.

Duncan Campbell, Make It New, John, Tramway (2010). Reproduced courtesy of Tramway.

Friends and family opening of The Modern Institute's Osborne Street gallery, March 2010. Photograph: Sarah Lowndes, reproduced courtesy of Sarah Lowndes.


Front cover image: Richard Wright, installing *No Title* (2009), The Turner Prize, Tate Britain, 2009. Photograph: Arthur Lambert, reproduced courtesy of Richard Wright.

Back cover image: Cathy Wilkes, (installation detail), *I Give You All My Money*, The Turner Prize, Tate Britain, London, 2008. Photograph: Andy Keate, reproduced courtesy of The Modern Institute/Toby Webster Ltd.

# INDEX

426

437